ANTON CHEKHOV'S PLAYS

THE SEA GULL

UNCLE VANYA

THE THREE SISTERS

THE CHERRY ORCHARD

Backgrounds

Criticism

➤➤➤ A NORTON CRITICAL EDITION ◄◄◄

ANTON CHEKHOV'S PLAYS

THE SEA GULL
UNCLE VANYA
THE THREE SISTERS
THE CHERRY ORCHARD
Backgrounds
Criticism

➤➤➤ ◄◄◄

Translated and Edited by

EUGENE K. BRISTOW

INDIANA UNIVERSITY

W · W · NORTON & COMPANY · INC · *New York*

FIRST EDITION

ACKNOWLEDGMENTS

Eric Bentley: "Craftsmanship in *Uncle Vanya*," from *In Search of Theater*, by Eric Bentley (New York: Alfred A. Knopf, 1953), pp. 342–64. Copyright © 1949 by Eric Bentley. Reprinted by permission of the author and Atheneum Publishers.

Robert Brustein: Foreword from *Chekhov: The Major Plays*, translated by Ann Dunnigan (New York: New American Library, 1964), pp. vii–xxii. Copyright © 1964 by Robert Brustein. Reprinted by arrangement with The New American Library, Inc., New York, New York.

Francis Fergusson: From "*Ghosts* and *The Cherry Orchard*: The Theater of Modern Realism," in *The Idea of a Theater: A Study of Ten Plays, the Art of Modern Drama in Changing Perspective* (Princeton, N.J.: Princeton University Press, 1949), pp. 161–77. Copyright © 1949 by Princeton University Press; Princeton Paperback, 1968. Reprinted by permission of Princeton University Press.

John Gassner: "The Duality of Chekhov," from *Chekhov: A Collection of Critical Essays*, edited by Robert Louis Jackson (Englewood Cliffs, N.J.: Prentice-Hall, 1967), pp. 175–83. Reprinted by permission of the publisher.

Ronald Hingley: From *Russian Writers and Society, 1825–1904* (New York: McGraw-Hill, 1967). Copyright © 1967 by Ronald Hingley. Used with permission of McGraw-Hill and of George Weidenfeld and Nicholson. From *Chekhov, a Biographical and Critical Study* (London: George Allen & Unwin Ltd., 1966; originally published 1950), pp. 236–39. Reprinted by permission of the publisher.

David Magarshack: From *Chekhov the Dramatist* (New York: Hill & Wang, 1960). Copyright © 1952, 1960 by David Magarshack. Reprinted by permission of Farrar, Straus & Giroux, Inc.

Siegfried Melchinger: "Stage Production in Europe" from *Anton Chekhov* (New York: Frederick Ungar, 1972), pp. 159–66. Copyright © 1972 by Frederick Ungar Publishing Co., Inc. Reprinted by permission.

Vsevolod Meyerhold: "The Naturalistic Theatre and the Theatre of Mood," translated by Nora Beeson, from *Tulane Drama Review*, IV, 4 (May 1960), pp. 134–41. Reprinted by permission of *Tulane Drama Review*. (Written in 1906 and originally published in *Theatr. Kniga o novom teatre: sbornik statej* [St. Petersburg, 1908].)

Nicholas Moravčevich: "Chekhov and Naturalism: From Affinity to Divergence," from *Comparative Drama*, IV (Winter 1970–71), pp. 219–40. Copyright © 1970 by the Editors of Comparative Drama. Reprinted by permission of the Editors of Comparative Drama.

Vladimir Nabokov: From *Nikolai Gogol* (New York: New Directions, 1961; originally published 1944), pp. 63–70. Reprinted by permission of the publisher.

Charles B. Timmer: "The Bizarre Element in Chekhov's Art" from *Anton Čechov: 1860–1960* edited by T. Eekman (Leiden: E. J. Brill, 1960). Reprinted by permission of the publisher.

Georgy Tovstonogov: "Chekhov's *Three Sisters* at the Gorky Theatre," translated by Joyce Vining, from *TDR (The Drama Review)*, 13 (T42, winter 1968). Reprinted by permission of *TDR*.

Thomas G. Winner: "Chekhov's *Seagull* and Shakespeare's *Hamlet*: A Study of a Dramatic Device," from *The American Slavic and East European Review*, XV February 1956), 103–11. Reprinted by permission of the author and the publisher.

Library of Congress Cataloging in Publication Data

Chekhov, Anton Pavlovich, 1860–1904.

   Anton Chekhov's plays.

   (A Norton critical edition)

   Bibliography: p.

   CONTENTS: The sea gull.—Uncle Vanya.—The three sisters. [etc]

   I. Bristow, Eugene Kerr, 1927–

PG3456.A19B7   1977   891.7'2'3   77–21521

ISBN 0–393–04432–7

ISBN 0–393–09163–5 pbk.

For
"Prof" Lee Norvelle:
teacher, colleague, friend

Contents

Preface

"My Holy of Holies," Chekhov once wrote, "it's the human body, health, intelligence, talent, inspiration, love, and the most absolute freedom, freedom from coercion and falsehood in whatever [form] they may appear."[1] To these he consistently subscribed, and, as Robert Brustein puts it, "No one has even been able to write of him without the most profound affection and love; and he, the author, remains the most positive character in his fiction."[2]

My purpose is to bring together in one volume Anton Chekhov's last four plays—in new translations—as well as a selection of essays about Chekhov himself, his dramaturgy, the Russia of his day, and his legacy to our generation.

To illustrate both the abundance and variety of Chekhovian criticism, fourteen essays have been collected, one-fourth of them receiving publication in book form for the first time and almost half having first appeared within the past ten years. The authors represent different countries (Germany, the United Kingdom, imperial Russia, as well as the USSR and the United States), and also a number of professions. They include scholars, critics, and teachers; actors, stage directors, and producers; linguists and language teachers; novelists and playwrights. When read together, these essays testify—by their very diversity of insight, complexity in argument, and dissonance of conclusion—to the brilliance, impartiality, and tolerance of Anton Chekhov as critic, playwright, and person.

The essays have been grouped under two main headings, Backgrounds and Criticism. Backgrounds includes not only an essay pertaining to Chekhov's Russia but also two short Chekhov plays. The first, *Impure Tragedians and Leprous Playwrights*, is a satirical farce on the Russian theatre of the eighties. The second, *On the Injurious Effects of Tobacco*, is in two versions, the first written early in his career; the last, two years before his death. The two versions illustrate significant changes in Chekhov's dramaturgy and offer insights into the dramaturgy of his last four plays.

The essays in the Criticism section have been divided into four

1. Anton Chekhov, Letter to A. N. Pleshcheev, Moscow, October 4, 1888, in A. P. Chekhov, *Polnoe sobranie sočinenij i pisem v dvadcati tomax* [The complete works and letters in twenty volumes] (Moscow: Goslitizdat [State publishing house for belles lettres], 1944–51), Vol. XIV, p. 177. (Hereafter cited as *Complete Works*.)
2. Robert Brustein, Foreword to *Chekhov: The Major Plays*, tr. Ann Dunnigan (New York: New American Library, 1964), p. xxii.

sections: Dramaturgy; Language, Style, Performance; The Major Plays; and Legacy. The first three essays discuss Chekhovian architecture or play structure and illustrate important aspects of the playwright's development of character and thought. The essays under Language, Style, and Performance explicate Chekhovian language (both diction and sounds) and mood, and discuss the production of his plays in the theatre. Of particular interest are Vladimir Nabokov's definition of *poshlost'*, Ronald Hingley's essay on *nastroenie*, and Meyerhold's important piece on style. The four essays under the Major Plays, each pertaining to one of the plays collected in this volume, are ranked by critics as seminal criticism. The final two essays are John Gassner's American view of the Russian dramatist and Siegfried Melchinger's observations on stage productions in Europe.

My chief aim in translating these four major works has been to provide plays that are appropriate for production in the English-speaking theatre. The principles that have guided my aim and methods in translation are set forth in the introductory essay, "On Translating Chekhov."

I should like to express my appreciation and thanks to the late Professor Ernest J. Simmons for his advice and encouragement in the preparation of this volume, and especially for his insight pertaining to my translation of *The Three Sisters* in the spring of 1970; to John Benedict of W. W. Norton & Company, Inc., and his staff, especially John W. N. Francis and Emily Garlin for their careful reading of the entire manuscript, and Tanya Mairs, a native Russian, whose close vetting of each of my translations has proved invaluable; to the twenty-two members of the cast and the sixty-two members of the staff of the Indiana University Theatre production of *The Three Sisters*, in my translation and under my direction, in the spring of 1970, especially to my colleagues who aided in the production, as well as my personal staff; to my native-Russian teachers in the 1960s, especially Margaret Fedulova, Galina McLaws, Vera Oussenko, and Lydia Slavatinskaya, whose expertise in their courses in Russian language and literature was both exciting and exacting; to my wife, Norma, and our four children, Pam, Mike, Carol, and Mary Kate, for their help in reading proof and in sorting pages; and to Chancellor Herman B Wells and the Indiana University Foundation for a research grant in Russian theatre and drama (1964–65).

EUGENE K. BRISTOW

A Note on the Texts of the Plays

The standard Russian texts of Chekhov's plays are found in A. P. Chekhov, *Polnoe sobranie sočinenij i pisem v dvadcati tomax* [The complete works and letters in twenty volumes] (Moscow: Goslitizdat [State Publishing House for Belles Lettres], 1944–51). Moreover, the article "Dve rannie redakcii p'esy *Tri sestry*; stat'ja i publikacija [Two early editions of the play *The Three Sisters*; essay and publication]," by A. R. Vladimirskaya, in *Literaturnoe nasledstvo* [Literary Heritage], vol. 68, A. P. Chekhov (Moscow and Leningrad, 1960), pp. 1–86, proved useful since it pertains to the major emendations, based on two early Chekhovian manuscripts discovered since 1953 by Russian editors. In addition to these sources, the following editions of Chekhovian works and letters were consulted:

A. P. Chekhov, *Sobranie sočinenij v dvenadcati tomax* [Collected Works in twelve volumes] (Moscow: Goslitizdat, 1954–57).

A. P. Chekhov, *Čajka* [*The Seagull*], edited with an Introduction and notes by P. Henry (Chicago: Russian Language Specialties, 1965). (Bradda Books edition in Russian.)

A. P. Chekhov, *Djadja Vanja* [*Uncle Vanya*], edited with notes by J. M. C. Davidson (Cambridge, Mass.: Schoenhof's Foreign Books, 1963). (Bradda Books edition in Russian.)

A. P. Chekhov, *Tri sestry* [*The Three Sisters*], edited with an introduction and notes by J. M. C. Davidson (Chicago: Russian Language Specialties, 1962). (Bradda Books edition in Russian.)

A. P. Chekhov, *Višnëvyj sad* [*The Cherry Orchard*], edited with Notes by J. M. C. Davidson (London: Bradda Books, 1962).

A. P. Chekhov, *P'esy* [Plays] (London: Bradda Books, n.d.).

A. P. Chekhov, *Sobranie sočinenij v dvenadcati tomax* [Collected works in twelve volumes] (Moscow: Goslitizdat, 1963).

The following three language references in Russian, similar in purpose to the English *OED*, were useful.

V. I. Dal', *Tolkovyj slovar' živogo velikorusskogo jazyka* [Explanatory dictionary of the living great Russian language], 4 vols. (Moscow, 1955). (Collected and printed from the second edition, 1880–82.)

Institut Jazykoznanija Akademija Nauk SSSR [Linguistics Institute of the Academy of Sciences, USSR], *Slovar' russkogo jazyka* [Dictionary of the Russian language], 4 vols. (Moscow, 1957).

Tolkovyj slovar' russkogo jazyka [Explanatory dictionary of the Russian language], edited by D. N. Ushakov, 4 vols. (Moscow, 1935).

A Note on Transliteration and Pronunciation

Although there is no generally accepted system of transliterating the Russian alphabet, my guide has been J. Thomas Shaw's pamphlet, *The Transliteration of Modern Russian for English-Language Publications*, in which four systems are devised, each arranged according to a particular purpose. In transliterating *personal and place names* in the text, I have used System I; in the footnotes, System III. Moreover, in the texts of the plays, a few original Russian words *qua* words have been retained, and in those rare instances Professor Shaw's System I has been followed. In the footnotes, however, System III has been employed.

The pronunciation guide should be viewed as only approximate, since most of the letters/sounds are pronounced in more than one way. An accurate pronunciation of a letter/sound is governed by the place of stress or where the letter/sound occurs in the word. Stress is marked by an acute accent over the vowel. There are instances when the letter used in the correct spelling of a word has a sound that is not typical in terms of the correct pronunciation. For example, the *v* in the name Treplyov has the sound of *f*, whereas the *v* in the name Treplyova has the typical sound associated with the letter *v*. When these instances occur, the name (without the acute accent) is repeated in lower-case inside parentheses, e.g. (treplyóf), with the proper acute accent added.

For instance, in *The Sea Gull*:

Irína Nikolaevna (nikaláevna) Arkádina, by marriage Treplyóva
Konstantin (kanstantín) Gavrilovich (gavrílavich) (Gavrílych)
Treplyov (treplyóf)

In the second line of the example above, both spellings of the patronymic are given, i.e., Gavrilovich (gavrílavich) (Gavrílych), since both spellings occur in Chekhov's original. It may be noted, however, that in spoken conversation, the second spelling is closer to the correct pronunciation.

Cryllic	System I	System III	Pronunciation
Аа	a	a	*fá*ther; *má*ma
Бб	b	b	*b*ank; to*p*
Вв	v	v	*v*et; dea*f*
Гг	g	g	*g*et; brea*k*
Дд	d	d	*d*addy; ve*t*
Ее	e[1]	e	*m*et; *y*eah
Ёё[2]	yo	e	*bó*rder; *yo*re
Жж	zh	ž	*vi*sion; pu*sh*

1. All footnotes in this section, unless otherwise indicated, are from J. Thomas Shaw, *The Transliteration of Modern Russian for English-Language Publications* (Madison: University of Wisconsin Press, 1967), pp. 10–11. In System I, the spelling ye- may be used initially (e.g., Yevtushenko). It should *not* be used intervocalically (*Alexeev*, not *Alexeyev*; *Dostoevsky*; not *Dostoyevsky*).

2. This symbol is considered not a separate letter of the Russian alphabet but a pronunciation variant of *e*. The rules for its use are very complex. In System I, where pronunciation is emphasized, it should be transliterated as *yo* (e.g., in

Cryllic	System I	System III	Pronunciation
Зз	z	z	zeal; miss
Ии	i	i	cheese; if
Йй	y	j	unstressed vowel
Кκ	k	k	kept
Лл	l	l	log
Мм	m	m	mama
Нн	n	n	no
Оо	o	o	órder; alóne; artístic
Пп	p	p	page
Рр	r	r	rake
Сс	s	s	miss
Тτ	t	t	ten
Уy	u	u	spoon
Фф	f	f	form
Хx	kh	x	a voiceless velar fricative; the Russian equivalent of the German ach
Цц	ts	c	a voiceless alveolar affricate; its
Чч	ch	č	chief
Шш	sh	š	shoe
Щщ	shch	šč	fish chówder
Ъъ	—³	″⁴	the hard sign has no sound value, but influences the sound of the preceding consonant
Ыы	y	y	one of the hard tonic vowels, placed high as in beat, placed back as in boot, but spread in place of rounded
Ьь	—³	′⁵	the soft sign has no sound value, but influences the sound of the preceding consonant
Ээ	e	è	vet; yet
Юю	yu	ju	you; sue
Яя	ya	ja	artistic; its; yah; yip

Combinations of Letters

-ый	-y	-yj	(in names)
-ий	-y	-ij	(in names)
-ия	-ia	-ija	
-ье	-ie	-′e	
-ьи	-yi	-′i	
кс	x	ks	

such names as *Alyosha, Lyova,* in fiction); in Systems II, III, and IV, it should ordinarily be transliterated as *e,* but if it is important to distinguish this symbol from *e,* it may be transliterated as ë.
3. Simply omitted, with no indication of omission.
4. The symbol ″ is used to transliterate the Russian letter ъ (the hard sign). The symbol ″ for the hard sign is preferable to the symbol ' ' (used for double quotation marks).
5. The symbol ′ is used to transliterate the Russian letter ь (the soft sign). The symbol ′ for the soft sign is preferable to the symbol ' (used for the single quotation mark and the apostrophe).

Introduction: On Translating Chekhov[1]

Translating Russian plays is a complex game in which each participant defines his own boundaries, makes his own rules, and keeps his own score. What is out-of-bounds for one may be "in" for the next. No single opinion concerning the aim of translation prevails; so the game is played without controlling principles. Part of the difficulty stems from the very nature of translation; part, from the components of theatre; and part, from the translator's bias.

The exact balance of sound, sense, and feeling that has been achieved in one language may be transferred only rarely to another. In Chekhov's plays the vocal sound moves in the same rhythmical direction as the action it accompanies, the event it describes, or the emotion it evokes. His dialogue, often described in musical terms, gains part of its effect from language structure. At times the English will effectively approximate the Russian, as in the three-syllable exchange between Ranevskaya and Lopakhin in *The Cherry Orchard*: *"Kto kupíl?"* (Who bought it?) *"Ja kupíl."* (I bought it.) Usually, however, the special rhythmic flow is lost. For example, the feminine endings of Anya's speech to Ranevskaya blend sound with sense and create a gentle glide in Russian that vanishes in the hard consonant endings of English: *"Mílaja, dóbraja, xoróšaja mojá máma, mojá prekrásnaja, ja ljubljú tebjá . . ."* (Dear, good, kind my mama, my precious, I love you . . .) The loss, though undeniable, has often been exaggerated. "The Italian proverb, *Traduttore, traditore* (translator, traitor)," as Albert Guérard points out, "is a victim's hyperbole."[2] Yet the impossibility of total translation affords an excuse for literalists to rely upon the letter and for stylists to revel in the spirit.

Theatre, at best, is a synthesis of art and craft. Most of its components—actors, director, language, audience—are, as William Becker puts it, "too human in character to be anything but highly imperfect."[3] At times in the commercial theatre, for example, limitations may be clearly illustrated by the difference between translation and adaptation. Translation is the faithful rendition that is handed to the producer; adaptation is the final result after the script has been rewritten, rehearsed, and produced. At any point in the process, the literal translation may be "adapted," in deference to the limiting conditions of theatre.

Even within the skin of his own language, every person translates

1. Portions of this essay were published as a lead article, "On Translating Chekhov," in "New Books in Review," *The Quarterly Journal of Speech*, LII (October 1966), 290–94.

2. Albert Guérard, "Translation," in *Dictionary of World Literature*, ed. Joseph T. Shipley, rev. ed. (Paterson, N.J.: Littlefield, Adams, 1964), p. 425.

3. William Becker, "Some French Plays in Translation," *Hudson Review*, IX, 2 (Summer 1956), 279.

what he sees, or reads, from his own experience. *The Cherry Orchard*, for example, was not the same in the minds of its directors at the Moscow Art Theatre—Konstantin Stanislavsky and Vladimir Nemirovich-Denchenko—or in Chekhov's. To its directors, the play was a tragedy; to its author, "a comedy, in places even a farce. . . ."[4] Though the directors eventually had their way, the author insisted that "not once had either one read through my play carefully."[5] Perhaps Chekhov's complaint sums up the difficulty of translating Russian plays, since the apparent shift between the letter and the spirit of any given translation may be attributed, in large measure, to the translator's bias. The components of theatre and the nature of translation serve only to complicate the problem.

In a splendid essay on directing, "Seeing the Point," Stark Young supplies the translator with a workable solution. Borrowing from Plato, he notes that "most men are blind to the fact of their ignorance of the essential character of each individual thing. They do not see . . . what, if the thing were freed from all but its own characteristic, would remain, and would be the point of it, and would define its existence in the midst of a multitude of things like and unlike. What men are least apt to do is to see the point."[6]

Like the stage director, the translator should see the point of the original, as it is revealed not only in structure and language but also in character and thought. Seeing the point requires that the translator make the distinction, to take Elder Olson's phrase, between "speech as action (*praxis*) and speech as meaningful (*lexis*)."[7] In *The Three Sisters*, for example, Olga's inability to direct her anger governs the meaning of several speeches in Act III, and the tension apparent in the original should be made distinct in the translation. As the director may freely convert, moment by moment, the point of the script into his theatrical milieu, so may the translator freely transform, in a mathematical sense, the point of the original into his own language.

Given the director's aim, the translator then faces the choice of time and place. Should his language, for example, approximate the English of Chekhov's day, or that of contemporary speech? How much of the Russian environment should be preserved? To re-create classic dramas, is it necessary, in Stravinsky's words, "to *cool* them, to bring them closer by making them more distant,"[8] or to natural-

4. Anton Chekhov, Letter to M. P. Alexeeva (Lilina), dated September 15, 1903, in *Complete Works*, XX, 131.
5. Anton Chekhov, Letter to O. L. Knipper, dated April 10, 1904, in *Complete Works*, XX, 265.
6. Stark Young, "Seeing the Point," in *Theatre Practice* (New York: Charles Scribner's Sons, 1926), pp. 108–9.

7. Elder Olson, "William Empson, Contemporary Criticism and Poetic Diction," in *Critics and Criticism, Ancient and Modern*, ed. R. S. Crane (Chicago: University of Chicago Press, 1952), p. 71.
8. Statement attributed to Igor Stravinsky in *Reinhardt, Jessner, Piscator oder Klassikertod* by Herbert Ihering (Berlin: E. Rowolt, 1929), pp. 14–15.

ize them by substituting new images that achieve effects similar to those in the original? In short, the degree to which the translator's words succeed in realizing his intent is measured by the response of his audience.

> A jest's prosperity lies in the ear
> Of him that hears it, never in the tongue
> Of him that makes it.
> [*Love's Labour's Lost*, V, ii, 879–72]

Chekhov's words *qua* words are deceptively simple. A second-year student of Russian, for example, may be assigned several of his short stories; a third-year student, one of his major plays. Yet Chekhov has interlaced his language with threads of folk song, folklore, poems, and literary allusions that stitch point to patterns of meaning that are easily understood or felt only by audiences familiar with the Russian language and environment. Though Chekhov's intent is quite different, his technique is similar to the running gag in comedy sketches. A fable by Krylov or a line from Pushkin will occur and recur with increasing complexity in his tapestry of sound and image. Although the allusion may be translated, its effectiveness may be diminished and, in a few instances, completely lost on its new audience. Two or three examples that come readily to mind occur in *The Three Sisters*.

Early in the play, the first words spoken by Masha are the opening lines of the Prologue to *Ruslan and Lyudmila* (1820) by A. S. Pushkin (1799–1837), who is considered Russia's greatest poet:

> By the curved seashore stands an oak tree green;
> A golden chain to that oak is bound . . .
>
> [p. 107]

She then repeats the second line. Chekhov's selection of these particular lines is appropriate at all levels: structure; character; thought; diction; music; spectacle. These lines introduce a long fairy tale which, in turn, is based upon seventeenth-century popular narrative, and thus in *The Three Sisters* they clarify the beginning of the Vershinin-Masha-Kulygin triangle in terms of awe, mystery, ecstasy of new love.

At the end of the first act, these same two lines are repeated by Masha. In my translation, however, the third and fourth lines of the poem have been added to the first and second lines at the end of Act I:

> And linked to the chain with a scholarly mien
> A tomcat is seen going round and round and . . .
>
> [p. 118]

Even though the third and fourth lines are not in Chekhov's play, they were added to complete the poetic image that Chekhov used and which is well known among educated Russians (these Pushkin lines are probably as well known in Russia as, say, Hamlet's "To be or not to be" soliloquy is to us.) Moreover, the introduction of these third and fourth lines at the end of Act I clarifies the repetition by Masha in the fourth act, in which she scrambles the poem and refers to "a tomcat green" (p. 155). Then, too, immediately before Masha repeats the lines at the end of Act I, Fedotik's humming top (his gift to Irina) has been set in sound and in motion, and thus the images of the cat circling the tree, as well as that of Masha and the love cycle, are reinforced both visually and aurally. Moreover, the image of the tomcat chained to, and circling round, the oak tree underscores both the repetition (act one) and the final effect (act four) of Masha's love: first, for her husband Kulygin (about four years before the play opens); second, for Vershinin (lasting about three and a half years) during the course of the play.

Shortly after the introduction of the Pushkin poem in *The Three Sisters*, Solyony—responding to an insult flung at him by Masha ("you loathsome, vulgar person")—quotes lines from *The Peasant and the Workman* (1815), a fable by I. A. Krylov (1769–1844):

> Before he had time to let out a yell,
> The bear was squeezing him to hell
>
> [p. 108]

In Act IV, these same two lines by Krylov are repeated twice: first, by Solyony; second, by Chebutykin (p. 150). Thus, Chekhov has linked Solyony and his action to the action of the bear; the *he* in the lines is associated with Tuzenbakh, who is killed by Solyony in a duel.

In Act I, immediately after Solyony quotes Krylov, two persons enter with a cake (a gift to Irina) from Mikhail Ivanych Protopopov, the Chairman of the local District Council. It is tempting to associate Protopopov with the two lines in the Krylov fable, particularly with the bear in the fable. That is, the common nicknames of *Mikhail* are *Misha* and *Mishka*, which are also common names for *bear* (*medved'*). The action of Protopopov, who is never seen but is talked about, resembles the action of the bear in Krylov's fable: Act I, a cake arrives from Protopopov, who is not invited to the name-day party for Irina; Act II, the bells of his troika are heard, and Natasha accepts his invitation for a drive; Act III, Natasha's second child, Sofya, has been born (Protopopov is perhaps the father), and Chebutykin declares that it is common knowledge Protopopov is having an affair with Natasha; Act IV, the Prozorov family is outside in the garden; Protopopov is sitting inside the house, playing with Sofya; and Andrey (Natasha's husband) is pushing Natasha's first child, Bobik, in the baby carriage.

Allusions to men of letters and their works (both Russian and European) occur frequently in Chekhov's major plays, and these have been identified in the textual notes. One literary concept threaded verbally into three of the plays (and is directly exemplified in several major characters in all four plays) is that associated with the words *superfluous* (*lišnij*) and *free loader* (*prizival*). Moreover, in *The Three Sisters*, Chekhov's early introduction of the concept occurs with the speech by the old doctor Chebutykin: "It's a fact, you know, I've never worked at all. Not a lick of work since leaving the university, why, I haven't lifted a finger. I haven't even read through a single book. The only thing I read are newspapers. . . . Here . . . according to the newspapers, I know there was, for instance, a man named Dobrolyubov, but what he wrote about— I don't know . . ." (p. 107). N. A. Dobrolyubov (1836–1861) was an important social and literary critic whose work added significantly to literature and criticism which centered on the "superfluous person" theme—a theme peculiar to Russia throughout the nineteenth century. Since the "superfluous person" theme is an important theme of *The Three Sisters* (as well as of the other three plays), its subtle introduction by Chekhov in these early moments testify to his wit and craftsmanship.[9]

Another word that recurs frequently in *The Cherry Orchard* (and is related to *superfluous*) is *nedotëpa*, translated as *silly galoot*. The word is defined in the Russian standard-language dictionary as an "awkward, clumsy [blundering] . . . person."[1] Magarshack finds *duffer* as perhaps the best British equivalent, defined by the *OED* as, "a person without practical ability or capacity, or, generally, a stupid or foolish person."[2] The word recurs in Chekhov's notebook, e.g., "Chekhov gave Varya, 'the perfect fool,' the family name of Nedotyopina. Another reference . . . 'nedotëpa—on the cross (in a graveyard) someone has written: Here lies a nedotëpa.' "[3] Something of the difficulty in finding the right phrase in English for "Èx, ty, nedotëpa" (translated here as "Oh, you silly galoot, you") may be seen in the following typical translations: Dunnigan, "Ach, you . . .

9. Since Chekhov disagreed with a narrow interpretation of reality, as well as with an insistence upon the idea that social concerns should take precedence over literary and artistic principles, both viewpoints advocated by N. A. Dobrolyubov, the Dobrolyubov named by the old doctor may well have been, for example, A. M. Dobrolyubov (1876–?), a symbolist poet who turned to religion early in his career and whose chief legacy was perhaps his adherence to models of French symbolism .

1. Institut Jazykoznanija Akademija Nauk SSSR [Linguistics Institute of the Academy of Sciences USSR], *Slovar' russkogo jazyka* [Dictionary of the Russian language] (Moscow, 1957), II, 609. (Hereafter cited as *Dictionary*.)
2. David Magarshack, *Chekhov the Dramatist* (New York: Hill and Wang, 1960), p. 285.
3. Ibid.

addlepate!"; Fen, "Oh, you . . . you're daft!"; Garnett, "Ech! I'm
good for nothing."; Hingley, "You're just a—nincompoop."; Magarshack, "Ugh, you—nincompoop!"; Pitcher, "You, you're an absolute
wash-out!"

There are several words and phrases in Chekhovian drama that are
embedded in the Russian language and milieu and that offer difficulty in finding the right English word or phrase. For example, in
The Three Sisters, near the end of Act I, Masha cries out: "Oh, my,
life is beautiful; where, oh where, has ours gone to? Oh, what the
hell—why not? (*"Èx-ma, zizn' malinovaja, gde naša ne propadala!"*)
(p. 117). The first word is normally used in the expression of "delight, ecstasy, sudden surprise, regret, irritation, etc."[4] The adjective
malinovaja, which modifies *life* (*žizn'*), has as its root noun *malina*,
which has several meanings: (1) the raspberry shrub; (2) the fragrant, sweet, usually red flower, the berry of this shrub; (3) a hot
broth made out of the dried berries, used for medicinal purposes, or
tea made from these berries; (4) the color *crimson*; (5) the sound
mellow. Moreover, there is a *malinovaja nalivka*, a kind of brandy.[5]
The phrase *gde naša ne propadala* sounds—in spoken Russian—exactly like the phrase *gde naše ne propadalo*, an expression "which is
used on entering that action to which is connected risk."[6] The verb
propadat' has several meanings, e.g., to be missing; to vanish; to perish; to be wasted. Thus, the phrase *gde naša ne propadala*, as printed,
has the meaning, "where has our [life] gone to?"; but in spoken
Russian, the phrase sounds like the expression—which may be
translated as "Why in the hell not [do it]?"—which is said prior to
entering an action connected with risk. Consequently, in Masha's
exclamation Chekhov has managed in the original Russian to combine a multitude of meanings and feeling tones, chief of which are:
delight, ecstasy, surprise, regret, irritation; life is fragrant, sweet, hot
crimson, mellow, lovely; where has our life gone to, vanished, perished, been wasted; Oh, why in the hell not do it? This last meaning, or feeling tone, is probably related to Masha's emotions
pertaining to Vershinin, and the "risk" she feels is perhaps that of
reliving the same pattern of the love cycle, having gone through that
pattern once with the teacher she married. This pattern is revealed
in Masha's very next speech, i.e., the repetition of the lines from
Pushkin's work (p. 118). Something of the difficulty in translating
Chekhov—and accounting, in large measure, for frequently wide
variations—is revealed in the typical translations of these particular
phrases: Dunnigan, "Why not, it's a rosy life, and we only live

---

4. *Dictionary*, IV, 1059.
5. Ibid., II, 297.
6. V. I. Dal' *Tolkovyj slovar' živogo
velikorusskogo jazyka* [Explanatory dictionary of the living Great Russian lan-
guage] (Moscow, 1955, reprint of 2nd
ed., 1880–82), I, 402; III, 501; *Dictionary*, III, 684.

once!"; Guthrie-Kipnis, "A toast. Here's to our empty life—to hell with it."; Hingley, "Eat, drink and be merry—after all, we only live once."; Magarshack, "Oh, life is sweet—what the hell—."

Another abstruse phrase occurs in *The Cherry Orchard*, in Lopakhin's second speech in Act I: "*so svinym rylom v kalašnyj rjad,*" translated here as "Like a pig's nozzle showing up in a row of wedding cakes" (p. 166). The word *kalač* incorporates the meaning of a small loaf of white wheat bread, often "baked in the form of castles. . . ."[7] In his notes to the Bradda edition of *The Cherry Orchard* in Russian, J. M. C. Davidson discusses two comparable English proverbs: "You cannot make a silk purse out of a sow's ear" and "like a bull in a china shop." The second emphasizes that "Lopakhin is out of place and liable to upset the order surrounding him, but misses the idea of the pig's snout of which he is so conscious and which is predominant in the original Russian."[8] Typical English translations, arranged in chronological order since 1912, are: Calderon, "a silk purse out of a sow's ear, you might say"; Garnett, "like a pig in a bun shop"; Young, "Like a pig rooting in a pastry shop"; Yarmolinsky, "a pig in a pastry shop, you might say"; Magarshack, "like a jackdaw in peacock's feathers"; Corrigan, "like a crown in peacock's feathers"; Fen, "But you can't make a silk purse out of a sow's ear"; Dunnigan, "like a pig in a pastry shop"; Hingley, "barging in like a bull in a china shop"; Guthrie-Kipnis, "talk about a pig in clover."

Several words or phrases in Chekhov's plays required substantial changes. The more important ones are discussed here. In the fourth act of *The Three Sisters*, for example, Kulygin, in the original Russian, says: "One time in a seminary, a teacher wrote *čepuxa* [nonsense] on a student's essay, and the student read *renixa*—he thought it had been written in Latin." The word *čepuxa* (nonsense), written in Cyrillic cursive can be read as *renixa* in Latin. To transfer directly the point of the joke from the Russian to English is impossible; thus, the words, "and began declining *hoki, hoko,* etc.," were added by the translator to create a similar joke based on Latin and English: "And the student was certain it was Latin and began declining: *hoki, hoko, hoko, hokum, hokum*" (p. 146). To prepare for the *hokum* joke, the translator translated Masha's lines in Act II, i.e., "*ili že vsë pustjaki, tryn-trava*" (literally "or else everything is nonsense, it doesn't matter") as: "or else everything is nonsense, hokum" (p. 125). Moreover, when *čepuxa* occurs in *The Cherry Orchard*, it has been translated as "stuff and nonsense" (p. 172).

Another interesting phrase occurs in the first act of *The Cherry Orchard*, i.e., "*oblezlyj barin,*" translated here as "that used-up, old

7. *Dictionary*, II, 23.
8. *Višnëvyj sad (The Cherry Orchard)*, ed. J. M. C. Davidson (London: Bradda Books, 1962), p. 73.

gentleman," in reference to Trofimov (p. 177). The colloquial word
oblezlyj is defined: "(1) with falling out, [or] with extremely sparse
hair. . . . (2) with peeled-off paint, plaster, etc., frayed, faded."[9] It
was tempting to translate this phrase as "that used-up, old gentleman who looks like a plucked chicken." In Simeonov-Pishchik's
phrase in the same act, i.e., "*propadaj moja telega, vse četyre kolesa*,"
"Get lost my cart, all four wheels" (p. 172), the phrases, "Oh, my,
that's something!" and "as the saying goes," were added by the
translator to clarify the colloquial expression which implies, "Come
what may, I can't help falling for her."[1]

The last four major changes occur in *Uncle Vanya*. In the second
act, Dr. Astrov says, "There's an assistant of mine who never says
'*idët*,' but '*idët'*.'" (p. 70). The word *idët* can be translated as
"O.K.," "right," or "it's a deal"; the word *idët'* is mispronounced
in that the sound for *t* is "soft," not "hard." The sentence, translated here as "There's an assistant of mine who never says 'all right,'
but 'all rat,'" has received various translations: Dunnigan, "I've got
a medical assistant who never says right, but 'roight.'"; Fen, "I've
got an unqualified assistant who never says 'all right' but always
'aw-right.'"; Garnett, "I have an assistant who never says 'right,'
but 'roight.'"; Hingley, "I have an assistant who can't say 'what
do you,' always says 'wodger.'"; Magarshack, translation omitted.
A few moments later, Sonya enters, and, finding the men drunk, she
says, "*Podruzilis' jasnye sokoly* (literally, "The pure falcons became
friends.") This idiom *jasnyj sokol* ("pure falcon") is a term of
endearment for youngsters and men, and refers to a person who
exhibits beauty, bravery, or courage, boldness. The word *jasnyj* in
connection with *sokol* has no definite meaning.[2] My translation
reads: "Our boys got together for a little fuss" (p. 70). At the end
of the second act, the watchman says, "Hey you, Zhuchka (*zhúchka*),
Malchik (*málchik*)! Good dogs, you! Zuchka!" (p. 76). The phrase
Good dogs, you, was inserted to identify *Zuchka* and *Malchik* as
nicknames for dogs. In Act III, Sonya says, "It's eating away my
heart and soul" (p. 77). The sentence in Russian reads: "*Èto
takoe stradanie!*" (literally, "It is such suffering!") Typical translations are: Dunnigan, "It's such agony!"; Fen, "It's such a torment!"; Garnett, "That's such agony!"; Hingley, "It's breaking my
heart."; Magarshack, "Oh, I can't bear it!"

Like Ibsen, Chekhov relates every moment in a play to all other
moments in that play, and translators as well as directors should
be wary of cutting, transposing, or "improving" Chekhovian drama.
Constance Garnett, for instance, corrected Lopakhin's misquotations
from *Hamlet*, missing the point that the name *Ophelia* is distorted

9. *Dictionary*, II, 737.   2. *Dictionary*, IV, 260, 1078.
1. Davidson, p. 75.

to incorporate a Russian word meaning, "hops, *intoxication.*" Translators have since corrected Mrs. Garnett, usually giving the Russian name *Okhmeliya*, or substituting an English distortion, "Amelia" (Hingley and Guthrie-Kipnis), or "Aurelia" (Yarmolinsky and Dunnigan). Though they were an overstatement of Chekhov's subtle point and were eventually dismissed, Ronald Hingley's translations illustrate the wittiness intended in the original: "Ophelia—hop along and get thee to a nunnery" and "Nymph, in thy orisons be all my sins—and double gins—remembered."[3]

An important part of Chekhov's milieu resides in the social system of estates and the bureaucratic system associated with the Table of Ranks. Although both systems are discussed in Ronald Hingley's essay "Chekhov's Russia," several major points related to the plays may be made here in regard to the system of estates. In *The Sea Gull*, for example, Treplyov, Arkadina's son, says early in the first act: "I have no talent, no money, and according to my passport, I'm a petty bourgeois from Kiev. My father, you know, belonged to the Kievan petty bourgeoisie, even though he was a famous actor" (p. 9). The estate of the petty bourgeoisie (*meščane*), termed "burghers" by Hingley, consisted of almost 45 percent of the urban population in Russia and was one level above the estate of the peasantry. Something of the bitterness between Arkadina and her son is rooted in the social conflict between estates; even though Arkadina is a member of the gentry, her husband, Treplyov's father, passed on to his son his own socially inferior identification. This aspect of the conflict between mother and son is clearly revealed in their devastating quarrel in Act III (pp. 32–33), wherein each cuts to the very center of the other's personal weakness in a scene that ends with both in tears.

In *The Three Sisters*, one of the major sources of conflict between the sisters and Natasha is the conflict between estates. Both the sisters and their brother Andrey are members of the gentry, whereas Natasha is a member of the petty bourgeoisie (*meščane*). Thus, when Andrey marries Natasha he is marrying far beneath his class, and this action in turn fosters irreconcilable barriers between sisters and brother. At one point in the second act, Masha—in referring to Natasha—cries out, "*Meščanka!*" (a female member of the *meščane*), which has been translated here as "Common fishwife!" (p. 130). In *The Cherry Orchard*, too, the various feeling tones of inferiority, resentment, etc., experienced by Lopakhin—a highly successful businessman although his father and grandfather were serfs on the Ranevskaya estate—reside largely in the social conflict of estates. Gaev, Ranevskaya's brother and a member of the gentry,

3. *The Oxford Chekhov*, tr. and ed. Ronald Hingley (London: Oxford University Press, 1964), III, 335.

scarcely conceals his dislike of Lopakhin. Moreover, the aunt who could save the orchard, Gaev points out, "doesn't care one iota for us. First of all, my sister married a lawyer, not a nobleman" (p. 178).

A language characteristic associated with the socially inferior estates or ranks in the bureaucratic system was the *s* sound. In *Uncle Vanya*, for example, Dr. Astrov says, "Yes, sir, I held her, sir ("*Da-s, obnimal-s*") . . ." (p. 89). The addition of the *s* sound to a word is the effect (in Chekhov's Russia, now considered obsolete) "of giving . . . an inflection of courtesy, deference, or servility or . . . for the expression of a joke, [or] irony."[4] It occurs frequently in Chekhov's work and has been translated, according to sex and marital status, as *sir, ma'am, madam, miss*. In this particular instance in *Uncle Vanya*, as Davidson points out, the effect is "exaggerated politeness, and hence scornful."[5] The *s* sound is also "an abbreviation of *sudar'*," or *sir* (*ma'am*, etc.), as Birkett and Struve explain, "and was often added in the old days by persons of low social standing, especially of the official class, in addressing their superiors; also by servants speaking to their masters."[6]

In translating these plays, I raised questions similar to those raised by a stage director in the pre-rehearsal planning phases and devoted a proportion of time that was more than equal to the time given over to choosing the actual words and their arrangements. That is, I spent more time in understanding the structure of action in each play in the original language—not only by numerous readings but also by listening to, as well as seeing, productions of the plays in Russian. An example or two from each of the four plays may illustrate the process and its results.

In *The Sea Gull*, for example, early in Act I, Treplyov says, "What we need are new forms [in the theatre]. We've got to have new forms. And if there aren't any, then we'd be better off to have nothing at all" (pp. 8–9). Treplyov's arguments for, and dedication to, new forms in theatre have their foundation in the new art and literary movements in Russia at the turn of the century. For example, Vsevelod Meyerhold (1874–1940), who originated the role of Treplyov in the 1898 production by the Moscow Art Theatre, was subsequently a major stage director in the new theatre movement in Russia. A few moments later in Act I, Treplyov's mother, the famous actress Arkadina—in responding to her son's play being enacted—says, "This is something decadent" (p. 13). (The name *decadent* was applied to the very same literary movement of the 1890s that today is usually called *symbolist*.) In Act IV, Treplyov arrives at

4. *Dictionary*, IV, 10.

5. *Dyadya Vanya (Uncle Vanya)*, ed. J. M. C. Davidson (Cambridge, Mass.: Schoenhof's Foreign Books, 1963), p. 100.

6. *Anton Chekhov: Selected Short Stories* (in Russian), ed. G. A. Birkett and Gleb Struve (Oxford: Clarendon Press, 1961), p. 127 .

the first of two major discoveries, i.e., "the issue is neither a question of old nor of new forms, but that a person simply writes, never thinking about the kind of forms, he writes because it pours freely out of his own soul" (p. 47). This major discovery is immediately followed by Nina's *rap on the window*; hence, the subsequent interaction between Nina and Treplyov leads to his second major discovery, i.e., whereas Nina has the makings of a true, productive life in the theatre, he keeps on "drifting in a maelstrom of dreams and images, not knowing why it has to be or for whose sake" (p. 49), and eventually to his final decision to destroy whatever remains of his literature and his own life. As is apparent in *The Sea Gull*, Chekhov was interested in the "decadent" drama, especially in plays by Maurice Maeterlinck (1862–1949) such as *The Blind* (*Les Avengles*, 1890), *The Intruder* (*L'Intruse*, 1890), and *Aglavaine et Selysette* (1896), all of which he had read. However, he apparently dismissed Russian imitators of the new European literary movement. Chekhov is said to have "disapproved of the decadents, calling them insincere clowns, senseless imitators of foreign writers."[7] It seems that in the symbolic uses of the sea gull, the water images, etc., Chekhov was centrally concerned with questions associated with art and literature, and much of what he personally subscribed to in answer to the question of what goes into the makings of art and literature has been incorporated into his play. His use of the lake, for example, is both as emblem and as symbol. At the end of Act I, Dr. Dorn says, "Oh, you bewitching lake!" (p. 18). The lake is the last major agent introduced in this act, according to some critics, who stress the meanings associated with *bewitching* (*koldovskoe*) lake, e.g., witchcraft, magic, and folk legends of good and evil powers.

In *Uncle Vanya*, early in Act I, the old servant Marina says: "Higgledy-piggledy! The professor gets up at twelve o'clock while the samovar's been boiling since morning, the whole time just waiting for him. Without them here, we always ate dinner between twelve and one, like decent people everywhere, but with them here it's after six in the evening. At night the professor reads and writes, and suddenly, after one o'clock in the morning, the bell . . . Good gracious me, what is it? Why, it's tea he's after! So you must wake up people for it, put on the samovar . . . Higgledy-piggledy!" (p. 57). The key word in this speech is, of course, *porjadki*, translated here as *higgledy-piggledy*, or topsy-turvy—the usual order in the normal life of the estate is being turned upside down. Before the old, retired professor and his young and beautiful second wife, Yelena, arrived on the estate (before the play begins), life followed

---

7. Evtixij Karpov, "Dve poslednie vstreči s A. P. Čexovym [Two last encounters with A. P. Chekhov]," in *Čexov i teatr* [Chekhov and theatre], ed. E. D. Surkov (Moscow, 1961), p. 374. (Hereafter cited as *Chekhov and Theatre*.)

its daily routine. Vanya, his mother, and his niece, Sonya, whose dead mother was the professor's first wife, had been working steadily to make the estate a profitable venture for the professor. Dr. Astrov, Vanya's friend and the man Sonya secretly loves, has been a casual visitor to the estate, in order to recoup from his hard work as district physician. After the arrival of the professor and Yelena, abnormal conditions begin to occur, which are further complicated in the course of the play. Coveting the professor's wife, Vanya (he's forty-seven to Yelena's twenty-seven) discovers that his years of work have gone for nought since the professor, an art scholar, for twenty-five years has "been pouring from one empty pot into the next" (p. 58). Vanya has come to the realization that his life is not only practically over but also worthless. His hopes (false) for a meaningful life with Yelena fade with each passing moment. By the second act, in the early-morning hours of the day following that of the first act, Yelena complains to Vanya: "Everything's going to rack and ruin in this house. Your mother hates everything except her pamphlets and the professor. The professor is so completely upset he doesn't trust me, and he's afraid of you. Sonya is irritated with her father, she's irritated with me, and she hasn't talked to me for two whole weeks. You hate my husband, and you openly treat your own mother with contempt. I'm so completely upset I've been ready to cry twenty times today. . . . Everything's going to rack and ruin in this house" (p. 68). The topsy-turvy conditions intensify in the third act, which takes place at one o'clock in the afternoon, when Yelena, on a mission to see if Dr. Astrov loves Sonya (he does not), finds herself being kissed by the doctor. At that moment Vanya enters and is crushed by what he sees. Sonya, a few moments later, learns from Yelena that Astrov does not love her. In the middle of the third act, the professor arrives, having summoned everyone for a conference. "I've invited you here, ladies and gentlemen, to announce that an inspector general is coming to see us" (p. 83). These lines by the professor are a paraphrase of the opening sentence in *The Inspector General* (Revizor, 1836) by Nikolay Gogol (1809–52), and the remainder of Act III is a parallel—at various levels of irony, humor, and frantic activity—of the famous Gogol comedy.

In Gogol's play, the corrupt mayor (*gorodničij*) of a provincial town summons his equally corrupt officials to announce that an inspector general (*revizor*), or an official appointed by the central government to investigate government management in the provinces, is traveling incognito with the aim of making inquiries into their illegal management. An impoverished young clerk from Petersburg is mistaken for the inspector general, is fêted and bribed by the mayor and his officials, and leaves town the next day after writing a letter describing the mistaken identity. His letter is brought by the postmaster to the other officials, who, shocked by the disclosure, begin to tally up their losses. Their activity is cut short by the entrance of a gendarme who announces the arrival of the real inspector general.

Among many interpretations of Gogol's play, Vladimir Nabokov's is perhaps the most provocative, and sheds light on Chekhov's third-act parallel in *Uncle Vanya*. "Gogol's play is poetry in action, and by poetry I mean the mysteries of the irrational as perceived through rational words. True poetry of that kind provokes—not laughter and not tears—but a radiant smile of perfect satisfaction, a purr of beatitude—and a writer may well be proud of himself if he can make his readers, or more exactly some of his readers, smile and purr that way."[8] "The play begins with a blinding flash of lightning and ends in a thunderclap," Nabokov goes on to say. "In fact it is wholly placed in the tense gap between the flash and the crash."[9] In a similar way, the last half of Act III in *Uncle Vanya* begins with a flash of lightning, i.e., with the professor's announcement that he plans to sell the estate, and ends in a thunderclap, when Vanya twice fires a gun at the professor and misses both times. And the frantic and humorous activity of the major characters in Chekhov's comedy resembles the frantic and humorous activity of the major characters in Gogol's comedy.

At the opening of Act I of *The Three Sisters*, the sisters are on stage: Masha, in a black dress, is seated reading a book; Irina, dressed in white, stands lost in thought; Olga, wearing the dark blue uniform dress of a teacher, is correcting student exercise books and is walking to and fro. It is noon. Olga speaks the opening lines: "Father died exactly one year ago, on this very day, the fifth of May, on your saint's day, Irina. It was bitter cold, it was snowing at the time. I felt as if I could never live through it. You had fainted, and you lay there as though dead. And yet, and yet a year has gone by, it's easier to look back on it now. You've even started wearing white, and your face is radiant. [*The clock strikes twelve.*]" (p. 103). In this play, often considered by critics as Chekhov's best work, it is apparent from the opening, as well as from subsequent, moments that Chekhov is centrally concerned with duration and time in terms not only of definition and measurement but also of the nature of existence itself. References to calendars, dates, days, hours, time of day and night, seasons of the year, together with actual clocks and watches, are threaded aurally and visually, together with the mutability and rhythm of characters, actions, language, into the space and time art that a play in performance is. The daily rituals of eating, drinking, interacting combine with the larger rituals associated with

8. Vladimir Nabokov, *Nikolai Gogol* 55. (New York: New Directions, 1944), p.   9. Ibid., p. 42.

individual rites of passage: celebration of a saint's day in the first act; recent births (Bobik between the first and second acts, Sofya between the second and third acts); and death (Tuzenbakh in the fourth act). Group rituals occur throughout, including a rite of intensification in Act II (Carnival Week), as well as that of fighting the town fire in Act III, and the arrival (Act I) and departure (Act IV) of the soldiers. Characters try to capture moments and events; in effect, they try to stop or alter the inexorable flow of time with photography (first and fourth acts), with memories of the past and dreams of the future, with the fleeting human emotional states of love, jealousy, hate, friendship. And by the same means, the characters attempt to reassure themselves and others of their identities and of their very existence.

The periods of time, as well as the locale and space, covered in the play, are rather complex. For my translation and production of the play in 1970, I set forth the following in the program notes:

Act One. Drawing room in the Prozorov house. Twelve o'clock noon. Spring of 1897.

Act Two. Same as in Act One. Eight o'clock in the evening. Winter of 1899.

Act Three. Room shared by Olga and Irina in the Prozorov house. Between two and three o'clock in the morning. Summer of 1900.

Act Four. The old garden outside the Prozorov house. Twelve o'clock noon. Autumn of 1900.

Whereas one period of time covered in the whole play is about three and a half years, another period could span but one year in that all four seasons of the year (one for each act) are depicted. A third period of time may also be interpreted as lasting only twenty-four hours: from noon on the first day to eight o'clock that night, to between two and three o'clock the next morning, and finally to noon of the second day. The change of locale, too, begins with the security of the drawing room at high noon (and the happiness of a saint's day party), shifts to less space at night (and the disappointment of a cancelled celebration), then moves to even less space (a bedroom) in the early-morning hours (and a fire that may destroy the town), and finally ends outside the house (and outside the security of home) at high noon (and the farewell parting of friends).

Early in Act I of *The Cherry Orchard*, Anya (the daughter of Ranevskaya) and Varya (Ranevskaya's adopted daughter) are alone on stage.

ANYA. Well, then, how are things going here? Have you paid the interest [on the estate]?

VARYA. Not a chance in the world.

ANYA. Dear God in heaven, dear God . . .
VARYA. The estate will be sold in August . . .
ANYA. Dear God in heaven . . .
LOPAKHIN. [*looks in through the door and bleats like a calf*] Meh-meh-meh . . . [*Goes out.*] [p. 169]

Critical opinions, as well as directorial interpretations, concerning Lopakhin's action at this moment are varied. The usual directorial interpretation has been to give Lopakhin some kind of realistic motivation and action to perform, e.g., Lopakhin enters dragging a trunk through the room. Then, too, directors sometimes simply cut the lines and action. Some critics, like David Magarshack, interpret this moment in terms of psychology and realistic intent. That is, Lopakhin, feeling like "a pig's nozzle showing up in a row of wedding cakes" (p. 166), has arrived at the estate with a plan to save the orchard from the auction block. Thus, he overhears the conversation of the sisters, and (in Magarshack's words) "is unable to control his excitement and, thrusting his head in at the door, bleats to show his contempt for their search for a solution of the problem that he believes he has solved already."[1] Other critics, like Harvey Pitcher, view this moment as typical of one Chekhovian technique, i.e., comic deformalization. That is, just prior to Lopakhin's bleating, the tone of the dialogue is serious, troubled; whereas, with Lopakhin's sudden bleating the tone changes immediately to a moment of frivolity, piquancy. Thus, the bleating, in Pitcher's words, "deformalizes the dialogue; it varies the emotional key."[2]

During the second act of *The Cherry Orchard*, which takes place outside near an old chapel, Lyubov Andreevna Ranevskaya and her brother Gaev (owners of the estate), Anya, Trofimov (a student and friend), Varya, Lopakhin, and Firs (the old servant) have all gathered, just after the sun has set.

All are sitting, deep in thought. Silence. All that can be heard is FIRS, *who mumbles quietly. Suddenly a sound is heard far off in the distance, as if coming from the sky. It is the sound of a string breaking that dies away sadly.*
LYUBOV ANDREEVNA. What was that?
LOPAKHIN. I don't know. Somewhere far off in the mines a bucket must have broken loose. But it's somewhere far, far away.
GAEV. Perhaps it was a bird of some kind . . . like a heron.
TROFIMOV. Or an eagle owl . . .
LYUBOV ANDREEVNA. [*shudders*] It was unpleasant, and I don't know why. [Pause.]

1. Magarshack, Preface to *Chekhov the Dramatist*, p. x.
2. Harvey Pitcher, *The Chekhov Play; A New Interpretation* (New York: Harper & Row, 1972), p. 170.

FIRS. It was just the same before the troubles—and the owl kept hooting and the samovar humming without stopping. [p. 188]

The sound, which is repeated at the end of the last act (p. 211), is discussed at some length by the characters on-stage, each giving his or her own interpretation (Anya, for example, weeps). Thus, when the sound recurs it has adequately been prepared for interpretation by the reader or audience. Moreover, the effect was used by Chekhov in several short stories, and the sound itself apparently was heard by Chekhov in his youth when he lived in the Donets Basin, "the mining area of Russia, where a bucket falling in a distant mine-shaft would produce this strangely evocative sound."[3] Although numerous precise meanings have been given to this sound effect, it seems perhaps that Chekhov did not aim for specificity. In his letter to Olga Knipper-Chekhova (his wife), dated March 18, 1904, Chekhov advised: "Tell Nemirovich [one of the directors of the Moscow Art Theatre] that the sound in Acts Two and Four of *The Cherry Orchard* must be shorter, a great deal shorter, and the feeling must be as though from a great distance. What a lot of bother about nothing, not being able to come to an understanding with a trifle, with a sound, although it's described so clearly in the play."[4] As to the causes of emotions in these four plays, Elder Olson's description of the four classes was particularly helpful. "(1) the precedent context, not of words merely, but of the action as a whole up to a given point; (2) the particular speech-action, together with its implications; (3) the speech as diction; (4) ornament."[5] My chief concern, then, in the initial phases of translation dealt more with the first two classes than the last two. In short, "seeing the point" of each moment in the script was my primary goal.

Moreover, my task was to give—moment by moment in each play—as many options for interpretation in English as are similarly created by Chekhov in the Russian. For example, Treplyov's uncle in *The Sea Gull* has speech habits peculiar to the nature of his character, e.g., the consistent repetition of certain hackneyed phrases —translated as "it's perfectly clear," "and all that sort of thing," or "when all's said and done"—a characteristic mode that is perhaps reminiscent of his former bureaucratic life in the civil service, as well as related to his age, to the kinds of questions he raises, to the decisions he makes, etc. Even though it was tempting to give Sorin greater variety in his choice of words—thus, making his speeches more "readable" or "interesting"—care was taken to keep his repetitions consistent in translation and, in this way, provide equivalent options for interpretation in English as are given in the Russian.

3. *Ibid.*, pp. 182, 218.
4. *Complete Works*, XX, 251.
5. Olson, pp. 71–72.

Another example that comes readily to mind is the repetitious phrase *"vsë ravno"* (translated as "it doesn't matter") in *The Three Sisters*. The phrase itself, together with its variants, is said over thirty times, becoming—by the end of the play—a major musical theme. Again, consistency in translation was essential to making Chekhov's point in English.

The choice of words and their arrangement, Elder Olson's third and fourth classes, was governed (once consistency in the first and second classes was observed) by the aim of approximating in English the colloquial or standard expression found in the original. No attempt was made to use English appropriate to the last century, and the latest slang was avoided. The guiding principle was to approximate in modern English the tone and feeling of each character as conditioned by his or her action and intention. All Russian personal and place names were retained, as were German, Latin, and French words, phrases, and sentences.[6]

Moreover, the Russian conventions of punctuation have been rather consistently followed. This is especially true in instances pertaining to Chekhov's notorious suspensions (. . .) that are liberally deployed. Although some translators like Ronald Hingley have omitted all these dots—he has noted that when the dots have been retained, "there are occasions when the page of a translated text appears to be suffering from a severe attack of measles"[7]—I believe that these Chekhovian dots have both point and purpose and are significantly related to both structure and character, as well as to language and thought. Ronald Hingley may see "measles," but I see impressionism, almost pointillism. I did not follow, however, the principle Stark Young employed in his translations of Chekhov's *The Three Sisters*: "Let Chekhov . . . have it his own way—let him, for example, repeat a word when he chooses to repeat it, invert the word-order when he chooses, and so on."[8] Had I followed this principle with Chekhov, the points in the original would easily have been lost in the English.

Throughout the plays I have kept certain elements as signs to the reader or to the audience that the scene is indeed Russian, not midwest American. The chief element is the transliteration of personal and place names as they appear in the original. To keep the flavor of the original in production, however, the actors should be trained to pronounce the names in phonetically accurate Russian. The Russian language has numerous variants of personal names which reveal

6. See "A Note on Transliteration and Pronunciation," above.
7. Hingley, p. xvii.
8. Stark Young, "Chekhov in Translation," in Anton Chekhov, *The Three Sisters*, tr. Stark Young (New York: Samuel French, 1941), p. vii.

the attitude of the speaker toward the person he refers to, and I have indicated in the textual notes the various nuances associated with the names. Even though such nuances will generally be lost on audiences who do not know Russian, the actors may make up something of the difference by characterizing the attitudes.

Essentially, my goal has been to search for a style, or a manner, that translates the distinctive Russian elements in Chekhovian drama into terms appropriate to American theatrical art. Part of the magnificence of his drama resides in its special Russian quality, and his style—in translation—perhaps depends ultimately upon the proper fusion of convention and point. Moreover, I am convinced that "naturalizing" his plays, or coming up with American or British images in place of the Russian, produces elements that diminish his powers of dramatic art. The way to Chekhov's Russia is neither the Brighton Line nor the New York Central, and the translator buying either ticket will reach Moscow about as fast as the three sisters.

The past months with Chekhov's plays have given me the pleasure of seeing into Chekhov's world, and whatever new insights these translations provide may be attributed to my being "exposed to the *lues Boswelliana,* or disease of admiration."[9] Few playwrights can match Chekhov's genius, exceed his vision, or speak with greater clarity to our age.

9. T. B. Macaulay, review of *A History of the Right Honourable William Pitt . . .* by Francis Thackeray (London, 1827), in *The Edinburgh Review,* 58 (January 1834), 508.

The Texts of
The Plays

The Sea Gull

Three short stories by Chekhov have been cited by critics as closely related to *The Sea Gull: A Dreary Story* (1891), *My Life* (1896), and *Ionych* (1898). In the first-named story, the Nina plot line is clearly related, whereas the second and third stories supply an environment similar to the background of the action in *The Sea Gull*. That is, the universe of a provincial intelligentsia is depicted, wherein the chief interest of the characters is focused on literature and the theatre. Other sources that Chekhov apparently drew upon are Shakespeare's *Hamlet* (discussed in an essay by Thomas G. Winner in this volume), *The Wild Duck* (1884) by Henrik Ibsen (1828–1906), Guy de Maupassant (1850–93), and autobiographical incidents in the author's life.

The association of Nina with the dead sea gull suggests, critics point out, a parody of Ibsen's play; Donald Rayfield, however, sees this association also as a "parody of Trigorin's way of poeticizing the ugliness of reality."[1] That is, if Nina is cast in the role of the sea gull, or victim, then Trigorin need not consider her a human being. Guy de Maupassant is twice referred to in the play: first, Treplyov notes the French author's response upon first seeing the Eiffel Tower (p. 8); second, in Act II, Dr. Dorn and then Arkadina read aloud from Maupassant's personal writings, *On the Water* (*Sur l'eau*, 1888). Maupassant's work is an account of a sailing trip along the Mediterranean coast, during which he jotted down what he saw and what he thought. Arkadina takes over the reading from *On the Water*. " 'And it stands to reason that for society people to mollycoddle novelists and to lure them into their homes is just as dangerous as for the corn merchant to breed rats in his storehouses. . . . Thus, when a woman has picked out a novelist whom she desires to capture, she engulfs him by means of compliments, adulation, and favors . . .' " (p. 19). Arkadina stops reading and contends that Russian women are different from the French (her own paramour, Trigorin the writer, is not far away), in that the former are always madly in love with the writer. When Nina enters, Arkadina reads several lines to herself and then reports that "the next isn't one bit interesting or even true" (p. 20). What Arkadina does not read aloud from *On the Water* is a fairly accurate description of her own relationship with Trigorin. "Like water which, drop by drop, cuts through the hardest rock, praise tumbles down at every word on the susceptible heart of the man of letters. Then, as soon as she perceives that he is touched, moved, won over by this constant flattery, she isolates him, she severs bit by bit all his ties he may have elsewhere, and imperceptibly she gets him accustomed to come to her place, to make him pleased to be there, and to install his thoughts there."[2]

1. *Chekhov; The Evolution of his Art* (London: Elek Books, 1975), p. 205.
2. Guy de Maupassant, *Oeuvres Com-* pletes (Paris: L'édition d'art H. Piazza, 1968), XIII, 169.

Events in Chekhov's own life, biographers delight in pointing out, bear directly on several incidents and characters in the play. The origin of the shot sea gull was apparently closely connected to an actual event that took place in April 1892; during a hunting trip with his friend Isaac Levitan, the impressionist painter, Chekhov was forced to kill a woodcock that had been winged by Levitan. The first suicide attempt by Treplyov seems related to the suicide attempt by Levitan, to whose bedside the author hastened in October 1895. There, on an estate in the Novgorod area, about two hundred miles from the Finnish Gulf, Chekhov had the opportunity of viewing a large lake with a number of sea gulls.

When the character Trigorin jots down in his notebook an idea for a story, "A man happens to come by, sees her and, having nothing else to do, destroys her like that sea gull there" (p. 28), the story line seems connected to an actual event: I. N. Potapenko, the writer, and Chekhov's friend, Lika Mizinova, had a love affair which resulted in the birth of a child. Critics emphasize, however, that the resemblance between the Nina-Trigorin story line and the Mizinova-Potapenko life event does not necessarily mean that the characters in the play are modeled on the persons in life. In fact, Trigorin's attitude toward the art and craft of writing is much closer to that of Chekhov himself than to Potapenko's. The incident of Nina's gift to Trigorin, the medallion with the inscription (p. 29), probably came from a similar event in Chekhov's own life, involving his friend Lydia Avilova.[3] Another young woman with whom Chekhov was acquainted, the actress Lydia Yavorskaya, has been suggested as the prototype for Arkadina. Chekhov not only praised her work at the Korsh Theatre but also helped to advance her career.[4]

Two or three references to the theatre of Chekhov's day are explained here. Early in Act I the young writer Treplyov, in describing his mother's career, says: "but just try and praise Duse in her presence. . . . And you'd better go to into ecstasies over her incredible acting in *The Lady with the Camellias* or in *The Fumes of Life*" (p. 8). Duse was the Italian actress Eleanora Duse (1859–1924), who was internationally ranked among the best actresses of her time. The first-named play, best known as *Camille*, by Alexandre Dumas *fils* (1824–95), was first produced in 1852. Its innumerable productions throughout Europe and America during the nineteenth century, as well as its frequent revivals in this century, proved popular not only with audiences but also with countless theatre managers and actresses. *The Fumes of Life* was dramatized by Boleslav Mikhaylovich Markevich (1822–84) from his own novel, *The Abyss*. Originally produced by Mikhail Valentinovich Lentovsky (1843–1906), the drama, in Chekhov's own view, was written "with a broom and smells badly."[5]

As in all his works, Chekhov usually selected the names of his characters in terms of their bent or disposition (and sometimes in terms of his own

3. For a description of Chekhov's relationship with Lydia Avilova, see Ernest J. Simmons, *Chekhov: A Biography* (Boston: Little, Brown, 1962), passim; and Ronald J. Hingley, *A New Life of Anton Chekhov* (New York: Alfred A. Knopf, 1976).

4. T. L. Shchepkina-Kupernik, "O Chekhova" [On Chekhov], in *Chekhov and Theatre*, p. 243.

5. *Chekhov and Theatre*, pp. 188–89, 381.

attitude toward the characters)—a tradition in dramatic literature that dates from the ancient Greek and Roman drama. For example, Nina's name, *Zarechnaya*, incorporates in Russian the meaning of "over" or "beyond the river"; hence, the first verbal reference to Nina (p. 6) connects her to the water image in the play. Her first name is a variant of the Hebrew name *Hannah* "full of grace, mercy, and prayer." *Konstantin* is related to the Latin name meaning "unwavering" or "firm," whereas his last name incorporates the root of a Russian verb with a series of related meanings, chief of which are: "flutter," "blow around," "wear out," "fray," "prattle," "talk nonsense."

The pronunciation of the characters' names, together with the appropriate stress:

Iŕna Nikolaevna (nikaláevna) Arkádina, by marriage Treplyóva
Konstantin (kanstantín) Gavrilovich (gavrílavich) (Gavrílych) Treplyov (treplyóf)
Pyótr (Petrúsha) Nikolaevich (nikaláevich) Sórin
Nína Mikhaylovna (mikháylavna) Zaréchnaya
Ilyá Afanásevich Shamraev (shamráef)
Polina (palína) Andréevna
Másha, Márya (Máshenka) Ilínishna
Borís Alexéevich Tregórin
Yevgény Sergéevich (Sergéich) Dorn
Semyón Semyonovich (semyónavich) Medvedenko (medvédenka)
Yakov (yákaf)

Other personal and place names (in alphabetical order) in the play: Grokholsky (grakhólsky); Izmailov (izmáilaf); Kharkov (khárkaf); Matryóna; Molchanovka (malchánafka); Slavyánsky; Suzdaltsev (súzdaltsef); Trezór; Turgenev (turgénef); Yeléts; Yelisavetgrad (yelisavetgrát).

The Sea Gull

A Comedy in Four Acts

LIST OF CHARACTERS

IRINA NIKOLAEVNA ARKADINA, *by marriage Treplyova, an actress*
KONSTANTIN GAVRILOVICH TREPLYOV, *her son, a young man*
PYOTR NIKOLAEVICH SORIN, *her brother*
NINA MIKHAYLOVNA ZARECHNAYA, *a young girl, daughter of a rich landowner*
ILYA AFANASEVICH SHAMRAEV, *a retired army lieutenant, manager of Sorin's estate*
POLINA ANDREEVNA, *his wife*
MASHA, *her daughter*
BORIS ALEXEEVICH TRIGORIN, *a novelist*
YEVGENY SERGEEVICH DORN, *a doctor*
SEMYON SEMYONOVICH MEDVEDENKO, *a schoolteacher*
YAKOV, *a workman*
A COOK
A MAIDSERVANT

The action takes place on SORIN's *country estate. Between the third and fourth acts there is an interval of two years.*

Act One

Part of the park on SORIN's *estate. A broad avenue leads from the view of the audience into the depths of the park toward a lake. A platform stage—pieced together and hastily built for a home performance—has been placed across the avenue in such a way that the lake cannot be seen. To the left and right of the platform stage is shrubbery. There are a few chairs and a small table. The sun has just set.* YAKOV *and other workmen are on the platform stage behind the lowered stage curtain. The sounds of coughing and hammering can be heard.* MASHA *and* MEDVEDENKO, *returning from a stroll, enter from the left.*

MEDVEDENKO. Why is it you always wear black?
MASHA. Because I'm in mourning for my life. I'm unhappy.
MEDVEDENKO. And why? [*Deep in thought.*] I don't understand it . . . You enjoy good health, and even if your father isn't wealthy, still he's pretty well-to-do. Why, my life is far more difficult than yours. I receive a sum total of twenty-three rubles a month—and don't forget you must then deduct my payment to the pension

5

fund—but I still don't go around in mourning. [*They sit down.*]

MASHA. It isn't a question of money. Even a poor man can be happy.

MEDVEDENKO. That's in theory, but in practice it turns out like this. There's my mother, two sisters, my little brother, and me—all on a salary totaling twenty-three rubles. We have to eat and drink, don't we? We must have tea and sugar, don't you think? And what about tobacco? Just try and wriggle out of that one.

MASHA. [*looking around at the platform stage*] The play is going to start soon.

MEDVEDENKO. Yes. Zarechnaya will be acting, and the play was written by Konstantin Gavrilovich. They are in love with each other. And tonight their souls will unite in their striving to render one and the same artistic creation. But my soul and yours have no mutual points of contact. I love you, my longing for you is so deep I can't bear to stay home, and so every day I walk six versts[1] here and six versts back. And what do I get from you? Only complete indifference. Well, it makes sense. I don't have money, my family is large . . . Who's willing to marry a man who doesn't have enough to eat himself?

MASHA. Stuff and nonsense. [*Takes snuff.*] Your love touches me, but I can't love you in return—that's all. [*Holding out her snuff box to him.*] Help yourself.

MEDVEDENKO. I don't feel like it. [*Pause.*]

MASHA. It's so muggy. I imagine there'll be a thunderstorm tonight. You either philosophize or talk about money the whole time. According to you, there's no greater misfortune than poverty. As far as I'm concerned, it's a thousand times easier to go in rags and live as a beggar than . . . However, you'll never understand that . . .

SORIN *and* TREPYLOV *enter from the right.*

SORIN. [*leaning on his walking stick*] Living in the country is somehow wrong for me, dear boy, and it's perfectly clear I'll never get used to it. Last night I went to sleep at ten o'clock and woke up this morning at nine, feeling—just from sleeping too long—as if my brains were pasted to my skull and all that sort of thing. [*Laughs.*] And after dinner I accidentally fell asleep again, and now every joint in my body aches. I feel as if I'm going through a nightmare, when all's said and done . . .

TREPLYOV. True, you ought to live in town. [*Having seen* MASHA *and* MEDVEDENKO.] My good people, when the play begins we'll call you, but you shouldn't be here now. Go away, please.

SORIN. [*to* MASHA] Marya Ilinichna, be kind and ask your dear Papa to give orders that the dog be turned loose. Otherwise, it howls. My sister didn't sleep the whole night again.

---

1. A former Russian unit of measurement, the equivalent of about thirty-five hundred feet.

MASHA. You can tell my father yourself, because I won't talk to him. Don't ask me to, please. [*To* MEDVEDENKO.] Let's go!

MEDVEDENKO. [*to* TREPLYOV] You be sure and tell us, won't you, before it begins.

MEDVEDENKO *and* MASHA *go out.*

SORIN. Well, it means that dog will howl the night long again. That's the way the story goes, you see. I've never lived the way I'd like to in the country. Oh, I used to take a twenty-eight-day leave and come here to get some rest and that's all there is to it. No sooner did I get here than they'd start nagging me to death with all sorts of nonsense, so that from the first day on I felt like clearing out. [*Laughs.*] I've always gone away from here feeling tremendously pleased . . . Well, now that I'm retired, there's no other place to go to, when all's said and done. Like it or not, you must live . . .

YAKOV. [*to* TREPLYOV] Konstantin Gavrilych, we're on our way for a swim.

TREPLYOV. All right, just come back and be in your places in ten minutes. [*Looks at his watch.*] We are going to begin shortly.

YAKOV. Yes, sir. [*Goes out.*]

TREPLYOV. [*taking in the sage at a glance*] See, that's a theatre for you. The curtain, the first set of wings, the second set, and beyond that—open space. No scenery at all. You have a clear and open view of both the lake and the horizon. The curtain goes up at eight-thirty sharp, just as the moon is rising.

SORIN. Magnificent.

TREPLYOV. If Zarechnaya is late, then, of course, the whole effect will be wasted. She should be here, it's time. Her father and stepmother keep watch over her, and getting out of her own home is as hard for her as breaking out of prison. [*Adjusts his uncle's necktie.*] Your hair and beard look disheveled. You ought to have a trim, wouldn't you say . . .

SORIN. [*combing his beard*] The tragedy of my life. When I was young I looked the same. As if I did nothing but drink—and that's all there is to it. And women never cared one whit for me. [*Sitting down.*] Why is my sister in a bad mood?

TREPLYOV. Why? She's bored. [*Sitting down beside him.*] Jealous. She's already turned against me, against the performance, and against my play because she isn't acting in it, and Zarechnaya is. She doesn't even know my play, but she already hates it.

SORIN. [*laughs*] You sure can make things up, really . . .

TREPLYOV. Look, she's already annoyed that on this tiny stage Zarechnaya is going to score a success, not she. [*Having looked at his watch.*] My mother—the psychological joke. There's no question she's talented, she's intelligent, she's capable of sobbing her eyes out over a little book, she can rattle off all of Nekrasov[2] by heart for you, she'll care for someone who's sick like an angel—but just try and praise Duse in her presence. Oh my, oh my! You must praise her—and her alone—you must write about her and shout it to the skies. And you'd better go into ecstasies over her incredible acting in *The Lady with the Camellias* or in *The Fumes of Life.* But because she's here in the country, where there's none of this narcotic praise, she is bored and angry, so we are all her enemies, we are all to blame. At the same time she's superstitious, afraid of three lighted candles[3] and the number thirteen. And she's as tightfisted as they come. She has seventy thousand rubles in a bank in Odessa[4]—I know this for a fact. But try to get a loan from her, and she'll break down and cry.

SORIN. You've got it in your head that your mother isn't going to like your play, and you're getting all upset and that's all there is to it. Calm down. Your mother adores you.

TREPLYOV. [*tearing off the petals of a flower*] She loves me, she loves me not, she loves me, she loves me not, she loves me, she loves me not. [Laughs] You see, my mother does not love me. Why, of course! She wants a life to live, to fall in love, to wear brightly colored blouses, and here I am—twenty-five years old and I constantly remind her she is no longer a young woman. When I'm not around, she's only thirty-two. But if I am around, she is forty-three, and that's why she hates me. What's more, she knows I refuse to accept the theatre. She loves the theatre and thinks she is serving mankind and the sacred purpose of art, but in my opinion the theatre of today is in a rut, engrained with conventionalism. When the curtain rises on a room with three walls, illuminated by artificial light, and we see those great talented artists, those priests and priestesses of a sacred art, depict how people eat, drink, love, walk around, and wear their jackets. When out of deadly scenes and shallow phrases they try to fish up a moral —a tiny, comfortable, easy-to-grasp moral, useful for consumption in the home. When in a thousand different ways they go on treating me to one and the same thing over and over and over again—then I run and I keep on running, just as Maupassant ran away from the Eiffel Tower, which choked his brains with its vulgarity.

SORIN. It's impossible to do without the theatre.

TREPLYOV. What we need are new forms. We've got to have

2. N. A. Nekrasov (pronounced *nekrásaf*) (1821–78) idealized the Russian peasantry in his poems, expressing the essence of the poverty, suffering, and nobility in their lives.
3. A fairly widespread superstition: if three lights (be they candles, lamps, or torches) are burning, one must be snuffed out; otherwise, misfortune will occur; moreover, this practice is especially observed by actors and actresses.
4. Odessa (*adéssa*), the most significant Black Sea port in tsarist Russia, was the fourth largest city in population by 1897 and was known as a good theatre town.

new forms. And if there aren't any, then we'd be better off to have nothing at all. [*Looks at his watch.*] I love my mother, deeply love her, but she leads a rattlebrained life, forever flitting here and there with that novelist, and her name is always being dragged through the newspapers—and all this wears me out. Sometimes when I simply feel selfish like any ordinary human being, then I'm sorry my mother is a famous actress, and I think I'd be a much happier person if she were an ordinary woman. Imagine if you can, Uncle, a more absurd and desperate situation than this. As it's usually happened, only celebrities would be her guests, actors and writers, and in their midst was I—a nobody, and they put up with me only because I'm her son. But who am I really? What am I? I left the university in my third year "owing to circumstances," as the editors say in the newspapers, "over which we have no control." I have no talent, no money, and according to my passport, I'm a petty bourgeois from Kiev.[5] My father, you know, belonged to the Kievan petty bourgeoisie, even though he was a famous actor. And there you have it. As it's usually happened, when all those actors and writers in her drawing room were kind enough to pay attention to me, I felt they were simply measuring the degree of my insignificance—I would guess what they were thinking—and suffered deeply from humiliation . . .

SORIN. By the way, please tell me what kind of person this novelist is. I can't figure him out. He never says anything.

TREPLYOV. He's an intelligent person, simple, dropping somewhat —you know—into melancholia. Very decent, really. He's a good deal under forty, but he's already famous and chock-full of everything he wants . . . As far as his writing goes . . . well, how can I put it? Winsome, gifted . . . but . . . after Tolstoy or Zola[6] you'd never feel like reading Trigorin.

SORIN. But I love literary people, dear boy. Time was I desperately wanted two things out of life. I wanted to get married, and I wanted to become a writer, and I haven't managed to do one or the other. Yes. If you're only a minor writer, it must feel gratifying, when all's said and done.

TREPLYOV. [*listens*] I hear footsteps . . . [*Embraces his uncle.*] I can't live without her . . . Even the sound of her footsteps is beautiful . . . I'm happy, madly happy. [*Goes quickly to meet* NINA ZARECHNAYA, *who is entering.*] My enchanting darling, dream of my life . . .

NINA. [*agitatedly*] Oh, I'm not late . . . Surely, I'm not late . . .

TREPLYOV. [*kissing her hands*] No, no, no . . .

NINA. I've been upset and worried the whole day, and I've felt terribly frightened! I was afraid my·father wouldn't let me go . . . But

---

5. Kiev (*kief*), on the Dnieper River, ranked seventh in urban population at the end of the nineteenth century.

6. L. N. Tolstoy (1828–1910), the Russian writer; Émile Zola (1840–1902), the French novelist.

just now he went out with my stepmother. The sky was red, the moon was starting to come up, and I drove my horse hard, fast, as fast as I could. [*Laughs.*] I'm glad, so glad that I did. [*Presses* SORIN's *hand warmly.*]

SORIN. [*laughs*] Your eyes look as if you'd been crying . . . Aha, aha! That's not right!

NINA. It's fine . . . You see how hard it is for me to breathe. I'll leave in half an hour. I must hurry. I can't stay any longer, I can't. For God's sake don't try and keep me. My father doesn't even know I'm here.

TREPLYOV. In fact it's time to begin. We must go and call everyone.

SORIN. I'll go and that's all there is to it. This very minute. [*Goes to the right, singing.*] "Into France two grenadiers . . ."[7] [*Looks around.*] Once I started to sing like that, and a certain assistant public prosecutor said to me, "Your Excellency,[8] you have a strong voice . . ." Then he thought it over and added "But . . . disgusting." [*Laughs and goes out.*]

NINA. My father and his wife won't let me come here. They say this place is Bohemian . . . They're frightened I might become an actress . . . But I ache to return to this lake, as if I were a sea gull. . . . My heart is full, so full of you. [*Looks around.*]

TREPLYOV. We are completely alone.

NINA. I thought I heard someone . . .

TREPLYOV. No one. [*A kiss.*]

NINA. What kind of tree is this?

TREPLYOV. An elm.

NINA. Why is it so dark?

TREPLYOV. Night has come. Everything is growing dark. Don't go away so early, I implore you.

NINA. I can't stay.

TREPLYOV. What if I came to your place, Nina? I'd stand in the orchard all night long and look at your window.

NINA. You couldn't possibly, the night watchman would see you. Trezor still isn't used to you and he'd start barking.

TREPLYOV. I love you.

NINA. Tss . . .

TREPLYOV. [*having heard footsteps*] Who's there? Is it you, Yakov?

YAKOV. [*behind the stage*] Yes, sir.

TREPLYOV. Get in your places, everyone. It's time. Is the moon rising?

YAKOV. Yes, sir.

TREPLYOV. Do you have the methylated spirits? And the sulfur? When the red eyes appear, there has to be a smell of sulfur. [*To*

---

7. *Die Grenadiere* by Heinrich Heine (1797–1856), music by Robert Schumann (1810–56).

8. "Your Excellency," the form of address used to Sorin by a subordinate, is an indication of the high rank in the civil service, equivalent to the rank of major general in the military, attained by Sorin before his retirement.

NINA.] You can go now. Everything's all set. Do you feel nervous? . .

NINA. Yes, very. I'm not afraid of your mother. She's all right. What terrifies me is Trigorin . . . I feel so ashamed acting in front of him . . . A famous writer . . . Is he young?

TREPLYOV. Yes.

NINA. Oh, his stories are marvelous!

TREPLYOV. [*coldly*] I don't know, I've never read them.

NINA. It's so difficult to act in your play. There are no living characters in it, none.

TREPLYOV. Living characters! You mustn't depict life as it is, or as it should be, but life as it appears in your dreams.

NINA. There's very little action in your play. It's just reading lines. And I believe a play must certainly have love in it . . . [*They both go behind the platform stage.*]

  POLINA ANDREEVNA *and* DORN *enter.*

POLINA ANDREEVNA. It's getting damp. Go back and put on your galoshes.

DORN. It's too hot for me.

POLINA ANDREEVNA. You don't take care of yourself. And it's simply stubbornness. You are a doctor, and you know perfectly well that damp air is harmful to you, but you just want to make me feel miserable. Yesterday you willfully kept sitting outside on the veranda the whole evening long . . .

DORN. [*singing*] "Don't ever say that our youth is wasted."

POLINA ANDREEVNA. You were so carried away in talking with Irina Nikolaevna . . . you didn't even notice how cold it was. You might as well own up to it, you like her . . .

DORN. I'm fifty-five years old.

POLINA ANDREEVNA. Stuff and nonsense. That isn't old for a man. You are so beautifully preserved that women still fall for you.

DORN. Then what is it you want me to do?

POLINA ANDREEVNA. You're all more than ready to fall on your knees before an actress. Everyone of you!

DORN. [*singing*] "Once again I stand before you . . ." If artists are well loved by society and are treated differently from, let's say, people in business, then that's in the order of things. It's called idealism.

POLINA ANDREEVNA. Women have constantly fallen in love with you. They've always thrown themselves at you. Do you call that idealism, too?

DORN. [*having shrugged his shoulders*] Well, hmm?[9] There's been a lot that was good in our relationship—women's and mine. What they loved mostly about me was the fact I'm a first-rate physician. Ten or fifteen years ago, you remember, I was the only decent

---

9. The expression *čto ž*, translated here as "well, hmm," usually incorporates a physical movement such as shrugging the shoulders.

obstetrician in the whole district. And then I've always been an honest person.

POLINA ANDREEVNA. [*seizes him by the hand*] Oh, my darling!

DORN. Not so loud. Someone's coming here.

ARKADINA, *arm-in-arm with* SORIN, TRIGORIN, SHAMRAEV, MEDVEDENKO, *and* MASHA *enter.*

SHAMRAEV. Her acting was simply amazing. I saw her at the fair in Poltava[1] in 1873, and it was pure ecstasy! Absolutely marvelous acting! Would you mind letting me know where the comic actor Chadin is now, Pavel Semyonych Chadin? When he played Rasplyuev he was simply inimitable. Better even than Sadovsky,[2] I swear he was, my dear honored lady. Where is he now?

ARKADINA. You're forever asking about all sorts of antediluvians. How on earth should I know where they've gone to! [*Sits down.*]

SHAMRAEV. [*having sighed*] Pashka Chadin! Oh, there's no one acting today who's even comparable. The stage has gone downhill, Irina Nikolaevna! In times gone by there were mighty oak trees, but we see only tree stumps today.

DORN. That's true, there are very few actors gifted with brilliance nowadays, but the average actor today is much, much better than he used to be.

SHAMRAEV. I just can't agree with you. Oh, well, it's all a question of taste anyway. *De gustibus aut bene, aut nihil.*[3]

TREPLYOV *enters from behind the platform stage.*

ARKADINA. [*to her son*] When are you going to start, my dear son?

TREPLYOV. In a minute. I beg you, be patient.

ARKADINA. [*reciting from Hamlet*] "My son! Thou turn'st my eye into my very soul. And there I see such black and grained spots as will not leave their tinct!"

TREPLYOV. [*from Hamlet*] "And why did you give yourself to vice and seek love in the abyss of crime?" [*A small horn is heard playing behind the platform stage.*] Ladies and gentlemen, we are going to begin! I beg your attention! [*Pause.*] I shall begin. [*Taps with a stick and speaks in a loud voice.*] Oh, you venerable shades of olden days, you who drift over this lake in dark of night, rock us to sleep and let us dream of what it shall be in the course of two hundred thousand years!

SORIN. There won't be anything in two hundred thousand years, nothing.

---

1. Poltava (*paltáva*), a city in the Ukraine, was noted for its brisk commercial life in the nineteenth century.
2. Pável (*páshka*) Semyónych Chádin, apparently a fictitious actor invented by Chekhov. Rasplyuev (*rasplyúef*), a character in *Krechinsky's Wedding*, the first play in the trilogy by Alexander Sukhovo-Kobylin (1817–1903), first produced in 1855 at the Maly Theatre in Moscow. Sadovsky (*sadófsky*), a family of famous Russian actors, of whom the first, Prov Mikhalylovich Sadovsky (1818–72), originated the role of Rasplyuev at the Maly Theatre.
3. Shamraev confuses two Latin sayings, i.e., *De gustibus non est disputandum* ("About taste—it's no matter for debate") and *De mortuis aut bene aut nihil* ("About death—either it's good, or it's bad"), and comes up with "About taste —either it's good, or it's bad."

TREPLYOV. All right, then let them show us what that nothing is.

ARKADINA. Yes, let them. We've been rocked to sleep.

The curtain on the platform stage is raised, and a view of the lake is seen. The moon over the horizon is reflected in the water. Dressed all in white, NINA ZARECHNAYA *is sitting on a huge stone.*

NINA. Men and women, the lions, the eagles and the partridges, the antlered deer, the geese, the spiders, the silent fishes living in the sea, the starfishes and those creatures invisible to the eye—in a word, all who live, all who live, all, all having gone through their sad life cycles—are now extinct . . . A thousand centuries have gone by on this earth without one single living thing, and this poor moon has turned on its lantern in vain. On this meadow no one awakens to the cry of the cranes, and the May beetles are heard no longer in the lime groves. Cold, cold, cold. Empty, empty, empty. Frightful, frightful, frightful. [*Pause.*] The bodies of all living creatures have disappeared into dust, and eternal matter has changed them into stones, into water, into clouds, while the souls have all united into one. That one soul of the world is I . . . I . . . In me may be found the soul of Alexander the Great, of Caesar, of Shakespeare, of Napoleon, and the soul of the nethermost leech. The consciousness of all humanity, together with the instincts of animals, have united in me. And I remember all, all, all, and I relive in my very being the lives of each and every one. [*Will-o'-the-wisps appear.*]

ARKADINA. [*quietly*] This is something decadent.

TREPLYOV. [*beseechingly and with reproach*] Mama!

NINA. I am lonely. I open my lips to speak once in a hundred years, and my voice resounds despondently in this barren, desolate place, and no one hears . . . And you, pale lights, you do not hear me . . . Towards morning the stagnant marsh will give you birth, and you will roam until the break of day—without thought, without will, without one quiver of life. Fearing that life will spring up once more in you, the devil, the father of eternal matter, creates each moment in you, as he does in the stones and in the water, an exchange of atoms, and so you keep on changing, forever changing. In the whole universe only the spirit, and the spirit alone, endures—constant and immutable. [*Pause.*] Like a prisoner cast into a deep, empty well, I do not know where I am or what awaits me. All is hidden from me except my struggle with the devil, the origin of material forces. In this stubborn and cruel struggle I am destined to conquer, and after that material matter and the spirit will unite in beautiful harmony, and the Kingdom of Universal Will shall ensue. But all this will take place little by little, in the course of a long, long succession of millennia, when the moon, and bright Sirius, and the earth itself have all turned to dust . . . And until that time, there is only horror, horror . . . [*Pause. Against the background of the lake, two red spots appear.*] Here, my mighty adversary, the devil, draws near. I see his terrifying crimson eyes . . .

ARKADINA. It reeks of sulfur. Is that really necessary?

TREPLYOV. Yes.

ARKADINA. [*laughs*] Yes, it's a stage effect.

TREPLYOV. Mama!

NINA. He is bored without humanity . . .

POLINA ANDREEVNA. [*to Dorn*] You've taken off your hat. Put it on or you're going to catch a cold.

ARKADINA. The doctor here has taken off his hat to the devil, the father of eternal matter.

TREPLYOV. [*having flared up, in a loud voice*] The play is over and done with! Enough! Curtain!

ARKADINA. What is it you're angry about?

TREPLYOV. Enough, that's all! Curtain! Bring down the curtain! [*Having stamped his feet.*] Curtain! [*The curtain is lowered.*] It's my fault! I lost sight of the fact that only a chosen few can write plays and get them produced in the theatre. I've tried to break into a monopoly! Me . . . I . . . [*Wants to say something more, but waves his hand and goes out left.*]

ARKADINA. What's the matter with him?

SORIN. Irina, you shouldn't injure a young man's pride like that.

ARKADINA. What is it I said to him?

SORIN. You've hurt his feelings.

ARKADINA. He warned us in advance himself. He said his play was a joke, and so I treated it like a joke.

SORIN. Nonetheless . . .

ARKADINA. Now it turns out he's written a masterpiece of art! Well, tell me another one! And so it wasn't for a joke that he staged this show and virtually drenched us with his sulfur. It was a demonstration . . . He simply wanted to teach us how to write and what to act in. This is getting pretty boring, after all. These continual little sallies against me, these little digs, if you please, would make anyone sick and tired. A capricious, conceited little boy.

SORIN. He wanted to give you pleasure.

ARKADINA. Yes? Then why didn't he choose some ordinary play— why did he make us sit through these decadent ravings? For the sake of a joke I'm even ready to listen to ranting and ravings, but what we have here are pretensions to new forms, to a brand-new era in art. There are no new forms available, as I see it, just a bad temper.

TRIGORIN. Every person writes as he likes and as he is able.

ARKADINA. Let him write as he likes and as he is able. Just let him leave me in peace.

DORN. Jupiter, you are getting angry . . .

ARKADINA. I'm not Jupiter, but a woman. [*Lights a cigarette.*] I'm not getting angry. I'm only annoyed that a young person passes his time away in such a boring way. I didn't want to hurt his feelings.

MEDVEDENKO. No one has the basis to separate spirit from matter, because the spirit itself may be the sum total of material atoms. [*Eagerly, to* TRIGORIN.] But here's a subject, wouldn't you say, you could write a play about the way we teachers live and then get it produced on stage. A difficult life we live, difficult!

ARKADINA. That's a good point, but let's stop talking about plays and atoms. It's a glorious evening, it is! Do you hear the singing, ladies and gentlemen? [*Listens.*] How very nice it sounds!

POLINA ANDREEVNA. It's on the other side of the lake. [*Pause.*]

ARKADINA. [*to* TRIGORIN] Sit down beside me. About ten or fifteen years ago, music and singing were heard continuously on the lake almost every night. On the lake shore there are six country estates. Oh, I do remember the laughter, the noise, the shootings, and romances, oh, romances all the time . . . The *jeune premier*⁴ and idol of all six estates at the time was that man over there—I give you [*nods toward* DORN] Doctor Yevgeny Sergeich. Nowadays he's still charming, but at that time he was irresistible. Oh, my conscience is starting to bother me. Why did I ever hurt my poor boy's feelings? I'm worried. [*Loudly.*] Kostya!⁵ My son! Kostya!

MASHA. I'll go and look for him.

ARKADINA. Thank you, my dear.

MASHA. [*goes to the left*] Hullo! Konstantin Gavrilovich! Hullo! [*Goes out.*]

NINA. [*entering from behind the platform stage*] It seems clear we aren't going to continue, so I may as well come out. Good evening! [*Kisses* ARKADINA *and* POLINA ANDREEVNA.]

SORIN. Bravo! Bravo!

ARKADINA. Bravo, bravo! We fell in love with you, we did. The way you look and with that marvelous voice of yours, it's a sin for you to stay in the country. You probably have a gift for acting. Do you hear? You must go on the stage. It's your duty!

NINA. Oh, it's my dream! [*Having sighed.*] But it won't ever come true.

ARKADINA. Who knows? Here, let me introduce you. This is Trigorin, Boris Alexeevich.

NINA. Oh, I'm so glad . . . [*Embarrassed.*] I always read you . . .

ARKADINA. [*making her sit down beside them*] Don't be shy, my dear. He's a celebrity, but he has a simple soul. You see, he feels shy himself.

DORN. I suppose the curtain could be raised now. Otherwise, it's spooky.

SHAMRAEV. [*in a loud voice*] Yakov, my dear man, just pull up the curtain! [*The curtain is raised.*]

4. Young romantic lead.
5. Kostya (*kóstya*) is an affectionate nickname for *Konstantin*.

NINA. [*to* TRIGORIN] It's a strange play, wouldn't you say?

TRIGORIN. I didn't understand a thing in it. All the same, I watched it with pleasure. You acted so sincerely. And the scenery was beautiful. [*Pause.*] There's probably a lot of fish in that lake.

NINA. Yes.

TRIGORIN. I love to fish. There's no greater delight for me than to sit on the shore towards evening and watch the bobber.

NINA. But I think that for anyone who'd experienced the delight of creating, all other pleasures simply couldn't exist.

ARKADINA. [*laughing*] Don't talk to him that way. Whenever any-one says something nice to him, he doesn't know which way to turn.

SHAMRAEV. I remember in Moscow once, at the opera house, the famous Silva hit a low C. As luck would have it, the bass from our church choir was sitting in the gallery at the time. All of a sudden—and you can imagine our complete amazement—we heard coming from the gallery, "Bravo, Silva!"—a whole octave lower . . . Like this [*in a low bass*]: "Bravo, Silva . . ." The audience sat dumfounded. [*Pause.*]

DORN. The angel of quietude just flew by.[6]

NINA. And it's time for me to go. Good-bye.

ARKADINA. Go where? Why so early? We just won't let you go.

NINA. Papa is waiting for me.

ARKADINA. Oh, he's really something, isn't he . . . [*They kiss.*] Well, it can't be helped. I'm sorry, very sorry to let you go.

NINA. If you only knew how hard it is for me to leave!

ARKADINA. Someone ought to take you, my little one.

NINA. [*frightened*] Oh, no, no!

SORIN. [*beseechingly to her*] Stay, please do!

NINA. I can't, Pyotr Nikolaevich.

SORIN. Stay just an hour and that's all there is to it. Well, what about it, all right . . .

NINA. [*having thought a moment, through tears*] I can't possibly. [*Presses his hand and goes out quickly.*]

ARKADINA. An unlucky girl, really. Her late mother, they say, left to her husband her entire enormous fortune, every single kopek, and now this girl has nothing at all because her father in turn has willed everything to his second wife. It's outrageous.

DORN. Yes, if you want to do him justice, you must admit her dear papa is really a first-rate louse.

SORIN. [*rubbing his hands, which are cold*] Let's just go, dear friends, why don't we? It's getting damp, you know. My legs are hurting.

ARKADINA. You must have wooden legs, you can scarcely walk. Well, let's go, my ill-starred old man. [*Takes him by the arm.*]

SHAMRAEV. [*holding out his hand to his wife*] Madame?

---

6. A favorite Russian remark whenever a pause occurs in conversation.

SORIN. I hear that dog howling again. [*To* SHAMRAEV.] Be kind, Ilya Afanasevich, and give orders that the dog be turned loose.

SHAMRAEV. I can't possibly, Pyotr Nikolaevich, I'm afraid thieves might break into the storehouse. I've got millet in there. [*To* MEDVEDENKO, *who is walking next to him.*] Yes, a whole octave lower: "Bravo, Silva!" And you know, he wasn't even a professional singer—he was simply a member of the church choir.

MEDVEDENKO. How much of a salary does a choir member get, anyway?

> *Everyone goes out, except* DORN.

DORN. [*alone*] I don't know. Maybe I don't really understand anything or maybe I've lost my mind, but I liked that play. There's something in it, all right. When that little girl spoke of her loneliness, and later on when those red eyes of the devil appeared, I got so excited my hands were trembling. It was fresh, innocent . . . There, I think he's on his way here. I want to tell him as many pleasant things as I can think of about the play.

TREPLYOV. [*enters*] They've already gone. No one's here.

DORN. I am.

TREPLYOV. Mashenka's looking for me over the entire park. An unbearable creature.

DORN. Konstantin Gavrilovich, I liked your play tremendously. It was somewhat strange, and I didn't hear the end, but all the same it made an enormous impression on me. You are a gifted person, and you must continue. [TREPLYOV *firmly presses* DORN's *hand, then impulsively embraces him.*] Phew, how high-strung. Tears in the eyes . . . What was it I wanted to say? You chose a subject from the field of abstract ideas. And rightly so, because a work of art must continually express some kind of significant thought or other. Only the serious is really beautiful. How pale you are!

TREPLYOV. Then you say I should continue?

DORN. Yes . . . But you must depict only what is important and eternal. You know, I've spent a varied sort of life, I've been a person of taste, and I am satisfied. But if I'd ever experienced the soaring of the spirit that artists feel at the time of creative work, then it seems to me I'd despise this material shell of mine and whatever's peculiar to it, and that's all there is to it. I'd fly away from this earth, as far as I could possibly go, on to the very heights.

TREPLYOV. I'm sorry, but where is Zarechnaya?

DORN. And one thing more. There must be a clear and definite thought in a work of art. You must know what it is you're writing for. Otherwise, if you go along that picturesque road without a definite aim, you will lose your way and your talent will destroy you.

TREPLYOV. [*impatiently*] Where is Zarechnaya?

DORN. She's gone home.

TREPLYOV. [*agitated*] What on earth can I do? I want to see her . . . I've got to see her . . . I'm going . . . [MASHA *enters.*]

DORN. [*to* TREPLYOV] Calm down, my friend.

TREPLYOV. But all the same I'm going. I've got to see her, I must.

MASHA. You ought to go home, Konstantin Gavrilovich. Your mama is expecting you. She's worried.

TREPLYOV. Tell her I've gone. And I beg all of you, just leave me in peace! Leave me alone! Don't follow me around, either!

DORN. Come, come, come, dear boy . . . You mustn't go on that way . . . It's not right.

TREPLYOV. [*through tears*] Good-bye, Doctor. Thank you . . . . [*Goes out.*]

DORN. [*having sighed*] Oh, youth, youth!

MASHA. When there's nothing more to be said, then people say, "Oh, youth, youth . . ." [*Takes snuff.*]

DORN. [*takes her snuffbox and hurls it into the bushes*] That's degrading! [*Pause.*] It seems there's music in the house. We must go in.

MASHA. Wait.

DORN. What is it?

MASHA. I want to tell you something once more. I feel like talking . . . [*Agitated.*] I don't love my own father . . . but I like you a lot. Deep in my heart and soul, I feel somehow you are close to me . . . Then help me.[7] Help me or I'll do something stupid. Help me before I make a mockery of my own life and ruin it . . . I can't go on any longer . . .

DORN. What is it? How can I help you?

MASHA. My heart is breaking. No one, no one can ever know how miserable I feel! [*Lays her head on his chest, quietly.*] I'm in love with Konstantin.

DORN. How troubled everyone is, how worried and anxious! And so much, so much love . . . Oh, you bewitching lake! [*Gently.*] But what can I do, my dear child? What? What?

CURTAIN

Act Two

A lawn for croquet. In the background on the right is a house with a large veranda. The lake with the sparkling sun reflecting in it is seen to the left. There are flower beds. It is noontime and hot. ARKADINA, DORN, *and* MASHA *are sitting on a bench in the shade of an old lime tree, next to the croquet lawn.* DORN *has an open book on his lap.*

---

7. In an early version of *The Sea Gull*, it was suddenly revealed at the end of Act I that Masha's biological father was Dr. Dorn; on the advice of Nemirovich-Danchenko, Chekhov deleted this fact in subsequent versions. See Vladimir Nemirovich-Danchenko, *My Life in the Russian Theatre*, tr. John Cournos (New York: Theatre Arts Books, 1968), pp. 57–58.

ARKADINA. [*to* MASHA] Here, let's get up. [*They both rise.*] Let's stand side by side. You are twenty-two, and I'm almost twice your age. Yevgeny Sergeich, which one of us looks younger?

DORN. You, of course.

ARKADINA. There you are, miss . . . And what's the reason? Because I work, I feel, and I'm constantly on the run, while you stay forever in the same old place, and you're not really living . . . And I have a rule—never take a look into the future. I never think about old age or about death. What is to be, will be. There's no escaping it.

MASHA. And I feel as if I'd been born long, long ago. I drag my life behind me like an endless train . . . And there are many times I don't even have the will to go on living. [*Sits down.*] Of course, it's all stuff and nonsense. I must give myself a good shaking, throw every bit of this off.

DORN. [*sings quietly*] "Go and tell her, my flowers . . ."

ARKADINA. Then I'm as proper as an Englishman. My dear, I keep myself in tune, as the saying goes, I'm always dressed and have my hair done *comme il faut.*[8] Can you imagine I'd let myself go out of the house, even into the garden here, in just a dressing gown and without my hair properly done? Never. That's why I've kept looking the way I have for so long. Because I've never been a fat, sluggish frump, and I've never let myself go as many women have . . . [*With her hands on her hips, paces up and down the lawn.*] There you are. Spry as a chick. Why, I could play the role of a fifteen-year-old girl.

DORN. Well, miss, nonetheless I'll go on just the same. [*Takes the book.*] We'd stopped with the corn merchant and the rats . . .

ARKADINA. And the rats. Go on reading. [*Sits down.*] By the way, give it to me, and I'll read. My turn. [*Takes the book and skims through it to catch sight of the place.*] And the rats . . . Here it is . . . [*Reads.*] "And it stands to reason that for society people to mollycoddle novelists and to lure them into their homes is just as dangerous as for the corn merchant to breed rats in his storehouses. And yet they continue to thrive. Thus, when a woman has picked out a novelist whom she desires to capture, she engulfs him by means of compliments, adulation, and favors . . ." Well, perhaps that's the way with the French, but there's nothing of the sort with us. We just don't work out a plan of action. Our women—even before they set out to capture a writer—are usually up to their ears in love themselves, if you please. To go no further, if you took Trigorin and me . . .

> Leaning on his walking stick, SORIN *enters with* NINA *at his side.* MEDVEDENKO *follows, rolling an empty wheelchair.*

SORIN. [*in a caressing tone of voice, as if speaking to a child*] Yes? Are we happy? Are we enjoying ourselves today, when all's said and done? [*To his sister.*] We are happy! Father and stepmother

8. In a proper, suitable manner.

have gone to Tver,[9] and now we're free for three whole days.

NINA. [*sits down next to* ARKADINA *and embraces her*] I'm so happy! Now I belong to you.

SORIN. [*sits down in his wheelchair*] She's very nice and beautiful today.

ARKADINA. Well-dressed, very attractive . . . How clever you are to look the way you do. [*Kisses* NINA.] We'd better be careful. Too much praise could put a jinx on you. Where is Boris Alexeevich?

NINA. He's down by the bathhouse, fishing.

ARKADINA. Why he isn't sick and tired of it, I'll never know! [*About to continue reading.*]

NINA. What is it you have?

ARKADINA. Maupassant's "On the Water," my dearest. [*Reads several lines to herself.*] Well, the next isn't one bit interesting or even true. [*Closes the book.*] I'm worried, deeply distressed in my soul. Tell me, what's the matter with my son? Why is he so dejected and grim? He spends days on end at the lake, and I scarcely ever see him.

MASHA. He's sick at heart. [*To* NINA, *timidly.*] I beg you, will you read something from his play?

NINA. [*having shrugged her shoulders*] Do you want me to? But it isn't one bit interesting.

MASHA. [*restraining her delight*] When he reads something himself, his eyes flash and his face turns pale. His voice is beautiful and sad. He has the manner of a poet.

SORIN *is heard snoring.*

DORN. Good night!

ARKADINA. Petrusha!

SORIN. Ah?

ARKADINA. Are you asleep?

SORIN. Not in the least. [*Pause.*]

ARKADINA. You're not receiving medical treatment at all, and it isn't right, my dear.

SORIN. I'd be very happy to, but the doctor here won't do anything.

DORN. Treatment for a man of sixty!

SORIN. Even at sixty you want to go on living.

DORN. [*irked*] Oh! well, then take valerian drops.

ARKADINA. He ought to go to a spa somewhere or other. I think it would be good for him.

DORN. Well, hmm? He might go. And then again he might not.

ARKADINA. Try and make sense out of that.

DORN. No problem at all. It's very clear. [*Pause.*]

MEDVEDENKO. Pyotr Nikolaevich ought to give up smoking, I think.

SORIN. Stuff and nonsense.

DORN. No, it isn't. Wine and tobacco take possession of our per-

9. Now Kaliningrad, located northwest of Moscow, this ancient town has a history dating to the origins of Russia.

sonality. After a cigar or a glass of vodka, you are no longer Pyotr Nikolaevich but Pyotr Nikolaevich plus someone else. Your own personality, your "I," disseminates rapidly, and you even look upon yourself as a third person—as *he*.

SORIN. [*laughs*] It's all right for you to talk. You've had your day, but what about me? I served in the department of justice for twenty-eight years, but I haven't really lived. I haven't really experienced anything when all's said and done. Isn't it perfectly clear I'd like to go on living? You've had your fill of life, so you can afford to be indifferent. That's why you're more inclined to philosophize. But I want to go on living, and that's exactly why I drink sherry at dinner and smoke cigars. That's all there is to it. That's it and that's all there is to it.

DORN. A person should take life seriously. But to look for medical care at sixty and to feel sorry for yourself because there was little in your youth that you reveled in—why that's frivolity pure and simple, if you'll excuse me for saying so.

MASHA. [*rises*] It's time for lunch, I expect. [*Walks with an indolent and flaccid gait.*] My leg's gone to sleep . . . [*Goes out.*]

DORN. She'll go and soak up a couple of glasses before lunch.

SORIN. She has no personal happiness, poor thing.

DORN. Nonsense, your Excellency.

SORIN. You reason like a person who's had all the good things in life.

ARKADINA. Oh, what could possibly be more boring than this mellifluous boring life in the country. It's hot, it's quiet, nobody does anything, everybody sits around and talks philosophy . . . It's nice to be with you, my friends, I even enjoy listening to you, but . . . to sit in your own hotel room and study your part—how much better it would be, so much better!

NINA. [*ecstatic*] Oh, yes, it would! I know exactly what you mean.

SORIN. It's better in town, of course. You sit in your study, the footman lets no one in unannounced. There's a telephone . . . there are cabs in the street, and that's all there is to it . . .

DORN. [*sings*] "Go and tell her, my flowers . . ."

SHAMRAEV *enters, followed by* POLINA ANDREEVNA.

SHAMRAEV. Here they all are. Good afternoon! [*Kisses* ARKADINA'S *hand, then* NINA'S.] I'm so very glad to see you all in such good health. [*To* ARKADINA.] My wife tells me you intend to drive into town with her today. Is that right?

ARKADINA. Yes, we're intending to.

SHAMRAEV. Hmm . . . That's splendid, but how is it you're going to travel, my dear esteemed lady? We're hauling rye today, and all the workmen are busy. And if I may ask, what horses are you going to use?

ARKADINA. What horses? How on earth should I know—what horses!

SORIN. We have carriage horses, I know we do.

SHAMRAEV. [*agitated*] Carriage horses! But where am I going to get collars for them? Where, I ask you, where? I'm shocked! I can't even understand it, my dear most esteemed lady! Excuse me, I deeply respect your talent, I'm ready to give you ten years of my life, but I can't give you horses, I can't!

ARKADINA. But what if I have to go somewhere? Strange business!

SHAMRAEV. My dear esteemed lady! You don't have any idea of what it means to manage an estate!

ARKADINA. [*flaring up*] Oh, that's an old story! In that case, I'm leaving for Moscow this very day. Tell them to hire horses for me in the village, or else I'll go to the station on foot!

SHAMRAEV. [*flaring up*] In that case, I resign! Go and find yourself another manager! [*Goes out.*]

ARKADINA. It's like this every summer I've been here. Someone insults me every summer! I'll never set foot here again, never! [*Goes out to the left, where the bathhouse is assumed to be. After a minute she is seen crossing into the house, followed by* TRIGORIN *carrying fishing rods and a pail.*]

SORIN. [*flaring up*] Of all the gall, the nerve of that man! Damned if I'm going to take any more of it! It makes me sick and tired when it's all said and done. Send all my horses here right now, at once!

NINA. [*to* POLINA ANDREEVNA.] To turn down Irina Nikolaevna, the famous actress! Wouldn't you say that every desire of hers, even the slightest whim, is more important than your whole estate? It's simply beyond belief!

POLINA ANDREEVNA. [*in despair*] What can I do? Put yourself in my place. What can I do?

SORIN. [*to* NINA] Let's go in and see my sister . . . We'll all beg her not to leave. It's the right thing to do, don't you think? [*Looking in the direction in which* SHAMRAEV *has gone.*] I can't stand that man! He's a tyrant!

NINA. [*stopping him from getting up*] Sit down, sit down . . . We'll take you there . . . [MEDVEDENKO *and she push the wheelchair.*] Oh, how terrible it is! . .

SORIN. Yes, yes, it is terrible . . . But he won't go away, I'll talk with him right away. [*They go out. Only* DORN *and* POLINA ANDREEVNA *remain.*]

DORN. What bores people turn out to be. As a matter of fact, your husband ought to be thrown out on his neck, but you know how it's going to end finally. That old woman Pyotr Nikolaevich and his sister will beg your husband's pardon. Just wait and see!

POLINA ANDREEVNA. He sent the carriage horses for work in the fields, you know. And misunderstandings like this go on every day. If you only knew how it worries and upsets me!

It's making me ill. See, I'm trembling . . . I can't stand his rudeness, I can't. [*Beseechingly.*] Yevgeny, my dear lovely man, take me into your own home . . . Our time is passing by, we are young no longer, and if at the end of our lives we could only stop hiding, stop telling these lies . . . [*Pause.*]

DORN. I'm fifty-five now. It's late, too late, to change the way I live.

POLINA ANDREEVNA. I knew it. You refuse me because you've other women besides me who are close to you. You can't take all of them into your house, can you? I see it clearly now. Forgive me, but you're sick and tired of me.

NINA *appears near the house. She is picking flowers.*

DORN. No, I'm not.

POLINA ANDREEVNA. I'm tormented by jealousy. You're a doctor, of course, and you can't possibly escape women. I see it clearly now . . .

DORN. [*to* NINA, *who walks up to them*] How's everything in there?

NINA. Irina Nikolaevna is weeping, and Pyotr Nikolaevich is having an asthma attack.

DORN. [*rises*] I'd better go and give them both valerian drops . . .

NINA. [*gives flowers to him*] Here, for you!

DORN. *Merci bien.* [*Goes toward the house.*]

POLINA ANDREEVNA. [*going with him*] What darling flowers! [*Near the house, in a toneless voice.*] Give me those flowers! Give me those flowers! [*Having received the flowers, she tears them up and throws them aside. They both go into the house.*]

NINA. [*alone*] How strange to see a famous actress weeping, and for such a frivolous reason, too! And isn't it strange to find a celebrated writer, beloved by the public and written about in all the newspapers, photographs of him are always on sale, his writings are translated into foreign languages, and yet what does he do? Why, he goes fishing the whole day long and is thrilled because he's caught two minnows! I used to think that famous people were proud and unapproachable. I thought they despised the mob and, by using their glory and the luster of their names, they revenged themselves on those who placed nobility of birth and wealth higher than anything else. But here they are weeping, going fishing, playing cards, laughing, and getting angry—just like everybody else . . .

TREPLYOV. [*enters without a hat, carrying a gun and a dead sea gull*] Are you alone here?

NINA. Alone. [TREPLYOV *puts the sea gull at her feet.*] What does this mean?

TREPLYOV. Today I did something contemptible. I killed this sea gull, and now I place it at your feet.

NINA. What's the matter with you? [*Picks up the sea gull and looks at it.*]

TREPLYOV. [*after a pause*] Soon, in the same way, I shall kill myself.

NINA. I don't recognize you anymore.

TREPLYOV. Yes, ever since I stopped recognizing what you are. You've changed toward me, your eyes are cold, my presence even embarrasses you.

NINA. For some time now you've been growing irritable. You don't make much sense when you talk—it's as if you speak in symbols. And I suppose this sea gull here is obviously a symbol, too, but—forgive me—I don't understand it . . . [*Puts the sea gull on the bench.*] I'm much too simple to understand you.

TREPLYOV. It all started on that very evening my play flopped. What a stupid fiasco that was. Women never forgive failure. I've burned it all, everything down to the last shred. If you only knew how unhappy I am! Your coldness is terrifying. It's beyond belief. I feel as if I'd suddenly awakened to see this lake here completely dried up or gone forever into the ground. You just said you were much too simple to understand me. Oh, what is there to understand? My play was disliked. You despise my inspiration, and you consider me mediocre, a nonentity, exactly like plenty of others . . . [*Having stamped his foot.*] How well I understand it, oh, how well! I feel as if a nail had been driven into my brain. Oh, damn it together with my pride that is sucking my lifeblood, sucking it like a viper . . . [*Having seen* TRIGORIN, *who is walking and reading his notebook.*] Here comes a veritable genius, he walks like Hamlet, and carries a book, too. [*Mockingly.*] "Words, words, words . . ." This sun has scarcely reached you, and you're beginning to smile. The coldness in your eyes is melting fast in its rays. I won't disturb you anymore. [*Goes out quickly.*]

TRIGORIN. [*writes in his notebook*] Takes snuff and drinks vodka . . . Always in black. The schoolteacher loves her . . .

NINA. Good afternoon, Boris Alexeevich!

TRIGORIN. Good afternoon. Circumstances have an unexpected way of turning out, don't they? So it seems we're leaving today. I don't think you and I will ever meet again. And I'm sorry. I don't often meet young girls—girls who are both young and attractive. I've forgotten what it feels like to be eighteen or nineteen. I can't imagine it clearly, and that's why young girls in my novels and stories are usually false. I'd like to live in your place—if only for an hour—to understand the way you think and what sort of pretty little thing you actually are.

NINA. And I'd like to live in your place for a while.

TRIGORIN. Why?

NINA. To understand how it feels to be a famous, gifted writer. What does it feel like to be famous? How does it affect you, being well known?

TRIGORIN. How? Probably, in no way at all. I've never thought about it. [*Having thought about it*.] One of two things. Either you exaggerate my fame or fame is something that is not felt.

NINA. But if you read about yourself in the newspapers?

TRIGORIN. When they praise me, it's all right. But when they assail me, then I'm in a bad mood for two days.

NINA. A marvelous world! If you only knew how I envy you! The destinies of people differ so much. Some can scarcely drag out their tedious, inconspicuous existence, each one resembling the next, and all of them unhappy. Others, like you for instance —oh, you're one in a million—your destiny is to live an exciting and brilliant life, filled with meaning . . . You are fortunate . . .

TRIGORIN. I am? [*Shrugging his shoulders*.] Hmm . . . Here you speak of fame, of happiness, of some kind of brilliant and exciting life, but for me all those fine words—forgive me for saying so— are very much like jelly, which I never eat. You're very kind and still so very young.

NINA. Your life is beautiful!

TRIGORIN. What's especially good about it, anyway? [*Looks at his watch*.] I must go now and write. Excuse me, I just don't have time . . . [*Laughs*.] You've stepped on my favorite corn, as the saying goes, and here I am starting to get excited and a little angry. All right, then, let's talk. We'll talk about my brilliant and beautiful life . . . Well now, miss, what shall we begin with? [*Having thought a moment*.] There are some persistent notions that dominate a person's mind, for instance, when someone thinks constantly about the moon day and night. Well, I have my own kind of moon. Day and night one persistent thought obsesses me—I must write, I must write, I must . . . I no sooner finish one story than for some reason or other I must write the next, then a third, and after that a fourth . . . I write endlessly, exactly as relay horses run, and I can't do it differently. So I ask you, what's particularly beautiful or brilliant about that? Oh, what a senseless and remote way to live! Here I am with you, I'm overwrought, but at the same time I keep remembering—with every passing moment—that my unfinished story awaits me. I see that cloud over there, the one that looks like a grand piano. And I think—I must remember and use it somewhere in a story—that a cloud floated by looking like a grand piano. I smell heliotrope around here. And quicker than I can shake a whisker, I've jotted it down in my mind—a saccharine smell, the widow's color, remember and use for a description of a summer evening. I catch myself listening to every phrase or word I say, and everything you say, too, and I hurry as fast as I can to lock up all these words and phrases in my literary storeroom—they might fill the bill sometime! When I finish my work, I run off to the theatre or go fishing.

That's where I ought to rest and forget myself, but—lo and behold—I can't because a heavy cast-iron cannon ball is starting to toss and turn around in my head. It's a new subject for a story. And it pulls me back to my desk, where I must hurry once more to write and write. And that's the way it goes—always and forever—I have no peace from myself, and I feel that I am consuming my own life. For the sake of the honey that I give away to someone out there, I steal the pollen of my best flowers, pick the flowers themselves, and then trample down their roots. Don't you think I've gone mad? Do you think my close friends and acquaintances treat me as they do someone who is healthy? "What are you scribbling now?" they ask. "What are you favoring us next with?" It's the same thing over and over again, and it seems to me that this attention from those I know, the constant praise and elation, it's all a false front. They're really deceiving me as they would someone who's ill. Sometimes I fear they're just ready to creep upon me from behind, grab me, and carry me off—just like Poprishchin[1]—to the madhouse. In the years of my youth—my better years—when I was just beginning, my writing was nothing but endless agony. A minor writer, especially if he isn't very lucky, looks upon himself as awkward, blundering, superfluous. His nerves are on edge, ready to snap, and he can't stop hovering around people associated with literature and art—unrecognized, disregarded by everybody, afraid to look anyone straight in the eye, just like a passionate gambler who hasn't any money. I've never seen a single one of my readers, but for some reason or other I've always pictured them in my mind as skeptical and unfriendly. I was afraid of a theatre audience—it was terrifying to me—and whenever I had to stage a new play of mine, it seemed to me every time that the dark-haired people in the audience were in a hostile mood and the fair-haired people were coldly indifferent. Oh, how terrible it was! What agony I went through!

NINA. But don't you find moments of elation and happiness in both inspiration and the very process of creation? Surely you must.

TRIGORIN. Yes. I find pleasure when I'm writing. And reading proofs, too, but . . . once it's off the presses I can't stand it, and it's not so much that it's a mistake as that it should never have been written at all. I feel irritable, rotten in my soul . . . [*Laughs.*] And after the public reads it, you hear, "Yes, winsome and gifted . . . winsome but a long way from Tolstoy"— or else "An excellent piece but *Fathers and Children* by Turgenev is better."[2] And so to my dying day everything will be

---

1. Poprishchin (*paprishchin*) is the leading character in *Memoirs of a Madman* (1835) by N. V. Gogol (1809–52).

2. This novel, whose title is usually trans- lated as *Fathers and Sons* and published in 1862 by I. S. Turgenev (1818–1883), is considered by most critics to be his finest.

winsome and gifted, winsome and gifted—nothing more. When I die, those people I knew will walk past my grave and say: "Here lies Trigorin. He was a good author, but he was not as good as Turgenev."

NINA. Forgive me, but I just can't accept what you're saying. You are simply spoiled by success.

TRIGORIN. By what success? I've never pleased myself. I dislike myself as a writer. Worst of all, I feel dazed and often I don't understand what I write . . . I love this water here, the trees and the sky. I've a feeling for nature. It arouses passion in me— an overwhelming urge to write. But you know I'm not just a painter of landscapes. You know I'm still a citizen, too. I love my country and its people. I feel that if I really am a writer my duty is to speak up about the people and their sufferings, and about their future, to speak up about science and learning, about the rights of man, and so on and so on. I speak up about everything, I hurry on—people drive me from all sides, they get angry. I rush from one side to the next like a fox hunted down by dogs. I see that both life and science keep on striding ahead, onward and forward. And I keep dropping behind, always too late, like the peasant who has missed the train. When it's all said and done, I feel that I have the ability just to describe landscapes, and that everything else is false—false to the marrow of my bones.

NINA. You've been working too long and too hard, and you've neither the time nor the inclination to realize your own significance. Go ahead and be dissatisfied with yourself, but others see you as great and beautiful. If I were a writer like you, I'd give my whole life to the people. But I'd realize at the same time that their only happiness would consist of rising up to where I am— and they'd pull me along in a chariot.

TRIGORIN. Come now, in a chariot . . . Who do you think I am, Agamemnon, perhaps? [*They both smile.*]

NINA. For the sake of happiness like that, being a writer or an actress, I would endure poverty, disillusionment, and the hatred of those close to me. I'd live in an attic and eat nothing but rye bread. I'd suffer dissatisfaction with myself in realizing my own fame . . . genuine, resounding fame . . . [*Covers her face with her hands.*] My head's going round and round . . . Phew! . .

ARKADINA. [*from inside the house*] Boris Alexeevich!

TRIGORIN. They're calling me . . . Probably to pack up my things. But I don't want to go away. [*Looking around at the lake.*] See, it's really a paradise! . . wonderful!

NINA. Do you see that house and orchard on that shore over there?

TRIGORIN. Yes.

NINA. That estate belonged to my mother when she was alive. I was born there. I've lived my whole life near this lake, and I know every little island on it.

TRIGORIN. It's very nice here. [*Having seen the sea gull.*] But what's this?

NINA. A sea gull. Konstantin Gavrilych killed it.

TRIGORIN. A beautiful bird. I don't feel like leaving, really. See if you can't talk Irina Nikolaevna into staying on here. [*Writes in his notebook.*].

NINA. What are you writing down?

TRIGORIN. Oh, making some notes . . . A subject crossed my mind just now . . . [*Pocketing his notebook.*] A subject for a short story. A young girl has lived her whole life on the shores of a lake. A girl like you. She loves the lake, like a sea gull, and she's as happy and free as a sea gull, too. A man happens to come by, sees her, and, having nothing else to do, destroys her like that sea gull there. [*Pause.*]

ARKADINA *appears at a window of the house.*

ARKADINA. Boris Alexeevich, where are you?

TRIGORIN. I'm on my way. [*Goes, turning back now and again to look at* NINA. *By the window, he speaks to* ARKADINA.] What is it?

ARKADINA. We're staying on here.

TRIGORIN *goes into the house.*

NINA. [*goes to the footlights. She is lost in thought for a few moments and then speaks*] It's a dream!

CURTAIN

Act Three

The dining room in SORIN'S *house. To the right and left are doors. A sideboard. A cupboard with medical supplies. A table in the middle of the room. A suitcase and hatboxes. Preparations for a trip are visible.* TRIGORIN *is eating his lunch.* MASHA *is standing by the table.*

MASHA. I'm going over all this because you're a writer. You can use it if you want to. I can tell you in all honesty. If he had injured himself seriously, I wouldn't have gone on living for a single moment. Oh, I'm still brave enough to face up to things. I've made up my mind here and now to tear this love out of my heart, tear it out by the very roots.

TRIGORIN. And how will you do it?

MASHA. I'm going to get married. To Medvedenko.

TRIGORIN. You mean the schoolteacher?

MASHA. Yes.

TRIGORIN. It's not clear to me why you feel you must.

MASHA. To love without any hope, to go on year after year just waiting for something . . . But once I get married, I won't have time for love. New responsibilities will smother all the old concerns.

And anyway, don't you see, it will be a change. Shall we have another drink, or not?

TRIGORIN. But won't that be too much for you?

MASHA. Well, if that isn't something! [*Fills up their glasses.*] Don't look at me like that. Women drink more often than you realize. A few drinks openly as I do, but most of them drink in secret. Yes, they do. And it's always vodka or brandy. [*Clinks glasses with him.*] All the very best to you! You're a fine person, easy to know. I'm sorry we must go our separate ways. [*They both drink.*]

TRIGORIN. As far as I'm concerned, I don't want to leave.

MASHA. Then go and ask her to stay on here.

TRIGORIN. No, there's no way of keeping her here now. Her son's been far too tactless in his behavior. First, he goes and shoots himself, and now they're saying he intends to challenge me to a duel. Whatever for, I'd like to know? He does nothing but sulk, snort, and make pronouncements about new forms . . . But there's plenty of room for all, both the old and the new—why shove and push?

MASHA. Well, there is jealousy, too. Oh, it's none of my business, anyway. [*Pause.* YAKOV, *with a suitcase, goes from the left to the right.* NINA *enters and stops by the window.*] My schoolteacher just isn't very bright, but he's a kind man, he's very poor, and he loves me deeply. I feel sorry for him. And I'm sorry for his old mother. Well, sir, let me wish you the best of everything. Don't think badly of me. [*Shakes his head warmly.*] Thank you so much for your kind interest in me. Send me your books, and be sure to autograph them. Just don't write "to my dear lady," but put it simply: "To Marya, who doesn't remember her origins, who doesn't know for certain why she's alive on this earth." Good-bye! [*Goes out.*]

NINA. [*holding out her hand with the fist closed to* TRIGORIN] Odd or even?

TRIGORIN. Even.

NINA. [*having sighed*] So it's no. I've only got one chickpea seed in my hand. I was trying to figure out my fortune. Should I go on the stage or not? If only someone would give me some advice.

TRIGORIN. It's really impossible to give advice in this case. [*Pause.*]

NINA. We're going to part now and . . . perhaps we won't ever see each other again. I beg you to take this little medallion as a keepsake. I had your initials engraved . . . and on this side is the name of your book, *Days and Nights*.

TRIGORIN. What a splendid thing to do! [*Kisses the medallion.*] A charming present!

NINA. Think of me from time to time.

TRIGORIN. I will. I'll remember you the way you were on that bright and sunny day—do you recall?—a week ago, when you were wearing that light-colored dress . . . We were talking . . . there was a white sea gull lying on the bench at the time.

NINA. [*deep in thought*] Yes, a sea gull . . . [*Pause.*] We can't talk anymore. Someone is coming . . . Before you go away, give me a minute or two of your time, I beg you . . .

> She goes out left. At the same time ARKADINA enters from the right with SORIN, who is wearing a dress coat with the star of an order on it, then YAKOV, who is preoccupied with the packing.

ARKADINA. Then just stay at home, old man. With that rheumatism of yours do you think you can ride hither and yon and go visiting people? [*To* TRIGORIN.] Who was it that left just now? Nina?

TRIGORIN. Yes.

ARKADINA. Pardon, we bothered you . . . [*Sits down.*] I think I've packed everything. I'm worn out.

TRIGORIN. [*reads the inscription on the medallion*] "*Days and Nights* page 121, lines 11 and 12."

YAKOV. [*clearing the table*] Do you want me to pack your fishing rods, too?

TRIGORIN. Yes, I'll have to have them again. But give the books away to someone.

YAKOV. Very good, sir.

TRIGORIN. [*to himself*] Page 121, lines 11 and 12. What on earth can those lines be? [*To* ARKADINA.] Are my own books in your house here?

ARKADINA. In brother's study, in the corner bookcase.

TRIGORIN. Page 121 . . . [*Goes out.*]

ARKADINA. Really, Petrusha, you ought to stay home . . .

SORIN. You are going away, and it would be hard for me to stay home without you.

ARKADINA. But in town what is there?

SORIN. Oh, nothing particular, but nonetheless. [*Laughs.*] There will be a stone-laying affair for the new Council building, and all that sort of thing . . . If only for an hour or two, I'd like to break loose from this fish-like existence—this gudgeon way of life—and begin to feel alive once more. Oh, I've been lying around much too long, and I've gotten as stale as an old used-up cigar holder. I've told them to have the horses ready at one o'clock, so then we can leave at the same time.

ARKADINA. [*after a pause*] Well, you stay on living here, do. Don't let it get you down, and don't catch a cold. Keep an eye on my son. Take care of him. Put him on the right track. [*Pause.*] Here I'm going away, and I don't even know why Konstantin shot himself. It seems to me the chief reason was jealousy, and the sooner I get Trigorin out of here the better.

SORIN. How can I tell you? There were other reasons, too. It's perfectly clear. He's a young person, very bright, living in the country, really in the backwoods, without money, without position, without a future. Not a single thing to do. Having nothing to do makes him feel ashamed and frightened. I love him deeply, and he's attached to me, but all the same—when it's all said and done —it seems to him that he is superfluous in this house, simply a parasite, a freeloader. It's perfectly clear, his pride . . .

ARKADINA. Oh, the grief he brings me. [*Deliberating.*] Maybe he ought to enter the civil service, or something . . .

SORIN. [*whistles, then indecisively*] It seems to me the best thing to do would be for you . . . to give him a little money. To begin with, he needs to dress like a member of the human race, and that's all there is to it. Just take a good look, he's been wearing one and the same jacket for three whole years—he walks around without an overcoat . . . [*Laughs.*] What's more, it wouldn't hurt him to kick up his heels and have some fun . . . To go abroad, or something . . . That doesn't cost so much.

ARKADINA. All the same . . . Perhaps, I could find enough for the suit, but to go abroad . . . No, and at this time I can't even pay for the suit. [*Decisively.*] I don't have money! [SORIN *laughs.*] None!

SORIN. [*whistles*] Just so, ma'am. Forgive me, my dear, don't be angry. I believe you . . . You are a magnanimous woman, positively noble-hearted.

ARKADINA. [*through tears*] I don't have money!

SORIN. If I had the money, it's perfectly clear I'd give it to him myself, but I have absolutely nothing, not five kopeks. [*Laughs.*] My manager collects my whole pension and spends it on running the estate. He farms, raises cattle, tends to the bees, and my money goes to waste. The bees all die, the cattle all die, and they don't let me use the horses when I need them . . .

ARKADINA. Yes, I do have money, but you know I'm an actress. My costumes alone are enough to ruin me.

SORIN. You are kind, my dear . . . I respect you . . . Yes . . . But something's not right with me again . . . [*Staggers and sways.*] My head's going round and round. [*Holds onto the table.*] I feel faint, and that's all there is to it.

ARKADINA. [*frightened*] Petrusha! [*Trying to support him.*] Petrusha, my dear . . . [*Shouts.*] Help me! Help! . . [TREPLYOV, *with his head bandaged, and* MEDVEDENKO *enter.*] He feels as though he's going to faint.

SORIN. It's nothing, nothing . . . [*Smiles and drinks water.*] It's gone now . . . and that's all there is to it . . .

TREPLYOV. [*to his mother*] Don't be scared, Mama, it isn't dangerous. This often happens to Uncle now. [*To his uncle.*] Uncle, you must go and lie down.

SORIN. A little while, yes . . . But all the same I'm going into town . . . I'll go lie down and then I'll be ready to go . . . it's perfectly clear . . . [*Goes, leaning on his walking stick.*]

MEDVEDENKO. [*gives him support with his arm*] Here's a riddle.[3]

---

3. The riddle of the Sphinx that Oedipus solved.

In the morning on four legs, at noontime on two, in the evening on three . . .

SORIN. [*laughs*] That's it exactly. And at night on his back. Thank you, I can walk by myself . . .

MEDVEDENKO. Well, come now, why stand on ceremony! . . [SORIN *and he go out.*]

ARKADINA. Oh, he really scared me!

TREPLYOV. He can't enjoy good health living in the country. It gets him down. If only you could open those tight fists of yours, Mama, show some generosity all of a sudden and lend Uncle fifteen hundred or two thousand rubles. Then he could live in town for a whole year.

ARKADINA. I don't have any money. I am an actress, not a banker. [*Pause.*]

TREPLYOV. Change the bandage for me, Mama. You do it very well.

ARKADINA. [*takes idioform and a box of bandage material out of the cupboard*] The doctor is late.

TREPLYOV. He promised to be here at ten, but it's already noon.

ARKADINA. Sit down. [*Takes the bandage off his head.*] You look as though you're wearing a turban. Yesterday in the kitchen some newcomer or other asked about you. He wanted to know what your nationality was. Why, it's almost entirely healed up. What's left doesn't amount to much. [*Kisses him on the head.*] And when I'm gone you're not going to go click-click again, are you?

TREPLYOV. No, Mama. That was a moment of mad despair, when I could no longer control myself. It won't happen anymore. [*Kisses her hand.*] You've hands of gold. I remember, it was so long ago, when you were still acting on the imperial stage[4]—I was a little boy at the time—there was a fight outside in the yard. A washerwoman who lived in the house had been terribly beaten up. Remember? When they picked her up she was unconscious . . . You took care of her until she was well. You brought medicine and washed her children in a tub. Don't you remember?

ARKADINA. No. [*Puts on a new bandage.*]

TREPLYOV. Two ballet dancers were living in the very same house where we lived at that time . . . They used to come and drink coffee with you . . .

ARKADINA. Now, that I remember.

TREPLYOV. Oh, they were such devout women. [*Pause.*] Lately, these last few days here, I've loved you as I did when I was a child —tenderly and with all my heart. I've no one left now except you. Only just tell me why, why have you fallen under the influence of that man?

ARKADINA. You don't understand him, Konstantin. This man's a superior person . . .

TREPLYOV. Nonetheless, when they announced to him that I was

4. Arkadina had been employed as an actress in the imperial court theatres in St. Petersburg or Moscow.

planning to challenge him to a duel, his superiority didn't stop him from playing the coward. He is going away. An ignominious escape!

ARKADINA. What nonsense! I begged him myself to leave here.

TREPLYOV. A superior person! There, you see, we're almost ready to quarrel because of him, and where is he now? Somewhere in the drawing room or in the orchard laughing at us . . . developing Nina's character, trying to convince her once and for all that he is a genius.

ARKADINA. It's sheer delight for you, isn't it, to say unpleasant things to me. I respect that man, and I beg you not to express your wicked thoughts about him when I'm around.

TREPLYOV. And I don't respect him. Oh, you'd like me to consider him a genius, too. Forgive me, but I can't lie—his books make me sick.

ARKADINA. That's jealousy. People who claim talents they don't possess have nothing left to them except to malign those who are truly gifted. Some consolation, you must admit!

TREPLYOV. [*ironically*] Truly gifted, indeed! [*Furiously.*] As far as that goes, I'm more gifted than all of you put together. [*Tears off the bandage on his head.*] You people with your narrow-minded, run-of-the-mill conventions have grabbed the leadership in art today. And you consider only what you do yourselves as genuine and legitimate. Everything else you squeeze out and suppress. I refuse to acknowledge you or your leadership! I just won't accept either you or him!

ARKADINA. Decadent! . .

TREPLYOV. Go on, go back to your winsome theatre and act in those pitiful, vapid plays!

ARKADINA. I've never once acted in plays like that. Leave me alone! Why, you don't even have the talent to write a pitiful little skit. You petty bourgeois from Kiev! Freeloader!

TREPLYOV. Miser!

ARKADINA. Ragamuffin! [TREPLYOV *sits down and weeps quietly.*] You nonentity, you! [*Walking up and down in agitation.*] Don't cry. You don't need to cry . . . [*Weeps.*] You don't have to . . . [*Kisses his forehead, cheeks, and head.*] My dear child, forgive me . . . Forgive your guilty mother. Forgive me, I'm so miserable.

TREPLYOV. [*embraces her*] If you only knew! I've lost everything. She doesn't love me, and now I can't write . . . All my hopes have gone down the drain . . .

ARKADINA. Don't lose heart . . . Everything will settle itself. He's going away soon, and she'll fall in love with you again. [*Wipes away his tears.*] There, that's enough. We've stopped quarreling and made up.

TREPLYOV. [*kisses her hands*] Yes, Mama.

ARKADINA. [*gently*] Then make up with him. There's no need for a duel . . . You know there isn't, don't you?

TREPLYOV. All right . . . One thing, Mama, don't insist on my meeting with him. That would be hard for me . . . beyond my strength . . . [TRIGORIN *enters*.] There, you see . . . I'm going now . . . [*Quickly puts the medical supplies into the cupboard.*] Oh, the doctor can do the bandage later on . . .

TRIGORIN. [*looks through the book*] Page 121 . . . lines 11 and 12 . . . Here it is. . . . [*Reads.*] "If ever you have need of my life, then come and take it."

TREPLYOV *picks up the bandage from the floor and goes out.*

ARKADINA. [*having glanced at the clock*] They will bring the horses soon.

TRIGORIN. [*to himself*] "If ever you have need of my life, then come and take it."

ARKADINA. All your things have been packed up, I hope?

TRIGORIN. [*impatiently*] Yes, yes . . . [*Deliberating.*] Why do I hear so much sorrow in this cry sent by someone so pure in soul? Why does it wring so much pain in my own heart? . . "If ever you have need of my life, then come and take it." [*To* ARKADINA.] Let's stay on here for one more day! [ARKADINA *shakes her head negatively*.] Let's stay!

ARKADINA. My dear, I know what's holding you here. But you must find the strength to control yourself. You're a little intoxicated, you must try and sober up.

TRIGORIN. You must be sober, too, be smart, be reasonable, I beg you. Look at all this like a genuine friend . . . [*Presses her hand.*] You're capable of sacrifice . . . Then be my friend, and let me go . . .

ARKADINA. [*greatly upset*] Have you fallen for her that much?

TRIGORIN. Something draws me to her! Perhaps this is just what I need.

ARKADINA. The love of a provincial girl? Oh, how little you know yourself!

TRIGORIN. Sometimes people are asleep when they walk. That's what it is with me now. I'm talking with you, but I feel as if I were asleep and seeing her in my dreams . . . Sweet, marvelous dreams have taken hold of me . . . Let me go . . .

ARKADINA. [*trembling*] No, no . . . I'm an ordinary woman. You can't talk to me like that . . . Don't torment me, Boris . . . It terrifies me . . .

TRIGORIN. If you wanted to, you could be extraordinary. The love of a young girl, charming, poetic, carrying me off into the realm of dreams—only that kind of love, no other, can bring happiness on this earth! I've never experienced love like that . . . When I was young I didn't have time. I kept haunting editorial offices, struggling to stay alive . . . It is here now, that kind of love has come at last, it draws me to her . . . What's the sense of trying to escape it?

ARKADINA. [*furiously*] You have lost your mind!

TRIGORIN. So be it.

ARKADINA. You've all arranged things today simply to torment me! [*Weeps.*]

TRIGORIN. [*clutches his head*] She doesn't understand! She doesn't even want to understand!

ARKADINA. Do you think I'm so old and hideous already that you can talk to me about other women without one trace of embarrassment? [*Embraces and kisses him.*] Oh, you've gone mad! My handsome, glorious . . . You are the last page of my life! [*Falls on her knees.*] Oh, my happiness, my pride, my paradise . . . [*Embraces his knees.*] If you desert me—if only for one hour—I'll never live through it, I'll lose my mind. My wonderful, splendid, my sovereign master . . .

TRIGORIN. Someone could come in here. [*Helps her to rise.*]

ARKADINA. Let them. I'm not ashamed of my love for you. [*Kisses his hands.*] My treasure, you outrageous beast, you'd like to behave like someone gone mad, wouldn't you, but I don't want you to, I won't let you . . . [*Laughs.*] You are mine . . . mine . . . And this forehead is mine, and these eyes are mine, and this beautiful, silken hair is mine . . . You are all mine. You are so gifted, so brilliant, the best of all our writers today. You are Russia's one and only hope . . . How much sincerity you have, simplicity, freshness, healthy humor . . . In one stroke of your pen, you can express what is both significant and distinctive—be it a person or a landscape. Your people are so very much alive. Oh, it's impossible to read your books without feeling sheer ecstasy! You think I'm praising you to the skies? I would flatter you? Well, just look at me in my eyes . . . Go ahead and look . . . Do I resemble a liar? Besides, you can see I'm the one person who can appreciate you. The only one who will tell you the truth, my dear, marvelous . . . You're going with me, aren't you? Yes? You're not going to desert me, are you? . .

TRIGORIN. I have no will of my own . . . I've never had any will of my own . . . Sluggish, ready to crumble to pieces, always submissive. How on earth can that ever be pleasing to a woman? Take me, carry me off, but just don't let me go one single step away from you . . .

ARKADINA. [*to herself*] He is mine now. [*Nonchalantly, as if nothing had taken place.*] If you want to, though, you can stay on here. I'll go by myself, and you can meet me later on. Let's say in a week. After all, why must you hurry off somewhere?

TRIGORIN. No, let's go together.

ARKADINA. As you like. If it's together, it's together, then . . . [*Pause.* TRIGORIN *writes in his notebook.*] What are you doing?

TRIGORIN. An expression I heard this morning. It was a good one. "A girlish pine forest . . ." Might come in handy sometime.

[*Stretches.*] It means we're going, then? Again the railway coaches, stations, eating buffet style, slices of beef, talk and more talk . . .

SHAMRAEV. [*enters*] I've the honor to announce, I'm sorry to say it, that the horses are ready. The time has come, my dear honored lady, to go to the station. The train arrives at five minutes after two. So, Irina Nikolaevna, you'll do me a favor, won't you, and don't forget to find out about the actor Suzdaltsev? Where is he now? Whether he's alive? Whether he's in good health? Once upon a time we did a lot of drinking together, he and I . . . In *The Mail Robbery* he was simply inimitable . . . At that time too in Yelisavetgrad,[5] I remember, he was working with the tragedian Izmailov, who was also a singular person in his own right. No reason to hurry, my dear honored lady, you've still got about five minutes left. One time they were playing conspirators in a certain melodrama, and when they were suddenly discovered, they were supposed to say, "We're caught like rats in a trap" but Izmailov said, "We're caught like traps in a rat . . ." [*Shouts with laughter.*] Traps in a rat! . .

> While SHAMRAEV *is speaking,* YAKOV *bustles around the suitcases; the* MAIDSERVANT *brings* ARKADINA *her hat, cloak, umbrella, gloves; everyone helps* ARKADINA *get them on. The* COOK *peeps out from behind the door on the left, and a little while later on he dubiously comes in.* POLINA ANDREEVNA *enters, followed by* SORIN *and* MEDVEDENKO.

POLINA ANDREEVNA. [*carrying a small basket*] Here are some plums for you to take for the road . . . They're very sweet. Maybe you'll feel like indulging yourself . . .

ARKADINA. You're very kind, Polina Andreevna.

POLINA ANDREEVNA. Good-bye, my dear! If things hadn't gone the way you wanted, then forgive us, please. [*Weeps.*]

ARKADINA. [*embraces her*] Everything was just fine, everything. But you shouldn't cry, really.

POLINA ANDREEVNA. Our time is slipping away!

ARKADINA. What on earth can be done about it!

SORIN. [*enters from the door on the left, wearing a hat and an overcoat in the style of a cape, and carrying a cane; crossing through the room, he speaks*] Sister, it's time to go, or you'll be late when all's said and done. I'll go and sit in the carriage. [*Goes out.*]

MEDVEDENKO. And I'll be going on foot to the station . . . to see you on your way. I'll step lively . . . [*Goes out.*]

ARKADINA. Until we meet again, my darlings . . . If we're all still alive and in good health, we'll meet again this summer . . . [*The*

5. A city in the Ukraine now called Kirovograd.

MAIDSERVANT, YAKOV, *and the* COOK *all kiss her hand*.] Don't forget me. [*Gives the* COOK *a ruble*.] Here's a ruble for the three of you.

THE COOK. Thank you most kindly, ma'am. A happy journey to you! You're more than good to us.

YAKOV. May God grant you many happy moments!

SHAMRAEV. We'd feel overjoyed if you'd write to us every now and then. Good-bye, Boris Alexeevich!

ARKADINA. Where is Konstantin? Tell him I'm leaving. We must say good-bye. Well, think kindly of me. [*To* YAKOV.] I gave the cook a ruble. It's for the three of you.

> *Everyone goes out on the right. The stage is empty. Offstage there are the usual sounds that occur when persons are being seen off. A* MAIDSERVANT *returns, takes the basket of plums from the table, and again goes out.*

TRIGORIN. [*having returned*] I've forgotten my stick. No doubt it's out on the veranda. [*Starts to go and meets* NINA, *who is entering at the door on the left.*]

NINA. I had a feeling we'd see each other again. [*Excitedly.*] Boris Alexeevich, I've made my mind up once and for all, the die is cast—I shall go on the stage. When tomorrow comes I won't be here, no, I'm leaving my father, deserting everything and everyone, I'm beginning a new life . . . I'm leaving, just like you, for . . . Moscow. We will meet there.

TRIGORIN. [*having glanced around*] Stop at the Slavyansky Bazaar[6] . . . Send me word at once . . . Molchanovka, at the House of Grokholsky . . . I've got to run . . . [*Pause.*]

NINA. A minute more, just one . . .

TRIGORIN. [*in an undertone*] You are beautiful, so . . . Oh, how happy I am just to think we'll see each other soon! [*She bends her head on his chest.*] I'll look once more on these marvelous eyes, this indescribable, loving smile . . . your gentle face, your look of angelic purity . . . my dearest . . . [*A prolonged kiss.*]

CURTAIN

> *Between the third and fourth acts there is an interval of two years.*

Act Four

One of the drawing rooms in SORIN'S *house, changed by* KONSTANTIN TREPLYOV *into a study. To the right and to the left are doors which lead into the interior rooms. Directly up-*

---

6. Or the Slavonic Bazaar, a well-known hotel in Moscow.

stage is a glass door opening onto the veranda. In addition to the usual drawing-room furniture, there are, in the corner on the right, a writing table; by the door on the left, a Turkish divan, a bookcase with books; and books may be seen on the window sills and chairs. It is evening. A single lamp is burning under a lampshade. Half-light. The rapidly changing sounds of wind in the trees and the howling of wind in the chimneys. The watchman is heard tapping.[7] MEDVEDENKO *and* MASHA *enter.*

MASHA. [*calling*] Konstantin Gavrilych! Konstantin Gavrilych! [*Looking about.*] There's no one here. The old man never lets a minute go by without asking, "Where's Kostya, where is he . . ." He can't live without him . . .

MEDVEDENKO. Loneliness scares him. [*Listening.*] What horrible weather! It's been going on like this for almost two whole days and nights.

MASHA. [*turns up the light in the lamp*] Waves are breaking on the lake. Gigantic ones.

MEDVEDENKO. It's pitch-dark in the garden. They should've been told to tear down that theatre outside. It stands there in the garden, naked and deformed like a skeleton, and its curtain keeps on flapping in the wind. Yesterday evening when I was passing by, I thought I heard someone weeping inside.

MASHA. Oh, go on with . . . [*Pause.*]

MEDVEDENKO. Masha, let's go home!

MASHA. [*shakes her head*] I'm going to stay here for the night.

MEDVEDENKO. [*pleadingly*] Masha, let's go, let's! Our baby must be hungry.

MASHA. Stuff and nonsense. Matryona will feed him. [*Pause.*]

MEDVEDENKO. I feel sorry for him. It'll be his third night without his mother.

MASHA. You've become dull and boring. In the old days at least you used to put out a pretty good line of philosophy, but nowadays you keep coming up with "Off to the baby," or "Off to the home"—one minute it's baby, the next it's home—and that's the most anybody ever gets out of you.

MEDVEDENKO. Masha, let's go!

MASHA. You can drive off yourself.

MEDVEDENKO. Your father won't give me the horses.

MASHA. He will too. Go ahead and ask, he'll give them to you.

MEDVEDENKO. Then maybe I'll go ahead and ask. Can I count on you coming home tomorrow?

MASHA. [*takes snuff*] All right, tomorrow then. How you keep at it . . . [TREPLYOV *and* POLINA ANDREEVNA *enter.* TREPLYOV *is carrying pillows and a blanket, and* POLINA ANDREEVNA *some*

7. The watchman was a member of the staff on Russian estates. At night, in making his rounds, he tapped on a wooden device to signal the inhabitants that "all was well" and to warn trespassers that the estate was guarded.

linen, which they place on the Turkish divan. Then TREPLYOV
goes to his table and sits.] What's this for, Mama?

POLINA ANDREEVNA. Pyotr Nikolaevich asked that a place be fixed up
for him in Kostya's room.

MASHA. Let me . . . [Makes the bed.]

POLINA ANDREEVNA. [having sighed] Old persons are like the little
ones . . . [Goes to the writing table and, leaning on her elbows,
looks at the manuscript. Pause.]

MEDVEDENKO. Well, then, I'm on my way. Good-bye, Masha.
[Kisses his wife's hand.] Good-bye, Mamasha.[8] [Wants to kiss
his mother-in-law's hand.]

POLINA ANDREEVNA. [irritated] Come on! Off you go, if you're
going.

MEDVEDENKO. Good-bye, Konstantin Gavrilych.

TREPLYOV silently shakes his hand. MEDVEDENKO goes out.

POLINA ANDREEVNA. [glancing at the manuscript] No one ever
thought or even so much as guessed that you'd turn out to be a
genuine writer, Kostya. And yet here you are, thank the Lord, and
even the journals have started sending you money. [Passes her
hand over his hair.] You've grown handsome, too . . . Dear
Kostya, you're a good boy, be a little nicer to my Mashenka! . .

MASHA. [making the bed] Let him alone, Mama.

POLINA ANDREEVNA. [to TREPLYOV] She's a sweet little girl.
[Pause.] A woman doesn't yearn for a thing, Kostya, except for
an adoring look. I know that myself.

TREPLYOV gets out of his chair and goes out silently.

MASHA. There, you've gone and made him angry. You just had to
keep at it, didn't you!

POLINA ANDREEVNA. I'm sorry for you, Mashenka.

MASHA. Oh, that helps me a lot!

POLINA ANDREEVNA. My heart aches for you. I see everything, you
know, and I can understand.

MASHA. It's so much nonsense. Love without hope, why that only
happens in novels. Stuff and nonsense. What you can't do is let
yourself go, you just can't sit by the seashore and wait for something, expect the weather to change . . . Whenever love gets into
your heart, you've got to drive it out. You know they've promised
to send my husband to another district. When we've moved
there, I won't remember a thing . . . I'll tear it out of my heart by
the roots.

Two rooms away a melancholy waltz is being played.

POLINA ANDREEVNA. Kostya is playing. He must feel miserable.

MASHA. [without a sound, dances two or three turns of the waltz]
The chief thing, Mama, is not to see him face to face. If only
they'd give my Semyon the transfer, and once there and a month
goes by I won't remember a thing. Believe me. It's all so much
stuff and nonsense.

8. Mamasha (mamásha) is a term of endearment for Mama.

The door on the left opens. DORN *and* MEDVEDENKO *wheel in* SORIN.

MEDVEDENKO. I've got six of them at home now. And flour's up to two kopeks a pound.

DORN. Just try and wriggle out of that one.

MEDVEDENKO. Oh, it's all right for you to laugh. You've got so much money even the chickens have stopped nibbling.[9]

DORN. Money? I've been in practice for thirty years, a practice which gave me no peace, my friend, when neither day nor night belonged to myself, and what did I manage to save in all that time? Only two thousand rubles, and what's more, I ran through the last kopek of that on a trip abroad not too long ago. I don't have a single thing.

MASHA. [*to her husband*] Haven't you gone yet?

MEDVEDENKO. [*feeling guilty*] Why blame me? When they don't even let me have the horses!

MASHA. [*with bitter disappointment, in an undertone*] Would to God I'd never laid eyes on you!

The wheelchair comes to a stop in the left half of the room. POLINA ANDREEVNA, MASHA, *and* DORN *sit down nearby.* MEDVEDENKO, *woebegone, walks away to one side.*

DORN. My, I'd say you've changed things a lot in here! Out of a drawing room you've made a study.

MASHA. It's more convenient for Konstantin Gavrilych to work in here. He can go out into the garden, whenever he feels like it, and do some thinking there.

The WATCHMAN *is heard tapping.*

SORIN. Where is sister?

DORN. Gone to the station to meet Trigorin. She'll be right back.

SORIN. If you've found it necessary to send for my sister, it must mean I'm seriously ill. [*Having been silent for a while.*] That's the way the story goes, you see, I'm seriously ill, and in the meantime not one whit of medicine is given to me.

DORN. And what is it you want? Valerian drops? A little baking soda? Quinine?

SORIN. Here it comes, the same old philosophy. Oh, am I in for it now! [*Nodding his head in the direction of the Turkish divan.*] That made up for me?

POLINA ANDREEVNA. For you, Pyotr Nikolaevich.

SORIN. And I thank you.

DORIN. [*singing*] "Oh, the moon sails tonight across the heavens . . ."

SORIN. I've come up with a subject for a story I'd like to give to Kostya. It ought to be called thus: "The Person Who Was Bound and Determined To." "*L'homme, qui a voulu.*"[1] Once upon a time in my youth I was bound and determined to become a writer

---

9. Literally, "Your money isn't gobbled up by the hens."   1. "The man who has willed."

—and I never became one. I was bound and determined to speak beautifully—and I spoke hideously [*mocking himself*]: "and that's all there is to it, and all that sort of thing, maybe so and then maybe not . . . ," and when you were supposed to wrap up everything into a tidy summary, I used to keep on wrapping up and up until I broke out in a cold sweat. I was bound and determined to get married—and I never did. Bound and determined to live in town my whole life—and here I am, ending it all up in the country and that's all there is to it.

DORN. He was bound and determined to become a state councilor[2] —and he became one.

SORIN. [*laughs*] I didn't really make any special effort for that. It happened all by itself.

DORN. To come right out and say you're dissatisfied with life at sixty-two—you must admit that's not very big of you.

SORIN. What a persistent fellow you are. Just understand that I want to live.

DORN. That's asinine. Every life must come to an end. That's what nature itself decrees.

SORIN. You keep on talking like someone who's chock-full of everything he wanted out of life. You're chock-full, and that's why nothing touches you now. Just doesn't matter to you. But when your turn comes, you'll be afraid to die, too.

DORN. The fear of death is an animal fear . . . something you've got to repress. Only those who believe in life eternal are consciously afraid of death, and what scares them is the knowledge of their own sins. Now you, in the first place, can scarcely be called a person who believes, and in the second place, what sort of sins have you committed? You served in the justice department for twenty-five years—that's all.

SORIN. [*laughs*] Twenty-eight . . .

TREPLYOV *enters and sits on a small bench at* SORIN's *feet. The whole time* MASHA *doesn't take her eyes from him.*

DORN. We're interfering with Konstantin Gavrilovich and his work.

TREPLYOV. No, it's nothing. [*Pause.*]

MEDVEDENKO. Permit me to ask you a question, Doctor; what city outside this country did you like most of all?

DORN. Genoa.

TREPLYOV. Why Genoa?

DORN. You find superbly crowded streets there. In the evening when you go out of your hotel, you see that the entire street is swarming with people. You are then set in motion aimlessly in the crowd—here one moment, over there the next—zigzagging this way and that, your life linked together with the mass, blending in with it psychologically. And you start to believe that a single world

2. Permanent State Councilor was rank number four in the Table of Ranks in the civil service; this rank was equivalent to the status of major-general in the military.

soul is indeed possible, very much like the one Nina Zarechnaya enacted in your play once upon a time. By the way, where is Zarechnaya nowadays? Where is she and how is she?

TREPLYOV. She must be alive and well.

DORN. I was told that apparently she started to lead a sort of peculiar life. What's up?

TREPLYOV. That's a long story, Doctor.

DORN. Well, you can make it short. [*Pause.*]

TREPLYOV. She ran away from home and took up with Trigorin. That's something you already know, isn't it?

DORN. Yes, I know it.

TREPLYOV. She had a child. The child died. Trigorin fell out of love with her and returned to his former devotions, as might have been expected. Not that he had ever deserted them, however, but in keeping with his lack of character, he somehow managed to play both ends and the middle. As far as I'm able to understand what's been told to me, Nina's personal life has been a miserable failure.

DORN. But what about her stage career?

TREPLYOV. Even worse, it seems. She made her theatrical debut at some holiday resort or other near Moscow and then left for the provinces. In those days I never let her out of my sight, and for some time thereafter, wherever she appeared, there I was too. She kept on tackling the biggest parts, but she played them crudely, tastelessly, complete with the proverbial caterwauling and garish gesturing. Oh, there were moments when she gave forth cries of anguish with talent, when she died with talent, but that's all they ever were. Just moments.

DORN. Then you'd say, after all, there is a gift?

TREPLYOV. It was difficult to see, for certain. Yes, there must be. I saw her, but she didn't want to see me. The chambermaid refused me entrance into her hotel room. I understood the way she felt, so I didn't insist on a meeting. [*Pause.*] What else can I say to you? Afterwards, when I'd returned home here, I received some letters from her. The letters were intelligent, warm, provocative. She never complained, but I felt that she was profoundly unhappy—not one line that didn't reveal tightly stretched nervous tension. Even her imagination seemed a bit shattered. She kept signing her letters: "The Sea Gull." In the same way that the miller in *The Mermaid*[3] kept saying that he is a raven, so did she in her own letters keep on repeating that she was a sea gull. She's here now.

DORN. Here, what do you mean, here?

TREPLYOV. In town, at the inn. She's been living in one of the rooms there for about five days or so. I've already gone to visit her

---

3. A dramatic poem, *Rusalka* (1832), by A. S. Pushkin (1799–1837) that was never finished. In the poem, the miller's daughter (betrayed by a prince) throws herself into the Dnieper River and becomes a *rusalka*. Her father goes mad with grief over his daughter's death.

there, and Marya Ilinishna here has gone too, but she won't allow anyone to come in. Semyon Semyonovich is positive he saw her yesterday after dinner in the fields nearby, no more than two versts from here.

MEDVEDENKO. That's right, I did see her. She was walking away from here, on her way to town. I made my bow and asked her why she hasn't come to visit us. She said she was going to.

TREPLYOV. She won't come. [*Pause.*] Her father and step-mother won't have a thing to do with her. They've got watchmen stationed everywhere, just to keep her from going anywhere near the estate. [*Walks off with the* DOCTOR *toward his writing table.*] How very easy it is, Doctor, to be a philosopher on paper, and how difficult it is making it work out in practice!

SORIN. The girl was simply fascinating.

DORN. What's that, sir?

SORIN. The girl, I said, was simply fascinating. State Councilor Sorin was even in love with her for a little while.

DORN. You lecherous old man. [SHAMRAEV *can be heard laughing.*]

POLINA ANDREEVNA. It seems our travelers have come from the station . . .

TREPLYOV. Yes, I can hear Mama.

ARKADINA *and* TRIGORIN *enter, followed by* SHAMRAEV.

SHAMRAEV. [*entering*] We're all getting older and older, weathered as we are under the impact of nature's elements, but you, my dear honored lady, you remain forever young . . . Your bright-colored blouse, vivacity . . . grace . . .

ARKADINA. Look what you're trying to do again, you tedious person, you, casting an evil spell on me!

TRIGORIN. [*to* SORIN] Hello, Pyotr Nikolaevich! How is it you're always coming down with something? That's very bad! [*Having seen* MASHA, *happily.*] Marya Ilinishna!

MASHA. You recognized me? [*Shakes his hand.*]

TRIGORIN. Married?

MASHA. Long, long ago.

TRIGORIN. Are you happy? [*Bows to* DORN *and* MEDVEDENKO, *then hesitatingly walks to* TREPLYOV.] Irina Nikolaevna said you've forgotten the past completely and stopped being angry.

TREPLYOV *holds out his hand to* TRIGORIN.

ARKADINA. [*to her son*] Boris Alexeevich here has brought the journal with your new story.

TREPLYOV. [*takes the journal; to* TRIGORIN] Thank you. You're very kind.

They sit down.

TRIGORIN. Your admirers send their regards to you . . . In Petersburg and Moscow a great deal of interest is being expressed in you, and I'm always getting questioned about you. Oh, they keep on asking: what's he like, how old is he, does he have dark or light hair. For some reason or other, everyone thinks you're no longer a young person. And no one even knows your real name, since you publish your works under a pseudonym. You are as mysterious as the Man in the Iron Mask.[4]

TREPLYOV. Will you be staying for long with us?

TRIGORIN. No, I'm thinking of leaving for Moscow tomorrow. I must. I'm in a hurry to finish my story, and after that I've promised to get something ready for a collection of stories. In a word, it's the same old thing. [*While they are conversing,* ARKADINA *and* POLINA ANDREEVNA *put a card table in the middle of the room and open it.* SHAMRAEV *lights the candles and sets up chairs. A game of lotto[5] is brought from the cupboard.*] The weather has scarcely greeted me kindly. The wind is cruel. Tomorrow morning, if it quiets down, I'll set out for the lake to fish. By the way, I must take a look around the garden and that place where they produced your play. Do you remember? I've come up with an idea for a story, and the only thing I need do is trigger my memory of the place of action.

MASHA. [*to her father*] Papa, let my husband take a horse! He must go home.

SHAMRAEV. [*mimics*] A horse . . . to go home . . . [*Sternly.*] You've seen it yourself, the horses have just returned from the station. You can't just drive them again right away.

MASHA. But you know there are other horses . . . [*Seeing that her father is silent, she waves her hand.*] Trying to deal with you is like . . .

MEDVEDENKO. I can just walk home, Masha. Really and truly . . .

POLINA ANDREEVNA. [*having sighed*] To walk home, in this kind of weather . . . [*Sits at the card table.*] If you please, ladies and gentlemen.

MEDVEDENKO. You know its only six versts . . . Good-bye . . . [*Kisses his wife's hand.*] Good-bye, Mamasha. [*His mother-in-law reluctantly holds out her hand for him to kiss.*] I wouldn't have troubled anyone, but the baby . . . [*Bows to everyone.*] Good-bye . . . [*Goes out. His gait is apologetic.*]

SHAMRAEV. He can make it on foot all right. He's no general.

POLINA ANDREEVNA. [*taps on the table*] If you please, ladies and gentlemen. We've no time to lose, they'll be calling us to supper soon enough.

---

4. During the reign of Louis XIV in France, Mattioli, minister of Duke Charles Ferdinand of Mantua, was imprisoned for a number of years, dying in the Bastille in 1703. His imprisonment is the origin of numerous stories and historical studies associated with "the man in the iron mask."

5. Lotto is similar to bingo. In a recent essay, "*The Seagull's* Second Symbolist Play-Within-the-Play," W. Gareth Jones argues that the lotto game in this fourth act is closely related to Treplyov's symbolist play in the first act, comes up with an intricate numerological interpretation of the lotto numbers, and concludes that Chekhov's miniature drama (the lotto game) artfully demonstrated in 1896 what Maurice Maeterlinck (1862–1949) subsequently defined as *le tragique quotidien.* (*SEER*, 53, no. 130 [January 1975], 17–26.)

SHAMRAEV, MASHA, *and* DORN *sit at the table.*

ARKADINA. [*to* TRIGORIN] When the long autumn evening set in, they play lotto here. Will you look at that—it's the same old lotto we used to play with Mother, who's gone now, when we were children. You'd like to play a game with us before supper, wouldn't you? [*Sits down with* TRIGORIN *at the table.*] A boring game, but if you get used to it, it turns out all right. [*Deals out three cards to each player.*]

TREPLYOV. [*turning the pages of the journal*] He has read his own story, but he hasn't even cut the pages of mine. [*Puts the journal down on the writing table, then sets out for the door on the left. Walking past his mother, he kisses her on the head.*]

ARKADINA. How about you, Kostya?

TREPLYOV. Forgive me, I don't feel like it somehow . . . I'll pass the time in walking. [*Goes out.*]

ARKADINA. The stake is ten kopeks. Put it down for me, Doctor.

DORN. Yes, ma'am.

MASHA. Have all the stakes been put down? I'm beginning . . . Twenty-two!

ARKADINA. All right.

MASHA. Three!

DORN. So that's it, ma'am.

MASHA. Everyone put down three? Eight! Eighty-one! Ten!

SHAMRAEV. Slow down.

ARKADINA. What a reception they gave me in Kharkov,[6] goodness gracious me, my head hasn't stopped whirling yet!

MASHA. Thirty-four! [*A melancholy waltz is being played offstage.*]

ARKADINA. The students got together an ovation . . . Three baskets of flowers, two garlands, and see here . . . [*Unfastens a brooch from her breast and throws it on the table.*]

SHAMRAEV. Yes, that's something, that is . . .

MASHA. Fifty! . .

DORN. Exactly fifty?

ARKADINA. I wore a striking outfit . . . Say what you will, when it comes to dressing, I'm no fool.

POLINA ANDREEVNA. Kostya is playing the piano. The poor boy feels miserable.

SHAMRAEV. He's been getting a first-rate roasting in the newspapers.

MASHA. Seventy-seven!

ARKADINA. Why on earth should he pay any attention!

TRIGORIN. He just isn't lucky. He still can't seem to hit the right note. There's something far-fetched, undefined, even resembling at times a delirious nonsense. Not one living character can be found in his writings.

MASHA. Eleven!

---

6. A large city in the northeastern part of the Ukraine.

ARKADINA. [*having glanced around at* SORIN] Petrusha, are you getting bored? [*Pause.*] He's asleep.

DORN. The Honorable State Councilor is asleep.

MASHA. Seven! Ninety!

TRIGORIN. If I had lived on an estate like this, by the lake, would I have ever turned to writing? I would have overcome this passion of mine and I'd have done nothing but go fishing.

MASHA. Twenty-eight!

TRIGORIN. To catch perch or ruff—what a glorious feeling!

DORN. But I believe in Konstantin Gavrilych. There's something there, all right! There's something there, all right! He thinks in images, his stories are striking, vivid, and they move me deeply. The only regret is that he doesn't have any clearly defined aims. He makes an impression, and nothing more. But you know, you don't travel far by impression alone. Irina Nikolaevna, are you glad you have a son who's a writer?

ARKADINA. Just imagine, I still haven't read him. Somehow I never have the time.

MASHA. Twenty-six!

> TREPLYOV *enters quietly and goes to his writing table.*

SHAMRAEV. [*to* TRIGORIN] That thing of yours, Boris Alexeevich, is still with us.

TRIGORIN. What thing?

SHAMRAEV. Konstantin Gavrilych shot a sea gull once, and you charged me with the responsibility of getting it stuffed.

TRIGORIN. I don't remember. [*Pondering.*] I don't remember!

MASHA. Sixty-six! One!

TREPLYOV. [*opens wide the window and listens*] How dark it is! I don't understand why it is I feel so restless.

ARKADINA. Kostya, close the window, or it will blow in on us. [TREPLYOV *closes the window.*]

MASHA. Eighty-eight.

TRIGORIN. I have the game, ladies and gentlemen.

ARKADINA. [*happily*] Bravo! Bravo!

SHAMRAEV. Bravo!

ARKADINA. That man has all the luck. No matter where he is or what he's doing. [*Rises.*] And now let's go and get a bite of something or other. Our celebrity hasn't dined today. After supper we'll continue. [*To her son.*] Kostya, leave your manuscripts, let's go and eat.

TREPLYOV. I don't want to, Mama, I'm chock-full.

ARKADINA. Do as you please. [*Wakes up* SORIN.] Petrusha, time for supper! [*Takes* SHAMRAEV *by the arm.*] I'll tell you all about my reception in Kharkov . . .

> POLINA ANDREEVNA *puts out the candles on the table, then she and* DORN *wheel out* SORIN'S *chair. Everyone goes out the door on the left.* TREPLYOV *alone remains on stage at his writing table.*

TREPLYOV. [*gets ready to write; runs over what he has already written*] I've talked and talked a lot about new forms, yet I feel now that I too am slipping little by little into a conventional rut. [*Reads.*] "The placard on the fence proclaimed . . . The white face, framed by dark hair . . ." Proclaimed, framed . . . That's inept. [*Crosses out.*] I'll begin where the hero is awakened by the sound of rain, and all the rest must be tossed out. The description of the moonlit evening is long and much too precious. Trigorin has worked out his own devices, it's easy for him . . . He'd have the broken neck of a bottle glistening on the dike and the shadow of the mill wheel looming darker and darker—and there it is, the moonlit evening all set.[7] And what do I have? The tremulous light, and the soft glimmer of the stars, and the faraway sounds of a piano, dying off in the calm, fragrant air . . . That's agonizing. [*Pause.*] Yes, I'm invariably coming more and more to the conviction that the issue is a question neither of old nor of new forms, but that a person simply writes, never thinking about the kind of forms, he writes because it pours freely out of his soul. [*Someone raps on the window next to the table.*] What's that? [*Glances out the window.*] Nothing can be seen . . . [*Opens the glass door and looks out into the garden.*] Someone ran by down the steps. [*Calls.*] Who's out here? [*Goes out. Sounds can be heard of him walking quickly along the veranda. A half-minute later he returns with NINA ZARECHNAYA.*] Nina! Nina! [NINA *puts her head on his chest and, bursting into tears, restrains her sobbing.* TREPLYOV *is deeply moved.*] Nina! Nina! It's you . . . you . . . I've had a feeling, I knew you'd come here, I've longed for you, ached for you the whole livelong day. [TREPLYOV *takes off her hat and cape.*] My warmhearted girl, my beloved, she's come here. We won't weep, no, we won't.

NINA. Someone is here.

TREPLYOV. No one.

NINA. Lock the doors, or else they'll come in.

TREPLYOV. No one will come in.

NINA. I know Irina Nikolaevna is here. Lock the doors . . .

TREPLYOV. [*locks the door on the right with a key and goes to the door on the left*] There's no lock here. I'll block the door with an armchair. [*Places an armchair next to the door.*] Don't be frightened, no one will come in.

NINA. [*looks at his face intently*] Just let me look at you. [*Looks around.*] It's warm, nice . . . This place used to be the drawing room. Have I changed very much?

TREPLYOV. Yes . . . You've grown thinner, and your eyes have become bigger. Nina, somehow it's strange to see you as I do. Why is it you didn't let me come into your place? Why haven't you come here before? I know you've been living here almost a week

---

7. Chekhov used this particular image in his story *The Wolf* (1886) and mentioned it as a literary device to his brother Alexander in a letter dated May 10, 1886.

. . . I've gone to your place several times every day, I've stood outside under your window like a beggar.

NINA. I've been afraid you hated me. Every night I've had the same dream: you look at me and you don't recognize me. If you only knew! From the first moment I arrived, I kept walking over here . . . by the lake. I've gone by your home many times, and each time I've decided not to come in. Let's sit down. [*They sit down.*] We'll sit and talk, yes, talk. It's nice here, it's warm, cozy . . . Do you hear it—the wind? In Turgenev there's a passage: "Fortunate is the person on a night like this who can sit with a roof overhead, who has a warm corner."[8] I am a sea gull . . . No not right. [*Rubs her forehead.*] What was I talking about? Yes . . . Turgenev . . . "And may the Lord help all homeless wanderers . . ." It's nothing. [*Sobs.*]

TREPLYOV. Nina, you're weeping again . . . Nina!

NINA. It's nothing, it gives me relief . . . I've gone two whole years without crying. Yesterday, late at night, I went into the garden, to see if our theatre was intact. And there it still stands. I wept for the first time in two years, and I felt relieved, I felt much more cleansed in my soul. See, I'm no longer weeping. [*Takes him by his hand.*] And so you've already become a writer . . . You are a writer, I am an actress . . . We've fallen, you and I, right smack in the middle of the whirlpool . . . When I was a child, I lived a happy life—I'd wake up in the morning and start singing. I loved you, I dreamed about fame, and now? Tomorrow, early in the morning, I must go to Yelets[9] third-class . . . with peasants, and in Yelets cultured businessmen will bedevil me with their little gallantries. Life is shabby!

TREPLYOV. Why go to Yelets?

NINA. I took an engagement for the whole winter. It's time to leave.

TREPLYOV. Nina, I damned you, hated you, tore up your letters and photographs, but every moment I realized that my soul is bound forever to you. I didn't have the strength to fall out of love with you, Nina. Ever since I lost you and began to get published, life for me has been unbearable. I am tormented . . . It seems as if my youth has suddenly been torn away, and it seems to me I've already lived ninety years on this earth. I used to call for you, I used to kiss the very ground you walked on. No matter where I looked, everywhere your face appeared before me. That tender smile which once shone on me in the best years of my life . . .

NINA. [*distraught*] Why is he talking this way, why is he talking this way?

TREPLYOV. I am lonely. There's no one close to warm me, I am cold as if I were in a cave, and no matter what I write, everything, it's all dry, stale, gloomy. Stay here, Nina, I beg you, or else let me go

8. The quotation is from the epilogue to Turgenev's novel *Rudin* (1856).

9. A town in central Russia 230 miles south of Moscow.

with you! [NINA *quickly puts on her hat and cape*.] Nina, why?
For God's sake, Nina . . . [*Looks as she dresses herself. Pause*.]

NINA. My horses are standing at the garden gate. Don't see me off,
I can make it myself . . . [*Through tears*.] Give me some
water . . .

TREPLYOV. [*gives her water to drink*] Where are you off to now?

NINA. To town. [*Pause*.] Is Irina Nikolaevna here?

TREPLYOV. Yes . . . On Thursday Uncle was not well, so we tele-
graphed her to come.

NINA. Why do you say you kissed the very ground I walked on? I
ought to be killed. [*Bends toward the table*.] I'm so weary! If
I could rest . . . rest! [*Raises her head*.] I am a sea gull . . . No,
not right. I am an actress. So, yes! [*Having heard the laughter
of* ARKADINA *and* TRIGORIN, *she listens, then runs to the door on
the left and looks through the keyhole*.] He's here too . . . [*Returns to* TREPLYOV.] So, yes . . . It's nothing . . . Yes . . . He
didn't believe in the theatre, he kept on laughing at my dreams,
and little by little I too stopped believing and my spirit sank . . .
Here too were worries of love, jealousy, continual fear for my
little one . . . I turned into someone trivial, a nonentity, I acted
out my roles without a single thought in my head . . . I didn't
know what to do with my hands, how to stand on the stage, or to
control my voice. You can't understand a condition like this,
when you instinctively know you are acting horribly. I am a sea
gull. No, not right . . . Do you remember, you shot down a sea
gull? A man happens to come by, sees her, and, having nothing
else to do, destroys her . . . A subject for a short story. That's not
right . . . [*Rubs her forehead*.] What was I talking about? . . I
was talking about the stage. I'm not the same now as I used to be
. . . I'm a genuine actress now, I revel in the joy of playing roles,
I'm enraptured. When I'm on the stage, I'm drunk with delight,
and I feel myself beautiful. And now, while I've been living here,
I go for walks all the time, I keep on walking and I think, I think
and feel how with each passing day my mind and soul keep growing stronger . . . I know now, Kostya, I've come to realize that in
our work—it doesn't matter whether we play roles on stage or
whether we write—the important thing is neither fame nor
glamor nor what I used to dream about, but it's knowing how to
endure. Know how to bear your cross and have faith. I have faith,
and it's not so painful to me. And when I think about my profession, then I'm no longer afraid of life.

TREPLYOV. [*sadly*] You've found your path, you know where
you're going, but I still keep on drifting in a maelstrom of dreams
and images, not knowing why it has to be or for whose sake. I
don't have faith, and I don't know what my profession is all
about.

NINA. [*listening*] Tss . . . I'm going. Good-bye. When I become a
great actress, come and see me on the stage. Promise? And now

. . . [*Presses his hand.*] It's late. I can scarcely stand up . . . I'm exhausted, I want something to eat . . .

TREPLYOV. Stay, I'll give you some supper . . .

NINA. No, no . . . Don't see me on my way, I'll get there by myself . . . My horses are close by . . . And so she brought him with her? Well, hmm, it doesn't matter. When you see Trigorin, don't tell him a single thing . . . I love him. I love him even more strongly than before . . . A subject for a short story . . . I love him. I love him passionately. I love him desperately. How good it was before, Kostya! Do you remember? What a serene, warm, joyous life, how pure. What feelings we used to have, feelings like tender, elegant flowers . . . Do you remember? . . [*Recites.*] "Men and women, the lions, the eagles and the partridges, the antlered deer, the geese, the spiders, the silent fishes living in the sea, the starfishes and those creatures invisible to the eye—in a word, all who live, all who live, all, all having gone through their sad life cycles are now extinct. A thousand centuries have gone by on this earth without one single living thing, and this poor moon has turned on its lantern in vain. On this meadow no one awakens to the cry of the cranes, and the May beetles are heard no longer in the lime groves . . ." [*Embraces* TREPLYOV *impulsively and runs out through the glass door.*]

TREPLYOV. [*after a pause*] It'd be very bad if someone met her in the garden and told Mama. It might upset Mama . . .

> In the next two minutes of silence, he tears up all of his manuscripts and throws them under the table. Then he unlocks the door on the right and goes out.

DORN. [*trying to open the door on the left*] Strange. The door seems to be locked . . . [*Enters and puts the armchair in its place.*] An obstacle race.

> [ARKADINA *and* POLINA ANDREEVNA *enter, followed by* YAKOV, *who carries bottles, and* MASHA; *then* SHAMRAEV *and* TREGORIN.]

ARKADINA. Put the red wine and beer for Boris Alexeevich here, on the table. We shall play as we drink. Let's sit down, ladies and gentlemen.

POLINA ANDREEVNA. [*to* YAKOV] Bring tea now as well. [*Lights the candles and sits at the card table.*]

SHAMRAEV. [*leads* TRIGORIN *to the cupboard*] Here's that thing I was talking about just now . . . [*Gets the stuffed sea gull out of the cupboard.*] You wanted it done.

TRIGORIN. [*looks at the sea gull*] I don't remember! [*Having thought about it.*] I don't remember!

> On the right, offstage, there is a gunshot. Everyone flinches.

ARKADINA. [*frightened*] What was that?

DORN. It's nothing. Probably just something that burst in my medicine case. Don't upset yourself. [*Goes out the door on the right, returns in half of a minute.*] Just as I thought. A bottle of ether burst. [*Sings.*] "Once again I stand before you, enchanted . . ."

ARKADINA. [*sitting at the table*] Whew, I was frightened. It brought to mind once more how . . . [*Covers her face with her hands.*] Everything went black before my eyes . . .

DORN. [*turning the pages of a journal, to* TRIGORIN] About two months ago a certain article was printed here . . . a letter from America, and I wanted to ask you, incidentally . . . [*Takes* TRIGORIN *by the waist and leads him to the footlights.*] since I'm very much interested in this question . . . [*Drops his voice, in an undertone.*] Take Irina Nikolaevna somewhere, away from here. The fact is, Konstantin Gavrilovich has shot himself . . .

CURTAIN

Uncle Vanya

The chief source of *Uncle Vanya* (1895–97) is an earlier Chekhov play, *The Wood Demon* (*Lešij*, 1889), which originally consisted of material the author had planned for a novel in 1888–89. Even though Chekhov claimed to have written *Uncle Vanya* in 1890, most critics agree that it was probably reworked from *The Wood Demon* at about the same time that the author was writing *The Sea Gull*, i.e., in 1895. It was published in 1897. Approximately two-thirds of *Uncle Vanya* consists of the very same dialogue as in *The Wood Demon* (both plays are compared in an essay collected in this volume), although the second play is better structured as a play than is the earlier version.

Like the background of *The Sea Gull*, the environment of *Uncle Vanya* is centered on the life style of a provincial estate, wherein the wanton and wasteful destruction of the land and its resources is paralleled by the destruction that takes place in the lives of the characters.

Two or three references to Russian provincial life can be explained here. For example, in Act II, Yelena and Sonya patch up their quarrel, and Yelena says: "Let's drink to our friendship. . . . Well, it means we're friends now, close friends (literally, "Let us drink to *Brudershaft* [brotherhood or fellowship]." . . . Well, that means—*na ty?*" (or, "we will use the familiar second person when we address each other?") (p. 74). The action when drinking to friendship (*Brudershaft*) usually requires linking arms and touching glasses. In the same act, Dr. Astrov dances and sings:

> "Dance away, my stove, dance away, my shed,
> There's no place for the master to go to bed." [p. 70]

The origin of this song is unknown, but critics suggest that it may be a *častuška*, a topical and funny folk verse which corresponds in part to our limerick. In Act III, Dr. Astrov explains his ecological map to Yelena and refers to the "hermitages of Old Believers" (p. 79). (Sometimes referred to as Old Ritualists or Schismatics, they split from the Russian Orthodox Church in 1667 over the revision of Russian church books, preferring the older versions.) As he is getting ready to leave in the last act, Dr. Astrov says, "My trace horse has gone lame somehow" (p. 94). The two trace horses are harnessed (in traces or straps) outside the two shafts between which the middle horse is harnessed. The two trace (side) horses gallop, whereas the middle horse trots. This is standard practice for the troika in Russia and Hungary.

As in *The Sea Gull*, Chekhov chose appropriate names for his characters in *Uncle Vanya*. For example, in keeping with his high purpose to preserve the earth's resources, the hard-working doctor received as his last name a Russian word that suggests "stars." *Yelena*, the first name of the professor's beautiful wife, is the Russian equivalent of the Greek *Helen. Ivan* or *Uncle*

Vanya is the equivalent of our *John* or *Uncle Johnny*—perhaps the most common of names. The professor's last name contains a root of the Russian word for *silver*, as well as a root of the Russian verb meaning "to drop with a bang." His daughter's first name, *Sonya*, is a variant on the Greek name *Sophia* ("wisdom"). Her dead mother's name, *Vera*, is Latin for "true," and her mother's patronymic, *Petrovna*, is a variant of the Greek word *Peter* ("rock," "stone").

The pronunciation of the characters' names, together with the appropriate stress:

> Alexándr Vladimirovich (vladímiravich) Serebryakov (serebryakóf)
> Yeléna Andréevna
> Sófya (Sónya) Alexandrovna (alexándravna)
> Mária Vasílevna Voynitskaya (vaynítskaya)
> Iván (Ványa) Petróvich Voynitsky (vaynítsky)
> Mikhaíl Lvóvich Astrov (ástraf)
> Ilyá Ilích Telégin
> Marína Timofeevna (timaféevna)

Other personal and place names (in alphabetical order) are: Ayvazovsky (ayvazófsky); Batyushkov (bátyushkaf); Grigóry Ilích; Iván Iványch; Kharkov (khárkaf); Konstantin (kanstantín) Trifimovich (trifímavich) Lakedemonov (lakedemónaf); Lenochka (lénachka); Malitskoe (málitskae); Pável Alexéevich; Petrúshka; Rozhdestvennoe (razhdéstvennae); Sofi (safí); Sónechka; Túla; Véra Petróvna; Yefím.

Uncle Vanya

Scenes from Country Life in Four Acts

LIST OF CHARACTERS

ALEXANDR VLADIMIROVICH SEREBRYAKOV, *a retired professor*
YELENA ANDREEVNA, *his wife, aged twenty-seven*
SOFYA ALEXANDROVNA* (*SONYA*), *his daughter by his first marriage*
MARIA VASILEVNA VOYNITSKAYA, *widow of a Privy Councilor,*[1] *mother of the professor's first wife*
IVAN PETROVICH VOYNITSKY, *her son*
MIKHAIL LVOVICH ASTROV, *a doctor*
ILYA ILICH TELEGIN, *an impoverished landowner*
MARINA, *an old nurse*
A WORKMAN

The action takes place on SEREBRYAKOV'S *estate.*

Act One

A garden. Part of the garden and the veranda are visible. A table set for tea has been placed in the pathway under an old poplar tree. There are benches and chairs, and a guitar is lying on one of the benches. Not far from the table is a swing. It is between two and three o'clock on a cloudy and gloomy afternoon. MARINA, *a heavy-set old woman with neither the ability nor inclination to move with ease, sits by the samovar and knits a stocking.* ASTROV *is walking near her.*

MARINA. [*pours a glass of tea*] Take some tea, my pet.
ASTROV. [*takes the glass reluctantly*] Somehow or other I don't feel like it.
MARINA. Maybe a drop or two of vodka?
ASTROV. No. I don't drink vodka every day. Besides it's too muggy. [*Pause.*] How many years have gone by, *nyanka,*[2] that we've known each other?
MARINA. [*deliberating*] How many years? Oh, Lord help me recollect . . . You came here, into these parts . . . when? . . So-nechka's[3] mother, Vera Petrovna, was still living. You used to visit us during her last two winters . . . So it must be about eleven years have gone by! [*Having thought a moment.*] But maybe even more . . .

---

1. In the civil service, the third rank, equivalent to the rank of lieutenant-general in the military.

2. Pronounced *nyánka.* A colloquial word for *nyanya* (*nyánya*), "nanny" or nurse.
3. A term of endearment for *Sonya.*

ASTROV. Have I changed a good deal since then?

MARINA. A good deal. At the time you were young, as handsome as they come, but now you've started putting on years. Those good looks of yours aren't the same anymore. And I might as well say it —nowadays you keep on drinking your drop or two of vodka.

ASTROV. Yes . . . In ten years I've become a different person. And the reason for it? Been working too long and too hard, *nyanka*. From morning till night always on the go, I get no peace, and at night I lie under the bedcovers, scared they may drag me out to a patient. All the time we've known each other I've never had a free day, not one. How can I help but put on years? And life itself is boring, stupid, sordid . . . drags you down, a life like this. You're surrounded by eccentric people, no matter where you look, it's one foolish person after the next. Live around them two or three years, and little by little you become strange yourself, and you never notice it. A fate you can't escape. [*Twisting his long moustache.*] Phew, see this, I've grown a colossal moustache . . . An asinine moustache. I've become eccentric too, *nyanka* . . . I haven't turned stupid, not yet, thank the Lord, my brains still work, but somehow or other my feelings seem dead to the world. There's nothing I want, nothing I need, no one I even love . . . Except you, perhaps, you're the only one I may love. [*Kisses her on the head.*] When I was a child, I had a *nyanka* like you.

MARINA. Maybe you'd like something to eat?

ASTROV. No. The third week of Lent I went to Malitskoe on account of the epidemic . . . Spotted typhus . . . In the huts the villagers were stretched out every which way . . . Mud and grime, reeking smells, smoke, even calves on the floor alongside the sick people . . . Little pigs on the spot, too . . . I kept at it the whole day, didn't sit down once or take a bite to eat, and when I came home, they didn't give me a moment's peace and rest. A switchman from the railroad was brought in. I put him on the table to operate, and he went and died on me under the chloroform. Just when I didn't need it, my feelings came back again, and I was tortured so much by my conscience I felt I'd deliberately killed him . . . I sat down, closed my eyes—just like this—and I began to think. Will those people who live after us, in the course of a hundred or two hundred years, those people we're clearing the way for now, will they remember and speak kindly of us? Why, *nyanka*, you know they won't remember!

MARINA. People won't remember, but God will.

ASTROV. Thanks. Thanks a lot. You said it very well.

VOYNITSKY *enters.*

VOYNITSKY. [*Comes out of the house. He has had a good nap after lunch and appears rumpled. He sits down on a bench and adjusts his stylish tie.*] Yes . . . [*Pause.*] Yes . . .

ASTROV. Had a good sleep?

VOYNITSKY. Yes . . . Very good. [*Yawns.*] From the moment the professor and his spouse came here to live, our life has been knocked smack out of kilter . . . I sleep at the wrong time, eat all kinds of rich sauces for lunch and dinner, drink wine . . . bad for the health, every bit of it! In the old days there wasn't one free minute, Sonya and I kept working—believe you me, we did—but now only Sonya keeps working, while I sleep, eat, drink . . . That's very bad!

MARINA. [*having nodded her head*] Higgledy-piggledy! The professor gets up at twelve o'clock, while the samovar's been boiling since morning, the whole time just waiting for him. Without them here, we always ate dinner between twelve and one, like decent people everywhere, but with them here it's after six in the evening. At night the professor reads and writes, and suddenly, after one o'clock in the morning, the bell . . . Good gracious me, what is it? Why, it's tea he's after! So you must wake up people for it, put on the samovar . . . Higgledy-piggledy!

ASTROV. How much longer are they going to stay?

VOYNITSKY. [*whistles*] A hundred years. The professor's decided to settle down here.

MARINA. See, that's the way things are nowadays. The samovar's been on the table for two whole hours, and they've up and gone for a walk.

VOYNITSKY. They're coming, they're coming . . . Don't get upset.
Voices are heard. Returning from a stroll, SEREBRYAKOV, YELENA ANDREEVNA, SONYA, *and* TELEGIN *enter from the depths of the garden.*

SEREBRYAKOV. Excellent, excellent . . . Simply marvelous scenery.

TELEGIN. Out of this world, your Excellency.[4]

SONYA. And tomorrow, Papa, we're off to the forest preserve. Want to come?

VOYNITSKY. Time for tea, ladies and gentlemen!

SEREBRYAKOV. My friends, would you be so kind as to have my tea sent to me in the study! There are still one or two things I must do today.

SONYA. You'll like it at the forest preserve, no question about it . . .
YELENA ANDREEVNA, SEREBRYAKOV, *and* SONYA *go into the house.* TELEGIN *goes to the table and sits near* MARINA.

VOYNITSKY. It's hot and it's muggy, but our great man of letters is dressed in overcoat and galoshes, carries an umbrella, and is wearing gloves.

ASTROV. It proves he's taking care of himself.

VOYNITSKY. Oh, how lovely she is, lovely! I haven't seen a more beautiful woman in my whole life.

TELEGIN. Whether I drive through the fields, Marina Timofeevna, or walk in a shady garden, or look at this table, I experience inexpressible bliss! The weather is charming, the birds are singing, we

---

4. Telegin's form of address to the professor is an indication of Serebryakov's high rank in the civil service.

live together in peace and harmony—what more do we need? [*Accepting a glass of tea.*] I'm much obliged to you, much obliged.

VOYNITSKY. [*dreamily*] Her eyes . . . A marvelous woman!

ASTROV. Ivan Petrovich, at least say something.

VOYNITSKY. [*listlessly*] What is it you'd like me to say?

ASTROV. What's new, anything?

VOYNITSKY. Nothing. Everything's old. I'm still the same as I was, even worse perhaps, because I've grown lazy. I don't do anything. I only fret and fume like the proverbial old crabapple, while my dear *Maman*, the lazy old crow, keeps on squawking about the emancipation of women. With one eye she fastens on the grave, with the other she searches through her books of learning for the dawn of a new life.

ASTROV. And the professor?

VOYNITSKY. And the professor, the same as before, from morning until deep into the night, sits in his study and writes.

> "With crinkled brow and toiling brain
> Our epic odes we phrase and rhyme with everlasting might,
> But neither we nor they can e'er obtain
> One bit of praise from anywhere no matter what we write."[5]

Poor, unfortunate paper! He'd be better off to write his autobiography. Oh, what a superb subject that would be! A retired professor, don't you get it, an old dried-up biscuit, a learned, smoke-cured fish . . . he has gout, rheumatism, migraine, his liver is swollen with jealousy and envy . . . this learned, smoke-cured fish lives on the estate of his first wife, lives there against his will because he hasn't the money to live in town. He goes on and on, grumbling about his misfortunes, although really he's been remarkably lucky. [*Nervously.*] Only think how lucky! The son of a common sexton, schooled in theology, he picked up his university degrees and got his professorship. He became "your Excellency," the son-in-law of a senator[6] and so on, and so on. All that really doesn't matter, of course, but you'd better take stock of this. A person lectures and writes about art for precisely twenty-five years, but he understands precisely nothing about art. For twenty-five years he's gone on chewing up and spitting out everyone else's ideas about realism, naturalism, and every other kind of nonsense. For twenty-five years he's been lecturing and writing what intelligent people have known about for a long time and what stupid people have no interest in. To put it bluntly, for twenty-five years he's been pouring from one empty pot into the next. And at the same time what incredible conceit, what cocksure pretensions!

---

5. These lines are from the satire *Somebody Else's Doctrine* (*Čužoj tolk*, 1794) by I. I. Dmitriev (1760–1837), in which the main character lacks talent in writing poetry.

6. A member of the Senate would have ranked very high in the Russian civil service—higher than a general in the military.

He's retired and not one living soul even knows who he is. He's completely unheard of. To put it bluntly, for twenty-five years he's taken over someone else's job. And just look at him. He prances around like a demigod!

ASTROV. Well, I'd say offhand you envy him.

VOYNITSKY. Yes, I do envy him! See how successful he's been with women! Why, not one Don Juan was ever that successful! His first wife, my sister, an excellent, gentle creature—as pure as that blue sky—a noble, generous woman with far more admirers than he's had students. Why, she loved him as only the angels, purity incarnate, can love those who are as pure and excellent as themselves. My own mother, his mother-in-law, still worships him. He still inspires her with feelings of reverent awe. His second wife, beautiful and intelligent—you've just seen her—married him when he was already an old man and gave him her youth, her beauty, her freedom, the radiance that is hers alone. And for what? Why?

ASTROV. She is faithful to the professor?

VOYNITSKY. Unfortunately, yes.

ASTROV. Why do you say, unfortunately?

VOYNITSKY. Because fidelity like hers is false from beginning to end. You find a lot of rhetoric in it, but no logic. To deceive an old husband you can't endure—that's immoral. To try to suppress your own feelings of life, vitality, and youth—that's not immoral.

TELEGIN. [*in a tearful voice*] Vanya, I don't like it when you talk like this. Look here, now, really . . . Whoever betrays a wife or a husband is someone who, consequently, is an unfaithful person, one who might even betray his own native land!

VOYNITSKY. [*with annoyance*] Plug up your fountain, Waffles!

TELEGIN. If you don't mind, Vanya. On the very day after our wedding, my wife ran away with a man she adored, by reason of my unprepossessing appearance. Since then I've always lived up to my responsibility. I still love her and I'm faithful to her. I help her in whatever way I can. I've given everything I own to the education of the children she's had by her lover. I've been deprived of happiness, but I still have my pride. And she? Her youth has gone by, her beauty under the influence of nature's laws has withered away, her lover has died . . . What does she have left?

> SONYA *and* YELENA ANDREEVNA *enter. A moment or so later* MARIA VASILEVNA *enters with a book; she sits and reads; tea is given to her and she drinks it without looking around.*

SONYA. [*in haste, to the nurse*] Over there, nyanechka,[7] some persons from the village have just come. Go and talk to them, and I'll take care of the tea myself . . . [*Pours tea. The nurse goes out.* YELENA ANDREEVNA *takes her cup and drinks, sitting in the swing.*]

ASTROV. [*to* YELENA ANDREEVNA] I'm here, you know, to see your

---

7. Pronounced *nyánechka.* A term of endearment for *nyanya.*

husband. You wrote that he was very sick, rheumatism and something else, but it turns out he's hale and hearty.

YELENA ANDREEVNA. Last night he was depressed and complained about pains in his legs, but today there's nothing wrong . . .

ASTROV. And I just galloped thirty versts at breakneck speed. Oh, well, forget it, it isn't the first time. To make up for it I'll stay until tomorrow and at least I'll get a good sleep—*quantum satis.*[8]

SONYA. Oh, that's marvelous. You hardly ever stay with us. I don't suppose you've had dinner?

ASTROV. No, miss, I haven't.

SONYA. Then you can stay and have dinner here, too. Nowadays we have dinner after six. [*Drinks tea.*] The tea's cold!

TELEGIN. The temperature in the samovar has dropped significantly.

YELENA ANDREEVNA. It's all right, Ivan Ivanych, we'll drink it cold.

TELEGIN. Beg your pardon, ma'am . . . It's not Ivan Ivanych, but Ilya Ilich, ma'am . . . Ilya Ilich Telegin, or, as some people call me, by reason of my pockmarked face, Waffles. Sometime back I served as Sonechka's godfather and blessed her, and his Excellency, your spouse, knows me very well. Nowadays I live here, ma'am, on this estate, ma'am . . . You may have been so good as to notice I eat dinner with you every day.

SONYA. Ilya Ilich is our helper, our right hand. [*Tenderly.*] Let me pour more tea for you, Godfather.

MARIA VASILEVNA. Oh!

SONYA. What is it, Grandmother?

MARIA VASILEVNA. I forgot to tell Alexandr . . . it completely escaped me . . . today I received a letter from Kharkov, from Pavel Alexeevich[9] . . . He sent his own new pamphlet . . .

ASTROV. Interesting?

MARINA VASILEVNA. Interesting, but somehow strange. He refutes the very point that he himself defended seven years ago. It's awful!

VOYNITSKY. Nothing awful about that. Drink your tea, *Maman.*

MARIA VASILEVNA. But I want to talk!

VOYNITSKY. For fifty years now we've been talking and talking and reading pamphlets. It's high time we stopped.

MARINA VASILEVNA. For some reason you find it unpleasant to listen to me when I speak. Forgive me, Jean,[1] but you've changed so much in the last year that I don't even know you anymore . . . You used to be a person with definite convictions, a shining personality . . .

VOYNITSKY. Oh, yes! I used to be a shining personality, whose light never illuminated a single person, not one . . . [*Pause.*] I used to be a shining personality . . . You couldn't have come up with a

---

8. "As much as is needed."
9. Kharkov (*khárkaf*) is a large city in the northeastern part of the Ukraine.
1. In the early years of the nineteenth century, the upper classes in Russia employed French extensively. The practice diminished in succeeding decades.

deadlier joke! I'm forty-seven now. Up to last year I did what you are doing. I deliberately tried to cloud my vision with the same sort of scholarship that you use, so that I lost sight of life as it's really and truly lived. And I thought I was doing what was right. But now, if you only knew! I can't sleep at night because of the disappointment and the anger I feel at how stupidly I let time glide by. Oh, the years I wasted when I could have had everything I can't have now because I am too old.

SONYA. Uncle Vanya, this is boring.

MARIA VASILEVNA. [*to her son*] It sounds like you're holding your own former convictions responsible for something or other . . . Don't blame them, blame yourself. You've forgotten that convictions by themselves mean nothing, a dead letter . . . Something useful ought to have gotten done.[2]

VOYNITSKY. Something useful? Not everyone is capable of being a writer *perpetuum mobile*, like your Herr Professor.

MARIA VASILEVNA. And what precisely do you mean by that?

SONYA. [*pleadingly*] Grandmother! Uncle Vanya! I beg you!

VOYNITSKY. My lips are sealed, sealed and with my apologies. [*Pause.*]

YELENA ANDREEVNA. What lovely weather today . . . It's not too hot . . . [*Pause.*]

VOYNITSKY. In lovely weather like this a man could hang himself . . .

　　　　TELEGIN *tunes the guitar.* MARINA *walks near the house and calls the chickens.*

MARINA. *Tsip, tsip, tsip*[3] . . .

SONYA. *Nyanechka*, what did the people from the village come for?

MARINA. It's the same thing, as always. They were going on again about the waste land. *Tsip, tsip, tsip* . . .

SONYA. Which one are you after?

MARINA. The speckled hen has walked off with her chicks . . . The crows might steal them . . . [*Goes out.*]

　　　　TELEGIN *plays a polka. All listen in silence.* A WORKMAN *enters.*

WORKMAN. Is the gentleman who's a doctor here? [*To* ASTROV.] Please, Mikhail Lvovich, they've come for you.

ASTROV. From where?

WORKMAN. From the factory.

2. In Chekhov's day, as Simon Karlinsky points out, a second meaning for the sentence "Something useful ought to have gotten done" existed. That is, "Something for the cause ought to have gotten done." The "cause" consisted of "socially useful actions" to alleviate the suffering of the Russian people. The "cause" as claimed by Maria Vasilevna in this act, as well as by Serebryakov, who repeats the same thought in his charge (translated as "Ladies and gentlemen, you must get down to work. Something useful ought to get done.") to the family in Act IV (p. 93), is an ironic comment on the actions of Serebryakov, Yelena Andreevna, and Maria Vasilevna. (*Anton Chekhov's Life and Thought: Selected Letters and Commentary*, tr. Michael Henry Heim and Simon Karlinsky [Berkeley: University of California Press, 1975], p. 28.)

3. The Russian equivalent of the American "chick, chick, chick."

ASTROV. [*with annoyance*] I thank you kindly. Oh, well, I must go then . . . [*Looks around for his cap.*] Oh, that's damned annoying . . .

SONYA. It's not a bit pleasant, I know . . . When you're through at the factory, why don't you come back here for dinner?

ASTROV. No, it will be too late. Where is it possible . . . Whereabouts could I . . . [*To the* WORKMAN.] Look here, my good man, go and fetch me a glass of vodka. [WORKMAN *goes out.*] Where is it possible . . . whereabouts could I . . . [*He has found his cap.*] In one of Ostrovsky's plays there's a person with a thick moustache and very thin wit . . . That's me. Well, ladies and gentlemen, I have the honor . . . [*To* YELENA ANDREEVNA.] If you happen to drop by my place sometime, with Sofya Alexandrovna here, I'd be sincerely happy. My estate isn't large by any means, a little more than eighty acres, but if you're interested there's a model orchard and a nursery which you won't find within a thousand versts around here. And right next to my place there's a government forest preserve . . . The forester there is an old man and sick most of the time, so that I really look after the whole place.

YELENA ANDREEVNA. I've been told how very much you love the forests. Of course, you can do a world of good that way, but doesn't it interfere with your real calling? After all, you are a doctor.

ASTROV. God alone knows what our real calling is.

YELENA ANDREEVNA. And is it interesting?

ASTROV. Yes, the work is interesting.

VOYNITSKY. [*with irony*] Very!

YELENA ANDREEVNA. [*To* ASTROV] You're still a young man, you look no more than, well . . . thirty-six—thirty-seven . . . and surely it isn't as interesting as you claim it is. Trees, trees, nothing but trees. Seems to me, that's the very same image, one very much like the next.

SONYA. No, it's extremely interesting. Mikhail Lvovich plants new forests every year, and he's already received a bronze medal and a diploma for his work. He's doing everything he can to stop the devastation of the old forests. If you listen closely to him, you'll agree with him completely. He says that the forests glorify our earth, they teach a person the meaning of beauty and kindle a spirit of majesty. The forests make the climate less severe. In countries where the climate is mild, less energy is spent in the struggle with nature, and so there we find a gentler, more understanding person. There too people are beautiful, pliant, and responsive; their speech is elegant, and their movements are graceful. Both science and art thrive among them, their philosophy is never somber, their attitude toward women is fully refined, noble . . .

VOYNITSKY. [*laughing*] Bravo, bravo! . . All of this is very nice but it's not convincing. [*To* ASTROV.] So, my friend, let me go on burn-ing firewood in my stoves and building my barns out of trees.

ASTROV. You can burn peat in your stoves and build your barns out of stone. Well, I'll go along with your cutting down forests when you absolutely need to, but why must you devastate them? The forests in Russia are cracking under the axe. Millions upon millions of trees are being wasted, the homes of the animals and birds are choked out, the rivers grow shallow and dry up, the marvelous landscape is disappearing, gone forever, and it's all because the lazy person doesn't have sense enough to bend down and pick up his fuel from the earth. [*To* YELENA ANDREEVNA.] Isn't that true, madam? Only a thoughtless barbarian could burn beauty like this in his stove and destroy what we ourselves can't create. Man is endowed with reason and with the power of crea-tion so he can increase what is given to him, but up to this mo-ment he hasn't created—he's destroyed. The forests diminish year after year, rivers dry up, wildlife is coming to an end, the climate is spoiled, and with every passing day the earth keeps growing poorer and uglier. [*To* VOYNITSKY.] I see that look of irony on your face. What I've been saying doesn't seem serious to you, and . . . and perhaps it's only an idea an eccentric might come up with. But when I walk past the forests belonging to the villages, the for-ests I saved from being cut down, or when I hear the sounds of the young forests I planted with my own hands, then I realize that the climate is partly in my power too. And if in the course of a thou-sand years humankind finds happiness, I realize that I too will be partly responsible for it. When I plant a young birch and then see its leaves turn green and the way it sways in the wind, my soul is filled with pride, and I . . . [*Having seen the* WORKMAN, *who has brought a glass of vodka on a tray.*] However . . . [*Drinks.*] It's time for me. When it's over and done with, it's probably an idea an eccentric might come up with. I have the honor to say good-bye! [*Goes to the house.*]

SONYA. [*takes him by the arm and goes with him*] When is it you're coming to see us?

ASTROV. I don't know . . .

SONYA. Not again for a whole month? . .

> ASTROV *and* SONYA *go into the house.* MARIA VASILEVNA *and* TELEGIN *remain near the table.* YELENA ANDREEVNA *and* VOY-NITSKY *walk to the veranda.*

YELENA ANDREEVNA. And you, Ivan Petrovich, have behaved abys-mally again. Why did you have to upset Maria Vasilevna by talk-ing about the *perpetuum mobile!* And today at lunch you quarreled with Alexandr again. It's so trivial, really it is!

VOYNITSKY. What if I hate him!

YELENA ANDREEVNA. You have no reason to hate Alexandr. He's the same as anyone else. No worse than you.

VOYNITSKY. If only you could see your face, the way you move . . . Even to go on living seems too much of an effort for you! Oh, much too much!

YELENA ANDREEVNA. Oh, much too much and how boring it is, too! Everyone chides my husband, they all look at me with such sympathy. "How unfortunate you are, you have an old husband!" This concern for me—oh, how well I understand it! How was it Astrov said it just now? All of you are thoughtlessly destroying the forests, and soon nothing will be left on earth. In the same way you are thoughtlessly destroying humankind, and soon, thanks to you, there will be neither loyalty nor purity nor the talent for self-sacrifice left on this earth. Why is it you can't be indifferent to women who do not belong to you? Because—and the doctor is right—there's a devil of destruction inside every one of you. You don't care one whit for the forests, for the birds, for the women, or even for each other.

VOYNITSKY. I don't like this kind of philosophy.

YELENA ANDREEVNA. That doctor of yours looks tired and on edge. It's a handsome face. Apparently Sonya is attracted to him. She's fallen in love with him, and I can understand why she has. He's been here three times since my arrival, but I'm shy and not once have I spoken with him as I should, and I haven't been particularly kind to him. He must think I'm spiteful. You and I are good friends, Ivan Petrovich, and it's probably because we're both tedious, boring people! Tedious! Don't look at me the way you do, I don't like it.

VOYNITSKY. What other way can I look at you if I love you? You are my happiness, my life, my youth! I know my chances of your returning my love are next to nothing, equal to zero. There's nothing I want—only let me look at you, hear your voice . . .

YELENA ANDREEVNA. Shush, they may hear you! [*They go into the house.*]

VOYNITSKY. [*following her*] Just let me talk about my love, don't drive me away, and this and this alone will make me the happiest person in the world . . .

YELENA ANDREEVNA. This is torture . . .

> Both go into the house. TELEGIN strikes the strings and plays a polka. MARIA VASILEVNA jots down something on the margin of the pamphlet.

CURTAIN

Act Two

The dining room in SEREBRYAKOV's *house. Night. The watchman can be heard tapping in the garden.*[4] SEREBRYAKOV *is*

---

4. See note 7, p. 38 (*The Sea Gull*).

*sitting in an armchair in front of an open window, he is doz-
ing.* YELENA ANDREEVNA *is sitting next to him, and she too is
dozing.*

SEREBRYAKOV. [*having awakened*] Who's there? Is it you, Sonya?

YELENA ANDREEVNA. It's me.

SEREBRYAKOV. You, Lenochka[5] . . . Oh, this pain is excruciating!

YELENA ANDREEVNA. Your blanket's fallen on the floor. [*Wraps it
around his legs.*] I'll shut the window, Alexandr.

SEREBRYAKOV. No, it feels muggy to me . . . I dozed off just now
and dreamed that my left leg belonged to someone else. I woke up
from the torture of this pain. No, it isn't gout, it's closer to rheumatism. What time is it now?

YELENA ANDREEVNA. Twenty minutes past twelve. [*Pause.*]

SEREBRYAKOV. In the morning look for Batyushkov[6] in the library.
I believe we have him here.

YELENA ANDREEVNA. What?

SEREBRYAKOV. Look for Batyushkov in the morning. I remember we
had him here. But why is it so hard for me to breathe?

YELENA ANDREEVNA. You're tired. It's the second night you've gone
without sleep.

SEREBRYAKOV. They say that Turgenev's *angina pectoris*[7] came from
his gout. I'm afraid I might come down with it, too. Oh, this
damnable old age, I loathe it. To hell with it. Since I started putting on years, I've reached the point where I find myself detestable. I'm sure all of you must detest the very sight of me.

YELENA ANDREEVNA. You keep harping about your old age, as if we're
all to blame because you're old.

SEREBRYAKOV. And you more than anyone else detest me. [YELENA
ANDREEVNA *moves and sits down farther away.*] Of course, you're
right. I'm not a fool and I can understand it. You're a young,
healthy, beautiful woman, you want to live your life, while I'm
an old man, practically a corpse. Well, hmm? Don't think I don't
understand, I do. And, of course, it's foolish I'm even still alive.
But only wait a little, I'll set you all free soon. I won't drag on for
long.

YELENA ANDREEVNA. I'm growing weary . . . For God's sake, be
quiet.

SEREBRYAKOV. It turns out that, thanks to me, everyone is growing
weary, getting bored, destroying their own youth, and I am the
only one who thoroughly enjoys life, who is satisfied. Why, yes, of
course.

YELENA ANDREEVNA. Be quiet, please! You've worn me out, completely.

---

5. A nickname for *Yelena.*
6. K. N. Batyushkov (1787–1855), a notable Russian poet.
7. Literally, "quinsy of the chest; pains
of short duration, together with feelings
of anxiety and fear." I. S. Turgenev
(1818–83), the Russian novelist.

SEREBRYAKOV. I've worn every one of you out, completely. Of course.

YELENA ANDREEVNA. [*through tears*] I can't stand it! What do you want from me? Tell me.

SEREBRYAKOV. Nothing.

YELENA ANDREEVNA. Well, then, be quiet. I beg you.

SEREBRYAKOV. It's a strange thing, whenever Ivan Petrovich or that old idiot, Maria Vasilevna, begin talking your head off, then it's all well and good, everyone listens. But if I so much as say one word, everyone begins feeling down in the dumps. Even my voice is detestable. Well, let's say I am detestable, I'm an egotist, I'm a despot, but can it be that even in my old age I don't have the right to be a little wrapped up in myself? Can it be I don't deserve it? Can it really be, I ask you, don't I have the right to a tranquil old age, to people paying attention to me?

YELENA ANDREEVNA. No one is disputing your rights. [*The window bangs in the wind.*] The wind has picked up, I'll close the window. [*Closes the window.*] It's going to rain now. No one is disputing your rights. [*Pause*].

In the garden the WATCHMAN *taps and sings a song.*

SEREBRYAKOV. You work your whole life for the sake of scholarship, you get accustomed to your own study, to the lecture hall, and to your esteemed colleagues. Then suddenly, for no reason at all, you find yourself buried in this tomb, where every day you see foolish people and listen to their good-for-nothing talk, talk, talk . . . I want to live, I love success, fame, I love making a fuss in the world, and here—it's like being sent into exile. To devote every single minute to yearning for the past, watching step by step the success of others, fearing death . . . I can't stand it! I don't have the strength! And even now they don't want to forgive me for being old.

YELENA ANDREEVNA. Wait a little while, have patience. In the course of five or six years, I too will be old.

SONYA *enters.*

SONYA. Papa, you were the one who insisted that Dr. Astrov be sent for, but now that he's come, you won't let him see you. It's inconsiderate. We've only bothered the man for nothing . . .

SEREBRYAKOV. What's your Astrov going to do for me? He knows as much about medicine as I—about astronomy.

SONYA. A whole medical faculty can't be sent for, simply for the sake of your gout.

SEREBRYAKOV. I won't even speak to that man, he behaves like God's divine fool.

SONYA. Do what you like. [*Sits.*] It doesn't matter to me.

SEREBRYAKOV. What time is it now?

YELENA ANDREEVNA. It's after twelve.

SEREBRYAKOV. It's muggy . . . Sonya, give me the drops on the table.

SONYA. There you are. [*Gives him the drops.*]

SEREBRYAKOV. [*irritably*] Oh, not these, really! You can't ask for a single thing!

SONYA. Don't by naughty, please. Some people may very well like it, but spare me that pleasure, if you please! I don't care for it. And I don't have the time, either. I must get up early tomorrow to look after the mowing.

> VOYNITSKY *enters, wearing a dressing gown and carrying a candle.*

VOYNITSKY. There's a storm brewing outside. [*A flash of lightning.*] There you are, see! Hélène and Sonya, go to sleep. I've come to take over for you.

SEREBRYAKOV. [*frightened*] No, no! Don't leave me with him! No. He'll talk my head off!

VOYNITSKY. But they've got to have some peace and rest! It's the second night in a row they've gone without sleep.

SEREBRYAKOV. Let them go to sleep, but you leave too. I thank you. I beg you. In the name of our past friendship, no objections, please. We can talk later.

VOYNITSKY. [*with an ironic smile*] Our past friendship . . . Past . . .

SONYA. Be quiet, Uncle Vanya.

SEREBRYAKOV. [*to his wife*] My dear, don't leave me with him. He'll talk my head off.

VOYNITSKY. This is even becoming funny.

> MARINA *enters, carrying a candle.*

SONYA. You ought to go to sleep, *nyanechka*. It's quite late.

MARINA. The samovar hasn't been cleared from the table. Not likely I'll be getting to sleep soon.

SEREBRYAKOV. Not one of you can sleep, everyone is growing weary, I'm the only one who's having a delightful time.

MARINA. [*goes to* SEREBRYAKOV, *tenderly*] What is it, my pet? That pain again? Why, my own legs get to hurting so, you'd think they'll never quit. [*Arranges his blanket.*] It's that old illness of yours. Sonya's mother, Vera Petrovna, God rest her soul, time and again never got to sleep for nights, killing herself with work and grief[8] over it . . . She loved you so much, she did . . . [*Pause.*] Old folks are just like the little ones; children always want someone who has feelings for them. But there's no one who feels a thing for old folks. [*Kisses* SEREBRYAKOV *on the shoulder.*] Come to your bed, my pet . . . Come along, dearest . . . I'll pour some lime-flower tea[9] for you and warm your feet . . . and pray to God for you . . .

SEREBRYAKOV. [*deeply moved*] Let's go, Marina.

MARINA. My own legs get to hurting so, why you'd think they'll never quit. [*She and* SONYA *lead him out.*] Vera Petrovna always used to kill herself with work and grief over it, she was always

---

8. The Russian verb *ubivaecja* has colloquial meanings (in addition to the meaning "kill"): "drive to the point of exhaustion" and "experience a huge grief."
9. Tea made from the flower of the lime tree and used for medicinal purposes.

crying . . . Sonyushka, you were still a little girl and pretty silly at the time . . . Come, my pet, come . . .

SEREBRYAKOV, SONYA, *and* MARINA *go out.*

YELENA ANDREEVNA. He's worn me out, completely. I can scarcely stand.

VOYNITSKY. He's worn you out and I've worn myself out. It's the third night I've gone without sleep.

YELENA ANDREEVNA. Everything's going to rack and ruin in this house. Your mother hates everything except her pamphlets and the professor. The professor is so completely upset he doesn't trust me, and he's afraid of you. Sonya is irritated with her father, she's irritated with me, and she hasn't talked to me for two whole weeks. You hate my husband, and you openly treat your own mother with contempt. I'm so completely upset I've been ready to cry twenty times today . . . Everything's going to rack and ruin in this house.

VOYNITSKY. Let's leave philosophy alone!

YELENA ANDREEVNA. Ivan Petrovich, you're educated and intelligent, and you must realize, surely, that the world is being destroyed not by plunder or by fire, but by hatred, rancor, and all these tiffs and spats . . . Your concern should be to stop squawking and help bring the people in this house together, in peace and harmony.

VOYNITSKY. First you help me bring myself together, in peace and harmony! My dearest . . . [*Bends down to kiss her hand.*]

YELENA ANDREEVNA. Leave me alone! [*Pulls her hand away.*] Go away!

VOYNITSKY. In a moment the rain will be over, and everything in nature will be renewed and breathe with ease. I alone will not feel renewed by the storm. Day and night, like an evil spirit, one thought keeps haunting me, the thought that my life has been lost, gone forever. I have no past life, it's stupidly been used up on things that don't matter. And the present is so absurd, it terrifies me. There you see it, my life and my love. Where can I put them? What am I to do with them? My feelings are wasting away in vain, like a ray of sunlight falling into a pit, and I too am wasting away.

YELENA ANDREEVNA. When you talk to me of your love, somehow I feel dull, and I don't know what to say. Forgive me, there's nothing more I can say to you. [*Wants to go.*] Good night.

VOYNITSKY. [*blocking her way*] If you only knew how I'm tortured by the thought that in this very house another life, side by side with my own, is wasting away. And it's yours. What is it you're waiting for? What damned philosophy is stopping you? You must realize, you must . . .

YELENA ANDREEVNA. [*looks at him intently*] Ivan Petrovich, you are drunk!

VOYNITSKY. Maybe, maybe . . .

YELENA ANDREEVNA. Where's the doctor?

VOYNITSKY. He's in there . . . spending the night in my room. Maybe, maybe . . . anything may be, anything!

YELENA ANDREEVNA. So you've been drinking today? Why do you do it?

VOYNITSKY. It gives you the feeling that you're alive at least . . . Don't stop me, Hélène!

YELENA ANDREEVNA. You didn't drink before, never. And you have never talked so much before . . . Go to sleep! You bore me.

VOYNITSKY. [bends down to kiss her hand] My dearest . . . you marvelous woman, you!

YELENA ANDREEVNA. [with annoyance] Leave me alone, I find all this detestable. [Goes out.]

VOYNITSKY. [alone] She's gone . . . [Pause.] Ten years ago I used to meet her at my late sister's place. At that time she was seventeen, and I was thirty-seven. Why is it I didn't fall in love with her then and ask her to marry me? You know, it could have happened that way! And she would've been my own wife now . . . Yes . . . The storm would've awakened the two of us just now. She'd be frightened by the thunder, and I'd hold her in my arms and whisper, "Don't be afraid, I am here." Oh, what marvelous ideas, so wonderful, I'm even starting to laugh . . . But, dear God, I'm getting all mixed up . . . Why is it I'm old? Why is it she doesn't understand me? Her rhetoric, her idle moralizing, her nonsensical, idle thoughts about the world being destroyed—how much I hate all this. [Pause.] Oh, the ways I've been deceived! I used to worship that professor, that pitiable, gout-infected old man, I worked like an ox for him! Sonya and I squeezed the last drop out of this estate. Like tight-fisted peasants we drove hard bargains over our vegetable oil, our peas and cottage cheese. We scrimped and cut corners ourselves, so that from the kopeks we saved thousands of rubles were sent to him. I took pride in him and in his scholarship, I lived and breathed this man. Everything he wrote, every pronouncement he made, seemed to me inspired by genius . . . Dear God, and now? There he is, retired, and the sum total of his life can be seen now. Not one page of his work will remain after he's gone, he is completely unknown, he is nothing! A bubble of soap! And I've been deceived . . . I see it clearly—foolishly deceived . . .

ASTROV enters, wearing a frock-coat, without waistcoat or tie; he is tipsy; TELEGIN, with a guitar, follows him.

ASTROV. Play!

TELEGIN. Everyone is sleeping, sir!

ASTROV. Play! [TELEGIN begins to strum softly. To VOYNITSKY.] Are you alone here? No ladies around? [Arms akimbo, he sings softly.]

"Dance away, my stove, dance away, my shed,
There's no place for the master to go to bed . . ."

The storm woke me up. Grand little rain. What's the time?

VOYNITSKY. Damned if I know.

ASTROV. I thought I heard Yelena Andreevna's voice.

VOYNITSKY. She was here a moment ago.

ASTROV. A dazzling woman. [*Inspects bottles on the table.*] Medicines. What prescriptions don't we find here! Why, from Kharkov, Moscow, and Tula[1] . . . Every town in Russia must be bored to death with his gout. Is he really ill or is he pretending?

VOYNITSKY. He is ill. [*Pause.*]

ASTROV. Why are you so gloomy today? Feeling a little sorry for the professor, is that it?

VOYNITSKY. Leave me alone.

ASTROV. Or is it perhaps you're in love with the professor's wife?

VOYNITSKY. She is my friend.

ASTROV. Already?

VOYNITSKY. What does this "already" mean?

ASTROV. A woman can be a man's friend only in this order: first, an acquaintance; then, a mistress; and afterwards, a friend.

VOYNITSKY. A petty and vulgar philosophy.

ASTROV. How's that? Yes . . . I must own up I've become a petty and vulgar person. As you see, I'm even drunk. I usually drink too much like this once a month. When I'm in this condition, I become shamelessly arrogant, even insolent. Oh, there's nothing I feel I can't do then! I tackle the most difficult operations and do them superbly. I sketch out the most all-embracing plans for the future. At such times I no longer consider myself eccentric and I believe I bring monumental benefits to all humankind . . . Monumental! And at such times I have my very own philosophical system, and all of you, brothers, come across to me as such tiny insects . . . microbes. [*To* TELEGIN.] Waffles, play!

TELEGIN. I'd be happy to, dear friend, with all my heart and soul, but you remember, don't you, everyone in the house is asleep!

ASTROV. Play! [TELEGIN *strums softly.*] We must have a drink. Come on, I think we still have some cognac left over there. As soon as it's daylight, we'll drive over to my place. "All rat?" There's an assistant of mine who never says "all right," but "all rat." A terrible scroundrel. So, "all rat?" [*Having seen* SONYA, *who is entering.*] Excuse me, I don't have my necktie. [*Goes out quickly;* TELEGIN *follows him.*]

SONYA. Uncle Vanya, you've gone and gotten drunk with the doctor again. Our boys got together for a little fuss. Well, he's always ready for one, but what on earth provoked you? At your age it just doesn't suit you.

1. An industrial city located about 120 miles south of Moscow.

VOYNITSKY. Age hasn't a thing to do with it. When there's no real life to live, you must get by with illusions. It's better than nothing, after all.

SONYA. Our hay's been cut, it rains every day, everything lies rotting in the fields, and you busy yourself with illusions. You've completely deserted the estate . . . I'm left to work alone, and I'm down to my last ounce of strength, completely . . . [*Frightened.*] Uncle, you have tears in your eyes!

VOYNITSKY. What tears, what? It's nothing . . . nonsense . . . You looked at me just now the way your mother used to . . . My dear . . . [*Avidly kisses her face and hands.*] My sister . . . my dear sister . . . where is she now? If she only knew! Oh, if she only knew!

SONYA. What? Knew what, Uncle?

VOYNITSKY. It's difficult, it isn't right . . . It's nothing . . . Later on . . . It's nothing . . . I'm leaving now. [*Goes out.*]

SONYA. [*knocks on the door*] Mikhail Lvovich! Are you asleep? A moment only!

ASTROV. [*through the door*] Be right there! [*After waiting a short while, he enters; he now is wearing his waistcoat and tie.*] What can I do?

SONYA. You can go on drinking if you don't find it detestable, but I beg you, don't let my uncle drink. It's bad for him.

ASTROV. All right. We won't drink anymore. [*Pause.*] I'll leave for my place right now. It's all settled and signed. It will be daylight by the time they've finished the harnessing.

SONYA. It's raining. Wait until morning.

ASTROV. The storm is going past, we'll just catch the edge of it. I'm going. And please don't ask me to treat your father again. I tell him it's gout, and he says it's rheumatism. I ask him to lie down, he sits up. And today he wouldn't speak to me at all.

SONYA. He's spoiled. [*Looks in the sideboard.*] Like something to eat?

ASTROV. I think so, yes.

SONYA. I love to snack at night. I think we've something left in the sideboard. In his day and age, they say, he was tremendously successful with women, and the ladies simply spoiled him. Here, take some cheese. [*They stand by the sideboard and eat.*]

ASTROV. I haven't eaten anything today, I've only been drinking. Your father is a difficult person. [*Gets a bottle out of the sideboard.*] May I? [*Drinks a glass.*] No one is here, and so I can speak candidly. You know, I don't think I could live through a single month in your house. The air would strangle me . . . Your father is totally bound up in his gout and his books, your Uncle Vanya with his depression, your grandmother, and finally there's your stepmother . . .

SONYA. What about my stepmother?

ASTROV. Everything about people should be the finest there is—their faces, what they wear, the way they think, their heart and soul. She is a fine woman, no quarrel here, but . . . you know she only eats, sleeps, goes for walks, and charms everyone of us with her beauty —and nothing more. She doesn't have any responsibilities, other persons work for her . . . It's so, isn't it? There's no integrity in a life of idleness. [*Pause.*] Oh, perhaps I'm much too severe. Like your Uncle Vanya, I'm disappointed with life, both of us have turned into a pair of grumpy old men.

SONYA. Are you dissatisfied with life, then?

ASTROV. In general, I love life, but I can't bear the life we live, this provincial, boxed-in life in Russia, and I despise it with all my heart and soul. As for my own personal life, God in heaven, there's definitely nothing good about it. You know, when you go through a forest on a dark night and you happen to see a small light shining in the distance, then you don't notice your sheer exhaustion, nor the darkness around you, nor even the way thorny branches keep lashing your face . . . I go on working—as you well know—as no one else in the district works. Fate never stops lashing me, there are times I suffer unbearably, and yet there is no light at all in the distance for me. I no longer expect anything for myself, I don't care, really care, for people . . . I haven't loved anyone for a long time.

SONYA. No one?

ASTROV. No one. Oh, I do care for your *nyanka* in a special way—in memory of the old days—but she's the only one. The peasants are all very much alike, backward and living in filth. And I find it difficult to get along with intellectuals. They wear me out. All of those good people we know are trivial and superficial in whatever they think and however they feel. And they never see farther than their own noses—they are plainly and simply stupid. Even those with more brains and with more to offer are hysterical, absorbed with analysis and introspection . . . They're constantly complaining, hating, and spreading malicious lies. They sneak up to a person, look at him sideways, and then declaim: "Oh, he is a psychopath," or, "He's a phrasemonger!" And when they don't know the kind of label to stick on my forehead, they declare, "Oh, he is a strange one, strange!" I love the forests—that's strange. I don't eat meat—that's strange too. They no longer can relate decently, freely, or directly with nature or with people . . . No relationship, none at all! [*About to take a drink.*]

SONYA. [*stops him*] No, I ask you, I beg you, don't drink anymore.

ASTROV. Why?

SONYA. It doesn't become you at all! You are a gracious person, your voice is gentle . . . And I can say that you, unlike all the people I know—you are a fine, good person. Why on earth be like the usual run of people, the ones who drink and gamble? Oh, don't be like that, I beg you! You've said time and again that people don't create but only destroy what God in heaven has given them. Why on earth, why, are you destroying yourself? You don't have to, you don't, I beg, I implore you.

ASTROV. [*holds out his hand to her*] I won't drink anymore.

SONYA. Give me your word .

ASTROV. My word of honor.

SONYA. [*holds his hand firmly*] Thank you!

ASTROV. *Basta!*[2] I'm not drunk now. As you see, I'm completely sober, and I'll stay that way until the end of my days. [*Looks at his watch.*] So, so, let's go on. As I was saying, my time has already gone by, it's too late for me . . . I've started putting on years, I've worked too long and too hard, I've become petty and vulgar, as sordid as one can be. My feelings are gone, dead to the world, and I really don't think I could ever grow close to another person. There's no one I love, and . . . no one I ever shall love. What still fascinates me is beauty. I'm not indifferent when it comes to that. I think that if, say, Yelena Andreevna wanted to, she could turn my head in a single day . . . But that isn't love, you see, or devotion . . . [*Covers his eyes with his hand and shudders.*]

SONYA. What is it?

ASTROV. Nothing . . . During Lent a patient of mine died under chloroform.

SONYA. It's time to forget about that. [*Pause.*] Tell me, Mikhail Lvovich . . . if I had a friend or a younger sister, and if you knew that she . . . well, let's say, that she were in love with you, what would you do about it?

ASTROV. [*having shrugged his shoulders*] I don't know. Probably nothing. I'd make sure she understood I couldn't fall in love with her . . . Besides, I've got other things on my mind, not that. At any rate, if I'm going to go, it's time. I'll say good-bye, my dear, or we won't stop until morning. [*Holds her hand.*] I'll go through the drawing room, if I may, or else I'm afraid your uncle might delay me. [*Goes out.*]

SONYA. [*alone*] He had nothing to say to me . . . I still don't know what's in his heart and soul, but why is it I feel so happy? [*Laughs from happiness.*] I told him, "You are a gracious person, you are noble, your voice is so gentle . . ." Oh, surely that wasn't out of place, was it? His voice vibrates, caresses . . . there, I can feel it in the air. But when I told him about a younger sister, he didn't understand . . . [*Wringing her hands.*] Oh, it's terrible I'm homely, terrible! I know I'm homely, I know, I know . . . Last Sunday as we were coming out of church, I heard them talking about me, and one woman said, "She is kind, really a generous girl, but it's a shame that she is so homely . . ." So homely . . .

YELENA ANDREEVNA *enters.*

2. "Enough!"

YELENA ANDREEVNA. [*opens the window*] The storm is over. How good the air is! [*Pause.*] Where's the doctor?

SONYA. He's gone. [*Pause.*]

YELENA ANDREEVNA. Sofi!

SONYA. What?

YELENA ANDREEVNA. How long are you going to be mad at me? We've never hurt each other. Then why on earth do we have to be enemies? It's time we stopped . . .

SONYA. I wanted to myself . . . [*Embraces her.*] Let's stop being angry.

YELENA ANDREEVNA. Oh, that's perfect. [*Both are deeply moved.*]

SONYA. Has Papa gone to bed?

YELENA ANDREEVNA. No, he's sitting up in the drawing room . . . We don't talk to each other for weeks and weeks and only God in heaven knows why . . . [*Having seen that the sideboard is open.*] What's this?

SONYA. Mikhail Lvovich has been having supper.

YELENA ANDREEVNA. And some wine is here . . . Let's drink to our friendship.

SONYA. Yes, let's do.

YELENA ANDREEVNA. Out of the same wineglass . . . [*Pours the wine.*] It's better this way. Well, it means we're friends now, close friends?

SONYA. Close friends. [*They drink and kiss each other.*] I've been wanting to settle our differences and become friends for a long time now, but somehow I always felt ashamed . . . [*Weeps.*]

YELENA ANDREEVNA. Why is it you're crying?

SONYA. It's nothing, no reason.

YELENA ANDREEVNA. Come, enough, that will do . . . [*Weeps.*] How eccentric I've become, and I've started crying too . . . [*Pause.*] You're angry with me because you think I married your father for what I could get out of it . . . If you can put your faith in vows, then I swear to you—it was for love that I married him. He fascinated me, as a scholar and a famous person. The love I felt wasn't real. It was artificial, but you see, at the time it seemed very real to me. I'm not to blame for it. Yet from the very day of our wedding, you haven't stopped chastising me with those intelligent, skeptical eyes of yours.

SONYA. Come, peace, peace! Let's forget what's past.

YELENA ANDREEVNA. You don't have to look that way—it doesn't become you. You must have faith in people, or else you can't possibly live. [*Pause.*]

SONYA. Tell me in all honesty as a friend . . . Are you happy?

YELENA ANDREEVNA. No.

SONYA. I knew that. One more question. Tell me frankly, wouldn't you rather have a husband who is young?

YELENA ANDREEVNA. What a little girl you still are. Of course I'd rather. [*Laughs.*] Well, ask me something else, ask me . . .

SONYA. Do you like the doctor?

YELENA ANDREEVNA. Yes, very much.

SONYA. [*laughs*] I have a foolish look on my face . . . don't I? See, he's gone, but I keep hearing his voice and the way he walks. I can glance at a dark window and see his face reflected there. Let me tell you everything I feel and think about . . . But I can't talk so loudly, I feel ashamed. Let's go to my room, we'll talk there. I seem foolish to you, don't I? Confess . . . Tell me something about him . . .

YELENA ANDREEVNA. What should I say?

SONYA. He is intelligent . . . He knows how to do everything, he's able to do anything . . . He treats those who are ill, he plants forests too . . .

YELENA ANDREEVNA. Oh, it isn't in the forests he plants or in the medicine he practices . . . My dear, don't you see? He is gifted. And you know, don't you, what being gifted means? Courage, freedom of mind, breadth of vision . . . As he plants a tree he is already figuring out what it will be like in the course of a thousand years; he already sees glimmerings of happiness for humankind. People like that are rare and must be loved . . . He drinks, he's frequently crude, but what's wrong with that? A gifted person in Russia can't be completely immaculate. Only think what kind of life this doctor maintains. Lakes of mud where roads should be, difficult if not impossible to get through, freezing weather, frost, enormous distances, crude, savage peasants, poverty and illness surrounding him. A person who works and struggles day after day in circumstances like these can scarcely reach the age of forty and remain completely immaculate and sober . . . [*Kisses her.*] I wish you the best with all my heart and soul, you deserve happiness . . . [*Rises.*] And I'm a tedious person, an incidental character . . . In my music, in my husband's house, in my romantic affairs— wherever you look in fact, I have only been an incidental character. To tell the truth, Sonya, if you really think about it, I'm a very, very unhappy woman. [*Walks in agitation about the stage.*] There's no happiness for me on this earth. None! What are you laughing about?

SONYA. [*laughs, having covered her face*] I'm so happy . . . happy!

YELENA ANDREEVNA. I want to play the piano . . . I'd like to play something now.

SONYA. Go ahead, play. [*Embraces her.*] I can't sleep . . . Go ahead, play!

YELENA ANDREEVNA. In a moment. Your father isn't sleeping. When he is sick, music irritates him. Go and ask him. If it's all right with him, I'll play. Go on.

SONYA. Right away. [*Goes out.*]

The WATCHMAN *is heard tapping in the garden.*

YELENA ANDREEVNA. It's been a long time since I've played. I'll play the piano and cry, cry like a foolish girl. [*Through the window.*] It's you tapping, Yefim, isn't it?

WATCHMAN'S VOICE. It's me!

YELENA ANDREEVNA. Stop tapping, the master isn't well.

WATCHMAN'S VOICE. I'll leave right away! [*Whistles.*] Hey you, Zhuchka, Malchik! Good dogs, you! Zhuchka! [*Pause.*]

SONYA. [*having returned*] We can't!

CURTAIN

Act Three

The drawing room in SEREBRYAKOV'S *house. Three doors, right, left, and in the center. Daytime.* VOYNITSKY *and* SONYA *are sitting and* YELENA ANDREEVNA *is walking about the stage, thinking about something.*

VOYNITSKY. Herr Professor has been so good as to express the wish for all of us to meet here in this drawing room at one o'clock today. [*Looks at his watch.*] It's 12:45. He wants to reveal something to the world.

YELENA ANDREEVNA. Probably, it's something or other to do with business.

VOYNITSKY. He has no business, none. He writes nonsense, grumbles, and feels jealous. Nothing more.

SONYA. [*in a tone of reproach*] Uncle!

VOYNITSKY. Well, there, I'm sorry. [*Points to* YELENA ANDREEVNA.] Just look at her, will you, meandering around, swaying from side to side, ready to drop from sheer laziness. It's very sweet, very!

YELENA ANDREEVNA. There you go, buzz, buzz the whole day long— aren't you sick and tired of it! [*With anguish.*] I'm dying from boredom, I don't know what I can do.

SONYA. [*shrugging her shoulders.*] So little to do? There's plenty if only you wanted to.

YELENA ANDREEVNA. For example?

SONYA. You could help with the estate, you could teach, you could help treat those who are ill. So little to do? Look, when you and Papa weren't here, Uncle Vanya and I used to go to the market ourselves and trade our flour.

YELENA ANDREEVNA. I don't know how to. Besides, I'm not one bit interested. It's only in ideological novels that you find people going out to teach and heal the peasants. How could I, for no reason whatsoever, suddenly run off to teach or to heal?

SONYA. But what I don't understand is why you just don't go and begin teaching. Wait a while, and you'll get accustomed to it. [*Embraces her.*] Don't stay bored, my dear. [*Laughs.*] You are bored, you can't find a thing to do with yourself, but boredom and idleness are infectious. See for yourself. Uncle Vanya does nothing except trot after you like a shadow. I dropped my own work and ran off to you just to talk. I've gotten so lazy I can't stand it! Doctor Mikhail Lvovich hardly ever used to see us before, once a month, and it was hard to talk him into a visit. But now he drives here every day. He's completely deserted both his forests and his medicine. You are undoubtedly a witch.

VOYNITSKY. Why is it you're dejected? [*Exhilarated.*] Well, my dear, wonderful woman, be reasonable! The blood of a mermaid flows in your veins, then be a mermaid! At least once in your life, have a will of your own and fall recklessly in love up to your ears with some water sprite or other—and dive headlong into a whirlpool so that Herr Professor and the rest of us can only throw up our hands.

YELENA ANDREEVNA. [*with anger*] Leave me in peace! How vicious you can be! [*Wants to leave.*]

VOYNITSKY. [*not letting her go*] Well, well, light of my life, forgive me . . . Excuse me. [*Kisses her hand.*] Peace.

YELENA ANDREEVNA. You agree, don't you, even an angel would run out of patience.

VOYNITSKY. As a sign of peace and agreement I'll bring a bouquet of roses in a moment. I got them ready for you this morning . . . Autumn roses, lovely roses, and sad . . . [*Goes out.*]

SONYA. Autumn roses, lovely roses, and sad . . . [*Both look out the window.*]

YELENA ANDREEVNA. There, it's September already. How can we ever live through the winter here! [*Pause.*] Where is the doctor?

SONYA. In Uncle Vanya's room. He's writing something. I'm glad Uncle Vanya went out, I must talk to you.

YELENA ANDREEVNA. What about?

SONYA. What about? [*Puts her head on* YELENA ANDREEVNA'S *breast.*]

YELENA ANDREEVNA. There, it's all right now, no more . . . [*Strokes her hair.*] No more.

SONYA. I am homely.

YELENA ANDREEVNA. You have pretty hair.

SONYA. No! [*Looks around to glance at herself in the mirror.*] No! When a woman is homely, they keep telling her, "You have pretty eyes, you have pretty hair." I've been in love with him for six whole years, I love him more than my own mother. Every waking moment I hear the sound of his voice, feel the touch of his hand, and I keep looking at the door, expecting him to walk in at any moment. And here, you see, I always run to you, just to talk about him. Now he's here every day, but he doesn't look at me, he doesn't even see me . . . It's eating away my heart and soul. I have no hope left, none, none at all! [*Desperately.*] Oh, dear God, give me strength . . . I've prayed the whole night long . . . Time after time I go up to him, begin talking to him, I keep looking into his eyes . . . I've no pride, I don't even have the strength to control myself . . . Yesterday I couldn't get hold of myself and I told Uncle Vanya I was in love . . . And all the servants know I love him. Everyone knows it.

YELENA ANDREEVNA. And he?

SONYA. No. He doesn't notice me.

YELENA ANDREEVNA. [*deliberating*] He is a strange person . . . You know something? Let me talk to him . . . I'll be careful, nothing more than an inkling here and there . . . [*Pause.*] Really, how much longer can you stand this uncertainty . . . Let me do it! [SONYA *nods her head in agreement.*] Oh, that's perfect. Does he love you or doesn't he—it won't be hard to find out. Don't feel embarrassed, darling, and don't worry. I'll question him so carefully he won't even notice it. We must only find out: yes or no? [*Pause.*] If it's no, then let him stop coming here so often. Right? [SONYA *nods her head in agreement.*] It's easier when you don't see him. We won't put it off any longer, we'll start our cross-examination right away. He was going to show me some kind of drawings . . . Go and tell him I want to see him.

SONYA. [*greatly agitated*] Will you tell me the whole truth?

YELENA ANDREEVNA. Yes, of course. It seems to me that the truth, no matter what it may be, isn't so terrible, after all, as this uncertainty. Have faith in me, darling.

SONYA. Yes . . . Yes . . . I'll say you want to see his drawings . . . [*Walks and stops near the door*] No, uncertainty is much better . . . at least there's still hope . . .

YELENA ANDREEVNA. What are you saying?

SONYA. Nothing. [*Goes out.*]

YELENA ANDREEVNA. [*alone*] No, there's nothing worse than knowing another person's secret and not being able to help. [*Deliberating.*] He isn't in love with her, that's clear, but why on earth shouldn't he marry her? She is homely, but she'd be a perfect wife for a country doctor at his age. She's an intelligent girl, so kind, pure . . . No, that isn't it exactly, not at all . . . [*Pause.*] I understand this poor girl. In the middle of outrageous boredom, where there are no people, only gray specks hovering all around, and petty and vulgar talk, talk, talk is heard, where the only thing they know is how to eat, drink, sleep—now and then he appears, different from the others, good looking, interesting, fascinating— just like a clear moon rising out of the darkness . . . To give in to the charm of a person like that, to forget yourself . . . I think I'm a little fascinated myself. Yes, I am bored without him, and here I am smiling as I think about him . . . That Uncle Vanya says I seem to have mermaid's blood in my veins. "At least once in your life have a will of your own . . ." Well, hmm? Maybe that's what I should do . . . If only I could fly off, free as a bird, fly away from all of you, from your sleepy faces and your constant talk, to forget that you, everyone of you, even exist in the world . . . But I am a

coward and I'm shy . . . My conscience would never let me rest . . .
You know, he comes here every day, I can guess why it is, and I
already feel guilty. I'm ready to fall on my knees before Sonya,
beg her to forgive me, cry and cry . . .

ASTROV. [*enters with a cartogram*] Good afternoon! [*Shakes hands.*]
You wanted to see my art work?

YELENA ANDREEVNA. You promised to show me your work yesterday . . . You're not busy now?

ASTROV. Oh, of course not. [*Spreads the cartogram out on the card
table and fastens it with drawing pins.*] Where were you born?

YELENA ANDREEVNA. [*helping him.*] In Petersburg.

ASTROV. And where did you receive your education?

YELENA ANDREEVNA. At the Conservatory.[3]

ASTROV. Then I don't think you'll find this interesting.

YELENA ANDREEVNA. Why say that? I don't know the countryside,
it's true, but I've read a lot.

ASTROV. I have my own table here in the house . . . in Ivan Petrovich's room. When I'm completely exhausted, practically dead but
still breathing, I'll drop everything, run over here, and have a little
fun for an hour or two with this stuff . . . Ivan Petrovich and Sofya
Alexandrovna keep on clicking the abacus to settle their accounts,
and I sit next to them at my own table, smearing my paints. And
I'm warm, it's peaceful, and the cricket chirps. But I can afford
this pleasure very seldom, just once a month . . . [*Pointing to the
cartogram.*] Now, take a look here. It's a picture of our district as
it was fifty years ago. The dark and light green paints stand for
the forests. Half of the total area was covered with forests. Where
the red cross-hatching is placed over the green, there elk and wild
goats used to live . . . I show both flora and fauna here. On this
lake there were swans, geese, ducks, birds of all sorts, and birds
galore, as the old folks say, so many you couldn't count 'em, flying
thick as clouds in the sky. Besides the villages and country places,
you can see scattered here and there different isolated settlements, tiny farms, hermitages of Old Believers, water mills . . .
There were countless horned cattle and horses. That's seen in
blue. In this region, for instance, where the blue is pretty thick,
there were herds upon herds of horses, an average of three to every
household. [*Pause.*] Now let's take a look lower down. That
shows what it was like twenty-five years ago. Here only a third of
the district is under forest. The wild goats are gone, but there are
elk. The green and blue paints grow paler and paler. And so on,
and so on. Let's cross over to the third part, a picture of the district as it is now. The green lies here and there, no longer continuous, but in patches. The elk, and the swans, and the wood

3. The St. Petersburg Conservatory,
founded in 1862 by Anton Grigorevich
Rubinstein (1829–94) and Carl Schu-
berth. Rubinstein remained as its director
and professor until 1867. Among his first
students was P. I. Tchaikovsky (1840–
93). Thus Yelena, who at the end of Act
II is not allowed by her aging husband
to play the piano, perhaps wastes her talent as a musician.

grouse have all disappeared . . . Not one trace remains of the former settlements, tiny farms, hermitages, and water mills. In general, it's a picture of gradual and unmistakable degeneration, and apparently only some ten or fifteen years remain before it will become complete. You'll say it's the result of cultural influences, that naturally the old life had to give way to the new. Yes, I can understand that. If highways and railroads were running in place of these devastated forests, if mills, factories, and schools had been built, our people would have become healthier, richer, more intelligent. But, you see, nothing of the sort has taken place. We find the very same swamps and mosquitoes, the very same scarcity of roads, the same poverty, typhus, diphtheria, and fires in the district . . . What we have here is a degeneration, the result of a downhill struggle for existence. People don't have the strength for it, they're backward and ignorant, and they have no awareness of self, none. And so everything degenerates. If a man is freezing, hungry, and sick, and if he wants to save what's left of life and to protect his children, then instinctively and unconsciously he grabs at anything to stop the hunger and to keep warm. And so he destroys everything and never thinks about tomorrow . . . Now almost everything has been destroyed, but nothing at all has been created in its place. [*Coldly.*] I can see by your face that this doesn't interest you.

YELENA ANDREEVNA. But I understand so little about it . . .

ASTROV. There's really nothing to understand, it simply doesn't interest you.

YELENA ANDREEVNA. To be quite candid, my thoughts were somewhere else. Forgive me. I must put you through a little cross-examination, and I feel embarrassed. I don't know how to begin.

ASTROV. Cross-examination?

YELENA ANDREEVNA. Yes, a cross-examination but . . . a rather harmless one. Let's sit down! [*They sit down.*] It concerns a certain young person. Let's speak to each other in all honesty, like friends, openly and in plain words. We'll have our talk and then forget whatever was said. Yes?

ASTROV. Yes.

YELENA ANDREEVNA. It concerns my stepdaughter, Sonya. Do you like her?

ASTROV. Yes, I respect her.

YELENA ANDREEVNA. Do you like her as a woman?

ASTROV. [*after a pause*] No.

YELENA ANDREEVNA. Two or three more words, and that's the end. There's nothing you've noticed, then?

ASTROV. Nothing.

YELENA ANDREEVNA. [*takes him by the arm*] You don't love her, I can see it in your eyes . . . She is suffering . . . Understand that she is and . . . stop coming here.

ASTROV. [*rises*] My time has already gone by . . . Besides, I've no time for . . . [*Having shrugged his shoulders.*] When could I have the time? [*He is embarrassed.*]

YELENA ANDREEVNA. Ugh, what an unpleasant conversation! I'm so upset, I feel as if I'd been dragging a couple of tons around with me. Well, thank the Lord, it's over and done with. Let's forget it, it's as if we hadn't talked at all, and . . . and you leave now. You're an intelligent man, please understand . . . [*Pause.*] I've even started to blush.

ASTROV. If you'd spoken to me a month or two ago, perhaps I would have considered it, but now . . . [*Shrugs his shoulders.*] And if she's suffering, then of course . . . There's just one thing I don't understand: what made you go through with this cross-examination? [*Looks into her eyes and threatens with his finger.*] Oh, you're a sly one!

YELENA ANDREEVNA. What do you mean by that?

ASTROV. [*laughs*] A sly one! Let's say Sonya is suffering, I'll go along with that, but what's the point of your cross-examination? [*Stopping her from speaking, exhilarated.*] Come now, don't look so surprised, you know perfectly well why I've been coming here every day . . . You know perfectly well why I've been coming and whom I expect to see. My dear bird of prey, don't look at me like that. I'm an old sparrow . . .

YELENA ANDREEVNA. [*bewildered*] Bird of prey? I don't know what you're talking about.

ASTROV. You beautiful, fluffy weasel, you . . . You must have your victims! Here I've done nothing for a whole month, I dropped everything, I desperately look for you—and you're terribly pleased, aren't you, terribly . . . Well, why not? I am conquered, as you knew I would be, and without a cross-examination. [*Having crossed his arms and bowed his head.*] I surrender. Here I am, eat me!

YELENA ANDREEVNA. You've gone out of your mind!

ASTROV. [*laughs through his teeth*] You're shy . . .

YELENA ANDREEVNA. Oh, I'm better, far better than you think! I swear it to you! [*Wants to leave.*]

ASTROV. [*blocking her way*] I'm going away today, I won't be coming back here, but . . . [*Takes her by the arm, looks around.*] Where can we see each other? Tell me quickly, where? Someone may come in here, tell me quickly. [*Passionately.*] What a marvelous, wonderful woman . . . one kiss . . . just let me kiss your fragrant hair . . .

YELENA ANDREEVNA. I swear it to you . . .

ASTROV. [*stopping her from speaking*] Why swear anything? There's no need to swear. No need for superfluous words . . . Oh, how beautiful you are! What hands! [*Kisses her hands.*]

YELENA ANDREEVNA. Enough, enough, no more . . . go away . . . [*Takes away her hands.*] You're forgetting yourself.

ASTROV. Tell me, yes, tell me where we can meet tomorrow? [*Takes *her by the waist.*] You see, we can't escape it, we must see each other. [*Kisses her.*]

> At this moment VOYNITSKY *enters, carrying a bunch of roses, and stops by the door.*

YELENA ANDREEVNA. [*not seeing* VOYNITSKY] Have mercy . . . leave me alone . . . [*Lays her head on* ASTROV'S *chest.*] No! [*Wants to leave.*]

ASTROV. [*holding her by the waist*] Come to the forest preserve tomorrow . . . by two o'clock . . . Yes? Yes? You'll come?

YELENA ANDREEVNA. [*having seen* VOYNITSKY] Let me go! [*Distraught and embarrassed, she moves away to the window.*] This is terrible.

VOYNITSKY. [*puts roses on a chair. Greatly upset, he wipes his face and around his collar with a handkerchief.*] It's nothing . . . Yes . . . It's nothing . . .

ASTROV. [*inwardly displeased*] The weather today, my esteemed Ivan Petrovich, isn't too bad. This morning it was dark and cloudy and looked as if it might rain, but now the sun is out. Speaking in all honesty, it's turned out to be an excellent autumn . . . and the winter crops are coming along fairly well. [*Rolls up the cartogram into cylindrical shape.*] There's just one thing, however, the days are getting shorter . . . [*Goes out.*]

YELENA ANDREEVNA. [*quickly goes up to* VOYNITSKY] You must try everything you can think of, use every bit of your influence, so my husband and I can get away from here this very day! Do you hear? This very day!

VOYNITSKY. [*wiping his face*] Hmm? Well, yes . . . good . . . I saw everything, Hélène, everything . . .

YELENA ANDREEVNA. [*nervously*] Do you hear? I must get away from here this very day!

> SEREBRYAKOV, SONYA, TELEGIN, *and* MARINA *enter.*

TELEGIN. Somehow, your Excellency, I'm not feeling too well myself. See, the last two days I've been ailing. Something to do with my head, that is, er . . .

SEREBRYAKOV. But where are the others? I don't care at all for this house. It's a labyrinth, that's what it is. Twenty-six enormous rooms, everyone scatters off in different directions, and you can never find a single person. [*Rings.*] Ask Maria Vasilevna and Yelena Andreevna to come here.

YELENA ANDREEVNA. I am here.

SEREBRYAKOV. Ladies and gentlemen, sit down, I beg you.

SONYA. [*going up to* YELENA ANDREEVNA, *impatiently*] what did he say?

YELENA ANDREEVNA. Later on.

SONYA. You're trembling, aren't you? And you're upset? [*Stares inquisitively into her face.*] I understand . . . He said he wouldn't be coming here again . . . Yes? [*Pause.*] Say it, yes?

YELENA ANDREEVNA *nods her head in agreement.*

SEREBRYAKOV. [*to* TELEGIN] You can still get along with bad health, it doesn't make much difference, I suppose. But if there's one thing I can't swallow, it's this whole system of country life. I feel as if I'd been knocked right off the earth onto some sort of alien planet. Sit down, ladies and gentlemen, I beg you. Sonya! [SONYA *does not hear him, she is standing, hanging her head sadly.*] Sonya! [*Pause.*} She doesn't hear. [*To* MARINA.] Nyanya, you sit down too. [*The* NURSE *sits and knits a stocking.*] Ladies and gentlemen, I beg you. Hang your ears, as the saying goes, on the nail of attention. [*Laughs.*]

VOYNITSKY. [*greatly upset*] Perhaps I'm not needed? May I go?

SEREBRYAKOV. No, you are needed here more than anyone else.

VOYNITSKY. What do you want from me?

SEREBRYAKOV. "Want from you . . ." What are you angry about? [*Pause.*] If I've offended you in some way or other, please excuse me.

VOYNITSKY. Oh, drop that tone, and let's move on to the business at hand . . . What is it you need?

MARIA VASILEVNA *enters.*

SEREBRYAKOV. There is *Maman*, too. I'll begin, ladies and gentlemen. [*Pause.*] I've invited you here, ladies and gentlemen, to announce that an inspector general is coming to see us. All joking aside, by the way, the matter is serious. Ladies and gentlemen, I've brought you together here to ask your help and advice, and, knowing your customary kindness, I hope that I shall receive it. I'm a scholar, I live with books, and practical life has always been foreign to me. I can't manage without the instruction of experienced persons, and I beg your help, Ivan Petrovich, you too, Ilya Ilich, and you, *Maman* . . . The fact is, *manet omnes una nox*,[4] that is to say, we are all mortal. I am old and I'm ill, and so I consider it a good time to arrange matters concerning my property insofar as they concern my family. My life is over and done with, and I'm not thinking about myself, but I have a young wife and an unmarried daughter. [*Pause.*] It's out of the question for me to go on living in the country. We weren't born for country life. And it's out of the question to live in town on the income we get from this estate. If the forest were sold, let's say, that would be an extraordinary measure, and one we certainly couldn't do year after year. We must find ways and means that would guarantee us a steady, more or less definite income figure. One such measure has come to mind, and I have the honor to propose it for your discussion. I'll pass over the details and set it out in rough outline. Our estate gives on the average no more than two percent. I propose to sell it. If we invest the proceeds in shares, we will receive from four to five percent. And I think there may even be a

4. From Horace, *Odes*, I, 28, 15: "a night awaits us all."

surplus of several thousand rubles, which would enable us to buy a small dacha[5] in Finland.

VOYNITSKY. Stop for a moment . . . I think my ears are deceiving me. Repeat what you said.

SEREBRYAKOV. To invest the money in shares and, with whatever surplus remains, to buy a dacha in Finland.

VOYNITSKY. Not about Finland . . . There was still something else you said.

SEREBRYAKOV. I propose to sell the estate.

VOYNITSKY. That's it exactly. You will sell the estate, superb, a brilliant idea . . . And where do you plan to put my old mother and me? And what are you doing with Sonya here?

SEREBRYAKOV. We'll discuss all this in good time. It can't be decided right away.

VOYNITSKY. Stop for a moment. It's clear I haven't had one drop of common sense up till now. Up till now I was stupid enough to think that this estate belonged to Sonya. My late father bought this estate as a dowry for my sister. Up till now I've been naïve, I didn't know we were following Turkish law,[6] and I thought the estate had passed from my sister to Sonya.

SEREBRYAKOV. Yes, the estate does belong to Sonya. Who's arguing about that? Without Sonya's consent I'd never think of selling it. Besides, I propose doing it for Sonya's benefit.

VOYNITSKY. This is incredible, absolutely incredible! Either I've lost my mind, or . . . or . . .

MARIA VASILEVNA. Jean, don't contradict Alexandr. Believe me, he knows better than we do what is good and what is bad.

VOYNITSKY. No, give me some water. [*Drinks water.*] Say what you please, whatever you please!

SEREBRYAKOV. I don't understand why you're upset. I'm not saying my project is ideal. If everyone finds it good for nothing, I certainly won't insist on it. [*Pause.*]

TELEGIN. [*embarrassed*] Your Excellency, I nourish for learning not only a deep respect, but also a family feeling. The brother of the wife of my brother Grigory Ilich, it's possible you may know him, Konstantin Trofimovich Lakedemonov, was a master of arts . . .

VOYNITSKY. Stop for a moment, Waffles, we're talking serious business . . . Wait a while, later on . . . [*To* SEREBRYAKOV.] Here, you ask him. This estate was bought from his uncle.

SEREBRYAKOV. Ah, why should I question him? What's the purpose?

VOYNITSKY. This estate was bought, at the existing prices of that time, for ninety-five thousand rubles. My father paid only seventy thousand, and a mortgage of twenty-five thousand was left. Now listen to what I have to say . . . This estate would never have been bought if I hadn't given up my inheritance in favor of my sister,

---

5. Pronounced *dácha*. A summer house located outside the city, used by urban residents on vacation.

6. Vanya is correct in this specific instance, i.e., in the 1890's a Turkish husband retained the dowry if his wife died.

whom I loved with all my heart. What's more, I worked like an ox for ten years and paid off the whole debt . . .

SEREBRYAKOV. I regret that I started this conversation.

VOYNITSKY. This estate is free from debt and in proper order only by virtue of my personal efforts. And here when I've grown old, they want to throw me out on my neck!

SEREBRYAKOV. I don't understand what you're trying to get at!

VOYNITSKY. For twenty-five years I've been running this estate, I've worked, I've sent the money to you like the most conscientious manager, and all this time not once did you thank me. All this time, when I was young and even today, I've been getting from you a salary of five hundred rubles a year—a beggar's wages! And not once did it cross your mind to give me at least one more ruble!

SEREBRYAKOV. Ivan Petrovich, how was I to know, really? I'm not a practical person, and I don't understand things like this. You could have raised it yourself, as much as you liked.

VOYNITSKY. Why on earth didn't I steal? Why don't all of you despise me because I didn't steal? It would have been fair and square, and I wouldn't be a beggar now!

MARIA VASILEVNA. [*sternly*] Jean!

TELEGIN. [*greatly upset*] Vanya, my dear friend, you shouldn't, you shouldn't . . . I'm trembling . . . Why on earth spoil good relations? [*Kisses him.*] You shouldn't.

VOYNITSKY. For twenty-five years I've been sitting like a mole in these four walls with this mother of mine . . . All our thoughts and feelings were centered on you alone. In the daytime we kept talking of you and your work, we were proud of you, and we even pronounced your name with reverence. We wasted our nights by reading journals and books that now I deeply despise!

TELEGIN. You shouldn't, Vanya, you shouldn't . . . I can't stand it . . .

SEREBRYAKOV. [*angrily*] What is it you're after? I don't understand it.

VOYNITSKY. We looked upon you as towering over the rest of us, and your articles we knew by heart . . . But now my eyes have been opened! I can see everything clearly. You write about art, but there isn't a single thing in art you understand. All your works, which I used to love, aren't worth so much as a copper kopek! You have hoodwinked all of us!

SEREBRYAKOV. Ladies and gentlemen! Oh, calm him down, no more! I'm leaving!

YELENA ANDREEVNA. Ivan Petrovich, I demand that you shut up! Do you hear?

VOYNITSKY. I won't shut up! [*Blocking* SEREBRYAKOV's *way.*] Stop for a moment, I haven't finished! You wasted my life! I've never lived, really lived! Thanks to you I've destroyed the best years of my life, they've gone for nothing! You are my bitterest enemy!

TELEGIN. I can't stand it . . . I can't . . . I'm leaving . . . [*Greatly agitated, he goes out.*]

SEREBRYAKOV. What do you want from me? And what right do you have to speak to me in that tone? A nonentity, that's what you are! If the estate is yours, then take it, I don't want it!

YELENA ANDREEVNA. I'm getting out of this miserable inferno this very minute! [*Screams.*] I've taken it as long as I can!

VOYNITSKY. My life is over and done with! I'm gifted, intelligent, courageous . . . If I'd lived a normal life, I might have turned out as a Schopenhauer, a Dostoevsky[7] . . . I'm talking so much nonsense! I'm going out of my mind . . . *Matushka*, I've lost heart and soul! *Matushka!*[8]

MARIA VASILEVNA. [*sternly*] Listen to Alexandr!

SONYA. [*kneels in front of the* NURSE *and presses close to her*] Nyanechka! Nyanechka!

VOYNITSKY. *Matushka!* What can I do? No, you don't have to say it! I know what I must do, I know it myself! [*To* SEREBRYAKOV.] You'll remember me all right! [*Goes out through the middle door.* MARIA VASILEVNA *follows him.*]

SEREBRYAKOV. Ladies and gentlemen, what on earth is this all about, I'd like to know? Take this madman away from me! I can't stand to live with him under the same roof! He lives in there [*points to the middle door*], practically right next to me . . . Let him remove himself into the village, into a cabin on the estate, or I'll move out of here myself, but I can't stay with him in the same house . . .

YELENA ANDREEVNA. [*to her husband*] We're going away from here today! The preparations should be made this very minute.

SEREBRYAKOV. A complete nonentity, that's what he is!

SONYA. [*on her knees, turns to her father, nervously, through tears*] You must have some compassion, Papa! Uncle Vanya and I are so unhappy! [*Holding back her despair.*] You must have some compassion! Remember, when you were younger, Uncle Vanya and Grandmother used to translate books for you at night, copy out your papers . . . every single night, for nights on end! Uncle Vanya and I kept working without resting, we were afraid to waste a single kopek on ourselves, and we sent everything to you . . . We earned every bit of our daily bread! I'm not saying it the right way, not the right way at all, but you must understand us, Papa. You must have some compassion!

YELENA ANDREEVNA. [*agitated, to her husband*] Alexandr, for God's sake, straighten it out with him . . . I beg you.

SEREBRYAKOV. Very well, I'll straighten it out with him . . . I'm not holding him responsible for a single thing, I'm not angry, but you

---

7. Arthur Schopenhauer (1788–1860), German philosopher; F. M. Dostoevsky (*dastaéfsky*) (1821–81), the great Russian novelist.

8. Voynitsky cries out *matuška* (*mátushka*), an old-fashioned (sometimes poetic) word for *mother*.

must agree that his behavior, to say the very least, is strange. If you like, I'll go and see him [*Goes out through the middle door.*]

YELENA ANDREEVNA. Be more gentle with him, calm him down . . . [*Goes out, following him.*]

SONYA. [*pressing close to the* NURSE] Nyanechka! Nyanechka!

MARINA. It's nothing, my child. The ganders will cackle, and then they'll stop . . . cackle and then stop . . .

SONYA. *Nyanechka!*

MARINA. [*strokes her head*] You're trembling as if you'd been out in the freezing cold! Now, now, poor motherless child, God is merciful. Some lime tea or raspberry, and it will pass . . . Don't grieve, poor motherless child . . . [*Looking at the middle door, irritably.*] Ugh, listen to the ganders raise the dust, the devil take them! [*A shot offstage.* YELENA ANDREEVNA *is heard screaming.* SONYA *shudders.*] Oh, go to the devil, you![9]

SEREBRYAKOV. [*runs in, reeling and frightened*] Stop him! Stop him! He's gone out of his mind!

   YELENA ANDREEVNA *and* VOYNITSKY *struggle in the doorway.*

YELENA ANDREEVNA. [*trying to take the revolver from him*] Give it to me! Give it to me, I tell you!

VOYNITSKY. Let go, Hélène! Let me go! [*Having freed himself, he runs in and looks for* SEREBRYAKOV.] Where is he? Ah, there he is! [*Fires at him.*] Bang! [*Pause.*] Didn't I hit him? Missed him again?! [*Angrily.*] Oh, damn, damn . . . damn it to hell . . .

   He throws the revolver on the floor and sits down on a chair, exhausted. SEREBRYAKOV *looks stunned.* YELENA ANDREEVNA *leans against a wall, feeling ill and ready to faint.*

YELENA ANDREEVNA. Take me away from here. Take me away, kill me if you must, but . . . I can't stay here, I can't!

VOYNITSKY. [*in despair*] Oh, what am I doing! What am I doing!

SONYA. [*quietly*] Nyanechka! Nyanechka!

CURTAIN

Act Four

VOYNITSKY'S *room, which serves as both his bedroom and the estate office. By the window is a large table with account books and papers of every kind; a tall stand-up desk, cupboards, and scales. A somewhat smaller table for* ASTROV; *on it is equipment for drawing and painting; alongside is a portfolio. A cage with a starling in it. On the wall is a map of Africa; clearly, no one has need of it here. An enormous sofa, upholstered in oilcloth. To the left, a door leading to a room. To the right, a door into the entrance hall. Near the door, right, is a mat for the peasants to stand on so as not to bring*

---

9. Refers to the person who fired the shot.

dirt into the room.[1] An autumn evening. It is quiet. TELEGIN *and* MARINA *are sitting opposite each other and are winding stocking wool.*

TELEGIN. Better hurry up, Marina Timofeevna, they'll be calling us in a moment to say good-bye. They've already ordered the horses to be brought to the house.

MARINA. [*tries to wind the wool faster*] Only a little bit left.

TELEGIN. They're going to Kharkov. They're going to live there.

MARINA. It's better that way.

TELEGIN. They've gotten pretty scared . . . Take Yelena Andreevna. "I don't want to live here one more hour . . ." she says, "We've got to get away, I mean it . . ." "W'ell live in Kharkov for a little while," she says, "take a look around, and then send for our things . . ." They're going without all their things. They weren't destined to live here, Marina Timofeevna, that's what it comes down to, they just weren't destined . . . it was ordained by fate.

MARINA. It's better that way. All the noise they raised a while back, the shooting, why, it's downright shameful!

TELEGIN. Yes, a subject deserving the brush of Ayvazovsky.[2]

MARINA. Would that my eyes had never seen it. [*Pause.*] We'll start living again like it was, in the old way. Our breakfast by eight in the morning, dinner at noon, and in the evening we sit down to supper. Everything right and proper the way it ought to be with decent people . . . with Christians. [*With a sigh.*] It's been a long time since an old sinner like me has sat down to noodle soup.

TELEGIN. Yes, it's been quite some time since noodle soup was made in this place. [*Pause.*] Quite some time . . . This morning, Marina Timofeevna, I was walking in the village, and a storekeeper yelled after me, "Hey, you freeloader, you!" And that really gnawed at me!

MARINA. Don't you pay a bit of attention, my pet. All of us are freeloaders in the sight of God. The same with you, Sonya, and Ivan Petrovich, not one of us sits without something to do, we all keep working! All of us . . . Where is Sonya?

TELEGIN. In the garden walking with the doctor. They're looking for Ivan Petrovich. They're afraid he might still lay hands on himself.

MARINA. And where is his revolver?

TELEGIN. [*in a whisper*] I hid it in the cellar!

MARINA. [*with an ironical grin*] Sin after sin after sin!

VOYNITSKY *and* ASTROV *enter from outside.*

VOYNITSKY. Leave me alone. [*To* MARINA *and* TELEGIN. Get out of here. At least leave me alone for one hour! I can't take this constant supervision.

---

1. Peasants, upon coming into the living quarters of landowners, were normally required to remain on the mat by the door.

2. I. K. Ayvazovsky (1817–1900), famous as a painter of seascapes.

TELEGIN. This very minute, Vanya. [*Goes out on tiptoe.*]

MARINA. It's the gander himself, gaw-gaw-gaw! [*Collects her wool and goes out.*]

VOYNITSKY. Leave me alone!

ASTROV. With the greatest pleasure. I should have left here long ago, but I'll say it again, I'm not leaving until you give back what you took from me.

VOYNITSKY. I haven't taken anything from you.

ASTROV. I'm talking to you seriously. Don't keep me waiting. It was time for me to leave hours ago.

VOYNITSKY. I have not taken a single thing from you. [*Both sit.*]

ASTROV. Is that so? All right, I'll wait a little longer, and then, I hope you'll excuse me, we shall have to use force. We'll tie you up and search you. I say this in all seriousness.

VOYNITSKY. Do as you like. [*Pause.*] I've made a fool of myself, a damn fool. To shoot two times and not once hit the target! It's something I'll never forgive myself for!

ASTROV. If you had an itch to go shooting, well, you ought to have shot yourself in the head.

VOYNITSKY. [*having shrugged his shoulders*] It's strange. I tried to commit a murder, but they don't arrest me or drag me into court. It must mean they consider me mad. [*A bitter laugh.*] I am a madman. But those who cover up their mediocrity, stupidity, and blatant coldheartedness behind the mask of a professor or a scholarly magician, why, they aren't mad. And those who marry old men and then deceive them in front of everybody, why they aren't mad either. I saw you, I saw the way you held her in your arms!

ASTROV. Yes sir, I held her, sir, and this is for you. [*Thumbs his nose.*]

VOYNITSKY. [*looking at the door*] No, the earth itself is mad if it can still keep you around!

ASTROV. Now that's downright stupid.

VOYNITSKY. Well, why not? I'm mad, I'm irresponsible, so I must have the right to say stupid things.

ASTROV. Pretty old stuff and nonsense. You're not mad, you're simply eccentric. A laughing stock full of beans.[3] I used to think that every eccentric person was sick and abnormal, but now I've come to the opinion that being eccentric is the normal condition of mankind. You are completely normal.

VOYNITSKY. [*covers his face with his hands*] I feel ashamed! If you only knew how ashamed I am! This feeling of shame is sharp, so much so it can't compare with physical pain. [*In agony and despair.*] I can't take it! [*Leans on the table.*] What can I do? What can I do?

ASTROV. Nothing.

VOYNITSKY. Give me something, anything! Oh, dear God . . . I'm

3. Literally, "a clown full of peas"; said of a ridiculous person who is foolishly dressed, or a shallow person who serves as a universal laughingstock.

forty-seven years old. Let's say I live to be sixty, that leaves me thirteen more years. That's a long time. How can I get through those thirteen years? What will I do, what can I fill them with? Oh, you can understand . . . [*Fervently squeezes* ASTROV'S *arm.*] you can understand what it would mean to live the rest of your life in some new way. If you could wake up one clear, quiet morning and feel that you're beginning your life over again, that the entire past is forgotten, scattered to the winds like smoke. [*Weeps.*] To begin a new life . . . Give me a hint, tell me how to begin . . . what to begin with . . .

ASTROV. [*with annoyance*] Oh, come on, now! What do you mean, a new life! Our situation, yours and mine, is hopeless.

VOYNITSKY. Yes?

ASTROV. I'm sure of it.

VOYNITSKY. Then give me something at least . . . [*Points to his heart.*] I'm burning up in here.

ASTROV. [*shouts angrily*] Stop it! [*Mollified.*] Those who come after us, in the course of a hundred or two hundred years, and who will despise us for making our lives so stupid and so tasteless, perhaps they will find ways to be happy, but as for us . . . You and I have only one hope. The hope that when we lie sleeping in our graves, visions will come to us, perhaps even pleasant ones. [*Having sighed.*] Yes, brother. In the entire district there were only two decent, educated persons—you and I. But some ten years or so of this contemptible, provincial existence have dragged us down completely. Its rotten air has poisoned our blood, and we have become just as petty and vulgar as everyone else. [*With animation.*] You won't get off the hook by trying to talk me out of it. You give back what you took from me.

VOYNITSKY. I didn't take anything from you.

ASTROV. You took a small bottle of morphine out of my traveling medical bag. [*Pause.*] Listen, if you've made up your mind once and for all to finish yourself off, then go to the forest and shoot yourself there. But give me back the morphine, or there will be all sorts of talk and guesswork and people will think that I gave it to you . . . It's going to be enough for me to do your postmortem . . . You don't think I'll find that exciting, do you?

    SONYA *enters.*

VOYNITSKY. Leave me alone!

ASTROV. [*to* SONYA] Sofia Alexandrovna, your uncle stole a small bottle of morphine out of my medical bag and he won't give it back. Tell him that it's . . . not very smart, after all. Besides, I can't stay another minute. It's time for me to go.

SONYA. Uncle Vanya, did you take the morphine? [*Pause.*]

ASTROV. He took it. I'm sure of it.

SONYA. Give it back. Why go on frightening us? [*Tenderly.*] Give it back, Uncle Vanya! I imagine I'm just as unhappy as you, but I'm not going to give in to despair. I accept the way things are

and I'll go on accepting them until my life comes to its own na-
tural end . . . You must have patience too. [*Pause.*] Give it back.
[*Kisses his hands.*] Dear, kind Uncle, give it back, my dear!
[*Weeps.*] You're a kind man, you'll think about us and give it
back, won't you. You must accept the way things are, Uncle
Vanya, you must accept them!

VOYNITSKY. [*gets the bottle out of the desk and gives it to* ASTROV]
There, take it! [*To* SONYA.] But we must hurry and get to work,
we must do something quickly, or I can't go on . . . I can't . . .

SONYA. Yes, yes, to get to work. As soon as we see them on their
way, we'll sit down and start working . . . [*Nervously sorts through
some papers on the table.*] We've let everything slide by.

ASTROV. [*puts the bottle into his medical bag and tightens the
straps*] Now I can start on my way.

YELENA ANDREEVNA. [*enters*] Ivan Petrovich, are you here? We
are leaving now . . . Go and talk to Alexandr, he wants to say
something to you.

SONYA. Go on, Uncle Vanya. [*Takes* VOYNITSKY *by the arm.*] Let's
go. You and Papa must settle your differences and be friends
again. It's what you must do.

    SONYA *and* VOYNITSKY *go out.*

YELENA ANDREEVNA. I'm going away. [*Gives* ASTROV *her hand.*]
Good-bye.

ASTROV. Already?

YELENA ANDREEVNA. The horses have been brought to the house.

ASTROV. Good-bye.

YELENA ANDREEVNA. You promised me today you'd leave this place.

ASTROV. I remember. I'm going in a moment. [*Pause.*] Are you
scared? [*Takes her by the hand.*] It is really so terrible?

YELENA ANDREEVNA. Yes.

ASTROV. Perhaps you ought to stay! Hmm? Tomorrow at the forest
preserve . . .

YELENA ANDREEVNA. No . . . It's settled . . . And that's why I have
the courage to look at you now. Because it's settled once and for
all that we're going away . . . There's something I will ask of you
—think of me as a better person. What I'd like is for you to respect me.

ASTROV. Oh! [*An impatient gesture.*] Stay here, I beg you. You'd
better own up you have nothing in the world to do, no purpose in
life, nothing to occupy your mind, and sooner or later, as a matter
of course, you're going to cave in to the way you feel—that's exactly what's in store for you. It would be much better if it took
place here in the lap of nature . . . not in Kharkov or somewhere
like Kursk.[4] At least it's poetic here, even the autumn is beautiful . . . There's the forest preserve and run-down country houses
like the places Turgenev describes . . .

---

4. A town in middle Russia about 150 miles north of Kharkov.

YELENA ANDREEVNA. How funny you really are . . . I'm angry with you, but nonetheless . . . I shall remember you with pleasure. You're an interesting, singular person. We'll never see each other anymore, so why on earth should I hide it? I was indeed a little fascinated by you. Well, let's shake hands and say good-bye as friends. Remember me kindly.

ASTROV. [*having shaken hands*] Yes, you'd better be on your way . . . [*Deliberating.*] You seem to be a good, sincere person, but there's still something strange about your very nature. The instant you and your husband arrived here, all of us who were doing our work, scampering hither and yon creating something, we all had to drop everything and spend the whole summer just looking after your husband's gout and you. You both—he and you—infected everyone of us with your idleness. I was carried away, I hadn't done a thing for a whole month, and all this time people have gotten sick and the villagers have been grazing their cattle in my forests, among the saplings I planted . . . And so, no matter where you and your husband set foot, you bring destruction everywhere . . . I'm joking, of course, but nonetheless . . . it's strange. And I'm thoroughly convinced that, if you had remained here, the devastation would have been enormous. I would've wasted away, and as for you . . . you would have paid for it too. Well, you'd better be on your way. *Finita la commedia!*[5]

YELENA ANDREEVNA. [*takes a pencil from his desk and quickly hides it*] I take this pencil to remember you by.

ASTROV. Somehow it's strange . . . we've gotten to know each other and suddenly for some reason . . . we'll never see each other anymore. That's the way everything goes in the world . . . While there's no one here, before Uncle Vanya enters with a bouquet, let me . . . kiss you . . . good-bye . . . Yes? [*Kisses her on the cheek.*] Well, there . . . Very good too.

YELENA ANDREEVNA. I wish you the best of everything. [*Having looked around.*] Oh, come what may, at least for once in my life! [*Embraces him impulsively and then both at once quickly move away from each other.*] I must leave.

ASTROV. Then go quickly. If the horses are at the door, you'd better set off.

YELENA ANDREEVNA. I think they're coming in here. [*Both listen.*]

ASTROV. *Finita!*

> SEREBRYAKOV, VOYNITSKY, MARIA VASILEVNA, *carrying a book,* TELEGIN, *and* SONYA *enter.*

SEREBRYAKOV. [*to* VOYNITSKY] Let bygones be bygones. After all that's happened, I've lived through so much and turned over so many things in my mind these last few hours, I believe that I could write an entire treatise on how people ought to live for the edification of posterity. I readily accept your apologies and in

---

5. "The comedy is finished!"

turn I beg you to excuse me. Good-bye! [*He and* VOYNITSKY *kiss each other three times.*]

VOYNITSKY. You'll be receiving regularly the same amount you received before. Everything will be just as it was.

YELENA ANDREEVNA *embraces* SONYA.

SEREBRYAKOV. [*kisses* MARIA VASILEVNA's *hand.*] *Maman* . . .

MARIA VASILEVNA. [*kissing him*] Alexandr, have your photograph taken again and send it to me. You know how very much you mean to me.

TELEGIN. Good-bye, your Excellency! Don't forget us!

SEREBRYAKOV. [*having kissed his daughter.*] Good-bye . . . Good-bye, all of you! [*Shaking hands with* ASTROV.] I thank you for your pleasant company . . . I respect your way of thinking, your enthusiasm, and your fervent impulses, but let an old man introduce just one observation into his farewell greetings. Ladies and gentlemen, you must get down to work. Something useful ought to get done![6] [*A general bow.*] The best to everyone! [*Goes out, followed by* MARIA VASILEVNA *and* SONYA.]

VOYNITSKY. [*fervently kisses* YELENA ANDREEVNA's *hand*] Good-bye . . . Forgive me . . . We'll never see each other again.

YELENA ANDREEVNA. [*moved*] Good-bye, my dear. [*Kisses him on the head and goes out.*]

ASTROV. [*to* TELEGIN] You might tell them, Waffles, to bring my horses around to the door at the same time.

TELEGIN. At your service, my dear friend. [*Goes out. Only* ASTROV *and* VOYNITSKY *remain.*]

ASTROV. [*clears his paints from the table and puts them into a suitcase*] Why don't you go and see them on their way?

VOYNITSKY. Let them go away, but I . . . I can't do it. I feel terribly depressed. I must hurry and get myself occupied with something . . . Work, that's what I must do, work! [*Rummages among the papers on the table.*]

A *pause. Harness bells are heard.*

ASTROV. They've gone. I'd say the professor is glad! You won't lure him back here now no matter what bait you use.

MARINA. [*enters*] They've gone. [*Sits in an armchair and knits a stocking.*]

SONYA. [*enters*] They've gone. [*Wipes her eyes.*] God grant everything goes well for them. [*To her uncle.*] Well, Uncle Vanya, let's do something.

VOYNITSKY. Work, that's what we must do, work . . .

SONYA. It's been a long, long time since we sat down at this table together. [*Lights the lamp on the table.*] There doesn't seem to be any ink . . . [*Takes the inkwell, goes to the cupboard, and fills it.*] I feel sad now that they've gone.

6. See note 2, p. 61.

MARIA VASILEVNA. [*enters slowly*] They've gone! [*Sits and becomes absorbed in her reading.*]

SONYA. [*sits at the table and turns the pages of the account book*] First of all, Uncle Vanya, we'll make out the bills. It's terrible how we let them slide by. Someone sent for his account again today. Begin writing. You make out one account, and I'll do another . . .

VOYNITSKY. [*writes*] "The billing . . . to Mr. . . ." [*Both write in silence.*]

MARINA. [*yawns*] I'm ready to go beddy-bye . . .

ASTROV. It's quiet and peaceful. Pens are scratching, the cricket chirping. It's warm and cozy . . . I don't feel like leaving here. [*Harness bells are heard.*] Well, they're bringing my horses . . . And so what's left is to say good-bye to you, my friends, say good-bye to my desk and—get going! [*Puts the cartograms into the portfolio.*]

MARINA. And what's all the hustle and bustle about? You ought to sit a spell.

ASTROV. I can't.

VOYNITSKY. [*writes*] "And two rubles seventy-five kopeks remain from your old debt . . ."

A WORKMAN *enters.*

WORKMAN. Mikhail Lvovich, the horses have been brought to the house.

ASTROV. I heard them. [*Gives him the medical bag, suitcase, and portfolio.*] Here, take them. See that you don't mash the portfolio.

WORKMAN. Very good, sir. [*Goes out.*]

ASTROV. Well, miss . . . [*Goes to say good-bye.*]

SONYA. When shall we see you again?

ASTROV. Not before summer, most likely. Hardly this winter . . . If something happens, of course, let me know—I'll be here. [*Shakes hands.*] Thank you for your bread, your salt,[7] your kindness . . . in fact, thank you for everything. [*Goes to the* NURSE *and kisses her on the head.*] Good-bye, old woman.

MARINA. And so you're on your way without tea?

ASTROV. I don't want any, *nyanka.*

MARINA. Maybe, a drop or two of vodka?

ASTROV. [*indecisively*] Oh, perhaps . . . [MARINA *leaves. After a pause.*] My trace horse has gone lame somehow. I noticed it yesterday when Petrushka[8] was leading him to water.

VOYNITSKY. You should have him reshod.

ASTROV. I'll have to drop by the blacksmith's in Rozhdestvennoe.[9] There's no escaping it. [*Goes to the map of Africa and looks at*

---

7. Traditional emblems of hospitality.
8. Apparently one of the workers attached to the estate.
9. Apparently a village near Dr. Astrov's estate.

it.] Ah, way down there in Africa, I'll bet there's a blazing heat wave now—a terrible scorcher!

VOYNITSKY. Yes, probably so.

MARINA. [*returns with a tray on which there is a glass of vodka and a piece of bread*] There you are. [ASTROV *drinks the vodka*.] Your health, my pet. [*Bows low*.] And you should take some of the bread.

ASTROV. No, I'm all right the way it is . . . And so, all the very best to you! [*To* MARINA.] Don't see me to the door, *nyanka*. You don't have to.

> He goes out. SONYA *follows, carrying a candle to see him off.* MARINA *sits down in her own armchair.*

VOYNITSKY. [*writes*] "February second, oil, twenty pounds . . . February sixteenth, again oil, twenty pounds . . . Buckwheat meal . . ." [*Pause*.]

> *Harness bells are heard.*

MARINA. He's gone. [*Pause*.]

SONYA. [*returns and places the candle on the table*] He's gone . . .

VOYNITSKY. [*counts on the abacus and jots it down*] In all . . . fifteen . . . twenty-five . . .

> SONYA *sits and writes.*

MARINA. [*yawns*] Oh, our sins . . .

> TELEGIN *enters on tiptoe, sits by the door, and quietly tunes his guitar.*

VOYNITSKY. [*to* SONYA, *passing his hand over her hair*] My child, I'm terribly depressed! Oh, if you only knew how it breaks my heart!

SONYA. Well, what do you do then? You must go on living! [*Pause*.] Uncle Vanya, we shall keep on living. We shall live through a long, long procession of days and everlasting evenings. We shall patiently endure the trials we are destined to meet. We shall work for the sake of others, now and when we are old, never knowing peace or rest. And when our own hour has come, we shall die without complaining; and there, beyond the grave, we shall say that we have suffered, we have wept, our life has been hard and bitter, and God will take pity on us. And you and I, my dear Uncle Vanya, we shall see a life which is bright, beautiful, and fine. We shall rejoice and look back on our present misfortunes with a feeling of tenderness, with a smile—and we shall rest. I believe, Uncle, I believe in it fervently, passionately . . . [*Kneels before him and lays her head on his hand. In a tired voice*.] We shall rest! [TELEGIN *quietly plays the guitar*.] We shall rest! We shall hear the angels, we shall see the whole sky shining like diamonds. We shall see all these earthly evils, all our sufferings, drowned in mercy that will fill the whole world, and our life will then grow quiet and gentle and sweet as a caress. I believe, I believe in it . . . [*Wipes his tears with a handkerchief*.] Poor, poor Uncle

Vanya, you are crying . . . [*Through tears.*] You've never known happiness in your life, but wait, Uncle Vanya, wait a little while . . . We shall rest . . . [*Embraces him.*] We shall rest! [*The* WATCHMAN *taps.* TELEGIN *plays quietly.* MARIA VASILEVNA *writes on the margin of her pamphlet.* MARINA *knits a stocking.*] We shall rest!

THE CURTAIN SLOWLY FALLS

The Three Sisters

Unlike the other major plays, the environment in *The Three Sisters* is the life style of a Russian provincial city of about one hundred thousand inhabitants. In fact, in a letter to the writer Maxim Gorky (1868–1936) Chekhov suggested that the action could take place in a city like Perm, located in central Russia. Life in a provincial city permeates much of the play, chiefly in the characters of Natasha (whose onstage action is readily perceived) and Protopopov (although he is never seen, he is the prime mover of several events offstage), as well as in the dreams of the sisters to escape the humdrum, meaningless existence which is partly expressed in the Russian concept of *poshlost'* (defined in Vladimir Nabokov's essay in this volume).

Although the play is threaded with instances of *poshlost'*, three important ones are discussed here. For example, early in Act II, Vershinin, Masha, and Tuzenbakh are talking a "little philosophy" (pp. 124–125), each one searching for the meaning of happiness in life. Their discussion concludes in three final speeches.

> MASHA. It seems to me that man must have faith, or he must look for faith. Otherwise, his life is empty, empty . . . To live and not to know the reason why cranes fly, why children are born, why stars are in the sky . . . Either you know the reason why you are living, or else everything is nonsense, hokum. [*Pause*.]
> VERSHININ. All the same, it's a shame when youth is over . . .
> MASHA. As Gogol says, "It's a dreary world we live in, ladies and gentlemen!" [p. 125]

Masha's quotation is the concluding sentence in *The Story of How Ivan Ivanovich Quarreled with Ivan Nikiforovich* (1835) by Nikolay Gogol (1809–52). In Gogol's story the two Ivans are friends but become enemies over a trivial incident that flowers into a grand fight, complete with aberrant behavior and lawsuits—all written in the style of the grotesque. Near the end of Gogol's story, aptly subtitled(in Victor Erlich's words) "A Tale of Two Idiots Told by an Idiot,"[1] the provincial "idiot" narrator disappears and is replaced by a more thoughtful narrator who concludes the story. The two Ivans have grown old. "Each is reduced to ludicrous fixation, kept alive only by the 'positive information' that tomorrow, or next week, the case will be settled in his favor. The weather, the seedy town, the two absurd old men, blend into a dreary, all too subhuman spectacle."[2] Thus, Chekhov links the Gogolian universe of *poshlost'* to his own world of *The Three Sisters*.

Early in Act III, with the fire raging throughout the town, the old army doctor Chebutykin stumbles drunk into the bedroom shared by Olga and

1. Victor Erlich, *Gogol* (New Haven: Yale University Press, 1969), p. 71. 2. Ibid., p. 73.

Irina. In a touching monologue, Chebutykin describes his own ineptness as a physician and the shoddy hypocrisy of his fellow club members. "Petty and vulgar [*poshlost'*], mean [*nizost'*]! And that woman, the one I killed on Wednesday, came back to my mind . . . and everything came back to my mind, and in my heart and soul I felt twisted, corrupt, ugly . . ." (p. 136). The third instance occurs in Act IV, when Andrey, outside the Prozorov house to wheel his own child Bobik (his rival Protopopov sits inside the house playing with perhaps his own child Sofya), tries to explain Natasha to Chebutykin. "A wife is a wife. She is pure, honest, and perhaps kind. But there's something in her that corrupts, makes her something of a petty, blind animal, rough and hard-skinned. In any case she is not human. . . . I love Natasha, it's so, but sometimes she seems to me absolutely petty and vulgar [*poshlost'*]" (p. 149). A reference to the illusion of happiness which is partly linked to the concept of *poshlost'* occurs immediately after the trio [Vershinin, Masha, Tuzenbakh] conclude their Act II discussion of happiness in life.

> CHEBUTYKIN. [*reading the newspaper*] Balzac was married in Berdichev. [IRINA *hums quietly*.] Better write that down in my little book. [*Writes*.] Balzac was married in Berdichev.
>   IRINA. [*lost in thought, she sets out the cards for a game of patience*] Balzac was married in Berdichev. [p. 125]

The musical line of dialogue, twice repeated, is an historical fact. Honoré de Balzac (1799–1850), the famous French writer, married Madame de Hanska on March 14, 1850, in the parochial church of St. Barbara in Berdichev in the Ukraine. Balzac's long courtship (lasting almost seventeen years) of the woman to whom he had pledged eternal love was finally concluded in marriage, biographers suggest, when his doctors told her that Balzac would never recover from his illness. Less than six months later, during the night of August 18–19, 1850, he died. Even though Balzac and Madame de Hanska had been lovers during the greater part of the seventeen-year courtship, and although she had been free to marry Balzac (her husband died in 1841), her consistent refusal, his persistent request, and their life together could also be interpreted as slithering inside, outside, and around the universe of *poshlost'*.

Linked to the forces of darkness (Natasha and Protopopov) is Captain Solyony, whose character contains aspects of *poshlost'*. In Act II, Solyony warns Tuzenbakh of his impending death by referring to the works of two famous Russian authors as well as to a famous Russian poet.

> SOLYONY. [*declaiming*] "I am strange, but who is not strange! Do not be angry, Aleko!" . . . I've never had anything against you, Baron. But I have the disposition of Lermontov. [*Quietly*.] I even look a little like Lermontov. [p. 128]

The first line, "I am strange, but who is not strange!", is from the play *Woe from Wit* (*Gore ot uma*, 1822–24) by A. S. Griboedov (1795–1829). It is from a speech (Act III) by Chatsky, the central character, who—as a witty, honest, thoughtful person—is surrounded by persons in Moscow society characterized by dullness, hypocrisy, and "gamesmanship." Moreover, Chatsky is a prototype of the "superfluous person" theme in Russian literature. Solyony apparently sees himself as a "hero" opposing everyone—just as Chatsky opposes, and is opposed by, the group he comes into contact with. The second line, "Do not be angry, Aleko!", is a paraphrase of a line from *The Gypsies* (1824), a narrative poem by A. S. Pushkin (1799–1837), in which the hero, Aleko, enraged with jealousy, kills his wife, Zemfira, and her young lover. The line in the poem, "Be angry if you must/I'm singing the song ["Old Husband"] ·about you," is said by Zemfira to Aleko just before she leaves to meet her lover. Like the avenger Aleko, Solyony sees himself as the "winner" in the love triangle of Solyony-Irina-Tuzenbakh. Solyony's reference to the likenesses shared by M. Yu. Lermontov (1814–41) and himself is appropriate to the action in the play. The famous Russian poet is associated with romanticism in Russian literature; moreover, he enjoyed dueling and even died in a duel. In a letter to I. A. Tikhomirov dated January 14, 1901, Chekhov explains the relationship: "Solyony thinks that he resembles Lermontov; but of course he does not. . . . The connection with Lermontov is huge, but only in the opinion of Solyony (*Complete Works*, XIX, 18). The love affair between Masha and Vershinin achieves its promise of completeness in Act III.

> VERSHININ. My lust for living runs full rein . . . [*Sings.*]
>
> "All ages are obedient to love,
> Its passions are good to . . ." [*Laughs.*]
>
> MASHA. Tram-tam-tam . . .
> VERSHININ. Tam-tam . . .
> MASHA. Tra-ra-ra?
> VERSHININ. Tra-ta-ta. [*Laughs.*] [pp. 138–139]

What Vershinin sings consists of lines 1 and 3, Stanza 29, Chapter VIII of Pushkin's *Eugene Onegin* (1823–31), and the music is probably from the three-act opera composed in 1879 by P. I. Tchaikovsky (1840–93), with a libretto by the composer and Konstantin S. Shilovsky. The declaration of love is continued with nonsense sounds, during which Masha agrees to the consummation of their affair. Thus, near the end of Act III, when Vershinin calls from offstage, "Tram-tam-tam!" Masha answers, "Tra-ta-ta!" (p. 143), and then exits.[3]

For the opening production at the Moscow Art Theatre in January 1901, Chekhov gave several instructions, among which the following are important. Early in Act III, an alarm bell sounds. In a letter to Olga Knipper dated January 17, 1901, Chekhov described both the mood and the effects of Act III: "Of course, Act Three should be conducted quietly on the stage in order to feel that people are tired, that they want to go to bed. What's all this about noise? It's shown where the bells are to ring offstage" (*Com-plete Works*, XIX, 21). Later in Act III, when Natasha enters with a candle (p. 141), Chekhov explains her strange business. "You write that in Act·III Natasha is making the rounds of the house, it's night, she puts out the lights

3. Anton Chekhov, Letter to Olga Knipper, January 20, 1901, *Complete Works*, XIX, 24.

and looks for thieves under the furniture. But it seems to me, it would be better for her to cross the stage in a straight line, not looking at anybody or anything, *à la* Lady Macbeth, with a candle—that way it's quicker and more frightening" (*Complete Works*, XIX, 8). Shortly after Natasha enters and exits in Act III, Masha says, "My dear sisters, I've something to confess" (p. 142). In a letter to Olga Knipper dated January 21, 1901, Chekhov gave the following directions: "My dear, Masha's repentance in Act III isn't repentance at all, but only a frank talk. Do it with feeling, but not desperately, don't shout, smile if only now and then, and in general, do it so that the tiredness of the night is felt. And make it feel you're smarter than your sisters, or that you think yourself smarter at least. About your "tram-tam-tam," do as you know best. You're my sensible woman" (*Complete Works*, XIX, 25). V. V. Luzhsky, who played the role of Andrey in the original production, recalled that Chekhov first saw the rehearsals for *The Three Sisters* in the autumn of 1901, after it had opened the previous season. Chekhov made (in Luzhsky's words) "observations so detailed that he even personally staged the scene of the fire in the third act. He remained dissatisfied with me at rehearsals, sent for me, and in great detail, with pauses and explanations, went through the role of Andrey. . . . He demanded that in the last monologue (p. 152) Andrey should be very excited. 'He must be just about ready to threaten the audience with his fists!' " (V. V. Luzhsky, *Chekhov and Theatre*, p. 353.)

Two other items of Russian milieu can be explained here. In Act II, the event is Carnival Week (p. 119), during which the days immediately prior to Lent, corresponding to Shrovetide, were days of festivity that in Russia featured pancakes and masquerades. Thus, the references in this act to pancakes, frying, mummers, etc., reveal common Russian activities during Carnival Week. Later in Act II, the characters onstage sing, "Oh, you, porch, my porch . . ." (p. 129). This is a well-known Russian folk song. In Russian productions of this play, Andrey, Tuzenbakh, and Chebutykin dance during the song, which is accompanied by guitar music played by Fedotik and Rode. The word *seni*, translated here as *porch*, is defined as "a room between the dwelling part of the house and the [outer] porch in wooden peasant houses and in old municipal houses" (*Dictionary*, IV, 107).

Of the numerous deletions made in the final version of this play, the following shed light on the action and the characters. These deletions are given in chronological order. After Chebutykin's speech in Act I, concluding with the sentence "God only knows" (p. 107), the following words were cut: "I haven't done anything my whole life, I've never had time to do anything my whole life" (*Complete Works*, XI, 588). The following passage was cut in Masha's speech in Act I, following "Oh, how she dresses" (p. 111): "You're from Moscow, you know what I mean. I can't stand the way they dress here; women of fashion here simply insult me" (*Complete Works*, XI, 588). The following passage in Vershinin's speech after the sentence "Well, just imagine that!" was cut by Chekhov; the stage direction "[*Laughs.*]" and the sentence "You know so much that is simply superfluous" were substituted: "In the first place, it's doubtful that any one of us holds a point of view sufficiently correct to discern what is superfluous from that which is necessary. And in the second place" (*Complete Works,* XI, 588). In Act II the following passage in Andrey's speech after the sentence "Come back tomorrow morning, pick up the papers here" (p. 121) was cut from the final version: "You see, I remember everything; I haven't forgotten anything. I have a colossal memory, and, with such a memory, any other person in my place long ago would have stretched himself across all Moscow, like your rope. Or across all Russia" (*Complete Works,* XI, 589). In Act II, after Tuzenbakh's question "Well, how is it possible for me to convince you?" (p. 125), the following passage was cut: "We live our present lives, and the future will live its own life, one exactly like ours—no better and no worse . . ." (*Complete Works,* XI, 589). In Act III, after Andrey's statement "it's simply capriciousness on your part" (p. 143), the following was cut: "or even better, the childish tricks of old maids. Old maids aren't fond of their sisters-in-law and never have been fond of them, that's the truth" (*Complete Works,* XI, 589). In Act IV, after Masha's sentence "Here, now, I am boiling inside" (p. 148) the following passage was cut: "The person I'd like to give a whipping good and proper is Andrey, our brother. The laughingstock stuffed full of beans" (*Complete Works,* XI, 589). In Act IV, after Masha's sentence "we are left alone, to begin our life over again" (p. 157), the following passage was cut by Chekhov from the final version, at the request of Olga Knipper, who complained of problems acting it: "I shall go on living, sisters. One must live. [*Looks up.*] There are migrating birds up there, they fly past every spring and fall, already for thousands of years, and they don't know the reason why, but they fly and they'll go on flying for ever and ever, for thousands and thousands of years—until at last God reveals his secrets to them."[4] In Act IV, after the sentence "The band plays softer and softer" (p. 157), the following stage direction was cut by Chekhov: "*at the depths of the stage [is heard] a noise, a crowd is seen, they are watching as the body of the baron, who has been killed in the duel, is carried by.*"[5] When Stanislavsky objected to this action as one that would be difficult to stage—e.g., what do the sisters do?—Chekhov agreed: "Of course, you are a thousand times right, to show Tuzenbakh's body is not at all proper. I felt that myself when I wrote it, and I spoke to you about it, if you remember" (*Complete Works,* XIX, 20). A few days later, in a letter to Olga Knipper dated January 20, 1901, Chekhov brought the matter up again: "I said at the time that to carry Tuzenbakh's body on your stage would be awkward, but Alekseev [Stanislavsky] was firmly convinced that without the body it was absolutely impossible. I wrote him that the body should not be carried past, I don't know if he received my letter" (*Complete Works,* XIX, 24).

Chekhov's choice of names for his characters is appropriate. For example, the first names of the sisters enhance their natures: *Olga,* from the Teutonic word for *holy*; *Masha,* a variant of *Mary,* from the Hebrew for *bitter*; *Irina,* a variant of the Greek *Irene,* or *peace. Andrey* is the Greek *Andrew,* or *manly.* The name *Vershinin* incorporates the Russian root word *vershina,*

4. A. R. Vladimirskaya, "Dve rannie redakcii p'esy *Tri sestry*; Stat'ja i publikacija" [Two Early Editions of the play *The Three Sisters*; Essay and Publication], in *Literaturnoe nasledstvo* [Literary Heritage], Vol. 68, *A. P. Chekhov* (Moscow and Leningrad, 1960), p. 86.
5. Ibid.

which means "summit," "top," "crest," "peak," "apex." The name *Solyony*, on the other hand, incorporates the Russian word for *salt*. Protopopov's first and last names were the same as those of the literary critic Mikhail Protopopov (1848–1915), whom Chekhov thoroughly disliked. Chekhov's offstage Protopopov, however, received a patronymic that differed from that of the critic.

The pronunciation of the characters' names, together with the appropriate stress:

Ándrey Sergéevich (Sergéich) Prozorov (prózaraf)
Natálya Ivanovna (ivánavna) (Natásha)
Ólga (Ólyushka, Ólya, Ólga Sergéevna, Ólechka)
Másha (Márya, Mária Sergéevna, Máshka, Máshenka)
Irína (Arínyshka, Arísha)
Fyódor (Fédya) Ilích Kulýgin
Alexándr Ignátevich (Ignátich) Vershínin
Nikolay (nikaláy) Lvóvich Túzenbakh
Vasíly Vasílevich (Vasílich) Solyony (salyóny)
Iván Romanovich (ramánavich) (Romanych) (ramánych) Chebutýkin
Alexéy Petróvich Fedótik
Vladímir Karlovich (kárlavich) Rode (radé)
Ferapónt
Anfísa

The pronunciation of other words (in alphabetical order) : Aleko (aléka); Andryúsha; Andryushánchik; Basmánny; Berdichev (berdíchef); Bóbik; Boloshoy (balshóy); chekhartmá; cheremshá; Chitá; Dobrolyubov (dabralyúbaf); Kirsanovsky (kirsánafsky); Kokhane (kakháne); Kolotilin (kalatílin); Kozyrev (kózyref); Krásny; Lermontov (lérmantaf); Márfa; mátushka; Moskovsky (maskófsky); Nemétskaya; Novo-Devichy (nóvadévichy); nyánechka; Potapych (patápych); Protopopov (pratapópaf), Mikhaíl Iványch; Pyzhihov's (pýzhikaf's); Saratov (sarátaf); Sofochka (sófachka); Skvorstsov (skvartsóf); Spiridónych; Stanislav (stanisláf); Testov's (téstaf's); Tsitsikár; Zásyp.

The Three Sisters

A Drama in Four Acts

LIST OF CHARACTERS

ANDREY SERGEEVICH PROZOROV
NATALYA IVANOVNA, *his fiancée, later his wife*
OLGA ⎫
MASHA ⎬ *his sisters*
IRINA ⎭
FYODOR ILICH KULYGIN, *a high-school teacher,* MASHA's *husband*
ALEXANDR IGNATEVICH VERSHININ, *a lieutenant-colonel, battery commander*
BARON NIKOLAY LVOVICH TUZENBAKH, *a lieutenant*
CAPTAIN VASILY VASILEVICH SOLYONY
IVAN ROMANOVICH CHEBUTYKIN, *an army doctor*
ALEXEY PETROVICH FEDOTIK, *a second lieutenant*
VLADIMIR KARLOVICH RODE, *a second lieutenant*
FERAPONT, *a watchman from the District Council, an old man*
ANFISA, *an old nurse of eighty years*

The action takes place in a provincial town.

Act One

In the house of the PROZOROVS. *A drawing room with columns, behind which is seen a ballroom.*[1] *Noon. Outdoors it is sunny and bright. In the ballroom the table is being set for lunch.* OLGA, *wearing the dark-blue uniform dress of a teacher in the girls' high school, is correcting student exercise books the whole time, either standing or walking to and fro.* MASHA, *in a black dress, sits with her hat on her knees and reads a little book.* IRINA, *in a white dress, stands lost in thought.*

OLGA. Father died exactly one year ago, on this very day, the fifth of May, on your saint's day, Irina. It was bitter cold, it was snowing at the time. I felt as if I could never live through it. You had fainted, and you lay there as though dead. And yet, and yet a year has gone by, it's easier to look back on it now. You've even started wearing white, and your face is radiant. [*The clock strikes twelve.*] At that time too the clock was striking. [*Pause.*] I remember, as they took Father to the cemetery, the band was playing; at the

---

1. A ballroom was a standard part of upper-class houses in nineteenth-century Russia.

graveside they fired a salute. He was a general, the commander of a brigade, and yet almost no one at all came to the funeral. Of course, it was raining at the time. A heavy rain and snow.

IRINA. Why bring back those memories?

In the ballroom, behind the columns, BARON TUZENBAKH, CHEBUTYKIN, *and* SOLYONY *appear near the table.*

OLGA. It's warm today, so warm we can keep the windows wide open, and yet not a single bud has appeared on the birch trees. Father was given command of the brigade, and together we all left Moscow eleven years ago. I can remember perfectly well the beginning of May in Moscow. By this time in Moscow everything is in full bloom, it's warm, everything is bathed in sunlight. Eleven years have gone by, and I remember everything there as if we had just left yesterday. Oh, dear God in Heaven! This morning I woke up, I saw at once the sunlight everywhere, I saw at once that it was springtime, and I felt my heart would break with joy. I wanted desperately to go home again.

CHEBUTYKIN. The hell you say!

TUZENBAKH. Of course, it's all nonsense.

MASHA, *having become thoughtful over her book, quietly whistles a tune.*

OLGA. Don't whistle, Masha. How can you! [*Pause.*] After being at the high school day after day and then giving private lessons until dinner, I have headaches constantly. And my thoughts, why I've even started to think like an old woman. In fact, the past four years I've worked at the high school, day after day I've felt my strength and my youth drain away, drop by drop. And just one dream keeps growing stronger and stronger, one dream . . .

IRINA. To leave for Moscow. To sell the house, put an end to everything here, and off to Moscow . . .

OLGA. Yes! As soon as possible, off to Moscow.

CHEBUTYKIN *and* TUZENBAKH *laugh.*

IRINA. Brother will probably become a professor. It doesn't matter because he won't live here. The only complication is poor Masha.[2]

OLGA. Masha will come to Moscow for the whole summer, every year.

MASHA *quietly whistles a tune.*

IRINA. Pray to God it will all work out. [*Looking out the window.*] The weather is marvelous today. I'm so happy deep inside, so excited, and I don't know why. Early this morning I remembered that today is my name day[3] and suddenly I felt like shouting for joy, and I remembered when we were children, when Mama was still alive. And what wonderful ideas took hold of me, what wonderful ideas!

---

2. That is, Masha will not be able to go because she is married and her school-teacher husband, Kulygin, has a position in this provincial town.

3. On saint's day—the day of the saint whose name a person has been given is normally the day of celebration for that person.

OLGA. You're so radiant today, you look absolutely beautiful. And Masha too is beautiful. Andrey would be good-looking if only he hadn't put on so much weight, it just doesn't suit him. And I've started putting on years, I'm getting terribly thin, and it's all because, well, it must be that I get so angry with the girls in school. But today I am free, I'm here at home, and my head doesn't ache. I feel younger than I did yesterday. I am only twenty-eight years old, it's just that . . . Everything is right and fine, everything has been ordained by God, and yet I can't help thinking that if I were married and sitting at home all day it would be better, far better. [*Pause.*] I would love my husband.

TUZENBAKH. [*to* SOLYONY] You're talking so much nonsense I'm sick of listening to you. [*Coming into the drawing room.*] I forgot to tell you. Today our new battery commander Vershinin will pay you a visit. [*Sits at the piano.*]

OLGA. Oh, well, hmm! I'm delighted.

IRINA. Is he old?

TUZENBAKH. No, not at all. No more than forty, perhaps forty-five. [*Plays quietly on the piano.*] Apparently a rather nice fellow. He's no fool—no question about that. The only thing is, he does talk a great deal.

IRINA. Is he an interesting person?

TUZENBAKH. Oh, he gets by. Only there's a wife, a mother-in-law, and two little girls. On top of that, it's his second marriage. Everywhere he goes, he says he has a wife and two daughters. Mark my words, he'll say it here. His wife is a bit half-witted, with her hair in a long braid like a schoolgirl, chatters only about high-and-mighty things, constantly philosophizing, and every now and again attempts suicide, evidently just to needle her husband. I would have left a woman like that a long time ago, but Vershinin continues to put up with it, and the only thing he does is complain.

SOLYONY. [*coming out of the ballroom into the drawing room with* CHEBUTYKIN] With one hand I can pick up only fifty pounds, but with two hands I can pick up three and a half, or even more than four times as much. From this I conclude that two persons are not twice, but thrice, as strong as one, even stronger . . .

CHEBUTYKIN. [*reading the newspaper as he walks*] For falling hair . . . Eight and a half grams of naphthaline into a half-bottle of alcohol . . . Dissolve and use every day . . . [*Jots it down in a notebook.*] We'll jot it down, sir! [*To* SOLYONY.] Now then, as I was saying to you, a cork is driven into a little bottle; and then you must run a little glass tube through it . . . After that, you take a pinch of ordinary alum,[4] the most common alum you can find . . .

IRINA. Ivan Romanych, dear Ivan Romanych!

CHEBUTYKIN. What is it, my child, light of my life?

4. A colorless or white liquid used in medicine as either (internally) an emetic or (externally) to stop bleeding.

IRINA. Tell me, why is it I'm so happy today? Just as if I were sailing, and over me the broad blue sky with great white birds floating by. Why is it I feel this way, why?

CHEBUTYKIN. [*kissing both her hands, tenderly*] My wonderful white bird . . .

IRINA. When I woke up this morning, I got up and washed, and then suddenly everything in the world became clear to me. I know now the way people must live. Dear Ivan Romanych, I know everything. A person must toil, work by the sweat of his face, no matter who he may be, and in this—and this alone—is found the meaning and the purpose of his life, his happiness, his ecstasy. How right and good it is to be a workman who gets up before sunrise and breaks stones on the road, to be a shepherd, to be a teacher who teaches children, to be an engineer on the railroad . . . Dear God in Heaven, to say nothing of people, it's better to be an ox, or a common ordinary horse—far better—so long as you go on working, than to be the kind of young woman who wakes up at twelve o'clock noon, then drinks her coffee in bed, then takes two hours getting dressed . . . Oh, that's awful! Just as some people thirst for a cool drink on a hot day, so do I in the same way—I thirst for work. And Ivan Romanych, if I don't get up early, if I don't work, then refuse me your friendship.

CHEBUTYKIN. [*tenderly*] I shall refuse it, I shall . . .

OLGA. Father taught us to get up at seven o'clock. So now Irina still wakes up at seven, but she lies in bed at least until nine, thinking about something or other. And see how serious she looks! [*Laughs.*]

IRINA. You still think of me as a little girl, and it seems so strange to you if I look the least bit serious. After all, I am twenty years old!

TUZENBAKH. This longing for work, oh, dear God in Heaven, how clear that is to me! I've never worked, not once in my life. I was born in Petersburg, a city cold and idle, in a family that understood neither work nor worry. On coming home from military school, I remember there was even a valet to pull off my boots. At the time I was a bit silly—I'd say and do the first thing that came to mind—and my mother would always look adoringly at me. And she was always surprised when other people looked at me in a different way. I was protected against work. Only I doubt that the protection was completely successful, I really do! The time has come, something huge and immense is coming nearer and nearer to all of us—a strong, exhilarating storm is beginning to gather, it's on its way, it's almost here, a storm that will soon cleanse our whole society—sweep away all the laziness, the indifference, the prejudice against work, the rotten boredom. I shall work, and in another twenty-five or thirty years every person will be working. Everyone!

CHEBUTYKIN. Well, I'm not planning to work.

TUZENBAKH. You don't count.

SOLYONY. In another twenty-five years you won't be alive on this earth, thank the Lord. In only two or three years you will die of a stroke, or I will lose my temper and plant a bullet in your forehead, my angel.[5] [*Takes a small bottle of scent out of his pocket and sprinkles his chest and his hands.*]

CHEBUTYKIN. [*laughs*] It's a fact, you know, I've never worked at all. Not a lick of work since leaving the university, why, I haven't lifted a finger. I haven't even read through a single book. The only thing I read are newspapers . . . [*Takes another newspaper out of his pocket.*] Here . . . according to the newspapers, I know there was, for instance, a man named Dobrolyubov, but what he wrote about—I don't know . . . God only knows . . . [*A knock is heard from the floor below.*] There . . . They're calling me downstairs, someone has come to see me. I'll be right back . . . Wait a bit . . . [*Goes out hurriedly, combing his beard.*]

IRINA. He's up to something.

TUZENBAKH. Yes, he looked so pompous when he went out, evidently he is going to bring you a present very soon.

IRINA. Oh, that's annoying!

OLGA. Yes, it's terrible, really. He's always doing foolish things.

MASHA. "By the curved seashore stands an oak tree green;
    A golden chain to that oak is bound . . .
    A golden chain to that oak is bound . . ." [*Rises and hums quietly.*]

OLGA. You are unhappy today, Masha. [MASHA, *humming, puts on her hat.*] Where are you going?

MASHA. Home.

IRINA. It's not right . . .

TUZENBAKH. To walk out on a name-day party!

MASHA. It doesn't matter . . . I'll come back this evening. Goodbye, my precious . . . [*Kisses* IRINA.] Once more, the best of everything, be happy. In the old days when Father was alive, there were always up to thirty or forty officers around at our name-day parties. It was noisy, but today there's no more than a man and a half. It's quiet, just as if we were in a desert . . . I'm going . . . I'm depressed today, unhappy, so don't you listen to me. [*Laughing through her tears.*] Later on we'll have a little talk, but for now, good-bye, my dear. I'm off somewhere, any place at all.

IRINA. [*displeased*] Oh, who do you think . . .

OLGA. [*with tears*] I understand you, Masha.

SOLYONY. If a man talks philosophy, then you'll come up with philosophistry or at least sophistry; but if a woman talks philosophy, or two women, then it will be so much twiddle-twaddle.

MASHA. What is it you wanted to say, you terrible, loathsome person?

SOLYONY. Nothing at all.

5. Solyony's remarks are directed to Tuzenbakh.

"Before he had time to let out a yell,
The bear was squeezing him to hell." [*Pause.*]

MASHA. [*to* OLGA, *angrily*] Stop blubbering!

Enter ANFISA *and* FERAPONT *with a cake.*

ANFISA. This way, pet, come in, your feet are clean. [*To* IRINA.] From the District Council, from Protopopov, Mikhail Ivanych . . . A cake.

IRINA. Thank you. Please give him our thanks. [*Takes cake.*]

FERAPONT. What is it?

IRINA. [*louder*] Please give him our thanks!

OLGA. *Nyanechka*, give him some cake, dear. Ferapont, go on, and they'll give you some cake.

FERAPONT. What is it?

ANFISA. Let's go, Ferapont Spiridonych, my pet. Let's go . . . [*Goes out with* FERAPONT.]

MASHA. I don't like Protopopov at all, this Mikhail Potapych or Ivanych. He should not be invited here.

IRINA. I didn't invite him.

MASHA. Good for you.

Enter CHEBUTYKIN, *followed by a* SOLDIER *with a silver samovar; rumble of surprise and dissatisfaction.*

OLGA. [*covering face with her hands*] A samovar![6] It's terrible! [*Goes to the table in the ballroom.*]

IRINA. Oh, Ivan Romanych, darling, what on earth are you doing!

TUZENBAKH. [*laughs*] I told you so.

MASHA. Ivan Romanych, you should be ashamed of yourself!

CHEBUTYKIN. My dearest ones, my precious ones, you are all I have, you mean more to me than anything in the world. I am going to be sixty soon, I'm an old man, a lonely worthless old man . . . I've nothing—nothing right or good in me—except this love I feel for you, and if it weren't for you, then I'd have died a long time ago . . . [*To* IRINA.] My dearest little child, I've known you since the very day you were born . . . I carried you in my arms . . . I loved your dead mama . . .

IRINA. But why on earth do you give me expensive presents like this?

CHEBUTYKIN. [*through tears, angrily*] Expensive presents . . . Oh, the hell with it! [*To the orderly.*] Take the samovar away . . . [*Mockingly.*] Expensive presents . . .

The ORDERLY *carries the samovar into the ballroom.*

ANFISA. [*passing through the drawing room*] My dear ones, there's a colonel, a stranger to us! He's got his coat off already, my little ones, he's on his way here. Arinushka,[7] now you be kind and respectful like . . . [*Going out.*] And it's about time we had lunch . . . Oh, dear Lord . . .

---

6. Pronounced *samavár*. According to Russian custom, Chebutykin's expensive gift to Irina on her name day is inappropriate; a gift of this value would normally be presented on the occasion of a silver or golden wedding anniversary.

7. A mispronunciation of *Irinushka*, an intimate nickname.

TUZENBAKH. It's Vershinin, no doubt. [VERSHININ *enters.*] Lieutenant-colonel Vershinin.

VERSHININ. [*to* MASHA *and* IRINA] I have the honor to introduce myself: Vershinin. I'm glad, very, very glad to be in your home at last. Oh, my, how you have changed! My! My!

IRINA. Sit down, please. We're delighted to see you.

VERSHININ. [*cheerfully*] Oh, I am glad, very glad, indeed! But there were three sisters, you know. I remember—three little girls. I don't remember their faces, but Colonel Prozorov, your father, had three small daughters—that I remember perfectly well. I saw them with my own eyes. How time flies! My, my, how time flies!

TUZENBAKH. Alexandr Ignatevich is from Moscow.

IRINA. From Moscow? You are from Moscow?

VERSHININ. Yes, that's where I'm from. Your dead father was battery commander there, and at the same time I was brigade officer. [*To* MASHA.] Now, your face—I think I remember a little.

MASHA. But you—I don't remember at all.

IRINA. Olya! Olya! [*Shouts into the ballroom.*] Olya, come here! [OLGA *enters from the ballroom into the drawing room.*] Lieutenant-colonel Vershinin, it just happens, comes from Moscow.

VERSHININ. I think you are Olga Sergeevna, the oldest . . . and you are Maria . . . And you are Irina—the youngest . . .

OLGA. You are from Moscow?

VERSHININ. Yes. I studied in Moscow and began military service in Moscow, I served there a long time, and at last I received command of the battery here—I've moved here, as you can see. I don't remember you exactly, I only remember there were three sisters. Your father I have preserved in my memory; I have only to close my eyes to see him as though he were alive. I used to visit you in Moscow . . .

OLGA. I thought I remembered everyone, and now, all of a sudden . . .

VERSHININ. My name is Alexandr Ignatevich . . .

IRINA. Alexandr Ignatevich, you are from Moscow . . . Why it's so surprising, so unexpected!

OLGA. We are going to move there, you see.

IRINA. We're hoping to be there by this coming fall. It's our own home town, we were born there . . . On Old Basmannaya Street . . .
Both laugh out of happiness.

MASHA. And now suddenly, so unexpectedly, we see someone from home. [*Lively.*] Now I remember! You recall, don't you Olya, at home they used to talk about the "lovesick major." You were a lieutenant at the time, and you'd fallen in love with somebody, and for some reason or other everybody nicknamed you the "major" . . .

VERSHININ. [*laughs*] Yes, that's right . . . the "lovesick major," that's what . . .

MASHA. At the time you only had a moustache . . . You look older now! [*Through tears.*] Much, much older.

VERSHININ. Yes, when they called me the "lovesick major," I was still a young man, I was in love. It's not the same now.

OLGA. But you don't have a single gray hair, not one. You may have grown older, but you'll still not old.

VERSHININ. Nevertheless, I'm already forty-two. Have you been away from Moscow a long time?

IRINA. Eleven years. Oh, why on earth are you crying, Masha, you foolish girl . . . [*Through tears.*] Now I'll start crying too . . .

MASHA. I'm all right. And on what street did you live?

VERSHININ. On Old Basmannaya.

OLGA. So did we . . .

VERSHININ. I lived on Nemetskaya Street[8] at one time. I used to walk from Nemetskaya Street to the Krasny Barracks.[9] On the way there you cross over a dark and dreary bridge, and under the bridge the water rages and roars. When you're by yourself, it can break your heart. [*Pause.*] But here you have a broad, wonderful river! A marvelous river!

OLGA. Yes, only it's cold. Here it is cold and the mosquitoes . . .

VERSHININ. You're not serious! Why, it's a good Russian climate here, healthy, exhilarating. The forest, the river . . . and here too are the birch trees. Lovely, unassuming birches, I love them best of all the trees. It's good to live here. Only it is strange, the railway station is twenty versts[1] away . . . And no one knows the reason for it.

SOLYONY. But I know the reason for it. [*All look at him.*] Because if the station were nearby, then it would not be far away; but if it is far away, then, that means, it cannot be nearby.

An awkward silence.

TUZENBAKH. You're something of a clown, Vasily Vasilich.

OLGA. Now, just now, everything came back, I remember you, I remember.

VERSHININ. I knew your dear mother.

CHEBUTYKIN. She was a good woman, God rest her soul.

IRINA. Mama is buried in Moscow.

OLGA. In Novo-Devichy[2] . . .

MASHA. Just imagine, I've started to forget what she looked like, her face. In the same way they won't remember us. We shall be forgotten.

VERSHININ. Yes. We shall be forgotten. That will be our destiny, and there's nothing you can do about it, nothing. Whatever seems to us serious, significant, so very important today will—in the course of time—be forgotten or seem unimportant. [*Pause.*]

8. Literally, "German Street."
9. Literally, "Red Barracks."
1. A former Russian unit of measurement, the equivalent of about thirty-five hundred feet.
2. A famous monastery in Moscow, where a number of notables (including Chekhov himself) are buried.

And isn't it interesting that right now we actually don't know at all what people in the future will regard as noble or important and what they will regard as pitiful or ridiculous. Didn't the discoveries of Copernicus, or let's say Columbus, didn't these discoveries appear in the beginning rather unnecessary and ridiculous, while some sort of empty nonsense, written by a fool, appeared to be the everlasting truth? And it may happen that our present life, which we have come to terms with, will—in the course of time—appear strange, inconvenient, and stupid—by no means pure enough, even terribly sinful, perhaps . . .

TUZENBAKH. Who knows? It's quite possible, isn't it, that people in the future will call our age noble, great, and will remember our lives with honor and respect. Nowadays you don't find torture racks or public executions, and you certainly don't see invasions today. And yet at the same time, look at all the suffering there is in the world!

SOLYONY. [*in a thin voice*] *Tsip, tsip, tsip*[3] . . . Don't feed the Baron any mush, just give him a chance to talk philosophy.

TUZENBAKH. Vasily Vasilich, I beg you, leave me alone . . . [*Sits in another place.*] It's boring to me, after all.

SOLYONY. [*in a thin voice*] *Tsip, tsip, tsip* . . .

TUZENBAKH. [*to* VERSHININ] However much suffering you see nowadays, and there is still too much of it, our society still has achieved a higher level of moral strength than you will . . .

VERSHININ. Yes, yes, of course.

CHEBUTYKIN. You said just now, Baron, that they'll call our age great, but people are still small . . . [*Rises.*] Take a good look at how small I am. You are only trying to console me when you say that my life is great, something clear and comprehensible.

Behind the scenes is heard the playing of a violin.

MASHA. That's Andrey playing, our brother.

IRINA. He's the scholar in our family. There's no question that he'll become a professor. Papa was a military man, but his son chose a scholar's career for himself.

MASHA. In keeping with Papa's wishes.

OLGA. We've started teasing him today. It seems he's a little bit in love.

IRINA. With one of the local girls. She will be here today, in all probability.

MASHA. Oh, how she dresses! It's not that her clothes are simply ugly or outmoded, it's just that they turn out pathetic. Some sort of strange, bright-yellowish skirt, with a cheap vulgar fringe on it, and a red blouse. And her cheeks are scrubbed clean. My, how scrubbed they are! Andrey is not in love—I won't admit to that, he has taste, after all. It's simply that he is teasing us, he's playing the fool. Yesterday I heard that she is going to marry Proto-

---

3. Sounds made by domestic fowl.

popov, the chairman of the District Council. Good for her . . .
[*At the side door.*] Andrey, come out here! Come, my dear, just
for a minute!

ANDREY *enters.*

OLGA. This is my brother, Andrey Sergeich.

VERSHININ. Vershinin.

ANDREY. Prozorov. [*Wipes his perspiring face.*] You're the new
battery commander here?

OLGA. Can you imagine, Alexandr Ignatich is from Moscow.

ANDREY. No! Well, I congratulate you, my sisters won't give you any
peace and quiet now.

VERSHININ. So far I've managed to make your sisters sick and tired
of me.

IRINA. Just look at the little picture frame Andrey gave me today.
[*Shows the picture frame.*] You see, he made it himself.

VERSHININ. [*looking at the picture frame and not knowing what
to say*] Yes . . . it's something . . .

IRINA. And see the little frame above the piano. He also made that.

ANDREY *waves his hand and moves away.*

OLGA. He's the scholar in our family, and he plays the violin, and
makes different things on the fretsaw—in a word, he is a master
of whatever he touches. Andrey, don't leave! He has the habit of
always walking off. Come here!

MASHA *and* IRINA *take him by the arms and, laughing, bring
him back.*

MASHA. Come on, come!

ANDREY. Leave me alone, please.

MASHA. Isn't he funny! Once upon a time, they called Alexandr
Ignatevich the "lovesick major," and he didn't get a bit angry.

VERSHININ. Not at all!

MASHA. And I plan to call you: the "lovesick fiddler"!

IRINA. Or the "lovesick professor"! . .

OLGA. He's in love! Andryusha's in love!

IRINA. [*clapping her hands*] Bravo, bravo! Encore! Andryushka's[4] in
love!

CHEBUTYKIN. [*comes up behind* ANDREY *and puts both his arms
around his waist*] Nature brought us into the world for the sake
of love alone! [*Roars with laughter; he holds the newspaper the
whole time.*]

ANDREY. Now, that's enough, enough . . . [*Wipes his face.*] I
didn't get to sleep all night, so I'm a little out of sorts today, as
the saying goes. I read until four o'clock, then I lay down, but
nothing came of it. I thought about this and that, and when dawn
came, the sun simply crawled into my bedroom. While I'm here
this summer, I want to translate a certain English book.

VERSHININ. So you read English?

ANDREY. Yes. Father, God rest his soul, overpowered us all with

4. An intimate nickname.

learning. It's funny and a little stupid, but all the same I must admit I started putting on weight right after Father died. And in one year I've grown fat, just as if my body has been freed of tremendous pressure. Thanks to Father, my sisters and I know French, German, and English, and Irina also knows Italian. But how much we paid for it!

MASHA. To know three languages in this town is an unnecessary luxury. It's not even a luxury, but some sort of unnecessary appendage, like a sixth finger. We know so much that is simply superfluous.

VERSHININ. Well, just imagine that! [*Laughs.*] You know so much that is simply superfluous. You know, I can't visualize a place so dull and dismal where intelligent men and women are not necessary. Let's say, that among the one hundred thousand inhabitants of this town, which is—quite naturally—backward and coarse, that there are only three persons like you. Obviously, you three will never win the battle over the ignorant and uneducated masses[5] surrounding you. And, in the course of your lifetime, you will find yourselves giving in little by little until you disappear in that crowd of one hundred thousand. Life will simply devour you. And yet, all the same, you will not vanish completely. You will have made a beginning. After you're gone, perhaps six more like you will appear, then twelve, and so on, until at last people like you will have become a majority. In the course of two hundred, three hundred years, life on this earth will be inconceivably beautiful, wonderful. Man stands in need of a life like that, and if it isn't here yet, then he must feel it intuitively, wait, dream, prepare for it, he must see and know more than his father and his grandfather ever did. [*Laughs.*] And you complain that you know so much that is simply superfluous.

MASHA. [*takes off her hat*] I will stay for lunch.

IRINA. [*with a sigh*] Really, all of that should have been written down . . .

ANDREY *is gone; he left without being noticed.*

TUZENBAKH. In the course of many years, you say, life on this earth will be beautiful, wonderful. That's true. But, in order to take part in it now, if only from a distance, it's necessary to prepare for it, it's necessary to work . . .

VERSHININ. [*rises*] Yes. But what a lot of flowers you have! [*Looking around.*] And a marvelous apartment. I envy you! I've spent my whole life in two-by-four apartments with two chairs, one sofa, and stoves that always smoked. That's what I've missed my whole life—flowers like these here . . . [*He rubs his hands.*] Oh, well! Why talk about it!

TUZENBAKH. Yes, it's necessary to work. No doubt you're thinking: the German is getting sentimental. But I'm a Russian, word of

5. Literally, "dark masses," with the implied meaning "ignorant and uneducated masses."

honor. Why, I don't even speak German. My own father belonged to the Russian Orthodox Church . . . [*Pause.*]

VERSHININ. [*walks about the stage*] I sometimes think: what if you were given the chance to live your life over again, but this time knowing full well you were going to? If that one life which you've already lived through were, as the saying goes, a first draft only—and your second chance is the final copy! Then I think that each of us would try, more than anything else, never to repeat himself. I mean, he would create a different set of conditions in his life, arrange for himself an apartment like this, with flowers and lots of light . . . I have a wife, two little girls. Besides, my wife is a lady in declining health, and so forth and so forth. Well, if you were given the chance to live your life over again, then I would not get married . . . No, no!

Enter KULYGIN, *dressed in the uniform coat of a teacher.*

KULYGIN. [*goes to* IRINA] Dear sister, allow me to congratulate you on the day of your saint and to wish you sincerely, from my soul, health and all that which is possible to wish a girl of your years. And then to offer you, as a present, this little book here. [*Gives little book to* IRINA.] The history of our high school over a fifty-year period, written by me. A trivial little book, which was written when I'd nothing better to do, but you read through it all the same. How do you do, ladies and gentlemen, how do you do! [*To* VERSHININ.] Kulygin, teacher at the local high school. Councilor to the State.[6] [*To* IRINA.] In this little book you will discover the list of all those who completed their work in our high school in the past fifty years. *Feci, quod potui, faciant meliora potentes.*[7] [*Kisses* MASHA.]

IRINA. But, you know, at Easter you gave me the very same little book.

KULYGIN. [*laughs*] It's not possible! In that case give it back, or better yet, give it to the Colonel. Take it, Colonel. Read it some time whenever you're bored.

VERSHININ. Thank you. [*Prepares to leave.*] I am very pleased to have made your acquaintance . . .

OLGA. You are leaving? No, no!

IRINA. You must stay for lunch with us. Please.

OLGA. I beg you!

VERSHININ. [*bows*] It seems I've dropped in on a name-day party. Forgive me, I didn't know, I haven't even congratulated you . . . [*Goes with* OLGA *into the ballroom.*]

KULYGIN. Today, ladies and gentlemen, is Sunday, a day of rest. Let us rest, let us enjoy ourselves, each according to his age and to his situation. The carpets should be taken away for the summer and put away until winter . . . in Persian powder or naphthaline

---

6. Literally, "court councilor," rank number seven in the Table of Ranks, equivalent to lieutenant-colonel in the military.

7. "Do what you can, let those who are able do it better."

. . . The Romans were healthy because they knew how to work and they knew *how to rest*; they had *mens sana in corpore sano*.[8] Their life flowed in accordance with certain forms. Our director at the high school says: The chief thing in every life—the chief thing is its form . . . Whatever loses its form, then that one will come to nothing—and in our daily lives it is the very same thing. [*Takes* MASHA *by the waist, laughing.*] Masha loves me. My wife loves me. And the window curtains should go out with the carpets . . . Today I'm in high spirits, I'm in a marvelous mood. Masha, at four o'clock today we are to be at the director's house. A walk is being arranged for the teachers and their families.

MASHA. I am not going.

KULYGIN. [*hurt*] Masha, my dear, why?

MASHA. Later . . . [*Angrily.*] All right, I'll go, only leave me alone, please . . . [*Walks away.*]

KULYGIN. Then later on we will spend the evening at the director's house. Notwithstanding his bad health, this man tries, more than anything else, to be sociable. An excellent, bright personality. A magnificent person. Yesterday after the meeting he said to me: "I am tired, Fyodor Ilich! I am tired!" [*Looks at the wall clock, then at his own watch.*] Your clock is seven minutes fast. Yes, he said, "I am tired!"

A violin is heard behind the scenes.

OLGA. Ladies and gentlemen, come along to lunch, please! There is a pie!

KULYGIN. Ah, my dear Olga, my dear! Yesterday I worked from morning until eleven o'clock at night, I was tired and today I feel happy. [*Goes into the ballroom to the table.*] My dear . . .

CHEBUTYKIN. [*puts newspaper into his pocket and combs his beard*] A pie? Magnificent!

MASHA. [*to* CHEBUTYKIN, *sternly*] Only see here: don't drink anything today. You hear me? It's bad for you to drink.

CHEBUTYKIN. Come now! That thing's over and done with a long time ago. It's been two years since my last drinking bout. [*Impatiently.*] Oh, *matushka*,[9] what does it matter, anyway!

MASHA. All the same, don't you dare drink. Don't you dare. [*Angrily, but in such a way that her husband does not hear.*] Oh, to hell with it, why must I spend another long dull evening at the director's!

TUZENBAKH. I just wouldn't go if I were in your place . . . Very simple.

CHEBUTYKIN. Don't go, my precious.

MASHA. Yes, don't go . . . This life is damnable, unbearable . . . [*Goes into the ballroom.*]

CHEBUTYKIN. [*follows her*] Well, now!

SOLYONY. [*going into the ballroom*] Tsip, tsip, tsip . . .

8. "A healthy spirit in a healthy body."
9. An old-fashioned, sometimes poetic word for *mother*.

TUZENBAKH. Enough, Vasily Vasilich. No more!

SOLYONY. *Tsip, tsip, tsip* . . .

KULYGIN. [*cheerfully*] Your health, Colonel! I am a teacher, and I'm right at home here, being Masha's husband . . . She is kind, very kind . . .

VERSHININ. I'll take a little of that dark vodka . . . [*Drinks.*] Your health! [*To* OLGA.] It's good, so good being here with you! . .

In the drawing room only IRINA *and* TUZENBAKH *remain.*

IRINA. Masha is out of sorts today. She got married when she was eighteen, and her husband seemed to her then the cleverest of men. It isn't the same now. He's the kindest, but he isn't the cleverest.

OLGA. [*impatiently*] Andrey, come in here, won't you!

ANDREY. [*behind the scenes*] At once. [*Enters and goes to the table.*]

TUZENBAKH. What are you thinking about?

IRINA. Oh, nothing in particular. I don't like that Solyony of yours. I'm afraid of him. Whatever he says is only so much nonsense . . .

TUZENBAKH. He's a strange person. I'm both sorry for him and annoyed, but I'm more sorry. I think he's shy . . . Whenever we're alone together, he can be very clever and friendly enough; but in company he's coarse and goes around with a chip on his shoulder. Don't go, let them get seated at the table. Let me be with you for a while. What are you thinking about? [*Pause.*] You're twenty years old, I'm not yet thirty. How many years we have ahead of us still, a long, unbroken procession of days, each one filled with my love for you . . .

IRINA. Nikolay Lvovich, dear, don't talk to me about love.

TUZENBAKH. [*not listening*] I have a passionate thirst for life, for struggle, for work, and this thirst in my soul is bound up with my love for you, Irina. And as it turns out, since you are fine and beautiful, then life to me is fine and beautiful too. What are you thinking about?

IRINA. You say that life is fine and beautiful. Yes, but what if it only seems so! We three sisters certainly haven't found life either fine or beautiful up to now, life has devoured us like weeds in the garden . . . I'm starting to cry. I shouldn't . . . [*Quickly wipes her face, smiles.*] I should work, work. That's the reason we're unhappy, the reason we see life as dark and dreary. It's because we've never known what it is to work. We were born of people who despised work . . .

NATALYA IVANOVNA enters; she is in a pink dress with a green belt.

NATASHA. Oh, no, they're sitting down to lunch already . . . I'm late . . . [*In passing she glances at the mirror, then she tidies herself.*] I think my hair looks all right . . . [*Having seen Irina.*] Dear Irina Sergeevna, I congratulate you! [*Kisses her firmly and in a pro-*

longed way.] You have many guests, really I feel ashamed . . .
How do you do, Baron!

OLGA. [*coming into the drawing room*] Well, Natalya Ivanovna is
here. How do you do, my dear! [*They kiss.*]

NATASHA. Congratulations on this name day. You have so many
people here, I feel awfully embarrassed . . .

OLGA. That will do, they're all old friends. [*In a startled undertone.*] You are wearing a green belt! My dear, it's not right!

NATASHA. You don't mean it's unlucky, do you?

OLGA. No, it simply isn't suitable . . . and somehow it looks
strange . . .

NATASHA. [*in a tearful voice*] Yes? But you see it isn't green, but
kind of a dull color. [*Follows* OLGA *into the ballroom.*]
In the ballroom they are sitting down for lunch; in the drawing room there is not a single person.

KULYGIN. I wish you, Irina, a nice fiancé. It's about time you were
married.

CHEBUTYKIN, Natalya Ivanovna, I wish you a little fiancé, too.

KULYGIN. Natalya Ivanovna already has a little fiancé in mind.

MASHA. I'll take a little glass of wine! Oh, my, life is beautiful;
where, oh where, has ours gone to? Oh, what the hell—why not?

KULYGIN. You receive a three minus for bad behavior.

VERSHININ. This brandy is very good. What's it made of?

SOLYONY. Cockroaches.

IRINA. [*in a tearful voice*] Oh, no, that's disgusting! . .

OLGA. At dinner there will be roast turkey and apple pie. Thank the
Lord, today I am home for the whole day, in the evening, home
. . . Ladies and gentlemen, come again this evening . . .

VERSHININ. Allow me to come too in the evening!

IRINA. Please do.

NATASHA. They don't stand on ceremonies here.

CHEBUTYKIN. Nature brought us into the world for the sake of
love alone. [*Laughs.*]

ANDREY. [*angrily*] Stop it, gentlemen! Aren't you tired of it?
FEDOTIK *and* RODE *enter with a huge basket of flowers.*

FEDOTIK. Why they're already at lunch.

RODE. [*loudly, mispronouncing the* r *sound*] Already at lunch?
Yes, they're already at lunch . . .

FEDOTIK. Wait a minute! [*Takes a photograph.*] One! Wait,
hold still for one more . . . [*Takes a second photograph.*] Two!
It's all right now!
They take the basket and go into the ballroom, where they
are noisily greeted.

RODE. [*loudly*] Congratulations, I wish you everything, everything!
The weather outside is enchanting, simply magnificent. I've been
walking all morning with some of the high-school boys. I teach
gymnastics at the high school . . .

FEDOTIK. You may move now, Irina Sergeevna, you may move! [*Taking a photograph.*] You are positively beautiful today. [*Takes a humming top from his pocket.*] Here, by the way, is a top . . . A wonderful sound . . .

IRINA. How fascinating!

MASHA. "By the curved seashore stands an oak tree green;
  A golden chain to that oak is bound . . .
  And linked to the chain with a scholarly mien
  A tomcat is seen going round and round and . . ."
[*Tearfully.*] Now, why on earth do I keep saying this? Those lines have been bothering me since early morning . . .

KULYGIN. There are thirteen at the table!

RODE. [*loudly*] Ladies and gentlemen, don't tell me you believe in superstitions? [*Laughter.*]

KULYGIN. If there are thirteen at the table, then it means that someone here is in love. It isn't you, Ivan Romanovich, by any chance, is it . . . [*Laughter.*]

CHEBUTYKIN. I'm an old sinner, but why on earth Natalya Ivanovna here should be embarrassed—I absolutely don't understand it.
  Loud laughter. NATASHA *runs out of the ballroom into the drawing room, followed by* ANDREY.

ANDREY. Come now, don't pay any attention to them! Wait . . . wait, I beg you . . .

NATASHA. I feel ashamed . . . I don't know what's the matter with me, but they keep on laughing at me. I know it's not right to leave the table that way, but I can't help it . . . I can't . . . [*Covers her face with her hands.*]

ANDREY. My precious, I beg you, I beseech you, don't get upset. I assure you they're simply joking, joking out of kindness. My precious, my sweetheart, they're kind, warmhearted people, all of them, and they love both of us Come to the window, they can't see us here . . . [*Looks around.*]

NATASHA. I'm not used to being with a group of people! . .

ANDREY. Oh, to be young, how marvelous, how wonderful it is to be young! My precious, my sweetheart, don't get upset, don't! . . Believe me, believe me . . . Oh, I feel so good, my soul is filled with love, ecstasy . . . Oh, they can't see us here, they can't! Why is it I fell in love with you, why, when did I fall in love? Oh, there's nothing that's clear to me, nothing. My precious, my pure, innocent sweetheart, be my wife! I love you, love . . . as I've never loved anyone before . . . [*Kisses her.*]
  Two officers enter and, having seen the pair kissing, stop in astonishment.

CURTAIN

Act Two

*The setting is the same as in Act One. Eight o'clock in
the evening. Behind the scenes the sound of an accordion is
barely heard outside on the street. There is no light.* NATALYA
IVANOVNA *enters, wearing a dressing gown and carrying a
candle. She walks and stops at the door which leads to* AN-
DREY'S *room.*

NATASHA. Andryusha, what are you doing? Are you reading? It's nothing, I was only wondering . . . [*Walks, opens another door and,
having looked in the room, closes it.*] If a light is burning . . .

ANDREY. [*enters with a book in his hand*] What is it, Natasha?

NATASHA. I'm looking in case a light is burning . . . It's Carnival
Week, the servants aren't behaving as they should, so you must
keep your eyes peeled to make sure nothing goes wrong. Yesterday
at midnight I walked through the dining room, and there I saw a
candle burning. Who lit it? Why, I couldn't even get a straight
answer out of them. [*Puts down the candle.*] What time is it?

ANDREY. [*having glanced at his watch*] A quarter past eight.

NATASHA. And Olga and Irina still not here. Haven't come in yet.
Poor things, they're still working. Olga is at the faculty meeting,
Irina at the telegraph office . . . [*Sighs.*] I spoke to your sister
only this morning. "Irina, darling," I was saying, "Take care of
yourself." But she just won't listen. A quarter past eight, you say?
I'm afraid our Bobik[1] isn't a bit well. Why is it he's so cold? He
had a fever yesterday, and today he is cold all over . . . I'm so
afraid!

ANDREY. It's nothing, Natasha. The boy's in good health.

NATASHA. All the same let's put him on a diet, it would be better.
I'm afraid. And tonight, they tell me, the mummers will be here
something after nine o'clock. It would be better, Andryusha, if
they just didn't come.

ANDREY. I don't know, really. You know they've been asked.

NATASHA. This morning the little fellow woke up, looked at me, and
suddenly smiled. That means he recognized me. "Bobik," I said.
"How do you do, dear, how do you do!" And he laughed. Children understand, they understand perfectly. Well, that means,
Andryusha, I'll say the mummers should not be allowed in.

ANDREY. [*irresolutely*] Well, that's for my sisters to say, isn't it?
They run the house, you know.

NATASHA. And so they do. I'll speak to them. They are kind . . .
[*Going.*] I've ordered yogurt for dinner. The doctors say you
should be given nothing but yogurt. Otherwise, you will never get
thin. [*Stops.*] Bobik is cold. I'm afraid it's too cold for him in
his room, perhaps. He must go into a different room, at least

1. The nickname of Natasha's first child was a popular nickname for male dogs
in Russia.

until there's warmer weather. Irina's room, for example, is just right for the baby. It's dry, and there's sun the whole day. She must be told she can share Olga's room for the time being . . . It doesn't matter since she's not at home in the daytime, she only spends the night there . . . [*Pause.*] Andryushanchik,[2] why are you so quiet?

ANDREY. Well, I was thinking . . . There's nothing much to say, I guess . . .

NATASHA. So . . . I wanted to tell you something . . . Oh, yes, Ferapont's come here from the Council, he's asking for you.

ANDREY. [*yawns*] Send him in. [NATASHA *goes out.* ANDREY, *bending over the candle, which she has forgotten, reads his book.* FERAPONT *enters. He is dressed in an old, tattered coat with the collar turned up; his ears are bound.*] Hello, old friend. What is it you want to say?

FAREPONT. The Chairman sent a book and some sort of paper. Here . . . [*Gives book and parcel to* ANDREY.]

ANDREY. Thanks. Good. Why is it you didn't come earlier? It's past eight, you know.

FERAPONT. What is it?

ANDREY [*louder*] I said, you came late, it's already past eight.

FERAPONT. Exactly so. I got to the place, it was still light, but they wouldn't let me in, not a bit. The master is busy, they said. Oh, well, hmm. If he's busy, he's busy. I'm in no rush. [*Thinking that* ANDREY *has asked him about something.*] What is it?

ANDREY. Nothing. [*Looking at the book.*] Tomorrow is Friday, we won't have a meeting, but it doesn't matter, I'll go in . . . and keep busy. It's boring at home here . . . [*Pause.*] Dear old man, it's strange, isn't it, the way everything changes—the way life cheats you! I was bored today, and having nothing to do, I happened to pick up this book here. It's my old university lectures, and I started to laugh . . . Dear God in heaven, I am secretary at the District Council, the very same Council where Protopopov presides, I am secretary, and the most that I can hope for, the very most—is to become a member of the District Council myself. For me to be a member of the local District Council, me, who dreams every night that I am a professor at Moscow University, a famous scholar of whom all Russia is proud!

FERAPONT. I can't know . . . My hearing's not good . . .

ANDREY. If you heard all right, then I doubt if I'd be talking to you in this way. I must talk to someone. My wife doesn't understand me. I'm afraid of my sisters for some reason or other. I'm afraid they'll make fun of me, put me to shame . . . I don't drink, I'm not fond of taverns, but how I would love to be in Moscow right now, to be sitting in Testov's Restaurant or in the Bolshoy Moskovsky,[3] my dear fellow.

FERAPONT. But in Moscow, as a builder was saying at the Council

---

2. An intimate nickname for *Andrey*.   3. Two restaurants in Moscow.

the other day, some merchants were eating pancakes in Moscow. One of them who ate up forty pancakes, it seems as if he died. If it wasn't forty, then it was fifty. I don't remember.

ANDREY. You are sitting in Moscow, in a huge hall of the restaurant, you don't know anybody, and no one knows you, and at the same time you don't feel that you're a stranger. But here you know everybody and everybody knows you, and you are a stranger, a stranger . . . A stranger and alone.

FERAPONT. What is it? [*Pause.*] And that very same builder said—maybe he was lying—it seems as if a rope or cable is stretched all across Moscow.

ANDREY. For what purpose?

FERAPONT. I can't know. The builder said it.

ANDREY. Nonsense, hokum. [*Reads the book.*] Have you ever been to Moscow?

FERAPONT. [*after a pause*] Never was. God did not grant it. [*Pause.*] All right for me to go?

ANDREY. You can go. Take care. [FERAPONT *goes out.*] Take care. [*Reading.*] Come back tomorrow morning, pick up the papers here . . . Go along . . . [*Pause.*] He's gone. [*A bell sounds.*] Yes, things to do . . . [*Stretches and in no hurry goes to his room.*]
Behind the scenes a NURSE *sings, rocking a child to sleep. Enter* MASHA *and* VERSHININ. *While they are chatting, a* MAIDSERVANT *lights the lamp and candles.*

MASHA. I don't know. [*Pause.*] I don't know. Of course, habit means a lot. After father died, for example, it was a long time before we got used to the idea of doing without a single orderly in the house. But apart from habit, I think I was quite fair in saying what I did. Perhaps in other places it isn't true, but in our town it's the military who turn out as the most decent, the most noble and well-bred.

VERSHININ. I'd like something to drink. I'd like some tea.

MASHA. [*having glanced at the clock*] They'll bring it in very soon. My marriage was arranged when I was eighteen, and I was afraid of my own husband. You see, I had barely finished school at the time, and he was a teacher. At the time he seemed to me terribly scholarly, clever, and important. But how it's not the same at all, unfortunately.

VERSHININ. Just so . . . yes.

MASHA. I'm not speaking about my husband. I've grown used to him. But among civilians in general, there are so many ill-bred people, coarse, impolite, and unkind. Any sort of coarseness is upsetting to me, I feel insulted, and I find it unbearable to see people who lack sensitivity—who are neither gentle nor polite and kind. Whenever I'm around teachers, friends of my husband, I simply can't bear it.

VERSHININ. Yes, ma'am . . . But it seems to me it doesn't matter. In this town, at least, the military and the civilians are very much the same, equally uninteresting. It doesn't matter! If you talk long enough to any one of the educated persons in this town—I don't care if he's a civilian or an army man—then you soon discover that he is sick and tired of his wife, sick and tired of his house, sick and tired of his estate, sick and tired of his horses . . . A Russian likes nothing better than to think and discourse in a noble and exalted way. But tell me, why is it that in his everyday life his actions are anything but noble and exalted? Why?

MASHA. Why?

VERSHININ. Why is it he's sick and tired of his children, sick and tired of his wife? And why is it his wife and his children are sick and tired of him?

MASHA. You are a little out of sorts today.

VERSHININ. Perhaps. I didn't have dinner today, I've eaten nothing since morning. One of my daughters isn't feeling well, and when my little girls are sick, I live in fear, I'm tormented by the thought of their having a mother like that. Oh, if you could have seen her today! Why, she's nothing, absolutely worthless! We started quarreling at seven this morning, and at nine I slammed the door and walked off. [*Pause.*] I never talk about this, and strange as it seems, I complain only to you alone. [*Kisses her hand.*] Don't be angry with me. Except for you—and you alone—I have no one, no one . . . [*Pause.*]

MASHA. Listen, listen to the noise in the stove. It wailed like that in the chimney just before father died. Exactly like that.

VERSHININ. Are you superstitious?

MASHA. Yes.

VERSHININ. That's strange. [*Kisses her hand.*] You're a wonderful, marvelous woman. Wonderful, marvelous! It's dark here, but I can see your eyes shining.

MASHA. [*sits in another chair*] There's more light over here . . .

VERSHININ. I love you, love you, love you . . . I love your eyes, I dream about the way you move . . . Wonderful, marvelous woman!

MASHA. [*laughs quietly*] When you talk to me like that, somehow or other I laugh, even though it frightens me too. Don't say any more, I beg you . . . [*In a low voice.*] But anyway, please go on, it doesn't matter to me . . . [*Covers her face with her hands.*] It doesn't matter to me. They're coming in here, talk about something else . . .

    IRINA *and* TUZENBAKH *enter through the ballroom.*

TUZENBAKH. I have three names, three. They call me Baron Tuzenbakh-Krone-Altshauer, but I am a Russian, Russian Orthodox, like you. There's precious little German left at all, oh, maybe something of the patience and stubbornness that I keep boring you with. Look at the way I walk you home each evening.

IRINA. Oh, I am tired, tired!

TUZENBAKH. And every day I shall show up at the telegraph office and walk you home. I shall show up every day for ten, twenty years, until you drive me away . . . [*Having seen* MASHA *and* VER-SHININ, *overjoyed.*] Is that you? How are you?

IRINA. There, I'm home, home at last. [*To* MASHA.] A lady came to the office just now to telegraph her brother in Saratov,[4] to say her son died today. And she couldn't remember the address at all. So she sent it without an address, simply to Saratov. She was crying. And I was rude to her, for no reason, no reason at all. "I don't have time," I said. It turned out so stupidly. Are the mummers coming tonight?

MASHA. Yes.

IRINA. [*sits in an armchair*] I must rest. I am tired.

TUZENBAKH. [*with a smile*] When you come home from work, you seem so young, wistful, somehow sick at heart . . . [*Pause.*]

IRINA. I am tired. No, I do not like the telegraph office, not one bit.

MASHA. You've become thinner . . . [*Whistles.*] And a little younger, too, your face has begun to look like a little boy's.

TUZENBAKH. That's the way she's wearing her hair.

IRINA. I must look for a different job, this one is beyond me. Everything I've wanted so much, all I've dreamed of, it isn't in the job I'm doing. It is work without poetry, without thought . . . [*A knock on the floor.*] The doctor is knocking. [*To* TUZENBAKH.] Rap back, dear . . . I can't . . . I am tired . . . [TUZENBAKH *knocks on the floor.*] He's going to be up here shortly. Look, something or other had better be done. The doctor and our own Andrey were at the club yesterday and they lost again. In town they're saying Andrey lost two hundred rubles.

MASHA. [*indifferently*] What on earth can be done now!

IRINA. He lost two weeks ago, he lost in December. Maybe, just maybe, the sooner he loses everything, the sooner we can leave this town. Dear God in Heaven, I dream of Moscow every night, I think I must be going mad. [*Laughs.*] We will move there in June, but until June that still leaves . . . February, March, April, May . . . almost half a year!

MASHA. Only we'd better make sure that Natasha doesn't find out a thing about the losses.

IRINA. As far as I can see, it doesn't matter to her.

CHEBUTYKIN, *who has just gotten out of bed—he rested after dinner—enters the ballroom and combs his beard; then he sits at the table and takes a newspaper out of his pocket.*

MASHA. There, he's just come up . . . Has he paid for the apartment?

IRINA. [*laughs*] No. Not one kopek for eight months. Apparently, he's forgotten.

MASHA. [*laughs*] Doesn't he look important sitting there!

Everyone laughs. A pause.

IRINA. Why are you quiet, Alexandr Ignatich?

4. Capital city of Saratov and port on the Volga, five hundred miles upstream from the Caspian Sea.

VERSHININ. I don't know. I'd like some tea. Half my life for a glass of tea! I haven't eaten at all since morning . . .

CHEBUTYKIN. Irina Sergeevna!

IRINA. What is it you want?

CHEBUTYKIN. Come here, please. *Venez ici.*[5] [IRINA *goes and sits at the table.*] I can't do a thing without you.

    IRINA *sets out the cards for a game of patience.*

VERSHININ. Well, hmm? If they won't give us tea, at least let's talk a little philosophy.

TUZENBAKH. Let's. About what?

VERSHININ. About what? Let's dream a little . . . for example, about that life which will come after us, in about two hundred or three hundred years.

TUZENBAKH. Well, hmm? Oh, after we're gone, they will fly in balloons, change the style of their jackets, perhaps discover a sixth sense and develop it. But life itself will remain very much the same as before, a hard life, full of secrets and happiness. And a thoussand years from now, man will be sighing much the same as before, "Ah, how difficult life is!" And yet he will be afraid of death and as unwilling to die as he is nowadays.

VERSHININ. [*having thought a little*] How shall I say it? It seems to me that everything here on earth must change, little by little. And those changes are already taking place right before our very eyes. In the course of two hundred, three hundred, or even a thousand years—the length of time doesn't matter—a new, a happy life will appear. We won't share in this new life, of course, but we're living for it, we're working for it, yes, even suffering for it. We are creating that new life now. That's the sole purpose, the reason, for our existence, and, if you'd like, for our own happiness.

    MASHA *laughs quietly.*

TUZENBAKH. What are you up to?

MASHA. I don't know. I've been laughing the whole day through, ever since morning.

VERSHININ. I finished school where you did, although I didn't go on to the Academy.[6] I do read a great deal, but I don't know how to choose books. So I probably don't read what I ought to. All the same, the longer I live, the more I want to know. My hair is getting gray, I'm almost an old man, but I know so little, oh, how little—how little I know! And yet it seems to me I know what is most important, what is really true. I have grasped it firmly. If I could only prove to you this one thing—there isn't going to be any happiness for us, there shouldn't be, and there won't be, not for us . . . The only thing we must do is to work and keep on working. But as for happiness, that is for those who will come after us—

5. "Come here."
6. Before 1914 there were twenty military schools, a school in almost all of the major cities, in Russia; the Military (subsequently the General Staff) Academy was founded in 1832.

long, long after us. [*Pause.*] Not for me, no, but at least for the
descendants of my descendants.

> FEDOTIK *and* RODE *appear in the ballroom; they sit and sing
> quietly, strumming on the guitar.*

TUZENBAKH. According to you, no one must even dream of happiness! But what if I am happy!

VERSHININ. No, you're not.

TUZENBAKH. [*having thrown up his arms and laughed*] Obviously,
we don't understand each other. Well, how is it possible for me to
convince you? [MASHA *laughs quietly.* TUZENBAKH, *holding up
his finger.*] Go ahead, laugh! [*To* VERSHININ.] You can have
your two hundred, your three hundred years, I don't care if it's a
million years. Life does not, will not change. Life will remain the
very same as it has always been, constant, following its own laws—
laws which don't concern you or at least you'll never get to know
them. Those birds that migrate from place to place, cranes, for example, fly and keep on flying: And whatever thoughts, great or
small, that may wander through their heads, they'll go on flying
and they'll never know where they're going or the reason why.
They fly and will go on flying however many philosophers may
turn up among them. And let them talk as much philosophy as
they want, so long as they keep on flying . . .

MASHA. All the same, there must be some point, some meaning?

TUZENBAKH. Some point . . . Look, there, it's snowing. Where's the
meaning in that? [*Pause.*]

MASHA. It seems to me that man must have faith, or he must look
for faith. Otherwise, his life is empty, empty . . . To live and
not to know the reason why cranes fly, why children are born, why
stars are in the sky . . . Either you know the reason why you are
living, or else everything is nonsense, hokum.

> *Pause.*

VERSHININ. All the same, it's a shame when youth is over . . .

MASHA. As Gogol says, "It's a dreary world we live in, ladies and
gentlemen!"

TUZENBAKH. And I say, it's difficult to argue with you, ladies and
gentlemen! Oh, well, what the . . .

CHEBUTYKIN. [*reading the newspaper*] Balzac was married in
Berdichev.[7] [IRINA *hums quietly.*] Better write that down in my
little book. [*Writes.*] Balzac was married in Berdichev. [*Reads
newspaper.*]

IRINA. [*lost in thought, she sets out the cards for a game of patience*] Balzac was married in Berdichev.

TUZENBAKH. The die is cast. You know, Maria Sergeevna, I have
handed in my resignation.

MASHA. I heard. And I see nothing good in it. I don't like civilians.

---

7. For an interpretation of this musical
line of dialogue, see "The Bizarre Element in Chekhov's Art" by Charles B.
Timmer, p. 282, below.

TUZENBAKH. It doesn't matter . . . [*Rises.*] I'm not good-looking, what sort of military man am I, do you suppose? So, it doesn't really matter, anyway . . . I shall be going to work. Even if it's only one day in my life, I shall work to the point that when I come home in the evening, I'll roll into my bed tired and go to sleep immediately. [*Going into the ballroom.*] I'd say that workers must sleep soundly!

FEDOTIK. [*to* IRINA] Just now at Pyzhikov's on Moscow Street I bought some colored pencils for you. And, here, this little pen-knife . . .

IRINA. You are so used to treating me like a little girl, but I've grown up, you know . . . [*Takes pencils and penknife, happily.*] How charming they are!

FEDOTIK. And for myself I bought a knife . . . Here, take a look . . . one blade, still another blade, a third, this one to clean your ears, these are scissors, this one to clean your nails . . .

RODE. [*loudly*] Doctor, how old are you?

CHEBUTYKIN. Me? Thirty-two. [*Laughter.*]

FEDOTIK. I'll just show you another kind of patience . . . [*Sets out the cards for a game of patience.*]

> The samovar is brought in. ANFISA *sits by the samovar. A little later* NATASHA *enters and also bustles at the table.* SOLYONY *enters, and after greeting everyone, he sits at the table.*

VERSHININ. Listen to that wind!

MASHA. Yes, I'm sick and tired of winter. I've already forgotten what summer is like.

IRINA. The game is working out, I see. We shall go to Moscow.

FEDOTIK. No, it isn't working out. See, the eight has fallen on the two of spades. [*Laughs.*] That means you won't be going to Moscow.

CHEBUTYKIN. [*reads the newspaper*] Tsitsikar.[8] Smallpox is raging there.

ANFISA. [*going up to* MASHA] Masha, have some tea, *matushka.* [*To* VERSHININ.] Please, Your Honor . . . excuse me, my pet. I've forgotten your name . . .

MASHA. Bring it here, *nyanya.* I won't go in there.

IRINA. *Nyanya!*

ANFISA. Com-ming!

NATASHA. [*to* SOLYONY] Little babies understand perfectly. "How do you do, Bobik," I said. "How do you do, darling!" He looked up at me in that special way. You think I'm saying this only because it's the mother in me. But no, no, I assure you! This is an extraordinary child.

SOLYONY. If that child were mine, I'd fry him in a skillet and eat him all up. [*With glass in hand, he goes into the drawing room and sits in a corner.*]

8. A city in northeast China, now called Chichihaerh in Heilungkiang province.

NATASHA. [*having covered her face with her hands*] Rude, ill-bred man!

MASHA. A happy person doesn't even notice whether it's winter or summer. If I were in Moscow, it seems to me I wouldn't concern myself about the weather, I'd be indifferent . . .

VERSHININ. The other day I was reading the diary of a certain French minister. It was written when he was in prison. He'd been convicted for his part in the Panama Canal affair.[9] In the diary he mentions with delight, even with ecstasy, the various birds he can see from his prison window—birds which he hadn't noticed before when he was a minister. Of course, now that he's been freed from prison, he will return to his old habit. He won't even notice the birds, just as he did before. In the very same way, you won't even notice Moscow when you go to live there. We have no happiness, and we never will, we only long for it.

TUZENBAKH. [*takes box from the table*] Where on earth is the candy?

IRINA. Solyony ate it up.

TUZENBAKH. All of it?

ANFISA. [*serving tea*] A letter for you, my pet.

VERSHININ. For me? [*Takes letter.*] From my daughter. [*Reads.*] Yes, of course . . . Excuse me, Maria Sergeevna, I'll leave quietly. I won't have tea. [*Rises, upset.*] It's always the same story . . .

MASHA. What is it? Can you say?

VERSHININ. [*quietly*] My wife has taken poison again. I must go. I'll leave without being noticed. All this is terribly unpleasant. [*Kisses* MASHA's *hand.*] My dear, wonderful, lovely woman . . . I'll go out this way quietly . . . [*Goes out.*]

ANFISA. Where is it he's going? And I've just given his tea . . . He's something, he is.

MASHA. [*becoming angry*] Leave me alone! Here you are, picking, picking. There isn't a bit of rest from you . . . [*With her cup, she goes to the table.*] I'm sick and tired of you, old woman!

ANFISA. Why is it you feel hurt? My dearest!

ANDREY'S VOICE. Anfisa!

ANFISA. [*mimicking*] Anfisa! There he sits . . . [*Exits.*]

MASHA. [*at the table in the ballroom, angrily*] Move over, won't you! [*Mixes up the cards on the table.*] Oh, you've spread your cards everywhere. Drink your tea!

IRINA. You are malicious tonight, Mashka.

MASHA. Well, if I'm malicious tonight, then don't talk to me. Don't touch me!

CHEBUTYKIN. [*laughing*] Don't touch her, don't touch . . .

MASHA. You are sixty years old, but you—like any little naughty boy —you always come up with something, just for the hell of it.

9. The "affair" refers to the French Company, organized to build the Panama Canal, the financial arrangements of which resulted in bankruptcy in 1888 and eventual convictions of politicians charged with fraud.

NATASHA. [*sighs*] Masha dear, why do you use expressions like that in your conversation? With all your good looks, I can tell you straight out that you would be simply enchanting in decent, fashionable company, if it weren't for these words of yours. *Je vous prie pardonnez moi, Marie, mais vous avez des manières un peu grossières.*[1]

TUZENBAKH. [*suppressing laughter*] Give me . . . Give me . . . There, it seems, there's cognac . . .

NATASHA. *Il paraît, que mon Bobik déjà ne dort pas,*[2] he's awake. He isn't well tonight. I'll go to him, excuse me . . . [*Exits.*]

IRINA. And where did Alexandr Ignatich go?

MASHA. Home. Something out of the ordinary with his wife again.

TUZENBAKH. [*crosses to* SOLYONY, *a decanter of cognac in his hands*] You sit alone all the time, thinking about something—and no one knows what it is. Well, let's make peace. Let's drink some cognac. [*They drink.*] Tonight I must play the piano all night, no doubt play all sorts of nonsense . . . Oh, what the hell!

SOLYONY. Why do you say "Let's make peace"? I haven't quarrelled with you.

TUZENBAKH. You always make me feel as if something has happened between us. Although I must admit there's something strange about you.

SOLYONY. [*declaiming*] "I am strange, but who is not strange! Do not be angry, Aleko!"

TUZENBAKH. And what's Aleko got to do with it . . . [*Pause.*]

SOLYONY. When I am alone with someone or other, then it's all right, I am like anyone else. But when I'm together with a group of people, I'm despondent, shy, and . . . I talk all sorts of nonsense. All the same I'm more decent and noble, much more so than a lot of others, a lot. And I'm able to prove I am.

TUZENBAKH. I often get angry with you, you're constantly needling me when we're together with a group, but I still find you likable somehow. Oh, what the hell, I'm going to get drunk tonight. Let's drink!

SOLYONY. Let's drink. [*They drink.*] I've never had anything against you, Baron. But I have the disposition of Lermontov. [*Quietly.*] I even look a little like Lermontov . . . as they say . . . [*Gets bottle of scent from his pocket and pours it on his hands.*]

TUZENBAKH. I'm handing in my resignation. *Basta!*[3] I've been thinking it over for five years, and I've made up my mind at last. I shall be going to work.

SOLYONY. [*declaiming*] "Do not be angry, Aleko . . . Forget, forget your dreams . . ."

> *While they are speaking,* ANDREY *quietly enters and sits down by a candle.*

---

1. "I beg you to excuse me, Marie, but you are slightly uncouth."
2. "It seems my Bobik is no longer asleep." Natasha's word order is Russian, not French.
3. "Enough!"

TUZENBAKH. I shall be going to work . . .

CHEBUTYKIN. [*coming into the drawing room with* IRINA.] And they treated you also to real food of the Caucasus: onion soup, and for the main course—*chekhartma*, roast meat.

SOLYONY. *Cheremsha* is not meat at all, but a plant in the nature of our onion.

CHEBUTYKIN. No, sir, my dear boy. *Chekhartma* is not an onion, but roast meat of lamb.

SOLYONY. But I tell you, *cheremsha* is an onion.

CHEBUTYKIN. But I tell you, *chekhartma* is lamb.

SOLYONY. But I tell you, *cheremsha* is an onion.

CHEBUTYKIN. Why on earth should I quarrel with you? You have never been to the Caucasus, and you have never eaten *chekhartma*.

SOLYONY. I have never eaten it, because I cannot stand it. There's such a smell from *cheremsha*, exactly like garlic.

ANDREY. [*beseeching*] Enough, gentlemen! I beg you!

TUZENBAKH. When will the mummers arrive?

IRINA. They promised to come here at nine. That means very soon now.

TUZENBAKH. [*embraces* ANDREY, *singing*] "Oh, you, porch, my porch, my new porch . . ."

ANDREY. [*dances and sings*] "New porch, of maple wood . . ."

CHEBUTYKIN. [*dances*] "Latticed, like a sieve!" [*Laughter.*]

TUZENBAKH. [*kisses* ANDREY] Oh, the hell with it, let's have a drink, Andryusha, let's drink to our friendship. And I'll go with you, Andryusha, to Moscow, to the University.

SOLYONY. To which one? In Moscow there are two universities.

ANDREY. In Moscow there is one university.

SOLONY. And I tell you—there are two.

ANDREY. Even if there are three, so much the better.

SOLYONY. In Moscow there are two universities. [*Sounds of murmuring and hissing.*] In Moscow there are two universities: the old one and the new one. If you don't care to listen, if my words annoy you, then I can stop talking. I can even go into another room . . . [*Goes out through one of the doors.*]

TUZENBAKH. Bravo, bravo! [*Laughs.*] Ladies and gentlemen, let's begin, I'll sit down and play! That Solyony is funny . . . [*Sits at piano, plays a waltz.*]

MASHA. [*dances waltz by herself*] The Baron is drunk, the Baron is drunk, the Baron is drunk!

    Enter NATASHA.

NATASHA. [*to* CHEBUTYKIN] Ivan Romanych! [*Says something to* CHEBUTYKIN, *then quietly goes out.*]

    CHEBUTYKIN *touches* TUZENBAKH *on the shoulder and whispers something to him.*

IRINA. What is it?

CHEBUTYKIN. It's time for us to go. Take care of yourselves.

TUZENBAKH. Good night. Time to go.

IRINA. Let me . . . But what about the mummers? . .

ANDREY. [*having become confused*] The mummers won't be coming. Don't you see, my dear, Natasha says that Bobik isn't a bit well, and that's why . . . In a word, I don't know, it doesn't matter to me at all.

IRINA. [*shrugging her shoulders*] Bobik's not well!

MASHA. Where, oh where, has our life gone? Oh, what the hell—why not? They're driving us out, it's come to that, so we must go. [*To* IRINA.] Bobik isn't the one who's sick, but it's she herself . . . Right here! [*Strikes forehead with finger.*] Common fishwife!

> ANDREY *goes out the right door to his room;* CHEBUTYKIN *goes with him; in the ballroom they say good-bye.*

FEDOTIK. It's a shame! I'd counted on staying through the evening, but if the little child is sick, then, of course . . . Tomorrow I'll bring him some toys . . .

RODE. [*loudly*] After dinner today I expressly took a good long nap, I thought I'd be dancing the whole night. Now it's only nine o'clock, you know!

MASHA. Let's go outside, we can talk it over there. We'll decide what to do.

> *There is heard:* "Good-bye! Take care of yourself!" *The happy laughter of* TUZENBAKH *is heard. Everyone is leaving.* ANFISA *and the* MAIDSERVANT *clear the table and put out the lights. The* NURSE *is heard singing to the child.* ANDREY, *wearing a coat and hat, enters quietly with* CHEBUTYKIN.

CHEBUTYKIN. I didn't have time to get married because life flashed by like lightning. Yes, and because I was madly in love with your mother, who was already married . . .

ANDREY. A person shouldn't get married. No, he shouldn't because it's so humdrum.

CHEBUTYKIN. That's true, but just consider loneliness. However much you may try to reason it out, loneliness is a terrible thing, my dear boy . . . Although, in reality . . . of course, it doesn't matter at all!

ANDREY. Let's go as soon as possible.

CHEBUTYKIN. Why on earth hurry? We have time.

ANDREY. I'm afraid my wife may stop us.

CHEBUTYKIN. Ah!

ANDREY. I don't plan on playing tonight, I'll only sit and watch. I don't feel well . . . What can I do, Ivan Romanych, for shortness of breath?

CHEBUTYKIN. Why ask me! I don't remember, my dear boy. I don't know.

ANDREY. Let's go through the kitchen.

> *Sound of a bell, then another; voices are heard, laughter. They go out.*

IRINA. [*enters*] What is it?

ANFISA. [*in a whisper*] The mummers! [*Sound of bell.*]

IRINA. Tell them, *nyanechka*, tell them there's no one at home. Oh, let them excuse us.

> ANFISA *goes out.* IRINA, *deep in thought, walks around the room; she is upset.* SOLYONY *enters.*

SOLYONY. [*perplexed*] No one's here . . . And where is everybody?

IRINA. They've left for home.

SOLYONY. Strange. You're alone here?

IRINA. Alone. [*Pause.*] Good-bye.

SOLYONY. A little while ago I didn't behave as I should. I lost control, I was tactless. You aren't like the others, you are noble and pure, you can see the truth . . . You alone and only you alone can understand me. I love you deeply, love you boundlessly . . .

IRINA. Good-bye! Please go.

SOLYONY. I cannot live without you. [*Following her.*] Oh, blessed light of my life! [*Through tears.*] Oh, joy of my life! Your eyes, your wonderful, glorious, heavenly eyes—eyes I've never seen in another woman . . .

IRINA. [*coldly*] Stop it, Vasily Vasilich!

SOLYONY. I speak of love to you for the first time, and I feel as if I a not here on this earth, but on another planet. [*Rubs his forehead.*] Well, it doesn't matter, anyway. You can't force someone to love you, of course . . . But I won't have any successful rivals . . . I won't have it . . . I swear to you by all that is holy, I shall kill any rival . . . Oh, you marvelous woman!

> NATASHA, *carrying a candle, walks across the stage.*

NATASHA. [*looks through one door, into another, and then walks by the door which leads to her husband's room*] There's Andrey. Oh, let him read. You must excuse me, Vasily Vasilich, I didn't know you were here, I'm not dressed for company . . .

SOLYONY. It doesn't matter to me. Good-bye! [*Goes out.*]

NATASHA. And you are tired, aren't you dear, my poor little girl! [*Kisses* IRINA.] You must go to bed a little earlier.

IRINA. Is Bobik asleep?

NATASHA. Asleep. But it's a restless sleep. By the way, my dear, I've been wanting to speak to you, but it's always either you're not here, or I've not had the time . . . The nursery Bobik is in now, it seems to me it's cold and damp. But your room is such a good one for the child. My dearest darling, move into Olya's room for the time being!

IRINA. [*not understanding*] Where?

> *There is heard the sound of a troika with little bells approaching the house.*

NATASHA. You and Olya will be in one room for the time being, and Bobik will have your room. He's such a sweetie, today I said to him: "Bobik, you are mine! Mine!" And he looked at me with his darling little eyes. [*A bell.*] It must be Olga. How late she is! [*The* MAIDSERVANT *goes to* NATASHA *and whispers in her ear.*]

Protopopov? What an eccentric man he is. Protopopov is here, he's inviting me to go for a drive with him in his troika. [*Laughs.*] How strange these men are . . . [*A bell.*] Someone's just arrived. Perhaps I'll go for a little ride, no more than quarter of an hour . . . [*To* MAIDSERVANT.] Tell him I'll be right down. [*A bell.*] It's ringing . . . It must be Olga. [*Goes out.*]

> *The* MAIDSERVANT *runs off;* IRINA *sits lost in thought; enter* KULYGIN, OLGA, *after them* VERSHININ.

KULYGIN. Well, that's one for you! You said you were going to have a party.

VERSHININ. Strange, I left a little while ago, not more than half an hour, and they were expecting the mummers . . .

IRINA. Everyone left.

KULYGIN. And Masha left? Where did she go? And why is Protopopov downstairs waiting in his troika? Who is it he's waiting for?

IRINA. Don't ask me any questions . . . I am tired.

KULYGIN. Well, just listen to our little whimsy . . .

OLGA. The meeting just now ended. I am exhausted. Our headmistress is sick, and now I'm to take her place. My head, my head is aching, oh my head . . . [*Sits.*] Andrey lost two hundred rubles at cards yestereday . . . The whole town is talking about it . . .

KULYGIN. Yes, and that meeting tired me out, too. [*Sits.*]

VERSHININ. My wife took it into her head to frighten me just now, she almost poisoned herself. Everything's turned out all right, and I'm glad I can relax now . . . So it's come to that, we must go? Well, hmm, then allow me to wish you good night. Fyodor Ilich, let's go out somewhere! I can't stay at home, I just can't . . . Let's go!

KULYGIN. I am tired. I'm not going. [*Rises.*] I am tired. Has my wife gone home?

IRINA. She's probably there.

KULYGIN. [*kisses* IRINA'S *hand*] Good-bye. Tomorrow and the day after we can rest the whole day. Good night. [*Going.*] I'd like some tea very much. I'd counted on staying through the whole evening in some pleasant company—o, *fallacem hominum spem!*[4] Accusative case of the exclamatory . . .

VERSKININ. That means I'll go somewhere alone. [*Goes out with* KULYGIN, *whistles.*]

OLGA. Oh, my head is aching, my head . . . Andrey lost . . . The whole town is talking . . . I'll go lie down. [*Going.*] Tomorrow I'm free . . . Oh, dear God in Heaven, how pleasant that will be! Tomorrow, free, the day after, free . . . Oh, my head is aching, my head . . . [*Goes out.*]

IRINA. [*alone*] Everyone has gone. No one is left.

> *In the street there is the sound of an accordion; the* NURSE *is singing a song.*

NATASHA. [*goes through the ballroom, dressed in a fur coat and*

4. "O, the deceit of human hope."

cap, followed by the MAIDSERVANT] I will be back in half an hour.
I'll only be driving a little while. [*Goes out.*]
IRINA. [*left alone, with anguish and longing*] To Moscow! Moscow! Moscow!

CURTAIN

Act Three

The room of OLGA *and* IRINA. *To the left and the right are
beds, blocked off by screens. Between two and three o'clock
in the morning. Behind the scenes an alarm bell is striking
because of a fire that began some time ago. It is apparent
that in the house no one has yet gone to bed.* MASHA *is lying
on the sofa; she is dressed, as usual, in a black dress. Enter*
OLGA *and* ANFISA.

ANFISA. Right now they're sitting below under the stairs . . . I told
them—"Please, upstairs." I said, "You don't call sitting there
right, do you?" They are crying. "*Papasha,*"5 they're saying. "We
don't know where he is." "God help us," they keep on saying.
"He's not burned up." Oh, the ideas they come up with! And
those others outside . . . they've also lost all their clothes.

OLGA. [*takes dresses out of the wardrobe*] Here, take this gray
dress . . . And this one here . . . Also the blouse . . . And take this
shirt, *nyanechka* . . . What a terrible thing this is, dear God in
Heaven! Kirsanovsky Lane is all burned up, apparently . . . Take
this . . . Take this . . . [*Throws the dresses into her hands.*] The
poor Vershinins were frightened to death . . . Their place almost
burned down. Let them spend the night with us . . . We can't
possibly let them go home . . . At poor Fedotik's place everything
was burned, nothing is left, nothing . . .

ANFISA. You'd better call Ferapont, Olyushka, or I won't be able to
carry . . .

OLGA. [*rings*] You keep ringing but no one answers . . . [*At the
door.*] Come up here, whoever is there! [*In the open door is
seen a window, red from the glow; the sound of the fire engine
going past the house is heard.*] Oh, it's terrible, terrible! And how
tiring it is! [FERAPONT *enters.*] Here, take these down . . .
There under the stairs the Kolotilin girls are standing . . . Give
the clothing to them. And give them this . . .

FERAPONT. Yes, ma'am. In the year eighteen and twelve Moscow
also burned down. Oh, dear Lord God in Heaven! The French
were surprised.6

5. Pronounced *papásha.* Affectionate, intimate form of address to an elderly person or an old man.
6. Ferapont refers to the ultimately dis-
astrous French invasion of Russia in
1812, in the course of which Muscovites
burned down their own city.

OLGA. Go along, on your way now.

FERAPONT. Yes, ma'am. [*Goes out.*]

OLGA. *Nyanechka*, my dear, give them everything. There's nothing we need, give them everything, *nyanechka* . . . I am tired, I can barely stand up . . . It's out of the question to let the Vershinins go home . . . The little girls can sleep in the drawing room, and Alexandr Ignatich downstairs where the Baron is . . . Fedotik at the Baron's too, or let him stay here in the ballroom . . . The doctor is drunk, terribly drunk—as if he'd done it on purpose tonight —so it's out of the question to put anyone in his room. And Vershinin's wife in the drawing room, too.

ANFISA. [*wearily*] Olyushka, dear, don't you drive me out! Don't drive me out!

OLGA. You're talking nonsense, *nyanya*. No one is driving you out, no one.

ANFISA. [*puts her head on* OLGA's *breast*] My own, my precious darling, I am working, I work hard . . . If I get weak, everyone will say: "Let her go." But where can I go? Where? I am eighty years old. Eighty-one years . . .

OLGA. You sit down, *nyanechka* . . . You are tired, dear, poor thing . . . [*Seats her.*] Rest, my dearest. Oh, how pale you are! [NATASHA *enters.*]

NATASHA. Downstairs they're saying we should set up a committee as soon as possible, to help those who lost their homes in the fire. Well, hmm? An excellent idea. As a matter of fact, we must help out poor people, that's the obligation of the rich. Bobik and Sofochka[7] have fallen asleep, they are sleeping as if nothing in the world were going on. We have, oh, so many people everywhere, no matter where you go the house is full. Right now in town there's influenza, I'm afraid the children might catch it.

OLGA. [*not listening to her*] You can't see the fire from this room, it's peaceful here . . .

NATASHA. Yes . . . Oh, I probably look a mess. [*In front of the mirror.*] They say I've put on weight . . . and it's not true! In no way at all! And Masha is sleeping, worn out, poor thing . . . [*To* ANFISA, *coldly.*] Don't you dare sit down in my presence! Get up! On your way now! [ANFISA *goes out; a pause.*] And why on earth you hold on to that old woman, I don't understand!

OLGA. [*having been struck dumb*] Excuse me, I too don't understand . . .

NATASHA. She has no purpose being here. She is a peasant, she should live in the country . . . I've never seen such mollycoddling! I like order in the house! Those who are superfluous should not remain in the house. [*Strokes* OLGA's *cheek.*] You, poor, poor thing, you're tired, aren't you! Our headmistress is tired, isn't she! You know, when my Sofochka grows up and goes to the high school, I shall be afraid of you.

7. Sofya is Natasha's second child.

OLGA. I won't be the headmistress.

NATASHA. They'll elect you, Olechka dear. It's all decided.

OLGA. I shall refuse. I can't . . . I don't have the strength for it . . . [*Drinks some water.*] You treated *nyanya* so rudely just now. . . . Forgive me, but I can't stand it . . . Everything went black before my eyes . . .

NATASHA. [*agitated*] Forgive me, Olya, forgive me . . . I didn't want to upset you.

    MASHA *rises, takes her pillow, and leaves, angrily.*

OLGA. Understand, my dear . . . we were brought up, perhaps, in a strange way, but I can't stand it. What happened just now, that kind of behavior depresses me, I begin feeling sick . . . I simply lose heart and soul!

NATASHA. Forgive me, forgive . . . [*Kisses her.*]

OLGA. Every sort of rudeness, even the slightest, even a tasteless word, pulls me apart inside . . .

NATASHA. I know I often say too much, it's true, but you agree, my dear, she should live in the country.

OLGA. She has been with us for thirty years.

NATASHA. But you know, don't you, she is unable to work now! Either I don't understand you, or else you just don't want to understand me. She is incapable of working, the only thing she does is sleep or sit.

OLGA. Then let her sit.

NATASHA. [*surprised*] What are you talking about, let her sit? But you know she's a servant, after all. [*Through tears.*] I don't understand you, Olya. I have a *nyanka*, I have a wet nurse, we have a maid, we have a cook . . . what on earth do we still have that old woman for? For what?

    Behind the scenes the fire alarm is struck.

OLGA. I have put on ten years in this night.

NATASHA. We must come to an understanding, Olya, once and for all. You are at the high school, I—am at home. You are in charge of teaching, I—am in charge of the house. And if I say something that has to do with the servants, then I know what I am talking about. I know what-I-am-talk-ing-a-bout . . . And by tomorrow you see that old thief gets out of here, that old hag . . . [*Stamps her feet.*] that witch! . . Don't you dare irritate me! Don't you dare! [*Remembering herself.*] Really, if you don't move downstairs, then we shall always be quarreling. It's terrible.

    KULYGIN *enters.*

KULYGIN. Where is Masha? It's time we were going home. The fire, they say, is dying down. [*Stretches.*] Only one block was burned down, but in the beginning, with that wind, you know, it seemed as if the whole town was going to burn. [*Sits.*] I am tired. Olechka, my dear . . . I often think—if it hadn't been for Masha, then I'd have married you, Olechka. You're a good person, very good . . . I am exhausted. [*Listens for something.*]

OLGA. What is it?

KULYGIN. The doctor's having a drinking bout, as if he'd done it on purpose tonight. He's terribly drunk. Tonight of all nights, on purpose! [*Rises.*] There, he's coming up here, I think . . . Do you hear? Yes, up here . . . [*Laughs.*] Oh, he's something, it's true . . . I'll go hide . . . [*Goes to the wardrobe and stands in the corner.*] Oh, he's a pirate, he is.

OLGA. He hasn't been drinking for two years, and here all of a sudden he's gone and gotten drunk . . . [*Goes with* NATASHA *to the upstage part of the room.*]

> CHEBUTYKIN *enters; as if sober, not reeling, he walks about the room, stops, looks, then goes to the washstand, and begins to wash his hands.*

CHEBUTYKIN. [*morosely*] To hell with them all . . . to hell . . . They think I am a doctor, I am able to cure every kind of illness, but I know absolutely nothing at all, I've forgotten everything I knew, I remember nothing, absolutely nothing at all. [OLGA *and* NATASHA, *unnoticed by him, go out.*] To hell with them. Last Wednesday I treated a woman at Zasyp—she died, and it's my fault she died. Yes . . . I knew something or other twenty-five years ago, but now I remember nothing at all. Nothing. Perhaps I am not really a person, but only pretend that I have hands, and feet, and a head. Perhaps I don't even exist at all, but it only seems to me that I walk, eat, sleep. [*He weeps.*] Oh, if only I no longer existed! [*Stops weeping, morosely.*] Who the hell knows . . . Day before yesterday they were talking at the club; they were saying, Shakespeare, Voltaire . . . I haven't read them, haven't read them at all, but I let it show on my face as if I had read them. And the others did so too, just like me. Petty and vulgar! Mean! And that woman, the one I killed on Wednesday, came back to my mind . . . and everything came back to my mind, and in my heart and soul I felt twisted, corrupt, ugly . . . I went and got drunk . . .

> *Enter* IRINA, VERSHININ, *and* TUZENBAKH. TUZENBAKH *is dressed in civilian clothes, new and fashionable.*

IRINA. Let's sit in here. No one will come here.

VERSHININ. If it hadn't been for the soldiers, the whole town would have burned down. Marvelous fellows! [*Rubs his hands with pleasure.*] The best on earth. Ah, what marvelous fellows, marvelous!

KULYGIN. [*going up to them*] What time is it, gentlemen?

TUZENBAKH. It's past three o'clock. It's getting light.

IRINA. Everyone is sitting in the ballroom, no one is leaving. And that Solyony of yours is sitting . . . [*To* CHEBUTYKIN.] Doctor, you ought to go to bed.

CHEBUTYKIN. It's nothing, miss . . . Thanks, miss. [*Combs his beard.*]

KULYGIN. [*laughs*] You've gone and gotten pickled, Ivan Romanych!

[*Slaps him on the shoulder.*] Marvelous fellow! *In vino veritas*,[8] as the ancients kept saying.

TUZENBAKH. Everyone is asking me to arrange a concert for the benefit of those who lost their homes in the fire.

IRINA. Well, who is there . . .

TUZENBAKH. It could be arranged if people wanted to. Marya Sergeevna, for example, plays the piano splendidly . . .

KULYGIN. She plays splendidly!

IRINA. She's already forgotten how. She hasn't played in three years . . . or four.

TUZENBAKH. There's absolutely no one here in this town who understands music, not one soul, but I, I understand. And I assure you, word of honor, that Maria Sergeevna plays splendidly, she's almost gifted.

KULYGIN. You are right, Baron. I love her very much, Masha. She's a fine woman.

TUZENBAKH. To be able to play so brilliantly, and at the same time, to realize that no one understands you, no one!

KULYGIN. [*sighs*] Yes . . . But is it proper for her to take part in the concert? [*Pause.*] Ladies and gentlemen, you know I know nothing about it. Perhaps it would be a good idea. I must confess that our director is a good person, even very good, most intelligent, but he does have his own points of view . . . Of course, it's none of his business, but all the same, if you want to, then I'll have a talk with him, if you like.

    CHEBUTYKIN *takes a porcelain clock in his hands and examines it.*

VERSHININ. I became filthy with dirt at the fire, so much so I must look like nothing on this earth. [*Pause.*] Yesterday I heard in passing that they want to move our brigade some place far away. Some say to occupied Poland; others—to Chita, it seems.

TUZENBAKH. I heard it too. Well, hmm? The town will become deserted, completely so by then.

IRINA. We shall leave too!

CHEBUTYKIN. [*drops the clock, which is broken*] Smashed to pieces, to pieces!

    Pause; everyone is upset and confused.

KULYGIN. [*gathering up the pieces*] To break such an expensive thing. Oh, Ivan Romanych, Ivan Romanych! You get zero minus for behavior!

IRINA. That was our Mama's clock.

CHEBUTYKIN. Perhaps . . . Mama's, so it was Mama's. Perhaps I didn't break it, but it only seems that I broke it. Perhaps it only seems to us that we exist, but we really aren't here at all. I don't know anything, nothing. No one knows anything, nothing. [*At the door.*] What are you looking at? Natasha is having a little affair

8. "In wine there is truth."

with Protopopov, and you don't see it . . . Here you sit, here, and you don't see anything, but Natasha is having a little affair with Protopopov . . . [*Sings.*] "Would you like to accept this date[9] . . ." [*Goes out.*]

VERSHININ. Yes . . . [*Laughs.*] How strange everything is, in reality! [*Pause.*] When the fire broke out, I ran off to my home as fast as I could. I got to our house and saw that it was all right, no harm done, beyond danger. But my two little girls were standing in the doorway, dressed only in their underclothing, their mother gone, people bustling around, horses and dogs running by, and on the faces of my little girls fear, terror, supplication, and I don't know what. When I saw their faces my heart sank. God in Heaven, I thought, what more must these little girls live through in the course of a long life! I picked them up, ran off, and all the time I was running, I kept thinking the very same thought—what more must they still live through on this earth! [*Fire alarm; pause.*] I got here, and their mother was here, shouting, angry. [MASHA *enters with a pillow and sits on the sofa.*] But when my little girls stood in the doorway, dressed only in their underclothing, and the street was red from the fire, the noise was terrible, then I thought that something like it must have happened many years ago, when the enemy unexpectedly invaded, looted, burned . . . And yet in reality, look at the difference, the difference between what is and what was! A little more time will pass—say, two hundred or three hundred years—and in the same way people will look back on our life today with terror and with derision. Everything today will seem somewhat boxed-in, both heavy, very uncomfortable, and strange. But in the future—oh, indeed what a life that shall be, what a life! [*Laughs.*] Forgive me, I seem to have dropped into philosophy once more. Allow me to continue, ladies and gentlemen. I want terribly to give my views, I'm in the mood for it now. [*Pause.*] It seems everyone has gone to sleep. So, as I was saying, what a life that shall be! You have only to imagine it . . . Today there are only three persons like you in the town, but in the generations to come there will be more people like you, forever increasing more and more, until the time will come when everything will change to your way of life. People will begin living the way you live, but by that time, your way will have become old-fashioned. People will be born who are better than you . . . [*Laughs.*] Today I feel in a special mood. My lust for living runs full rein . . . [*Sings.*]

> "All ages are obedient to love,
> Its passions are good to . . ." [*Laughs.*]

MASHA. *Tram-tam-tam* . . .
VERSHININ. *Tam-tam* . . .

9. These words, Chekhov explained, were sung in a operetta which he had once heard; he had forgotten both its name and the rest of the song. The word "date" in the lyric refers to the fruit of the date palm tree.

MASHA. *Tra-ra-ra?*

VERSHININ. *Tra-ta-ta.* [*Laughs.*]

  FEDOTIK *enters.*

FEDOTIK. [*dances*] Burned out, burned out! Gone, gone, everything's gone! [*Laughter.*]

IRINA. That's nothing to joke about! Has everything burned up?

FEDOTIK. [*laughs*] Gone, gone, everything's gone. Nothing at all remains. And the guitar is burned up, and my photography equipment is burned up, and all my letters . . . And that little notebook I wanted to give you—it's burned up, too.

  SOLYONY *enters.*

IRINA. No, please go away, Vasily Vasilich. It's forbidden to be in here.

SOLYONY. Why is it possible for the Baron, but forbidden to me?

VERSHININ. We must leave, really. How's the fire?

SOLYONY. It's dying down, they say. No, it's absolutely strange to me, why is it possible for the Baron, but forbidden to me? [*Takes out bottle of scent and sprinkles himself.*]

VERSHININ. *Tram-tam-tam?*

MASHA. *Tram-tam.*

VERSHININ. [*laughs, to* SOLYONY] Let's go into the ballroom.

SOLYONY. Very well, sir, we'll jot it down in so many words.

   "It's possible perhaps to make the point clear,
    But that might provoke the geese, I fear . . ."[1]

[*Glancing at* TUZENBAKH.] *Tsip, tsip, tsip* . . . [*Goes out with* VERSHININ *and* FEDOTIK.]

IRINA. Oh, that Solyony has filled this room with smoke . . . [*In perplexity.*] The Baron is asleep. Baron! Baron!

TUZENBAKH. [*waking up*] I am tired, really . . . The brick factory . . . I am not raving in my sleep, really. I will set off soon for the brick factory, I'll begin to work . . . I've talked to them already. [*To* IRINA, *tenderly.*] You are so pale, so beautiful, fascinating . . . It seems to me your pallor brightens up the darkness surrounding you, like a light . . . You're sad, you're displeased with life . . . Oh, come with me, let's go away together and work! . .

MASHA. Nikolay Lvovich, go away from here.

TUZENBAKH. [*laughing*] Are you here? I didn't see you. [*Kisses* IRINA's *hand.*] Good-bye, I'll go . . . I look at you now, and it comes back to me, that day a long time ago, on your saint's day —that day as you talked of the joy of work, you were cheerful, bright . . . Oh, the happy life I imagined at that time! Where is it now? [*Kisses her hand.*] There are tears in your eyes. Go to sleep, it's getting light already . . . Morning has come . . . If only I were allowed to give my life for you!

---

1. A paraphrase of the concluding lines from Krylov's "The Geese." Bernard Pares's translation is as follows: " 'Twould be hard to make my moral yet more clear/But that means vexing geese, I fear!" *Krylov's Fables*, tr. Bernard Pares (New York: Harcourt, Brace, n.d.), p. 108.

MASHA. Nikolay Lvovich, go away! Well, what about it, really . . .

TUZENBAKH. I'll go . . . [*Goes out.*]

MASHA. [*lying down*] Are you asleep, Fyodor?

KULYGIN. Ah?

MASHA. You had better go home.

KULYGIN. My dear Masha, my precious Masha . . .

IRINA. She is tired. You should let her rest, Fedya.

KULYGIN. I'll go presently . . . My good, fine wife . . . I love you, you and you alone . . .

MASHA. [*angrily*] Amo, amas, amat, amamus, amatis, amant.[2]

KULYGIN. [*laughs*] No, it's true, isn't she amazing. I have been married to you for seven years, but it seems that we were married only yesterday. Word of honor. No, it's true, you're an amazing woman. I am satisfied, I am satisfied, I am satisfied!

MASHA. And I am bored, bored, bored . . . [*Rises and speaks sitting up.*] Look, I can't get it out of my head . . . it's simply outrageous. It's like a nail driven into my head, I can't keep silent. What I'm talking about is Andrey . . . He's gone and mortgaged this house to the bank, and his wife has taken all the money. And you know the house doesn't belong to him alone, but to all four of us! He must realize it if he has any honesty at all.

KULYGIN. Why go on, Masha? What does it matter to you? Andryusha is in debt to everybody, well, and God help him.

MASHA. In any case it's outrageous. [*Lies down.*]

KULYGIN. We are not poor. I'm working, I go to the high school, then I give lessons . . . I am an honest person. Plain and simple . . . Omnia mea mecum porto,[3] as they say.

MASHA. I'm not demanding anything, but it's the injustice that makes me angry. [*Pause.*] On your way now, Fyodor.

KULYGIN. [*kisses her*] You are tired, rest for half an hour, and I'll sit outside, I'll wait for you. Sleep . . . [*Going.*] I am satisfied, I am satisfied. I am satisfied. [*Goes out.*]

IRINA. If the truth were said, our Andrey has been cut to pieces, lost whatever depth he had. Look how he's been used up, how he's aged beyond his years living around that woman! At one time he was working to be a professor, but yesterday he was boasting how at last he's become a member of the District Council. Oh, yes, he's a member of the Council, but Protopopov is the chairman . . . The whole town is talking about it, laughing at him, and he's the only one who knows nothing and sees nothing . . . And at this very moment while everyone is running off to the fire, he sits in his room and pays no attention, none. Only sits playing his violin. [*Nervously.*] Oh, it's terrible, terrible, terrible! [*Weeps.*] I can't, I can't stand it any longer! . . I can't, I can't! . . [OLGA *enters, clears up around her little table.* IRINA *sobs loudly.*] Throw me out, throw me out, I can't stand it any longer! . .

2. "I love, you love," etc.
3. "Everything I have that is mine I carry with me."

OLGA. [*frightened*] What is it, what? My dearest!

IRINA. [*sobbing*] Where? Where has it all gone? Where is it? Oh, dear God, dear God in Heaven! I've forgotten everything, forgotten . . . My head is all muddled up . . . I don't even remember the Italian for window or ceiling . . . I'm forgetting everything, every day I keep forgetting, and life is slipping away and will never come back, never, ever. And we shall never go to Moscow . . . I see that we won't go . . .

OLGA. Dearest, dearest . . .

IRINA. [*restraining herself*] Oh, I'm so unhappy. . . . I can't work, I won't work. Enough of working, enough! I was a telegraph clerk, now I work in the City Council. And I hate and despise everything they give me to do . . . I'm already twenty-three, I've been working for a long time, and my brain's drying up. I've grown thin, old, ugly, and nothing, nothing, nothing at all satisfies me. And time is slipping away, and you feel as if you're always moving away from a beautiful, genuine life, you're always moving further and further away into some kind of abyss. I've lost heart, why I'm still alive, why I haven't killed myself before now I don't understand . . .

OLGA. Don't cry, dear little one, don't cry . . . It hurts me too.

IRINA. I'm not crying, I'm not . . . Enough . . . Well, there, I've stopped crying. Enough . . . Enough!

OLGA. Dearest, I'm going to talk to you as a sister, as a friend, if you want my advice, marry the Baron! [IRINA *weeps quietly.*] You know you respect him, you think well of him, even highly . . . He's not good-looking, it's true, but he's so honest, pure . . . You know, don't you, a person doesn't marry for love, but only to do one's duty. At least, that's what I think, and I'd marry without love. If someone made me a proposal, so long as he were an honest person, it doesn't matter who, I'd marry him. I'd even marry an old man . . .

IRINA. All the time I expected that we'd move to Moscow, there I'd meet the right man for me, the one I've dreamed about, the one I've come to love . . . But it's all turned out as nonsense, all, all nonsense . . .

OLGA. [*embraces her sister*] My dear beautiful sister, I understand you, I do. When Baron Nikolay Lvovich resigned from the army and came to see us dressed in civilian clothes, he seemed so ugly to me I even started to cry . . . "Why are you crying?" he asked me. As if I could ever tell him! But if it's God's will for him to marry you, then I'd feel happy. You see that's a different matter, altogether different.

> *Natasha, with a candle, enters through the right door, walks across the stage, and goes out through the left door. She does not speak.*

MASHA. [*sitting up*] She keeps walking around, just as if she'd started the fire herself.

OLGA. Masha, you are silly and stupid. The most stupid in our family—it's you. Forgive me, please. [*Pause.*]

MASHA. My dear sisters, I've something I want to confess. It's tearing me apart inside, so I shall tell you two and then say nothing more to anyone, ever . . . I'll tell you now. [*Quietly.*] It's my secret, but you must know everything . . . I can keep silent no longer . . . [Pause.] I love, I love . . . I love that person . . . You saw him just now . . . Oh, why go on this way. To come to the point, I love Vershinin . . .

OLGA. [*goes behind her screen*] Stop it. It doesn't matter, I'm not listening.

MASHA. What can I do! [*Clutches her head.*] At the very beginning he seemed strange to me, then I felt sorry for him . . . then I fell in love . . . I fell in love with his voice, with his words, his misfortunes, his two little girls . . .

OLGA. [*behind the screen*] It doesn't matter, I'm not listening. Whatever stupid things you say, it doesn't matter, I'm not listening.

MASHA. Oh, you amaze me, Olya. I am in love, that's all there is to it. It's my fate. There's no other choice . . . And he loves me . . . It's all so frightening. Yes? It's not right, is it? [*Pulls* IRINA *by the hand, draws her to her.*] Oh, my dear . . . how is it we shall live through the rest of our lives, what shall become of us . . . When you read a novel this sort of thing seems old and everything in it—so, so clear. But when you fall in love yourself, then you see for yourself that no one really and truly understands, and each person must come to a decision by himself . . . My dear, dear sisters . . . I've confessed everything to you, now I shall keep silent . . . I shall be like Gogol's madman now[4] . . . silence . . . silence . . .

ANDREY *enters, followed by* FERAPONT.

ANDREY. [*angrily*] What do you want? I don't understand.

FERAPONT. [*in the doorway, impatiently*] Andrey Sergeevich, I have already told you about ten times.

ANDREY. In the first place, I am not Andrey Sergeevich to you, but your Honor!

FERAPONT. The firemen, your Worship,[5] they're asking if it's allowed to drive through the garden on the way to the river. Up to now they're driving the long way around, and to keep driving and driving—it's hurting pretty bad.

ANDREY. All right. Tell them, all right. [FERAPONT *goes out.*] They've made me sick and tired. Where is Olga? [OLGA *comes out from behind the screen.*] I've come up to see you, give me the key to the cupboard, will you? I lost mine. You have it, that little key.

4. A reference to Gogol's *The Memoirs of a Madman* (1835).
5. Andrey asks Ferapont to use the title of address associated with ranks eight to six; however, Ferapont responds with the title of address for ranks five to three in the Table of Ranks.

[OLGA *silently gives him the key.* IRINA *goes behind her own screen; pause.*] And what a tremendous fire! It's starting to die down now. Damn it, that Ferapont irritated me, and I said a stupid thing to him . . . Your Honor . . . [*Pause.*] Why is it you're quiet, Olya? [*Pause.*] It's time to give up all this nonsense and pouting the way you do, there's no reason for it. Masha, you're here, Irina is here. Well, that's excellent—let's talk about it, openly, frankly, once and for all. What do you have against me? What?

OLGA. Stop it, Andryusha. We'll talk about it tomorrow. [*Agitated.*] Oh, what an agonizing night!

ANDREY. [*he is very confused*] Don't, don't get upset. I am asking you quite calmly: what do you have against me? Tell me in plain words.

VOICE OF VERSHININ. *Tram-tam-tam!*

MASHA. [*rises, loudly*] *Tra-ta-ta!* [*To* OLGA.] Good-bye, Olya, God be with you. [*Goes behind screen, kisses* IRINA.] Sleep quietly . . . Good-bye, Andrey, Go away, they are tired . . . You can talk tomorrow . . . [*Goes out.*]

OLGA. Indeed, Andryusha, let's talk tomorrow . . . [*Goes behind her screen.*] It's time to go to sleep.

ANDREY. I'll just say something and then I'll leave. At once . . . In the first place, you have something against Natasha, my wife, and I've seen it from the very day of my wedding. If you want to know, Natasha is a beautiful and straightforward person, pure and noble—that is my opinion. My wife I love and respect, understand me, respect. And I demand that others respect her, too. I repeat, she is a pure, noble person, and all your displeasure with her, forgive me for saying so, it's simply capriciousness on your part. [*Pause.*] In the second place, you are angry it seems because I am not a professor, that I'm not devoting myself to scholarship. But I serve in the local government, I am a member of the District Council, and I consider my service there just as sacred and high-minded as any service to scholarship. I am a member of the District Council and I am proud of it, if you wish to know . . . [*Pause.*] In the third place . . . I have something else to say . . . I mortgaged the house, without asking your permission . . . I was wrong, I know, and I beg you to forgive me. My debts required me to do so . . . thirty-five thousand. I no longer play cards, I gave it up a long time ago, and the most important thing I can say in my defense, it's that you girls, you receive a pension, I just didn't have . . . earnings, so to say . . . [*Pause.*]

KULYGIN. [*in the doorway*] Masha isn't here? [*Alarmed.*] Where on earth is she? It's strange . . . [*Goes out.*]

ANDREY. They aren't listening. Natasha is a pure, splendid person. [*Walks to and fro on the stage, in silence, then stops.*] When I married, I thought that we were going to be happy . . . all of us, happy . . . But dear God in Heaven . . . [*Weeps.*] My dear sisters, my precious sisters, don't believe what I've said, don't believe me . . . [*Goes out.*]

KULYGIN. [*in the doorway, alarmed*] Where is Masha? Masha isn't here? A surprising thing. [*Goes out.*]

Alarm bell. The stage is empty.

IRINA. [*behind the screen*] Olya! Who is it knocking on the floor?

OLGA. It's the doctor, Ivan Romanych. He is drunk.

IRINA. What a restless night! [*Pause.*] Olya! [*Glances out from behind the screen.*] Have you heard? They are taking the brigade away from us, sending them some place far away.

OLGA. It's only a rumor.

IRINA. We shall be left alone then . . . Olya!

OLGA. Well?

IRINA. Dear, my precious, I respect the Baron, I think well of him, he is a fine person, I shall marry him, I agree, only let's go to Moscow! I implore you, let's go! There's no place on earth better than Moscow! Let's go, Olya! Let's go!

CURTAIN

Act Four

The old garden attached to the Prozorov house. A long avenue of fir trees at the end of which is seen the river. On the other side of the river—a forest. On the right is the terrace of the house. On it a table with bottles and glasses—it is apparent they have just been drinking champagne. Twelve o'clock noon. Now and then passers-by from the street go through the garden on their way to the river. About five soldiers pass through quickly.

CHEBUTYKIN, *in a complacent mood which does not abandon him in the course of the whole act, is sitting in an arm-chair in the garden, waiting for them to call him. He is wearing a military cap and has a stick.* IRINA, KULYGIN *with his order around his neck and without his moustache, and* TUZENBAKH *are standing on the terrace and saying good-bye to* FEDOTIK *and* RODE, *who are coming down the steps. Both officers are wearing marching uniforms.*

TUZENBAKH. [*kisses* FEDOTIK] You're a good friend, Fedotik, we always hit it off, didn't we. [*Kisses* RODE.] Once more . . . Good-bye, dear friend!

IRINA. Until we meet again!

FEDOTIK. No, it isn't till we meet again, but it's good-bye, we won't see each other again, ever!

KULYGIN. Who knows! [*Wipes his eyes, smiles.*] There, I was starting to cry.

IRINA. We shall meet again, some time.

FEDOTIK. After ten—fifteen years? By that time we shall scarcely know one another. We'll greet each other as though we'd just met . . . [*Takes a photograph.*] Stand there . . . Again, for the last time.

RODE. [*embraces* TUZENBAKH.] We won't see each other again, ever . . . [*Kisses* IRINA'S *hand.*] Thanks for everything, for everything!

FEDOTIK. [*irritated*] Hey, hold it a minute!

TUZENBAKH. God willing, we'll see each other. Write, write to us now. Be sure to write.

RODE. [*takes in the garden at a glance*] Good-bye, trees! [*Shouts.*] Gop-gop![6] [*Pause.*] Good-bye, echo!

KULYGIN. I expect you'll get married there, in Poland . . . Your Polish wife will hug you and say: "*Kokhane!*"[7] [*Laughs.*]

FEDOTIK. [*having looked at his watch*] There's less than an hour remaining. Solyony's the only one from our battery going on the barge. We're to march with the formation. Three batteries will leave today, three more tomorrow—and into the town will come silence and peace.

TUZENBAKH. And tedium, dull weary tedium.

RODE. But where is Maria Sergeevna?

KULYGIN. Masha is in the garden.

FEDOTIK. We'll say good-bye to her.

RODE. Good-bye, I must leave or I'll start crying . . . [*Quickly embraces* TUZENBAKH *and* KULYGIN, *kisses* IRINA'S *hand.*] It's been wonderful living here . . .

FEDOTIK. [*to* KULYGIN] Take this as a souvenir . . . a little book with a little pencil . . . We'll go to the river this way . . .

    FEDOTIK *and* RODE *go out, both glancing back.*

RODE. [*shouts*] Gop-gop!

KULYGIN. [*shouts*] Good-bye!

    At the back of the stage FEDOTIK *and* RODE *meet* MASHA *and say good-bye to her; she leaves with them.*

IRINA. They've gone . . . [*Sits on the lowest step of the terrace.*]

CHEBUTYKIN. And they forgot to say good-bye to me.

IRINA. And you, what about you?

CHEBUTYKIN. Yes, I somehow forgot it, too. Anyway, I'll see them soon; I leave tomorrow. Yes . . . One more little day remains. They'll retire me in a year, I'll come back here and live out the rest of my days near you . . . One more little year remains until my pension . . . [*Puts one newspaper into his pocket, takes out another.*] Yes, I'll come back to you here and change my ways, change them at the core . . . I'll turn into such a quiet, hon . . . honorable, proper little fellow . . .

6. This phrase, transliterated from the Russian, is an instruction or command to a dog or horse to jump. Rode here sim- ply wants to make an echo.

7. Meaning "beloved" in Polish.

IRINA. And you should change your ways, my dear. You ought to, somehow.

CHEBUTYKIN. Yes. That's the way I feel. [*Sings quietly.*] "Tarara . . . boom-di-yah . . . sitting on a curb today . . ."

KULYGIN. Incorrigible, Ivan Romanych! You are incorrigible!

CHEBUTYKIN. Yes, how about some lessons from you. You just might make me corrigible then.

IRINA. Fyodor shaved off his moustache. I can't bear to look at him!

KULYGIN. And why can't you?

CHEBUTYKIN. I could tell you what your physiognomy resembles right now, but I don't think I should.

KULYGIN. Well, hmm! It is accepted, it is *modus vivendi*.[8] Our director's had his moustache shaved off, and so when I became the inspector, I also shaved off mine. No one likes it, but it doesn't matter to me. I am satisfied. With a moustache or without a moustache, I am satisfied one way or the other. [*Sits.*]

> At the back of the stage ANDREY *wheels a baby carriage with a sleeping child in it.*

IRINA. Dear Ivan Romanych, my dearest, I'm terribly worried. You were on the boulevard yesterday; tell me what happened there.

CHEBUTYKIN. What happened? Nothing. Nothing but nonsense. [*Reads newspaper.*] It doesn't matter!

KULYGIN. They're saying, it seems, that Solyony and the Baron met yesterday on the boulevard near the theatre . . .

TUZENBAKH. Stop it! Oh, why on earth . . . [*Waves his hand and goes into the house.*]

KULYGIN. Near the theatre . . . Solyony started needling the Baron, and the Baron wouldn't take it and said something insulting . . .

CHEBUTYKIN. I don't know. It's all nonsense, hokum.

KULYGIN. One time in a seminary, a teacher wrote "hokum" on a student's essay, and the student was certain it was Latin and began declining: *hoki, hoko, hoko, hokum, hokum* . . . [*Laughs.*] Wonderfully funny. They're saying, it seems, Solyony is in love with Irina and has come to hate the Baron . . . That's understandable. Irina is a very fine girl. She is even a little like Masha, gets wrapped up in her own thoughts the very same way. Only, Irina, you're more gentle. You have to admit though Masha is very fine, too. I love her, Masha.

> At the back of the garden, behind the scenes, is heard, "Yo-ho! Gop-gop!"

IRINA. [*shudders*] Everything somehow frightens me today. [*Pause.*] All my things are ready to go, and after dinner I'll send everything off. Tomorrow the Baron and I shall marry, and tomorrow too we leave for the brick factory. And day after tomorrow I'll be settled at the school, a new life will begin. Somehow God will help me! When I took the examination for the

8. Literally, "a mode of living; a temporary compromise."

teacher's permit, I was crying, crying for joy . . . [*Pause.*] The cart will be here presently for my things . . .

KULYGIN. That's all very well, only it's not at all serious somehow. They're only ideas, but not much that's serious. Even so I wish you the very best with all my heart and soul.

CHEBUTYKIN. [*with tender emotion*] My wonderful, my fine . . . my precious . . . You've gone so far ahead I can't catch up to you. I'm left behind, like a bird of passage, one who's grown old, unable to fly. Fly, my dear ones, fly away, and God go with you. [*Pause.*] It's useless, Fyodor Ilich, to have shaved off your moustache.

KULYGIN. Enough, that will do! [*Sighs.*] Today's the day the army is leaving, and everything will go back the way it was before. No matter what people've been saying, Masha is a good, pure woman, I love her very much and I can thank my fate . . . Everyone's fate is very different . . . A certain Kozyrev is working in the excise office here. We went to school together, and they expelled him from the fifth class in the high school because he could‧ never understand *ut consecutivum*.⁹ Nowadays he is terribly poor, sick, and whenever I meet him, I say to him: "Hello, *ut consecutivum*!" "Yes," he says, "that's it exactly, *ut consecutivum*! And he coughs . . . Now I've been lucky my whole life, I am happy, here I even hold the Order of Stanislav,¹ second class, and now I am teaching others this *ut consecutivum*. Of course, I am a clever person, cleverer than lots of others, but that doesn't make for happiness . . .

In the house, "The Maiden's Prayer"² is being played on the piano.

IRINA. And tomorrow night I won't have to listen to that "Maiden's Prayer" anymore, and I won't have to meet Protopopov . . . [*Pause.*] And Protopopov keeps sitting there in the drawing room. He came today too . . .

KULYGIN. The headmistress still hasn't arrived?

IRINA. No. They've sent for her. If you only knew how difficult it is to live here alone, without Olya . . . She lives at the high school, she's the headmistress, and she has things to do all day long, but I'm alone. I'm bored to death, there's nothing to do, and I hate the room where I live . . . So I've decided once and for all that if it's not my fate to live in Moscow, then so be it. It's my fate, pure and simple, and you can't do anything about it . . . Everything is God's will, that's true. Nikolay Lvovich proposed to me . . . Well, hmm? I thought it over and decided. He's a fine person, very much so, such a fine . . . And suddenly it seemed as if my soul had grown wings, I cheered up, I felt relaxed, and I

9. A syntactical locution in Latin.
1. An award and decoration in the civil service.
2. In the original Russian, Chekhov does not identify directly the person who is playing this song; my assumption is that it is Natasha.

wanted desperately to work again, work . . . And yet, yet something happened yesterday, and I feel as if something mysterious is hanging over me now . . .

CHEBUTYKIN. Hokum. *Hoki, hoko, hokum.*

NATASHA. [*at the window*] The headmistress!

KULYGIN. The headmistress has arrived. Let's go. [*Goes with* IRINA *into the house.*]

CHEBUTYKIN [*reads newspaper, sings quietly*] "Ta-ra-ra . . . boom-di-yah . . . sitting on a curb today . . ."

> MASHA *approaches. At the back of the stage* ANDREY *is pushing the baby carriage.*

MASHA. There he sits, just sitting for a little while . . .

CHEBUTYKIN. And why not?

MASHA. [*sits*] Nothing . . . [*Pause.*] Did you love my mother?

CHEBUTYKIN. Very much.

MASHA. And she, you?

CHEBUTYKIN. [*after a pause*] That I don't remember anymore.

MASHA. Is my man here? That's the way our cook Marfa used to talk about her policeman: my man. Is my man here?

CHEBUTYKIN. Not yet.

MASHA. When you must take your happiness at odd moments, in little bits and pieces, then you lose it, just as I have, and little by little you begin to grow coarse, you become furious . . . [*Indicates her breast.*] Here, now, I am boiling inside . . . [*Looking at her brother* ANDREY, *who is pushing the baby carriage.*] There's our Andrey, little brother . . . All our hopes have vanished. Thousands of people raised the bell, a lot of work and money was spent, but suddenly it fell and smashed to pieces. Suddenly, for no reason, no reason at all. So it was with Andrey . . .

ANDREY. And when will they quiet down in the house, when? Such noise.

CHEBUTYKIN. Soon. [*Looks at watch.*] I have an old-fashioned watch, it strikes the hours . . . [*Winds up watch, it strikes.*] The first, second, and fifth batteries will leave at one o'clock sharp . . . [*Pause.*] And I, tomorrow.

ANDREY. Forever?

CHEBUTYKIN. I don't know. Perhaps I'll come back in a year. Although, damned if I know . . . It doesn't matter . . .

> There are heard, as if someplace faraway, the sounds of a harp and violin being played.

ANDREY. The town will become deserted. Exactly as if they'd spread a nightcap over it. [*Pause.*] Something happened yesterday near the theatre. Everyone is talking about it, but I don't know.

CHEBUTYKIN. Nothing. Stupidity. Solyony started needling the Baron, and the Baron lost his temper and insulted him, and it finally turned out that Solyony had to challenge him to a duel.

[*Looks at his watch.*] Seems it's about time now . . . At half-past twelve o'clock, in the government grove, there, the one you can see from here, on the other side of the river . . . *pif-paf.* [*Laughs.*] Solyony imagines he is Lermontov and even writes poems. Well, joking is one thing, but it's his third duel.

MASHA. Whose?

CHEBUTYKIN. Solyony's.

MASHA. And the Baron?

CHEBUTYKIN. What about the Baron? [*Pause.*]

MASHA. My head's all muddled up . . . All the same I say it should not be permitted. He might wound the Baron or even kill him.

CHEBUTYKIN. The Baron is a fine person, but one Baron more, one Baron less—what does it matter, anyway! Let them! It doesn't matter! [*Beyond the garden a shout:* "Yo-ho! *Gop-gop!*"] You can wait. That's Skvortsov shouting, he's the second. He's sitting in a boat. [*Pause.*]

ANDREY. If you want my opinion, to participate in a duel or to be present at one, even in the capacity of a doctor, is simply immoral.

CHEBUTYKIN. That only seems so . . . We aren't here, nothing is here on this earth, we do not exist, but it only seems that we exist . . . What does it matter, anyway!

MASHA. Talk, talk, that's all it is the whole day through . . . [*Going.*] Living as you do in a climate where it might start snowing any moment, and what do you do—keep on talking, that's what . . . [*Stopping.*] I'm not going into that house, I can't stand going in there . . . When Vershinin comes, tell me . . . [*Walks along the avenue.*] And the birds of passage are flying already . . . [*Looks up.*] Swans or geese . . . My dear, happy, lovely birds . . . [*Goes out.*]

ANDREY. Our house will be deserted. The officers are leaving, you are leaving, my sister is getting married, and I shall be left alone in the house.

CHEBUTYKIN. And your wife?

FERAPONT *enters with papers.*

ANDREY. A wife is a wife. She is pure, honest, and perhaps kind. But there's something in her that corrupts, makes her something of a petty, blind animal, rough and hard-skinned. In any case she is not human. I am talking to you as a friend, the only one I can tell what's in my heart and soul. I love Natasha, it's so, but sometimes she seems to me absolutely petty and vulgar. And that's the time I feel lost. I don't understand the reason why I love her so much, or at least, I did love her once . . .

CHEBUTYKIN. [*rises*] Tomorrow, my friend, I am leaving, per-haps we'll never see each other again, so here's my advice to you. You know, put on your hat, take your stick in your hand, and walk off . . . walk off, and go, go without once glancing back. And the farther you go, the better.

SOLYONY *walks across the back of the stage with two* OFFI-

CERS; *having seen* CHEBUTYKIN, *he turns to him; the* OFFI-
CERS *walk on.*

SOLYONY. Doctor, time to go! Already half-past twelve. [*Greets*
ANDREY.]

CHEBUTYKIN. Presently. I'm sick and tired of all of you. [*To*
ANDREY.] If someone asks for me, Andryusha, tell them I'll be
back presently . . . [*Sighs.*] Okho-kho-kho!

SOLYONY. "Before he had time to let out a yell,
The bear was squeezing him to hell."
[*Goes with him.*] What is it you're quacking about, old man?

CHEBUTYKIN. Come now!

SOLYONY. How are you feeling?

CHEBUTYKIN. [*angrily*] Like butter out of a cow.

SOLYONY. The old man is getting upset, needlessly. I'll permit myself
only so much, I'll just wing him like a woodcock. [*Takes out
scent and sprinkles it on his hands.*] Here I've poured out a
whole bottle today, but they still smell. My hands smell like a
corpse. [*Pause.*] Yes, sir . . . Remember the verses?

"But he, rebellious, seeks the storm,
As if in storms there is peace . . ."[3]

CHEBUTYKIN. Yes.

"Before he had time to let out a yell,
The bear was squeezing him to hell."

[*Goes out with* SOLYONY.]
Shouts are heard: "Gop-gop! Yo-ho!" ANDREY *and* FERA-
PONT *enter.*[4]

FERAPONT. The papers must be signed . . .

ANDREY. [*nervously*] Leave me alone! Leave me! I beg you! [*Goes
out with baby carriage.*]

FERAPONT. Why have papers, you know, if they don't get signed?
[*Goes out at the back of the stage.*]
Enter IRINA *and* TUZENBAKH, *wearing a straw hat.* KULY-
GIN *crosses the stage, shouting,* "Yo-ho, *Masha,* yo-ho!"

TUZENBAKH. It seems he's the only person in town who's overjoyed
to see the army go away.

IRINA. It's understandable. [*Pause.*] Now our town will be deserted.

TUZENBAKH. [*having glanced at his watch*] My dear, I'll come
back presently.

IRINA. Where are you going?

TUZENBAKH. I must go into town, after that . . . to see off my com-
rades.

3. The final two lines of a twelve-line
poem, *The Sail*, by M. Yu. Lermontov
(1814–41).

4. It should be noted that there is no
previous stage direction that Andrey
should leave the stage.

IRINA. That's not true . . . Nikolay, why is it you are so distracted today? [*Pause.*] What happened yesterday near the theatre?

TUZENBAKH. [*an impatient movement*] In an hour I'll return and be with you again. [*Kisses her hands.*] My beloved . . . [*Looks closely at her face.*] I've been in love with you for more than five years, and I still can't get used to it, you seem to me more beautiful all the time. What charming, marvelous hair! And your eyes, glorious! Tomorrow I shall carry you off, we shall go to work, we shall be rich, my dreams will come alive. You shall be happy. There is only one thing, one thing only—you don't love me!

IRINA. It's not in my power. I shall be your wife, faithful and obedient, but there is no love, none. What can I do! [*Weeps.*] I've never been in love in my life, not once. Oh, I have dreamed of love, dreamed for a long, long time, day and night, but my soul is like a beautiful piano that has been locked up and the key is lost. [*Pause.*] You look distressed.

TUZENBAKH. I didn't sleep the whole night. There's nothing in my life, nothing so terrifying that can frighten me, but it's only that key, that lost key, that torments me to the depths of my soul and gives me no sleep . . . Tell me something. [*Pause.*] Tell me something . . .

IRINA. What? What can I say? What?

TUZENBAKH. Something.

IRINA. Enough, no more, please! [*Pause.*]

TUZENBAKH. It doesn't make much sense, does it, when stupid little trifles sometimes become important in life, suddenly very important, for no reason, no reason at all. Oh, you laugh at them as before, still consider them as so much nonsense, but you keep going on and you feel you don't have the strength to stop them or yourself. Oh, we won't talk about that! I feel wonderful today. I feel as if it's the first time in my life I actually see these fir trees, the maples, and birches. And everything it seems is looking back at me, watching, questioning, waiting. What beautiful trees, and in reality, there ought to be a beautiful life to go with them. [*Shout: "Yo-ho! Gop-gop!"*] I must go, it's time . . . Look at that tree standing there, it's dried up, but see it sway in the wind together with the other trees. So it seems to me that if I should die, I too will take part in life in one way or another. Good-bye, my dear . . . [*Kisses her hand.*] Your papers that you gave me are lying on my table under the calendar.

IRINA. And I'll go with you.

TUZENBAKH. [*uneasily*] No, no! [*Quickly goes, stops in the avenue.*] Irina!

IRINA. What?

TUZENBAKH. [*not knowing what to say*] I haven't had my coffee today. Tell them to make me some . . . [*Quickly goes out.*]

IRINA *stands lost in thought, then goes to the back of the stage and sits on the swing.* ANDREY *enters with the baby carriage;* FERAPONT *appears.*

FERAPONT. Andrey Sergeich, the papers, you know, are not mine, but government ones. I did not think them up.

ANDREY. Oh, where is it, where did it go, my past life, the time when I was young and happy and clever, when I dreamed with grace and thought with ease, when both the present and my future were bright with hope? Why is it that we, just at the moment we've scarcely begun to live, why is it we become boring, dull, and uninteresting? Why is it we become lazy, indifferent, useless, and unhappy . . . Our town here has already existed for two hundred years, a hundred thousand people live in it, and yet there isn't a single person who doesn't resemble everybody else. There's not one saint either in the past or in the present, not one scholar, not one artist, not one person in the least out of the ordinary who could arouse envy or passionate desire for imitation . . . The only thing they do is eat, drink, sleep, and then they die . . . Others are born and they also eat, drink, sleep, and, to keep from being bored sick, they bring a little variety into their lives by resorting to malicious gossip, vodka, cards, and lawsuits. The wives deceive their husbands, and the husbands go on lying, pretend they see nothing, pretend they hear nothing. And the children are irresistibly oppressed by the shallow and vulgar triviality of their parents' lives. And the spark of God is extinguished in them, and they in turn become the very same pitiful corpses, each resembling the other, as their fathers and their mothers did before them . . . [*To* FERAPONT, *angrily.*] What do you want?

FERAPONT. What? The papers must be signed.

ANDREY. I'm sick and tired of you.

FERAPONT. [*handing him the papers*] Just now the porter from the Council finance office was saying . . . "It seems," he was saying, "last winter in Petersburg they had two hundred degrees of frost."

ANDREY. The present is detestable. But then, when I think of the future, I feel wonderful. I become relaxed, feel so free. Far off in the distance I see a light beginning to dawn. I can see freedom, I can see how my children and I will become free from idleness, free from drinking kvas[5] and eating goose with cabbage, free from naps after dinner, free from the wretched life of feeding on others . . .

FERAPONT. Two thousand people died from the frost, it seems. "The people," he was saying, "were terrified." Either in Petersburg, or in Moscow—I don't recollect.

ANDREY. [*seized by tender emotion*] My dear sisters, my marvelous sisters! [*Through tears.*] Masha, my sister . . .

---

5. Or kvass: a beer with a slightly acid flavor; homemade, i.e., by pouring water over a mixture of rye, barley, and other cereals, and letting it ferment.

NATASHA. [*in the window*] Who is it talking so loudly out there? It's you, Andryusha? You'll wake up Sofochka. *Il ne faut pas faire du bruit, la Sophie est dormée déjà. Vous êtes un ours.*[6] [*Getting angry.*] If you want to talk, then give the baby carriage to someone else. Ferapont, take the carriage from the master!

FERAPONT. Yes, ma'am. [*Takes baby carriage.*]

ANDREY. [*disconcerted*] I am talking quietly.

NATASHA. [*behind the window, caressing her little boy*] Bobik! You little imp, Bobik! Bad Bobik!

ANDREY. [*looking at the papers*] All right, I'll look over the papers, sign those that require it, and you take them to the Council again . . . [*Goes into the house, reading the papers;* FERAPONT *pushes the baby carriage to the back of the garden.*]

NATASHA. [*behind the window*] Bobik, what is Mama's name? Dear, dear Bobik! And who is this? It is Auntie Olya, say to your auntie: "Hello, Olya!"

    Strolling musicians, a man and a girl, playing on the violin and harp; VERSHININ, OLGA *and* ANFISA *come out of the house and listen for a moment in silence;* IRINA *approaches.*

OLGA. Our garden is like a public thoroughfare, they're always walking and driving through it. *Nyanya,* give these musicians something! . .

ANFISA. [*gives money to the musicians*] Go along and God be with you, dear ones. [*The musicians bow and exit.*] Bitter people. They would not be playing like that if they had full stomachs. [*To* IRINA.] Hello, Arisha! [*Kisses her.*] And so, my child, I go on living! Go on living at the high school in the government apartment, my precious, together with Olyushka—the good Lord took care of me in my old age. Sinner that I am, I've never lived like this . . . the apartment big, paid for by the government, and for me a whole room and my own bed. All of it paid for by the government. I wake up in the night and—oh, dear Lord, Mother of God, never was there a happier person than me!

VERSHININ. [*having looked at his watch*] We'll be going presently, Olga Sergeevna. It's time for me. [*Pause.*] I wish you the best . . . Where is Maria Sergeevna?

IRINA. She's somewhere in the garden . . . I'll go look for her.

VERSHININ. Would you be so kind? I'm in a hurry.

ANFISA. I'll go and look. [*Shouts.*] Mashenka, yo-ho! [*Goes with* IRINA *to the back of the garden.*] Yo-ho! Yo-ho!

VERSHININ. Everything comes to an end. So here we stand saying our last good-bye. [*Looks at his watch.*] The town gave us something like a luncheon, we drank champagne, the mayor made a speech; I ate and listened, but in my heart and soul I was here with you . . . [*Looks around the garden.*] I've come to feel at home with you.

OLGA. Shall we meet again sometime?

6. "Don't make a noise, Sophie is already asleep. You are a bear!"

VERSHININ. I don't believe we shall. [*Pause.*] My wife and two little girls will live here for the next two months or so. Please, if something happens or if they need . . .

OLGA. Yes, yes, of course. Don't worry. [*Pause.*] In the town tomorrow not a single soldier will be here, everything will have become a memory, and, of course, a new life will begin for us . . . [*Pause.*] Nothing turns out the way we want it to. I did not want to be a headmistress, but all the same I am one. That means we shall never live in Moscow . . .

VERSHININ. Well . . . Thanks to you for everything . . . Forgive me, if what I've done was not so . . . Too much, oh, I've talked much too much—and for that forgive me, don't think harshly of me.

OLGA. [*wipes eyes*] Why is it Masha doesn't come . . .

VERSHININ. What else can I say to you in saying good-bye forever? If I dropped into philosophy, what could I say? . . [*Laughs.*] Life is hard. To many of us it seems a bit faint, lonely, and without hope. Yet we must admit life is becoming easier and brighter all the time. The time will come—it's not far off, it seems—the time will come when everything will become clear and bright. [*Looks at watch.*] It's time for me, it's time! In the old days, people were busy fighting wars, filling out their existence with campaigns, invasions, victories. Nowadays all that has died out, and we are left with a huge empty place—with nothing at all to fill it. People are searching passionately for something, and of course, they will find it. Oh, if only it would come as soon as possible. [*Pause.*] If only, you know, we could add education to the drive for hard work—and the drive for hard work to education. [*Looks at watch.*] It's time for me, really it is . . .

OLGA. There, she's coming.

MASHA *enters.*

VERSHININ. I've come to say good-bye . . .

OLGA *walks off a little to the side, in order not to hinder the parting.*

MASHA. [*looking into his face*] Good-bye . . .

A *prolonged kiss.*

OLGA. Enough, that will do, please . . .

MASHA *sobs loudly.*

VERSHININ. Write me . . . Don't forget! Now, let me go . . . it's time . . . Olga Sergeevna, take her, it's already . . . time for me . . . I am late . . .

Deeply moved, he kisses OLGA'S *hand, then embraces* MASHA *once more and quickly goes out.*

OLGA. Enough, Masha! Stop it, dear . . .

KULYGIN *enters.*

KULYGIN. [*embarrassed*] Nothing, let her cry, let her . . . My fine Masha, my good Masha . . . You're my wife, and I'm happy, whatever has happened . . . I don't complain, and I don't give you one single reproach . . . Here is Olya as my witness . . . We'll start to

live once more as of old, and I won't say a single word, not even a
hint . . .

MASHA. [*restraining her sobbing*]

> "By the curved seashore stands an oak tree green;
> A golden chain to that oak is bound . . .
> A golden chain to that oak is bound . . ."

I am going out of my mind . . .

> "By the curved seashore . . . stands an oak tree green . . ."

OLGA. Get hold of yourself, Masha . . . Get hold . . . Give her some
water.

MASHA. I am not crying anymore . . .

KULYGIN. She's stopped crying . . . she is a good woman . . .
There is heard a faint shot, far off.

MASHA. "By the curved seashore stands an oak tree green;
> A golden chain to that oak is bound . . .
> A tomcat green . . . an oak tree green . . ."

I'm getting it all mixed up . . . [*Drinks water.*] My life is a failure . . . There's nothing I want now . . . I'll get hold of myself in a
moment . . . It doesn't matter . . . What does it mean, "By a
curved seashore"? Why is it those words keep going through my
mind? I'm all mixed up in my thoughts.

> IRINA *enters.*

OLGA. Get hold of yourself, Masha. Well, that's my good girl . . .
Let's go inside.

MASHA. [*angrily*] I never shall go in there. [*Sobs, but stops herself immediately.*] I no longer go into that house, and I never
shall go . . .

IRINA. Let's sit down together for a while, we don't need to talk.
Tomorrow, you know, I shall be leaving . . . [*Pause.*]

KULYGIN. Yesterday I took this moustache and beard from a certain
little boy in the third class . . . [*Puts on moustache and beard.*]
I look like the German language teacher . . . [*Laughs.*] Isn't that
true? Those boys are funny.

MASHA. You certainly do look like that German of yours.

OLGA. [*laughs*] Yes. [MASHA *weeps.*]

IRINA. That will do, Masha!

KULYGIN. Very much like . . .

> NATASHA *enters.*

NATASHA. [*to the* MAIDSERVANT] What? Protopopov, Mikhail
Ivanych, will sit with Sofochka, and let Andrey Sergeich push
Bobik in the carriage. What a fuss there is with children . . . [*To*
IRINA.] Irina, you are leaving tomorrow. What a shame it is. At
least stay another little week. [*Having seen* KULYGIN, *she screams.*
KULYGIN *laughs and takes off the moustache and beard.*] Oh, you,
what in the . . . you scared me to death! [*To* IRINA.] I've gotten

used to you, and do you think saying good-bye to you is going to
be easy? I'll order Andrey with his violin to move into your room—
let him saw away in there—and we can put Sofochka into his
room. A delightful, marvelous child! What a good little girl!
Today she looked at me with those eyes of hers and—out came,
"Mama"!

KULYGIN. A fine child, that's true.

NATASHA. That means tomorrow I will be alone here. [*Sighs.*]
First of all I'll order this avenue of fir trees cut down, then that
maple there . . . In the evenings it's so ugly . . . [*To* IRINA.] My
dear, that belt doesn't suit you at all . . . It's tasteless . . . You
must wear something or other a little brighter. And here I'll order
little flowers planted everywhere, little flowers, and there'll be
scent . . . [*Severely.*] Why is there a fork lying about on the
bench? [*Going to the house, to the* MAIDSERVANT.] Why is there
a fork lying about on the bench, I ask you? [*Shouts.*] Don't you
dare back talk me!

KULYGIN. She's off and running again!
    *Behind the scene the music being played is a march; everyone
    listens.*

OLGA. They are going away.
    CHEBUTYKIN *enters.*

MASHA. Our friends are going away. Oh, well, hmm . . . A happy
journey to them! [*To her husband.*] We must go home . . .
Where are my hat and cape?

KULYGIN. I took them into the house . . . I'll bring them at once.
[*Goes into the house.*]

OLGA. Yes, now we can all go to our homes. It's time.

CHEBUTYKIN. Olga Sergeevna!

OLGA. What? [*Pause.*] What?

CHEBUTYKIN. Nothing . . . I don't know how to tell you . . . [*Whispers in her ear.*]

OLGA. [*frightened*] It isn't possible!

CHEBUTYKIN. Yes . . . That's the story . . . I am tired, worn out, I
don't want to say any more . . . [*Irritated.*] Besides, it doesn't
matter!

MASHA. What happened?

OLGA. [*embraces* IRINA] A terrible day today . . . I don't know how
to tell you, my precious . . .

IRINA. What? Tell me quickly, what? For the love of God! [*Weeps.*]

CHEBUTYKIN. Just now in a duel the Baron was killed . . .

IRINA. [*weeps quietly*] I knew it, I knew it . . .

CHEBUTYKIN. [*at the back of the stage, he sits on the bench*] I a
tired . . . [*Takes newspaper out of his pocket.*] Let them cry
. . . [*Sings quietly.*] "Ta-ra-ra . . . boom-di-yah . . . sitting on a
curb today . . ." What does it matter, anyway!
    The three sisters stand, pressing next to one another.

MASHA. Oh, listen to the band playing! They are leaving us, one has gone, gone, gone forever, we are left alone, to begin our life over again. We must live . . . We must live . . .

IRINA. [*places her head on* OLGA's *breast*] The time will come when everyone shall know the reason for all this, the reason why people must suffer, there shall be no more secrets, ever, but for the time being we must live . . . we must work, we must only work! Tomorrow I shall go alone, I'll teach in a school, and I'll give my whole life to those who may need it. It is autumn now, soon winter will come, it will cover everything with snow, and I shall work, I shall work . . .

OLGA. [*embraces both her sisters*] Listen, listen to the band play— so joyfully, so happily, you want to live! Oh, dear God in Heaven! Time will pass, and we shall be gone forever. We won't be remembered, they'll forget what we looked like, forget our voices and how many of us there were. But our sufferings can turn to joy for those who live after us. In time happiness and peace will come to this earth, and people will remember and speak kindly and bless those of us who live now. Oh, my dear sisters, our life is not over yet. We shall live, we shall! The band plays so joyfully, so happily, and it seems that in a little while we shall know the reason we live, the reason we suffer . . . If only we knew, if only we knew!

> *The band plays more and more softly;* KULYGIN, *happy, smiling, brings the hat and cape,* ANDREY *wheels the baby carriage, in which Bobik is sitting.*

CHEBUTYKIN. [*sings quietly*] "Tara . . . ra . . . boom-di-yah . . . sitting on a curb today . . ." [*Reads newspaper.*] It doesn't matter! It doesn't matter!

OLGA. If only we knew, if only we knew!

CURTAIN

The Cherry Orchard

For the environment of his last play, Chekhov returned to the scene of his earlier major plays, that is, against the background of the life style on a provincial estate, the transition from the old order to the new takes place. Three of the four acts occur inside the house on the estate, and Chekhov in his letters explained the kind of house he had in mind. "It's an old manor house. Some time ago the people who lived there did so on a very rich scale, and this must be felt in the setting. A feeling of richness and cosiness" (*Complete Works*, XX, 154). About three weeks later, in a letter (November 5, 1903) to Stanislavsky—one of the directors of the first production at the Moscow Art Theatre—Chekhov expanded on his conception of the house.

> The house . . . consists of two stories and is large. . . . The house must be large and sturdy; whether of wood . . . or stone, it doesn't matter. It is very old and grand, people on vacation do not rent these houses; such houses are usually pulled down, and the material is utilized for the building of summer vacation homes. The furniture is old, has style, is sturdy. Debts and financial disaster have not touched the furnishings and furniture. When a house like this is purchased, then people reason thusly: it's cheaper and easier to build a new smaller one, than to repair this old one. [*Complete Works*, XX, 176–77]

In a similar way, Chekhov had fairly concrete ideas as to the nature of his characters as well as to who in the Moscow Art Theatre company should play them. For example, he was distressed that MKhAT had neglected to hire an older actress who could play Lyubov Andreevna Ranevskaya. "I spent three years preparing to write *The Cherry Orchard*," he complained to Nemirovich-Danchenko, "and for three years I've been telling you to engage an actress for the role of Lyubov Andreevna" (*Complete Works*, XX, 173). To his wife, the actress Olga Knipper, he explained the role of Ranevskaya:

> You will play Lyubov Andreevna since there's no one else who can. She isn't dressed luxuriously, but with great taste. She is intelligent, very kind, absent-minded; she feels deeply for everyone she meets; always has a smile on her face. . . . No, I never wanted to make Ranevskaya someone who has calmed down. It would take death to calm a woman like that. But perhaps I don't understand what you intended to say. It's not difficult to play Ranevskaya; it's only necessary to strike the correct tone from the very beginning; it's necessary to come up with a smile and a style of smiling; it's necessary to know how to dress. Well, you'll succeed in all that if you've made up your mind to do so and with good health. [*Complete Works*, XX, 153, 164–65]

Ranevskaya's brother Gaev was apparently written with A. L. Vishnevsky (1861–1943) in mind. "Gaev is for Vishnevsky," Chekhov told his wife.

"Ask Vishnevsky to listen to how people play billiards and to write down as many billiard terms as possible. I don't play billiards, or I played once upon a time and have forgotten everything by now, and everything in the play is by mere chance. Later on I can arrange it with Vishnevsky, and I'll insert everything that's needed" (*Complete Works*, XX, 154). Eventually Stanislavsky played the role of Gaev.

Even though Chekhov had written the role of Lopakhin with Stanislavsky in mind, L. M. Leonidov (1873–1941) played it. "Stanislavsky will be a very good and original Gaev," Chekhov wrote his wife, "but at the same time who will play Lopakhin? You know, don't you, that the role of Lopakhin is central. If it doesn't succeed, then that means the whole play will flop. Lopakhin shouldn't be played by someone who shouts, and he doesn't inevitably have to be a [typical] merchant. He is a gentle person" (*Complete Works*, XX, 169). In an earlier letter, Chekhov had declared that Lopakhin was "not a merchant in the vulgar meaning of that word" (*Complete Works*, XX, 167). Chekhov explained to Stanislavsky:

> When I wrote the role of Lopakhin, I thought that it was your role. If for some reason or other you don't like it, then take Gaev. Lopakhin, it's true, is a merchant but an honest person in all its meanings, and he must behave as one who is completely decent and intelligent. He is not one bit petty, without tricks, and it seemed to me that with you in this role, which is central in the play, you would be brilliant. If you take Gaev, then give Lopakhin to Vishnevsky. It won't be an artistic Lopakhin, but at least it won't be petty. Luzhsky [V.V., 1869–1931] will be a cold foreigner in this role. Leonidov will make him a tight-fisted peasant [*kulaček*]. In the selection of an actor for this role, don't lose sight [of the fact] that Lopakhin was loved by Varya, a serious and religious girl; she wouldn't fall in love with a tight-fisted peasant. [*Complete Works*, XX, 170]

In a letter to Nemirovich-Danchenko, Chekhov expanded on his conception of Lopakhin. "Lopakhin has a white waistcoat and yellow boots. Waving his arms as he walks, he takes wide steps, and while walking he thinks; he walks in a straight line. His hair is not short, and that's the reason he so often throws back his head; he absent-mindedly combs his beard, from back to front, i.e., from his neck to his mouth" (*Complete Works*, XX, 172). Leonidov recalled that Chekhov told him that Lopakhin must resemble in part a merchant, in part a professor of medicine at Moscow University. Later, at a rehearsal after the performance of Act III, Chekhov told Leonidov: "Listen, Lopakhin doesn't shout. He is rich, and rich people never shout" (*Chekhov and Theatre*, p. 351).

As to the role of Anya, Chekhov believed that it should be played by a young actress who "looks like a little girl and speaks in a young, resounding voice" (*Complete Works*, XX, 172). Although the role was eventually played by Maria Petrovna Lilina (1866–1943), the wife of Stanislavsky, Chekhov did not want her to play the role since "she will be an old-fashioned girl with a squeaky voice and nothing more" (*Complete Works*, XX, 180). In place of playing Anya, Lilina would be much better in the role of Varya, Chekhov thought. Listing the characteristics of Varya, Chekhov noted: "somewhat crude and somewhat stupid, but very kind" and "a figure in a black dress, a nun, a foolish girl, a crybaby, and so on, and so on" (*Complete Works*, XX, 154, 172). In a letter to Nemirovich-Danchenko, Chekhov compared Ranevskaya's two daughters in terms of what he had written and what he feared was happening to them in rehearsal:

> I'm afraid Anya will have a tone of voice much too teary (you for some reason or other think she resembles Irina [in *The Three Sisters*]). . . . Not once does Anya weep in my play, nowhere does she speak in a tearful tone; in the second act she has tears in her eyes, but her tone is joyful, lively. Why in your telegram do you say that there are many weeping persons in the play? Where are they? The only one is Varya, but that's because Varya is a crybaby by nature, and her tears shouldn't create feelings of depression in the auditorium. In my play you'll often see the expression "through tears," but that shows only the mood of the characters, and not their tears. [*Complete Works*, XX, 162–63]

As to the secondary characters, Chekhov noted that "Sharlotta speaks pure, not broken, Russian. . . . occasionally mixing up hard and soft consonants at the ends of words and confusing adjectives of the masculine and feminine gender. Pishchik is a Russian, crippled with gout, old age, and chock-full of the good things in life . . . dressed in a long peasant coat . . . boots without heels" (*Complete Works*, XX, 172). For the production of the play, Stanislavsky decided to introduce the sounds of nature and a train in Act II. Chekhov objected to the sounds and agreed to a train providing there was no sound. (*Complete Works*, XX, 189–90.) Chekhov was not particularly pleased with the production by the Moscow Art Theatre. Writing to Olga Knipper in March 1904, Chekhov reported that Lulu and K. L. [relatives of his wife] had been to see *The Cherry Orchard*: "Both of them say that Stanislavsky [as Gaev] plays loathsomely in Act IV, that he drags out everything in a painful way. How terrible this is! An act, which must last twelve minutes at a maximum, takes you forty minutes. I can say only one thing: Stanislavsky has been the undoing of my play. Oh, well, never mind him" (*Complete Works*, XX, 258).

As in all his major plays, Chekhov incorporated literary allusions that enrich the texture of *The Cherry Orchard*. Three allusions are discussed here. In Act II, just after the characters who are sitting outside near an old chapel have finished talking about "the sound of a string breaking that dies away sadly" (p. 188), a passer-by, slightly drunk, enters and recites:

"Oh, my brother, my suffering brother . . . come out to the Volga, whose moan . . ." [p. 188].

The first phrase, "Oh, my brother, my suffering brother," is part of the opening line of a poem (1881) by S. Ya. Nadson (1862–87), in which is expressed the faith that love shall overcome the evil existing in the world and usher in a new age cleansed of war, slavery, and falsehood. The second part of the recitation—"come out to the Volga, whose moan . . ."—is part of a line from a famous poem, "Reflections at the Main Entrance" (1858), by N. A. Nakrasov (1821–78), in which the poet observes a group of village peasants arrive at the front door (guarded by a doorman) of an important official in St. Petersburg. They petition for an audience to hear their grievances; the official is sleeping; the doorman refuses admittance; and they go away peacefully. The section beginning "Come out to the Volga, whose moan is heard" introduces a poetic image that compares the great sorrow of the people (*narod*) flooding all Russia to the lesser springtime overflow by the Volga into the surrounding fields. In keeping with the Chekhovian dramaturgical principle of balancing, e.g., characters, dialogue, ideas, emotional keys, etc., Nadson's expression of faith is contrasted with Nekrasov's sorrowful moans of the Volga and the Russian people.

In Act III, during the party given by Ranevskaya, the station master recites "The Sinful Woman" (1857) by Aleksey Tolsoy (1817–75). The group listens to him, "but he has recited only a few lines when the sounds of a waltz come from the entrance hall and the reading is broken off" (p. 196). The poem of about two hundred lines narrates the sudden religious conversion of a beautiful sinner to a new Christian life by John of Galilee and Christ without benefit of psychological motivation or dialogue on the part of the converters. The poem begins with a feast at a rich house in Palestine, and thus the opening lines of the poem parody Ranevskaya and her strong attachment to her lover in Paris, as well as the party given on the very day of the auction of the estate. The opening lines of the poem are:

> The crowd is seething, happily laughter sounds
> With lutes ringing, the clashing of cymbals resounds
> Around and about growing flowers and plantings green
> Between the pillars are seen . . .[1]

To get the play accepted by the censorship office, Chekhov made two important changes in Act II. The first deleted passage (restored after 1917) reads: "everyone can see that the workers are detestably fed, sleep without suitable bedding, thirty to forty in a room with bedbugs everywhere, the stench, the dampness, and the moral corruption" (p. 187). The following passage was substituted in its place: "the great majority of us, ninety-nine out of a hundred, live like wild persons, at the slightest provocation swearing and shoving fists into mouths, eat revolting food, sleep in mud and bad air" (*Complete Works*, XI, 600). The second deleted passage (restored after 1917) reads: "To own human souls—it has transformed every one of you, don't you see, those who lived before and those living today. And so your mother, your uncle, and you no longer realize that you are living in debt, at the expense of other people, at the expense of the very people you will allow no farther than the entrance to your home" (pp. 189–200). The following passage was substituted in its place: "Oh, it's terrible, your orchard is frightening. When in the evening or at night you walk in the garden, then the old bark on the trees gives out a glow and it seems the cherry trees are apparently dreaming of what happened one or two hundred years ago, and painful visions weigh them down. Why talk about it?" (*Complete Works*, XI, 600.)

As in all his major plays, Chekhov selected appropriate names for his characters in *The Cherry Orchard*. For example, the first name of Ranev-

---

1. A. K. Tolstoy, *Sobranie sočinenij* 507.
[Collected works] (Moscow, 1963), I,

skaya is the Russian word for *love*, whereas her patronymic, *Andreevna*, means "daughter of manly." Her last name incorporates the name of Nevsky, or "of the Neva," accorded to Novgorod's prince, Alexander, who won a great battle on the Neva River in the thirteenth century; hence, the aristocratic tone of *Lyubov Andreevna Ranevskaya*. Her brother, Gaev, has been given a first name which is a variant of the Latin *Leo*, meaning "lion; brave as a lion," a parody on his disposition or the bent of his character. The name *Yepikhodov* incorporates the Russian word meaning "motion, speed, run"; whereas the double last name *Simeonov-Pishchik* implies "a broad comic figure," Magarshack points out. "The first half of it is impressively aristocratic and the second farcical (its English equivalent would be Squeaker)" (*Chekhov the Dramatist*, p. 284).

The pronunciation of the characters' names, together with the appropriate stress:

Lyubov (lyubóf) Andréevna Ranevskaya (ranéfskaya) (Lyúba)
Ánya
Várya (Varvára Mikhaylovna) (mikháylavna)
Leonid (leanít) Andréevich (Andréich) Gaev (gáef) (Lyónya)
Yermolay (yermaláy) Alexéevich (Alexéich) Lopakhin (lapákhin)
Pyótr (Pétya) Sergéevich (Sergéich) Trofimov (trafímaf)
Boris (barís) Borisovich (barísavich) Simeonov (simeónaf)-Píshchik
Sharlótta Ivanovna (ivánavna)
Semyón Pantaléevich (Pantaléich) Yepikhodov (yepikhódaf)
Dunyásha (Avdótya) Fyodorvna (fyódaravna)
Fírs Nikolaevich (nikaláevich)
Yásha

The pronunciation of other Russian words (in alphabetical order), together with the appropriate stress, are: Anastásy; Ánichka; dácha; Dáshenka; Deriganov (derigánaf); Grísha; Kardamonov (kardamónaf); lezgínka; Lopakhina (lapákhina); mamásha; Mamochka (mámachka); Mentóne; nyánya; papásha; Petrúshka; Pólya; Ragúlins; Yaroslavl (yaraslávl); Yashnevo (yáshneva); Yefímyushka; Yegór; Yevstigney (yefstignéy); Znoykov (znóykaf).

The Cherry Orchard

A Comedy in Four Acts

LIST OF CHARACTERS

LYUBOV ANDREEVNA RANEVSKAYA, *a landowner*
ANYA, *her daughter, age seventeen*
VARYA, *her adopted daughter, age twenty-four*
LEONID ANDREEVICH GAEV, *brother of Mrs. Ranevskaya*
YERMOLAY ALEXEEVICH LOPAKHIN, *a merchant*
PYOTR SERGEEVICH TROFIMOV, *a student*
BORIS BORISOVICH SIMEONOV-PISHCHIK, *a landowner*
SHARLOTTA IVANOVNA, *a governess*
SEMYON PANTELEEVICH YEPIKHODOV, *a clerk*
DUNYASHA, *a maidservant*
FIRS, *an old manservant, age eighty-seven*
YASHA, *a young manservant*
A PASSER-BY
A STATIONMASTER
A POST OFFICE CIVIL SERVANT
GUESTS *and* SERVANTS

The action takes place on the estate of MRS. RANEVSKAYA.

Act One

A room that still goes by the name of the nursery. One of the doors leads to ANYA'S *room. It is dawn and the sun will soon come up. It is May. The cherry trees are in flower, but in the orchard it is cold, there is morning frost. The windows in the room are closed. Enter* DUNYASHA *with a candle and* LOPAKHIN *with a book in his hand.*

LOPAKHIN. The train's arrived, thank the Lord. What's the time?

DUNYASHA. Almost two o'clock. [*Extinguishes the candle.*] It's already light.

LOPAKHIN. How late was the train, how many hours? About two, at least. [*Yawns and stretches himself.*] Of all the stupid tricks to pull, damned if I haven't gone and done it again. I came here on purpose so I could meet them at the station, and before you know it, I slept right through it . . . Went dead to sleep sitting up. Annoying, that's what . . . If only you might've awakened me.

DUNYASHA. I thought you'd left. [*Listens.*] There, I think they're coming now.

LOPAKHIN. [*listens*] No . . . they've got luggage to get, and one

165

thing or another . . . [*Pause.*] Lyubov Andreevna has been living five years abroad, and I don't know what she's become now . . . She's a very fine person. An obliging person, simple. I remember when I was a youngster about fifteen, my father—he's dead now but at the time he was a shopkeeper in the village here—hit me in the face with his fist. The blood ran out of my nose . . . We had come to the yard here for some reason, and he'd been drinking. Lyubov Andreevna, as I remember right now, was still very young, such a slim woman she was. She led me over to the washstand here in this very room, the nursery. "Don't cry, little peasant," she says "it will heal before your wedding . . ." [*Pause.*] Little peasant . . . It's true my father was a peasant, and here I am in a white waistcoat and yellow boots. Like a pig's nozzle showing up in a row of wedding cakes . . . It's just that I'm rich, lots of money for sure, but if you really think about it and look into it, you'll know I'm just a peasant through and through . . . [*Turns the pages of the book.*] I read this book and didn't catch on to a single thing. I was reading and fell right to sleep. [*Pause.*]

DUNYASHA. The dogs didn't sleep the whole night. They can sense their masters are coming.

LOPAKHIN. What is it with you, Dunyasha, such . . .

DUNYASHA. My hands are shaking. I'm going to faint.

LOPAKHIN. You're really delicate, Dunyasha, too much so. You dress yourself like a lady, and your hair is fixed up the same way. You can't do things like that. Better remember who you are.

YEPIKHODOV *enters, carrying a bouquet. He wears a jacket and brightly scrubbed high boots that squeak loudly. Entering, he drops the bouquet.*

YEPIKHODOV. [*picks up the bouquet*] Here's what the gardener sent, he says to put them in the dining room. [*Gives the bouquet to* DUNYASHA.]

LOPAKHIN. And bring me some kvas.[1]

DUNYASHA. Yes, sir. [*Goes out.*]

YEPIKHODOV. There's morning frost right now, three degrees of frost, but the cherry trees are all in bloom. I can't approve of our climate. [*Sighs.*] I can't. Our climate just can't promote the most suitable time. Here, Yermolay Alexeich, be so kind as to let me append to you, I bought myself these boots the day before yesterday, and they, I make bold to assure you, they squeak so it's beyond the realm of possibility. What should I lubricate them with?

LOPAKHIN. Leave me alone. I'm sick and tired of you.

YEPIKHODOV. Every day some catastrophe happens to me. But I don't grumble. I'm used to it, and I even smile. [DUNYASHA *enters and gives* LOPAKHIN *kvas.*] I'm going. [*Stumbles against a chair, which falls.*] There . . . [*As if he is celebrating it.*] There you see, excuse the expression, the kind of circumstance I bump

1. See note 5, p. 152 (*The Three Sisters*).

into, by the way . . . It's simply even out of this world! [*Goes out.*]

DUNYASHA. Oh, Yermolay Alexeich, I must confess Yepikhodov made a proposal to me.

LOPAKHIN. Oh!

DUNYASHA. I really don't know how . . . he's a mild sort of person, but those times he starts talking, you can't figure out a thing he says. Oh, it's very fine and there's plenty of feeling in it, only nothing makes a bit of sense. I'm pretty sure I like him. He's madly in love with me. He's an unlucky person, and there's something or other every day. That's why they keep teasing him, calling him "Two-and-Twenty Hard Knocks . . ."

LOPAKHIN. [*listening*] There, I think they're coming . . .

DUNYASHA. They're coming! Oh, what's the matter with me . . . I've gotten colder all over.

LOPAKHIN. They're coming, it's a fact. Let's go and meet them. Will she recognize me, I wonder? It's been five years since we've seen each other.

DUNYASHA. [*agitated*] I'm going to faint right now . . . Oh, I know I'm going to faint!

    Two carriages are heard driving up to the house. LOPAKHIN *and* DUNYASHA *quickly go out. The stage is empty. The sound of hubbub begins in the adjoining rooms. Leaning on a stick,* FIRS *hurriedly goes across the stage. He has been to the station to meet* LYUBOV ANDREEVNA. *He wears old-fashioned livery and a high hat. He keeps saying something to himself, but not a single word can be understood. The noise offstage keeps growing louder. A voice is heard saying: Let's go through here." Enter, all walking through the room,* LYUBOV ANDREEVNA, ANYA, *and* SHARLOTTA IVANOVNA *with a small dog on a chain—all are in traveling clothes—*VARYA, *wearing an overcoat and a scarf over her head,* GAEV, SIMEONOV-PISHCHIK, LOPAKHIN, DUNYASHA *with a bundle and an umbrella, and servants with luggage.*

ANYA. Let's go through here. Mama, do you remember what room this is?

LYUBOV ANDREEVNA. [*jubilantly, through tears*] The nursery!

VARYA. How cold it is, my hands are growing numb. [*To* LYUBOV ANDREEVNA.] Your rooms are the very same as they were, Mamochka,[2] white and violet.

LYUBOV ANDREEVNA. The nursery, my dear, beautiful room . . . I slept here when I was a little girl . . . [*Weeps.*] And now I'm like a little girl again . . . [*Kisses her brother and* VARYA, *then her brother again.*] Varya is just the same as she's always been, she still looks like a nun. And I recognized Dunyasha . . . [*Kisses* DUNYASHA.]

GAEV. The train was two hours late. That's something, isn't it? What a way to manage things, wouldn't you say?

2. Intimate nickname for *Mama*.

SHARLOTTA. [*to* PISHCHIK] My dog eats nuts, too.

PISHCHIK. [*surprised*] What do you think of that!

All go out except ANYA *and* DUNYASHA.

DUNYASHA. We've been waiting and expecting you for so long . . . [*Takes off* ANYA's *overcoat and hat.*]

ANYA. I haven't slept four whole nights on the way . . . now I feel terribly cold.

DUNYASHA. You went away during Lent, it was snowing and there was a frost then, but now? My dear! [*Laughs and kisses her.*] I've been waiting so long for you, my precious darling . . . I must tell you right now, I can't stand it another minute . . .

ANYA. [*listlessly*] Not something again, surely . . .

DUNYASHA. Right after Holy Week the clerk Yepikhodov made a proposal to me.

ANYA. You keep going on about the same thing . . . [*Adjusting her hair.*] I've been losing all my hairpins . . . [*She is very exhausted, she even staggers and sways.*]

DUNYASHA. I really don't know what to think. He's in love with me, he loves me so!

ANYA. [*looks through the door into her own room, affectionately*] My own room, my windows, it's just as if I'd never gone away. I'm home, home! Tomorrow morning I'll get up and run out to the orchard . . . Oh, if only I could fall asleep! I didn't get one wink of sleep the whole way coming back, I wore myself out worrying.

DUNYASHA. Pyotr Sergeich arrived the day before yesterday.

ANYA. [*jubilantly*] Petya!

DUNYASHA. He's asleep in the bathhouse, it's where he's living. "I'm afraid," he says, "of getting in their way." [*Having looked at her pocket watch.*] He ought to be wakened, but Varvara Mikhaylovna gave the word not to. "Don't you go and wake him," she says.

VARYA *enters; she has a bunch of keys on her belt.*

VARYA. Dunyasha, bring some coffee quickly . . . *Mamochka* is asking for some.

DUNYASHA. It won't be a minute. [*Goes out.*]

VARYA. Well, thank the Lord, you've all come back. You're home again. [*Adoringly.*] My precious is here, my beautiful darling has come back!

ANYA. I've had a horrible time of it.

VARYA. I can well imagine!

ANYA. I left just before Easter. It was cold at the time. Sharlotta kept on talking and doing her silly conjuring tricks the whole way there. Why you tacked Sharlotta onto me, I'll never know . . .

VARYA. You couldn't have gone all alone, my precious. At seventeen!

ANYA. We finally got to Paris and found it cold and snowing. My French was terrible. Mama was living on the fifth floor, and when

I came to her place, some French people were visiting, ladies and an old priest with a little book. It was filled with smoke and not one bit cozy. All of a sudden I felt sorry for Mama, so sorry for her, I took her head in my arms and pressed her close to me and simply couldn't let go. Afterwards Mama tried to make everything up to me, she was gentle and sweet and she kept crying. . .

VARYA. [*through tears*] Don't go on talking about it, don't . . .

ANYA. She'd already sold her dacha near Mentone,[3] and she had nothing left, nothing. I didn't have anything either, not a single kopek. We scarcely had enough to get here. But Mama just can't understand it! Whenever we sit down for dinner at the station, she keeps demanding the most expensive things and tipping the waiters a ruble each. Sharlotta's the same way. Yasha keeps demanding his share, too, it was simply terrible. Yasha is Mama's servant, you know. We brought him here with us . . .

VARYA. I've seen the scoundrel.

ANYA. Well, then, how are things going here? Have you paid the interest?

VARYA. Not a chance in the world.

ANYA. Dear God in heaven, dear God . . .

VARYA. The estate will be sold in August . . .

ANYA. Dear God in heaven . . .

LOPAKHIN. [*looks in through the door and bleats like a calf*] Meh-meh-meh . . . [*Goes out.*]

VARYA. [*through tears*] Oh, I'd like to give him something . . . [*Threatens with her fist.*]

ANYA. [*embraces* VARYA, *quietly*] Varya, has he proposed to you? [VARYA *shakes her head.*] Surely he loves you . . . Why don't the two of you talk it out, what on earth are you waiting for?

VARYA. I don't think anything will come of it. He has so many things to do he hasn't one bit of time for me . . . and he doesn't pay one bit of attention to me, either. God help him, I've had enough. It bothers me just to see him . . . Everyone is talking about our wedding and offering congratulations, but in fact there's nothing to it. It's all like a dream . . . [*In a different tone of voice.*] You have a brooch that looks something like a little bee.

ANYA. [*sadly*] Mama bought it. [*Goes into her own room and speaks happily like a child.*] You know in Paris I flew up in a balloon!

VARYA. My precious is here, my beautiful darling has come back! [DUNYASHA *has already returned with a coffee pot and is preparing coffee.* VARYA *stands near the door.*] I spend the whole day managing the house, my precious, but I keep dreaming and dreaming. I'd like to see you married to a rich person, and then I wouldn't feel troubled at all. I could start out to a cloister, and then on to Kiev[4] . . . to Moscow, and so I'd keep walking

---

3. Summer vacation home. Mentone is located on the Mediterranean coast of France.

4. See note 5, p. 9 (*The Sea Gull*).

from one holy place to the next . . . I'd keep on walking and walking. What a blessed way to live! . .

ANYA. The birds are singing in the orchard. What time is it now?

VARYA. It must be past two. It's time for you to go to sleep, my precious. [*Going into* ANYA's *room.*] What a blessed way to live!

YASHA *enters with a rug and a traveling bag.*

YASHA. [*goes across the stage, delicately*] Is it possible for one to go through here, Miss?

DUNYASHA. A person wouldn't recognize you, Yasha. You've become something else since you've been abroad.

YASHA. Hmm . . . and who are you?

DUNYASHA. When you left here, I was about as big as this . . . [*Indicates distance from the floor.*] I'm Dunyasha, the daughter of Fyodor Kozoedov. You can't remember me!

YASHA. Hmm . . . Saucy little cucumber! [*Looks around and embraces her. She screams and drops a saucer.* YASHA *quickly goes out.*]

VARYA. [*in a dissatisfied tone of voice, in the doorway*] What's going on now?

DUNYASHA. [*through tears*] I broke a saucer . . .

VARYA. It's a good sign.

ANYA. [*coming out of her room*] Mama ought to be warned in advance that Petya's here . . .

VARYA. I gave word not to wake him.

ANYA. [*deep in thought*] Six years ago father died, and a month later our brother Grisha drowned in the river. He was a beautiful little boy, just seven years old. Mama couldn't stand it anymore, and she went away, she went away without so much as a backward glance . . . [*Shudders.*] How well I can understand her, if she only knew! [*Pause.*] But Petya Trofimov was Grisha's tutor, and he might bring to mind . . .

FIRS *enters, wearing a jacket and white waistcoat.*

FIRS. [*goes to the coffee pot, anxiously*] The mistress will sup in here . . . [*Puts on white gloves.*] Is the coffee prepared? [*To* DUNYASHA, *sternly.*] You there! And the cream?

DUNYASHA. Oh, dear God in heaven . . . [*Goes out quickly.*]

FIRS. [*bustling around the coffee pot*] Oh, you silly galoot, you . . . [*Mumbles to himself.*] She's come back from Paris . . . Once upon a time the master himself used to go to Paris . . . by carriage . . . [*Laughs.*]

VARYA. What is it, Firs?

FIRS. What can I do for you, please? [*Jubilantly.*] My mistress has come back! Home, home at last! I'm even ready to die now . . . [*Weeps from joy.*]

LYUBOV ANDREEVNA, GAEV, *and* SIMEONOV-PISHCHIK *enter.*
PISHCHIK *wears a long peasant coat[5] made out of thin*

---

5. Pishchik is wearing typical outdoor peasant clothing, i.e., the *poddëvka*, which is fitted at the waist, and, probably, long wide trousers tucked into his high boots.

cloth and high boots. Entering, GAEV *moves his arms and body as if he were playing billiards.*

LYUBOV ANDREEVNA. How does it go? Let me remember a bit . . . "Off the yellow into the corner pocket! Bank shot into the middle!"[6]

GAEV. An english shot into the corner! Once upon a time, sister, you and I used to sleep here in this very room, and now I'm fifty-one, fifty-one years old. Strange, isn't it . . .

LOPAKHIN. Yes, time flies.[7]

GAEV. How's that?

LOPAKHIN. Time flies, I was saying.

GAEV. This place reeks of patchouli.[8]

ANYA. I'm going to sleep now. Good night, Mama. [*Kisses her mother.*]

LYUBOV ANDREEVNA. My beloved little girl. [*Kisses her hands.*] You're glad you're home, aren't you? I just can't get hold of myself.

ANYA. Fare you well, Uncle.

GAEV. [*kisses her face and hands*] God be with you. Oh, you look so much like your mother! [*To his sister.*] When you were her age, Lyuba, you were exactly like she is.

> ANYA *gives her hand to* LOPAKHIN *and* PISHCHIK, *goes out, and shuts the door to her room.*

LYUBOV ANDREEVNA. She's completely exhausted.

PISHCHIK. Most likely it's the long trip.

VARYA. [*to* LOPAKHIN *and* PISHCHIK] Well, hmm, gentlemen? It's after two and time you said your good-byes.

LYUBOV ANDREEVNA. [*laughs*] You're the same as you've always been, Varya. [*Draws* VARYA *to her and kisses her.*] I'll just drink some coffee, then we'll all go away. [FIRS *puts a little cushion under her feet.*] Thank you, my dear. I'm used to coffee now. I drink it day and night. Thank you, my dear old man. [*Kisses* FIRS.]

VARYA. I must go and see if they've brought in all the things . . . [*Goes out.*]

LYUBOV ANDREEVNA. It can't really be me sitting here, can it? [*Laughs.*] I want to jump up, leap around, and wave my arms. [*Covers her face with her hands.*] But suddenly I feel I may only be sleeping! God can see I love my country, I love it warmly. I couldn't even see it from the train—I was crying the whole time. [*Through tears.*] All the same I must drink my coffee. Thank you, Firs, thank you, my dear old man. I'm so glad you're still alive.

FIRS. The day before yesterday.

---

6. Since it is not clear whether Chekhov himself intended an accurate correspondence with the game as it was played in his day, I have kept my translation of the billiard terms literal.

7. There is no stage direction pertaining to Lopakhin's return onstage; it is assumed that he enters with Lyubov Andreevna, Gaev, and Simeonov-Pishchik.

8. A perfume made from an East Indian mint.

GAEV. He's hard of hearing.

LOPAKHIN. I must start for Kharkov pretty soon, after four this morning. Damned annoying! I wanted to have more of a look at you, talk awhile . . . You're the same as you've always been, a magnificent person.

PISHCHIK. [*breathes heavily*] Even prettier . . . Wearing Parisian clothes . . . Oh, my, that's something! "Get lost, my cart," as the saying goes, "all four wheels . . ."

LOPAKHIN. Your brother, Leonid Andreich here, keeps talking about me, saying I'm a peasant, a scoundrel grabbing with both hands, but it doesn't matter what he says, not a bit. Let him go on talking. The only thing I want is for you to believe in me as you used to and look at me with your beautiful, gentle eyes as you did in times gone by. Oh, merciful God in heaven! My father was a serf, belonging to your grandfather and after him your father, but you—you personally—did so much for me once I've forgotten all that and I love you as if we were flesh and blood . . . even more than my own flesh and blood.

LYUBOV ANDREEVNA. I can't sit any longer, not the way I feel . . . [*Jumps up and walks in great agitation.*] I'm so happy I can't stand it . . . Go ahead and laugh at me, I know I'm silly . . . My own dear little bookcase . . . [*Kisses the bookcase.*] My own little table . . .

GAEV. Oh, when you were gone *nyanya*[9] died.

LYUBOV ANDREEVNA. [*sits down and drinks her coffee*] Yes, may God in heaven be with her. They wrote me.

GAEV. And Anastasy died. Petrushka—the squint-eyed fellow—left me and now he's with the police chief in town. [*Takes a box of hard candy out of his pocket and sucks one.*]

PISHCHIK. My daughter Dashenka . . . sends her regards to you . . .

LOPAKHIN. I want to tell you something very pleasing and cheerful. [*Having glanced at his watch.*] I'm on my way right now, there's no time to talk . . . Oh, well, I can get to it in two or three words. As you already know, your cherry orchard is being sold to pay off debts. The auction is set for August twenty-second, but you mustn't worry, my dear, you can sleep in peace. There's a way out . . . Here's my plan. I beg your close attention! Your estate is located only twenty versts[1] from town, the railroad goes nearby, and if the cherry orchard and the land by the river were broken up into residential lots and then leased for summer homes, you'll have an income, at the very least, of twenty-five thousand rubles each year.

GAEV. Excuse me, I've never heard such stuff and nonsense.

LYUBOV ANDREEVNA. I don't quite understand you, Yermolay Alexeich.

LOPAKHIN. You will get from the tenants, at the very least, twenty-

9. See note 2, p. 55 (*Uncle Vanya*).
1. A former Russian unit of measurement, the equivalent of about thirty-five
hundred feet.

five rubles a year for every plot of about three acres, and if you advertise right away, I'm willing to bet whatever you like that you won't have a sliver of land left by autumn. Every bit of it will be grabbed up. In short, I congratulate you. You are saved. It's a marvelous place for building, and the river is deep. Only one thing, of course, it must be cleaned up a little, whipped into shape . . . For example, you'll have to pull down all the old buildings, let's say, and this house here, which is no longer of any use, cut down the old cherry orchard . . .

LYUBOV ANDREEVNA. Cut down? My dear, forgive me, but you don't know what you're talking about. If there's anything at all in this whole district that's still exciting, even incredible, that one thing is our cherry orchard.

LOPAKHIN. The only thing incredible about that cherry orchard is that it's damn big. There's only one crop every two years, and when it comes there's plenty of cherries around, but nobody will buy them.

GAEV. This orchard is even mentioned in the *Encyclopedia*.[2]

LOPAKHIN. [*having glanced at his watch*] If we don't think of something or come up with an idea, the cherry orchard and the whole estate will be sold at auction on August twenty-second. You can make up your minds to it! There's no other way out, I swear it to you. None at all, none.

FIRS. In times before, about forty or fifty years ago, the cherries were dried, soaked, marinated, and jam was made, and it used to be . . .

GAEV. Be quiet, Firs.

FIRS. And it used to be they'd send cartloads of dried chereries off to Moscow and to Kharkov.[3] Oh, there was money galore! And dried cherries at that time were soft and juicy, sweet and a good smell to them . . . They knew a way of doing it at that time . . .

LYUBOV ANDREEVNA. And where on earth is that way now?

FIRS. They've forgotten. No one remembers it.

PISHCHIK [*to* LYUBOV ANDREEVNA] What's in Paris? How did it go? Did you eat frogs?

LYUBOV ANDREEVNA. I ate crocodiles.

PISHCHIK. What do you think of that . . .

LOPAKHIN. Until recently you'd find only gentlemen and peasants in town, and now people for the summer are showing up. All the cities, even the very smallest, are surrounded now with summer places. You might even say, in the course of about twenty years, these people will multiply beyond the wildest dreams. Nowadays the summer resident only drinks tea on his balcony, but you know it might happen he'll take up farming his own plot of ground, and

---

2. Probably the *Brockhaus and Efron Encyclopedic Dictionary*, which was issued by F. A. Brockhaus–I. A. Efron joint-stock publishing company in the period from 1890 to 1907 and which consisted of eighty-six volumes (eighty-two books and four supplements).

3. Kharkov (khárkaf), is a large city in the northeastern Ukraine.

then your cherry orchard will become happy, rich, sumptuous . . .

GAEV. [*exasperated*] I've never heard such stuff and nonsense.

VARYA *and* YASHA *enter.*

VARYA. *Mamochka*, there are two telegrams for you. [*Picks out a key and noisily opens an old bookcase.*] Here they are.

LYUBOV ANDREEVNA. They're from Paris. [*Tears up the telegrams without reading them.*] Paris is over and done with . . .

GAEV. Oh, Lyuba, do you know how old this bookcase is? Last week I pulled out the bottom drawer, I looked and saw some figures scorched on it. The bookcase was made exactly one hundred years ago. That's something, isn't it? Ah! We could celebrate its anniversary. It's an inanimate object, but all the same it's a receptacle for books, after all.

PISHCHIK. [*surprised*] One hundred years . . . What do you think of that! . .

GAEV. Yes . . . It's quite a thing . . . [*Having touched all parts of the bookcase.*] Dear, honored bookcase! I hail your existence. For more than one hundred years your very being has been directed to the shining ideals of cardinal good and justice. Your silent appeal to fruitful labor has never lessened in the course of a hundred years, upholding [*through tears*] in generations of our line personal courage and faith in a better future and nurturing in us the ideals of cardinal good and social consciousness. [*Pause.*]

LOPAKHIN. Yes . . .

LYUBOV ANDREEVNA. You're the same as you've always been, Lyonya.

GAEV. [*a little embarrassed*] Off the ball right into the corner pocket! An english shot into the middle!

LOPAKHIN. [*having glanced at his watch*] Well, time for me to go.

YASHA. [*handing medicine to* LYUBOV ANDREEVNA] Perhaps you'll take your pills now . . .

PISHCHIK. No need to take medicines, my dearest . . . Oh, no damage comes from it, no benefit, either . . . Here, let me have them . . . honored lady. [*Takes the pills, pours them into the palm of his hand, blows on them, puts them in his mouth, and drinks them down with kvas.*] There!

LYUBOV ANDREEVNA. [*frightened*] Why, you've lost your mind!

PISHCHIK. I've taken all the pills.

LOPAKHIN. It's a hog with a hollow leg!

Everyone laughs.

FIRS. The gentleman was visiting us in Holy Week and ate half a bucket of cucumbers . . . [*Mumbles to himself.*]

LYUBOV ANDREEVNA. What is it he's saying?

VARYA. He's been mumbling that way for three years now. We've become used to it.

YASHA. Old as Methuselah, I'd say.

SHARLOTTA IVANOVNA, *in a white dress, walks across the stage. She is very thin and tightly laced, with a lorgnette on her belt.*

LOPAKHIN. Forgive me, Sharlotta Ivanovna, I haven't had time yet to say how do you do to you. [*Wants to kiss her hand.*]

SHARLOTTA. [*taking her hand away*] If you were permitted to kiss my hand, why you'd want to go right to the elbow next, and then the shoulder . . .

LOPAKHIN. It's not my lucky day. [*Everyone laughs.*] Sharlotta Ivanovna, show us a trick or two!

LYUBOV ANDREEVNA. Yes, Sharlotta, show us a trick!

SHARLOTTA. I don't want to. I'd like to go to sleep. [*Goes out.*]

LOPAKHIN. We'll see each other in three weeks. [*Kisses* LYUBOV ANDREEVNA'S *hand.*] In the meantime, good-bye. It's time for me. [*To* GAEV.] Until we meet again. [*Kisses* PISHCHIK.] Until we meet again. [*Shakes hands with* VARYA, *then with* FIRS *and* YASHA.] I don't want to leave. [*To* LYUBOV ANDREEVNA.] If you make up your mind about those summer places and decide to go ahead with it, just give me the word and I'll loan you fifty thousand or so. Think about it seriously.

VARYA. [*angrily*] You're on your way, why don't you just leave now!

LOPAKHIN. I'll go, I'll go . . . [*Goes out.*]

GAEV. Grabbing peasant. Nevertheless, I beg your pardon . . . Varya's going to marry him. He's Varya's dear fiancé.

VARYA. You're talking much too much, Uncle dear.

LYUBOV ANDREEVNA. Well, hmm, Varya, I shall be very glad. He's a good person.

PISHCHIK. A person, if the truth were said . . . who's most worthy . . . And my Dashenka . . . keeps saying also that . . . she keeps saying all sorts of words. [*Snores, but immediately wakes up.*] Be that as it may, my honored lady, if you'll oblige me with . . . a loan of two hundred and forty rubles . . . I can pay the interest due on the mortgage tomorrow . . .

VARYA. [*frightened*] We don't have it, we don't!

LYUBOV ANDREEVNA. As a matter of fact, I have nothing.

PISHCHIK. It'll turn up. [*Laughs.*] I never lose one bit of hope. Oh, time and again, I think everything's lost, gone, I've had it, and then—lo and behold—they built a railroad right through my land and . . . then went and paid me for it. Wait and see, something or other will happen—if not today, then tomorrow . . . Dashenka is going to win two hundred thousand . . . She has a lottery ticket.

LYUBOV ANDREEVNA. The coffee is finished, we can get some peace and rest.

FIRS. [*brushes* GAEV'S *clothes, reprovingly*] Again you've put on the wrong trousers. Oh, what on earth am I going to do with you!

VARYA. [*quietly*] Anya is sleeping. [*quietly opens the window.*] The sun's come up now, and it isn't cold. Look, *Mamochka*, what marvelous trees! And the air, too, dear God in heaven! The starlings are singing!

GAEV. [*opens another window*] The orchard is all in white. You haven't forgotten, Lyuba, have you? That long avenue over there keeps running straight, straight as a cord stretched tight. It shines brightly on moonlit nights. You remember, you haven't forgotten, have you?

LYUBOV ANDREEVNA. [*looks through the window at the orchard*] Oh, my childhood, days of my innocence! In this very nursery I used to sleep, I used to look out at the orchard from here, and when I woke up each morning I felt happy, so happy. At that time too the orchard was exactly the same, nothing at all has changed. [*Laughs jubilantly.*] All in white, all! Oh, my orchard! After the dreary, rainy autumn and cold winter, I find you young once more, filled with happiness, and I know the angels in heaven have not deserted you . . . If only the heaviness I feel in my heart, the millstone I carry now, were suddenly taken away forever, if only I could forget my past!

GAEV. Yes, and the orchard will be sold to pay off debts. Strange, isn't it . . .

LYUBOV ANDREEVNA. Just look, our own mama is walking in the orchard . . . in a white dress! [*Laughs jubilantly.*] See, it's Mama.

GAEV. Where is she?

VARYA. God be with you, *Mamochka*.

LYUBOV ANDREEVNA. There's no one, it just seemed to me I saw her. To the right, as the path turns to the summerhouse, there's a white small tree bending down—it looks like a woman . . . [TRO-FIMOV *enters, wearing spectacles and dressed in a threadbare student's uniform.*] What a splendid orchard! Row upon row of white blossoms, the light blue sky . . .

TROFIMOV. Lyubov Andreevna! [*She looks around at him.*] I'll only pay my respects and then go away at once. [*Ardently kisses her hand.*] I was told to wait until morning, but I didn't have the patience . . .

  LYUBOV ANDREEVNA *looks at him, bewildered.*

VARYA. [*through tears*] It's Petya Trofimov . . .

TROFIMOV. Petya Trofimov, former tutor of your Grisha . . . Can it be I've changed so much?

  LYUBOV ANDREEVNA *embraces him and weeps quietly.*

GAEV. [*embarrassed*] Enough, Lyuba, that'll do.

VARYA. [*weeps*] You see, Petya, I told you to wait until tomorrow.

LYUBOV ANDREEVNA. My Grisha . . . my little boy . . . Grisha . . . my son . . .

VARYA. What could we do, *Mamochka*? It was God's will.

TROFIMOV. [*gently, through tears*] There, there . . .

LYUBOV ANDREEVNA. [*weeps quietly*] My little boy is gone, drowned . . . and for what? Whatever was it for, my friend? [*More quietly.*] Anya is sleeping in there, and I go on talking in a loud voice . . . making so much noise . . . Well, Petya? Why do you look so homely now? Why have you started putting on years?

TROFIMOV. An old peasant woman on the train called me "that used-up old gentleman."

LYUBOV ANDREEVNA. You were no more than a boy then, a sweet young student, but now your hair is getting thin and you're wearing spectacles. Don't tell me you're still a student? [*Walks toward the door.*]

TROFIMOV. No doubt I'll be a student forever and ever.

LYUBOV ANDREEVNA. [*kisses her brother, then* VARYA] Well then, better go to sleep . . . You've started putting on years, too, Leonid.

PISHCHIK. [*follows her*] So now we're going to sleep . . . Oh, my gout! I'll stay the night here . . . Lyubov Andreevna, my darling, if you could help me out tomorrow morning, you know . . . two hundred and forty rubles . . .

GAEV. Oh, he keeps harping on the same old string.

PISHCHIK. Two hundred and forty rubles . . . to pay the interest due on the mortgage.

LYUBOV ANDREEVNA. I have no money, dear.

PISHCHIK. I'll pay it back, my dear . . . a trifling sum . . .

LYUBOV ANDREEVNA. Well, all right, Leonid will give you the amount . . . Leonid, you give it to him.

GAEV. Give it to him, Me? Oh, sure, open your pocket and see what comes!

LYUBOV ANDREEVNA. What on earth can we do? Give him the money . . . he needs it . . . He'll pay it back.

> LYUBOV ANDREEVNA, TROFIMOV, PISHCHIK, *and* FIRS *go out;* GAEV, VARYA, *and* YASHA *remain.*

GAEV. My sister still hasn't lost the habit of scattering all her money to the winds. [*To* YASHA.] Step out of the way, dear fellow, you smell like a dunghill biddy.[4]

YASHA. [*with an ironical smile*] You're just the same as you've always been, too, Leonid Andreevich.

GAEV. How's that? [*To* VARYA.] What did he say?

VARYA. [*to* YASHA] Your mother's come from the village. She's been sitting in the servants' lodgings since yesterday. She wants to see you . . .

YASHA. She can go to the devil, for all I care!

VARYA. Oh, you insolent pup, I'd be ashamed!

YASHA. She's a big help, isn't she? She might have come here tomorrow. [*Goes out.*]

VARYA. *Mamochka* is just the same as she was, she hasn't changed one whit. If she were given free rein, she'd give away everything.

GAEV. Yes . . . [*Pause.*] If plenty of remedies are prescribed for some sort of disease, it means the disease can't possibly be cured. I keep on thinking, stewing my brains over it, and I've come up with a lot of remedies, plenty of them. Of course, that means I really don't have a single one that would work. It would be fine to receive some sort of inheritance, it would be nice to marry our Anya

---

4. Literally, "There's the smell of a hen [coming] from you."

off to a rich person, it would be fine to leave for Yaroslavl[5] and try our luck with our dear aunt, the countess. Our auntie is rich, you know, very much so.

VARYA. [*weeps*] If only God would help.

GAEV. Stop blubbering. Our auntie is very rich, but she doesn't care one iota for us. First of all, my sister married a lawyer, not a nobleman . . . [ANYA *appears in the doorway*.] She did not marry into the nobility, and you can't say she's led a particularly upright and godly life. She is kind and good, a glorious person, really, and I love her very much. But whatever excuses you think of to justify what she's gone through, you must still admit she's an immoral woman. You're conscious of it in her slightest movement.

VARYA. [*in a whisper*] Anya is standing in the doorway.

GAEV. How's that? [*Pause*.] You know, it's surprising, but something landed in my right eye . . . I've started to see poorly. And on Thursday when I was at the district court . . .

    ANYA *enters*.

VARYA. Why on earth aren't you asleep, Anya?

ANYA. I can't fall aleep. I just can't.

GAEV. My little darling. [*Kisses* ANYA's *face and hands*.] My dear child . . . [*Through tears*.] You're not simply my niece, you're my angel, you mean everything to me. Believe me, believe . . .

ANYA. I believe you, Uncle. Everyone loves and respects you . . . but you must keep quiet, dear Uncle, only keep quiet. What were you saying just now about my mama, about your own sister? Whatever in the world made you say it?

GAEV. Yes, yes . . . [*Covers his face with her hand*.] It's terrible, really it is! Dear God in heaven! Dear God help me! And the speech I made today—to the bookcase . . . so very foolish! And only when I finished did I realize it was so foolish.

VARYA. It's true, dear Uncle, you ought to keep quiet. Just keep quiet, that's all.

ANYA. If you'll stop talking, you will feel more at peace with yourself.

GAEV. I'll keep quiet. [*Kisses* ANYA's *and* VARYA's *hands*.] I'll keep quiet. Only there is this business matter I should bring up. On Thursday I was at the district court, well, a bunch of us got together and talk started about this thing and that, skipping around from here to there; and it seems we might arrange a loan on promissory notes and pay the interest to the bank.

VARYA. If only God will help!

GAEV. On Tuesday I'll go and talk it over with them once more. [*To* VARYA.] Stop blubbering. [*To* ANYA.] Your mother is going to talk with Lopakhin. Of course, he won't turn her down . . . After you've had some peace and rest, you will leave for Yaroslavl to see the countess, your grandmother. In this way we'll be

5. An old Russian town on the Volga.

working from three sides—and so our whole business drops nicely into the hat. I'm convinced we'll pay off the interest . . . [*Puts a piece of candy into his mouth.*] I give you my word of honor, I'll swear by anything you want, this estate will not be sold! [*Excitedly.*] I swear by my own happiness! Here, take my hand and then you can call me a good-for-nothing rapscallion if I even so much as let the estate come up for auction! I swear it with all my heart and soul!

ANYA. [*a peaceful mood having returned to her, she is happy*] What a good person you are, Uncle, and so smart too! [*Embraces her uncle.*] I'm at peace now! At peace and so happy!

FIRS *enters.*

FIRS. [*reproachfully*] Leonid Andreich, have you no fear of God? When is it you're going to sleep?

GAEV. At once, at once. You can leave, Firs. I, yes, it's perfectly all right, I can undress myself. Well, my children, time to say bye-byes . . . We'll save the details until tomorrow, and now you go off to sleep. [*Kisses* ANYA *and* VARYA.] I'm a man of the eighties . . . No one pays tribute to those days, but I still went through plenty in life for my convictions, I can tell you I did. The peasant has reason to love me. You must get to know the peasant, I say. You must know how to . . .

ANYA. You're starting again, Uncle!

VARYA. You better keep quiet, Uncle dear.

FIRS. [*angrily*] Leonid Andreich!

GAEV. I'm coming, I'm coming . . . Lie down and go to sleep. Off two cushions right into the middle! I pocket the white . . . [*Goes out.* FIRS *quickly toddles after him.*]

ANYA. I'm at peace now. I don't want to go to Yaroslavl and I don't love my grandmother, but I still feel at peace. Thanks to Uncle. [*Sits down.*]

VARYA. We must go to sleep. I'm going to. Oh, something unpleasant happened here when you were gone. Only some old servants still live in the old servants' lodgings, as you well know—Yefimyushka, Polya, Yevstigney, and there's Karp, too. They started letting some rascals and passers-by spend the night there. I kept silent. Only then I began hearing a rumor they were spreading that I'd given orders to feed them nothing but dried peas. Out of stinginess, if you can imagine . . . Yevstigney was behind it all . . . All right, I think, if that's the way it is—then just you wait. I call in Yevstigney . . . [*Yawns.*] He shows up . . . "What are you up to," I say, "Yevstigney . . . you're such a fool . . ." [*Having glanced at* ANYA.] Anichka![6] [*Pause.*] She's fallen right to sleep . . . [*Takes* ANYA *by the arm.*] Come to your bed . . . Come along! . . [*Leading her.*] My precious has gone to sleep! Come along . . .

They go. A shepherd is heard playing on a reed pipe far be-

6. A term of endearment for *Anya*.

yond the orchard. TROFIMOV *crosses the stage and, having
seen* VARYA *and* ANYA, *stops.*

VARYA. Tsss . . . she's sleeping . . . sleeping . . . Come along, darling.

ANYA. [*quietly, half-asleep*] I'm so tired . . . those bells keep ringing
. . . Uncle . . . dear . . . and Mama and Uncle . . .

VARYA. Come, darling, come along . . . [*They go into* ANYA'S
room.]

TROFIMOV. [*deeply moved*] Light of my life! My springtime!

CURTAIN

Act Two

*A field. A very small, old chapel—bent out of shape and de-
serted a long time ago. Near it are an old bench, a well, and
large stones that apparently were once used as tombstones. A
road to* GAEV'S *estate can be seen. Towering poplar trees loom
darkly on one side, where the cherry orchard begins. In the
distance is a row of telegraph poles, and far, far away on the
horizon—appearing indistinct—is a large town, clearly seen
only in very fine, clear weather. It is shortly before sunset.*
SHARLOTTA, YASHA, *and* DUNYASHA *are sitting on the bench.*
YEPIKHODOV *stands nearby and plays the guitar, as the others
sit lost in thought.* SHARLOTTA, *wearing an old peaked cap,
has taken a gun from her shoulder and is adjusting the buckle
on the sling.*

SHARLOTTA. [*in a thoughtful mood*] I don't have a genuine passport.[7] I don't know how old I am, but I keep on thinking I'm
very young. When I was a small little girl, my father and *mamasha* used to travel from fair to fair and give shows—very good
ones too. Oh, I used to jump around, doing *salto-mortale*[8] and all
sorts of tricks. And when *papasha* and *mamasha*[9] died, a certain
German woman took me into her home and started teaching
me. All right. I grew up and then became a governess. But where
I come from and who I am—I don't know . . . Who were my parents, maybe they weren't even married . . . I don't know. [*Takes a
cucumber out of her pocket and begins eating it.*] I don't know
anything. [*Pause.*] I'd really like to start a conversation, but
there's no one to start with . . . I don't have anybody at all.

YEPIKHODOV. [*plays the guitar and sings*]

"What care I for the world and its tumult,
What care I for my friends or my foes . . ."[1]

---

7. An "internal" passport, not for crossing the borders of Russia into foreign
lands, but for movement within Russia.
8. Literally, "complete somersault."

9. Affectionate terms for *mother* and
father.
1. The words from a popular ballad at
the turn of the century.

How pleasant it is to play the mandolin!

DUNYASHA. It's a guitar, not a mandolin. [*Looks at herself in a small mirror and powders herself.*]

YEPIKHODOV. To a man who's lost his mind and fallen in love, this is a mandolin . . . [*Croons.*]

"Oh, how much my heart will burn
With the heat of your love in return . . ."

YASHA *joins in.*

SHARLOTTA. It's terrible the way these people sound . . . phew! Like jackals.

DUNYASHA. [*to* YASHA] All the same, what luck to go visiting abroad.

YASHA. Yes, of course. I can't possibly disagree with you on that point. [*Yawns, then lights a cigar.*]

YEPIKHODOV. It makes good sense. A long time ago everything abroad shaped up and achieved its full build.

YASHA. Goes without saying.

YEPIKHODOV. I'm a well-developed person, and I read all sorts of wonderful books. But I can't comprehend at all the direction I personally want to take, that is, to go on living or to shoot myself, personally speaking. But nonetheless I always carry a revolver on me. Here it is . . . [*Indicates the revolver.*]

SHARLOTTA. So much for that. Now I'm on my way. [*Slings on her gun.*] Yepikhodov, you are a very intelligent man and dreadfully frightening. Women must fall madly in love with you. Brrr! [*Walks.*] These intellectuals are all so stupid, there's no one to talk to . . . I feel alone all the time, all alone, I don't have anybody at all and . . . and who I am, what on earth I'm here for, is beyond me . . . [*Goes out without hurrying.*]

YEPIKHODOV. Personally speaking, and I'm not going to touch on other topics, I must explain something about myself, by the way. That is, fate treats me without one bit of remorse, like a storm regards a small ship. If, let us assume, I'm mistaken, then why is it I wake up this morning—and I'm saying this by way of illustration —I look, and perched on my chest is a spider of dreadful dimensions . . . That's how big. [*Indicates size with both hands.*] And also if I pick up some kvas so I can have a good drink, what do I see inside? Something or other extremely indecent like a cockroach. [*Pause.*] Have you read Buckle?[2] [*Pause.*] Avdotya Fyodorovna, I wish to bother you for a couple of words or so.

DUNYASHA. Go ahead and talk.

YEPIKHODOV. I'd find it most desirable if it were with you privately . . . [*Sighs.*]

DUNYASHA. [*embarrassed*] Very well . . . Only first of all bring me my cape . . . it's somewhere near the cupboard . . . It's a little damp here . . .

2. Henry Thomas Buckle (1821–62), English liberal historian and sociologist, author of *A History of Civilization in England*.

YEPIKHODOV. Very good, miss . . . I'll bring it, miss . . . Now I know what I can do with my revolver . . . [*Takes the guitar and goes out playing.*]

YASHA. Two-and-Twenty Hard Knocks! A stupid man, just between you and me. [*Yawns.*]

DUNYASHA. God forbid he doesn't shoot himself. [*Pause.*] I've grown so uneasy, I'm always in a dither. I was still a little girl when the master and mistress took me into their place, and now I've lost the habit of living the way common people do. Here, you can see my hands, white as white can be, just like a lady's. I've grown fragile, so delicate, refined and ladylike, everything in the world frightens me . . . terribly so. And if you deceive me, Yasha, I just don't know what it will go and do to my nerves.

YASHA. [*kisses her*] Saucy little cucumber! Every girl must remember who she is, to be sure, and there's nothing I dislike more than a girl who doesn't behave herself as she should.

DUNYASHA. I love you so terribly much. You're educated, there's nothing in the world you can't figure out. [*Pause.*]

YASHA. [*yawns*] Yes, miss . . . The way I look at it, if a girl loves anyone, it means she's immoral. [*Pause.*] It's pleasant to smoke a cigar in clean, pure air . . . [*Listens.*] Somebody's coming here . . . It's the ladies and gentlemen . . . [DUNYASHA *impulsively embraces him.*] You go on home as if you've gone to the river to bathe. Take that path, or else you'll meet them and they'll start thinking I made a point of going out with you. I can't take something like that.

DUNYASHA. [*quietly coughs*] I'm starting to get a headache from your cigar . . . [*Goes out.*]

YASHA *remains and sits down near the chapel.* LYUBOV AN-DREEVNA, GAEV, *and* LOPAKHIN *enter.*

LOPAKHIN. You must come to a decision once and for all—time waits for no one. Surely the question is quite simple. Do you agree to lease your land for summer cottages or don't you? You can answer in one word. Is it yes or no? Just one word!

LYUBOV ANDREEVNA. Who's smoking disgusting cigars out here . . . [*Sits down.*]

GAEV. Things became convenient once they built the railroad. [*Sits down.*] We made a short trip to town and had lunch . . . Off the yellow into the middle pocket! I'd like to go to the house first and play one game . . .

LYUBOV ANDREEVNA. You'll have time.

LOPAKHIN. Just one word! [*Beseechingly.*] Give me an answer, do!

GAEV. [*yawning*] How's that?

LYUBOV ANDREEVNA. [*looks in her purse*] Yesterday I had plenty of money, and today there's not much at all. Trying to save money, my poor Varya feeds all of us milk soup, and the old folks in the kitchen get nothing but dried peas. And yet I go on spending money thoughtlessly, somehow. [*Drops her purse, scattering gold coins.*] Now, they've fallen down . . . [*She is annoyed.*]

YASHA. Allow me, I'll go pick them up at once. [*Gathers up the coins.*]

LYUBOV ANDREEVNA. Please do, Yasha. Why on earth did I lunch in town . . . That good-for-nothing restaurant of yours with its music and tablecloths smelling of soap . . . Why did you drink so much, Lyonya, or eat so much? And talk so much? Today in the restaurant you were talking too much again, and every bit of it was out of place—about the seventies and the decadent movement. And to whom? Talking to the waiters about the decadents!

LOPAKHIN. Yes.

GAEV. [*waves his hand*] I'm incorrigible, that's obvious . . . [*Irritably, to* YASHA.] What are you doing, popping up in front of me all the time . . .

YASHA. [*laughs*] I can't listen to your voice without laughing.

GAEV. [*to his sister*] Either he, or I . . .

LYUBOV ANDREEVNA. You can leave, Yasha, on your way now . . .

YASHA. [*gives* LYUBOV ANDREEVNA *her purse*] I'm going right now. [*Scarcely able to contain his laughter.*] This very minute . . . [*Goes out.*]

LOPAKHIN. That rich fellow Deriganov is thinking about buying your estate. They say he's coming to the auction himself.

LYUBOV ANDREEVNA. Oh, where did you hear that?

LOPAKHIN. They're talking about it in town.

GAEV. Our auntie in Yaroslavl promised to send us money, but when, or how much, is beyond me. . . .

LOPAKHIN. How much will she send? A hundred thousand? Two hundred thousand?

LYUBOV ANDREEVNA. Well . . . about ten or fifteen thousand, and we're thankful to get that.

LOPAKHIN. You must forgive me, but I've never met people as rattlebrained as you two are, my friends, or so unbusinesslike and strange, too. You are told in plain language your estate is going to be sold, and it's just as if you don't understand it.

LYUBOV ANDREEVNA. But what is it we can do? You tell us, what?

LOPAKHIN. I keep telling you every day. Every day I keep on saying one and the same thing. Both the cherry orchard and the land must be leased for summer residences. You must do it right now, as soon as possible—the auction is practically under our nose. Try and grasp what I'm saying. When you decide once and for all on the summer cottages, you can raise whatever sum of money you'd like to and then you're safe and sound.

LYUBOV ANDREEVNA. Summer cottages and the people who go with them. Forgive me, but it's all so petty, so vulgar.

GAEV. I agree with you completely.

LOPAKHIN. I'm going to burst into tears, or shout, or fall on the ground and faint. I can't stand it! You've worn me out completely! [*To* GAEV.] You're an old woman!

GAEV. How's that?

LOPAKHIN. An old woman, that's what! [*Wants to leave.*]

LYUBOV ANDREEVNA. [*frightened*] No, don't go away, stay with us, dear. I beg you. Perhaps we'll think of something or other!

LOPAKHIN. What's there to think about?

LYUBOV ANDREEVNA. Don't go away, I beg you. When you're around it's more cheerful . . . [*Pause.*] I keep waiting for something, just as if the house were going to fall down on us.

GAEV. [*deep in thought*] Bank shot into the corner . . . Across into the middle . . .

LYUBOV ANDREEVNA. Oh, how very much we have sinned . . .

LOPAKHIN. What sins could you possibly have . . .

GAEV. [*puts a piece of candy into his mouth*] They say I've eaten up my fortune in candy . . . [*Laughs.*]

LYUBOV ANDREEVNA. Oh, my sins, my sins . . . I've always scattered money to the winds, impulsively, like someone out of her mind, and I married a man who did nothing but build up debts. My husband died of champagne, he reveled in drinking, and then I was unlucky enough to fall in love with someone else. I began living with him. And just at that time—it was my first punishment, a blow that drove me mad with grief—here in this very river . . . My little boy was drowned. I went abroad, left forever, never to return —never to see this river again . . . I just closed my eyes and ran, losing all sense of what I was doing or who I am, and *he* followed me . . . callously, brutally. I bought a dacha near Mentone because it was there he fell sick, and for the next three years I knew neither rest nor peace, nursing him day and night. He wore me out completely, my soul dried up. And last year, when the dacha was sold to pay off debts, I left for Paris. It was there he robbed me, deserted me, and began living with another woman. I tried to poison myself . . . It was all so stupid and degrading . . . And suddenly I felt a longing to come home to Russia, home to my own land and my little girl . . . [*Wipes away her tears.*] Oh, Lord, dear Lord in heaven, be gracious, forgive me my sins! Don't punish me anymore! [*Takes a telegram out of her pocket.*] This came today from Paris . . . He begs forgiveness and implores me to return . . . [*Tears up the telegram.*] That's music coming from somewhere, I think. [*Listens.*]

GAEV. It's our celebrated Jewish orchestra. You remember, don't you, the four violins, flute, and double bass?

LYUBOV ANDREEVNA. It still exists, then? We ought to send for them sometime and arrange an evening party at the house.

LOPAKHIN. [*listens*] I can't hear anything . . . [*Sings quietly.*]

"For the right amount of money, oh, the Germans can
Change a solid Russian into a Frenchy man."³ [*Laughs.*]

What a play I saw at the theatre yesterday. Really a lot to laugh at.

LYUBOV ANDREEVNA. And probably there wasn't anything funny in
it. Going to see plays isn't what you people should do. Try looking
at yourselves a little more often and see what gray lives you all
lead. How much of what you say is unnecessary.

LOPAKHIN. That's very true. You can be honest and say we all lead
the life of a fool . . . [*Pause.*] My *papasha* was a peasant, an
idiot. He didn't understand anything, so he taught me nothing and
just beat me when he was drunk, always with a stick, too. As a
matter of fact, I'm just as big a lunkhead and idiot myself. I never
learned anything, and my handwriting's miserable. The way I write
I'm ashamed to let people see it. Just the way a pig might write.

LYUBOV ANDREEVNA. You should get married, my friend.

LOPAKHIN. Yes . . . That's very true.

LYUBOV ANDREEVNA. To our own Varya. She's a fine girl.

LOPAKHIN. Yes.

LYUBOV ANDREEVNA. Her parents are common people. She works the
whole day long, but what's really important is that she loves you.
And you know you've liked her for a long time.

LOPAKHIN. Well, hmm? I've nothing against it . . . She's a fine girl.
[*Pause.*]

GAEV. They offered me a job in a bank. Six thousand rubles a year
. . . Have you heard?

LYUBOV ANDREEVNA. Oh, you're not up to it! You can stay as you
are . . .

　　　FIRS enters, bringing a coat.

FIRS. [*to* GAEV] Be so good as to put this on, sir, it's damp here.

GAEV. [*puts on coat*] You're bothering me, old man.

FIRS. No use going on . . . This morning you left without saying
one word to me. [*Looks him over.*]

LYUBOV ANDREEVNA. Oh, the years you've put on, Firs, the years!

FIRS. What can I do for you?

LOPAKHIN. They're saying you look so much older!

FIRS. I've been living a long time now. They were going to get me
married before your *papasha* was even in the world yet . . .
[*Laughs.*] When freedom came for the serfs,⁴ I was already the
head valet. I did not accept freedom at that time, so I kept on
with the master and mistress . . . [*Pause.*] Oh, I remember everyone was glad, but what they were glad about, why, they didn't
even know themselves.

LOPAKHIN. Oh, it was very good in the old days. At least they used
to flog them.

FIRS. [*not having heard him*] Yes, the good old days. The peasants

3. Critics have been unable to trace the origin of these lines.
4. Literally, "When freedom came." The references in this speech are to the reforms of the 1860's, which began with the emancipation of the serfs in 1861.

were attached to the master, and the master to the peasants, but nowadays they are all mixed up, and you can't tell one from the other.

GAEV. Keep quiet for a moment, Firs. Tomorrow I must go to town. I was promised an introduction to a certain general who might give us money on a promissory note.

LOPAKHIN. Nothing will come out of it. And you won't pay the interest, either, you can rest assured of that.

LYUBOV ANDREEVNA. He's just ranting and raving again. There aren't any generals, none.

TROFIMOV, ANYA, *and* VARYA *enter.*

GAEV. Oh, here come the children.

ANYA. Mama's sitting down.

LYUBOV ANDREEVNA. [*affectionately*] Come, come along . . . my darlings . . . [*Embraces* ANYA *and* VARYA.] If you both only knew how much I love you. Sit down beside me, that's the way.

　　All sit down.

LOPAKHIN. Our eternal student always takes good care of the young ladies.

TROFIMOV. It's none of your business.

LOPAKHIN. He's going to be fifty soon, but he's still a student.

TROFIMOV. You can stop your asinine jokes right now.

LOPAKHIN. What's a peculiar fellow like you getting angry about, anyway?

TROFIMOV. Oh, don't keep on pestering me, that's all.

LOPAKHIN. [*laughs*] Permit me, if you will, one question. What do you think about me?

TROFIMOV. I, Yermolay Alexeich, this is what I think. You are a rich man, and you're going to be a millionaire soon. In the economy of nature one form of matter is exchanged for another, and so we find indispensable the beast of prey which devours everything that lands on its path. In that way you too are indispensable.

　　All laugh.

VARYA. Oh, Petya, you'd better tell us about the planets.

LYUBOV ANDREEVNA. No, let's go on with what we were saying yesterday.

TROFIMOV. What was it about?

GAEV. Pride.

TROFIMOV. We talked a long time yesterday, but we didn't get anywhere. The proud person in your sense of the word has something mystical inside. Maybe you're even right the way you see it. But if we reason it out simply and not try to be one bit fancy, then what sort of pride can you possibly take or what's the sense of ever having it, if man is poorly put together as a physiological type and if the enormous majority of the human race is brutal, stupid, and profoundly unhappy? We must stop admiring ourselves. What we ought to do is just keep on working.

GAEV. We're going to die, so it doesn't matter.

TROFIMOV. Who knows for certain? Besides, what does "to die" really mean? It may be that man has a hundred senses and at death only the five known to us are lost, while the remaining ninety-five go on living.

LYUBOV ANDREEVNA. How intelligent you are, Petya!

LOPAKHIN. [*ironically*] Terribly!

TROFIMOV. Humankind strides on, perfecting its strength. All that lies beyond us now will become one day comprehensible and within our grasp. The one thing we must do is to work and do all we can for those who seek the truth. Here in Russia very few people really work now. The educated people I know, the vast majority at any rate, aren't in search of a single thing, and they certainly don't do anything. So far they lack even the ability for real work. They call themselves the intelligentsia, but they speak to their servants as inferiors and treat their peasants as if they were animals. They are poor students, they read absolutely nothing serious, and they do precisely nothing. They only talk about science, and as for art, they understand next to nothing. They are all very serious people with stern expressions on their faces. They discuss nothing but important matters and like to philosophize a great deal, while at the same time everyone can see that the workers are detestably fed, sleep without suitable bedding, thirty to forty in a room with bedbugs everywhere, the stench, the dampness, and the moral corruption . . . Obviously all our fine talk has gone on simply to hoodwink ourselves and other people as well. Show me the day nurseries that they're talking so much about. And where are the libraries? Why, they just write about nurseries and libraries in novels, while in fact not a single one even exists. What does exist is nothing but dirt, vulgarity, and a barbarian way of life . . . I dislike these terribly serious faces, they frighten me, and I'm afraid of serious conversations, too. We'd be better off if we all would just shut up for a while!

LOPAKHIN. You know, I get up before five in the morning, and I work from morning till night. Now, I've always got money on hand—my own and other people's—and so I can see what kind of people are around. You have only to start doing something or other to realize how few honest, decent people there are. Sometimes when I can't get to sleep, I keep thinking, "Dear Lord in heaven, you gave us these enormous forests, boundless fields, broad horizons, and living among them we really ought to be giants ourselves . . ."

LYUBOV ANDREEVNA. Now you find giants indispensable . . . Oh, they are very nice only in fairy stores; anywhere else they can scare you. [YEPIKHODOV *crosses at the depth of the stage, playing his guitar.* LYUBOV ANDREEVNA *is deep in thought.*] There goes Yepikhodov . . .

ANYA. [*deep in thought*] There goes Yepikhodov . . .

GAEV. The sun has set, ladies and gentlemen.

TROFIMOV. Yes.

GAEV. [*in a low voice, as if reciting*] Oh, nature, marvelous nature, shining with eternal radiance, beautiful yet unfeeling, you whom we name as mother, in whom are united both the living and the dead, you give life and you destroy . . .

VARYA. [*beseechingly*] Uncle dear!

ANYA. Uncle, you're starting again!

TROFIMOV. You'd better try a bank shot off the yellow into the middle.

GAEV. I'll keep silent, silent.

> *All are sitting, deep in thought. Silence. All that can be heard is* FIRS, *who mumbles quietly. Suddenly a sound is heard far off in the distance, as if coming from the sky. It is the sound of a string breaking that dies away sadly.*

LYUBOV ANDREEVNA. What was that?

LOPAKHIN. I don't know. Somewhere far off in the mines a bucket must have broken loose. But it's somewhere far, far away.

GAEV. Perhaps it was a bird of some kind . . . like a heron.

TROFIMOV. Or an eagle owl . . .

LYUBOV ANDREEVNA. [*shudders*] It was unpleasant, and I don't know why. [*Pause.*]

FIRS. It was just the same before the troubles—and the owl kept hooting and the samovar humming without stopping.

GAEV. What troubles are you talking about?

FIRS. Just before the serfs were given their freedom. [*Pause.*]

LYUBOV ANDREEVNA. You know, dear friends, evening has come. Let's go on our way. [*To* ANYA.] You have tears in your eyes . . . What is it, my little girl? [*Embraces her.*]

ANYA. No reason, Mama, it's nothing.

TROFIMOV. There's someone coming.

> *A passer-by appears, wearing a threadbare white peaked cap and an overcoat. He is slightly drunk.*

PASSER-BY. Permit me if you will one question. Can I go from here straight to the station?

GAEV. You can. Take that road.

PASSER-BY. I thank you from the bottom of my heart. [*Having coughed.*] Superb weather . . . [*Recites.*] "Oh, my brother, my suffering brother . . . come out to the Volga, whose moan . . ." [*To* VARYA.] Mademoiselle, could you allow a starving Russian thirty kopeks . . .

> VARYA *is frightened and shrieks.*

LOPAKHIN. [*angrily*] Even rascals ought to know how to behave properly.

LYUBOV ANDREEVNA. [*shocked and confused*] Take it . . . here. . . . [*Looks in her purse.*] There's no silver here . . . It doesn't matter, here's a gold coin for you . . .

PASSER-BY. I thank you from the bottom of my heart! [*Goes out.*]

> *There is laughter from those onstage.*

VARYA. [*frightened*] I'm going away . . . I'm going . . . Oh, there's nothing at home for the servants to eat, *Mamochka*, and you gave him a gold coin.

LYUBOV ANDREEVNA. I am foolish. What can be done with me, what! When we get home, I'll give you everything I have. Yermolay Alexeich, lend me something more, do! . .

LOPAKHIN. Yes, ma'am.

LYUBOV ANDREEVNA. Let's go, ladies and gentlemen, it's time. Oh, Varya, we've just signed, sealed, and absolutely promised you in marriage. Congratulations.

VARYA. [*through tears*] Mama, this is nothing to joke about.

LOPAKHIN. Oralia, get thee to a nunnery . . .

GAEV. Oh, my hands are shaking. I haven't played a billiard game in a long time.

LOPAKHIN. Oralia, oh nymph, remember me in thy orisons!

LYUBOV ANDREEVNA. Come along, ladies and gentlemen. We'll sit down soon for supper.

VARYA. Oh, how he scared me. My heart hasn't stopped pounding yet.

LOPAKHIN. I'd like to remind you, ladies and gentlemen, the cherry orchard will be up for.sale on the twenty-second of August. Think about it! . . Keep it in mind, do! . .

All go out except TROFIMOV *and* ANYA.

ANYA. [*laughing*] Thanks to that man who came by, Varya is scared, and we're alone now.

TROFIMOV. Varya's frightened we might suddenly fall in love, so she hasn't left us alone for days. With her narrow mind she can't possibly understand that we are above love. To give up all that is petty and unreal, which stops our being free and happy—that's the purpose and meaning of our lives. On then, ahead! We stride invincibly on to that bright star burning there in the distance! On then, ahead! Don't fall behind, my friends!

ANYA. [*throwing up her arms*] How wonderfully you speak! [*Pause.*] It's unbelievable here today!

TROFIMOV. Yes, the weather is striking.

ANYA. Whatever have you done to me, Petya? Why is it I no longer love the cherry orchard as I used to? I loved it so tenderly, and I thought no place on earth was better than our own orchard.

TROFIMOV. All Russia is our orchard. The land is vast and beautiful and filled with marvelous places. [*Pause.*] Just think, Anya, your grandfather and your great-grandfather and all your ancestors owned both land and serfs, they owned living souls. Don't you see that from every cherry tree in the orchard, from every leaf and every trunk, generations of human beings are gazing down at you, don't you hear their voices . . . To own human souls—it has transformed every one of you, don't you see, those who lived before and those living today. And so your mother, your uncle, and you no longer notice that you are living in debt, at the expense of other people, at the expense of the very people you will allow no farther than the entrance to your home . . . We are at least two hundred years behind the times, we haven't made any real headway yet, and we still don't have any clear idea about our relation to the past. We just philosophize, complain of boredom, or drink vodka. It's so clear, you see, that if we're to begin living in the present, we must first of all redeem our past and then be done with it forever. And the only way we can redeem our past is by suffering and by giving ourselves over to exceptional labor, to steadfast and endless work. You must realize this, Anya.

ANYA. The house we live in hasn't really been ours for a long time, and I'm going to leave it. I give you my word.

TROFIMOV. If you're given the keys to the household, throw them into the well and walk away, go. Be free like the wind.

ANYA. [*in exaltation*] How wonderfully you said everything!

TROFIMOV. Believe me, Anya, you must believe! I'm not yet thirty, I'm a young man, and I'm still a student, but I have already gone through so much! As soon as winter's come, I find myself hungry, ill, worried, poor as a beggar, and—the places fate has driven me, the places! Where haven't I been, where? And the whole time, every minute of the day and night, I've felt impressions of the future abound in my soul, visions I can't explain. I know happiness is coming, Anya, I can feel it. I already see it on the way . . .

ANYA. [*deep in thought*] The moon is rising.

YEPIKHODOV *is heard playing the guitar, the same sad song as before. The moon rises. Somewhere near the poplar trees,* VARYA *is looking for* ANYA *and is calling,* "Anya! Where are you?"

TROFIMOV. Yes, the moon is rising. [*Pause.*] There it is, happiness. There it comes, coming nearer, always nearer. I can already hear its footsteps. And if we don't see it, if we don't experience it, what does it matter? Other people will see it.

VARYA'S VOICE. [*offstage*] Anya! Where are you?

TROFIMOV. It's Varya again! [*Angrily.*] Oh, she is exasperating!

ANYA. Well, hmm? Let's go to the river. It's fine there.

TROFIMOV. Yes, let's go. [*They go out.*]

VARYA'S VOICE. [*offstage*] Anya! Anya!

CURTAIN

Act Three

The drawing room. In the distance, through the archway, the ballroom can be seen. The chandelier is lighted. The Jewish orchestra mentioned in the second act is heard playing in the entrance hall. It is evening. In the ballroom they are dancing a grand rond. *The voice of* SIMEONOV-PISHCHIK *is heard,*

"Promenade à une paire!" They enter the drawing room:
PISHCHIK *and* SHARLOTTA IVANOVNA *are the first couple;*
TROFIMOV *and* LYUBOV ANDREEVNA *the second;* ANYA *and the*
POST OFFICE CIVIL SERVANT, *the third;* VARYA *and the* STA-
TIONMASTER, *the fourth; and so on.* VARYA *is weeping quietly,
and as she dances, she wipes her tears away.* DUNYASHA *is in
the last couple. They walk around the drawing room, and*
PISHCHIK *shouts, "Grand rond, balancez!" and "Les cavaliers
à genoux et remerciez vos dames!"*[5] FIRS, *wearing a dress coat,
brings in a tray with seltzer water.* PISHCHIK *and* TROFIMOV
enter the drawing room.

PISHCHIK. I'm a pretty full-blooded man. I've had two strokes already so dancing is hard work for me, but, as the saying goes,

> "If you run with the pack,
> > you can trail.
> Keep silent or bark back,
> > · you can't fail.
> But you'd better get crack-
> > ing to jiggle and jaggle
> > and wiggle and waggle
> > > your tail."

I'm as healthy as a horse, however. My departed father was something of a joker—may the kingdom of heaven be his—and he used
to explain our origins like this. The ancient line of Simeonov-
Pishchik, he'd say, comes down from the very same horse that
Caligula had seated in the senate . . . [*Sits down.*] But my
trouble is I don't have any money, none! A hungry dog puts his
trust only in meat . . . [*Snores and then wakes up immediately.*]
That fits me to a . . . the only thing I keep thinking about is
money . . .
TROFIMOV. Indeed your build is somehow like a horse.
PISHCHIK. Well, hmm . . . a horse is a fine animal . . . You can sell
a horse . . .
*The sound of a billiard game being played in an adjoining
room is heard.* VARYA *appears in the ballroom underneath the
archway.*
TROFIMOV. [*teases*] Madame Lopakhina! Madame Lopkhina! . .
VARYA. [*angrily*] You're a used-up old gentleman!
TROFIMOV. Yes, I am a used-up old gentleman, and I'm proud of it!
VARYA. [*meditating bitterly*] Here we've gone and hired musicians,
but what are we going to pay them with? [*Goes out.*]
TROFIMOV. [*to* PISHCHIK] Just consider how much energy you've
used up in the course of your life trying to find money to pay the

---

5. *"Promenade à une paire!"*: "Promenade with your partner!" *"Grand Rond,
balancez!"*: "The great ring dance, get
set!" *"Les cavaliers à genoux et remerciez vos dames!"*: "Gentlemen, on your
knees and thank your ladies!"

interest on your loans. If you'd spent that same energy on something else, there's a good chance, when all's been said and done, you might have turned the world upside down.

PISHCHIK. Nietzsche . . . the philosopher . . . the greatest, very famous . . . a fellow of enormous intellect. Well, he says in his own works that it's all right to forge banknotes.

TROFIMOV. Then you've read Nietzsche?[6]

PISHCHIK. Well . . . Dashenka talked to me about it. Oh, the kind of situation I'm in right now, forging banknotes is about the only thing left for me to do . . . The day after tomorrow I must pay out three hundred and ten rubles . . . and what I've already got is one hundred and thirty . . . [*Feels his pockets, alarmed.*] The money is gone! I've lost my money! [*Through tears.*] Where's my money? [*Jubilantly.*] Here it is, inside the lining . . . You know, I even started to sweat . . .

    LYUBOV ANDREEVNA *and* SHARLOTTA IVANOVNA *enter.*

LYUBOV ANDREEVNA. [*hums a* lezginka][7] Why is Leonid taking so long? What's he doing in town? [*To* DUNYASHA.] Dunyasha, offer the musicians some tea . . .

TROFIMOV. I'd say the auction probably never took place.

LYUBOV ANDREEVNA. Oh, what on earth were we thinking of? Of all moments to send for the musicians. Of all moments to give a ball. The most inopportune of all . . . Well, it's nothing, really . . . [*Sits and hums quietly.*]

SHARLOTTA. [*gives a pack of cards to* PISHCHIK] Here's a pack of cards. Think of a card, any card you want.

PISHCHIK. I've thought of one.

SHARLOTTA. Now shuffle the pack. Very good. Now let me have them, oh my dear Mister Pishchik. *Ein, zwei, drei!*[8] And now just look. There it is, in your side pocket . . .

PISHCHIK. [*takes a card out of his side pocket*] The eight of spades, you're positively right! [*Surprised.*] What do you think of that!

SHARLOTTA. [*holds the pack of cards on the palm of her hand; to* TROFIMOV] Tell me quickly, what card is on top?

TROFIMOV. Well, hmm? Well, the queen of spades.

SHARLOTTA. And here it is! [*To* PISHCHIK.] Well, what do you say the top card is now?

PISHCHIK. The ace of hearts.

SHARLOTTA. And here it is! [*Claps her hands and the pack of cards disappears.*] Oh, what fine weather today! [*She is answered by a mysterious woman's voice that apparently comes from under the floor,* "Oh, yes, the weather is incredible, dear leady."] Oh, you're so fine, indeed you're my ideal . . .

    The voice, "I like you very much, too, dear lady."

---

6. Friedrich W. Nietzsche (1844–1900), German philosopher.
7. The music which in the Caucasus mountains accompanies a courtship dance in which the man dances with abandon around the woman, who moves with grace and ease.
8. German for "one, two, three."

THE STATION MASTER. [*applauds*] Bravo, our Miss Ventriloquist, bravo!

PISHCHIK. [*surprised*] What do you think of that! You're charming, Sharlotta Ivanovna, just charming . . . you know I've simply fallen in love . . .

SHARLOTTA. In love? [*Having shrugged her shoulders.*] How could you ever fall in love, really? *Guter Mensch, aber schlechter Musikant.*[9]

TROFIMOV. [*claps* PISHCHIK *on the shoulder*] Not bad for an old horse . . .

SHARLOTTA. I beg your attention, one last trick, if you please. [*Takes a lap robe from a chair.*] Here you see a very fine lap robe I'd like to sell . . . [*Shakes it.*] Isn't there anyone who'd like to buy it?

PISHCHIK. [*surprised*] What do you think of that!

SHARLOTTA. *Ein, zwei, drei!* [*Quickly raises the lap robe, which she had lowered and held like a curtain, and behind it stands* ANYA, *who curtsies, runs to her mother, embraces her, and runs back into the ballroom amid general excitement.*]

LYUBOV ANDREEVNA. [*applauds*] Bravo, bravo! . .

SHARLOTTA. Now once more! *Ein, zwei, drei!* [*Raises the lap robe and behind it stands* VARYA, *who bows.*]

PISHCHIK. [*surprised*] What do you think of that!

SHARLOTTA. That's all there is—the end! [*Throws the lap robe at* PISHCHIK, *curtsies, and runs off to the ballroom.*]

PISHCHIK. [*hurries after her*] Oh, you little scamp . . . Think you're something, don't you? Really something? [*Goes out.*]

LYUBOV ANDREEVNA. And Leonid still isn't back yet. I can't imagine what he's doing in town all this time! You know the whole thing must be finished by now, either the estate's sold or the auction didn't take place. Then why on earth keep us in the dark all this time!

VANYA. [*trying to comfort her*] Dear Uncle bought it, I'm convinced he did.

TROFIMOV. [*derisively*] Yes.

VARYA. Grandmother sent him the authority to buy it in her name and transfer the mortgage to her. It's for Anya's sake she's doing it. And with God's help I'm convinced dear Uncle will buy it.

LYUBOV ANDREEVNA. Grandmother in Yaroslavl sent fifteen thousand rubles to buy the estate in her name—she didn't trust us—and the money she sent won't even pay the interest. [*Covers her face with her hands.*] My fate is being decided today, my fate . . .

TROFIMOV. [*teases* VARYA] Madame Lopakhina!

VARYA. [*angrily*] Oh, it's the eternal student! He's been thrown out of the university two times so far.

LYUBOV ANDREEVNA. Why are you getting angry, Varya? He's teasing

9. German for "A good man, but a bad musician."

you about Lopakhin, oh well, hmm? If you want to, then go and
marry Lopakhin. He's a fine, interesting person. If you don't want
to, then don't marry him. No one is forcing you, darling . . .

VARYA. I look on this whole matter seriously, *Mamochka*, I must
tell you frankly. He is a fine person and I like him.

LYUBOV ANDREEVNA. Then go and marry him. What is it you're waiting for, I simply don't understand!

VARYA. *Mamochka*, I can't propose to him myself, I can't. For the
past two years everyone's been talking to me about him, and they
haven't stopped talking yet, but either he doesn't say anything or
else he jokes about it. And I can understand why. He's growing
rich, he's very busy, and he hasn't one bit of time for me. If only
I had the money, even a little, if it were only a hundred rubles,
I'd drop everything and walk off. I'd go as far as I could. I'd go
into a convent.

TROFIMOV. What a blessed way to live!

VARYA. [*to* TROFIMOV] Our student can't stop proving how smart he
is! [*In a gentle tone, in tears.*] Oh, Petya, you've grown so
homely, and you look old, so very old! [*No longer weeping, she
speaks to* LYUBOV ANDREEVNA.] I just can't go through life without things to do, *Mamochka*. I must be doing something or other
every single minute.

     YASHA *enters.*

YASHA. [*scarcely able to contain his laughter*] Yepikhodov's gone
and broken a billiard cue! . . [*Goes out.*]

VARYA. Why on earth is Yepikhodov here? And who gave him permission to play billiards? These people don't make any sense to
me . . . [*Goes out.*]

LYUBOV ANDREEVNA. Don't tease her, Petya. You can see, can't you,
she's unhappy enough without that.

TROFIMOV. She's much too much the fanatic. Why can't she stick
to things that concern her? She's kept on bothering me and Anya
the whole summer long, so afraid a love affair might come about.
Why should it matter to her, anyway? Not for a single moment
did I ever give any semblance of it, I'm far beyond vulgarity like
that. We are above love!

LYUBOV ANDREEVNA. And here I am beneath love, I suppose. [*In
great apprehension*] Why on earth isn't Leonid back? I'd just like
to know if the estate's sold or not. I can't believe this terrible thing
has gone as far as it has—it's so incredible I don't even know what
to think anymore, somehow I feel lost . . . I could scream right
now . . . or do something foolish. Save me, Petya. Say something
now, talk to me . . .

TROFIMOV. Does it really matter whether the estate is sold today or
not? It's over and done with, there's no turning back now, that
path's already overgrown. Get hold of yourself, my dear. And don't
go and deceive yourself now. At least for once in your life look
the truth right in the eyes.

LYUBOV ANDREEVNA. What truth? You can see, can't you, where the truth is and where it isn't, but it seems I've lost my sight, I see nothing. You confidently find answers for all the important problems, but tell me, my dear, isn't that because you're young, because you're not old enough for a single one of your problems to have brought about any substantial suffering? You look ahead so boldly, and you don't see or expect anything terrible to happen, and isn't that because life is still hidden from your young eyes? You are bolder, more honest, deeper than we are, but try and go into the heart of the matter—be at least halfway generous[1] and have mercy on me. You know I was born here, my father and my mother lived here, my grandfather, too. I love this house. Without the cherry orchard my life would lose its meaning, and if it must really be sold then go and sell me with the orchard . . . [*Embraces* TROFIMOV *and kisses him on the forehead.*] You see my son was drowned here . . . [*Weeps.*] Have pity on me, my fine, kind friend.

TROFIMOV. You know I feel for you with all my heart and soul.

LYUBOV ANDREEVNA. But that isn't the way to say it, it isn't the way at all . . . [*Takes out her handkerchief. A telegram falls on the floor.*] Today I feel I've lost heart and soul, you can't imagine how difficult it is for me. It's too noisy here for me. Every sound cuts deep inside and I feel I'm trembling all over, but I can't go to my room, I can't. All alone in the silence, it's terrifying. Don't condemn me, Petya . . . I love you as if you were one of my very own. I'd willingly let Anya marry you, I swear I would, my dear, only you must study and get your degree. You aren't doing a single thing, you just let fate throw you from one place to another, and that's what is so strange . . . Isn't it the truth? Yes? And you ought to do something or other with that beard to make it grow somehow . . . [*Laughs.*] Oh, you're funny, you really are!

TROFIMOV. [*picks up telegram*] I don't have the slightest desire to be good looking.

LYUBOV ANDREEVNA. That telegram is from Paris. I get one every day. Both yesterday and today. That wild creature has fallen ill again, and he's in trouble again . . . He begs forgiveness and implores me to go to him, and I really should go to Paris and spend some time near him. You disapprove, Petya, I can see from your face, but what else can be done, my dear, what can I really do? He is sick, he is alone and unhappy, and who is there to look after him? Who can stop him from doing the wrong things, and who will give him his medicine at the right time? Then why try to hide it or keep quiet about the way I feel? I love him, that's clear. I love him, I love him . . . That man's a millstone around my neck, I'm being dragged down with him, but I love that stone and I can't live without it. [*Presses* TROFIMOV's *hand.*] Don't think

1. Literally, "be generous at least in your fingernails."

badly of me, Petya, don't say anything to me, don't say anything . . .

TROFIMOV. [*through tears*] Forgive me for being outspoken, for God's sake, but you know he robbed you!

LYUBOV ANDREEVNA. No, no, no, you mustn't talk that way . . . [*Puts her hands over her ears.*]

TROFIMOV. That man is a good-for-nothing louse, and you're the only one who doesn't know it! He's a little, good-for-nothing louse, a nobody . . .

LYUBOV ANDREEVNA. [*having gotten angry, she controls herself*] You are twenty-six or twenty-seven years old, but you are still a schoolboy!

TROFIMOV. And even if I am!

LYUBOV ANDREEVNA. You ought to be a man—at your age you ought to have some understanding of people in love. And you ought to know what it is to love . . . You should fall in love yourself! [*Angrily.*] Yes, yes! And don't think you're so innocent and pure, you're simply an immaculate prude—that's what you are—a laughable eccentric boy, some kind of freak . . .

TROFIMOV. [*horrified*] What can she be saying!

LYUBOV ANDREEVNA. "I am above love!" You aren't above love, but —as our Firs keeps saying—you are just a silly galoot, that's all. At your age and not to have a mistress! . .

TROFIMOV. [*horrified*] This is terrible! What can she be saying? [*Having clutched his head, he goes into the ballroom.*] This is terrible . . . I can't stand it, I'm going . . . [*Goes out, but returns immediately.*] All is over between us! [*Goes out into the entrance hall.*]

LYUBOV ANDREEVNA. [*shouts after him*] Petya, wait a moment! You ridiculous boy, I was joking! Petya!

In the entrance hall there are the sounds of someone quickly running on the stairway and suddenly falling downstairs with a clatter. ANYA *and* VARYA *scream, which is followed immediately by the sound of laughter.*

LYUBOV ANDREEVNA. What's going on out there?

ANYA *runs in.*

ANYA. [*laughing*] Petya fell downstairs! [*Runs out.*]

LYUBOV ANDREEVNA. What an eccentric boy Petya is . . . [*Having stopped in the middle of the ballroom, the stationmaster recites "The Sinful Woman" by Aleksey Tolstoy. They listen to him, but he has recited only a few lines when the sounds of a waltz come from the entrance hall and the reading is broken off. All dance.* TROFIMOV, ANYA, VARYA, *and* LYUBOV ANDREEVNA *enter from the entrance hall.*] Now, Petya . . . now there, you dear innocent soul . . . Forgive me, I beg you . . . Let's dance . . . [*Dances with* PETYA.]

ANYA *and* VARYA *dance.* FIRS *enters and puts his walking stick near the side door.* YASHA *has also come in from the drawing room and is watching the dancing.*

YASHA. What do you say, Grandpa?

FIRS. I don't feel too well. In times gone by, why generals, barons, and admirals came to our dances, but now we send for the post office clerk and the stationmaster—and even they come against their will. Somehow I feel I've gotten weaker. My old master, who was their grandfather, used to dose every one of us with powdered sealing wax no matter what sickness we had. I've been taking sealing wax for about twenty years now, but it might even be more. Maybe I'm still alive because of it.

YASHA. Gramps, you make me sick and tired. [*Yawns.*] If only you'd go off and croak—the sooner the better.

FIRS. Oh, you . . . you silly galoot, you! [*Mumbles.*]

TROFIMOV *and* LYUBOV ANDREEVNA *dance in the ballroom and then into the drawing room.*

LYUBOV ANDREEVNA. *Merci.* I'd like to sit down for a while . . . [*Sits down.*] I'm tired.

ANYA *enters.*

ANYA. [*excitedly*] In the kitchen just now someone was saying that the cherry orchard was sold today.

LYUBOV ANDREEVNA. Sold? To whom?

ANYA. He didn't say. He's gone now. [*Dances with* TROFIMOV; *they go into the ballroom.*]

YASHA. It was just some old man wagging his tongue out there. We didn't know him.

FIRS. Oh, Leonid Andreich still isn't here, he hasn't come back yet. He's only wearing his lightweight overcoat, his "between-seasons" one, and before you can bat an eye he's going to catch cold. Oh, these green young things—they never learn.

LYUBOV ANDREEVNA. I'm going to die, I know it. Yasha, go and find out whom it was sold to.

YASHA. But he went away a long time back, it was an old man. [*Laughs.*]

LYUBOV ANDREEVNA. [*slightly annoyed*] Well, what are you laughing about? What's making you so happy?

YASHA. Oh, that Yepikhodov is really very funny. The man's so useless. Two-and-Twenty Hard Knocks.

LYUBOV ANDREEVNA. If the estate is sold, Firs, where will you go?

FIRS. Wherever you tell me, that's where I'll go.

LYUBOV ANDREEVNA. Why do you look like that? Aren't you feeling well? You ought to go lie down and sleep, you know . . .

FIRS. Yes . . . [*With an ironic smile.*] I'd go off to sleep, and if I'm not here who will there be to serve and keep things going the way they should? I'm the only one in charge of the whole house.

YASHA. [*to* LYUBOV ANDREEVNA] Lyubov Andreevna! Allow me to ask you something, if you'd be so kind! If you go to Paris again, do me a favor and take me with you, please. I can't stay here, it's absolutely impossible here. [*Looks around, in an undertone.*] I suppose it's needless to say it, you can see for yourself, this country is uncivilized and the people don't have any morals at all. Then there's the boredom, too. In the kitchen they feed you disgusting things, and to make it worse—that man Firs keeps walking around the whole time and mumbling all sorts of words that don't make much sense. Take me with you, if you'd be so kind!

PISHCHIK *enters.*

PISHCHIK. Please do me the favor . . . of this little waltz, oh gorgeous woman . . . [LYUBOV ANDREEVNA *goes with him.*] But I'll still take that one hundred and eighty rubles from you, my charming lady . . . Yes, I will . . . [*Dances.*] One hundred and eighty rubles . . . [*They go into the ballroom.*]

YASHA. [*quietly sings*] "If you could but know the excitement of my soul . . ."

In the ballroom a woman dressed in a gray top hat and checked trousers is seen jumping around and waving her arms. There are shouts of "Bravo, Sharlotta Ivanovna."

DUNYASHA. [*stops to powder*] The young mistress told me to dance. There are plenty of gentlemen and only a few ladies, but dancing makes my head spin around and my heart is pounding. Just now, Firs Nikolaevich, the clerk from the post office told me something that made me lose my breath.

The music subsides.

FIRS. What exactly did he tell you?

DUNYASHA. You are like a flower, he said.

YASHA. [*yawns*] Sheer case of ignorance . . . [*Goes out.*]

DUNYASHA. Like a flower . . . I'm such a delicate girl I just love hearing sweet words like that.

FIRS. You'll get swept off your feet before you know it.

YEPIKHODOV *enters.*

YEPIKHODOV. You don't want to look at me, Avdotya Fyodorovna . . . as if I were an insect of some kind. [*Sighs.*] Oh, that's life!

DUNYASHA. What do you want?

YEPIKHODOV. No doubt you are right, perhaps. [*Sighs.*] But, of course, if you look at it from one point of view—and I will allow myself to express myself this way, please excuse me for being so outspoken—you have completely reduced me to a state of mind. I know what luck I face. Every day some catastrophe or other happens to me, but I got used to that long, long ago, so that I look upon my fate with a smile on my face. You gave me your word, and even though I . . .

DUNYASHA. I beg you, let's talk a little later on, but now just leave me alone. I'm dreaming right now. [*Plays with her fan.*]

YEPIKHODOV. I have a catastrophe every day and—I'll permit myself to express myself this way—I just go on smiling, and sometimes I even laugh.

VARYA *enters from the ballroom.*

VARYA. Haven't you left yet, Semyon? Who do you think you are, really, don't you have any respect? [*To* DUNYASHA.] Be off, Dunyasha, you can leave. [*To* YEPIKHODOV] First you play billiards and break a cue, and now you walk around the drawing room as if you were a guest.

YEPIKHODOV. You can't make me—if you'll permit me to say—answer for it.

VARYA. I'm not making you answer for it, I'm just telling you. All you know how to do is walk from one place to the next, but you don't do one bit of work. We keep a clerk, but for what—it's beyond me.

YEPIKHODOV. [*offended*] Whether I work or ramble about, whether I eat or play billiards, these are issues up for discussion only by more reasonable and older people.

VARYA. How dare you talk to me that way! [*Having flared up.*] How dare you? Do you mean I'm not reasonable, is that it? Well, you can remove yourself, get out of here! This minute!

YEPIKHODOV. [*having become intimidated*] I beg you to express yourself in a delicate way.

VARYA. [*flying into a rage*] Get out of here this very minute! Out of here, out! [*He goes to the door and she follows him.*] Two-and-Twenty Hard Knocks! Out you go and never come in here again! Don't let me catch sight of you ever again! [YEPIKHODOV *goes out. Behind the door his voice is heard:* "I'm going to bring a complaint against you."] So you're coming back in here? [*Seizes the stick which* FIRS *placed near the door.*] Come on . . . come on . . . come on, I'll show you. . . . So you're coming back? You are, are you? Then take that . . . [*Flourishes the stick at the very moment* LOPAKHIN *enters.*]

LOPAKHIN. Thank you ever so much.

VARYA. [*angrily and derisively*] I'm very sorry!

LOPAKHIN. It's nothing, Miss. Thanks so much for your heartfelt generosity.

VARYA. Don't mention it. [*Walks away, then looks around and gently asks.*] I didn't hurt you, did I?

LOPAKHIN. No, it's nothing. There's going to be one whale of a swelling, though.

    Voices are heard in the ballroom: "Lopakhin's arrived! Yermolay Alexeich!"

PISHCHIK. Well, squint your eyes and bend your ears—it's him himself . . . [*Kisses* LOPAKHIN.] I caught a whiff of brandy on you, my dear old soul. We've been kicking up our heels around here too.

    LYUBOV ANDREEVNA *enters.*

LYUBOV ANDREEVNA. Then it's you, Yermolay Alexeich? What's taken you so long? Where is Leonid?

LOPAKHIN. Leonid Andreich came with me, he's on his way . . .

LYUBOV ANDREEVNA. [*agitated*] Well, what is it? Did the auction take place? Talk to me, tell me!

LOPAKHIN. [*embarrassed, fearing to betray his elation*] The auction was over by four . . . We were late for the train, and we had to wait until half past nine. [*Having sighed heavily.*] Phew! My head's starting to go round and round . . .

> GAEV *enters. He has his purchases in his right hand and wipes away his tears with his left hand.*

LYUBOV ANDREEVNA. Lyonya, what is it? Well, Lyonya? [*Impatiently, in tears.*] Tell me, for God's sake! Quickly . . .

GAEV. [*he can say nothing to her and only waves his hand; to* FIRS, *weeping*] Here, take these . . . It's anchovies and Kerch herrings . . . I've had nothing to eat today . . . How much I've had to go through! [*The door to the billiard room is open. The cracking of billiard balls is heard, and* YASHA's *voice:* "Seven and eighteen!" GAEV's *expression changes and he no longer weeps.*] I'm terribly tired. Give me a hand, Firs, I must change my clothes. [*Goes to his room through the ballroom, followed by* FIRS.]

PISHCHIK. What went on at the auction? Tell us now, do!

LYUBOV ANDREEVNA. Is the cherry orchard sold?

LOPAKHIN. It's sold.

LYUBOV ANDREEVNA. Who bought it?

LOPAKHIN. I bought it. [*Pause.* LYUBOV ANDREEVNA *is crushed. If she were not standing next to the armchair and table, she would have fallen. Varya takes the keys from her belt, throws them on the floor in the middle of the drawing room, and goes out.*] I bought it! Wait, ladies and gentlemen, be kind and wait one moment. My head's going round in circles, I can't talk . . . [*Laughs.*] When we got to the auction, Deriganov was already there. Leonid Andreich had only fifteen thousand rubles, and right away Deriganov bid thirty over and above the arrearage on the mortgage. I saw the shape things were in, so I took him on. I bid forty. He went to forty-five, I made it fifty-five. That's the way it went. He kept raising his offer by five thousand, I kept raising mine by ten . . . Well, it came to a finish at last. I bid ninety thousand rubles on top of the arrears, and I got it. The cherry orchard is mine now! Mine! [*Shouts with laughter.*] God in heaven, dear Lord God, the cherry orchard is mine! Tell me I'm drunk or out of my mind, that it's all a daydream I see before my eyes . . . [*Stamps his feet.*] Don't laugh at me! If only my father and grandfather could rise from their graves and see their Yermolay now—their Yermolay who was forever getting beaten, Yermolay who could scarcely read or write, who ran barefoot in the winter—if they could only see how this very same Yermolay went and bought this estate, the most beautiful spot in the world. I bought the estate where my grandfather and my father were slaves, where they weren't even allowed to go into the kitchen. I'm asleep, it's only a dream, it's only something that seems to be

. . . This is the fruit of your imagination, concealed in the shadows of uncertainty . . . [*Picks up the keys, smiling affectionately.*] She threw down the keys—she wants to show she doesn't run this house anymore . . . [*Jingles the keys.*] Well, it doesn't matter anyway. [*The orchestra is heard tuning up.*] Hey there, musicians, start playing. I want to hear you! Come on, all of you, come and see Yermolay Lopakhin slash the cherry orchard with his axe. Watch and see the trees come crashing down! We're going to build summer cottages, and our grandchildren and our great-grandchildren are going to see a new way to live around here . . . Music, start playing! [*The orchestra plays.* LYUBOV ANDREEVNA *has sunk into a chair and is weeping bitterly.* LOPAKHIN *speaks reproachfully.*] Why on earth, why didn't you listen to me before? My poor, fine friend, you can't turn round and go back now. [*In tears.*] Oh, if only this would pass by as quickly as possible, if only we could hurry and change our life somehow, this unhappy, helter-skelter way we live.

PISHCHIK. [*takes him by the arm, in an undertone*] She's crying. Let's go into the ballroom, let her be alone . . . Come, let's go . . . [*Takes him by the arm and leads him into the ballroom.*]

LOPAKHIN. What's going on? Say, you doing the music, play lively and clear! Let's start having things the way I want it. [*Ironically.*] Here comes the new landlord, the owner of the cherry orchard! [*Accidentally shoves a small table, nearly overturns the candelabra.*] I can pay for everything! [*Goes out with* PISHCHIK.]

  There is no one left in the ballroom or the drawing room except LYUBOV ANDREEVNA, *who sits all shrunken and is weeping bitterly. The orchestra plays quietly.* ANYA *and* TROFIMOV *enter quickly.* ANYA *goes to her mother and kneels down in front of her.* TROFIMOV *stays by the entrance to the ballroom.*

ANYA. Mama! . . Mama, are you crying? My dear, kind, beautiful Mama, my precious, I love you, I do . . . I give you my blessing. The cherry orchard is sold, it's gone now, it's true, so true, but don't cry, Mama. Your life is still ahead of you, and you haven't lost your beautiful, innocent soul . . . Come with me, my dear, let's go away from here, let's go! . . We shall plant a new orchard, far more splendid than this one. You shall see it, you shall know and find understanding, and happiness shall descend into your heart and soul—you shall know a quiet and profound joy—like the setting sun at the evening hour, and you shall smile, Mama! Come, my dear, let's go! Let's go! . .

CURTAIN

Act Four

The setting is the same as in the first act. There are no window curtains or pictures. The few remaining pieces of furniture have been piled into one corner, as if for sale. There is a feeling of emptiness. Suitcases, traveling bags, etc., have been piled up near the outer door at the rear of the stage. Through the open door, left, the voices of ANYA and VARYA can be heard. LOPAKHIN is standing, waiting. YASHA is holding a tray with glasses filled with champagne. In the entrance hall YEPIKHODOV is tying up a box. There is a rumble coming from offstage at the rear, the voices of the peasants who have come to say good-bye. GAEV's voice is heard: "Thanks, brothers, thank you."

YASHA. The peasants have come to say good-bye. The way I look at it, Yermolay Alexeich, such folks are decent enough, but they don't really know what's what.
    The rumble of voices subsides. LYUBOV ANDREEVNA *and* GAEV *come in through the entrance hall. She is not weeping; however, she is pale, her face is quivering, and she is unable to speak.*
GAEV. You gave them your purse, Lyuba. That's something you shouldn't do! You know you shouldn't!
LYUBOV ANDREEVNA. I couldn't help it! I simply couldn't help it! [*Both go out.*]
LOPAKHIN. [*in the doorway, calling after them*] Please, I ask you from the bottom of my heart, let's have one little glass since we must say good-bye. I didn't come up with the idea of bringing it from town, and I could only find one bottle at the station. Please, I beg you! [*Pause.*] Well, hmm, friends! Don't you want some? [*Walks away from the door.*] If I'd known, I wouldn't have bought it. Well, then, I'm not going to drink any, either. [YASHA *carefully puts the tray on a chair.*] You take some, Yasha, at least you.
YASHA. To those who are going away! And good luck to those who stay behind! [*Drinks.*] This champagne isn't the real stuff, you can take my word for it.
LOPAKHIN. Eight rubles a bottle. [*Pause.*] Damn, it's cold in here.
YASHA. They didn't start the fires today. It doesn't matter, we're going away. [*Laughs.*]
LOPAKHIN. What's so funny?
YASHA. I feel pleased, that's all.
LOPAKHIN. October has come, but it's sunny and quiet outside, like in the summer. Good weather for building. [*Having glanced*

at his watch, calls through the doorway.] Keep in mind, ladies and gentlemen, forty-six minutes before the train leaves. That means we must start for the station in twenty minutes. Better hurry up.

> *Trofimov, wearing an overcoat, enters from outside.*

TROFIMOV. I think it's time we set off. They've brought the horses to the door. Damned if I know where my galoshes are. They've disappeared. [*Calls through the doorway.*] Anya, my galoshes aren't here! Can't find them at all!

LOPAKHIN. I must go to Kharkov. I'll be going with you on the same train. I'll spend the whole winter in Kharkov. I've been shooting the breeze with you folks all the time, it really bothers me when I don't have things to do. I can't stand going without work, because I don't know what to do with my hands. You can see the peculiar way they dangle, just as if they belonged to someone else.

TROFIMOV. We're going away pretty soon, and you can get down to your useful labor again.

LOPAKHIN. How about it, have a little glass.

TROFIMOV. No, thanks.

LOPAKHIN. So you're going to Moscow, right?

TROFIMOV. Yes, I'll see them off and on their way in town, and tomorrow I'll start for Moscow.

LOPAKHIN. Yes . . . Well, hmm, the professors haven't started their lectures yet, I suppose, they must be waiting for you to show up!

TROFIMOV. It's none of your business.

LOPAKHIN. How many years have you been studying at the university?

TROFIMOV. Think of something new to say. That joke is old and flat. [*Looks for his galoshes.*] You know, don't you, we may not see each other anymore, so let me give you a word or two of advice. Don't wave your arms around! Get rid of that habit of waving your arms. Another thing too. When you count on building those summer homes and say that the owners in time will turn out to be independent farmers, you count so much on it— that's just the same as waving your arms around . . . Well, be that as it may, I still like you very much. You have delicate and gentle fingers like an artist has, and in the same way, you are delicate and gentle too in your soul . . .

LOPAKHIN. [*embraces him*] Good-bye, my friend. Thank you for everything. Let me give you some money for the trip, in case you need it.

TROFIMOV. Whatever for? I don't need it.

LOPAKHIN. You know you have nothing!

TROFIMOV. Yes, I have, and I thank you. I got something for a translation. It's here, in my pocket. [*Anxiously.*] But I still don't have my galoshes!

VARYA. [*from the adjoining room*] Oh, take your filthy things!

[*Throws a pair of rubber galoshes out on the stage.*]

TROFIMOV. Why are you so angry, Varya? Hmm . . . Oh, these aren't my galoshes!

LOPAKHIN. In the spring I seeded almost three thousand acres in poppies, and I just earned forty thousand rubles clear and clean. And when my poppies were in flower, what a picture of beauty that was! What I'm saying is this. I made forty thousand, so I'm offering you a loan because I can well afford to. So why stick your nose in the air? I'm a peasant . . . and I call a spade a spade.

TROFIMOV. Your father was a peasant, mine was a druggist, and these simple facts prove—exactly nothing. [LOPAKHIN *takes out his wallet.*] Oh, leave it alone, do . . . Even if you gave me two hundred thousand, I wouldn't take it. I'm a free person. And everything you value so highly and is held so dear by all of you, both rich and poor, not one of these things can sway me one iota. Why, they have as much power as a fluff of eiderdown floating in the air. I can make a go of it without you, I can even pass you by. I'm strong and proud. Humankind is on its way to a higher truth, to the greatest happiness possible on this earth, and I'm in the vanguard!

LOPAKHIN. Will you get there?

TROFIMOV. I will. [*Pause.*] I'll either get there or show others the way to get there.

> There is heard the sound of an axe striking a tree in the distance.

LOPAKHIN. Well, good-bye, dear boy. It's time to go. You and I stick our noses in the air and look down on each other, but life goes on without giving a hoot about us. When I work and keep at it steadily for some time, thoughts come more easily, and it seems to me I too know why I exist. But think how many people there are in Russia who just exist, brother, and for what—it's beyond me. Well, it doesn't matter, that isn't what keeps the wheels greased and spinning. Leonid Andreich has taken a job at the bank, they say, at six thousand a year . . . He just won't stick to it, you know, he's much too lazy . . .

ANYA. [*in the doorway*] Mama begs you not to cut down the orchard until after she's gone.

TROFIMOV. Yes, really, don't you have tact enough to see . . . [*Goes out through the entrance hall.*]

LOPAKHIN. All right, it'll take only a minute . . . Oh, these people, really. [*Goes out after him.*]

ANYA. Has Firs been sent to the hospital?

YASHA. I told them this morning. They've sent him, it stands to reason they have.

ANYA. [*to* YEPIKHODOV, *who is passing through the room*] Semyon Panteleich, please ask and find out if they've taken Firs to the hospital.

YASHA. [*offended*] I told Yegor this morning. Why keep on asking about it? You've brought it up ten times.

YEPIKHODOV. Firs has lived through so many years, my final and decisive opinion is that he's gone far beyond repair. It's time for him to meet his forefathers. And I can only envy him. [*He has put the suitcase down on a hatbox and has crushed it.*] Well, that's it, of course. I knew it'd turn out like that. [*Goes out.*]

YASHA. [*derisively*] Two-and-Twenty Hard Knocks . . .

VARYA. [*from behind the door*] Has Firs been taken to the hospital?

ANYA. Yes, he has.

VARYA. Why is it they didn't take the letter to the doctor?

ANYA. Then we must send it on after him . . . [*Goes out.*]

VARYA. [*from the adjoining room*] Where is Yasha? Tell him his mother's come and wants to say good-bye.

YASHA. [*waves his hand*] That's enough to make you lose your patience.

All this time DUNYASHA *has been fussing with the luggage. Now that* YASHA *is alone, she goes up to him.*

DUNYASHA. Why didn't you even glance at me once, Yasha? You are going away . . . You're walking out on me . . . [*Weeps and throws her arms around his neck.*]

YASHA. What are you crying about, hmm? [*Drinks champagne.*] I'll be in Paris again in six days. Tomorrow we'll take the express train, off we'll roll, and that's the last you'll see of us. I can't even believe it, somehow. *Vive la France!* . . It doesn't suit me here, I really can't stand this sort of life . . . and that's all there is to it. I've seen enough ignorance, oh, have I had my fill of it. [*Drinks champagne.*] What are you crying about, hmm? Behave yourself as you should, and you won't have to cry then.

DUNYASHA. [*looking in the small mirror, powders*] Send me a letter from Paris. You know I loved you, Yasha, I loved you so much! I'm a tenderhearted person, Yasha, through and through!

YASHA. Someone is coming. [*Fusses with a suitcase, quietly hums.*]

LYUBOV ANDREEVNA, GAEV, ANYA, *and* SHARLOTTA IVANOVNA *enter.*

GAEV. We ought to go. There's just a little time left. [*Looking at* YASHA.] Who is it in here reeks of herring?

LYUBOV ANDREEVNA. In about ten minutes we must be getting into the carriages . . . [*Looks around the room.*] Good-bye, my home. Fare thee well, dear old house of our forefathers. Winter will pass, spring will come in time, and then you won't be here anymore, you will be pulled down. Oh, the sights these walls have seen in days gone by! [*Kisses her daughter fervently.*] My treasure, how radiant you look, your eyes are shining like diamonds. Are you pleased, child? Really pleased?

ANYA. Really! This is the beginning of a new life, Mama!

GAEV. [*cheerfully*] Yes, indeed, everything is fine again. Before the cherry orchard was sold, we were all upset and worried ourselves sick, but afterwards, when the whole thing was settled once and for all, and not one chance of turning back, we all simmered down and even started to feel cheerful . . . I'm an employee of a bank now. I'm a financier . . . Off the yellow right into the middle. And Lyuba, in spite of everything, you are looking better, no doubt about it, none.

LYUBOV ANDREEVNA. Yes. My nerves are much better, that's true. [*Someone helps her put on her hat and coat.*] I'm sleeping fine. Take my things out, Yasha. It's time. [*To* ANYA.] My little girl, we'll see each other again soon . . . I'm going to Paris, and I'll live there on the money your grandmother from Yaroslavl sent to buy the estate—long live Grandmother! That money won't last for long.

ANYA. You'll come back soon, Mama, very soon . . . isn't that so? I'm going to study and pass my school examinations, and then I'll go to work and help you. Mama, we'll read all kinds of books together . . . isn't that so? [*Kisses her mother's hands.*] We shall read during the autumn evenings, we'll read through lots of books, and a new marvelous world will open up before us . . . [*Daydreams.*] Mama, come back . . .

LYUBOV ANDREEVNA. I will, my precious. [*Embraces her daughter.*]

LOPAKHIN *enters.* SHARLOTTA *quietly hums a song.*

GAEV. Happy Sharlotta, she's singing!

SHARLOTTA. [*picks up a bundle which resembles a baby in swaddling clothes*] Bye, bye, little baby mine . . . [*The crying of a baby is heard,* "Wah, Wah! . ."] Be quiet, my dear, my fine little boy. ["Wah! . . Wah! . ."] I feel sorry for you, so sorry! [*Throws the bundle down.*] Then please find me another job, won't you? I can't go on like this.

LOPAKHIN. We'll find something for you, Sharlotta Ivanovna, don't get upset.

GAEV. Everyone's discarding us. Varya's going away too . . . All of a sudden we're not needed.

SHARLOTTA. I don't have any place to live in town. I must go away . . . [*Hums.*] It doesn't matter . . .

PISHCHIK *enters.*

LOPAKHIN. What do I see? One of nature's miracles! . .

PISHCHIK. [*out of breath*] Phew, give me a chance to get my breath back . . . I'm bushed . . . My dear venerable friends . . . give me some water . . .

GAEV. You're after some money, I suppose? Your humble servant, I'm going to go now and leave my tempter behind me . . . [*Goes out.*]

PISHCHIK. It's been a while since I've been here . . . most beautiful lady . . . [*To* LOPAKHIN.] You're here too . . . I'm glad to see you . . . a fellow of most enormous intellect . . . Here, take

it . . . accept it, do . . . [*Gives* LOPAKHIN *money.*] Four hundred
rubles . . . I still owe you eight hundred and forty.

LOPAKHIN. [*bewildered, shrugs his shoulders*] It's like a dream . . .
Where on earth did you get it?

PISHCHIK. Wait a bit . . . I'm really hot . . . A most extraordinary
incident. Some Englishmen arrived at my place and found some
kind of white clay in the ground . . . [*To* LYUBOV ANDREEVNA.]
And four hundred for you . . . my beautiful stunning woman . . .
[*Gives her money.*] I'll give you the rest later on. [*Drinks
water.*] Just now a certain young man on the train was saying
that some sort of . . . great philosopher advises everybody to run
and jump off a roof . . . "Go ahead and jump," he says, and in
that lies the whole problem. [*Surprised.*] What do you think of
that! Give me some water! . .

LOPAKHIN. What sort of Englishmen were they?

PISHCHIK. I leased them the land with the clay in it for twenty-four
years . . . And now, please excuse me, I've no more time . . . Must
gallop farther on . . . I'm going to see Znoykov . . . and Kardamonov . . . I'm in debt to everybody . . . [*Drinks.*] I wish you
all a good day . . . I'll drop by on Thursday . . .

LYUBOV ANDREEVNA. We're just now moving our things to town,
and tomorrow I go abroad . . .

PISHCHIK. What's that? [*Becomes anxious.*] Why to town? Oh, yes,
now I see the furniture . . . suitcases . . . Well, it's nothing . . .
[*Through tears.*] It's nothing . . . People of mammoth intellect
. . . these Englishmen . . . It's nothing . . . all happiness to you
. . . God will help you . . . It's nothing . . . Everything in this
world must come to an end . . . [*Kisses* LYUBOV ANDREEVNA'S
hand.] And if the news gets to you that my end has come, just
recall this very . . . old horse and say, "Once on this earth there
was such-and-such a person . . . Simeonov-Pishchik . . . may the
kingdom of heaven be his . . ." Most remarkable weather today
. . . Yes . . . [*Goes out greatly troubled, but returns immediately to speak from the doorway.*] Dashenka sends her regards
to you! [*Goes out.*]

LYUBOV ANDREEVNA. Well, we can go now. I'm leaving with two
things weighing on my mind. My first worry is Firs and the fact
that he's ill. [*Having glanced at her watch.*] We have about five
minutes left . . .

ANYA. Mama, they've already sent Firs to the hospital. Yasha sent
him this morning.

LYUBOV ANDREEVNA. My other distress is Varya. She's accustomed to
getting up early and working, and now without anything to do—
she's like a fish out of water. She's become so thin and pale, and
she weeps all the time, poor darling . . . [*Pause.*] As you very well
know, Yermolay Alexeich, I've dreamed . . . of giving her in marriage to you. Besides, that's the way things seemed to look—you
were planning to get married. [*Whispers to* ANYA, *who nods to*

SHARLOTTA, *and they both go out.*] She loves you, you like her, and I don't know—I really don't—why it is you try to avoid each other. I simply can't understand it!

LOPAKHIN. I don't understand it, either, to tell the truth. Somehow it's all pretty strange . . . If there's still time, I'm all set to go ahead right now . . . Let's get it settled, finish it up, and—*basta.*[2] But I don't feel I can make a proposal unless you're here too.

LYUBOV ANDREEVNA. Oh, that's splendid. You know it'll take about a minute, no more. I'll call her now . . .

LOPAKHIN. By the way, we even have champagne. [*Having glanced at the glasses.*] Empty, someone's already drunk it all. [YASHA *coughs.*] That's really called lapping it up . . .

LYUBOV ANDREEVNA. [*vivaciously*] Wonderful. We'll leave you now . . . Yasha, *allez!*[3] I'll call her . . . [*In the doorway.*] Varya, leave everything and come here. Come along now! [*Goes out with* YASHA.]

LOPAKHIN. [*having glanced at his watch*] Yes . . . [*Pause.*]
Suppressed laughter and whispering are heard from behind the door. Finally VARYA enters.

VARYA. [*examines the luggage for a long time*] It's strange, I just can't seem to find . . .

LOPAKHIN. What are you searching for?

VARYA. I packed it away myself, and I can't remember. [*Pause.*]

LOPAKHIN. Where is it you're going now, Varvara Mikhaylovna?

VARYA. Me? To Ragulins' . . . I've agreed to look after their place . . . as the housekeeper. At least that's the impression I get.

LOPAKHIN. That's at Yashnevo, isn't it? About seventy versts away from here. [*Pause.*] And so life is over and done with in this house . . .

VARYA. [*examining the luggage*] Where on earth could it . . . Or, maybe, I packed it away in the trunk . . . Yes, life in this house is over and done with . . . And it will never come back here anymore . . .

LOPAKHIN. And I'm just now on my way to Kharkov . . . On the next train, you see. I've got plenty to do. I'm leaving Yepikhodov here to look after the work outside . . . I've hired him.

VARYA. Well, hmm!

LOPAKHIN. Last year at this time we had snow on the ground, if you recall, but now it's pretty quiet and plenty of sunshine. It's just cold, that's all . . . About three degrees of frost.

VARYA. I haven't looked. [*Pause.*] Besides, our thermometer's broken . . . [*Pause.*]
A voice from outside is heard calling through the door, "Yermolay Alexeich!"

2. See note 2, p. 73 (*Uncle Vanya*).
3. "Let's go!"

LOPAKHIN. [*as if he has been waiting a long time for this summons*] This very minute! [*Quickly goes out.*]

VARYA *sits on the floor, having laid her head on a bundle of clothing, and quietly sobs. The door opens, and* LYUBOV ANDREEVNA *enters warily.*

LYUBOV ANDREEVNA. Well? [*Pause.*] We must go.

VARYA. [*no longer is weeping and has wiped her eyes*] Yes, it's time, *Mamochka.* If I don't miss my train I can get to the Ragulins' today . . .

LYUBOV ANDREEVNA. [*in the doorway*] Anya, bundle up! [ANYA *enters, then* GAEV *and* SHARLOTTA IVANOVNA. GAEV *is wearing a warm overcoat with a hood. A* MAIDSERVANT *and* COACHMEN *enter and begin to fetch and carry.* YEPIKHODOV *bustles about and supervises those who carry the luggage.*] Now we can start on our way.

ANYA. [*jubilantly*] Yes, on our way!

GAEV. My friends, my dear, good friends! Deserting this home forever, how can I be silent, how can I refrain from expressing my feelings in saying good-bye, feelings that now fill my whole being . . .

ANYA. [*beseechingly*] Uncle!

VARYA. Uncle dear, you mustn't!

GAEV. [*despondently*] A bank shot off the yellow into the middle . . . I'll keep quiet . . .

TROFIMOV *enters, then* LOPAKHIN.

TROFIMOV. What about it, ladies and gentlemen, it's time to go!

LOPAKHIN. Yepikhodov, my overcoat!

LYUBOV ANDREEVNA. I'll just sit down one more minute. It's just as if I'd never noticed what the walls and ceiling of this house look like, and now I see them eagerly, with such a gentle love . . .

GAEV. I remember when I was six years old. I was sitting in this window on Trinity Sunday, and I saw my father going to church . . .

LYUBOV ANDREEVNA. Have they taken out all the things?

LOPAKHIN. Yes, it seems they have, everything. [*Putting on his coat, to* YEPIKHODOV.] Yepikhodov, be sure to look and see that everything's in the right order.

YEPIKHODOV. [*speaks in a hoarse voice*] You can rest assured, Yermolay Alexeich!

LOPAKHIN. What's the trouble with your voice?

YEPIKHODOV. I just now drank some water, I must have swallowed something or other.

YASHA. [*scornfully*] Sheer case of ignorance . . .

LYUBOV ANDREEVNA. We're going away, and not one soul will be left here . . .

LOPAKHIN. Until this coming spring.

VARYA. [*Pulls an umbrella out of a bundle and it looks as if she were going to strike someone.* LOPAKHIN *pretends that he is fright-*

ened.] Oh, you're not serious, you can't be . . . Why, the thought never entered my mind.

TROFIMOV. Ladies and gentlemen, let's go and get in the carriages . . . It's time, time! The train will soon be in!

VARYA. Petya, here they are, your galoshes, next to the suitcase. [*Through tears.*] And how filthy they are, and old . . .

TROFIMOV. [*putting on his galoshes*] On our way, ladies and gentlemen!

GAEV. [*greatly troubled and afraid of breaking into tears*] The train . . . The station . . . Across into the middle, bank shot off the white into the corner . . .

LYOBOV ANDREEVNA. On our way!

LOPAKHIN. Is everyone here? Nobody left behind? [*Locks the side door at left.*] Some things are stored in here, better keep it locked. Let's go! . .

ANYA. Good-bye, house! Fare thee well, old life!

TROFIMOV. Welcome, new life! . .

> He goes out with ANYA. VARYA looks around the room and goes out without hurrying. YASHA and SHARLOTTA, with her dog, go out.

LOPAKHIN. And so, till spring then. Come along, everybody . . . Until we meet again! . . [*Goes out.*]

> LYUBOV ANDREEVNA and GAEV are left alone. They seem to have waited for this moment and throw their arms around each other. They sob quietly, with restraint, afraid they might be overheard.

GAEV. [*in despair*] My sister, my sister . . .

LYUBOV ANDREEVNA. Oh, my beautiful orchard, my dear sweet orchard! . . My life, my youth, my happiness, good-bye! . . Good-bye! . .

ANYA. [*offstage, cheerfully and appealingly*] Mama! . .

TROFIMOV. [*offstage, cheerfully and excitedly*] Hullo! . .

LYUBOV ANDREEVNA. One last look at the walls and the windows . . . Our dear mother loved to walk in this room . . .

GAEV. My sister, my sister! . .

ANYA. [*offstage*] Mama! . .

TROFIMOV. [*offstage*] Hullo! . .

LYUBOV ANDREEVNA. We're on our way! . .

> They go out. The stage is empty. The sound of all the doors being locked is heard, then of carriages being driven away. It grows quiet. In the stillness a dull thud is heard, the striking of an axe into a tree. It sounds solitary and dolorous. Footsteps are heard. From the door, right, appears FIRS. He is dressed, as always, in a jacket and white waistcoat, and he is wearing slippers. He is ill.

FIRS. [*goes up to the door and touches the handle*] Locked. They've gone away . . . [*Sits on the sofa.*] They forgot me . . . It's nothing . . . I'll sit here for a while . . . And Leonid Andreich didn't put on his fur coat, I suppose, he must have gone away in his light one . . . [*Sighs anxiously.*] I just didn't look after it . . . Oh, these green young things—they never learn! [*Mumbles something that cannot be understood.*] Life just slipped by as if I'd never even lived . . . [*Lies down.*] I'll lie down for a while . . . You just don't have any strength, none, nothing's left, nothing at all. . . . Oh, you . . . silly galoot, you! . .

> *He lies motionless. A sound is heard far off in the distance, as if coming from the sky. It is the sound of a string breaking that dies away sadly. A stillness falls, and nothing is heard but the sound of an axe striking a tree far away in the orchard.*

CURTAIN

Backgrounds

RONALD HINGLEY

[Chekhov's Russia]

Geography

By the end of the nineteenth century the boundaries of the Russian Empire enclosed roughly the same huge area as that of its successor state the USSR. The differences were greatest on the western frontiers where Finland and Poland were both part of the territory ruled by the Tsar, Finland enjoying a large measure of autonomy, whereas Poland was a subject nation, especially after 1863. From 1815 to the end of the century Russia's western frontiers remained nearly stable, but in the south and east conditions were fluid, and vast new areas were added to the growing Empire.

* * *

By its very size imperial Russia seemed to threaten western Europe. It had some eight and a half million square miles of territory, of which about one quarter was in Europe and the remainder in Asia, so that it was larger than the entire north American continent. For a time the British Empire covered an even vaster expanse, but it was scattered over the globe. There was nowhere a continuous stretch of territory, ruled from a single centre, of comparable size to the Russian Empire. The sun did set on it—but not for many hours. Siberia above all caught the imagination of the world as a sort of European Russia writ even larger. With its vast coniferous forests, huge rivers, savage winter climate, extensive mountain ranges and general unsavoury repute, it seemed like another planet. Its area, one and a half times that of Europe including European Russia, was calculated to be greater than that of the face of the full moon.

* * * From the point of view of physical relief, European Russia and much of Siberia together form a huge plain flanked by mountains to east and south and extending from the western frontier through sixty degrees of longitude to the River Yenisey in central Siberia. A barrier, but not an important one, is imposed by the Ural Mountains (highest point, 6,210 feet), the boundary between Russia in Europe and Russia in Asia. The Valday Upland, rising to little more than 1,000 feet south-east of St Petersburg, and the Central Russian Upland, to the south of Moscow, formed even less of a barrier. It is on the southern and eastern frontiers that real obstacles are found. They begin in the south-west with the Carpathian Mountains and Crimean Upland, and continue in grander style with the Caucasian chain and—beyond the Caspian—the Pamir, Tien Shan,

Imperial Russia in the nineteenth century, showing the main rivers, lakes, seas, mountains, towns, and cities. From the western frontier to the River Yenisey in Central Siberia, the greater part of the Empire consisted of a vast plain. To the south and east the frontiers almost everywhere coincided with mountains, rivers, or seas.

Altay and Sayan ranges. Eastern Siberia is crossed by mountain chains, the Yablonovy, Stanovoy and others. Thus the southern border of the Empire was almost everywhere fenced off by mountains or seas.

* * * Russia has the two largest lakes in the world, so large that they are termed seas: the Caspian and the Aral. Apart from these she has the largest lakes in Asia (Baikal and Balkhash) and in Europe (Ladoga and Onega).

She is well stocked with rivers too, having the longest in Europe, the Volga (2,300 miles in length), and three in Siberia that dwarf even the Volga: the Ob (3,500 miles from the source of its chief tributary, the Irtysh), the Yenisey (3,700 miles from the source of the Selenga) and the Lena (2,670 miles).

Many important rivers of European Russia rise in a small area of the western midlands formed by the Valday and Central Russian Uplands. These include the Volga and its tributary the Oka, and also the Western Dvina, Dnieper and Don. Being close to each other and easily linked by portages in early times, and later by canal, the river system provided Russia with a valuable communication network, especially as most Russian rivers are slow-flowing and navigable far upstream. But many rivers become icebound for much of the year, flood heavily in spring and form shallows in summer. And Russians often felt that their rivers did not really lead anywhere. So many pour into landlocked or partly landlocked seas: the Caspian, Sea of Azov, Black Sea, Gulf of Riga, Gulf of Finland and the White Sea. Others, including the three longest rivers of Siberia, drain into the Arctic Ocean, not the most convenient of jumping-off points. Many Russian ports become ice-bound for long periods. So although Russians could move around effectively, if not very comfortably, inside their Empire by sledge, carriage or train, they sometimes felt claustrophobic about their restricted access to the world's sea routes.

* * * Vegetationally Russia consists of uneven broad zones running in roughly horizontal bands across European Russia and Siberia. In the extreme north are the Arctic wastes and tundra, thinly populated and of slight historical importance. South of those come the two most important vegetational zones: first the forest and then, to the south of that, the steppe—the word denotes a large treeless plain or prairie covered with herbaceous vegetation and having a dry climate.

Most of the forest zone is coniferous and is sometimes called, especially with reference to Siberia, the *tayga*. But in European Russia a wedge of mixed forest, coniferous and deciduous, stretches south of the coniferous belt from the western frontier and tapers off near Kazan on the Volga. Though smaller in area, the mixed forest is important as the cradle of the modern state, where Russia, centred on Moscow, made a second start after the decline of the old Russian state based on Kiev. Besides Moscow itself the area of mixed forest included such other historic cities as Novgorod, Nizhny Novgorod (now Gorky), Yaroslavl, Vladimir, Smolensk and St. Petersburg.

As one moved southwards there was no sudden change from forest to steppe. First came a transitional area, part woods and part steppe, sometimes termed the wooded steppe or meadow-grass steppe —found, for example in Oryol Province, scene of Turgenev's *Sportsman's Sketches*. South of it comes the steppe proper, also called feather-grass steppe. This in turn blends into arid (also called saline or wormwood) steppe, merging further to the south-east with the sand or stone deserts of Central Asia.

Not being fit for cultivation, the arid steppe was thinly populated, being the preserve of pastoral nomads. But the steppe proper and the wooded steppe are good crop-raising country, coinciding partly with the fertile black earth (*chernozem*) belt which stretches from the western frontier to the Altay foothills and reaches its greatest breadth of just under two hundred miles in European Russia. This became famous as one of the world's granaries and was supporting about a hundred people to the square mile at the beginning of the twentieth century. But the incursions of raiding horsemen had hampered cultivation of these lands until fairly late in Russian history, and insufficient rainfall made the raising of crops somewhat hazardous even on black earth.

* * * Poor conditions for growing food, the attacks of outside enemies, unsettled internal conditions and the exactions of central authority—all tended to make Russia a place where mere survival was an achievement. And there was also the Russian climate, which, as Yepikhodov rightly says in Chekhov's *Cherry Orchard* (1903–4), 'isn't exactly co-operative'.

Russia has an arctic climate in the extreme north, a subtropical climate on parts of the Black Sea coast, of Transcaucasia and of Central Asia, and a monsoon-type climate on the Pacific coast of the Far East. But these are only the fringes. The rest of the country, by far the greatest part of Russian territory, has a continental climate with long, cold winters and short, fairly hot summers. As one travels from west to east the range of temperature, between the cold of winter and the heat of summer, becomes ever wider. Eastern Siberia has an extreme continental climate. It can have heat waves in summer, but its winters are very severe, and it includes at Verkhoyansk what is often claimed as the cold pole of the northern hemisphere with a mean temperature in January of −58°F. and a lowest recorded temperature of −83.6°F. Over most of European Russia too, winter is the longest and perhaps most typically Russian season. The average number of days with a below-zero tempeature has been put at a hundred and forty and a hundred and fifty in Moscow and St Petersburg respectively, with a hundred and eighty in the middle Urals and a hundred and ninety in Archangel in the far north. Even in the southern port of Odessa the figure is as high as ninety.[1]

* * * The Russian winter can be monotonous, but is also awesome and picturesque. It is rendered more bearable by a tendency for the coldest days to be windless, at least in the north and centre. In the south blizzards are more common, so that the winters there can also be severe. But for Russian society in Moscow and St Petersburg, winter was a gay time with visits to the theatre and balls, and with sleighs whirring through the streets almost silent on the snow except for the tinkling of their bells. On fine days the low sun glittered blindingly on snow and ice. To Russian merchants winter was the time when heavy loads could be transported more easily than over the atrocious ruts and mire of the roads in spring and autumn. For the peasants field work came to an end in winter, but they might take seasonal jobs in a town and their families might have work to do at home, the organisation of cottage industries being widely developed.

The beginning of winter, with the arrival of the 'new road'—for sledges instead of carts—was a glad occasion, bringing the end of autumn slush. Another exhilarating event was the onset of spring, with the bleak, silent monochrome of winter rapidly giving way to colours, smells and bird song, while the breaking ice on the rivers thundered like an artillery barrage. For the farmer the summer was all too short, the sowing and reaping of a crop often being crowded into a mere hundred days. So spurts of intense effort were needed at sowing, haymaking and harvest time, in contrast to the long periods of winter inactivity.

The "Estates"

The Empire's population, both Russian and non-Russian, fell into a number of social categories according to a complicated system. In the first instance the vast majority of the inhabitants could be classed as native subjects. These comprised the entire population (including non-Russians) except for three relatively small groups: foreign nationals resident in Russia; the inhabitants of Finland; and

---

1. M. L. Schlesinger, *Land und Leute in Russland* [Land and people in Russia], 2nd ed. (Berlin, 1909), p. 238. [Unless otherwise noted, all translation in this essay is by Ronald Hingley—*Editor's note.*]

the peoples termed 'those of other race' (*inorodtsy*), consisting of Jews, but also of various primitive tribes.

Among the above the inhabitants of Finland were further subdivided into social classes according to a separate system which was inherited from Finland's period as a dependency of Sweden and need not be considered here. What must be explained now is the array of social groups into which the native subjects of the Empire, and also the Jews, were subdivided. To one or other of these groups (*sosloviya* or *sostoyaniya*), which may be termed estates, every individual was obliged at least in theory to belong. Each estate had its own special status in law and its own peculiar advantages or obligations.

There was thus no general category of Russian citizen. There were instead the estates of the gentry (hereditary and personal), clergy and peasantry. There were also several groups into which 'town-dwellers' were divided, those of: honorary citizens (hereditary and personal); merchants; craftsmen; and burghers (*meshchane*). But to make matters more complicated, only about half of the actual population of the towns consisted of members of these town-dwellers' estates, the remainder belonging to other estates, chiefly that of the peasantry. * * * The borderline between these groups was not always very precise, and membership of one estate need not exclude membership of another. It was customary also to speak of members of the armed forces as belonging to the military estates, though of course many officers were also members of the gentry. Officials were also often spoken of as forming an estate, though some of them belonged to that of the gentry as well.

Closer examination only confirms the unsystematic pattern presented by the Empire's social strata. In certain groups children automatically inherited the social status of their parents, as was the case with the hereditary gentry, hereditary honorary citizens, burghers and peasants. In other groups—those of the merchants, personal gentry and personal honorary citizens—status was not so transmitted. Most groups possessed a corporate organisation—the assemblies of the gentry; the merchants' guilds; the craft corporations; and the burghers' and peasants' communes. But the honorary citizens had no such organisation. Corporate organisations might exist below and up to the level of provinces, as they did in the case of the gentry. In one case there was overall control over a whole estate on an all-Russian level, since the whole clergy came under the supervision of the Holy Synod.

The legal position of the estates changed during the course of the century and the situation became more fluid. Originally the two estates of gentry and clergy were called privileged because their members enjoyed three advantages: freedom from conscription, from corporal punishment and from personal taxation. Hence the other estates were sometimes termed 'taxed'. With the restrictions on corporal punishment enacted in 1863, the introduction of universal liability to conscription in 1874 and the abolition of the poll-tax by 1887, the position changed. But other things being equal it was still worth being a gentleman rather than a member of the other estates. There was, it should be added, a certain amount of mobility between estates. For instance the attainment of sufficiently high military or civil rank automatically conferred entry to the gentry, as might the possession of sufficient funds to the estate of the merchants.

The relative size of the groups may be judged by the following figures showing the membership of the main estates or groups of estates as a percentage of the population at the end of the nineteenth century[2]:

Peasants	81.5 per cent
'Town-dwellers'	9 per cent
Military estates	6.5 per cent
Gentry	just over 1 per cent
Clergy	just under 1 per cent

Landowners and Gentlemen

The gentry's importance in Russian culture is completely out of proportion to its numbers—just over one per cent of the population at the end of the nineteenth century. Much Russian literature was written by landowners for landowners about landowners, and by the time of Turgenev the squire's country seat, such as the 'nest of gentlefolk' in the title of one of his novels, had become an established setting for Russian fiction.

Two overlapping concepts are involved here, those of landowner (*pomeshchik*) and gentleman (*dvoryanin*), the latter term denoting membership of one of the estates into which society was divided. It is sometimes rendered 'nobility', so that Turgenev's novel may be alluded to as *A Nest Of Noblemen,* but since the English word nobility implies possession of a title, the less misleading term gentry is preferred here.

Before 1861 a provision (sometimes circumvented, like all Russian provisions) existed whereby no one except a gentleman could own serfs, and as land tenure was usually combined with serf-

2. V. I. Kovalevsky, ed., *Rossija v konce XIX veka* [Russia at the end of the nineteenth century] (St. Petersburg, 1900), p. 67.

ownership, a large landowner at the time of serfdom was almost inevitably a member of the gentry class. After emancipation there was a continual decrease in the amount of land held by the gentry, whose holdings passed more and more to members of other classes. Thus Chekhov's *Cherry Orchard*, in which Lopakhin, the self-made son of a former serf, buys a vast estate from feckless genteel owners, seems to sum up over a hundred years of decline from the late eighteenth century under Catherine the Great, the gentry's golden age.

The estate of the gentry could be entered by non-gentlemen who attained high rank in the civil service or armed forces. Though the actual rank giving this right varied according to the regulations currently in force, the important point is that the estate was not exclusive, as some of its members would have liked to make it. Certain civil and military awards—those of St Vladimir and St George, as also the first class of other decorations—likewise conveyed the status of hereditary membership of the gentry. An inferior grade of gentry was that conferred by the status of personal, as opposed to hereditary, gentleman. Personal status was conferred by lower rank than that which gave hereditary gentry status, and, as the title implies, did not devolve to children.

The emperors tended to look to the gentry to resist revolution and support the *status quo*. One of Nicholas I's[3] police chiefs, Dubelt, summed up the position as follows: 'The landowner is the most reliable bulwark of the sovereign. . . . If his power is destroyed, the people will become a flood, endangering in time even the Tsar himself. . . . The landlord is the most faithful, the unsleeping watchdog of the state; he is the natural police-magistrate'.[4] The landowners' privileges were intended to preserve their loyalty and encourage them in the performance of specific services. Themselves exempt from flogging, conscription and personal taxation during the period when these inconveniences remained in force, they were responsible under serfdom for collecting poll-tax paid by their peasants, for drafting them into the army and for administering local justice—functions which all passed to the village commune or to the canton after 1861.

The gentry had an elaborate corporate organisation, including gentry assemblies at provincial and district level, presided over by marshals of the gentry who were chosen through a combination of election by their peers with appointment by the ministry of the interior. One of their duties was to see that delinquent gentlemen toed the line. Thus in Chekhov's story *My Life* (1896) the provincial

3. 1825–55 [*Editor's note*].
4. B. H. Sumner, *Survey of Russian History* (London, 1944), p. 142.

marshal of the gentry reports the hero, Misail Poloznev, to the governor of the province for working as a labourer—conduct unbecoming in a gentleman and son of the local architect.

After the local government reforms of 1864, the marshals of the gentry became *ex officio* chairmen of the assemblies of the newly instituted rural councils, the zemstvos. The institution of land captains appointed from among the gentry in 1889 * * * was another provision whereby the landowning gentry regained some of the control over peasant affairs lost at the time of emancipation.

* * * The Russians had a titled nobility or aristocracy, but it formed only a small section of the gentry as a whole. Their oldest hereditary title was that of prince (*knyaz*), and many Russian princes traced their descent from the semi-legendary founder of the Russian state, Ryurik, said to have died in 879 A.D. Others were descendants of Gedimin, Prince of Lithuania, or of Tatar or Georgian princes. Members of the Tsar's family held the title *veliky knyaz* (literally 'great prince'), for which grand duke is used in English. Prince was the only Russian title in use in the nineteenth century that dated from before Peter the Great[5] who introduced new grades of nobility: those of count (*graf*) and baron. The latter title was held by many members of the German nobility in the Russian Baltic, who so often reached high rank in the administration. When awarded to Russians it came to be granted to successful businessmen, so that princes and counts somewhat looked down on it.

By contrast with French and English practice, titles were inherited by all the children of a titled father, whence the large number of princes, princesses, counts and countesses scattered through the pages of Russian novels. It was also usual for property to be split among all the sons of a family, not left exclusively to an eldest son—hence a tendency for members of the aristocracy to be poorer than their rank suggests. There was thus nothing improbable in Dostoevsky beginning his *Idiot* by introducing a penniless Prince Myshkin almost in the role of beggar and suppliant, while if the name of a Prince Golitsyn cropped up in real life, the question was apt to be asked: 'Who is this Golitsyn? A rich one or a poor one?'[6]

* * * Peter the Great had compelled the gentry to dress like western Europeans by wearing what the peasants called 'German clothes', whereas clergy, merchants and peasants continued wearing traditional Russian dress. In the nineteenth century this differentiation by dress was maintained. Thus the heroine of Pushkin's *Young Lady as Peasant*, one of his *Tales of Belkin*, was able to pass herself off as a peasant girl only after getting her maids to run her up a

5. 1682–1725 [*Editor's note*].
6. Jerome Blum, *Lord and Peasant in*   *Russia from the Ninth to the Nineteenth Century* (Princeton, 1961), p. 376.

rustic shirt and *sarafan*[7] specially for the occasion. While remaining distinct from the clothing of other classes, the dress of the gentry did of course change according to changes in fashion. For ladies it was full skirts in the thirties and crinolines in the sixties. At the beginning of the nineteenth century men were wearing tail-coats. These continued to be formal wear, but were ousted for more ordinary occasions by frock-coats and later by jackets and dinner-jackets, as were top hats by bowlers. Waistcoats were considered essential wear for a gentleman. By the end of the nineteenth century, distinction of dress was becoming less marked in the sense that gentry and non-gentry townspeople were dressing more and more alike.

* * * As readers of Tolstoy's *War and Peace* will remember, French was a common means of communication for the Russian gentry at the beginning of the nineteenth century—in fact there were many Russian gentlemen who spoke it better than their own language. In a way Pushkin knew Russian better than anyone else before or since, but he regularly wrote to his Russian wife in French. Herzen[8] explains that his father wrote better French than Russian and would never so much as read a Russian book. He did once take up Karamzin's *History of the Russian State*, hearing that Alexander I[9] had read it, but soon laid it down, saying: 'All these Izyaslaviches and Olgoviches—what a bore!' (*My Past and Thoughts*, ch. v). After the discovery of Anna Karenina's adultery, her husband found it convenient to speak to her in French, for *vous* seemed chilly enough to express his disapproval, whereas the polite second-person plural would have meant too harsh a transition from the intimate form *ty*. As for Dostoevsky, being a rabid Russian nationalist he objected to the practice of bringing up genteel infants to speak French: 'Mummy doesn't know with what venom she is poisoning her child as early as the age of two, when she invites a French *bonne*[1] to look after him' (*Diary of a Writer*, May–June 1877).

In time the use of French declined socially, and by Chekhov's day it was almost becoming a genteel vulgarism. It is typical that some of Chekhov's non-approved characters, including Natasha in *Three Sisters* (1900–1901), should speak inaccurate French. The habit of using French names for Russian, for instance of addressing an Ivan as *Jean*, had also become a sign of social pretentiousness.

7. Russian peasant women's dress, without sleeves and buttoning in the front.
8. A. I. Herzen (1812–70), Russian revolutionary philosopher, left Russia in 1847 and published a free Russian weekly newspaper, *Kolokol* (*The Bell*, 1857), which was smuggled into Russia and widely read [*Editor's note*].
9. 1801–25 [*Editor's note*].
1. Nursery maid [*Editor's note*].

Towns

Though most Russians were countrymen, the population of the towns was growing fast in the eighteenth and nineteenth centuries—more than six times as rapidly as that of the countryside. The following figures show the increase of Russian urban population and the way in which it was rising as a percentage of the whole.[2]

Year	Number of town-dwellers	Percentage of whole population
1812	1,653,000	4.4
1835	3,025,000	5.8
1851	3,482,000	7.8
1867	8,157,000	10.6
1897	16,785,212	13.0

There were few large towns. In 1867 there were only four in the whole Empire with a population of over one hundred thousand (St Petersburg, Moscow, Warsaw and Odessa), and even then one of those was Polish. By 1897 the number (of towns in the Empire with a population over one hundred thousand) had risen to nineteen. These were, in descending order of size: St Petersburg, Moscow, Warsaw, Odessa, Lodz, Riga, Kiev, Kharkov, Tiflis, Vilna, Tashkent, Saratov, Kazan, Yekaterinoslav (now Dnepropetrovsk). Rostov-on-Don, Astrakhan, Baku, Tula and Kishinyov. By no means all the above towns were fully or even partly Russian, though all belonged to the Empire.

* * * Observers from western Europe hardly recognised Russian towns as towns at all. Less tactful foreigners, and some Russians too, described Moscow itself or even the whole Empire as one vast village. Observers also noted a lack of variety in Russian towns. Ample available space and danger of fire encouraged a tendency to sprawl, and the wide unpaved streets were often no better than those found in ordinary villages. Paved roads, sewage systems, street lighting and piped water were not unheard of, but even by the beginning of the twentieth century they were still restricted to small, prosperous sections of the larger towns.

Most houses were single-storied and made of wood, but stone-built apartment houses of several storeys were also going up in the towns where population pressure was greatest. It was common practice to rent apartments and houses rather than to own them, and the more salubrious might be occupied by wealthy officials, while the very poorest citizens might have to hire the corner of a room in some unsavoury doss-house. Among these that of Khitrov Market

2. Kovalevsky, p. 60.

in Moscow was a notorious haunt of tramps, prostitutes and thieves. Here professional beggar-women could hire emaciated babies by the day to attract alms from passers-by, and if the baby died during the course of the day they would continue exhibiting it so as to get their money's worth.[3]

Despite such grotesque examples of private enterprise, the general atmosphere of Russian towns was torpid. There were few shops as understood in western Europe, shopping often being done in markets consisting of small, ill-lit stores, each exactly like its neighbour and known as the trading rows. As in some villages, churches with painted domes and characteristic outlines might supply variety to the eye. And in provincial capitals the governor's residence, court of justice, administrative offices, gymnasiums (grammar schools), hospitals, theatres and so on provided a relatively imposing centre to the sprawling, ramshackle outskirts.

* * * Russian novelists were cautious about identifying provincial towns, preferring to call them 'the town of N.' (or any other letter of the alphabet). Or such places may, like the setting of Dostoevsky's *Devils* and the town in Chekhov's *My Life*, be called simply 'our town'. The identity of the town which forms the centre of Chichikov's intrigues in *Dead Souls* is concealed, but it was conceivably suggested to the author by Kursk. Similarly the identity of the provincial capital in *Three Sisters* is not revealed in the text of the play, though Chekhov did tell Gorky[4] that 'the action takes place in a provincial town such as Perm' (letter of 16th October 1900). The trouble is that there were so many Kursks and Perms in Russia with little to differentiate one from another. 'In Russia all towns are identical,' Chekhov once wrote to his sister from Yekaterinburg—now Sverdlovsk. 'Yekaterinburg is just like Perm or Tula. It's also like Sumy and Galyach' (letter of 29th April 1890). Even his home town, Taganrog, impressed Chekhov as boring, though it was a port on the sea of Azov with a polyglot population of sailors and merchants, including Greeks, Armenians and Bulgarians. It had quite a good theatre too and a passable library, but to Chekhov it was completely Asiatic, a place where people 'do nothing but eat, sleep and multiply and have no other interests' (letter of 7th April 1887). Chekhov's works abound in denunciations of provincial Russian towns so outspoken that it is no wonder if he was cryptic about their identity. One such speech is that delivered by Andrey Prozorov in Act Four of *Three Sisters*.

* * * Towns tended less to be organic growths than in western Europe, and to exist as the result of administrative policy. Catherine

3. Henri Troyat, *Daily Life in Russia under the Last Tsar*, tr. Malcolm Barnes (London, 1961), p. 61.

4. Maxim Gorky, pseudonym of Alexey Maximovich Peshkov (1868–1936), notable Russian writer [*Editor's note*].

the Great set up over two hundred towns in just over twenty years, being persuaded that Russia required a *bourgeoisie* such as it clearly did not possess, but mainly with the intention of strengthening administrative control over her far-flung Empire. It was easy to create a town by decree. 'To transform a village into a town, it was necessary merely to prepare an *izba*, or log-house, for the district court, another for the police-office, a third for the prison, and so on. . . . All this required very little creative effort.'[5] A hundred years after Catherine's death a Russian *bourgeoisie* had indeed come into being, and the usual claim that it was not very numerous is belied by statistics, since about half the urban population consisted of burghers, merchants and members of other bourgeois categories. But it is true that this was not a *bourgeoisie* on the European model and that it was not influential in affairs of state.

* * * Many town-dwellers were peasants temporarily or permanently absent from their villages. Members of the non-landowning gentry also tended to reside in towns, while landowners themselves often wintered in town, spending only part of the year on their estates. According to the 1897 census the peasants accounted for 38.8 per cent and the gentry for 6.2 per cent of all town-dwellers.[6] Most of the remainder, 44.3 per cent of the overall urban population, belonged to the estate of the burghers. Though no better translation of the word *meshchanin* suggests itself, it must be added that "burgher" conveys too solid an impression for a group which excluded merchants, a more prosperous category, and included small traders, owners of apartment-houses, craftsmen, factory workers and indeed more or less anyone who could not be fitted in elsewhere. The burghers had their own communes with elected elders— less vital institutions than the village commune, but by no means ornamental, since they too could exile offending members to Siberia.

* * *

The merchants (*kuptsy*) formed a special class within Russian society, and they included factory-owners as well as traders, so the term merchant may be misleading and it might be better to call them businessmen. Merchants did not form an estate in the same sense as did the gentry and clergy, since the status of merchant was more precarious. It was not hereditary, but was obtained by paying the dues required to join one of the two (before 1863 three) merchants' Guilds, of which the First Guild was for the wealthier, including those engaged in foreign trade, while the Second was for humbler operators. At the beginning of the twentieth century the First Merchant Guild numbered 30,000 members and the Second

5. D. Mackenzie Wallace, *Russia* (London, 1877), I, 261.
6. V. A. Aleksandrov, et al., eds., *Narody evropejskoj časti SSSR* [The peoples of the European part of the USSR], (Moscow, 1964), p. 326.

about 400,000. If a merchant was unable to meet his dues he would probably revert to being a burgher or peasant.

In contrast to gentry and officials, the merchants belonged with clergy and peasantry to the least europeanised part of the community. They were apt to sport huge beards and have the hair of their heads parted in the middle. The more old-fashioned continued to wear long black double-breasted coats buttoned down the middle in traditional Russian style, whereas gentlemen dressed in the European manner. Merchants did not usually speak any language except Russian. They might even be unable to read or write that, but it could be an expensive mistake to assume that such illiterates were poor businessmen. Many successful merchants were Old Believers, and also clung to the ways of old Moscow by keeping their wives and daughters in comparative seclusion. They liked to dispense hospitality, staging lavish banquets at vast expense with plenty of sturgeon, champagne flowing freely, and with luck a high official or a general or two among the guests to lend tone. Successful merchants built elaborately appointed houses and spent money on large ornate mirrors, grand pianos which were never played and other costly furniture. But all this was for show. When not entertaining, the host might occupy poky little rooms in some corner of the house with his family.

In the works of Russian literature best known outside Russia, Russian merchants do not figure prominently. One merchant in Russian literature familiar to the foreign theatre-goer is Lopakhin in Chekhov's *Cherry Orchard*, and for a fuller study of the merchant milieu in Chekhov the reader can turn to his story *Three Years* (1895).

* * *

* * * The general category of town-dwellers included, in addition to burghers and merchants, further subdivisions with smaller membership. These were honorary citizens, who might have either hereditary or life status. To this group were assigned for example sons of the clergy who had not entered the church, certain officials, and merchants who had made outstanding gifts to charity. The grade of honorary citizen was introduced in 1832 and conferred exemption from corporal punishment, recruitment and the poll-tax. Yet another estate, which existed in some towns, was membership of one of the craft corporations (*tsekhi*). But by the end of the nineteenth century formal distinctions between all estates were breaking down, and an individual might even not know his own social status until he needed a passport. As this suggests, Russian society was proceeding in the direction taken by western Europe.

* * *

* * * Provincial centres all possessed their gentry clubs and there were often clubs for professional people, small officials and merchants. Clubs might contain a restaurant, a reading-room and a large hall for staging elaborate receptions and balls—such as that described in the provincial gentry assembly hall in Chekhov's *Order of St Anne* (1895). But the main activity, according to literary and other evidence, was gambling over the card-table—often regarded as the main vice of the Russian privileged classes.

Another characteristic urban institution of increasing popularity was the practice of hiring country cottages (*dachi*) not far away from one's place of residence and preferably on a lake, river or sea accessible by railway. To such resorts urban husbands would pack off their wives and children for the summer, often themselves commuting to their place of work at special seasonal reduced fares. The *dacha* husband, a joke figure as one particularly vulnerable to cuckolding, became a staple feature of *fin-de-siècle* funny stories.

One practice not exclusive to Russian society was that of keeping open house on the afternoon or evening of a fixed day each week, when it was possible for friends of the family to drop in without any specific invitation. Hence such information as 'we receive on Thursdays', sometimes dispensed in Russian novels by the lady of the house, who usually took the leading role on social occasions. Such was the practice of polite society, but Russians of all classes were celebrated among foreigners for their hospitality, which erred if at all by its very excess. The celebration of namedays and birthdays of members of the family was one pleasant excuse for dispensing good cheer and another practice confined to urban Russia—as opposed to the village, where it was not much followed.

* * *

Officials

Imperial authority was enforced by a complex system of pressures and controls, some of which have been indicated already—the use made of the landowning gentry to keep the peasantry in line, and also of the Orthodox Church, conceived by authority as a bulwark of the state and custodian of its ideology.

The system of controls must now be further explored. This involves examining the civil service, * * * army, and also education, which was constantly under review with the aim of using it to combat revolution and produce malleable citizens. * * * Political opposition often reared its head within the very apparatus of control, especially in the law-courts, in the zemstvos, in education and above all in publishing. * * * It is important to note that imperial Russia was, after all, a going concern, even if its progress was a stumbling and painful affair. It did work, and it is the concern of the present [section] to show how, with particular reference to the imperial civil service.

* * * Foreign visitors were often struck by the vast numbers of officials who seemed to be found all over the place in imperial Russia, all wearing some kind of uniform, with dark green the dominant colour. Besides civil servants of various kinds, they also included many persons who would not automatically be regarded as functionaries in other societies, but who in Russia held official rank and wore uniforms. Members of the liberal professions were often employed by the state, and so many lawyers, doctors and architects held official rank. So did university professors, who, if sufficiently distinguished, might rate the title 'Your Excellency' like Professor Serebryakov in Chekhov's *Uncle Vanya*. Gymnasium (grammar school) masters, being state employees, also rated as officials, which is why a schoolmaster like Kulygin in Chekhov's *Three Sisters* may appear on the stage in uniform and even introduce himself as a 'court councillor'. Students, such as Trofimov in Chekhov's *Cherry Orchard*, also wore a uniform, though this provision was not in force throughout the period. But the idea that every other Russian was an official of some sort is an exaggeration. The total number of persons belonging to the class was only about one in two hundred and fifty of the population at the beginning of the twentieth century,[7] and they were naturally most thickly congregated in the two capitals where foreigners were likely to notice them.

* * * The imperial word for official, *chinovnik*, has become a term of abuse in Soviet Russia. If the evidence of nineteenth-century literature is anything to go on, this use of the word is thoroughly justified, for so many Russian authors portray the workings of the imperial bureaucracy as an indecorous farce. The first writer of note to explore the theme thoroughly as Gogol, himself briefly an official in St Petersburg. He produced two especially memorable studies—one comic, the play *The Inspector-General*, and the other tragi-comic, the story *The Overcoat*. Among many followers of Gogol the young Dostoevsky took up the theme with his wretched Makar Devushkin, hero of his first novel, *Poor Folk*, and with the fantastic twin heroes of his second novel, *The Double*.

A practice puzzling to the uninitated reader is that of calling civil servants of the first four ranks 'general', though they might never have donned military uniform or know one end of a gun from another. Civil service generals abound in Russian literature, as the result of which Virginia Woolf once claimed that, in a typical Russian novel, 'we open the door and find ourselves in a room full

7. Schlesinger, p. 60.

of Russian Generals'.[8] Such generals were often comic figures like General Pralinsky in Dostoevsky's *Nasty Anecdote* (1862), who intrudes on the wedding celebrations of a subordinate, gets helplessly drunk, collapses face down in a plate of blancmange and has to be put to bed on the nuptial couch. As this episode shows, authors did not always defer to rank when it came to ridiculing the civil service, though by common consent a lowish grade, that of titular councillor (class nine), was the most comic of all. The mere mention of a titular councillor was enough to create pleasurable tension in the reader, who could assume that some kind of slapstick comedy was likely to follow.

But were imperial officials really quite as funny as all that? Herzen did not think so, and he knew the milieu well, having himself been employed as a provincial official during exile to Vyatka and Novgorod. * * *

* * *

Among the points scored against officials in literature, sycophancy towards those of higher rank, as in Chekhov's early *Fat and Thin* (1883), is prominent. But the most common accusation is that of taking bribes. As Chekhov stated * * * in *My Life*: 'If you applied to the municipal offices, . . . the health centre or any other institution they would shout after you, "Remember to say thank you", and you would go back and hand over thirty or forty copecks.' It has been argued in defence of these exactions that civil servants were badly paid and that bribery, pretty well in accordance with a fixed tariff, had become a traditional way of supplementing inadequate incomes. The dishonest official was not the one who took bribes (since that was absolutely normal), but the one who hung on to a bribe when he could not perform the service for which it had been paid, or who would not stick to the usual tariff—like one of Gogol's officials, accused of taking bribes 'above his station'.

* * * The official class was a creation of Peter the Great, who in 1722 set up the celebrated hierarchy of fourteen official grades, termed the table of ranks, which remained in force with few alterations until 1917. These ranks had cumbrous titles borrowed from Prussian and other western European models, and care is needed in translating them from Russian. 'Privy councillor' is, for example, a tempting rendering for *tayny sovetnik*, and is in fact adopted below for want of a better alternative, but can give a misleading impression in English. The fourteen ranks are listed on the next page.

Classes eleven and thirteen fell into abeyance in the first half of the nineteenth century, and the military rank of major, formerly equivalent of collegiate assessor, was discontinued in 1884.

8. Virginia Woolf, "The Russian Point of View," in *The Common Reader: First*   *Series* (London, 1938), p. 177.

Class	Civilian Rank	Military Equivalent (after 1884)
1	Chancellor	Field Marshal
2	Actual Privy Councillor	General
3	Privy Councillor	Lieutenant-General
4	Actual State Councillor	Major-General
5	State Councillor	
6	Collegiate Councillor	Colonel
7	Court Councillor	Lieutenant-Colonel
8	Collegiate Assessor	Captain
9	Titular Councillor	Staff Captain
10	Collegiate Secretary	Lieutenant
11	Ship's Secretary	
12	Provincial (*gubernsky*) Secretary	Sub-Lieutenant
13	Provincial (*provintsialny*) Secretary	
14	Collegiate Registrar	

Each official had an appropriate honorific title with which he was addressed by subordinates and on official occasions. Classes one and two above were 'Your Supreme Excellency'; three, four and five rated as 'Your Excellency'; six to eight inclusive were 'Your Supreme Honour' and the remainder 'Your Honour'. Wives enjoyed these honorifics too, whence the occasions on which Anna Karenina is referred to as 'Her Excellency'.

Among the preoccupations of Russian officials was the award of various decorations called orders for which they might from time to time qualify. Most of these had several different grades, like that of St Vladimir with its four classes, even the lowest of which (class four) conferred hereditary membership of the gentry on the recipient. The order of St Anne (with three classes) was slightly less exalted—after receiving his St Anne class two, the hero of Chekhov's *Order of St Anne* planned to move on to the St Vladimir ladder and was rash enough to hint as much by making an execrable pun to the local provincial governor when, in accordance with etiquette, he paid a call to thank His Excellency for the award. * * *

* * * As already indicated, even the most exalted governmental organs had the function of executing the sovereign's will rather than of initiating policy. This is true of four bodies which must now be mentioned. The Senate was originally set up by Peter the Great in 1711 to supervise the whole administration and as the chief legislative, administrative and judicial organ. Its actual powers fell far short of this, especially in the period studied here, having decreased notably in the 1810s with the institution of the ministries (which were formally subordinate to it) and of the Committee of Ministers. But from 1864 onwards the Senate did operate as an effective court

of appeal besides discharging numerous minor functions. The Committee of Ministers functioned from 1802 to 1906 with the task of co-ordinating the work of different departments. Its capacity was mainly advisory, as was that of the Council of State, set up in 1810 to discuss, but not initiate, prospective legislation. A similar role was fulfilled by a shorter-lived body, the Council of Ministers, which met at the Tsar's discretion and under his presidency between 1861 and 1882.

The ministries, establishment of which was completed in 1811, played an important part in the administration. These have been described as 'state departments of the usual west-European type, each with a well-defined competence and each under the direction of a minister who was personally responsible for the legality of his actions'.[9] To this must be added a reminder that ministers were appointed and dismissed as and when the Tsar saw fit, and that he could take their advice or not as he wished.

* * *

It will be remembered that the reforms of Alexander II[1] included provisions for a new kind of local government, that of the zemstvos (rural councils) instituted by a law of 1864, and also of town councils (*gorodskiye dumy*) instituted by a law of 1870. These bodies were elective, albeit on a complex system with heavy weighting in favour of the gentry and of property owners. The zemstvos existed both on provincial and district level, having their headquarters in provincial and district capitals. Their members, elected for periods of three years, in turn elected executive boards, also for three years, to manage current business. Provincial councillors were elected by district councillors, and they also elected executive boards. The town councils had a similar organisation, being elected for four years and forming an executive board, and they also chose a mayor. Thus alongside state officials were functioning officials of a different kind—unpaid, self-consciously public-spirited and the repository of the hopes of liberal-minded Russians, who saw in these new institutions a school of practical democracy.

The rural councillors often saw themselves in this light too. So, unfortunately for them, did the central authority, which proceeded to hamper them in various ways. They did not even exist in all provinces, for by the end of the century they were functioning in only thirty-four. And the 'counter-reforms' of Alexander III[2] included a law of 1890 limiting their power and increasing their dependence on the state. They were in any case impeded by various powers of near-veto exercised by provincial governors, by the ulti-

9. Michael Karpovich, *Imperial Russia, 1801–1917* (New York, 1932), p. 18.

1. 1855–81 [*Editor's note*].
2. 1881–94 [*Editor's note*].

mate control of the ministry of the interior and by the difficulty of levying adequate taxes to meet their requirements. They were also compelled to accept the local marshal of the gentry (of district or province as the case might be) as chairman, thus confirming the gentry's dominant position. Still, peasants did find their way on to the councils, and incidentally often showed themselves more conservative than the representatives of the gentry on whom the government relied to keep them under control.

The councils were largely concerned with local economic needs— with the upkeep of roads and bridges, anti-famine precautions, medical care and elementary schools. By the end of the century they were employing many teachers and doctors, among whom they attracted the more radical-minded. Attempts by the councils to exercise wider political influence, outside the confines of local affairs, were carefully watched and thwarted by central authority. A certain tension existed between the local council with their new, progressive traditions, and the state officials, though the latter were by no means all the hidebound reactionaries of popular mythology.

* * *

The Army

The armed forces were an important pillar of the imperial Establishment, not least because of the tradition of appointing army generals to high administrative office. * * *

Though the Russian army in the first half of the nineteenth century was in many ways a backward and cruel institution, it also showed gleams of liberalism. Only perhaps in a land of surprises such as imperial Russia might one find guards officers, of all people, in the vanguard of a movement for reform. Yet this is what happened during the period of subversive secret societies which preceded the Decembrist revolt of 1825.[3] The campaigns following Napoleon's invasion of Russia in 1812 had opened the eyes of Russian soldiers serving in western Europe to the backwardness of their own country, showing them that forms of government other than the autocratic did exist elsewhere.

A Russian guards regiment, the Semyonovsky, had mutinied in 1820. Yet the guards were just as much of a social *élite* in Russia as elsewhere, 'quite fit to be compared with the German in the social position of their officer corps', as one authority states.[4] But officers

3. The Decembrist revolt is named after the month (December) in which a group of liberal noblemen, primarily officers in the army, led their regiments into the Senate Square in St. Petersburg, anticipating popular support that did not materialize. The revolt was put down by the incoming tsar, Nicholas I; about 120 persons were arrested and tried; five were hanged, and those remaining were sent to prison or exiled to Siberia [*Editor's note*].
4. Schlesinger, p. 361.

of less smart, non-guards regiments, normally dependent on their meagre pay, could not cut such a dash. One may contrast Lieutenant-colonel Count Vronsky, lover of Anna Karenina and owner of race horses and vast estates, with the less resplendent Lieutenant-colonel Vershinin, the battery commander in Chekhov's *Three Sisters*, who had an unpresentable wife with suicidal tendencies and spent all his life 'knocking around from one lot of rooms to another, with a couple of chairs and a sofa and stoves smoking all the time'.

* * *

Duels fought in defence of marital or regimental honour, reckless gambling, exciting love affairs and alcoholic orgies are among the features that lend glitter to the life of the Russian officer in nineteenth-century Russian fiction. There was another aspect to the officer's life, as Tolstoy himself did not conceal, and for an account more concentrated on the seamy side of the mess and less likely to stimulate recruiting than Tolstoy's, readers could turn to Kuprin's *The Duel* (1905).[5]

* * * Conditions were greatly improved by the army reforms of General D. A. Milyutin, who was minister of war from 1861 to 1881. In the law of 1874 he took the class bias out of conscription, to which all male citizens over the age of twenty-one now became liable, though in peace time it was not usually necessary to call up more than about a third of them, and certain categories—including the clergy, only sons and men who had brothers with the colours—were exempt. The period of active service was reduced to six years followed by a number of years in the reserve and militia. Further concessions gave advantage to those who had attended school and university. Thus university students were liable to only six months with the colours, while ex-pupils of the gymnasiums and other secondary schools need only serve eighteen months or three years, and pupils of primary schools need serve four. For university and secondary school graduates who cared to enlist voluntarily rather than take their chance of not being conscripted, the above terms were halved.

The army became a place where peasants first learned to read and write, for Milyutin was successful in putting army education on a sound footing. Discipline was made less harsh, corporal punishment being now confined, at least in theory, to penal units, though it was no uncommon thing even after the reforms for an officer to strike a soldier. Conditions remained bad by absolute standards, but the situation had been transformed by Milyutin's reforms if comparison is made with the early part of the century.

5. A. I. Kuprin (1870–1938) has often been compared to the American writer Jack London (1876–1916), since both were adept at stories of adventure and physical action [*Editor's note*].

Chekhov was sympathetically disposed towards the Russian army. According to Stanislavsky,[6] he sent his own military representative to supervise the rehearsals of *Three Sisters*, in which army officers figure so prominently. Chekhov wanted his officers shown as "charming, decent people," not as blimpish heel-clickers. If Stanislavsky is to be believed, he also used to become lyrical about the cultural mission performed by the Russian army when posted to remote parts of the country, to which it took 'knowledge, art, happiness and joy'.[7]

Like so much else in life, the Russian army had its good and bad sides, and the bracket between them, as befits the 'broad Russian nature', was especially wide.

Education

The progress of nineteenth-century Russian education follows the pattern of imperial development in general by showing fairly impressive improvement on modest beginnings. Thus all educational facilities had greatly expanded by the end of the century. For instance, in 1899 the Empire had nine universities with about 17,000 students, whereas back in 1809 there had been a mere 450 students in four universities[8] (these figures do not include the non-Russian universities of Helsingfors and Vilna). On the other hand, imperial education is less impressive if compared with that offered by the advanced countries of western Europe in the same period. An eloquent figure reflecting educational backwardness is the high proportion (seventy-four per cent) of citizens of the Empire between the ages of nine and forty-nine recorded as illiterate in the 1897 census.

* * *

Education of a more conventional type for a writer was received by Chekhov, who attended the gymnasium (grammar school) at Taganrog where Greek and Latin formed a large part of the curriculum. This was a most respectable form of education by the standards of the day, and Chekhov, though no outstanding pupil, was able to proceed to the University of Moscow. There he qualified as a doctor and unofficially as a writer by stories and sketches published during his student years.

Gorky received little formal education, being taught to read by the cook on a Volga steamer for whom he worked as pantry-boy. Of

6. Stanislavsky was the stage name of K. S. Alekseev (1863–1938), actor, stage director, and co-manager with V. I. Nemirovich-Danchenko (1858–1943) of the Moscow Art Theatre, which the two founded in 1898. All of Chekhov's major plays, except *The Sea Gull* and *Uncle Vanya*, received their première production at the Moscow Art Theatre [*Editor's note*].

7. Anton Chekhov, *The Oxford Chekhov*, tr. and ed. Ronald Hingley, (London, 1964), III, 314–16.

8. Michael T. Florinsky, *Russia: A History and An Interpretation* (New York, 1953), II, 726; Kovalevsky, p. 482.

this skill, once acquired, he made good use, besides receiving a rough but thorough education in the 'university of life'. He ironically gave the title *My Universities* to the section of his autobiography devoted to what would have been his student years if he had succeeded, as he had hoped, in gaining admission to the University of Kazan.

* * *

After the Crimean War, and increasingly during the rest of the period under review,[9] Russian universities became centres of political unrest. This was the age of student demonstrations, riots and strikes, supported by the more liberal university teachers, who risked dismissal by such displays of sympathy. Peasant disturbances at the time of emancipation and the Khodynka disaster of 1896[1] * * * were among occasions evoking student protests. Worse riots followed in St Petersburg University in 1899, sparked off by an official warning that unruliness would not be tolerated during the University's annual celebration on 8th February.[2] A student demonstration was dispersed by mounted police with whips, after which a general strike of students was declared and carried out in many other universities too. Student demonstrators were liable to harsh treatment, being sent down from the university in large numbers and often drafted into the army as privates—the deferment or curtailment of military service, to which they were entitled as students, conveniently lapsed when they were expelled. But this sort of thing only inflamed the situation, and in 1901 a former student assassinated the minister of education, N. P. Bogolepov, thus carrying academic protest to its ultimate limit.

Student unrest was due to political dissatisfaction aggravated by specific grievances, such as the disciplinary powers exercised by university inspectors and a virtual ban on free corporate activities. Many students were poor, as is not unknown in other countries, and they often lived in squalor, as does the student Raskolnikov in Dostoevsky's *Crime and Punishment.* Even Raskolnikov was better housed than many of his fellow-students, for at least he did not have to share his miserable garret in St Petersburg with anyone else.

Another well-known representative in literature of Russian uni-

9. To 1905 [*Editor's note*].
1. Mass festivities celebrating the coronation of Nicholas II (1894–1917) were held on the Khodynka Field in Moscow in 1896, wherein an estimated two thousand persons died by falling into ditches since the police were unable to control the crowds. That very same night the French embassy held a ball, and the Russian imperial party attended—an action that only intensified the feeling among many Russians that the imperial family and officials were simply inhuman [*Editor's note*].
2. The student strike on February 8, 1899, at St. Petersburg University was the first successful student strike; it spread throughout all institutions of higher learning in Russia within ten days, by which time all were closed down until the following autumn [*Editor's note*].

versity life is Peter Trofimov, the 'eternal student' in Chekhov's *Cherry Orchard*. There are references in the dialogue to him 'already having been sent down from the university twice', and 'having been landed in some pretty queer places', from which it seems clear that Soviet commentators are not being entirely fanciful when they claim Trofimov to have been conceived by Chekhov as a budding revolutionary. To portray him as such was impossible under censorship conditions of the time, as Chekhov implied in a letter to his wife: 'You see, Trofimov is in exile off and on, and gets chucked out of the university every so often, and how is one to depict that sort of thing?' (letter of 19th October 1903).

* * * So far as educational policy is concerned, a period of relative liberalism corresponding to the reign of Alexander II[3] was sandwiched between two slices of intolerance in the reigns of Nicholas I[4] and Alexander III[5], followed by some relaxations in the first part of Nicholas II's reign[6] and considerably more after 1905. But things were not quite so simple as that. During most of Alexander II's reign—from 1866 to 1880—the minister of education was an extreme reactionary, Count D. A. Tolstoy, whose views on education had little in common with those of his more famous namesake the novelist. D. A. Tolstoy's tenure of office did see a big increase in the number of schools and of the pupils attending them, but he kept a firm grip on appointments and syllabuses, particularly those of the gymnasiums (grammar schools). A feature of his policy was the emphasis laid on the study of Greek and Latin as a means of curbing political unrest. It was thought that concentration on these classical languages, especially on their syntax, might nip revolutionary sentiments in the bud—a vain hope because the gymnasiums in fact became centres of political disaffection, like the universities which many gymnasium pupils would later attend. Chekhov, the only nineteenth-century Russian writer of the very front rank to complete a full course at a gymnasium, never turned into a political firebrand, but was left with a distaste for Greek and Latin which apparently lasted him for life. Classicists may take some comfort from the fact that Chekhov, who received the most intensive classical education among leading Russian writers, also wrote exceptionally disciplined and elegant Russian prose, though how much credit for this can be given to the model of Cicero and Demosthenes is not clear. In his *Man in a Case* (1898) Chekhov has a brilliant description of a repulsive gymnasium teacher of Greek whose only pleasures in life are interfering with his colleagues' activities and rolling the Greek word *anthropos* round his tongue.

One aim of educational policy-makers in periods of political reac-

3. 1855–81 [*Editor's note*].
4. 1825–55 [*Editor's note*].
5. 1881–94 [*Editor's note*].
6. 1894–1917 [*Editor's note*].

tion was to make it impossible for pupils of humble social origin to enter the gymnasiums and universities. Increases in school and university fees, and insistence on irksome formalities were used from time to time to discourage lower-class children from claiming places in these establishments, which should be the monopoly of the gentry according to the more diehard social engineers. An official circular issued in 1887 proclaimed the need to keep out of the gymnasiums such undesirables as the children of coachmen, footmen, cooks, laundresses, small shopkeepers and similar people. This came out nearly ten years after Chekhov had received his leaving certificate from the Taganrog Gymnasium—otherwise he, being the son of a struggling shopkeeper, might have had to seek his schooling elsewhere.

* * * Despite attempts to use dead languages as a political narcotic, the gymnasiums did on the whole provide the best schooling widely available. They were first developed on any scale under Alexander I[7], when the initial aim was to provide every provincial capital with its gymnasium. By the end of the century this modest plan had been overfulfilled, and there were nearly two hundred gymnasiums in all. The gymnasium course was pretty well uniform throughout Russia, and had been expanded from four years to eight. Unsatisfactory pupils were kept down to do a second year in the same form—as happened to Chekhov in both the third and fifth forms—because of an inadequate performance in the annual examinations, a dreaded event. There were also pro-gymnasiums—similar institutions, offering the first part, four years, of the gymnasium course. Then there were also modern schools (*realnyye uchilishcha*). These placed emphasis on mathematics, science and modern languages, and they gave entry to technical colleges, whereas the gymnasiums proper provided their graduates with entry to the universities and preferential access to civil service posts. The above were all boys' schools, but girls too had their gymnasiums, being better served with secondary school education than they were at either university or primary level. Girls' gymnasiums offered a seven-year course with an extra year for those who wished to qualify as schoolmistresses. They also inflicted less Latin and Greek on their pupils.

* * *

In the same year the overall tally of primary schools throughout the Empire was nearly eighty thousand, with a total of nearly four million pupils. There was only one authority with wider control over primary education than that exercised by the Synod—the ministry of education itself, responsible in 1896 for some two-fifths of

7. 1801–25 [*Editor's note*].

the Empire's primary schools with nearly two-thirds of the pupils. At the same time the ministry of war was responsible for over ten thousand primary schools with some three hundred thousand pupils.[8]

Schools were set up by village communes, by town councils and also by the zemstvos, the zemstvo schools being of particular importance by the end of the nineteenth century. Many schools were founded by private individuals, including writers, and that established at Yasnaya Polyana by Tolstoy in 1859 became especially famous. A noted theorist of education, as of almost everything else in human life, Tolstoy also liked teaching peasant children and produced a fairly successful reading primer, his *ABC Book*, in 1872. Chekhov too founded schools for the peasants during his residence in the village of Melikhovo, south of Moscow, and his story *My Life* illustrates the sort of difficulties which this might involve.

* * * Besides the institutions mentioned above, Russia also possessed a variety of boarding-schools including the quaintly named 'pensions for well-born spinsters' for daughters of the gentry. There were Sunday schools designed to teach, not religious knowledge but reading and writing, and officially suspected as hotbeds of revolutionary agitation. And there were increasing numbers of technical and vocational colleges, including the Moscow Higher Technical School. It also became a common practice for factories to provide schools for the children of employees.

Even by the end of the period considered here, this rapidly growing system was on too small a scale for the gigantic Empire. With her large proportion of illiterates, Russia was still a long way from achieving universal primary education by 1904. And that of girls was particularly neglected. In 1896 less than a quarter of the overall number of primary school pupils were girls. No wonder that, according to a favourite proverb of the (male) Russian peasant: 'A woman is long on hair and short on brain'.

8. For figures in this paragraph, see Kovalevsky, pp. 476 ff.

Chekhov: Critic and Playwright

ANTON CHEKHOV

Impure Tragedians and Leprous Playwrights†

A Terribly—Horribly—Scandalously—Desperate Trrragedy

Lots of Acts   Even More Scenes

CAST OF CHARACTERS

MIKH. VAL. LENTOVSKY, *a man and entrepreneur*

TARNOVSKY, *a heart-wounding man; with devils, whales, and crocodiles on familiar speaking terms, addressing each other as "thou,"
etc. Pulse 225, temperature 109.04°*

PUBLIC, *a lady pleasing in every which way; eats everything that's
handed out*

KARL XII, King of Sweden; *has the manners of a fireman*

GENERAL ERENSWERD, *a terribly great man with the voice of a
mastodon*

DELAGARDI, *an ordinary man; plays his role with the unrestrained
familiarity . . . of a prompter*

STELLA, *sister of the entrepreneur*[1]

BURL, *a man who arrives on the shoulders of* SVOBODIN[2]

HANSEN[3]

OTHERS

Epilogue*

*The crater of a volcano. At a writing table, covered with
blood, sits* TARNOVSKY; *on his shoulders, in place of a head, is
a skull; brimstone is burning in his mouth; out of his nostrils*

† This play was first published in the journal *Budil'nik*, 1884, No. 4, under Chekhov's pseudonym, "The Brother of My Brother." It is a parody on the drama *Impure and Leprous*, written by K. Tarnovsky (who had translated it from the German) and produced at the theatre of M. V. Lentovsky (1843–1906). This translation is from the playscript (in Russian) published in *Chekhov and Theatre*, pp. 181–84.

1. Lentovsky's sister, who acted in his productions.
2. In the 1883–84 season, P. M. Svobodin worked in Lentovsky's theatre.
3. Hensen was ballet master at Lentovsky's theatre.
* *I wanted to put down* Prologue, *but the editor says that the more incredible, the better. Whatever he wants!* [*Typesetter's footnote.*]

jump little green devils who are smiling suspiciously. He dips his pen—not into an inkwell—but into lava, which is being stirred by witches. It's horrible. Flying through the air are the shivers that run up and down your spine. At the depths of the stage, trembling quakes are hanging on burning-hot hooks. Thunder and lightning. The calendar belonging to ALEKSEY SUVORIN [*the provincial secretary*] *is lying right there with the impartiality of a bailiff who predicts the collision of the earth with the sun, the annihilation of the universe, and the rising prices of drugs. Chaos, terror, fear . . . The remainder can be supplied by the reader's imagination.*

TARNOVSKY. [*gnawing his pen*] How's it possible to put something like that down on paper, daammmit to hell? Can't come up with a single thing! A *Journey to the Moon*—it's already been done . . . so has *A Hobo*[4] . . . [*Drinks boiling oil.*] Just got to come up with something more . . . something, so that the wives of businessmen in Zamoskvorets[5] will dream of devils three days in a row . . . [*Rubs his coronal bone.*] Hm . . . Go to it, you, o great brains! *He thinks; thunder and lightning; there is heard the salvo of a thousand cannons, executed from a drawing by Mr. Shekhtel; out of the cracks crawl a dragon, vampires, and snakes; into the crater falls a large box, out of which comes* LENTOVSKY, *who is dressed in a huge poster.*

LENTOVSKY. Hi, there, Tarnovsky!

TARNOVSKY. ⎫
WITCHES. ⎬ [*together*] All good health, Excellency![6]
OTHERS. ⎭

LENTOVSKY. Well, what do you say? Is the play ready, daammmit to hell? [*Waves a bludgeon.*]

TARNOVSKY. By no means, Mikhail Valentinych. See here, I'm thinking, I'm sitting and can't come up with a single thing. This piece of work you've handed on to me is much too tough! What you want is for my play to curdle the public's blood, for an earthquake to strike the hearts of the businessmen's wives in the Zamoskvorets, for my soliloquies to be so powerful they'll snap off the lights . . . But you will agree, won't you, that this demands a grander strength than even the great Tarnovsky can provide! [*Having praised himself, he is flustered.*]

LENTOVSKY. Ssstuff and nonsense, daammmit to hell! A bit more powder, Bengal lights, highflying soliloquies—and that's all there is to it! In the interests of costumes, take up—daammmit to hell—high society . . . Treachery . . . Prison . . . The girl the prisoner

<hr>

4. The titles of plays produced at Lentovsky's theatre.
5. Zamoskvorets was a district in Moscow wherein lived members of the merchant estate, petty bourgeoisie (*meščane*), and civil service officials on the lower rungs of the ladder system of ranks.
6. The Russian phrase translated as "All good health" was the standard form of greeting (in the pre-revolutionary Russian army) to the commanding officer by the rank and file.

loves is married off to the villain by brute force . . . The role of
the villain we'll hand over to Pisarev . . . Later on, an escape from
prison . . . Gunshots . . . I won't save on the powder . . . Later on,
a baby, whose noble birth is only revealed late in the show . . .
At the very end, gunshots again, a fire again, and the triumph of
virtue . . . To put it in one word, don't use your imagination,
but cook up something commonplace, just like Rocambole and the
Counts of Monte Cristo[7] . . .

> *Thunder, lightning,·hoarfrost, dew. The eruption of a volcano.* LENTOVSKY *is thrown outside.*

Act One

> *The* PUBLIC, USHERS, HANSEN, *and* OTHERS.

USHERS. [*taking off the* PUBLIC's *coats*] A little help from your
Honor! [*Not having received a tip, they grab the* PUBLIC *by their
coattails.*] O, black ingratitude!!! [*Are ashamed for the human
race.*]

ONE OF THE PUBLIC. What, Lentovsky's recovered?

USHER. He's started fighting again, that means he's well.

HANSEN. [*dressing in his dressing room*] I'll amaze them, I will!
I'll show them! They'll start talking in all the newspapers.

> *The act continues, but the reader is impatient; he thirsts
for the second act; this being so—curtain!*

Act Two

> *Palace of* KARL XII. *Behind his back,* VALTS[8] *is swallowing
swords and burning-hot coals. Thunder and lightning.* KARL
XII *and his* COURTIERS.

KARL. [*strides around the stage and rolls the whites of his eyes*]
Delagardi! You have betrayed your country. Hand over your sword
to the captain and march off to prison, if you please!

DELAGARDI. [*says a few words packed with emotion, and leaves.*]

KARL. Tarnovsky! You in your heart-wounding play have forced me
to live through ten superfluous years of my life! Hie yourself off
to prison, if you please! [*To the* BARONESS.] You are in love with
Delagardi and had a child by him. In the interests of the story
line in this play, I must not know this circumstance and must
marry you off to a man you don't love. Go and marry General
Erenswerd.

BARONESS. [*marrying the General*] Ah!

GENERAL ERENSWERD. I'll bake them in the oven till they're done!

---

7. *The Count of Monte Cristo*, a novel
by Alexandre Dumas *père*, was first published in 1844, and dramatizations soon
followed. Rocambole was the name of
the hero in several French adventure
stories.

8. Konstantin Fyodorovich Val'ts (1846–
1929) was chief engineer in charge of
theatre technology in the imperial theatres in Moscow. He also worked for
Lentovsky.

He is made superintendent of the prison, in which DELAGARDI
and TARNOVSKY *are locked up.*

KARL. Well, I'm free now, right up to the fifth act. I'm off to my
dressing room!

Acts Three and Four

STELLA. [*plays, as is her custom, not too badly*] Count, I love you!

YOUNG COUNT. And I love you, Stella, but I adjure you, in the name
of love, tell me, why in hell did Tarnovsky drag me into this long-
drawn-out mishmash? What am I needed for? What on earth
have I to do with the story line in this play?

BURL. But it was Sprut who caused all this! Thanks to him, I landed
in the army. He beat me, persecuted, bit me . . . and may I not be
Burl if it wasn't he who wrote this play! He's ready for anything,
just to bake me in the oven till I'm done!

STELLA. [*having learned of her origin*] I'll go and set father free!
On the way to the prison, she meets HANSEN. HANSEN *does an*
entrechat.

BURL. Thanks to Sprut, I landed in the army and I'm participating
in this play. No doubt it's this Sprut who is forcing Hansen to
dance, just to bake me in the oven till I'm done! Well, just you
wait!

The braces are falling. The stage collapses. HANSEN *executes
a leap which causes all the old maids in the audience to feel
faint.*

Acts Five and Six

STELLA. [*becomes acquainted with Papa in prison and, together,
they think up a plan to escape*] I'll save you, Father. But how can
it be done, so that Tarnovsky doesn't escape with us? Once he escapes from prison, he will write a new drama!

GENERAL ERENSWERD. [*tortures* BARONESS *and* PRISONERS] Since I am
the villain, then I must in no way resemble a person! [*Eats raw
meat.*]

DELAGARDI *and* STELLA. [*They escape from prison.*]

ALL. Grab them! Catch them!

DELAGARDI. Be that as it may, we shall escape nonetheless and remain all put together. [*A gunshot.*] Who gives a spit! [*Falls
dead.*] And who gives a spit about that, either! The author can
liquidate you; but he sure can resurrect you, too.

KARL *appears out of the dressing room and commands Virtue to triumph over Vice. General rejoicing. The Moon
smiles, and the Stars smile, too.*

PUBLIC. [*pointing* TARNOVSKY *out to* BURL] There he is, Sprut!
Catch him!

BURL. [*grabs* TARNOVSKY. TARNOVSKY *falls dead, but immediately jumps up. Thunder, lighting, hoarfrost,* The Murder of Coverley,[9] *a great migration of peoples, shipwreck, and the knitting together of all the parts.*]

LENTOVSKY. Nonetheless, I'm not yet satisfied. [*Vanishes.*]

ANTON CHEKHOV

On the Injurious Effects of Tobacco
(First Version, 1886) †

A Monologue for the Stage

DRAMATIS PERSONA

MARKEL IVANYCH NYUKHIN,[1] *the husband of his wife, who maintains a boarding school for girls*
The scene is the platform stage of a provincial club.

NYUKHIN. [*enters majestically, bows, adjusts his waistcoat, and majestically begins*] Dear ladies and dear gentlemen! It was proposed to my wife ,that I—for the purpose of charity—give a popular lecture of some sort or other. True erudition is modest and is not fond of showing off, but with the view of charity in mind, my wife agreed—so here I am before you. I am not a professor, and I am a stranger to university degrees, but it's no secret to any of you, that I . . . that I [*Squirms and quickly peeps at a piece of paper, which he fishes out of his waistcoat pocket.*] . . . that I, for thirty years without stopping, sacrificing health and the good things in life, I have been working on questions of a strictly scientific character, and sometimes I even write scientific articles for the organ of the local press . . . The other day I turned in to the editor a huge article entitled, "On the Injurious Effects of Teaism and Coffeeism on the Organism." For the subject of my lecture

9. *The Murder of Coverley*, a melodrama translated from the French.
† This monologue by Chekhov was completed February 14, 1886, and was originally published in the *Peterburgskaja gazeta* on February 17, 1886, over the signature. *A. Chekhonte*. This translation is made from *O vrede tabaka*, as published in A. P. Chekhov, *Sobranie sočinenij* [hereafter cited as *Collected Works*], IX (Moscow, GIKHL, 1963), 202–7. A comparison of this first version (1886) with Chekhov's last version (1902) sheds light on the development of Chekhovian dramatic technique from the early farces to the subsequent major plays.

1. The first syllable of the character's last name, *nyukh* (pronounced *nyúkhin*), means "scent, smell, flair." Thus, in the words of David Magarshack, "the rather comic name of . . . Smelly." *Chekhov the Dramatist* (New York: Hill & Wang, 1960), p. 153. The silly and exotic first name *Markel* (*márkel*) was eventually changed by Chekhov to *Ivan* (pronounced *iván*), or the common Russian equivalent of *John*, in the third version, and was retained in succeeding versions. The patronymic is pronounced *iványch*.

today I have chosen the injurious effects which come about in humankind by the consumption of tobacco. Of course, it is difficult to exhaust in one lecture the importance of the subject, but I shall try to be brief and speak only about what is very important . . . As an enemy of popularization, I shall be strictly scientific, and as for you, my listeners, I propose that you feel deeply into the full importance of the subject and treat my present lecture with proper respect . . . The person who is giddy, the one who is intimidated by the dryness of a strictly scientific address, then that person need not listen but should leave at once! . . [*Makes a majestic gesture and adjusts his waistcoat.*] Now then, I begin . . .

I ask your attention . . . I especially ask the attention of the gentlemen present here who are doctors, who may draw from my lecture a good deal of useful information, since tobacco, apart from its injurious activities, is also utilized in medicine. Thus, in the year eighteen hundred and seventy-one, on the tenth of February, it was prescribed to my wife in the matter of enemas [*Peeps at the paper.*] Tobacco is an organic body. It comes, in my opinion, from the plant Nicotiana Tabacum, which is related to the Solaneae family. It grows in America. Its chief component part consists of the horrible, pernicious poison, nicotine. Chemically it consists, in my opinion, of ten atoms of carbon, fourteen atoms of hydrogen and . . . two . . . atoms . . . nitrogen . . . [*He chokes and snatches at his chest, letting fall the paper.*] Some air! [*In order not to fall, he keeps his balance with his arms and legs.*] Oh! Hold it! Let me get my breath . . . Hold it . . . Just a moment . . . I'll stop this attack through will power alone . . . [*Beats his chest with his fist.*] Enough! Whew! [*A short pause, during* which NYUKHIN *walks about the stage, panting and puffing.*] For a long time . . . I've suffered these choking attacks . . . asthma . . . This illness of mine began in the year eighteen hundred and sixty-nine, on the thirteenth of September . . . on that very same day that my wife gave birth to the sixth daughter, Veronika . . . All my wife's daughters total nine exactly . . . as for a son—not one, for which my wife is overjoyed, since a son in a girls' boarding school in many respects would be inconvenient . . . In the whole school there is only one man—it's I . . . But the deeply esteemed, highly respected families who have entrusted the fate of their daughters to my wife can feel completely at ease in their minds, in regard to me . . . Or rather . . . In view of the shortage of time, we dare not wander away from the subject of the lecture . . . Now then, on what did I stop. Whew! The attack of asthma interrupted me at the most interesting place. But there is no evil without good. For my sake and for your sake, and especially for the sake of the gentlemen present here who are doctors, this attack may serve as an excellent lesson. In nature there exist no actions without cause . . . Let us look, then, for the cause of my attack today . . . [*Puts a finger to his forehead and thinks.*] Yes! The

sole remedy for asthma—it's the abstention from heavy and stimulating foods, and before coming here to the lecture, I allowed
myself to indulge somewhat to the point of gluttony. It should
be pointed out to you that at my wife's boarding school, today is
the day for pancakes. Every schoolgirl is to receive for dinner, in
place of roast, one whole pancake. Inasmuch as I am the husband
of my wife, it isn't I who should praise, it seems, this noble person, but I swear to you that nowhere is anyone fed such sensible,
hygienic, and well-planned meals, as in the boarding school of my
wife. I can personally testify to that, because in the boarding
school of my wife I have the honor to be the head of the housekeeping department. I buy provisions, check up on the servants,
submit the day's accounts to my wife every evening, bind and
stitch notebooks, invent insecticides, clean the air with a spray,
count linen, see to it that one toothbrush goes for no more than
five pupils and that no more than ten young ladies dry themselves
with one towel. Today my duty lay in issuing to the cook butter
and flour in such amounts that correspond precisely with the number of boarders. So, today pancakes were fried. You ought to note
that the pancakes were destined only for the pupils. For the members of the family of my wife a roast was prepared, for the purpose
of which there was the hind leg of a calf, which had been preserved
in the cellar since Friday of last week. My wife and I had arrived
at the conclusion that, if we didn't roast the leg today, it might
spoil by tomorrow. But, let's press on. Just listen to what happened later on! When the pancakes had been fried and counted,
my wife sent word to the kitchen, saying that five pupils were to
be punished for bad manners by being deprived of pancakes. In
this way it turned out that we had fried five superfluous pancakes.
What were we supposed to do with them? What? Give them to
our daughters? But my wife forbids our daughters to eat pasty
foods. Well, what do you think happened? What did we do with
them? [*Sighs and shakes his head.*] Oh, loving heart! Oh, angel
of kindness! She said, "Eat up these pancakes yourself, Markesha!"
And I ate them up, having downed a little glass of vodka beforehand. That, then, was the cause of the attack. *Da ist der Hund
begraben!*[2] Still however . . . [*Looks at his watch.*] We've forgotten ourselves and have wandered somewhat away from our subject.
Shall we continue . . . So, chemically nicotine consists of . . . of
. . . [*Nervously roots in his pockets and looks around for the
paper.*] I suggest that you remember this formula . . . A chemical
formula—it's a lodestar . . . [*Having seen the paper, he drops his
handkerchief on it. Picks up the handkerchief together with the
paper.*] I forgot to tell you that in the boarding school of my wife,
in addition to my housekeeping chores, I am responsible for teaching mathematics, physics, chemistry, geography, history, and object

2. Usually *Da liegt der Hund begraben*,
literally, There is (lies) the dog concealed"; colloquially, "There's the rub!,
That's the sore point!"

lessons. In addition to these studies, in the boarding school of my wife are taught the French, German, English languages, law of God, needlework, drawing, music, dancing, and behavior.

As you can see, the course of study is more than your secondary-school course. And the food! And the comfort! And what is really astonishing: all this for the most paltry fee! Full-time boarding-schoolgirls pay three hundred rubles; half-time—two hundred; and walkers—one hundred. For dancing, music, and drawing there is a separate fee, by arrangement with my wife . . . A beautiful boarding school! It's located on the corner of Cat Street and Five Dog Lane, in the house belonging to the widow of Staff Captain Mamashechkin. As to negotiations, it's possible to find my wife at home anytime, and the prospectus of the boarding school is sold by the porter at the door at fifty kopeks a copy. [*Looks at the paper.*] So, I invite you to remember the formula! Chemically, nicotine consists of ten atoms of carbon; fourteen, of hydrogen; two, of nitrogen. Take the trouble to jot it down. It is a colorless liquid with an ammoniacal odor. What's important for us, properly speaking, is the direct action of nicotine [*looks into his snuffbox*] on the nerve centers and muscles of the digestive canal. Oh, Lord God! Again they've poured something into it! [*Sighs.*] Well, what can be done with girls who are mean, low-down scamps? Yesterday they poured powder into my snuffbox, and today it's something pungent, something putrid. [*Sneezes and scratches his nose.*] You know, it's vile! This powder is doing the devil knows what to my nose. Brrr! . . Oh, they're mean, naughty! You, perhaps, in this delinquency of theirs discover a severe shortage of discipline in the boarding school of my wife. No, dear gentlemen, it's not the boarding school that is guilty. No! Society is guilty! You are guilty! The family must go hand in hand with the school, but, instead, what do we see? [*Sneezes.*] But let's forget it! [*Sneezes.*] Let's forget. Nicotine throws the stomach and intestines into a tetanic condition, that is, into a condition of tetanus! [*Pause.*] However, I notice smiles on many faces. Obviously, not all listeners sufficiently appreciate the complete, high-level significance of the subject which concerns us. There are even those persons who find it in their power to laugh when truths santified by exact science are announced from the platform! [*Sighs.*] Of course, I dare not rebuke you, but . . . to the daughters of my wife I always say, "Children, don't laugh at what is beyond laughter!" [*Sneezes.*] My wife has nine daughters. The eldest of them, Anna, is twenty-seven; the youngest, seventeen. Dear gentlemen! All that exists in nature of beauty, purity, and exaltation, all is collected in these nine young, immaculate creatures. Forgive me this agitation and this quivering in the voice: you see before you the happiest of fathers. [*Sighs.*] Oh, how hard it is nowadays to marry them off. Horribly hard! It's easier to find money for a third mortgage than it is to find a husband for only one daughter. [*Shakes his head.*] Ah, young people, young people! In your stubbornness, in your bent for material things, you deprive yourself of one of the sheerest of pleasures, the pleasure of family life! . . If you only knew how fine that life is! I have lived through thirty-three years with my wife, and I can say that they were the best years of my life. They flew by like one twinkling, happy moment. [*Weeps.*] How often I've brought pain to her by my weaknesses. The poor thing! Even though I've accepted punishment obediently, with what did I compensate for her anger? [*Pause.*] The daughters of my wife have taken so long in getting married because they are shy and because men never see them. My wife cannot give parties, she never invites anyone to dinner, but . . . I can let you in on a secret. [*Walks closer to the footlights and whispers.*] It's possible to see my daughters on high holidays at the home of their aunt, Natalya Semyonovna Zavertyukhina,[3] the very same person who suffers from falling sickness and collects old coins. Refreshments are served there, too. But with the shortage of time, we don't want to wander from our subject. I had stopped on tetanus. Or rather [*looks at his watch*], until the next time! [*Adjusts his waistcoat and majestically leaves.*]

ANTON CHEKHOV

On the Injurious Effects of Tobacco
(Last Version, 1902) †

A Monologue for the Stage in One Act

DRAMATIS PERSONA

IVAN IVANOVICH NYUKHIN, *the husband of his wife, who maintains a music school and a boarding school for girls*
   The scene is the platform stage of a provincial club.
NYUKHIN. [*has long burnsides without mustache; dressed in an old, shabby frock coat; enters majestically, bows, and adjusts his waistcoat*] Dear ladies and, in one way or another, dear gentlemen. [*Combing his burnsides.*] It was proposed to my wife, that I— for the purpose of charity—give a popular lecture of some sort or other. Well, hmm? If it's to be a lecture, then let it be a lecture

---

3. Natalya (*natálya*) Semyonovna (*semyónavna*) Zavertyukhina (*zavertyúkhina*). The aunt's last name incorporates the meaning "to begin to twirl, whirl, spin; to lose one's head."
† This monologue was originally published in Chekhov's *Collected Works* (*Sobranie sočinenij*), XIV, in 1903 and is the last version written by him, supposedly in September 1902. This translation is made from *O vrede tabaka*, as published in *Collected Works*, IX, 602–6.

—it doesn't matter to me anyway. I am not a professor, of course, and I am a stranger to university degrees, but nonetheless, all the same, here am I, for already thirty years without stopping, and it's even possible to say, for the sake of injury to my own health and so on, I've been working on questions of a strictly scientific character, which I turn over in my mind and sometimes even write, can you imagine it, scientific articles; that is, not quite scientific, but which are, excuse the expression, not unlike scientific, as it were. By the way, the other day an enormous article was written by me under the title, "On the Injurious Effects of Certain Insects." My daughters liked it very much, especially the part on bedbugs. I just read it through and tore it up. It doesn't matter, you know, whatever you may write, because you can't do without Persian powder.[1] Bedbugs are even in our piano . . . For the subject of my lecture today I have chosen, so to speak, the injurious effects which come about in humankind by the consumption of tobacco. I myself smoke, but my wife ordered me to lecture today on the injurious effects of tobacco, and, consequently, what else can you say but do it. If it's to be about tobacco, then let it be about tobacco—it doesn't matter to me anyway, and as for you, dear gentlemen, I propose that you treat my present lecture with proper respect, otherwise I can't be held responsible for the way it turns out. Be there anyone here who is intimidated by the dry, scientific lecture, or who just doesn't like it, then that person need not listen and should leave at once. [*Adjusts his waistcoat.*] I especially ask the attention of the gentlemen present here who are doctors, who may draw from my lecture a good deal of useful information, since tobacco, apart from its injurious activities, is also utilized in medicine. Thus, for example, if a fly is placed in a snuffbox, then it will expire, in all likelihood, from nervous disorder. Tobacco is, for the most part, a plant . . . When I lecture, I usually wink my right eye, but don't pay any attention to it; it comes from nervous excitement.[2] I am a very nervous person, generally speaking, but my eye began to wink in the year eighteen hundred and eighty-nine, on the thirteenth of September, the very same day that my wife gave birth, in one way or another, to her fourth daughter, Varvara. All my daughters were born on the thirteenth. Or rather [*having glanced at his watch*], in view of the shortage of time, we dare not wander away from the subject of the lecture. It should be pointed out to you, my wife maintains a music school and a private boarding school; that is, not quite a boarding school, but which is not unlike something of that sort. Confidentially speaking, my wife likes to complain about the lack of money, but she's socked away a little something, some forty or fifty thousand, and I don't have a kopek to my soul, not even part of one—well, what's the use of talking about it! In the boarding

1. An insecticide to ward off bugs.
2. *Èto ot volnenija*; literally, "it's from agitation."

school, I am the head of the housekeeping department. I buy provisions, check up on the servants, write down the expenses, bind and stitch notebooks, exterminate bedbugs, walk my wife's little dog, catch mice . . . Yesterday evening my duty lay in issuing to the cook butter and flour, because pancakes were intended. Well, sir, to put it in one word, today, when the pancakes had already been fried, my wife came to the cook and said that three pupils would not be eating pancakes, because they had swollen glands. In this way it turned out that we had fried several superfluous pancakes. What were we supposed to do with them? At first, my wife ordered them to be carried to the cellar, but then she thought; she thought and said: "Eat these pancakes yourself, you sloppy dummy." When she's out of sorts, that's what she calls me: sloppy dummy, or asp, or Satan. What kind of Satan am I, anyway? She is always out of sorts. And I didn't eat them, but I stuffed them down without chewing, because I am always hungry. Yesterday, for example, she didn't give me anything for dinner. "You sloppy dummy," she said, "What's the use of feeding you . . ." Still, however [*looks at his watch*], we've forgotten ourselves and have wandered somewhat away from our subject. Shall we continue. Though, of course, you'd be much more inclined now to listen to a love song, or some sort of symphony or other, or an aria . . . [*Sings and conducts.*] "In the thick of battle we do not bat an eye . . ." I can't really remember where that's from . . . By the way, I forgot to tell you that in the music school belonging to my wife, in addition to running the housekeeping department, my duties also include the teaching of mathematics, physics, chemistry, geography, history, solfeggio, literature, and so on. For dancing, singing, and drawing, my wife charges a special fee, though I'm also the one who teaches dancing and singing. Our music school is located in Five Dog Lane, number thirteen. That's why, in all likelihood, my life is so unfortunate, since the number of the house we live in is thirteen. And my daughters were born on the thirteenth, and in our house we have thirteen windows . . . Well, what's the use of talking about it! As to negotiations, it's possible to find my wife at home anytime, and the prospectus of the school, if you like, is sold by the porter at the door at thirty kopeks a copy. [*Takes several brochures out of his pocket.*] And here am I, if you like, able to share. Only thirty kopeks a copy! Who'd like one? [*Pause.*] No one wants a copy? Well, what about twenty kopeks! [*Pause.*] Isn't that the limit. Yes, house number thirteen! Nothing comes through for me, I'm putting on years, becoming stupid . . . Here am I giving a lecture, I look like I'm cheerful, but inside myself I'd like to cry out in full voice or fly away somewhere or other to the end of the world. And there's no one at all to complain to, I even want to start crying . . . You will say: your daughters . . . What daughters? I talk to them, but they only laugh . . . My wife has seven daughters . . . No, I'm sorry, it seems there are six . . .

[*Quickly.*] Seven! The oldest of them, Anna, is twenty-seven; the youngest, seventeen. Dear gentlemen! [*Looks around.*] I'm not happy, I've turned into a fool, a nonentity; but, in reality, you see before you the happiest of fathers. In reality, that's as it should be, and I dare not say otherwise. If only you knew! I've lived with my wife thirty-three years, and I can say those were the best years of my life, oh, by no means the best, but in general, that is. They've flown by, to put it in one word, like one twinkling, happy moment. As a matter of fact, damn them all, damn them to hell. [*Looks around.*] Or rather she, of course, still hasn't arrived, she isn't here, and it's possible to say whatever I like . . . I get terribly frightened . . . frightened when she looks at me. Well, like I was saying: my daughters have taken so long in getting married, because, in all likelihood, they are shy and because men never see them. My wife doesn't want to give parties, she never invites anyone to dinners, she is as tightfisted as they come, a bilious and pugnacious lady, and that's why no one ever stops by our place, but . . . I can let you in on a secret . . . [*Walks closer to the footlights.*] It's possible to see the daughters of my wife on high holidays at the home of their aunt, Natalya Semyonovna, the very same person who suffers from rheumatism and goes around in that yellow dress with black dots, just as if cockroaches were splattered all over her. Refreshments are handed out there, too. And when my wife isn't around there, then it's possible for this . . . [*Smacks himself on the neck.*] It should be pointed out to you, I get drunk on one glass, and from this comes such a good feeling in my soul, and at the same time, such sorrow that I can't possibly express; for some reason, memories of my youth come back, and for some reason, the longing to run away, oh, if you only knew, how much the longing! [*Carried away.*] To run away, to throw everything down, and to run without once looking back . . . Where to? It doesn't matter where . . . if only to run away from this rotten, vulgar, cheap life, which has turned me into an old, pitiful fool, an old, pitiful idiot, to run away from this stupid, petty, malicious, malicious, malicious money-grubber, from my wife, who tortured me for thirty-three years, to run away from music, from the kitchen, from the wife's money, from all this nonsense, pettiness and vulgarity . . . and to stop somewhere far, far away in the field and to stand there like a tree, a post, a garden scarecrow, under the wide sky, and the whole night through, watch how the silent, bright moon is hanging over you, and to forget, to forget[3] . . . Oh, how I long to remember nothing! . . How much I

3. This last version, although hilarious and ridiculous in parts, is shaped in great measure by Chekhov's introduction of *nastroenie*, or mood; by his heightening of Nyukhin's unconscious hatred for his wife; and by his coupling of both *nastroenie* and hatred with the absurd and farcical action of taking off his coat and stamping on it. By shedding and attempting to destroy his coat, Nyukhin acts out the dream (false) of casting aside his role of henpecked husband and of taking on an entirely new life style.

long to tear off this obscene old frock coat I wore thirty years ago at my wedding . . . [*tears off his frock coat*], in which I constantly give lectures for the purposes of charity . . . That's for you! [*Stamps on the frock coat.*] That's for you! I am old, poor, dilapidated, like this very same waistcoat with its shabby, used-up old back . . . [*Shows the back.*] I don't need anything! I'm superior to this, more clean and pure. Once upon a time I was young, intelligent, I studied at the university, I had dreams, I took for granted I was a human being . . . Now I don't need anything! Nothing except peace . . . except peace! [*Having glanced to the side, quickly puts on the frock coat.*] However, my wife is standing in the wings . . . She has arrived and is waiting for me there . . . [*Looks at his watch.*] Time has already passed . . . If she asks, then, please, I beg you, tell her that the lecture was . . . that the sloppy dummy, that is, I, conducted himself with dignity. [*Looks to the side, clears his throat.*] She is looking here . . . [*Having raised his voice.*] Proceeding from this proposition, that tobacco contains a horrible poison, of which I have only just spoken, under no circumstances is it proper to smoke, and I permit myself, in one way or another, to hope that this my lecture, "On the Injurious Effects of Tobacco," will be of service. I have said everything. *Dixi et animam levavi!*[4] [*Bows and majestically leaves.*]

4. "I have spoken and alleviated my soul."

Criticism

The Dramaturgy of
Anton Chekhov

DAVID MAGARSHACK

[Purpose and Structure in Chekhov's Plays]

* * *

The plays of Chekhov, like those of any other great dramatist, follow a certain pattern of development which can be traced through all its various stages. His last four plays, moreover, conform to certain general principles which are characteristic of the type of indirect-action drama to which they belong. Chekhov himself was fully aware of that. Already on November 3, 1888, in a letter to Aleksey Suvorin, he clearly stated that all works of art must conform to certain laws. "It is possible to collect in a heap the best that has been created by the artists in all ages," he wrote, "and, making use of the scientific method, discover the general principles which are characteristic of them all and which lie at the very basis of their value as works of art. These general principles will constitute their law. Works of art which are immortal possess a great deal in common; if one were to extract that which is common to them all from any of them, it would lose its value and its charm. This means that what is common to them all is necessary and is a *conditio sine qua non* of every work which lays claim to immortality."

Chekhov did not claim immortality for his plays. He was too modest for that. What he did claim for them, however, was something that any immortal work of art is generally supposed to possess, namely, the power so to influence people as to induce them to create a new and better life for themselves. * * *

The misinterpretation of Chekhov's plays by the Moscow Art Theatre led to constant conflicts between their author and its two directors. These conflicts became particularly violent during the production of *The Cherry Orchard*. "The production of *The Cherry Orchard*," Olga Knipper, Chekhov's wife and one of the leading actresses of the Moscow Art Theatre, wrote, "was difficult, almost agonising, I might say. The producers and the author could not understand each other and could not come to an agreement." Che-

259

khov himself wrote to Olga Knipper: "Nemirovich-Danchenko and Alekseev positively see in my play something I have not written, and I am ready to bet anything you like that neither of them has ever read my play through carefully." And to a well-known Russian producer Chekhov said: "Take my *Cherry Orchard*. Is it my *Cherry Orchard*? With the exception of two or three parts nothing in it is mine. I am describing life, ordinary life, and not blank despondency. They either make me into a cry-baby or into a bore. They invent something about me out of their own heads, anything they like, something I never thought of or dreamed about. This is beginning to make me angry."

* * *

* * * Chekhov was not, as is generally supposed, a great short-story writer who took up drama seriously only during the last seven or eight years of his all too short life. He was a born dramatist whose first works of importance were three full-length plays, two written in his late teens and the third in his early twenties. He took up short-story writing for two reasons: first, because he had to support a large family which was entirely dependent on him, and the writing of short stories was the quickest way of doing it; secondly, because the state of the Russian stage in the eighties and the nineties of the last century was such that no serious playwright could hope to have his plays performed, let alone earn a decent living in the theatre. Even Alexander Ostrovsky, whose reputation as a playwright had long been established, was not able to do so. It was indeed this hopeless position of the serious playwright in Russia towards the end of the nineteenth century that made Chekhov look on fiction as his "legal wife" and the stage as "a noisy, impudent and tiresome mistress." But the remarkable fact about a Chekhov short story is that it possesses the three indispensable elements of drama: compactness of structure (Chekhov's term for it was "architecture"), movement, that is dramatic development of plot, and action. "The reader," Chekhov wrote to the writer Ivan Leontiev on January 28th, 1888, "must never be allowed to rest; he must be kept in a state of suspense." The dialogue in Chekhov's short stories is essentially dramatic dialogue and that is what chiefly distinguishes them from the short stories of other fiction writers. Many of these short stories, particularly the early ones, have been adapted for the Russian stage, but the "adaptation" consisted mainly in lifting Chekhov's dialogue and using the descriptive passages as stage directions. Chekhov himself "adapted" five of his short stories for the stage on the same principle, that is, he merely lifted the dialogue, adding his own stage directions, and, if his story was too short, expanding it to the necessary length of a one-act play.

* * *

Chekhov, then, was a born playwright and his knowledge of the stage, too, was first-hand. As a boy in his native town of Taganrog he had often appeared on the amateur and professional stage and earned general recognition as a talented actor. * * *

His purely professional attitude towards drama * * * can further be gauged from the fact that he did not consider a play of his completed before it had been thoroughly revised by him at rehearsals. Thus he wrote on November 27th, 1889, to the poet Pleshcheev who had asked his permission to publish *The Wood Demon*, "I never consider a play ready for publication until it has been revised during rehearsals. Wait, please. It is not too late yet. When the play has been revised at the rehearsals, I shall take advantage of your kind offer without waiting for an invitation."

Chekhov's only reason for writing a play was the likelihood of its being performed on the stage. Moreover, when writing a play he usually bore in mind the actors who were most likely to appear in its leading parts and, as in the case of *Ivanov*, he never hesitated to alter a play radically if a different actor or actress took a part he had originally intended for someone else.

*   *   *

* * * Mention has already been made of Chekhov's views on the paramount importance of action in a play. What are the other general conditions that Chekhov regarded as necessary to an aspiring playwright? First of all comes a thorough, first-hand knowledge of the stage. "Beginning with the next season," Chekhov wrote to a fellow-dramatist in March 1889, "I shall start visiting the theatre regularly and educating myself scenically." To his eldest brother Alexander, who had sent him a general outline of a play he was proposing to write; Chekhov wrote: "Don't forget to visit the theatre a few times and make a thorough study of the stage. You'll then be able to compare and that is important." Another rule that Chekhov was never tired of enjoining on his fellow-dramatists was the need for originality. "Try to be original in your play," he advised his brother, "and, as far as possible, intelligent, but do not be afraid to appear silly. Complete freedom of expression is necessary, but remember that only he is free to express his views who is not afraid to write stupid things. Incidentally, love declarations, infidelities by husbands and wives, and tears shed by widows, orphans and other people have been described long ago." * * *

A play, in Chekhov's view, must above all be compact. "The more compact and the tighter a play is," he writes to a fellow dramatist, "the brighter and more expressive it is." He warns the same dramatist against becoming a professional playwright, that is to say, a playwright to whom the mere tricks of the stage are more important than the subject matter of his plays. A playwright, he insists, must above all be a poet and an artist. He must conquer the stage and not let the stage conquer him. All the same, so keen was Chekhov's perception of the requirements of the stage that in a letter to another fellow dramatist he coined the aphorism: "You must never put a loaded rifle on the stage if no one is going to fire it."

In addition to compactness and expressiveness, Chekhov laid great stress on "plasticity of phrase". He warned his brother against preciosity of language. He objected to the dialogue of one of Suvorin's plays because the language of its characters was "like a white silk dress which is all the time reflecting the sun and on which it hurts you to look. The words 'vulgarity' and 'vulgar'," he adds, "are old-fashioned now." Writing to Gorky in January 1899, Chekhov warned him against lack of gracefulness and restraint in his first play, defining "gracefulness" in these words: "When a man spends the least possible number of movements on some definite action, then that is gracefulness."

Another principle of writing plays Chekhov stuck to all through his career as a playwright concerned the elimination of what he called "the personal element." * * *

There is another piece of advice Chekhov gives to his brother which is characteristic of the external form of a Chekhov play and which might as well be noted here. Every full-length play of Chekhov's has four acts and the importance of each act in its relation to the play as a whole was defined by Chekhov as early as May 8th, 1889, in a letter to Alexander: "The first act," he wrote, "can go on as long as an hour, but the others must not last longer than thirty minutes. The climax of the play must occur in the third act, but it must not be too big a climax to kill the fourth act."

It was Chekhov's custom first to produce a rough draft of a play and then go on improving it. With *Ivanov* and *The Wood Demon* (*Uncle Vanya*) this procedure was much more drastic, the two plays in their final form undergoing vital alterations. This process of re-shaping a play Chekhov considered required much greater ability from the playwright than the initial process of writing the play. * * *

One more important aspect of Chekhov's attitude to the stage still remains to be elucidated, namely his views on the playwright's place in the theatre. It was undoubtedly Chekhov's great good fortune that among the greatest admirers of his genius was Nemirovich-Danchenko, one of the founders of the Moscow Art Theatre, who prevailed on Stanislavsky almost by main force to put on *The Sea Gull* during the Moscow Art Theatre's first season, thus being responsible for Chekhov's close association with one of the most progressive theatres in Russia. But this association with Stanislavsky and Nemirovich-Danchenko was also one of Chekhov's greatest misfortunes inasmuch as both producers were, at the outset of their stage careers at any rate, what is commonly known as producer-autocrats who brooked no interference either from their actors or from their authors and who quite honestly held the view * * * that they had a right to interpret a play any way they liked. Ordinarily this would have brought about an early break between Chekhov and the Moscow Art Theatre, for Chekhov would never have agreed to his elimination from the production of his plays and the complete disregard of his own interpretation of them. As early as 1887, he insisted on the playwright's right to have a deciding voice in anything that concerned the production of his plays. * * *

Holding such views, how did it happen that Chekhov let Stanislavsky and Nemirovich-Danchenko ride roughshod over his own conception of his plays? The answer to this question is simple: at the time his plays were being performed at the Moscow Art Theatre Chekhov was already a stricken man who could take no direct part in their production. He was condemned to live in the Crimea and the few rehearsals he managed to attend in Moscow were insufficient for him to correct the cardinal misunderstanding of his ideas by the two producers. (He did, however, take an active part in the rehearsals of *The Three Sisters* before the revival of the play in the autumn of 1901.) That was the reason for his frequent outbursts of anger during the rehearsals and his refusal to advise the actors how to play their parts. His stock reply to the actors, "You'll find it all in the text," was just an evasion forced on him by his complete helplessness to make his producers see the positive ideas he had taken so much pains to present in an artistic form. In face of such utter blindness on the part of his producers and their inability to raise themselves above the prevailing ideas of their time, Chekhov was powerless: he was too ill to do anything. The irony of it was that this cardinal misinterpretation of his plays seems to have agreed with the mood of that particular period in Russian history so that in spite of it the plays were (after a time) successful. There is, of course, the further fact that with so great a playwright as Chekhov the failure to grasp the ruling ideas of his plays, the inability to understand their structure, and even the plain distortion of their characters, leaves so much that is original and artistically true that the spectator has plenty left he can thoroughly enjoy. That, however, does not justify the view that Chekhov's outbursts of angry protests against the misinterpretation of his plays were merely the unaccountable tantrums of genius. Chekhov, as is plainly evident from his letters, does not belong to the type of writer who is devoid of critical ability. He was, in fact, a very profound literary critic as well as a man who possessed the invaluable capacity for self-criticism. It took him about seven years to work out his new formula of the play of indirect action, and there can be no doubt that he arrived at his new form of dramatic expression only after a careful and painstaking analysis of the technique of playwriting, including a thorough study of Greek drama,[1] a fact of some consequence to the understanding of the structure of his last four plays.

* * * There are, however, two characteristic features of Chekhov's indirect-action plays that must be considered. The first concerns the difference between the dialogue of Chekhov's early plays and that of his late ones. The dialogue of the early plays is remarkable for the directness of its appeal to the audience, while in the late plays its appeal is indirect and, mainly, evocative. Take, for example, the opening scene of *Ivanov*. As the curtain rises Ivanov is discovered sitting at a table in the garden of his house reading a book. It is evening, and a lamp is burning on the table. Borkin, the manager of his estate, who has been out shooting, comes in with a shotgun, steals up to Ivanov and takes aim at him. Ivanov jumps up with a start.

> IVANOV. What on earth are you doing, Michael? You made me jump. I'm upset as it is, and now you come along with your silly jokes. (*Sits down.*) Made me jump and looks as pleased as Punch about it.
> BORKIN (*roars with laughter*). All right, all right—I'm sorry, old man. (*Sits down beside Ivanov.*) I'm hot. Covered fifteen miles in about three hours—upon my word, I have. I'm dead beat. Feel my heart—it's pounding.
> IVANOV (*reading*). All right, later.
> BORKIN. No, feel it now. (*Takes Ivanov's hand and puts it to his chest.*) Do you hear? Thump-thump-thump-thump. That means that I have a weak heart. I may die suddenly any minute. Will you be sorry if I die?
> IVANOV. I'm reading—later——
> BORKIN. No, seriously, would you be sorry if I died suddenly?
> IVANOV. Don't pester me!
> BORKIN. Please, tell me: will you be sorry?
> IVANOV. I'm sorry you reek of vodka. That, Michael, is disgusting.
> BORKIN. (*laughs*) Do I? That's funny. . . .

Compare this with the opening scene of *The Sea Gull*, which also takes place in a garden in the evening. Again there are only two characters: Masha and Medvedenko, who have just returned from a stroll.

> MEDVEDENKO. Why do you always go about in black?
> MASHA. Because I'm in mourning for my life. I'm unhappy.

1. Among the large number of well-thumbed books Chekhov sent to the public library of his native town of Tagan- rog were the best available translations of the complete plays of the Greek dramatists.

MEDVEDENKO. Why? (*Wonderingly.*) I don't understand. I mean, there's nothing the matter with your health, and even if your father isn't rich, he's not badly off, either. My life is much harder than yours. I only get twenty-three roubles a month, and I have my insurance deducted from that. But I don't wear mourning, do I? (*They sit down.*)

MASHA. Money's not everything. Even a pauper can be happy.

MEDVEDENKO. That's all very well in theory, but in practice it's quite a different matter. I have to provide for my mother, my two sisters, my little brother and myself, and all on a salary of twenty-three roubles. We have to eat and drink, haven't we? We have to get tea and sugar, haven't we? And tobacco? It's a problem all right.

MASHA (*glancing at the stage*). The play will be starting soon.

MEDVEDENKO. Yes. Nina will be acting in it, and the play itself was written by Konstantin. They are in love. Tonight their souls will unite in the effort to give expression to one and the same artistic idea. But your soul and mine have no common points of contact. I'm in love with you. I long for you so terribly that I find it impossible to stay at home. Every day I walk four miles here and four miles back, but all I get from you is cold indifference. Well, I can't say I'm surprised at it. After all, I have no money, and I have a family to support. What's the use of marrying a man who can't even provide for himself?

MASHA. That's not important. (*Takes a pinch of snuff.*) I'm touched by your love, but I can't return it—that's all. (*Holds out the snuffbox to him.*) Help yourself.

MEDVEDENKO. Thank you, I don't feel like it. (*A pause.*)

The difference between these two scenes is not that the first one is active and the second one inactive. As a matter of fact, the second one requires a great deal more acting than the first one. The difference lies mainly in the different impact on the audience: the impact of the first is direct and immediate, the impact of the second is indirect and evocative, that is to say, since the characters in the second play are introspective, they arouse in the audience an emotional mood which is identical with their own. In other words, while in Chekhov's early plays the dialogue is mainly dramatic, it is mainly evocative or poetic in his last plays. * * *

Chekhov's dialogue is therefore a very subtle instrument for evoking the right mood in the audience and in this way preparing it for the development of the action of the play. * * * Tension in an indirect-action play is, therefore, one of the main motive forces of action. In a Greek play it arose out of the spectator's knowledge of the main dramatic events in the story. The play was, in the main, a mere dramatisation of a well-known legend, and the spectator's interest was aroused even before the appearance of the actors on the stage: he was all agog to see how the playwright and the actors would interpret the characters of a story that was rich in dramatic events which he knew and in which he even believed. Chekhov had to invent another method to convey this tension to his audience at the very beginning of the play. He did it by showing one of his main characters in a state of high nervous tension, like, for instance, Konstantin in the opening scenes of *The Sea Gull* or Voynitsky in the opening scenes of *Uncle Vanya*. Failure on the part of the actor to convey this highly overwrought state of the character he is representing will destroy this feeling of tension with the result that the play as a whole will become dull and flat, and this fact alone is indeed responsible for the impression that Chekhov's plays are devoid of action and movement, both of which * * * Chekhov esteemed above everything else in a dramatic work.

Another powerful impetus to action and movement is provided in an indirect-action play by the presence of "invisible" characters. In a Greek play it is mostly the gods who determine the fate of the characters. The presence of these "invisible" characters in a Chekhov play has been noted by many critics. * * * For instance, Nina's parents in *The Sea Gull*, Protopopov in *The Three Sisters*, and Mrs. Ranevsky's aunt and her Paris lover in *The Cherry Orchard*. In a play of direct action they would be allowed to take an active part on the stage, for they all occupy an important place in the plot and without them the final dénouement would be impossible. In an indirect action play, however, it is necessary that they, like the supernatural powers in a Greek play, should remain invisible, for their function is to supply a motive force for the action which is all the more powerful because the audience never sees them but is made to *imagine* them. * * *

The main elements through which action is expressed in an indirect-action play are: the "messenger" element, the function of which is to keep the audience informed about the chief dramatic incidents which takes place off stage (in a direct-action play this element is, as a rule, a structural flaw); the arrival and departure of the characters in the play round which the chief incidents that take place on the stage are grouped; the presence of a chorus which, as Aristotle points out, "forms an integral part of the whole play and shares in the action"; peripetia, that is, the reversal of the situation leading up to the dénouement, which Aristotle defines as "a change by which the action veers round to its opposite, subject always to the rule of probability and necessity", and which is the most powerful element of emotional interest in indirect-action plays and their main instrument for sustaining suspense and arousing surprise; and, lastly, background which lends depth to such plays.

The messenger element is perhaps the most difficult one to manage satisfactorily as it tends to impede the action and divert the attention of the audience from it. * * *

* * *

The messenger element must * * * concern itself strictly with the action of the play and contribute to its development. At the beginning of the play it serves the purely functional purpose of informing the audience about the events that have happened before the opening of the first scene, and at the end of the play it helps to sustain and to satisfy the curiosity of the audience. Chekhov's great art as a playwright is best revealed in the superb way in which he handles the messenger element. In the opening scene of *The Cherry Orchard* he reduces the narrative part to a minimum, and yet the situation is immediately clear; nor does the scene drag in the least: it is charged with tension and full of action[2].

* * *

The remarkable fact about *The Sea Gull* is that Chekhov dispenses with the messenger element in the first three acts altogether and when he comes to use it in the fourth act he can afford to take it at a more leisurely pace, for by that time the curiosity of the audience has been sufficiently aroused and he runs no risk of boring them. Still, he has to invent a special situation to make it more acceptable: he has to send Dorn away to Italy so as to make him ask all the right questions when the time comes for Konstantin to acquaint the audience with the highly dramatic events that have taken place in the interval between Act III and Act IV. Chekhov handles the scene with consummate skill.

* * *

The scene is completely natural (and the messenger element does not lend itself so easily to naturalness) and it is punctuated with what Stanislavsky used to call "pauses of tragic action", that is to say, pauses during which Konstantin has to *act* and not just sit silent and look embarrassed * * * He has to make the audience aware of the agonies he has been through, and he has to convey it all, to quote Chekhov himself, "with his tone of voice and *with his eyes*".

The arrival and departure element is one of the most indispensable elements in an indirect action play. It introduces action of a purely external kind, fills the stage with noise and bustle, and provides the producer with inexhaustible opportunities for stage effects of the most varied sort. The whole action of the play, in fact, leads up to and centres round this element, and Chekhov took the greatest possible advantage of it. In *The Sea Gull* it provides him with a magnificent climax in the third act and helps him to heighten the suspense in the last. In *Uncle Vanya* it helps him to contrive a

2. See p. 165, above [*Editor's note*].

most moving anti-climax in the last act. In *The Three Sisters* the entire action is built round it, and in *The Cherry Orchard* it gives him a fine dramatic opening and an ending of great poignancy. It is an element that is particularly welcome to producers who are incapable of dealing with indirect-action plays, and indeed it is the only element producers of Chekhov's plays have made full use of as a function of action.

The chorus element is another indispensable feature of the play of indirect-action. In Greek drama it was a special actor, or groups of actors, who gave expression to the moral and religious sentiments evoked by the action of the play. In the French pseudo-classical drama it was again a special actor who was entrusted with the task of passing a moral judgment on the characters, known in the Russian early pseudo-classical plays as the *raisonneur*, a somewhat tedious character spouting conventional moral sentiments. But quite often in a modern indirect-action play the rôle of the chorus is divided up between several characters, who stand apart from the main characters and are not directly involved in the action. In a Chekhov play, however, it is the characters themselves who provide the moral judgment on the action, and in it the chorus element therefore becomes an integral part of the whole play, as Aristotle urged the Greek playwrights to make it. His characters, as it were, assume the mantle of the chorus whenever their inner life bursts through the outer shell of their everyday appearance and overflows into a torrent of words. It is this spontaneous and almost palpable transmutation into speech of hidden thoughts and deeply buried emotions that is perhaps the most subtle expression of dramatic action in a Chekhov play. If not treated as such, it is liable to transform these flashes of self-revelation into static, isolated and disconnected statements of opinion. It is important to remember that no other great classical Russian playwright has employed this method of revealing the "inner man" of his character and that the notion, which is so common in England and America, that the Chekhov characters express themselves in such a way because they are "Russians" is entirely mistaken. Chekhov himself offered a very clear indication of his use of the chorus element in the opening scene of *The Three Sisters*, a play in which it is predominant. Indeed, the scenery of the first act of the play was conceived by Chekhov in the form of a Greek theatre: he divided the stage into two parts separated by a colonnade, the front part representing a drawing-room and the back part a dining-room. There are six characters in the opening scene, divided into two groups, each keeping to its own part of the stage, the three sisters in front of the columns and Chebutykin, Tuzenbakh and Solyony behind the columns. Their dialogue, too, is conducted in a sort of strophe and antistrophe manner. (There is a strong admixture of the messenger element in the dialogue of the sisters.)

Strophe	*Antistrophe*[3]
OLGA. It is just a year since father died—on this very day, the fifth of May—your birthday, Irina. It was dreadfully cold; it was snowing then. I felt as though I'd never be able to live through it and you were lying in a faint. But now a whole year has gone by and the thought of it no longer troubles us. You're wearing a white dress again, you look so radiant. (*The clock strikes twelve.*) Then, too, the clock struck twelve. (*Pause.*) I remember the military band playing at father's funeral, and they fired a salute at the cemetery. Though father was a General and a brigade commander, there were not many people at his funeral. It is true, it was raining then. Pouring with rain and snowing.	
IRINA. Why must you talk about it?	*In the dining-room behind the columns, Baron Tuzenbakh, Chebutykin and Solyony appear at the table.*
OLGA. It is warm today—the windows can be opened wide —but the birch-trees have not opened up yet. It is eleven years since father was given his brigade and left Moscow with us, and, I distinctly remember it, the flowers were in bloom in Moscow just at this time—at the beginning	

3. Strophe, literally, "a turning." In the ancient Greek theatre, the choral ode was often divided into groups of two stanzas each: (1) the stanza called the *strophe*; (2) the stanza called the *antistrophe*, literally, "a turning about (against)," which is a stanza in answer to the strophe [*Editor's note*].

of May—oh, it was so warm then, and everything was drenched in sunlight. Eleven years have passed and I can remember everything just as if we had left Moscow only yesterday. My goodness! When I woke up this morning and saw the bright sunshine—saw the spring—my heart leapt for joy, and I felt such a longing to be back home!

Masha, daydreaming over her book, whistles a tune softly.

OLGA. Don't whistle, Masha. How can you! I suppose it's because I'm at school all day and then giving lessons in the evenings that I'm getting these constant headaches and these thoughts, just as if I were old already. And, really, all these four years while I've been working at school I've felt as though my strength and my youth were draining out of me drop by drop. And one longing only grows stronger and stronger—

IRINA. To go to Moscow. Sell the house, finish with everything here and leave for Moscow.

OLGA. Yes! To Moscow as soon as possible.

CHEBUTYKIN. The devil you did!
TUZENBAKH. It's all nonsense, of course!

Chebutykin and Tuzenbakh laugh.

And the scene goes on till Tuzenbakh, clearly as a comment on the plans of the sisters, though actually addressing Chebutykin, says: "What nonsense you talk—I'm sick of listening to you." The two groups then join and the action of the play really starts. The end of the play, too, is composed entirely of a chorus scene in which only the three sisters take part.[4]

The most important elements so far as the structure, the "architecture," as Chekhov called it, of a play of indirect-action is concerned, is peripetia, the reversal of situation, which, according to Aristotle, "arises from the internal structure of the plot so that what follows should be the necessary or probable result of the preceding action." Aristotle illustrates this element by a reference to *Oedipus* where, he points out "the messenger comes to cheer Oedipus and free him from his anxiety about his mother, but by revealing who he (Oedipus) is, produces the opposite effect." This is the simplest and, no doubt, the most effective example of peripetia, but in Chekhov's plays of indirect-action this element assumes much more subtle forms. * * * It is so integral a part of the plot of the play. . . .

The background element of a Chekhov indirect-action play consists of the realistic touches which lend actuality and intimacy to the life of the characters in it as well as of the not so easily defined literary undertones which lend a greater depth to it. These "literary undertones" may derive from an old story or a play by Chekhov himself or some other Russian playwright, notably Ostrovsky, or, as in *The Sea Gull* from *Hamlet*, which forms, as it were, an enigma variation in the symphonic score of the play: it is always present but only in one or two instances does it emerge clearly and unmistakably. For instance, in "the play within the play," which, as in *Hamlet*, comes to an abortive end because of the passions it arouses, or in the two quotations from *Hamlet*, which * * * are an essential part of the dramatic action of the first act, though they are usually omitted in a performance of the play on the English stage.

These are the main basic elements through which action is expressed in Chekhov's last plays. Where Chekhov's genius as a playwright, however, finds its most brilliant expression is in the entirely original form he gave to the indirect-action type of drama by a completely new and infinitely subtle combination of its basic elements, and in this sense Chekhov can be said to be one of the greatest innovators in modern drama.

4. The final scene in the last act is arranged exactly like the opening scene in the first act. That is, in both scenes the three female characters downstage singing and dancing the strophe are balanced by three male characters upstage singing and dancing the antistrophe. In order to stress that a happy, new life is on its way and will be realized with the Revolution in October 1917, some Russian productions of the play since 1940 eliminate the male characters (Chebutykin, Kulygin, Andrey) in the final scene of Act IV and thereby cut out the balancing effect of Chekhov's antistrophe. Such Russian productions therefore create the effect of ·an optimistic future for the three sisters [*Editor's note*].

CHARLES B. TIMMER

The Bizarre Element in Chekhov's Art

A study in literature, whether on Gogol, Dostoevsky or Chekhov, is bound to involve a study in anti-reason: it cannot limit itself to a study of aesthetic laws only, unless we are prepared to assume that the grotesque, the bizarre, the absurd elements in the works of these authors are unexplainable phenomena.

The grotesque, the bizarre, the absurd—by using these words I realize that I am bringing to the foreground certain aspects of Chekhov's art, which to my knowledge did not thus far have the attention they undoubtedly deserve. It is certainly not my ambition to exhaust the subject in these notes; my purpose is merely to outline it and to make an attempt to trace the difference between the technique of the bizarre in Chekhov's last works and his use of the bizarre element in his early stories; for example, between a little scene like this in *The Cherry Orchard* (1903–4):

> *Varya*: The estate will be up for sale in August.
> *Anya*: Oh dear!
> *Lopakhin*: (*puts his head through the door and bleats*) M-e-e-e . . . (*Disappears*)"[1]

and "bizarre" stories like "On Christmas Eve" (1883), "At Sea" (1883), "Oysters" (1884), "The Mistress" (1882), "In the Home for Incurables and the Aged" (1884) and many others from Chekhov's early period, stories that are bizarre either in style or theme, or both. When we consider Chekhov's literary output as a whole, we cannot fail to notice one remarkable fact, namely, that the bizarre element is abundantly represented in the early, the "Chekhonte" stories, that it gradually disappears in his later and riper work, but reappears, more profusely than ever, in his plays.

But what really is the meaning of the bizarre in art and what is its function? When do we call a certain phenomenon, a situation, a statement *bizarre*?

The word defies precise definition. However, it is possible to mention one inherent quality—its irrelevancy—and one typical effect—its capability of producing bewilderment. In this it differs from the grotesque, which really is nothing but comical exaggeration, showing us the ludicrous side of "extreme situations"; it likewise differs from the absurd, which lies already wholly in the realm

---

1. Anton Chekhov, *Three Plays*, tr. Elisaveta Fen (London, 1953), p. 30.

of the irrational. the *bizarre* is not necessarily absurd: it is, as it were, a statement, or a situation, which has no logical place in the context or in the sequence of events, the resulting effect being one of sudden bewilderment; the bizarre brings about a kind of mental "airpocket": one gasps for breath, until the tension is relieved by laughter. The *absurd* is contrary to reason and does not necessarily contain this element of playful, whimsical strangeness, which is so characteristic for Chekhov in the youthful wantonness of his art, a strangeness, which comes so strikingly to light again in many characters and situations in his plays. It is difficult, if not impossible to draw a distinct line between such conceptions as "the absurd", "the bizarre", "the grotesque"; they often overlap and flow together. And besides, in all these matters the factor of personal appreciation by the reader or spectator and therefore of subjective interpretation influences the definition. A few examples by way of illustration, taken from Chekhov's Notebooks—this rich fund of grotesque, bizarre and absurd fancies and observations—, may throw some more light on the matter. Thus the following situation might be called simply "grotesque": "A shy young man came on a visit for the night; suddenly a deaf old woman of eighty came into his room, carrying a clyster-pipe[2] and administered a clyster to him; he thought that this must be the usual thing and so did not protest; in the morning it turned out that the old woman had made a mistake."[3] Here my contention that the characteristic quality of the grotesque lies in the exaggeration, in the hyperbolism of a *possible* situation, is clearly demonstrated by the English translation of this passage,[4] in which, possibly for reasons of modesty, the clyster-pipe is replaced by a cupping-glass and the victim is bled. Suppose another translator would go one step further and change the syringe for a cup of tea—then the grotesque element would have disappeared altogether. The bizarre element can be found in a statement like this: "When I become rich, I shall have a harem in which I shall keep fat naked women, with their buttocks painted green." This is a good example of that particular kind of "mental leap", so typical of the bizarre, with the clear-cut caesura in the logical sequence after the third section of this statement. Finally, the absurd is demonstrated in a note of the following kind: "N., a singer; speaks to nobody, his throat muffed up—he takes care of his voice,

---

2. An instrument for administering an enema [*Editor's note*].
3. *The Personal Papers of Anton Chekhov* (New York, 1948), p. 104. The translation of the Notebook is by S. S. Koteliansky and Leonard Woolf and is quoted with some corrections.
4. The passage referred to reads in the English translation "Suddenly a deaf old woman came into the room, carrying a cupping-glass, and bled him." Cf. A. P. Chekhov, *Polnoe sobranie sočinenij i pisem* [Complete collected works and letters] (hereafter cited as *PSSP*), XII, 284: "Vdrug vošla staruxa let 80, gluxaja, s klistirnoj kružekoj i postavila emu klistir."

but no one has ever heard him sing." Which, in my opinion, is a good example of irrational behaviour.

In the beginning of his career as a writer the bizarre element in Chekhov's work comes very close to the grotesque; wherever it appears in his later prose-writings and in his plays, it has more in common with the absurd. This is important and fully in harmony with the wellknown fact that the laughter in Chekhov's stories gradually dies down. In his early period it seems hardly likely that Chekhov used the bizarre deliberately as a consciously worked out technique: it rather appears that bizarre thoughts, statements, situations found their way in his work quite naturally, as the fruit of unbridled inspiration; they arose understandably from a youthful *brio*, playfulness and boldness in the author himself; they are, if I may quote Dylan Thomas, "A portrait of the artist as a young dog." More often than not the stories, in which the bizarre element is very evident, can be found in that group of narratives, which Chekhov himself did not include in his collected works and which form a part of his literary inheritance. The genuinely grotesque-bizarre stories are published under the penname "Chekhonte", a pseudonym rather bizarre in itself, at least for Russian ears.

* * * The bizarre in stories of this kind, as also in "On Christmas Eve," an early story, written in a pseudo-romantic vein, and in quite a few others is realized by way of a subtle mockery of the "terrible"; the element of horror is played with, rather flippantly sometimes, with the effect that horror becomes funny. Most of these stories have a definite point, with a surprising denouement, which does not however solve a problem or a mystery, but intensifies the comical effect of the narrative. Upon finishing his play *Ivanov*, Chekhov wrote in a letter to his brother Aleksandr: "This is the first play I wrote, ergo—I was bound to make mistakes. The subject is complicated and not stupid. Every act I end just like my stories: throughout the whole act everything goes on peacefully and smoothly, but towards the end I give the spectator a punch on the nose."[5] It is in this "punch on the nose," in this sudden uncovering of "green-painted buttocks", that the typical bizarre element in Chekhov's early work is revealed * * *.

* * * the bizarre gradually disappears in Chekhov's later work, or rather, it loses its grotesque aspect and approaches more and more that particular attitude towards things, which we call the absurd. Here it must be stated at once, however, that the absurd as such in Chekhov's art is always treated merely incidentally, never pro-grammatically, dogmatically or from the platform of a certain philosophy. For Chekhov life as such (existence) is neither absurd nor intelligible. The absurd elements in his stories should therefore

5. *PSSP*, XIII, 372.

not be confused with the absurd as idea. The absurd is the confrontation with the irrational; it is, what in relation to human judgment is considered as unreasonable. If we think of a scientist, whose knowledge in a certain field of science is unique and of immeasurable value to mankind, who suddenly dies in a car-accident, we may speak of an absurd occurrence, the absurd in this case consisting in the fact that such a tremendous wealth of knowledge and experience can be destroyed within a fraction of a second. Death in its finality is bizarre in so far as it causes bewilderment, it is absurd in so far as we consider it unreasonable. Chekhov had a wonderful feeling for the whole scale of subtle shades between the bizarre and the absurd in life and death. The long standing controversy, whether Chekhov was an optimist or a pessimist, with ardent partisans on both sides, loses its meaning, when we realize that Chekhov, like every sensitive artist, was torn between two contrary insights: that the world, or life as such, is unreasonable and at the same time, that man cannot leave off trying to find a reasonable explanation for this world, or, in the words of Albert Camus, this philosopher of the absurd (whose own death can stand as an example of absurdity): "Ce monde en lui-même n'est pas raisonnable . . . Mais ce qui est absurde, c'est la confrontation de cet irrationnel et de ce désir éperdu de clarté dont l'appel résonne au plus profond de l'homme."[6] Chekhov's dithyrambic dreams of a better life in the future, expressed in his last plays and in some of his stories, are no proof of his "optimism," but only of his desperate desire to find a solution to the problem of the antagonism, existing between absurd reality and rational ideality, his desire to bring about a peace between life as it is lived:—an apparently bizarre and senseless undertaking—and life as it could be projected in the mind—beauty, justice and harmony. On the other hand, if Chekhov were convinced that such a peace would a priori be impossible, that the search for a reasonable explanation of the world is an enterprise, foredoomed to failure, then we might be justified in calling him a pessimist; but he never made such a statement, on the contrary: somewhere, at some time in the future the solution will be found, he says. This is not optimism, but the firm conviction that life itself generates hope. Converted to secular values, we may compare Chekhov's faith with the "Credo quia absurdum"[7] of Tertullian, philosophically speaking the most optimistic statement ever made, if we put the stress on the "credo", but at the same time the most pessimistic one, if we realize that we

6. "This universe in itself is not rational. . . . What is absurd is the confrontation of this irrational and the mad desire for clarity whose appeal reverberates most deeply in man." Albert Camus, *Le mythe de Sisyphe* (Paris, 1942), p. 37.

Camus (1913–60) was a French writer and philosopher [*Editor's note*].
7. Belief because it is unreasonable. Quintus Septimius Florens Tertullianus (160?–230?) [*Editor's note*].

can never overcome the absurd, that we, as long as there is life, shall never be able to say: we believe in it, because it is reasonable. In other words: that faith can never be replaced by knowledge, Chekhov's dream of happiness "after two hundred years" is nothing else than this *désir éperdu de clarté*,[8] of which Camus speaks. In fact, hope and expectation are blended so masterfully in Chekhov's art with hopelessness and despair, the technique of evoking bizarre effects by letting hope clash on despondency is handled so skilfully, that we can say without hesitation that here we find the clue to that unique fascination, which emanates from his work and the spell it exercises on the reader. A perfect demonstration of this we find in stories like "Dreams" (1886), or "Happiness" (1887), in "Peasants" (1897), "In the Ravine" (1900) and many others. In the story "Happiness" an old shepherd is telling about the treasures, hidden, according to legend, somewhere in the vast Russian steppe. A young shepherd listens attentively to the old man's stories. "But, if you find the treasure, what are you going to do with it?" he asks in the end. The old man does not know; all through his long life he has dreamed of finding one of these legendary treasures, but the thought, what to do with it, has never occurred to him: that was not important. The young man also starts to wonder at the curious fact that only old men and women were so interested in thesse treasures, only the old kept constantly talking about them. At last the young shepherd falls silent and thinks about all the things he has heard in the course of the summernight. "He was not interested so much in happiness in itself, which he did not need, and which he could not comprehend, as in the fantastic, the fairytale side of human happiness . . . ," concludes Chekhov.

One of Chekhov's notions of the bizarre,—and probably one of the most important ones,—is that in an apparently hopeless life there is still hope, that, as I said before, life itself generates hope. That, if there is seemingly no way out,—there *is* nevertheless a way out: by being interested, fully, humanly interested in "the fantastic, fairytale side" of every situation. To the question of what life *means*, Chekhov had no other answer than: it is what it is, as in *Three Sisters*, when Masha asks: "Isn't there some meaning?" and Tuzenbakh answers: "Meaning? . . . Look out there, it's snowing. What's the meaning of that?"[9] In the same play the final conclusion of Andrey, when Chebutykin asks him: "What about your wife?" is: "My wife is my wife."[1] But even if every life is condemned to end in failure, even if it has many terrible aspects, it still is hopeful, because it is life, because it can be seen and felt and tasted and experienced, because it can be told. In the story "Peasants" this

8. Mad desire for clarity [*Editor's note*].   1. Ibid., p. 162.
9. Chekhov, *Three Plays*, p. 126.

hope, this life, this Chekhovian conception of indestructible continuation is impersonated in the little girl Sasha, who as an innocent witness of poverty and misery wanders through the whole story with eyes to see and to bear witness. The little girl is not a judge, she just observes and sees. The fact that in life there are eyes to see the injustice, the absurdity, is enough: this is all the hope there is. Well, and this is precisely the case with Chekhov himself: *he just sees.* And to see, really to see, with inquisitive, childlike eyes, means to discover the hidden relationships in life, to reveal its fairytale side. In many of Chekhov's stories it is the child, or the grown-up with the childlike mind that sees in this manner: it is the child and the artist, who possess this talent for discovering. And again, it is children and artists who have the genuine taste for the bizarre, the feeling for the absurd; it is they also, who can recreate it, because playfulness is an intrinsic part of their being * * * . In Chekhov's first long story "The Steppe" (1888) it is through the eyes of the little boy Yegorushka that the steppe and life in it are recreated. In the story "In Exile" (1892) it is the poor, illiterate Tartar with the mind of a child, who understands and grasps the "hidden relationships" and stammers the truth in his broken Russian: "The gentleman is a good soul, very good, and you are a beast, you are bad! The gentleman is alive and you are dead . . . God made man that he should be alive, that he should have happiness, sorrow, grief, and you want nothing, so you are not alive, but a stone! A stone wants nothing and so do you. . . ."[2]

When comparing the bizarre in Chekhov's work with the bizarre in Dostoevsky, we find some striking differences in their approach, both in technique and its application. In the great novels of Dostoevsky the bizarre element is mainly demonstrated in some of the secondary characters and they are always slices of enlarged humanity. Mentally, intellectually, the reader believes in a captain Lebyadkin ("Evil Spirits"), in a Lebedev ("The Idiot") and queer characters like these, although they possess a reality, built up out of isolated psychological components and the bizarre in them lies in their psychological hyperbolism. Lebedev in "The Idiot" is a vulgar scoundrel and a drunk, but at the same time a man, who prays at night for the salvation of the unfortunate comtesse Du Barry; he is a specialist in the exegesis of the Apocalypse, and in some casual, enigmatic remarks he gives a clue to the main theme of the whole novel. In the hundreds of characters in Chekhov's stories not one is in this sense 'enlarged' and hyperbolic; they always stay human in every respect; the bizarre with them—even with the queerest characters we meet in his plays—does not appear so much in what they

2. *The Stories of Anton Tchekov*, ed. Robert H. Linscott (New York, 1932), p. 180.

are, as well in what they do. Looking for the bizarre in Chekhov's work, we do not find it in the characters, but in their situation, in their mutual relationships. The reason for this may be found in the fact that Chekhov's characters nearly all are "whole", while Dostoevsky's characters are practically all "split personalities", or combined doubles; they are dramas, tragedies *in themselves*, while Chekhov's people through their interrelationship create tragedies and dramas *amongst themselves*. Chekhov's characters long for things they do not possess (Moscow, talent, love, gooseberries), or for what they are not and cannot be (famous, active, energetic) and the author knows how to uncover the bizarre element in such hopeless longing: in this respect the epithet of "a cruel talent" could be given to Chekhov also! But Dostoevsky's heroes are both mean and noble, both evil and good, both vulgar and highminded; alternatively the one or the other quality breaks out and suppresses the opposite impulse. Therefore the bizarre with Dostoevsky is one of inner conflict and of being; with Chekhov of outer conflict and of situation. In 1886 Chekhov wrote in a letter to his brother Aleksandr: "Heaven forbid that we indulge in the use of commonplaces! The best would be to avoid in your stories the description of the mental state of your heroes altogether. You must try to develop this state out of the actions of your heroes."[3] This is exactly the opposite of Dostoevsky's method, where the action is rather a result, the outcome of the mental state of the hero, of what I call his "inner conflict". Nikolay Chikildeev in the story "Peasants" had to give up his job as a waiter in a Moscow hotel because of ill health and returned with wife and child to his native village, where he slowly withers away. In the famous description of a night at the peasant-cottage Chekhov relates, how "Nikolay, who had not slept all night, got down from the stove. He took his dress-coat out of a green chest, put it on, and going to the window, stroked the sleeves, fingered the coat-tails—and smiled. Then he carefully removed the coat, put it away in the chest, and lay down again."[4] There is no question in Nikolay's bizarre behaviour in the middle of the night of a description of inner conflict: Nikolay is quite an ordinary man, but he is placed in an extraordinary situation, a man beyond hope and help, who attires himself at night with the only remaining attributes of his former happiness and dignity. In the given situation the bizarre lies in the fact that the ex-waiter, placed in the position of a parasite on the village-life, caresses as a symbol of liberty and human dignity an object, a waiter's dress-coat, which in fact should stand as a symbol for human servitude and humiliation.[5] It will be

3. *PSSP*, XIII, 215.
4. *The Portable Chekhov*, ed. Avrahm Yarmolinsky (New York, 1947), p. 339.
5. Cf. A. Derman, *O masterstve Chekhova* (On the mastery of Chekhov), (Moscow, 1959), p. 42.

clear, from an example like this, that the technique of the bizarre, as used by Chekhov in this passage, is quite a far cry from the overt and wanton caprices in his "Chekhonte" period; now the bizarre comes to us as a technique, subtly handled by a masterhand and only recognizable as bizarre through the intellectual cooperation of the reader.

In the confrontation with the bizarre man is conscious of his existence as an enigma. Although Chekhov, being through education a man of science himself, believed in the civilizing and beneficent powers of knowledge and enlightenment, his faith was not a blind faith in nineteenth century positivism and progress. Nobody saw clearer than Chekhov the danger of the so-called "intellectualism," nobody realized better the limits of pure rationalist thinking. Stories like e.g. "A Dreary Story" (1889), "Ward No. 6" (1892), or "The Black Monk" (1894) provide ample substance for this contention. Chekhov himself was a highly intelligent man, a keen observer, capable of putting two and two together in all the phenomena of life. But here he added one element to his intelligence—and in this we recognize his genius,—namely, his readiness to accept, to admit and to tolerate the statement that two and two can be five, at least to grant the possibility of such a statement, were it only as a form of protest. Protest against what? My answer would be: a protest against the *law*.

Amongst the few types of wholly negative characters in the work of Chekhov, a prominent place is given to the "man in a shell," of whom it is said that "the only things that were clear to him were. Government regulations and newspaper notices in which something was forbidden."[6] This man-in-a-shell type of the intelligentsia, this Belikov, has a close relative in a slightly different hero, one somewhat more sociable and congenial, but likewise inclined to terrorize his neighbourhood: the type of the Von Koren in the story "The Duel" (1891), or his pendant Lvov in the play *Ivanov* (1887–89). They are the personifications of what we may call the "guardians of duty", "the pillars of law and order"—men who are honest, correct, intelligent, but absolutely devoid of imagination, men with no feeling, no taste and no understanding at all for the *bizarre*. Both the story "The Duel" and the play *Ivanov* are built up around three heroes: in "The Duel" this trio is formed by Laevsky, Von Koren, and Samoylenko. In the play *Ivanov* we meet the same trio in the persons of Ivanov, Lvov and Lebedev. The positions of these three types are clear: Laevsky/Ivanov is the man fighting with, and eventually becoming the victim of the bizarre; Von Koren/Lvov is the man who does not admit the existence of the bizarre, while Samoylenko/Lebedev accepts the bizarre as an intrinsic part of life.

6. *The Portable Chekhov*, p. 356.

In the last act of *Ivanov*, when Ivanov, a prey to despair and harassed by self-accusations, informs his bride Sasha that he cannot marry her, when Lvov walks around as a Nemesis, firmly decided to unmask Ivanov once and for all, then the "fool" Lebedev, this apparent good-for-nothing, utters some words of plain common sense. In a conversation with his future son-in-law and friend Ivanov it is he, who exclaims: "Look at things simply, as everybody else does! In this world everything is simple. The ceiling is white, the boots are black, sugar is sweet. You love Sasha, she loves you. If you love her—stay with her, if you don't love her—go, we won't bear you any malice. It's really as simple as that!"[7]

With Chekhov just as with Shakespeare, we must above all things be attentive to what the "fool" has to say. The Lebedev-element, this third aspect of human intelligence, is innocence, presented—as is so often the case—in the disguise of foolishness. It is the voice of life itself as it is lived, when we are told: "In this world everything is simple!"—an observation which must sound the height of absurdity in the ears of pathetic Ivanovs, caught in a mess of guilt-complexes, or of the stern Lvovs who want to reduce life to a complicated system of regulations. But what we hear in Lebedev and Samoylenko, apart from a certain amount of *naïveté*, is the voice of confidence, this utter and stable confidence that cannot be shaken by all the horrors in the world. It is Chekhov's confidence in the regenerating powers of life. It is the voice of unassailable innocence in human intellect, of its inviolable virginity. It is the voice that will be heard "two hundred years from now . . ." The Lebedevs and Samoylenko's together with the little girl in "Peasants," with Lipa in "In the Ravine," with Gusev in the story of that name, with father Anastasy in "The Letter," with the Tartar in "In Exile,"—these are the ones, of whom I said that they are the children and artists, who see and accept the bizarre, who are free and possess the talent for discovering the hidden relationships.

However, it is not Chekhov's philosophy or outlook on life, that I am concerned with here. The problem of the grotesque-bizarre-absurd in his art is not a philosophical problem, but one of style and technique. I already pointed out that in the "Chekhonte" stories the bizarre element appears to be used as a series of outbursts of youthful spontaneity rather than a consciously applied literary technique. It was found that this element gradually disappears in his stories of a later date; whenever we find traces of it, it is used with much restraint and *con sordino*,[8] the technique is usually applied in the form of a quick, unexpected shifting of various moods. We only need to compare a story like "At Christmas Time" (1900) with one

7. Chekhov, *Three Plays*, p. 251.
8. With the mute—a direction in music [*Editor's note*].

of the "Chekhonte" stories to see the difference in function of the bizarre. At first glance this element seems to be present in this story as well with the same nonchalant brio as for instance in "For Stealing Apples" (1880), but soon it becomes clear that it is used in quite a different technique; while in the early story the bizarre was nothing but ornament, here it is the canvas, on which the story is embroidered.

But it is especially in the plays, and most of all in *Uncle Vanya, Three Sisters* and *The Cherry Orchard*, that we find the technique of the bizarre applied consciously and deliberately with an eye on the effect it will produce. The functions of the bizarre as consciously applied technique are manifold. In the first place there is the function of *retardation* of the action. A good example can be found in the last act of *Uncle Vanya*. In the stage-directions at the beginning of this act it says: *On the wall a map of Africa, obviously serving no useful purpose here.*[9] The "purpose" of this map, indeed a rather bizarre object in the study of an estate somewhere in the Russian province, becomes clear when Astrov takes his final leave. Astrov is firmly resolved to take his departure and to stay away for a long time to come, but he does not want to go at all. There really is nothing more to be said, but everybody feels the necessity of some remark being made, never mind what, only so that the final moment may be put off. It is then that Astrov walks up to the map of Africa and says: "I suppose down there in Africa the heat must be terrific now!" On this bizarre and quite irrelevant remark of the doctor in the prevailing situation Vanya reacts laconically with the words: "Yes, very likely."[1]

Apart from retardation the above example reveals another function of the bizarre and a very important one too, namely, to give a suggestion of indifference. It is well known, what importance Chekhov attached to "coldness", "non-attachment" in the creative process. The impact of emotions, of distress, delight, of grief and joy is felt much stronger, when they are suggested and not described. If, in the given situation, Astrov would have said: "How awful to have to leave you people; I don't want to go, but have to, you know!" or something of the kind, the impression on the spectator would be nil, because that would be exactly the thing he had expected. Instead, Astrov says: "I suppose down there in Africa the heat must be terrific now!" and this element of restraint, applied in a scene that is charged with emotions, greatly intensifies the impression on the spectator. The element of the bizarre as a technique to retard the action and restrain the emotions is used frequently by Chekhov in his plays.

9. Anton Chekhov, *The Seagull and Other Plays*, tr. Elisaveta Fen (London, 1954), p. 140.
1. Ibid., p. 150.

A third function of the bizarre is the communication of a hidden meaning. This end is often attained by way of an understatement. It may happen that one of the characters makes an apparently non-sensical remark, which stupefies the reader or spectator. In *Three Sisters* the old and doting doctor Chebutykin has the habit of reading aloud from some old newspaper he always carries around with him. In act II, in the midst of a lively conversation on the meaning of happiness, he suddenly, reading from his newspaper, remarks: "Balzac was married at Berdichev."[2] This in the given context seemingly quite senseless remark is repeated twice, showing that the author did not regard it as just a casual interjection by a drunk, but that these words were meant to communicate some hidden message, an allusion to something, which, however, is nowhere explained in the further development of the conversation. But what possible meaning could be concealed in the bizarre observation of an old, dilapidated country-physician, in a play, the action of which takes place around 1900, while the words "Balzac was married at Berdichev", read from a newspaper, point to an event that surely happened before Balzac's death in 1850? The theme of the play is the expectation of happiness: Vershinin projects the "coming happy life" in the future; the sisters believe that they will find happiness and fulfillment as soon as they will be in Moscow. When we remember that Berdichev is an ugly little bordertown in Western Russia the remark of Chebutykin becomes meaningful, without losing its bizarre character: it means to say that, if Balzac could find his happiness in such a doghole as Berdichev, it is quite unnecessary to go to Moscow to look for happiness, because it can be found anywhere, and further: why project your dreams of happiness in the future, when we only need to open some old newspaper in order to find ample proof of happiness and fulfilment in the past? The function of the bizarre in this instance is first to stupefy and to shock, to disrupt the logical sequence of thoughts by some eccentric observation, secondly to provide this observation with an undercurrent of deeper meaning. Another example of this technique we find in the long story "The Duel" (the scene, when doctor Samoylenko and Von Koren carry on an animated conversation about the "superfluous man" Laevsky). In the course of the conversation both get more and more excited. There is a third person in the room, a young deacon, a rather silly man who chuckles and giggles all the time, a man in whom we recognize once more one of these typical Chekhovian fools, who are not directly involved in the conflict, but who at unexpected moments come forward with their comments and who, in this respect, have a rather similar function to that of the "chorus" in the Greek tragedy. When the conversation between

Samoylenko and Von Koren reaches its climax and both are about ready to cut each other's throat, this little, insignificant deacon suddenly makes the casual observation: "Our Eminence does not travel by coach through his diocese, he always goes on horseback . . ." and then he compares the bishop in his humility and simplicity with a Biblical character. The interruption had nothing whatsoever to do with the conversation, there was no talk at all about bishops, coaches or horses and to all appearance the deacon's words are out of place and sheer nonsense. Yet it brings the conversation to a sudden stop, the heat of the quarrel has abated and the observation carried a hidden meaning as well: the hint to both hotheaded antagonists to follow the bishop's example and to be more humble.

In "Gooseberries" (1898) Chekhov makes the following observation: "What is terrible in life goes on somewhere behind the scenes . . ."[3] The bizarre is indeed quite frequently an eruption of the terrible on the smooth surface of common everyday life. Such an eruption takes place in the story "The Murder" (1895), in which the bizarre is an intrinsic part of the whole intrigue and a man is murdered, because during Lent he wanted to help himself at dinner to some oil; the instrument he is killed with is the oil-bottle.

Sometimes Chekhov does not leave the bizarre unexplained, but reveals the meaning of it in an exposé, for instance, in "The Lady with the Pet Dog" (1899), in the following fragment: "One evening, coming out of the physicians' club with an official with whom he (the hero) had been playing cards, he could not resist saying: 'If you only knew what a fascinating woman I became acquainted with at Yalta.'" The official has no better reply to this beginning of a lover's confidential confession than the sordid and bizarre words: "Dmitry Dmitrich! . . . You were right this evening: the sturgeon was a bit high!"[4] Whereupon Chekhov enters into a long explanation of why the hero was so infuriated by the vulgarity of the official's words.

A further function of the bizarre,—and this mainly in the plays again,—is to emphasize the salient features of certain characters, in other words, to show them in their absurdity. One of the most bizarre characters in Chekhov's plays is Solyony in *Three Sisters*, a sinister man, belonging to the family of the "men-in-a-shell," in so far as meanness and limitations are not only the result of social maladjustment, but also caused by his private inhibitions. He has a very important function in the drama and is, as his name indicates, the salt in the play. His condition of being a potential murderer Solyony can only cover up by spraying his hands frequently with perfume. Everything he says or does is absurd.

In order to give a note of the bizarre to his characters Chekhov

3. *The Portable Chekhov*, p. 381.   4. Ibid., p. 424.

often makes use of the attribute of gluttony. Quite a few of his early comical stories are based on this human weakness. But this element also appears in his later stories and in the plays. The official in "The Lady with the Pet Dog" could only think of sturgeon when his partner wanted to talk about his beloved; Pishchik, another bizarre character in *The Cherry Orchard* pours all the pills from a pill-box, brought by the valet to Madame Ranevskaja, into his hand and eats them. We also hear that during Easter week he had consumed a gallon and a half of cucumbers.[5] Solyony, in *Three Sisters*, referring to Bobik, Natasha's baby, remarks: "If that child were mine, I'd fry him in a frying pan and eat him,"[6] in which words he certainly betrays his radicalism. A little later it appears that he has eaten all the chocolates from a box of sweets on the table. Gaev, in *The Cherry Orchard*, frequently takes a box of caramels out of his pocket and sucks one.

Bizarre attributes are often used in drawing a character. Thus one notices Gaev's passion for billiards in *The Cherry Orchard* and his use of technical terms of the game, mostly in situations when he is confused and bewildered. Bizarre attributes, used in drawing Masha's character in *The Sea Gull*, are the black dress she wears and her opening-line in the play: "I am in mourning for my life";[7] in the case of Sorin, in the same play, it is his habit to use stock-expressions like: "and all that," "and all the rest of it," "and so on, and so forth,"[8] which are all that is left of *l'homme qui a voulu,*[9] the man, who in his youth had dreamt of becoming a literary man—and didn't . . . The pathos of an utterly lonely woman, the governess Sharlotta Ivanovna in *The Cherry Orchard*, is accentuated by her bizarre talent to amuse the company with card tricks; equally bizarre is the way she makes her appearance in the first act with a little dog on a line and introduces herself with the words: "My dog eats nuts too."[1]

All this shows that in Chekhov's plays the element of the bizarre both helps to build up a character and aids in preparing the surprise moment in the development of the action. Once they are firmly established as "queer characters," their quasi irrelevant observations cause a break in the dialogue. And here we touch upon one of the principal aspects of the bizarre, lying in the fact that, while all these observations and odd demeanours should normally bring about a certain bewilderment or at least some response in the others, this is not the case: more often than not there is no reaction at all, as if the others did not exist, as if the words were spoken in a void, as if all those persons were living in a vacuum, in other words: the

5. *The Plays of Anton Tchekov*, p. 72.
6. Ibid., p. 147.
7. Ibid., p. 3.
8 Ibid., p. 46.

9. The man who has willed [*Editor's note*].
1. *The Plays of Anton Tchekov*, p. 64.

bizarre is accepted, or rather tolerated, but not reacted upon. When in *The Cherry Orchard* the servantgirl Dunyasha, anxious to pour out her heart to her young mistress, says to Anya: "Yepikhodov, the clerk, made me a proposal just after Easter,"[2] the answer is: "I've lost all my hairpins." When in the second act of this play Sharlotta Ivanovna all of a sudden starts to complain about her fate and says: "Always alone, alone, nobody belonging to me . . . and who I am, and why I'm on earth, I don't know,"[3] there is no response from the others. When in the third act of *Three Sisters* Chebutykin has broken the clock and Irina says: "That was mother's clock", the old doctor declares in drunkenness: "Perhaps . . . Well, if it was hers, it was . . ."—and then continues: "What are you staring at? Natasha has got a little affair on with Protopopov, and you don't see it . . . You sit here and see nothing, while Natasha has a little affair on with Protopopov . . ."[4] The only reaction to this grave accusation comes from Vershinin, who says: "Yes" and then immediately resumes his conversation about his own affairs. Time and again we hear in Chekhov's stories and plays the desperate complaint: "To whom shall I tell my grief?"—which is used as motto in the story "Misery" (1886)—but there is no response and by this frequently used technique Chekhov succeeds in producing that oppressive atmosphere of human loneliness which is so typical for his art; the inability of people to understand each other, their complete lack of interest and attention is the core of all tragedy. Human coldness, indifference and careless cruelty—these form the main subject and the leading theme of many of Chekhov's stories and plays.

Finally, in some of the plays, especially in *Three Sisters*, Chekhov succeeds in attaining a bizarre effect by frequently putting quotations from other writers in the mouth of his characters. In many cases these quotations have a definite function in the play, both to reveal a character and to create a certain "mood," to evoke an atmosphere. Two of the best known of these functional quotations in *Three Sisters* are: "A green oak grows by a curving shore, and round that oak hangs a golden chain . . ."[5] which are the opening-lines of Pushkin's poem "Ruslan and Ljudmila", and: "He had no time to say 'Oh, oh!', before that bear had struck him low . . . ,"[6] two lines from Krylov's fable "The Peasant and the Farmhand," the first quotation being used by Masha, the second one by Solyony, and not just once, but several times on appropriate occasions, thus becoming something like motives, played by solo-instruments in a symphonic work. Apart from literary quotations Chekhov uses

2. Ibid.
3. Ibid., p. 80.
4. Ibid., p. 161.

5. Chekhov, *Three Plays*, p. 98.
6. Ibid., p. 99.

quotations, taken from actual life. An example of a quotation from life can be found in a letter by Olga Knipper to Anton Pavlovich, written in 1900, in reply to a complaint of the author that he was becoming bald. In this letter Olga Knipper writes: "I shall give you a fine recipe for falling hair. Take half a bottle of methylated spirit and dissolve in it two ounces of naphtalene, then rub the skin with this lotion . . ." Olga Knipper took her recipe so seriously that she hastened to write to Chekhov a few days later that she had made a mistake in it: it should not be two ounces of naphtalene, but only half an ounce. But Chekhov had already used the original passage in *Three Sisters*, first act, where he lets the *"fool"* Chebutykin read the recipe from his newspaper.[7] The motive for the well–known Tra-ta-ta conversation,—possibly the most mysterious and original "love-talk" in literature,—between Masha and Vershinin at the end of the third act of *Three Sisters* is likewise taken from real life and based on an actual experience Chekhov had in a restaurant. These examples,—and the notes in Chekhov's notebooks could easily provide further ample material,—show how keen an eye Chekhov had for the bizarre, how much value he attached to such phenomena and how anxious he was to apply this material in his art. I wonder, whether it is only a matter of coincidence that Chekhov's biographers managed to dig up such a remarkable variety of bizarre incidents in the life of the author. If we may believe one of his biographers, N. Teleshov, the bizarre did not even leave Chekhov on his deathbed: in the evening of July 15, 1904, in Badenweiler the doctor had ordered the sick man to drink a glass of champagne. Anton Pavlovich took the glass, remarked to his wife: "I have not tasted champagne in a long time," drank the glass to the bottom, lay down on his left side and died. "The oppressive silence of the night," Teleshov tells us, "was only disturbed by a large nightmoth that had flown in through the open window . . . After the doctor had gone, in the complete silence and stuffiness of the summernight, suddenly, with a terrific blow, the cork shot out of the half finished champagne bottle . . ."[8]

NICHOLAS MORAVČEVICH

Chekhov and Naturalism: From Affinity to Divergence

Once in the spring of 1901, while taking a carriage drive with Ivan Bunin along the Crimean shore in Yalta, Chekhov unexpectedly announced:

7. Ibid., p. 96. Cf. *Teatr, ežemesjačnyj žurnal dramaturgij i teatra* (Moscow, 1960), I: A. Vladimirskaya, *Zametki na poljax.*

8. N. Teleshov, *Zapiski pisatelja* (Moscow, 1950), pp. 86–87.

"Do you know how many more years they will read me? Seven."

"Why seven?" Bunin asked.

"Well, seven and a half."

"No," Bunin replied. "Poetry lives long, and the longer it lives the more powerful it becomes."

"My dear Sir," Chekhov chuckled, "You regard as poets only those who use such words as 'silvered distance,' 'accord,' or 'To battle, to battle in the struggle with darkness!' " . . . And then turning serious again, he continued: "Even though they may read me only seven more years, I have less than that to live: six."[1]

Chekhov was doubly wrong: he vastly underestimated both the peril of his illness and the extent of his future fame. Slightly over three years after this conversation he died, and almost seventy years since, his popularity and artistic stature still more than justify Bunin's prophecy.

As Chekhov's literary reputation in the West continued to grow over the past seven decades, the diversity of viewpoints in the realm of Chekhovian criticism engendered a wide range of unrelated, contradictory, and even mutually exclusive interpretations of the essence of the Chekhovian style. In one of the earlier studies, for example, W. H. Bruford defined the Chekhovian method as "psychological naturalism."[2] Francis Fergusson, however, came to a different conclusion; analyzing *The Cherry Orchard* he said that "Chekhov's poetry . . . is behind the naturalist surfaces; but the form of the play as a whole is 'nothing but' poetry in the widest sense. . . ."[3] Kenneth Tynan, in turn, challenged both of these views by maintaining that

the perfection of art in the theatre depends neither on naturalism nor on poetry. Drama has in its time borrowed tricks from both, but what it has built is a new and separate structure, whose foundation stones—the last acts of *The Master Builder* and *The Three Sisters*—are architectural triumphs of prose over naturalism.[4]

Maurice Valency diverged even further. He saw *The Three Sisters* as "Chekhov's masterpiece, the flower of impressionism in the drama."[5] Even earlier a synthesis of sorts that lumped together

1. Ernest J. Simmons, *Chekhov: A Biography* (Boston: Little, Brown, 1962), p. 525. Subsequent references to this book will be placed within parentheses in the text.
2. W. H. Bruford, *Anton Chekhov* (New Haven: Yale University Press, 1957), pp. 43, 45.
3. Francis Fergusson, *The Idea of a Theater* (Garden City, N.Y.: Doubleday, 1949), p. 178.
4. Kenneth Tynan, *Curtains* (New York: Atheneum, 1961), p. 70.
5. Maurice Valency, *The Breaking String* (New York: Oxford University Press, 1966), p. 219. Hereafter, references to Valency's book will be incorporated in the text within parentheses.

symbolism, realism and naturalism was attempted by John Gassner;
yet his statement that "if Maeterlinck's[6] plays are mood pieces, so
are the plays of Chekhov, who is considered a supreme realist or
naturalist,"[7] was also readily disputed by N. Efros who categori-
cally proclaimed that "Chekhov is an artistic realist; no other definition can be applied to him."[8] Finally, the stubborn complexity of
the *Ars Chekhoviana* prompted F. L. Lucas to conclude that "like
so many of the best writers since Homer, he merges in one the truth
of the realist, the self-control of the classic, and the imaginativeness
of the romantic,"[9] which only added to the already bulging Gordian
knot of "isms" attributed to the Chekhovian style.

In quest of the sword to cut it, let us return to the beginning.
Chekhov's early writings and personal pronouncements indicate that
in his formative years he often showed a distinct affinity for an
essentially naturalist world-view. In an article published in 1916 in
the St. Petersburg monthly *Vestnik Yevropi* (which in the 1880's
had first published Zola's naturalist manifestoes), Leonid Grossman
stated that the background influence on this dimension of Chekhov's style were his medical training and practice, his acquaintance
with Darwinian theory and Claude Bernard's principles of scientific
inquiry, his familiarity with Zola's efforts to follow these principles
in fiction, and his knowledge and appreciation of the writing tech-
niques of Flaubert and Maupassant.[1]

Not all of these points are easily verifiable. On the influence of
Chekhov's medical training, for example, there are two conflicting
accounts. In October of 1899, Chekhov wrote to his school friend,
Dr. Rossolimo:

> My work in the medical sciences has undoubtedly had a serious
> influence on my literary development; it significantly extended
> the area of my observations, enriched my knowledge, and only
> one who is himself a physician could understand the true value of
> all this for me as a writer. This training has also been a guide;
> and probably because of my closeness to medicine, I have man-
> aged to avoid many mistakes. Familiarity with the natural sci-
> ences and scientific method has always kept me on my guard, and
> I have tried, whenever possible, to take scientific data into con-

6. Maurice Maeterlinck (1862–1949), Bel-
gian playwright, poet, and essayist. See
Introduction, p. xxv, above [*Editor's
note*].
7. John Gassner, *Directions in Modern
Theatre and Drama* (New York: Holt,
Rinehart and Winston, 1966), p. 48.
8. N. Efros, "Chekhov and the Moscow
Art Theatre," in *Literary and Theatrical
Reminiscences*, ed. S. S. Koteliansky
(New York: George H. Doaran, n.d.),

p. 118.
9. F. L. Lucas, *The Drama of Chekhov,
Synge, Yeats, and Pirandello* (London:
Cassell, 1963), p. 123.
1. Leonid Grossman, "Naturalism Chekhova [The naturalism of Chekhov],"
Vestnik Europi [Herald of Europe], No.
7 (July 1914), pp. 218–47. [All translation in this essay, unless otherwise
noted, is by Nicholas Moravčevich—
Editor's note.]

sideration, and where that was impossible, I've preferred not to write at all.[2]

Yet Leontiev-Shcheglov stated in his reminiscences that in a conversation with him Chekhov once hinted that his scientific training frequently stifled his literary impulse, saying:

Now, for example, a simple person looks at the moon and is moved as before something terribly mysterious and unattainable, but an astronomer looks at it with entirely different eyes . . . With him there cannot be any fine illusions! With me, a physician, there are, also, few illusions. Of course, I am sorry for this . . . it somehow desiccates life. (Simmons, p. 480)

Nevertheless, Chekhov often invoked his medical knowledge in his judgments of literary plausibility. Though the writer in him was completely captivated by the artistry and scope of Tolstoy's *War and Peace*, the doctor did not fail to spot some factual improbabilities in the description of the wounded Prince Bolkonsky:

It is strange to read that the wound of the Prince—who was a wealthy man, served both day and night by a doctor, attended by Natasha and Sonya—gave out a cadaverous odor. . . .
If I was around Prince Andrey, I would have cured him.[3]

Study of medicine provided a solid basis for Chekhov's lifelong esteem of Darwin. With unusual severity he once mentioned in a letter to his brother that their friend Zembulatov deserved a dunce cap for his ignorance of Darwinism (Chekhov, XI, 19), and five years later he indignantly condemned the anti-Darwinian scribblings of a certain L. K. Popov on the staff of Suvorin's reactionary paper *New Times* (Chekhov, XI, 153).

Claude Bernard's name does not appear in Chekhov's papers, but the young author's perpetual concern for the scientific justification of his artistic insights shows to what extent he was influenced by the famous French physiologist. Writing to A. N. Pleshcheev about his story "An Attack of Nerves," Chekhov confidently declared: "As a doctor, I feel that I have described spiritual pain correctly, in agreement with all the rules of psychiatric science" (Chekhov, XI, 303).

Zola's demands for a complete surrender of intuition to scientifically collected data were at times too extreme for Chekhov, but in general he at that time had no quarrel with an artistic method based on faithful reproduction of materialistic phenomena. When in 1887 M. V. Kiseleva charged that Chekhov in writing dwelled too much

2. A. P. Chekhov, *Sobranie sočinenij v dvenadcati tomax* [Collected works in twelve volumes], (Moscow, 1957), XII, 356. Later references to these volumes will be found within parentheses in the text, with volume and page given.
3. Grossman, "Naturalism Chekhova," p. 222.

on the "dung hills" of life, without seeking the hidden "pearls" in them, he replied in a long letter that for him literature becomes art only insofar as it portrays life as it really is, adding:

> To a chemist nothing on earth is unclean. A writer must be as objective as a chemist, he must lay aside his personal subjective standpoint and must understand that dunghills play a very respectable part in a landscape, and that evil passions are as inherent in life as good ones. (Chekhov, XI, 113)

This was the closest that Chekhov ever came to Zola's views on the aim of artistic creativity. Yet, Chekhov's stress on objectivity did not stem from a blind acceptance of scientific determinism in literature. It was his meticulous concern for truth in depicting material reality, rather than a repudiation of artistic intuition that prompted him to compare a chemist and a writer. He felt at that time that literature must of necessity reflect the temporal reality of man, since that is his only window to the awareness of being. When, for instance, he encountered Paul Bourget's *The Disciple*, he wrote to Suvorin that he simply could not understand such a belated and deliberate crusade against materialism since

> in the first place, the materialistic movement is not a school or tendency in the narrow journalistic sense; it is not something passing or accidental; it is necessary, inevitable and beyond the power of man. . . . Outside matter there is neither knowledge nor experience, and consequently there is not truth. (Chekhov, XI, 357)

This, however, did not stop Chekhov from making occasional satiric comments on the deterministic excesses of various propagators of Zola's naturalist theories. Thus, with young Merezhkovsky[4] in mind, he once wrote to Suvorin:

> Those who have assimilated the wisdom of the scientific method and learned to think scientifically experience many alluring temptations. Archimedes wanted to turn the earth round, and the present day hotheads want through science to conceive the inconceivable, to discover the physical laws of creative art, to detect the laws and the formulae which are instinctively felt by the artist and are followed by him in creating music, novels, pictures, etc. . . . There probably is such a thing as the physiology of creative art, but we must nip in the bud our dreams of discovering it. . . . It is always a good thing to think scientifically, but the trouble is that scienific thinking about creative art will be bound to degenerate in the end into searching for the 'cells' or the 'centers' which control the creative faculty. (Chekhov, XI, 294)

4. Dmitry   Sergeevich   Merezhkovsky   with Symbolism [*Editor's note*].
(1865–1941), a Russian writer associated

During Chekhov's literary maturity, Zola's name appears in his correspondence mainly in connection with the Dreyfus affair, except in one letter to Suvorin, where Chekhov mentions that *Thérèse Raquin* is not a bad play.[5] His final statement on Zola, and one that well sums up his overall attitude toward the French author, followed the news of Zola's death in September of 1902. Writing to his wife, Chekhov said that though personally he wasn't particularly devoted to Zola as a writer, the turmoil of the Dreyfus affair[6] greatly enhanced his esteem of Zola as a man (Chekhov, XII, 500).

Flaubert's name appears in Chekhov's correspondence only once. In a letter to Suvorin Chekhov casually notes that Prince Urusov is a great admirer of the French master (Chekhov, XI, 535). Few other scattered references to the titles of Flaubert's books indicate that Chekhov was familiar with his work, but this is scarcely enough evidence to substantiate Grossman's assertion that the traces of *bovarism*[7] in the behavior of Anna Petrovna in "Anna on the Neck" or Natalia Prozorova in *The Three Sisters* are the result of Flaubert's direct influence.

Chekhov's references to Maupassant are more numerous and more informative. Early in 1891 he enthusiastically welcomed the appearance of Tolstoy's rendition of Maupassant's story "Françoise" in Suvorin's *New Times* (Chekhov, XI, 497). Five years later, Suvorin noted in his diary that Chekhov expressed a desire to attempt a new translation of Maupassant's tales, since he greatly esteemed his work (Simmons, p. 397). Shortly before, Chekhov himself had informed P. F. Yordanov (in connection with a gift of

5. E. D. Surkov, *Chekhov i teatr* [Chekhov and theatre], (Moscow, 1961), p. 82. Subsequent references to this work will be placed in the text within parentheses. [*Thérèse Raquin* by Émile Zola (1840–1902) was originally written as a novel (1867) and was consciously converted into a play (1873) by Zola as an example of naturalism—[*Editor's note*].

6. Captain Alfred Dreyfus, a republican and a Jew, was the victim of a clerico-royalist cabal in the French army. Accused of selling military secrets to Germany, Dreyfus was brought to trial in 1894, convicted, and sent to prison on Devil's Island. A re-trial was actuated in 1899 by public opinion, fostered by Émile Zola and Anatole France (pseudonym of Jacques Anatole François Thibault, 1844–1924). Dreyfus's life sentence was reduced to ten years, he was pardoned by President Loubet, and in 1906 he was restored to his due rank in the French army [*Editor's note*].

7. Gustave Flaubert (1821–80), French novelist, published his masterpiece, *Madame Bovary*, in 1857. In the novel, Emma Rouault, the beautiful and sensitive but restless daughter of a farmer, marries Charles Bovary, a physician. Raised in a convent and nurtured on the illusions depicted in romantic novels, Emma Bovary becomes disillusioned and embittered with her dull, weary life and eventually has two love affairs: the first is with Rodolphe Boulanger (identified by Vladimir Nabokov as a literary character personifying *poshlost'*); the second, with Léon Dupuis, a lawyer. Eventually Emma Bovary, who has spent her husband's money with abandon, is charged with debt and commits suicide. Her husband dies shortly thereafter, leaving their only daughter a legacy of only twelve francs. What Leonid Grossman apparently interprets as *bovarism* are two warring characteristics in the heroine: the first is the refined aesthetic taste for elegance; the second consists of the desires for sensual pleasures that diminish spiritual concerns [*Editor's note*].

books to the Taganrog library) that he was sending him, among other things, a 12-volume edition of Maupassant's stories, promising further translations and even a collection in French, which, he felt, any good library should have (Chekhov, XII, 121). Furthermore, two clear references to the French author appear in the text of *The Sea Gull*. In the first act Treplyov compares his revolt against the kind of art perpetrated by his mother and Trigorin to Maupassant's alleged revulsion and flight from the vulgarity of the Eiffel tower; and in the second act, Arkadina, while reading Maupassant's *Sur l'eau*, discovers a passage that resembles her and Trigorin's situation.

Chekhov's initial affinity for the naturalist mode of expression is even more apparent in his early works. Examining the structure of *Ivanov* (described by Chekhov as a play in which his "entire energy is concentrated on a few really powerful and striking scenes" [Chekhov, XI, 159]), Maurice Valency readily establishes a connection between a Chekhovian plotting technique and André Antoine's *quart d'heure*[8] dramatic capsule; also rooted in "the idea that a play was written for the sake of a few climactic scenes" (Valency, p. 84). Similarly, David Magarshack points out that Chekhov's early dramatic sketch *On the Highway* (1885), is a purely naturalistic *étude*.[9] Its action takes place in the interior of an old highway inn, dimly lit and tightly packed with peasants, pilgrims, alcoholics, laborers, and tramps, all driven indoors by a raging storm. Practically every ingredient of a naturalist milieu is present: the bleakness of the decor is aptly complemented by the depressiveness of the *Stimmung*,[1] the lower class characters are caught in their response to a raw, violent conflict, their authenticity is enhanced through meticulous attention to physical details and commonplace dialogue, and the threads of the action are deliberately left untied, so that the entire composition suggests a slice of life. Actually, the playlet is more than a match for Gorky's subsequent drama *The Lower Depths*[2] for it contains all its down-and-out flavor without its quasi-philosophical rhetoric and essentially romantic "cult of man." The Imperial censor, naturally, banned *On the Highway* as both gloomy and sordid,[3] which from the naturalist viewpoint was actually a compliment.

Traces of a naturalist technique can be occasionally spotted in some of Chekhov's "vaudevilles." The hard, cutting undertone in

8. Literally, "quarter of an hour." André Antoine (1858–1943), French actor, stage director, and theatre manager whose important contributions in the late nineteenth century led to reforms in the European theatre [*Editor's note*].

9. David Magarshack, *Chekhov, the Dramatist* (New York: Hill & Wang,

1960), p. 34. Later references to Magarshack's book will be noted in the text within parentheses.

1. Literally, "mood; state or frame of mind" [*Editor's note*].

2. 1902 [*Editor's note*].

3. A. M. Egolin and N. S. Tikhonov, eds., *Complete Works*, XI, 629.

the satire of *The Wedding*, for example, the play's surgically precise and economical characterization, its colloquial speech, fragmented dialogue, and the peculiar *Stimmung* of the sickeningly petty bourgeois milieu, all seem to take their edge from a clinical determinism in presenting human folly caught by an unblinking camera eye.

Still, the presence of naturalist elements in Chekhov's early works does not necessarily place him within the inner circle of the European naturalist camp. Eric Bentley has convincingly argued in *The Playwright as Thinker* that "Zolaist naturalism may be very important in the works of the writers who are on the whole not naturalistic."[4] The touchstone of Chekhov's artistic strength in his early years is the authenticity and force of his realism. The naturalist element in his early work was a controlled embellishment rather than the well-spring of his creativity. Chekhov remained throughout his life favorably inclined toward a materialistic view of reality, but he never absorbed a significant measure of that ideological dogmatism which characterized some of his naturalist contemporaries. Though it often appeared that he "looked upon social phenomena very much as the natural scientist rather than as the artist-sociologist" (Simmons, p. 169), he was still capable of appreciating the spontaneity of artistic intuition. In fact, he gradually became convinced that there is a basic unity between artistic and scientific forms of expression. This he expressed very clearly in a letter to Suvorin in which he pointed out that "in Goethe the naturalist lived in harmony along with the poet" (Chekhov, XI, 366).

Perhaps the most striking naturalist element in Chekhov's youthful aesthetic creed was his commitment to strict objectivity, which condemned concern with a "message," and denied any usefulness of a didactic stance in the presentation of reality. With Chekhov's subsequent mellowing (already apparent in his refusal to see the conflict between scientism and intuitive insight), this principle became less and less tenable, and in the second half of the 1880's the spirit of change began to permeate both his personal views and his works. It was a gradual yet steady process; more than five years separate his earliest doubt (1887) of the usefulness of objectivity in art and the first clear indication of his aesthetic transformation.

In a letter to Suvorin of November 25, 1892, Chekhov finally stated that the power of the great writers lay not in the strength of their objectivity but in the ultimate persuasiveness of their aim. He perceived that in their imaginative journeys

> they call upon us to go with them, and we feel not only with our reason but with the whole of our being that they have some aim. . . . The best of them are realists and depict life as it is, but

---

4. Eric Bentley, *The Playwright as Thinker* (New York: World, 1955), p. 8.

because every line they write is permeated, as with a juice, by a consciousness of an aim, you feel in addition to life as it is, also life as it should be, and it is that that delights you. (Chekhov, XI, 601)

This realization was a turning point in Chekhov's literary life; spiritually, it marked the end of his formative period and the beginning of his transcendence of the aesthetic dictates of naturalism. In practice, however, Chekhov's subordination of objectivity to artistic aims was not so abrupt. Several years of gradual adjustment both *precede* and *follow* the above statement (a fact that Magarshack, for example, overlooks [Magarshack, pp. 41–2]). His treatise *The Island of Sakhalin*, published in 1893, aptly illustrates this. Though originally conceived as a factual study of the living conditions in the Far Eastern penal colony visited by Chekhov in 1890, the monograph, in its final form, shows little resemblance to similar sociological inquiries. As E. J. Simmons points out,

> The high art of selectivity in the mass of material Chekhov was dealing with is everywhere in evidence; the facts, scenes and incidents are those calculated to impress and to move the readers. It is even possible to catch him at turning a dull but necessary passage from one of his learned sources into a thing of beauty. Any sensitive reader must conclude that though the book is essentially a scientific study, it could have been written only by a literary artist. (Simmons, p. 305)

The completion of *The Sea Gull* in the spring of 1896 marks the conclusion of both Chekhov's aesthetic shift and his stylistic uncertainty in dramatic expression. In his formative years Chekhov approached drama hesitantly; his main preoccupation was with the short story. Starting with *The Sea Gull*, his growing interest in theatre rapidly overshadowed his concern with fiction. All his significant stylistic innovations during the last eight years of his life were in playwriting, and most of them were trendsetters for the subsequent development of modern drama.

What are their most significant characteristics? The structural framework of Chekhov's great plays indicates a sharp departure from the traditional dramatic progression based upon direct plotting. Instead of encumbering his plays with an elaborate sequence of events and external intrigue, Chekhov usually concentrates on the effect of a single *theme* upon the thoughts and emotions of a group of finely drawn and subtly counterpointed characters. This theme or governing idea is usually introduced early in the action and kept alive by a particular symbolizing device (such as the sea gull, the Moscow motif, the cherry orchard, etc.) which, knit into the general stream of apparently aimless, commonplace conversation, manage through association to imbue even the most trivial bit of dialogue with significance beyond its nominal meaning. Instead of spurring the action, as dictated by the conventional rules of dramatic economy, Chekhovian dialogue usually meanders between the revelation of character and the conjuring of mood. The conventional protagonist is, in this kind of structure, obsolete. He is replaced by an ensemble, and his protracted struggle of will against an opposing force is supplanted by the epiphany of a collective pathos before an oppressive inevitability. Most of the overt, physical manifestations of conflict are relegated to the background; the psychological tension is frequently accentuated through verbal understatement and the interplay of non-verbal communication elements (such as pauses, gestures, off-stage sounds, silences, music). The dénouements are inconclusive and even seem to suggest a new beginning— the characters frequently not only survive the catastrophe, but are actually relieved that it came. Amid a hum and bustle of perennial family gatherings, of arrivals, celebrations, and departures, many of them remain perpetually preoccupied with the inner self; though involved in a dialogue, they continue to pursue their internal soliloquies, pausing from time to time not to listen but to gather more recollections from a memory directed solely inward.

To some critics this technique seemed Ibsenist. One of the earliest adherents of this view was Tolstoy. Despite his great fondness for Chekhov as a short story writer, Tolstoy (an arch-conservative in matters of dramatic structure and intent) bluntly dismissed *The Sea Gull* as "worthless nonsense, written as Ibsen writes. Words are piled on each other, and one does not know why."[5] Much later Martin Lamm also concluded, though without condemnation, that there is little point in denying the influence of Ibsen in the Chekhovian drama.[6] John Gassner and Maurice Valency have seen such influence in Chekhov's attitude toward symbolism,[7] and his use of "a comic style for the development of tragic theme" (Valency, p. 144), while Francis Fergusson noted that both Chekhov and Ibsen accept the literal and transcend it.[8]

Thus one would expect to find Chekhov praising Ibsen.[9] Yet, except for a single note addressed to the actor Vishnevsky,[1] all of

5. Martin Lamm, *Modern Drama* (Oxford: Basil Blackwell, 1952), p. 202.
6. Ibid., p. 201.
7. John Gassner, *Masters of the Drama* (New York: Dover, 1940), p. 513.
8. Fergusson, p. 161.
9. Henrik Ibsen (1828–1906), Norwegian dramatist [*Editor's note*].
1. The note said: "Since I am coming to Moscow soon, please set aside one seat for me for 'Pillars of Society' [1877]. I want to have a look at this amazing Norwegian play and will even pay for the privilege. Ibsen is my favorite author, you know." This statement was often misinterpreted in the past because it was usually taken literally. However, it is probably a joke, for all of Chekhov's other letters to Vishnevsky are in a vein of a bantering, light-hearted repartee. (The quotation is taken from *Selected Letters of Anton Chekhov*, ed. Lillian Hellman [New York: Farrar, Straus, 1955], pp. 318–19.)

Chekhov's statements about Ibsen are bluntly negative. Stanislavsky noted that Chekhov was plainly bored with the Moscow Art Theatre's production of *The Wild Duck*[2] and openly expressed his dislike by repeating several times: "Listen, Ibsen does not know life. It is not so in life" (Surkov, p. 280). His impression of *Hedda Gabler*[3] was no better, for after seeing it, he said: "See here, Ibsen is really not a dramatist at all!" (Surkov, p. 111). Describing Chekhov's reaction to *When We Dead Awaken*, Olga Knipper[4] also noted that he regarded Ibsen with mistrust since he found him too complex and given to philosophizing (Surkov, p. 330), and only four months before his death Chekhov himself wrote her that he had seen Ibsen's *Ghosts*, which he thought was a "wretched play" (Surkov, p. 163).

On the other hand, Chekhov's references to Hauptmann and Maeterlinck[5] are quite favorable. In the summer of 1899 Chekhov wrote to Suvorin that he had read Hauptmann's *Lonely Lives*, which amazed him with its novelty (Chekhov, XI, 337). A year later, while confirming the news of the Moscow Art Theatre's projected tour of the Crimea, he announced:

> They will give among other things Hauptmann's *Lonely Lives*, a magnificent play in my opinion. I read it with great pleasure, although I am not fond of plays. . . . (Chekhov, XII, 412)

After the performance, Chekhov confided to Stanislavsky that he preferred this work of Hauptmann to any of his own, adding, "he is a real dramatist. I am not one. Listen, I am a doctor" (Simmons, p. 504). A year later, in a letter to P. N. Kondakov, he repeated that Hauptmann is a great dramatist of whose work he is very fond (Surkov, p. 122).

Chekhov's references to Maeterlinck are equally enthusiastic. In the summer of 1897 (that is, prior to his earliest critique of Ibsen) Chekhov wrote to Suvorin:

> I am reading Maeterlinck. I have read his "Les Aveugles," "L'Intruse," and am reading "Aglavaine et Selysette." They are all strange, wonderful things, they make an immense impression, and if I had a theatre I would certainly stage "Les Aveugles." (Surkov, pp. 95–96)

2. 1884 [*Editor's note*].
3. 1890 [*Editor's note*].
4. *When We Dead Awaken* was written in 1899. Olga Leonardovna Knipper (1868–1959), one of the founding actresses of the Moscow Art Theatre, married Chekhov in 1901. She originated the following roles for productions of Chekhov's dramas at the Moscow Art Theatre: Arkandina in *The Sea Gull* (1898); Yelena Andreevna in *Uncle Vanya* (1899); Masha in *The Three Sisters* (1901); Ranevskaya in *The Cherry Orchard* (1904); and Sarra in *Ivanov* (1904) [*Editor's note*].
5. Gerhart Hauptmann (1862–1946), German playwright, whose *Lonely Lives* was written in 1891 [*Editor's note*].

The evidence of Chekhov's distaste for Ibsen's work and his acclaim of that of Hauptmann and Maeterlinck seriously undermines the critical notion of a significant Ibsenist influence upon the mature Chekhovian dramatic technique. Ibsen's keen sense for dramatic economy made him thrifty with words. Consequently, his dramatic structure occasionally displayed signs of virtuosity that displeased Chekhov, who preferred a looser, more leisurely approach to exposition. Ibsen improved the well-made-play form by constructing better plots, by improving characterization, by exposing significant issues in both the personal and social sphere, and by carefully defining the environment and mood, but he still remained largely a reformer *within* the confines of traditional dramatic expression. Chekhov, on the other hand, was a deliberate iconoclast whose lifelong quest for an existentially truthful art took him beyond the boundaries of the conventional dramatic structure. For all his personal gentleness, he was one of the most radical innovators of the modern drama, one of its subtlest and yet most far-reaching rebels. Robert Brustein is mistaken when he says that Chekhov only partially deserves such a name,[6] and David Magarshack even more so when he implies that the Chekhovian concept of indirect action reflects the influence of the classical dramatic structure (Magarshack, pp. 163–65).

Ibsen's structure is actually far closer to the classical pattern than is Chekhov's. Where Ibsen moves his characters through an intricate and cumulative plot constructed in a Sophoclean fashion, Chekhov lets his wander through a single dramatic situation which acts as a psychological catalyst. Ibsen's adherence to the linear dramatic progression and his frequent pat opposition of liberal and reactionary forces were in Chekhov's judgment unreal and over-manipulated. As Valency has remarked,

> To Chekhov, who could never quite manage a novel, Ibsen's method seemed novelistic; above all, it was too closely controlled for his taste. . . . Hauptmann, with his broader and more showy effects, and his wealth of detail, seemed to him much more to the purpose. (Valency, p. 145)

The composition of *Lonely Lives*, for example, pleased Chekhov because much of its surface detail possessed that fluidity and freedom of form which he himself was trying to perfect. With the struggle emerging through an inner state of tension for which no one is really responsible, with no major conflicts actually displayed, this play clearly suggests that human lives are frequently destroyed

---

6. Robert Brustein, *The Theatre of Revolt* (Boston: Little, Brown, 1962), p. 137.

by mere attrition, and Chekhov could not fail to respond with approval to a theme distinctly present in all his great plays.

Maeterlinck's work also pleased Chekhov because of its accent on internal life and the brooding sense of futility that envelops the visible action. In Maeterlinck's method of presenting a multitude of fleeting impressions and sensations which by means of complex contextual suggestion acquire exceptional depth, Chekhov saw an immense dramatic potential which he himself successfully utilized (though without Maeterlinck's symbolizing excesses and his near-absurd denial of external action and movement).

While Chekhov saw that the Ibsenist technique left little room for the presentation of the commonplace, random, accidental element in man's struggle against adversity, he also felt the need for greater verisimilitude between the reality of being and its artistic rendition than Hauptmann or Maeterlinck. He knew that everyday reality perpetually confronted man with both meaningful and inconsequential issues, he saw that frequently much of one's energy is spent in the very process of sifting, and he sensed that most often it is not a great ethical conflict that finally breaks a man, but the gradual encroachment of the commonplace, the accidental and the vulgar. In mastering means to present this truthfully Chekhov first experimented with the naturalist technique, until he eventually realized that determinism is a constricting force which prevents an author from penetrating into the shifting swells of the depicted phenomena and from experiencing the vast sensory lure of the reality's kaleidoscopical metamorphosis. His ultimate perception that the human scene observed through a coldly detached eye can easily become cluttered with documentary triteness, since such an approach concentrates more on the event at hand than on the participants' perception of it which gives it its meaning, finally opened the way for his shift from *naturalistic* veracity to *impressionist* selectivity. In principle Chekhov remained faithful to the concept of "life as it is," only now he no longer struggled to encompass the *entirety* of an experience or event in its representation. Instead, he selected and arranged its most characteristic elements in such a way that they fully evoked a sense of the whole.

Chekhov introduced his impressionist innovations gradually, and at first largely in his short stories. He was, for example, so pleased with the effects of this technique in his tale "The Wolf," published in March of 1886, that only a month later he advised his brother to follow his example:

> In descriptions of nature one ought to seize upon little particulars, grouping them in such a way that when you close your eyes after reading you see a picture. For example, you will get a moon-

lit night if you write that on the milldam, like a small bright star, glittered a bit of glass from a broken bottle, and there rolled by the round, black shadow of a dog or wolf, etc. (Chekhov, XI, 95)

Ten years later the same motif reappears at the end of *The Sea Gull*, where Treplyov, envious of Trigorin's style, bursts out:

> It's easy for him. . . . With him a broken bottleneck glitters on the dam and the mill wheel casts a black shadow—and there you have a moonlit night; but with me there's the shimmering light, the silent twinkling of the stars, the distant sounds of a piano dying away in the still, fragrant air. . . . It's agonizing.[7]

The pervasiveness of the visual detail in these descriptions of nature hints that Chekhov's innovative experiments in fiction could have been inspired by the impressionist manner of a professional landscape painter. And indeed Chekhov had such a friend with whom he not only exchanged ideas about art and literature but whose personal peccadilloes were occasionally absorbed into Chekhovian literary output as well.

The Sea Gull's plot contains several interesting episodes based on actual events from the life of the brilliant but eccentric artist Isaak Levitan,[8] one of the greatest Russian landscape painters of all time and a source of far deeper and steadier influence upon Chekhov's eventual shift toward impressionism than has generally been recognized.

As a Moscow Art School classmate and companion of Chekhov's older brother, Nikolai, Levitan met the young author while the latter was still a medical student and in his outlook on writing an enthusiastic supporter of literary objectivism and naturalist *vérité*. At the time this was very much in accord with Levitan's own preferences in the realm of painting, since under the influence of his master and mentor Savrasov,[9] he already manifested a distinct affinity for the forceful, uncompromisingly realistic and vibrantly natural manner of the French Barbizon[1] painters (Corot, Millet, Rousseau, Diaz, and Dupré), who were precursors of the Impressionists. As he became better acquainted with Chekhov and his work, Levitan readily perceived the extent of rapport between their respective attitudes toward creativity; and his spontaneous sense of kinship

7. A. P. Chekhov, *The Major Plays* (New York: Signet, 1964), p. 164.

8. Isaak Ilich Levitan (1860–1900) worked as a scene-painter and designer in 1885 at the Opera of S. I. Mamontov (1841–1918) in Moscow [*Editor's note*].

9. A. K. Savrasov (1830–1897), Russian painter associated with the artistic movement usually called the *peredvizhniki*

(travelers or wanderers); these painters were noted for their landscapes.

1. The name of a group of French landscape painters headed by Jean Corot (1796–1875); the name was apparently taken from the village of Barbizon, in the forest of Fontainebleau, where the group tended to congregate [*Editor's note*].

strongly enhanced his inclination to share with the young author his subsequent stylistic discoveries and insights.

That Chekhov greatly benefited from his close association with Levitan and his familiarity with Levitan's painting is apparent from a number of his works conceived after they met. In comparison with Chekhov's earlier writing, for example, the stories of his second and third collection (*The Motley Tales*, published in 1886, and *In the Twilights*, in 1887) clearly indicate that he has started to pay far greater attention to the spatial arrangement, visual details, and atmospheric coloring of the selected material. Levitan himself noted this with pleasure in a letter to Chekhov sent in the summer of 1888 from the Volga region where the painter went in search of a new inspiration:

> Dear Antosha . . . I once more read attentively your *Motley Tales* and *In the Twilights* and you astounded me as a landscapist. I am not talking about the multitude of very interesting thoughts, but about the landscapes in these tales—which are better than Savrasov's. The pictures of the steppe, the hillocks, sheep—they are all striking.[2]

The same stress on the paysage and the atmosphere later begins to appear in Chekhov's dramatic endeavor as well. At least a third of the action of *Ivanov*, written in the fall of 1887, takes place outdoors, and some of the play's most effective scenes (such as Ivanov's tiff with Doctor Lvov and Anna Petrovna in the first act, his hasty flight from home and her subsequent melancholy recount of their past) gain much of their dramatic power from the deft juxtaposition of the understated emotion and the accentuated ambiance. This is even more true of *The Wood Demon*, completed in 1889, in which the paysage and the atmosphere acquire such prominence that the author's numerous versions of the final act were seen by David Magarshack as an effort to transform the piece "from a melodrama into an idyll" (Magarshack, p. 143).

A few months before *The Wood Demon* was produced in Moscow (December 27, 1889), Levitan went on his first trip abroad visiting Germany, France and Italy. Paris, steeped in the excitement of that year's great World Exposition, was the focal point of his journey; its gaiety, cosmopolitanism, and art treasures completely overwhelmed him. Of all the city's artistic riches he was most profoundly affected by the 1889 Salon of French painting[3] which alongside works of the traditionally accepted neoclassical orienta-

2. V. Prytkov, *Chekhov i Levitan* (Moscow: Izd. Gos. Tretjakovskoj Galerei, 1948), p. 7.
3. At this showing, called the Paris Exhibition Universelle 1889, were examples of the new painting by Puvis de Cha-vannes (1824–98), Odilon Redon (1840–1916), and Paul Cézanne (1839–1906). The year 1889 is considered by art historians as a year of seminal events in the European modern art movement [*Editor's note*].

tion also displayed a number of those representative of the emerging modernist schools. Levitan's preferences were exclusively with the latter. The realists of the Barbizon School pleased him since their technique was similar to his own, but that very fact also lent their work a certain aura of *déjà-vu* things, from which he could learn but little. On the other hand, his encounter with the work of the Impressionists, and particularly that of Monet, proved to be an intense aesthetic revelation which undermined most of his previous stylistic concepts. Having perceived that the spontaneity of Monet's composition and the originality of his treatment of light and color contrasts was clearly a liberating alternative to the constricting narrowness of his previous realist concentration and the austere monotony of his color scheme, Levitan could not help being converted. The impact of the 1889 Salon upon him, according to his own later admission to a contemporary art critic, remained the greatest creative catalyst of his entire mature artistic development.[4]

Despite the concrete evidence of this significant stylistic change which was soon noticeable in Levitan's creative output, the vast majority of Russian critics and particularly those of the post-revolutionary Stalinist era preferred to ignore it. Only recently A. Yuferova ventured to mention that Levitan's Italian *études* painted after his departure from Paris were substantially different from those completed before his trip:

> Whereas until the 90's the grayish-brown gamut prevails in his paintings, and in rare works distinguished by the brightness of tone, the color is still very sharp, his new creations astonish one with their complexly fine and rich composition. Through the interplay of color blendings Levitan attains a particular spiritualization, a living tremulousness of the objects represented.[5]

Levitan's return from abroad provided Chekhov with a much needed opportunity to learn first hand about the basic principles of the impressionist technique in painting and see the results of their application on concrete artistic creations. Moreover, the spirited discussion of the artistic merits of the new method, in which Chekhov often participated while sitting in Levitan's studio and watching him work, helped the author realize to what extent the impressionist rendering of the visual phenomena was in accord with his own intuitive attempts to transcend the naturalist dictates in literary compositions. This gave him a firmer sense of direction in his hitherto casual stylistic experimentation and focused his creative efforts upon the concentrated quest for the verbal equivalents of that pic-

4. A. A. Rostislavov, *Levitan* (St. Petersburg: N. I. Butkovskaja, 1911), pp. 32–33.

5. A. A. Yuferova, *Isaak Ilich Levitan* (Leningrad: Xudožnik RSFSR, 1962), p. 16.

torial immediacy, vibrancy of light and color, and atmospheric completeness which so clearly distinguished Levitan's work of the early nineties.

Even the subject matter of Levitan's painting was readily absorbed by Chekhov in his exploration of the literary dimensions of the impressionist technique. The text of one of his best longer tales, "Three Years," for example, published in 1894 but composed earlier, contains a vivid description of Levitan's startling landscape "Quiet Cloister," produced and exhibited in 1891.

In one of the story's episodes, the protagonists of the piece, the wealthy Muscovites, Yulia Sergeievna and her husband Laptev, are shown attending an art exhibit. At first they are presented as members of a leisure class not especially sensitive to art, but simply involved in a routine social activity. But on this particular occasion, after a whole day of snobbish posturing, Yulia unexpectedly comes upon a small landscape which for the first time in her uneventful and unhappy life elicits from her a spontaneous, intensely sensory response of admiration and visceral understanding. The force with which this simple, peaceful paysage unleashes the tides of her emotional memory both stuns and saddens her, for in comparison with the perfectly captured milieu of the painting the vacuity of her real life existence appears even more unbearable. As all her attempts to explain the reasons for her great agitation to Laptev and Kostya find no response she withdraws back into herself distressed and bitter that this moment of extraordinary perceptiveness remains stubbornly untranslatable into words.

> After that, the gilded cornices, the Venetian mirrors with the floral design and other pictures like the one that hung over the piano, as well as her husband's and Kostya's discussions about art filled her with disgust and resentment, and sometimes even with hatred.[6]

By the mid-90's Levitan's influence upon Chekhov diminished largely because he was spending more and more time at the estate of his new friend and patron, the Moscow millionaire Savva Morozov, and because Chekhov, after much experimentation and two trips to the West (in the Spring of 1891 and the Fall of 1894), had already developed an independent understanding of the impressionist manner and his own means of utilizing it in the process of literary creation.

That Chekhov worked "systematically, intentionally and masterfully"[7] on strengthening various characteristics of the impressionist structure (such as vagueness in the overall plot development, con-

6. A. P. Chekhov, *Three Years* (Moscow: FLPH, n.d.), p. 100.
7. R. L. Jackson, ed., *Chekhov: A Col-* *lection of Critical Essays* (Englewood Cliffs, N.J.: Prentice-Hall, 1967), p. 54.

trasting prominence of details and trivia, absence of the authorial tendentiousness, and the pervasiveness of a general mood capable of provoking direct and immediate sensory response) throughout the period in which the stories "The Steppe" (1888), "A Dreary Story" (1889), "Three Years" (1894), and "My Life" (1896) were written, was already noted by Dmitry Chizevsky and in a less explicit way by several earlier critics. Comparing the illusion of truth in Chekhov's stories to the impression produced by a look into a stereoscope, Tolstoy concluded:

> Chekhov has his own manner, like the impressionists. You see a man daubing on whatever paint happens to be near at hand, apparently without selection, and it seems as though these paints bear no relation to one another. But if you step back a certain distance and look again, you will get a complete overall impression. Before you there is a vivid, unchallengeable picture of nature.[8]

Similarly, Ernest Simmons recalled that Chekhov the story-teller, like the impressionist painters before him, represented reality

> by a particular arrangement of selected scenes, situations and emotions rather than by an exact, detailed linear drawing, so that the total realistic impression conveyed would have greater depth and meaning.[9]

For all their astuteness, however, statements like these tend to remain ineffectual and tentative, for they either appear as random afterthoughts in studies concerned with issues unrelated to the question of Chekhov's impressionist affinities, or they fail to approach this subject organically, by encompassing the totality of Chekhov's aesthetic metamorphosis. This critical indifference toward the chronology of Chekhov's artistic growth has resulted in a general disregard of the fact that Chekhov's successful use of the impressionist technique in the short stories of the first half of the 1890's was but a necessary prelude for the far more important stylistic endeavor of transferring this newly acquired mastery into the realm of drama. It was the impressionist structure of *The Sea Gull*, produced in 1896, that marked the beginning of that far-reaching Chekhovian stylistic iconoclasm which so profoundly affected the development of twentieth century drama and made him one of the most significant theatrical innovators of the modern age. After all, the presence of impressionist detail in Chekhov's later short stories was nothing especially new; traces of that technique have graced the fiction of Maupassant, Flaubert, Tolstoy and even Dostoevsky long before Chekhov appeared as a writer. But the successful employment of

8. E. J. Simmons, *Introduction to Russian Realism* (Bloomington: Indiana University Press, 1965), p. 184.
9. Ibid.

the impressionist technique in drama was both new and revolutionary, and that accomplishment remains the cornerstone of Chekhov's creative greatness.

Of the contemporary dramatic critics only Maurice Valency and J. Chiari gave this fact a glint of just consideration. Observing the content of Chekhov's plays the former remarked that the author

> as an impressionist . . . was chiefly concerned with the surface and . . . made no obvious inference as to what, if anything, lay beneath it. His plays represent behaviour in meticulous detail, the thing done, and the thing said; the rest is left to the spectator. . . . It was a result of Chekhov's impressionistic attitude that he forebore the usual analysis of motive; it was also a mark of his extraordinary probity as a writer. (Valency, p. 230)

Chiari, however, sees the Chekhovian technique in a different light. Asserting that the "pure phenomenalism" of the Chekhovian surface reality is ultimately "translucent and transmuted," he explains that Chekhov proceeds impressionistically

> not in order to produce a complete picture as in a novel, but in order to produce a congruence of movement. He uses details like notes in a musical composition and always in order to rise from reality to imagination.[1]

Yet even correct perceptions of the stylistic aims of an author, such as these are, can pass unnoticed when they are not supported by ample evidence from a close textual analysis of his work. And since Valency and Chiari, like the earlier critics, unfortunately omit to provide this, the crucial proof that the so-called "Chekhovian" dramatic structure is impressionist throughout and not only in isolated touches and embellishments still remains to be presented. To do so let us carefully examine the content of *The Cherry Orchard*.

The very first set of the play's stage directions already betrays the extent of the author's impressionist concern with the pictorial and mood values of the landscape and atmosphere. Though the action to follow takes place in the "nursery" of Ranevskaya's country home, practically nothing is said about the room's interior. Instead, one's attention is directed entirely toward the resplendent outdoors:

> It is early morning: the sun is just coming up. The windows of the room are shut, but through them the cherry trees can be seen in blossom. It is May, but in the orchard there is morning frost. (Chekhov, XI, 309)

1. J. Chiari, *Landmarks of Contemporary Drama* (London: Herbert Jenkins, 1965), p. 38.

The result is a vibrant verbal étude in which the external scene appears as an integral, active part of the play's total milieu and not merely as a static embellishment of the salon-oriented plot. The existence of this peculiarly impressionist atmospheric continuum between the immediate plot-serving locale and the play's total ambience is even more noticeable in Chekhov's arrangement of the outdoor settings. His stage directions for the second act, which in its entirety takes place outdoors, provide both the objects usable in a utilitarian way within the narrow circle of the physical action (. . . a wayside shrine, a well, an old bench, some large stones which look like old tombstones . . . [Chekhov, XI, 326]), and a panoramic view of a vast rural scene pictorially and atmospherically realized as well as some of Levitan's best landscapes.

> . . . A road leading to Gaev's estate. On one side and some distance away is a row of dark poplars, and it is there that the cherry orchard begins. Further away is seen a line of telegraph poles, and beyond them, on the horizon, the vague outlines of a large town, visible only in very good, clear weather. The sun is about to set. (Chekhov, XI, 326)

The continuous hum of the off-stage sounds and musical fragments that accompany *The Cherry Orchard's* dialogue also lends to its action a mark of distinctly impressionist breadth and immediacy. The sound of the breaking string, for example, heard as a foreboding of disaster in the midst of the second act and repeated as a dolorous coda of the exodus of the dispossessed gentry at the end of the play, clearly betrays the author's aim to extend his theatrical rostrum far beyond the boundaries of the actual, visible incident. This concern for the atmospheric, tentative and peripheral histrionic details greatly enhanced his stylistic endeavor to treat the dramatic reality as a conglomerate of fluid and ephemeral rather than static and concrete phenomena and thus capture those evanescent tonalities of a chosen mood or situation which through the gateway of sensory incitement directly affect the sensibility. The frequency with which various spiritual states, events, and even objects are presented in the play in terms of what they *appear* to be rather than what they *are* is a further indication of Chekhov's impressionist tendency to shift the focus of representation from the essence of a particular phenomenon to that of a participant's perception of it. Both Dmitri Chizhevsky and Karl Kramer have aptly noted that after the mid-nineties the formulations beginning with "it seemed to . . ." became more and more frequent in Chekhov's descriptions of the psychological states of his short-story characters, which proves his enormous interest in situations characterized by "a displacement of actuality by the character's distorted or totally unrecognizable perception of it."[2] What, however, has thus far been neglected is the fact that Chekhov accomplished far more significant and striking effects with this impressionist device in his dramatic compositions than in his fiction. There where it is in the very nature of fiction to reveal subjective concepts of a certain objective reality largely through descriptive passages resulting from an omniscient authorial intrusion into the inner thoughts and feelings of a large number of characters, in drama it is simultaneously possible to plastically enact, externalize, and critically juxtapose both the objective reality and a number of its subjective renditions through the logical progression of action dependent upon the collective contribution to plot on the part of all of its participants.

This refractive interplay of the objective reality with a number of its delusionary counterparts forms the very core of *The Cherry Orchard's* action. At the very beginning of the play it is announced that the hopelessly indebted estate of Ranevskaya and Gaev is soon to be sold at an auction unless they find a way to save it. That is the objective reality of their situation. In three months time, between Ranevskaya's return from abroad with which the play opens, and the dreaded auction that takes place at the end of the third act, the proprietors simply fail to face up to that fact squarely and do something constructive. In the fourth act, after the inevitable has occurred, they accept it and leave. But while waiting for the crucial event they occupy themselves with a number of hopes, schemes and possibilities all impractical, delusionary, and futile, and from this ensemble-pathos the play derives most of its flavor and emotional significance. "I'm always dreaming and dreaming. If only we could marry you to some rich man" (Chekhov, XI, 314), says Varya to Anya as soon as the latter has returned home in the beginning of the play. The same wishful thought is soon repeated by Gaev, together with two additional possibilities: "It would be a good thing if somebody left us some money, or if one of us went to Yaroslavl and tried our luck with the old aunt, the Countess" (Chekhov, XI, 323). Later he further augments his repertory of solutions by hinting that some of his friends from the district court told him "it looks as if it might be possible to get a loan on promissory notes, in order to pay the interest to the bank" (Chekhov, XI, 324), and when that, of course, does not materialize, by announcing: "I was promised an introduction to some general who might lend us some money on a promissory note" (Chekhov, XI, 332).

Varya's response to the problem is equally ludicrous. As the housekeeper, she pinches pennies and feeds the servants only milk soups and dried peas, while she is perfectly aware that the estate is so deeply in debt that even at best the family's means are totally inadequate to cover merely the yearly interest on the mortgage. Ranevskaya is, on the one hand, quite capable of seeing objectively the uselessness of either Gaev's childish schemes or Varya's stinginess, and of dismissing them, but on the other, she is utterly incapable of applying the same rationality to her own actions. While the whole family lives on the money borrowed from Lopakhin, she gives a golden coin to a drunken tramp, lends 240 roubles to Simeonov-Pishchik to pay interest on his mortgaged estate, and even invites a band to play at a party, all the while saying how terrible it is to squander money so irresponsibly. Meanwhile, the only sensible solution of leasing the estate for summer residences, which Lopakhin keeps suggesting endlessly, is simply not considered even as a remote possibility by either Ranevskaya or Gaev. Thus the consistency of their blindness toward the objective reality eventually results in the irrevocability of their dispossession, and then the protracted "suffering of change" that precedes the catastrophe is brought to an an end.

The plurality of Chekhov's quick sketches of his characters' delusory, inconclusive, arbitrary responses to the demands of reality, together with the episodical arrangement of these *vignettes* within the boundaries provided by the opening announcement of the oncoming auction and its actual occurrence, lends to his dramatic structure an aura of plotlessness and ambiguity. Either unable or unwilling to see themselves and their situation clearly, the characters of *The Cherry Orchard* tend to pass their time in pursuit of memories, conceits, and trivia. The consequent crowding of the plot with random, incomprehensible details and events readily produces an atmosphere of complete bewilderment with reality. Thus in the beginning of the play, for example, Gaev says to Ranevskaya: "There was a time, sister, when you and I used to sleep here in this very room, and now I'm fifty-one, strange as it may seem . . ." (Chekhov, XI, 315). In the second act Sharlotta Ivanovna muses: "I haven't got a real passport, I don't know how old I am, but it always seems to me that I'm quite young. . . . But where I come from and who I am—I don't know . . ." (Chekhov, XI, 326). Shortly after that Yepikhodov announces: "I'm a cultivated fellow, I read all sorts of extraordinary books, but I am in no way able to make out my own inclinations, what it is I really want, whether, strictly speaking, to live or to shoot myself" (Chekhov, XI, 327). Upon her return home from abroad Ranevskaya exclaims: "Is this really me sitting here? . . . What if I'm just dreaming!" (Chekhov, XI, 316). Finally, old Firs, muttering about the long-gone serfdom days, concludes that life before the emancipation was far easier to comprehend. "The peasants kept to the gentry, and the gentry kept to the peasants; but now everything's separate, and you can't understand anything" (Chekhov, XI, 332).

By producing characters unable to comprehend and synthetize their present experiences, Chekhov managed to free himself from the conventional literary obligation to be didactic. Contrary to the views of a majority of Soviet critics (A. Derman, A. Roskin, V. Yermilov, M. Yelizarova, etc.) who saw Chekhov's works as realistic tendentiously progressive indictments of the decadent pre-revolutionary Russian society, his mature plays contain no conventional *raisonneurs*, no central figures which consistently act as the author's alter ego, and no ethical or aesthetic formulas of universal pretensions. Instead, he freely mixes the significant with the trivial, the exalted with the accidental, tentative and ambiguous. To accept Trofimov's speeches in *The Cherry Orchard*, for example, as announcements of Chekhov's own beliefs about the future (as the Russian critics have done), is to grossly overlook much of the satire and skepticism which went into the author's moulding of that "mangy gentleman" (Chekhov, XI, 322).

The events in which Chekhov's characters participate also leave an impression that they are in no way arranged and slanted to champion a particular authorial tendency. They are not only often incomprehensible to those involved but also tend to follow

> a formal principle that is in every respect opposed to 'frontality,' one in which everything is aimed at giving the representation the character of something overheard by chance, intimated by chance, something that has occurred by chance.[3]

The beginning of the third act of *The Cherry Orchard* illustrates this very well. As the dreaded auction takes place in town, a reception is in progress at the estate, an impromptu ball for which Ranevskaya says: "The band came at the wrong time, and the party started at the wrong time . . . Well . . . never mind . . ." (Chekhov, XI, 339).

These, and many additional examples, clearly indicate that Chekhov's adoption of the impressionist method was not accidental but deliberate. Only the impressionist technique could have provided his drama with that structural quality in which the microcosm of apparently haphazard detail could successfully suggest the macrocosm of the larger reality of life without sacrificing altogether the force of the artistic aim. However, it should also be emphasized at the end that his impressionist approach to writing was not a total break with

---

3. Arnold Hauser, *The Social History of Art* (New York: Alfred A. Knopf, 1952), II, 910.

the past. The new technique did not call for a purist repudiation of his past realist and naturalist affinities, but for their sublimation in the service of a deeper artistic truth than that of mere *sachlichkeit*.[4] Both realist and naturalist details played a vital role in that impressionist "trigger-process release of enormous forces by some tiny movement"[5] through which Chekhov managed subtly to convert the documentary fact into the truth of poetic vision. Absorbed by, but not lost in, the new literary structure, they, with their lifelike authenticity and directness, proved indispensable in Chekhov's rise toward the summit of artistic form—its ultimate invisibility.

4. Real; essential; objective; impartial [*Editor's note*].

5. Eric Bentley, *In Search of Theater* (New York: Vintage, 1953), p. 343.

Chekhov: Language, Style, Performance

RONALD HINGLEY

[*Nastroenie* and Atmosphere in Chekhov's Plays]

* * *

The quality of Chekhov's plays, so charged with emotional significance in spite of their surface innocence, has stimulated Russian critics to look for a suitable name to describe his technique. His drama has been called 'lyrical'; it has been called 'internal', as opposed to the earlier, 'external' variety, and it has also been called the 'drama of the under-water current', since the operative dramatic stresses are so often submerged. The most common description is 'the drama of *nastroenie*', a concept [of which] 'mood' or 'atmosphere' are the best English equivalents.

An examination of the plays shows that Chekhov's methods of presenting *nastroenie* are similar to those employed in the stories. The same use is made of memories of the past, hopes for the future, and the state of mind associated with unsuccessful love. Chekhov often chose to present situations particularly calculated to throw such sensations into relief. Leave-takings were very suitable for the purpose—for example, those involved in the departure of the regiment at the end of *Three Sisters*. It had been stationed for some years in the provincial town where the action takes place, so that, when it came to leave, intimate associations had to be broken off, with little prospect of them ever being renewed. The emotions attendant on such an occasion blended harmoniously into the Chekhov mood. Similar emotionally-charged partings are to be found in *Uncle Vanya* and *The Cherry Orchard*. Madame Ranevskaya's arrival at the beginning of the latter play shows that the reverse process is equally capable of evoking atmosphere. She arrives back in her home early one morning after an absence of several years and cannot restrain her tears at the sight of the old nursery where she slept as a little girl. She ranges from laughter to tears as she revives her memories of such varied things as her brother's habit of interspersing his conversation with imaginary billiard strokes, and the wonderful sight of the orchard in bloom.

In the plays, as in the stories, Chekhov also makes use of the beauties of nature in building up atmosphere. For example, the audience is not long allowed to forget the lake which figures so prominently in *The Seagull* that it has even been suggested that Chekhov regarded it as one of the *dramatis personae*. The cherry orchard plays an even more important part in conditioning the mood of the play to which it gives its name. 'White, white all over,' Madame Ranevskaya addresses her orchard on her return. 'Oh, my orchard! After a dark, foul autumn and a cold winter you are young again and full of happiness; the angels of heaven have not forsaken you.' Again and again the characters refer to the orchard. In the minds of Ranevskaya and her brother it is bound up with countless childhood memories. The old servant Firs remembers how forty or fifty years ago they used to send cherries by the wagon-load to Moscow and Kharkov, after subjecting them to a special preserving process—now nobody can remember the recipe. To Trofimov the orchard typifies an absolete social structure, but serves as a reminder of the beautiful life which he believes is possible on earth. . . .

Whereas all these characters relate the orchard to the past in their various ways, the businessman Lopakhin is more concerned with its future. Nobody listens to him when he points out that the cherry trees must be cut down so that summer bungalows can be built. Finally the orchard has to be sold, and it makes its last contribution to the atmosphere of the play at the very end when the curtain goes down to the sound of axes as the work of felling begins.

As anyone who has seen the play will remember, this is a particularly brilliant use of sound in the theatre. The same play provides many other examples, including the dance music which serves as a background to the third act—an eloquent commentary on the household crisis with which it coincides. An examination of the stage directions in the plays provides innumerable more illustrations of Chekhov's feeling for sound. Stanislavsky says that Chekhov himself sometimes used to confer with the sound-effects man to make sure that the noises produced were in exact accord with what he had in mind. At the beginning of the third act of *Three Sisters* an alarm is sounded in warning of a fire, and, according to Stanislvasky, Chekhov went to a lot of trouble experimenting with various apparatus in the hope of reproducing the typical and unmistakable "soul-searing" note of a church bell in a Russian provincial town. One remarkable sound effect has caused some embarrassment to producers, and illustrates the production of *nastroenie* on a more surrealist level. This is the 'distant, dying and mournful sound of a breaking string', which is heard twice in *The Cherry Orchard*. The play does not make it entirely clear how this noise is supposed to have originated, but Chekhov certainly regarded it as important in evoking the right sort of mood in his audience. Stanislavsky was a more than eager co-operator in producing sound effects, and often seems to have overdone it in Chekhov's opinion. His introduction of bird calls and croaking frogs were not always appropriate to the season in which the scene was supposed to be taking place, and his fondness for choruses of chirping crickets was a standing joke. There was plenty of scope for his ingenuity in correctly reproducing the sounds which actually appeared in the stage directions. It should not be thought, however, that the plays were swamped with sound effects, for Chekhov retained his usual sense of balance in this matter. The point is not so much that he used such effects—they appear to a greater or lesser extent in any play—but that he used them with unusual subtlety. They were a particularly useful method of creating atmosphere, and one which is interesting because it was not available to Chekhov in the short stories.

* * *

VSEVOLOD MEYERHOLD

The Naturalistic Theatre and the Theatre of Mood

* * *

The Moscow Art Theatre has two visages: the Naturalistic Theatre and the Theatre of Mood. The naturalism of the Moscow Art Theatre is a naturalism borrowed from the Meiningen players.[1] *Accuracy in reproducing nature* is its basic principle. On the stage everything has to be as real as possible—the ceilings, the stucco cornices, the stones, the wallpaper, the little stove doors, the ventilation holes, and so on.

On stage cascades a real waterfall and real rain falls. A little chapel is constructed of real wood, and a house is faced with fine plywood, its double frames stuffed with cotton. The windows covered with frost. All corners of the stage are clearly visible. The fireplaces, tables, and shelves are filled with a great quantity of small objects visible only with binoculars, which will engage the attention of the curious spectator for the entire act. The noise of the round moon creeping along its wire disturbs the audience. Through

---

1. A court theatrical company organized and directed by Georg II, Duke of Saxe-Meiningen (1826–1914); his third wife, the actress Ellen Franz (1839–1923); and Ludwig Chronegk (1837–91), an actor who was appointed stage director. Their annual tours, which began in 1874 and ended in 1890, and which included almost every major city in Europe, brought praise for their conception of the unified production of plays and for scenic investiture which featured pictorial realism [*Editor's note*].

the window a real ship can be seen in a fiord. Not only rooms are built on stage, but even several stories with real staircases and oaken doors. The stage is cluttered and confusing. There are footlights and many borders. The canvas which represents the sky is hung in a semicircle. In plays calling for a country estate, the floor is covered with papier-mâché dirt.

* * *

When performing historical plays, the Naturalistic Theatre conforms to the rule that the stage must be transformed into an exhibit of authentic museum pieces, or at least of exact copies made after period paintings or from photographs. The stage director and designer try to reproduce as exactly as possible the year, month, and day of the play's action, and find it insufficient, for example, that the play takes place simply "in the age of powder." Elaborate hedges, fantastic fountains, overgrown meandering paths, rose gardens, clipped chestnut and myrtle trees, crinolines and capricious coiffures—all these do not satisfy the naturalistic directors. They find it necessary to reproduce exactly the kind of sleeves worn in Louis XV's times, or to speculate how the coiffures during the reign of Louis XVI differed from those worn under Louis XV. Such directors do not want to stylize a period, but rather follow a fashion journal of the year, month, and day on which the action occurs.

Thus, the Naturalistic Theatre devised the method of *copying a historical style*. Such a method, naturally, does not observe the rhythmic architectonics of a play such as *Julius Caesar*, for example, with its plastic conflict between two opposing powers. And not one of the directors realized that a synthesis of "caesarism" could never be achieved with a kaleidoscope of realistic scenes and an imitation of historical costumes.

The actors' make-up is *overly realistic*—real faces as we see them in real life, an exact copy. The Naturalistic Theatre considers the face the actor's main expressive tool and consequently overlooks all other means of expression. The Naturalistic Theatre does not know the advantages of plasticity and does not compel its actors to train their bodies. The schools connected with the Naturalistic Theatre do not realize that physical sport should be a basic training, especially for plays such as *Antigone* and *Julius Caesar*, plays which because of their music belong to *another* kind of theatre.

Many excellently made-up faces remain in one's mind, but no postures or rhythmic movements. During a performance of *Antigone* the director somehow unconsciously arranged his actors to resemble frescoes and vase paintings, but he was not able to *synthesize* or *stylize* what he had seen in actual relics; he could only photograph. On the stage before us we could see a series of groupings, like a row of hill tops, but realistic gestures and movements, like ravines, disturbed the internal rhythm of the reproduction.

The actor in the Naturalistic Theatre is extremely nimble at transforming himself, but his methods do not originate from *plastic* action but from make-up and an onomatopoeic imitation of various accents, dialects, and voices. Instead of developing his esthetic sense to exclude all coarseness, the actor's task is to lose his self-consciousness. A photographic sense of recording daily trivia is instilled in the actor.

According to Gogol, the character Khlestakov "had nothing particularly distinctive," and yet Khlestakov is very clear-cut. *In the interpretation of images sharpness of outline is not at all necessary for clarity.*

* * *

The Naturalistic Theatre teaches the actor a crystal-clear, explicit mode of expression, never conscious underacting, or the play of allusions. And therefore, the Naturalistic Theatre smacks of *overacting.* Hints and insinuations are unknown in this kind of theatre. But even in this great period of naturalism some actors tried to bring moments of a new kind of acting to the stage as, for example, Vera Kommissarzhevskaia in her tarantella dance in *A Doll's House.*

The Naturalistic Theatre denies that the spectator has the ability to finish a painting in his imagination, or to dream as he does when listening to music. And yet the spectator possesses such an ability. In the first act of Yartsev's play *At the Monastery*[2] the interior of a monastery was shown and the curfew bells were heard. No window was shown on stage, but from the sound of the bells the playgoer imagined a courtyard covered with piles of bluish snow, fir trees as in the paintings by Nesterov[3] little paths leading from cell to cell, and the golden cupolas of a church. One spectator imagined such a picture, the second another, and the third still another. Mystery had taken hold of the playgoer, transporting him into the world of dreams. In the second act the director had a window showing the courtyard of the monastery but not those cells, those heaps of snow, nor the color of the cupolas. And the spectator was disenchanted and even enraged, for Mystery had disappeared and dreams were abused.

The Naturalistic Theatre consistently and consciously banished from the stage the power of Mystery. During the first performance

2. P. M. Yartsev (d. 1930), Russian theatrical critic, playwright, and stage director whose play *At the Monastery* was produced at the Moscow Art Theatre in 1904 [*Editor's note*].

3. M. V. Nesterov (1862–1942), Russian painter who started his career as a member of the *peredvižniki* (travelers or wanderers), established in 1870 [*Editor's note*].

of *The Sea Gull*,[4] in the first act, one could not see how the actors made their exit from the stage. Running across some boards, they disappeared into a black cloth thicket, into *somewhere* (at that time the designer still worked without the collaboration of the carpenter); but when *The Sea Gull* was given again in a new version, all the stage was clearly visible: a little summerhouse with real cupolas and real columns, and a ravine into which the actors made their exit seen by all. During *The Sea Gull*'s first performance, in the third act, a window was at the side of the stage, and no landscape could be seen; when the actors entered wearing galoshes, shaking their hats, shawls and kerchiefs, they conveyed the spirit of autumn, of freezing rain, puddles in the yard and boards squelching in the mud. When the play was restudied on a technically perfected stage, the window faced the audience and showed a landscape. Your imagination was lulled, and you did not imagine anything more than what the actors said about the weather outside. And the departure with horses and bells (the end of the third act in the first version) was only felt on the stage, yet was clearly pictured by the spectator's imagination; but according to the plan of the later performances, the audience had to see the horses with bells as well as the terrace from which the characters departed.

* * *

Somewhere Voltaire said: "*Le secret d'etre ennuyeux, c'est tout dire.*"[5]

When the spectator's imagination is not lulled to sleep but stimulated, then art becomes subtle. Why could the medieval plays be performed without any scenery? Because of the lively imagination of the audience.

The Naturalistic Theatre not only denies the playgoer the ability to dream, but even the ability to understand intelligent conversation on stage. All the scenes in Ibsen's plays are submitted to a tedious analysis which transforms the work of the Norwegian dramatist into something boring, dragging, and doctrinaire. Especially in the performance of Ibsen plays the method of the naturalistic stage director is clearly demonstrated. The play is divided into a series of scenes, and each separate part is *minutely analyzed*. This painstaking analysis is applied to the tiniest scenes of the drama. From these various, thoroughly-digested parts the whole is glued together again. This piecing together of the whole from its parts is called the art of the director, but I think the analytical work of the naturalist-director, this pasting together of the poet's, the actor's, the musician's,

---

4. Meyerhold, a member of the Moscow Art Theatre from 1898 to 1902, played the role of Treplyov in the 1898 production.

5. "The secret of being a bore is to say everything." François Marie Arouet de Voltaire (1694–1778), French philosopher and writer [*Editor's note*].

the painter's, or even the director's work, will never result in a unified whole.

The famous critic of the eighteenth century, Alexander Pope, in his didactic *Essay on Criticism* (1711), enumerating the reasons which prevent critics from giving sound judgment, among other reasons points out their habit of examining parts of a work when the critics' first duty should be to look from the point of view of the author at work *as a whole*.

The same could be said for the stage director. The naturalistic director, profoundly analyzing each separate part of a work, does not see the picture as a whole and, fascinated by his filigree work— the trimming of some scenes which present excellent material for his creative imagination with some pearls of "characterization"— destroys the balance, the harmony of the whole.

Timing is very important on the stage. If some scene which the author wanted short is drawn out, then the weight of the next scene, which the author considered very important, is lessened. Having to look for a long time at something which should be forgotten, the spectator is already tired when the important scene opens. Such a distortion of the harmony of the whole appeared in the interpretation of the Art Theatre's director in the third act of *The Cherry Orchard*. The author makes Ranevskaya's premonition of the threatening storm (the sale of the cherry orchard) the leitmotiv of the act. All the others around her live stupidly—they are dancing to the monotonous rattle of a Jewish orchestra, and as in a nightmare, whirl around in a tedious dance without amusement, or fervor, or grace, or even lust, not knowing that the earth on which they are dancing will be sold from under their feet. Only Ranevskaya foresees Evil, expects it, and for a moment stops the turning wheel, that night-marish dance of the puppets in their booth, as she lectures to the crowd on crime—how it is better not to be a "do gooder," for crimes may lead to holiness, whereas mediocrity leads nowhere. The act is divided into two parts: Ranevskaya's forebodings of the imminent Disaster (the fateful beginning of Chekhov's new mystic dramas), and the show booth of puppets (recently Chekhov had Sharlotta dance among the "residents" in the favorite costume of the puppet theatre—the black dress coat and checkered trousers). Speaking in musical terms this act is like a movement of a symphony with a sorrowful melody vacillating from *piano* to *forte* (Ranevskaya's mood), and a dissonant accompaniment—the monotonous strumming of the provincial orchestra and the dance of the living corpses. And so the scene with the tricks is only another discord in the melody of the tedious dance. That is to say, this scene must fuse with the dance, only to separate a minute later, and again to join with the dancing which should continuously serve as a background.[6]

The director of the Art Theatre showed how the harmony of this act can be destroyed. He created a scene with many details which proceeded slowly and laboriously. For a long time the spectator concentrated his attention on this scene and lost the leitmotiv of the act. And when the act had finished, only the melody of the background remained and the leitmotiv had disappeared.

In Chekhov's *Cherry Orchard*, as in the plays of Maeterlinck, an unseen hero exists on stage whose presence is felt whenever the curtain drops. When the curtain closed on the Moscow Art Theatre's performance of *The Cherry Orchard* the presence of such a protagonist was not felt. Only types were remembered. To Chekhov the characters of *The Cherry Orchard* were a means to an end and not a reality. But in the Moscow Art Theatre the characters became real and the lyrical-mystic aspect of *The Cherry Orchard* was lost.

If in the Chekhov plays the particulars distracted the director from the *whole* because the impressionistically-drawn figures of Chekhov lent themselves well to precise characterization, so in the plays by Ibsen the director had to explain to the public what seemed incomprehensible to him.

The performances of Ibsen plays above all aimed *to enliven the "boring" dialogue* with something—with eating a meal, arranging a room, introducing scenes of packing, moving about furniture, and so forth. In *Hedda Gabler*, in the scene between Tesman and Aunt Julia they ate breakfast together. I remember well how awkwardly the actor playing Tesman ate, but I hardly heard the thesis of the play.

In the Ibsen plays, apart from showing definite "patterns" of Norwegian life, the director emphasized every passage of dialogue which he considered *difficult*. The essence of Ibsen's *Pillars of Society*, for example, was drowned in the analytical work spent on less important scenes. And the playgoer who knew the play well from reading, saw in this performance a new play which he did not understand. The director made many minor scenes as important as the major ones, *but the sum total of these secondary scenes did not convey the essence of the entire play.* The emphasis on one particular moment catches audience attention and the rest of the act is lost in fog.

6. Such passing, jarring notes which jut out from the background the act's leitmotiv can be found in the stationmaster's reading poetry, in the scene of Yepikhodov's broken billiard cue, and Trofimov's fall on the stairs. And look how closely Chekhov interweaves the two melodies—the leitmotiv and the accompanying background.

ANYA. [*excitedly*] In the kitchen just now someone was saying that the cherry orchard was sold today.
LYUBOV ANDREEVNA. Sold? To whom?
ANYA. He didn't say. He's gone now. [*Dances with* TROFIMOV, *they go into the ballroom.*] [P. 197, *Editor's translation.*]

The fear of not showing everything, the fear of Mystery, transforms the theatre into a mere illustration to an author's words. "I hear the dog barking again," says one of the actors, and immediately the dog's bark is heard. The spectator is made aware of a departure with the sound of bells and horses' hoofs on a wooden bridge across a river. The falling of rain is heard on a tin roof, as well as birds, frogs, and crickets.

Let me relate a conversation between Chekhov and some actors. When A. P. Chekhov came for the second time to a rehearsal of *The Sea Gull* at the Moscow Art Theatre (September 11, 1898), one of the actors told him how frogs were going to croak, flies to buzz, and dogs to bark.

"Why all this?" asked Chekhov in a dissatisfied tone of voice.
"It's real," answered the actor.
"It's real," repeated Chekhov laughing, and after a pause said: "The stage is art. Kramskoy has a genre painting with wonderfully painted faces. How would it be if the nose were cut out from one of the faces and a real nose inserted? The nose will be 'real' but the pointing is spoiled."

One of the actors told Chekhov proudly that at the end of the third act of *The Sea Gull* the director was planning to bring all the household servants onto the stage including a woman with a crying child. Anton Pavlovich said: "That's not necessary. It's the same as if you were playing the piano *pianissimo* and suddenly the lid of the piano were to fall down." "It often happens in life that a *pianissimo* is suddenly interrupted by a completely unexpected *forte*," one of the actors tried to object. "Yes," said A. P., "but the stage requires a certain convention: you have no fourth wall. Besides that, the stage is art, the stage reflects the quintessence of life and nothing superfluous should be introduced." It is clear from this conversation what Chekhov himself thought about the Naturalistic Theatre. This theatre wanted a fourth wall and only absurdities resulted. The Naturalistic Theatre resembled a factory: everything on stage had to be "as in life" and transformed into a shop of museum pieces.

Stanislavsky felt that the theatrical sky could be made real to the public, and the entire administration worried about how to raise the roof of the theatre. And no one noticed that instead of repairing the stage the foundation of the Naturalistic Theatre was being demolished. For no one believed that the wind blowing the garlands in the first scene of *Julius Caesar* was not the stagehand, especially as the costumes of the actors were not blowing. In the second act of *The Cherry Orchard* the actors walked in "real" ravines, over "real" bridges, near a "real" chapel, and in the sky hung two great lumps covered with blue cloth the likes of which had never been seen in any sky. The hills on a battlefield (in *Julius Caesar*) were built so as to diminish gradually toward the horizon, but why did the actors not diminish in size when moving in the same direction as the hills?

> The stage sets in use today show landscapes of great depth but do not show the human figure in perspective to these landscapes. And yet this theatre pretends to reproduce nature accurately! Actors moving ten or even twenty meters back from the footlights are just as large and distinct as when standing directly at the footlights. According to the laws of perspective in painting, the further an actor moves upstage, if he has to be shown in his true size with the surrounding trees, houses, mountains, the smaller he should become, sometimes only a silhouette, sometimes even more indistinct.[7]

The trees used in the Naturalistic Theatre seem crude, unnatural, and much more artificial in their three dimensions than painted, two-dimensional trees. These are some of the absurd practices followed by the Naturalistic Theatre in its attempt to imitate nature. The fundamental aim of this theatre is to find rationality in any subject, to photograph, to illustrate with decorative painting the text of a dramatic work, and to copy a historical style.

Naturalism introduced a more complex staging technique in the Russian theatre, yet it is the Theatre of Chekhov, the second style of the Moscow Art Theatre, which demonstrated the power of *mood*; without this mood, or atmosphere, the theatre of the Meiningers would have perished long ago. But the development of the Naturalistic Theatre was not aided by this *new mood* originating from Chekhov's plays. The performance of *The Sea Gull* in the Alexandrinky Theatre did not dispel the author's mood, yet the secret was not to be found in the chirping of crickets, the barking of dogs, or in realistic doors. When *The Sea Gull* was performed in the Yermitazh building of the Moscow Art Theatre, the *machinery* was not working perfectly, and *technique* did not yet extend its feelers into all corners of the theatre.

The secret of Chekhov's mood lies in the *rhythm* of his language. This rhythm was felt by the actors of the Art Theatre during the rehearsals of the first Chekhov play, was felt because of the actors' love for Chekhov.

The Moscow Art Theatre would never have achieved its second style without the rhythmicality of Chekhov's words; the theatre of mood became its real character and was not a mask borrowed from the Meiningen players.

That the Art Theatre could under one roof shelter the Naturalis-

---

7. Georg Fuchs, *Die Schaubühne der Zukunst* [The stage of the future], p. 28.

tic Theatre and the Theatre of Mood was due, I am convinced, to
A. P. Chekhov who personally attended the rehearsals of his plays
and with the charm of his personality and with frequent conversations influenced the actors, their tastes, and their ideas about the
problem of art.

This new kind of theatre was created chiefly by a group of actors
known as "Chekhovian actors." They performed all the Chekhov
plays and can be considered the originators of the Chekhovian
rhythmic diction. Whenever I remember the active part taken by
these actors in creating *The Sea Gull*'s characters and mood, I
understand why I believe so strongly that the actor is the most
important element on a stage. Neither the sets, nor the crickets, nor
the horses' hoofs on the boards could create *mood*, but only the
extraordinary musicality of the performers who understood the
rhythm of Chekhov's poetry and could veil his work in lunar mist.

In the first two productions (*The Sea Gull* and *Uncle Vanya*) the
actors were perfectly *free* and the harmony was not disrupted. But
later, the naturalist-director made the ensembles more important
and lost the key to a Chekhov performance. Once the ensembles
became important, the work of the actors became passive; but instead of encouraging the lyricism of this *new key*, the naturalistic
director created atmosphere with external devices such as darkness,
sounds, accessories, and characters, and soon lost his sense of direction because he did not realize how Chekhov changed from subtle
realism to mystic lyricism.

Once the Moscow Art Theatre had decided how to produce Chekhov plays, it applied the same pattern to other authors. Ibsen and
Maeterlinck were performed "in the manner of Chekhov."

I have already written about Ibsen in the Moscow Art Theatre.
Maeterlinck was not approached by way of Chekhov's lyricism, but
rationally. The actors in *Les Aveugles* were treated as characters,
and Death appeared as a tulle cloud. Everything was very complicated, as was generally the case in the Naturalistic Theatre, and *not
at all symbolic*, as was Maeterlinck.

The Art Theatre could have extricated itself from the impasse in
which it found itself by using Chekhov's lyrical talent, but instead it
used more and more elaborate tricks, and finally even lost the key to
performing its very own author, just as the Germans had lost the
key to performing Hauptmann who besides his realistic plays had
written dramas (*Schluck und Jau* and *Und Pippa Tanzt*)[8] which
demanded an entirely different approach.

---

8. *Schluck and Jau*, 1900; *And Pippa Dances!*, 1906 *[Editor's note]*.

VLADIMIR NABOKOV

[A Definition of *Poshlost'*]

The Russian language is able to express by means of one pitiless word the idea of a certain widespread defect for which the other three European languages I happen to know possess no special term. The absence of a particular expression in the vocabulary of a nation does not necessarily coincide with the absence of the corresponding notion but it certainly impairs the fullness and readiness of the latter's perception. Various aspects of the idea which Russians concisely express by the term *poshlost'* (the stress- accent is on the puff-ball of the first syllable, and the final *t* has a moist softness that is hardly equalled by the French *t* in such words as *restiez* or *émoustillant*) are split among several English words and thus do not form a definite whole. On second thought, I find it preferable to transcribe that fat brute of a word thus: *poshlust*—which renders in a somewhat more adequate manner the dull sound of the second, neutral *o*. Inversely the first *o* is as big as the plop of an elephant falling into a muddy pond and as round as the bosom of a bathing beauty on a German picture postcard.

English words expressing several, although by no means all aspects of *poshlust* are for instance: "cheap, sham, common, smutty, pink-and-blue, high falutin', in bad taste." My little assistant, *Roget's Theaurus*, (which incidentally lists "rats, mice" under "Insects"—see page 21 of Revised Edition) supplies me moreover with "inferior, sorry, trashy, scurvy, tawdry, gimcrack" and others under "cheapness." All these however suggest merely certain false values for the detection of which no particular shrewdness is required. In fact they tend, these words, to supply an obvious classification of values at a given period of human history; but what Russians call *poshlust* is beautifully timeless and so cleverly painted all over with protective tints that its presence (in a book, in a soul, in an institution, in a thousand other places) often escapes detection.

Ever since Russia began to think, and up to the time that her mind went blank under the influence of the extraordinary regime she has been enduring for these last twenty-five years, educated, sensitive and free-minded Russians were acutely aware of the furtive and clammy touch of *poshlust*. Among the nations with which we came into contact, Germany had always seemed to us a country where *poshlust*, instead of being mocked, was one of the essential parts of the national spirit, habits, traditions and general atmosphere, although at the same time well-meaning Russian intellectuals of a more romantic type readily, too readily, adopted the legend of the greatness of German philosophy and literature; for it takes a super-Russian to admit that there is a dreadful streak of *poshlust* running through Goethe's *Faust*.

To exaggerate the worthlessness of a country at the awkward moment when one is at war with it—and would like to see it destroyed to the last beer-mug and last forget-me-not,—means walking dangerously close to that abyss of *poshlust* which yawns so universally at times of revolution or war. But if what one demurely murmurs is but a mild pre-war truth, even with something old-fashioned about it, the abyss is perhaps avoidable. Thus, a hundred years ago, while civic-minded publicists in St. Petersburg were mixing heady cocktails of Hegel and Schlegel (with a dash of Feuerbach),[1] Gogol, in a chance story he told, expressed the immortal spirit of *poshlust* pervading the German nation and expressed it with all the vigor of his genius.

The conversation around him had turned upon the subject of Germany, and after listening awhile, Gogol said: "Yes, generally speaking the average German is not too pleasant a creature, but it is impossible to imagine anything more unpleasant than a German Lothario, a German who tries to be winsome. . . . One day in Germany I happened to run across such a gallant. The dwelling place of the maiden whom he had long been courting without success stood on the bank of some lake or other, and there she would be every evening sitting on her balcony and doing two things at once: knitting a stocking and enjoying the view. My German gallant being sick of the futility of his pursuit finally devised an unfailing means whereby to conquer the heart of his cruel Gretchen. Every evening he would take off his clothes, plunge into the lake and, as he swam there, right under the eyes of his beloved, he would keep embracing a couple of swans which had been specially prepared by him for that purpose. I do not quite know what those swans were supposed to symbolize, but I do know that for several evenings on end he did nothing but float about and assume pretty postures with his birds under that precious balcony. Perhaps he fancied there was something poetically antique and mythological in such frolics, but whatever notion he had, the result proved favorable to his intentions: the lady's heart was conquered just as he thought it would be, and soon they were happily married."

Here you have *poshlust* in its ideal form, and it is clear that the terms trivial, trashy, smug and so on do not cover the aspect it takes in this epic of the blond swimmer and the two swans he fondled.

---

1. George Wilhelm Friedrich Hegel (1770–1831), the German philosopher; August Wilhelm Schlegel (1767–1845), German poet, critic, and translator; Ludwig Andreas Feuerbach (1804–72), German philosopher [*Editor's note*].

Neither is it necessary to travel so far both in space and time to obtain good examples. Open the first magazine at hand and you are sure to find something of the following kind: a radio set (or a car, or a refrigerator, or table silver—anything will do) has just come to the family: mother clasps her hands in .dazed delight, the children crowd around, all agog, Junior and the dog strain up to the edge of the table where the Idol is enthroned; even Grandma of the beaming wrinkles peeps out somewhere in the background (forgetful, we presume, of the terrific row she has had that very morning with her daughter-in-law); and somewhat apart, his thumbs gleefully inserted in the armpits of his waistcoat, legs a-straddle and eyes a-twinkle, stands triumphant Pop, the Proud Donor.

The rich *poshlust* emanating from advertisements of this kind is due not to their exaggerating (or inventing) the glory of this or that serviceable article but to suggesting that the acme of human happiness is purchasable and that its purchase somehow ennobles the purchaser. Of course, the world they create is pretty harmless in itself because everybody knows that it is made up by the seller with the understanding that the buyer will join in the make-believe. The amusing part is not that it is a world where nothing spiritual remains except the ecstatic smiles of people serving or eating celestial cereals or a world where the game of the senses is played according to bourgeois rules ("bourgeois" in the Flaubertian, *not* in the Marxist sense) but that it is a kind of satellite shadow world in the actual existence of which neither sellers nor buyers really believe in their heart of hearts—especially in this wise quiet country.

If a commercial artist wishes to depict a nice little boy he will grace him with freckles (which incidentally assume a horrible rashlike aspect in the humbler funnies). Here *poshlust* is directly connected with a forgotten convention of a faintly racial type. Kind people send our lonely soldiers silk hosed dummy legs modeled on those of Hollywood lovelies and stuffed with candies and safety razor blades—at least I have seen a picture of a person preparing such a leg in a certain periodical which is a world-famous purveyor of *poshlust*. Propaganda (which could not exist without a generous supply of and demand for *poshlust*) fills booklets with lovely Kolkhos[2] maidens and windswept clouds. I select my examples hurriedly and at random—the "Encyclopédie des Idées Reçues"[3] which Flaubert dreamt of writing one day was a more ambitious work.

2. The Russian word *kolxoz*, short for *kollektivnoe xozjajstvo*, literally, collective household or collective farm in the USSR. The word is sometimes transliterated as *kolkhoz* or *kolkoz*. What Nakhov refers to with his phrase "Kolkhos maidens and windswept clouds" is the propaganda photograph of "life on the *kolkoz*" popularized by the Soviet government in the 1930s and early 1940s [*Editor's note*].
3. Literally, "Encyclopedia of Accepted Views" [*Editor's note*].

Literature is one of its best breeding places and by *poshlust*-literature I do not mean the kind of thing which is termed "pulp" or which in England used to go under the name of "penny dreadfuls" and in Russia under that of "yellow literature." Obvious trash, curiously enough, contains sometimes a wholesome ingredient, readily appreciated by children and simple souls. Superman is undoubtable *poshlust*, but it is *poshlust* in such a mild, unpretentious form that it is not worth while talking about; and the fairy tales of yore contained, for that matter, as much trivial sentiment and naive vulgarity as these yarns about modern Giant Killers. *Poshlust*, it should be repeated, is especially vigorous and vicious when the sham is *not* obvious and when the values it mimics are considered, rightly or wrongly, to belong to the very highest level of art, thought or emotion. It is those books which are so *poshlustily* reviewed in the literary supplement of daily papers—the best sellers, the "stirring, profound and beautiful" novels; it is these "elevated and powerful" books that contain and distill the very essence of *poshlust*. I happen to have upon my desk a copy of a paper with a whole page advertising a certain novel, which novel is a fake from beginning to end and by its style, its ponderous gambols around elevated ideas, and absolute ignorance of what authentic literature was, is and always will be, strangely reminds one of the swan-fondling swimmer depicted by Gogol. "You lose yourself in it completely,"—says one reviewer;—"When the last page is turned you come back to the world of everyday a little thoughtful, as after a great experience" (note the coy "a little" and the perfectly automatic "as after a great"). "A singing book, compact of grace and light and ecstasy, a book of pearly radiance,"—whispers another (that swimmer was also "compact of grace," and the swans had a "pearly radiance, too"). "The work of a master psychologist who can skillfully probe the very inner recesses of men's souls." This "inner" (mind you—not "outer"), and the other two or three delightful details already mentioned are in exact conformity to the true value of the book. In fact, this praise is perfectly adequate: the "beautiful" novel is "beautifully" reviewed and the circle of *poshlust* is complete—or would be complete had not words taken a subtle revenge of their own and smuggled the truth in by secretly forming most nonsensical and most damning combinations while the reviewer and publisher are quite sure that they are praising the book, "which the reading public has made a (here follows an enormous figure apparently meaning the quantity of copies sold) triumph." For in the kingdom of *poshlust* it is not the book that "makes a triumph" but the "reading public" which laps it up, blurb and all.

The particular novel referred to here may have been a perfectly honest and sincere (as the saying goes) attempt on the author's part to write something he felt strongly about—and very possibly no commercial aspirations assisted him in that unfortunate process. The trouble is that sincerity, honesty and even true kindness of heart cannot prevent the demon of *poshlust* from possessing himself of an author's typewriter when the man lacks genius and when the "reading public" is what publishers think it is. The dreadful thing about *poshlust* is that one finds it so difficult to explain to people why a particular book which seems chock-full of noble emotion and compassion, and can hold the reader's attention "on a theme far removed from the discordant events of the day" is far, far worse than the kind of literature which *everybody* admits is cheap.

From the various examples collected here it will be I hope clear that *poshlust* is not only the obviously trashy but also the falsely important, the falsely beautiful, the falsely clever, the falsely attractive. A list of literary characters personifying *poshlust* (and thus namable in Russian *poshlyaki* in the case of males and *poshlyáchki* in the case of females—and rhyming with "key" and "latch-key" respectively) will include Polonius and the royal pair in Hamlet, Flaubert's Rodolphe and Homais, Laevsky in Chekhov's *Duel*, Joyce's Marion Bloom, young Bloch in A *la Recherche du Temps Perdu*,[4] Maupassant's "Bel Ami," Anna Karenina's husband, Berg in *War and Peace* and numerous other figures in universal fiction.

GEORGY TOVSTONOGOV

Chekhov's *Three Sisters* at the Gorky Theatre

A classic tends to age, disappear from active repertory, and then revive to meet the spiritual needs of a new audience, no less—and sometimes more—than do contemporary plays.

In recent years, Soviet theatre has increasingly produced the classics. Plays which not long ago saw little more than a dustrag have become the subject of violent debate, making new names for actors and directors.

Venerable academicians, learned literary scholars and theatre historians who have devoted their lives to the study of Russian classics react with divided feelings. They are pleased that their beloved plays once more meet the needs of the day, but are infuriated by what they see as the disrespect of the directors. Some of the older theatregoers are also unsatisfied with contemporary interpretations of the classics. They compare productions of thirty or forty years ago

---

4. Literally, "The Quest for Time That Has Gone By," or (in the well-known Moncrieff translation) "Remembrance of Things Past" [*Editor's note*].

with those staged today, and not only prefer the impressions of their youth, but consider today's approaches blasphemous.

I myself have the greatest respect for the productions done by Stanislavsky, Nemirovich-Danchenko, Meyerhold, Tairov, and Popov.[1] Even now, I remember them with delight and gratitude. But should all those productions, which had once impressed me so greatly, miraculously reappear just as they were played twenty-five or thirty years ago, I think they would evoke different emotional and intellectual reactions. Not because the productions had deteriorated. Because the audience has changed.

It seems to me that those who defend the old classic productions are confusing the works themselves with one way of producing them. A dramatic masterpiece dies when the theatrical form for it dies, and it revives when the theatre finds it a new form.

Of course, a classic cannot be torn from the times in which its author lived. Or from the culture and level of aesthetic appreciation of his audience, from the style of the actors who first performed it, from the technical possibilities of its theatre, from the political, social and moral ideas of its period—that is, from its conventions. The fact that Shakespeare's troupe consisted of only sixteen to twenty actors, that his performances took place in open daylight, and so on, had to affect his plays. Is it not because Shakespeare's theatre had no curtain that all his scenes begin with entrances and end with exits?

As the Comédie Française is heir to Molière's traditions, so Moscow's Maly Theatre is the home of Ostrovsky and the Moscow Art Theatre that of Chekhov: these theatres gave their authors their stage birth. But more than once, history has seen one theatre give life to a play, define the character of its performance for years, and then become the gravedigger of its beloved author.

Stanislavsky and Nemirovich-Danchenko strengthened the definition of Chekhov's drama as "theatre of mood" and the reputation of the writer himself as "a singer of melancholy." It is clear to an objective scholar of Chekhovian theatre that the pessimistic tone of the MKhAT productions derived from the particular period of social stagnation in which Russian society found itself. The form which the MKhAT found for Chekhov was the only accurate one possible at that time. When Nemirovich-Danchenko returned to *Three Sisters* almost forty years later [during the Stalinist period], he refused to revive his earlier and best production. It had become clear to him that, for 1940, the old play had to be given a new tone,

---

1. Vsevelod Yemilevich Meyerhold (1874–1940), famous stage director, was a member of the Moscow Art Theatre (see his essay, above). Alexandr Yakovlevich Tairov (1885–1950) founded the Kamerny (chamber) Theatre in Moscow in 1914 and served as artistic stage director. Alexey Dmitrievich Popov (1892–1961) was a stage director and playwright [*Editor's note*].

a new form. He firmly warned the performers away from "Chekhovianism," from dismal whinings, protracted rhythms, elegaic intonations—in short, from everything begotten by the MKhAT, which had already degenerated into cliché.

Twenty-five years went by. The production had set a new standard and begot a new tradition. In opposition to the notion of Chekhov as pessimist, another extreme attitude arose: interpreters began to look for traits of the fighting revolutionary in Chekhov's heroes. His protagonists were credited with a strong will and much energy, with courage and optimism. Historical and psychological truth was sacrificed to this conception. Thus, for example, Nina Zarechnaya in *The Sea Gull* was treated as a talented actress who had finally found her way. And this only because she says, in her last scene: "My morale improves every day," "I have faith . . . ," "I'm not afraid of life." As though words alone define the scope of a Chekhovian character!

Although they had denied Chekhov's heroes any right to melancholy, anguish or doubt, and had deprived them of their historical basis and psychological complexity, neither the theatres nor the critics had managed to modernize Chekhov. And Chekhov "the optimist" did not prove interesting to the contemporary audience, for Chekhov does not fit the Procrustean bed of monosyllabic definition.

By this time, Chekhov was being produced in theatres on all continents, in every language. It is possible that the freedom of foreign theatre from established Chekhovian traditions was conducive to his success abroad. But, in my opinion, the deciding factor lay in the fact that many men of theatre found Chekhov's plays thematically congenial, and saw in them the sources of modern dramatic form.

Many Chekhovian motifs, themes, problems, and conflicts have impregnated modern dramaturgy. Chekhov was the first Russian playwright to see the complexity and even impossibility of mutual understanding, to see man's difficulty in expressing all he thinks and feels. I think that the themes of spiritual loneliness and isolation, and of the futility of trying to reach another human soul, were suggested by Chekhov to the many foreign authors in whose writings they later appeared. All his plays begin in what is now called "non-communication." Chekhov found an extremely capacious and unprecedented form for expressing the complex inner life of a character. Nemirovich-Danchenko called it his "secondary level," his "undercurrent"—what we'd now call "subtext."

A classic play—or any good contemporary one, for that matter—should not be infused with ideas foreign or contradictory to the author's own. The theatre can single out and emphasize those facets of the work it finds most interesting. It can shift the accent, and make the previously unnoticed become significant. But one cannot single out, emphasize, or re-accent what is not in the play. And if the theatre ceases to be alert to qualitative changes which have taken place in the audience, it loses contact with life and thus with its public.

With these two basic positions in mind, the Leningrad Gorky Theatre produced a series of classic plays: Gorky's *The Barbarians, The Idiot* based on Dostoevsky and Griboedov's *Woe from Wit.* The experience of working on these plays helped me and the acting collective in our work on *Three Sisters.* And, as often happens, my conception for the play took shape unexpectedly, coming about in reaction to a production I had once seen abroad.

It is not for me to decide whether or not the Gorky Theatre was Nemirovich-Danchenko's "unknown company" which would "succeed in doing something amazing, daring, and true in the play, though we cannot even guess at what this something is." A new birth of Chekhov is yet to come. I can only say that all those who contributed to the production tried to abide by Nemirovich-Danchenko's wish that the tendency toward clichéd Chekhovianism be overcome.

In beginning work on the production, the last thing I wanted was to debate the Moscow Art Theatre production of twenty-five years before. In 1940, Nemirovich-Danchenko thought that the blame for a ruined life lay beyond the limits of human personality. Fine and noble people were victimized by the times and the social order. In its production, the MKhAT claimed that such people deserved another kind of life. These people knew the gross, crushing force of the banal, and longed for a better existence.

It was a natural interpretation for its time. But today I had the right to question it. Is it only environment that prevents people from living fully, intelligently, and beautifully? It is important to assert that it is not something or someone from outside that destroys, but that the Chekhovian characters themselves—intelligent, subtle, suffering people—destroy one another by their own passivity and irresolution. Of course, they became that way unknown to themselves and by force of the general laws of human society. But this cannot fully vindicate them, nor justify their indifference and cruelty.

How could Tuzenbakh, a man of rare spiritual beauty, be allowed to perish? After all, almost everyone knew of the impending duel. Why did even Irina, who had agreed to join her life to Tuzenbakh's, Irina—so delicate and sensitive a nature—not sense approaching disaster in Tuzenbakh's parting request to "say something to me"? How could she not tell her future husband, a few minutes before the fatal shot, that she loved him? The high moral principles which would not permit her to tell a lie became cruelty. And who knows—perhaps this urged Tuzenbakh on to his suicidal duel.

When it remains inactive, the spiritual perfection of Chekhov's heroes becomes its opposite. Occupied with their own emotional experiences and problems, these people lose their interest in the misfortunes and dramas of each other. They are kind, in general, and attentive, in general. But their squeamishness in the face of anything ugly, coarse, or evil, paralyzes their will, and they are unable to oppose these things. By running away from everything unpleasant, they desert the field of battle and surrender all their positions without a struggle.

Natasha brutishly throws out Anfisa, the eighty-year-old nurse who has spent thirty years in the Prozorov household. And Olga, who can be distressed by an indelicately spoken word, accepts all this in silence. It is only after the nurse has been pushed out the door that she, almost humbly, begs that her nerves be spared. . . .

Tuzenbakh is killed; Andrey is morally dead; Olga and Irina are forced from their home; and Masha's first and only love has been trampled. Who is to blame for all this? The coarse and bromidic, as personified by Natasha and the ever-present if invisible Protopopov, have won the day—because in their nobility of spirit and academic scrupulosity, the others did not even try to oppose them.

In one of his plays, Chekhov says: "You . . . must understand that the world will not be destroyed by fire, but by thieves."

In *Three Sisters*, I feel that Chekhov not only sympathizes with his heroes and loves them, but also judges them in anger. This lends their characters depth, scope, and complexity.

The theme of the intelligentsia and its approach to life is one of the most significant in literature. Both Chekhov and Gorky were concerned with the problem of the intelligentsia and its role in social history. With every period in history, attitudes toward the intelligentsia undergo radical changes. In my theatre the theme of the intelligentsia has been treated in a series of productions, beginning ten years ago with Gorky's *Barbarians*.

The production of *Three Sisters* followed a series of experiments which tested fresh modern readings of the classics. I staged each of these plays differently. The theatre used various means to reveal those themes and problems within each play which were relevant today. But from production to production, I became convinced that no worse service could be rendered a classic than to try to retain everyday detail with the accuracy of a museum, and to get carried away with the ethnography and exotica of ages past.

Everything shown on the stage acts on the audience by force of recognition. If the audience cannot relate a theatrical representation to its own living experience, interaction between the stage and the house dies. We cannot base a production on a limited group within the audience, i.e. on specialists in the history of minutiae of everyday living. Shakespeare already understood that. Historical detail appeared in productions at the Globe only insofar as it was intelligible to the Globe's audience. Today's audience is far better educated than its predecessors of the sixteenth and seventeenth centuries. But even today, the audience either does not know the social milieu of fifty years ago, or is indifferent to it. The art of externally reproducing past life is dying. And consequently, so are the means of expression of that theatre which was an imitator of life.

Chekhov's plays are saturated in the details of daily living which were familiar to his contemporaries. Characters drink tea and play lotto, dance the *grande ronde* to a Jewish orchestra and do card tricks, keep their accounts and receive guests. Chekhov infuses the atmosphere with a variety of sounds: the howl of a dog, the sound of a breaking string, coughing and snoring, a song on the far side of a lake, the blow of an axe, and so on and so forth. The lives of Chekhov's heroes are composed of a few important matters and thousands of trifles, lofty expatiations, complaints against fate, etc. But it is here, I think, that Chekhov shows himself an innovator in drama. It is in the useless map of Africa that hangs in Uncle Vanya's room, which becomes a poetic symbol of the absurdity of life. The blow of the axe demolishing the cherry orchard does not have an everyday meaning, but rather a symbolic one: the past is cut down and destroyed. The sound of keys turning in doors, of the heavy thump of the axe, would have been realistic details, and not obligatory—except that the old servant Firs has been forgotten and left in the empty house. And it is Firs that they are locking in and boarding up.

The fire in *The Three Sisters* seems to have no connection with the story of the Prozorovs and their friends. Yet Chekhov devoted almost all of the third act to it. Why? I think that the conflagration which he treats with such great mastery and authenticity is necessary to him—not as a genre scene, but as an artistic image, as reality heightened into symbol. The fire in the town is the fire in their souls. The Prozorov house didn't burn; but it became the smoldering ruin of dreams and hopes and ambitions. Andrey does not fight the fire; he plays the violin. Perhaps this is the most graphic indication of how ravaged and burnt out his soul is. And Irina is not impoverished by the real fire. But she screams and moans: "I can't take it anymore! I can't! I can't! Throw me out. Throw me out; I can't take it anymore! . . ."

In Chekhov, everything commonplace and realistic has a second meaning, imagaic and poetic. To stage Chekhov as though he were a mere annotator of manners is to impoverish and butcher the author. I find that the complexity of Chekhovian drama lies not only in the many levels of its content, but also in its form. To believe Chekhov means not to believe the literal meaning of his sentences and remarks.

Any classic play, and especially Chekhov, can be staged faithfully today only under one condition: freedom from the traditions which critical literature and stage history have imposed in regard to the characters of the play. It is correct, for example, to laugh at Kulygin, judge Solyony, and sympathize with Vershinin. But is it? In what way is Vershinin's military uniform better than Kulygin's teaching one? It is hardly correct to sympathize only with those who express themselves well, and deny sympathy to those who seem inarticulate.

All of Chekhov's heroes are dear to me, and all of them evoke conflicting feelings within me. I believe them all, except for Natasha. I believe that they suffer, and love, and desire that which is noble and good. But all of them excite opposite thoughts and feelings as well. It is a bitter shame that they are so criminally spineless, that their strength is paralyzed and their souls crippled by reflection. Of course, Kulygin is ridiculous and limited in his devotion to form and the school administration. But in spite of all that, his frequent "I am content" is an expression of pain, fear, and loneliness. He is a profoundly unhappy man. His love for Masha, and the tact with which he conceals his jealousy and grief, are deserving of sympathy. But this very love and tact and so on are somehow unpleasant, oppressively dull.

The characters of *Three Sisters* are caught up in a vicious circle. No one thought or deed can be evaluated by itself. Everything that anyone does is both good and bad.

This view of converging ideas is not dictated by a determination to stage Chekhov's play in a new way, whatever the cost. I feel that everything I have said above, and everything that the company tried to express in our production, is contained in the play.

I have seen Chekhov productions at home and abroad. Every director who stages Chekhov respectfully and rhapsodically throws up his hands when the conversation turns to psychological depth and complexity. In their productions all the complexities are introduced with an eye to contrasting the good and bad people, the enthusiasms of some and the ordinariness of others. Such direction reflects the notion that agonizing pauses, indefinite intonations, and inarticulate *mises-en-scène* will create Chekhovian insight and subtlety. I am deeply convinced that such external devices only create a semblance of richness of inner life in his characters and the mere appearance of psychological intensity.

Lee Strasberg became, in my opinion, a victim of the traditional idea of Chekhovian theatre. His *Three Sisters* was a collection of the most prevalent acting and directorial clichés. His stage was filled with everyday reality, done with photographic authenticity and combined with protracted rhythms. There was no room for Chekhov's imagery.

In my *Three Sisters*, I tried first of all to reveal the clear and definite movement of every scene. With the actors, I looked for the mainspring triggering the action of each character and of each scene. We found that all the characters firmly and actively asserted their right not to interfere in anything. Moral and spiritual paralysis —the result: objectivity. Each and every actor and character-image declines to grieve, think, or dream, but rather seeks (and clings to) any pretext and any chance for abandoning the necessity to attempt to do or accomplish anything. For many, their refuge proves to be conversations about the future, about the necessity of work, and the like.

Any melancholy atmosphere must come only as a result of the whole performance. It is totally unnecessary for each of its participants to be miserable and bored and idle.

In the fourth act, Kulygin tells a funny story: "A schoolmaster once wrote 'bunkum' on a pupil's essay and the boy thought it was Latin and started declining it. Bunkum, bunkum, bunkum, bunki, bunko, bunko."[2]—this senselessness, this unnatural confusion of what is real and what is false, in my opinion, constitutes the dramatic paradox of the play. The more the heroes' dreams are belittled and derided, the more the heroes themselves feel honest, decent and noble. And the process of their rise from humiliation is tragic. The higher the sisters' poetic nobility ascends from Natasha's common materialism, the more remote becomes the possibility of realizing their dream of returning to Moscow—the symbol of the genuine and meaningful life.

If you're going to sweep a house, your hands may get soiled. The protagonists of *Three Sisters* have a physical aversion to dirt. Their hands are antiseptically clean. And dirt and coarseness fill their house, and drive them out.

The 1903 production of *Three Sisters* showed how the force of coarseness and daily living blighted the lives of excellent people.

2. An interpolation by the translator, Joyce Vining. A literal translation of the passage reads: "In a certain seminary a teacher wrote on an essay *nonsense* [*čepuxa*], but the student read *renixa*— he thought it was written in Latin." Written in Cryllic cursive, *čepuxa* may be misread as *renixa*, written in Roman cursive. Thus, to produce a similar effect in English, Joyce Vining came up with the idea of declension. See the translation by Ronald Hingley, *Three Sisters*, in *The Oxford Chekhov*, III (London: Oxford University Press, 1964), 126 [*Editor's note*].

In 1940, *Three Sisters* was permeated with faith in a better future.

In 1965, it seemed right to us to stage *Three Sisters* as a play about human worth, and about the trials of every day. We wanted to direct our production against "the slave in man," as Chekhov put it, against the amazing ability of the intelligentsia to find justifications for its inertia and indifference.

Chekhov exploded the form of the theatre of his day from within. Externally, his plays are not far from the mainstream of the realistic play of manners of the turn of the century.

But today's audience has been brought up with movies and television. It has been educated to perception via montage. Its imagination differs from that of the Shakespearean audience, but is in no way inferior to it.

A convention of the old theatre is the fixed viewpoint of the audience. The actor-character moves across the stage, now approaching the audience, now receding from it. Each member of the audience is stationary, and cannot see phenomena from various angles. The constant convention of the film is the ever-changing viewpoint of the audience. The actor-character can be immobile in the film. By shifting the cameras, moving them closer or farther away, the film director shifts his audience, which is allowed to view phenomena from various angles.

Can cinematic illustration of life be used in the theatre? The experiment was tempting. And my *Three Sisters* was staged cinematically, in the familiar sense of the word, although we needed neither the technical methods of the other art nor its figurative language. The cinematic in the production was obtained by mobilizing the stage platform. By using both the revolving stage and small moving platforms, we were able to avoid changes in the *mise-en-scène* and yet present things from different angles, to focus or pan whenever we thought necessary. By shifting groups of characters without destroying the logic of their behavior or interrupting any flow of life, by presenting them from various angles, we enabled the audience to see things more completely. We could either stress or soften a scene to emphasize the essentials without making the actors heighten or mute anything. Chekhov has four acts, with three different places of action all thoroughly specified in his set descriptions. To what extent do those descriptions obligate the director today? It seems to me that we need consider essential only the basic definitions of the place of action. For the first and second acts—a living room; for the third—Olga's and Irina's room; for the fourth —a garden by the Prozorov house. None of the rest is important.

In our production, the rooms in the Prozorov house were not delimited by walls, ceilings, windows or doors. Furniture of the then popular redwood was distributed over all of our large stage. A crystal chandelier hung over the table. Near the center of the stage stood a lonely Empire column, which supported nothing. Sunlight poured in through windows placed upstage behind a gauze which

FLOOR PLANS

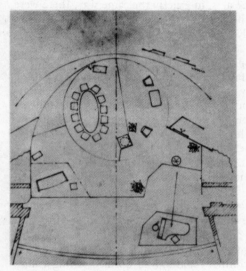

Act I

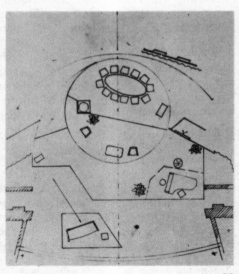

Act II

was hung along the circumference of the stage. The play of light and shadow on the column (caused by branches swaying behind the windows) and the soft twittering of birds created the atmosphere I wanted: spring, peace, and prosperity. A few minutes after the play had begun—more precisely, just before Vershinin's entrance—the light was cut on the windows behind the gauze, and they seemed to disappear. In the last three acts, in exactly the same way, there were illuminated windows in the Prozorov house, and an alley of birches (done three-dimensionally). And they disappeared in exactly the same way a few minutes after the act had begun. It seemed to me that these three-dimensional bits of scenery had served their purpose in indicating the place of action. All they could do further during the course of the play would be to distract the attention of the audience from the action itself. Dozens of spectators, whom we interrogated, did not even notice the disappearance of huge windows, whole walls of the house, and the long birch alley. No one in the audience felt that the interiors of the Prozorov house had disproportionately large room areas. We attributed this to the fact that we, and the designer Yunovich, rejected all reminders of the traditional box set.

We did not use the moving platforms often. During the first act only two lyric duets were drawn closer to the audience—Irina and Tuzenbakh, and Natasha and Andrey. There were four positions for the revolving stage during the first act: the initial one, with the table center stage; second, the dinner table moved upstage during Irina's scene with Tuzenbakh; third, when Natasha arrives, the dinner table returning to center stage, but brought closer to the audience; fourth, when Natasha runs from the table, the table again all the way upstage.

In order to delineate his intimate chamber scenes (Andrey's declaration of love, for example), Chekhov was obliged to put the dining table in the hall, behind the columns of the living room. The directors of early productions had to arrange circumstances which would justify the removal of unnecessary witnesses to the love scenes. Naturally, this led to partial reorganizations of the *mise-en-scène*. Fifty years ago, the actors would convey, by extremely conventional devices, that they had heard and seen nothing of what was going on right next to them. So that the lines of the individual scenes would not be drowned out, all the life around the table became soundless—by means of devices no less conventional. The moving platform made it possible and proper to employ a convention of the new theatre in lieu of the conventions of the old one. Our refusal to use a multitude of crosses[3] and to stop the life of

---

3. Movement on stage by actors in walking from one place to the next is said to be a "cross" or "crosses," usually written in cursive as an X [*Editor's note*].

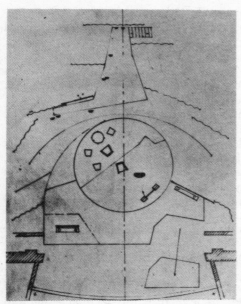

Act IV

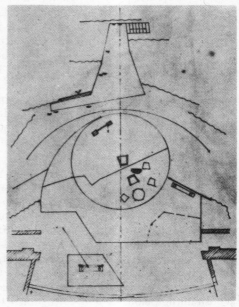

Act IV (*Finale*)

actors in the background made the atmosphere of the act immeasurably more believable and expressive. This convention helped create total truth to life.

In the second act, it seemed important to single out Masha's scene with Vershinin. They are happy. They are in love. But it is hard to talk about it, and is talk even necessary? In order that both of them be visible to the audience, they must be placed somewhat strangely, by convention. They could sit, shall we say, on a sofa. But elementary logic tells us that a sofa usually stands along a wall. Therefore, the sofa could only be placed squarely but upstage, or diagonally but to the left or right of house center. So we put the sofa on a wagon, and brought it almost to the very center of the covered orchestra. Masha and Vershinin were lit by the flicker from the embers in a fireplace. We didn't need the fireplace itself. And the hot and perpetually trembling flame that reflected on their faces, which already burned with that other flame of passion, relieved the actors of any necessity to sit close to one another. By bringing the actors as near as possible to the audience, they were obliged to remain almost motionless, and to feel love rather than act it. The audience became witnesses and accessories to the great mystery of the birth of feeling. Aside from all that, this solution guaranteed immunity from the banality to which love scenes are so prone.

It is hardly necessary to describe the production in detail. But I would like to discuss the play's finale. Olga, Irina and Masha watch the regiment leave the town, and move to follow them. A brisk, energetic march is playing, but the sisters are walking slowly— towards the revolving stage. The rhythm of the music becomes that not of a military but of a funeral march. The cast-iron grille of the gate drifts past them. In this way, it seems as though they are walking for a long time, and that for a long time they keep sight of those with whom the dream of a better life has been linked. I find the traditional staging—with the sisters watching the departure from behind the garden fence—to be too short and therefore less emotional than ours.

The revolving stage is more than a few years old, and the wagons were already in use in ancient Greek theatre. Neither the designer Yunovich nor I intend to take credit for that which we neither devised nor discovered. Only the experiment of applying the moving platform strikes us as a new perspective. And that's all. It is not for me to judge whether or not the experiment was successful.

The one thing of which I became firmly convinced after our production of *Three Sisters* is that today's Chekhov will not tolerate one stage second wasted on the reproduction of everyday detail. Verisimilitude alone is not worth much today. If Chekhov is not played with the idea of finding out what lies behind the external reproduction of life, and of revealing what lies behind the words and daily trivia and verisimilitude, then all the theatre's efforts will be fruitless.

Perhaps my experience in working on *Three Sisters* will prove useful to someone. But even for those who do not find my approach to the play persuasive, I have one bit of advice: Chekhov was ahead of his time, and the productions of his plays must not look to the past. And perhaps not even to the theatre of the present. Chekhov is a man of the future, and it is there that he must be sought.

Chekhov: The Major Plays

THOMAS G. WINNER

Chekhov's *Sea Gull* and Shakespeare's *Hamlet*: A Study of a Dramatic Device

Chekhov's use of literary allusions or echoes represents one of the most striking variations of the playwright's many evocative devices. Such devices, which stand outside the immediate action of his later plays, frequently are of symbolic significance and sometimes have a commentary function similar to that of the Greek chorus. Chekhov's use of literary or folklore allusions in his later plays is usually eclectic and may shift from author to author, folksong to folksong. Quotations from Shakespeare, especially from *Hamlet*, occur in various plays of Chekhov. But in *The Sea Gull* we find more than incidental background snatches from *Hamlet*. For *Hamlet* appears related to the total structure of the play, and it would seem that the image of *Hamlet* is, in the intent of the playwright, most intimately connected with the situations and characters of *The Sea Gull*.

It is the task of this paper to analyze the role of the Hamletian elements in *The Sea Gull* and to suggest their relationship to, and role in, the dramatic structure and intent of the play. These remarks are offered in a suggestive mood, since the complexity of the relationship of *Hamlet* and *The Sea Gull* could doubtlessly lead to various interpretations. But it is hoped that such a study will aid in clarifying a frequently puzzling aspect of *The Sea Gull*.

In Chekhov's works, in his notes and letters, we find ample evidence of his preoccupation with Shakespeare's tragedies. As early as 1882, Chekhov, at twenty-two years, reviewed an apparently poor performance of *Hamlet* in the Pushkin Theater in Moscow.[1] While attacking what he considered the misrepresentation of the character of Hamlet by the actor Ivanov-Kozelsky, he expressed strong praise for the play and its author, voicing the hope that Hamlet would aid in the much-needed rejuvenation of the Russian stage, even if played in mediocre fashion. "Better a badly acted Hamlet, than

---

1. This review, signed "Man Without Spleen," appeared in the journal *Moskva*, No. 3, 1882, and referred to the *Hamlet* performance of January 11, 1882. Cf. A. P. Chekhov, *Polnoe sobranie sočinenij i pisem* (Moscow, 1944–51), I, 489–91, 596–70, hereafter referred to as PS.

boring emptiness (*skučnoe ničego*)," he exclaimed. Hamlet, he said, had been represented as a whiner, especially in Act I, although "Hamlet was incapable of whining. A man's tears are valuable and must not be wasted (*nado dorožit' imi*) on the stage. Mr. Ivanov-Kozelsky," Chekhov complains, "was frightened of the ghost, so much so that one even felt pity for him. . . . Hamlet was a man of indecision, but he was never a coward."[2] This interpretation of Hamlet as a relatively strong personality must be kept in mind in considering the use Chekhov made of this character.

Unfortunately, we have no further record of any critical comment of Chekhov's concerning *Hamlet*, and thus much of our insight into Chekhov's interpretation of Shakespeare's much-disputed play must be left to inference. Incidental references to *Hamlet*, however, can be found frequently in Chekhov's letters and notebooks, revealing Chekhov's considerable preoccupation with this play.

References to *Hamlet* are frequent in Chekhov's creative writings. We know from his correspondence that in 1887 he was planning, in collaboration with his friend A. S. Lazarev-Gruzinsky, to produce what he called a "vaudeville" skit entitled *Hamlet, Prince of Denmark*.[3] However, the skit was never completed and there are no extant copies of a draft. The skit apparently was to serve primarily as a critique of existing Russian stage practices and while Chekhov's letters to Lazarev-Gruzinsky regarding this work reveal considerable information about his views of dramatic technique, they disclose nothing of his views on *Hamlet*. Chekhov's first "vaudeville," *Kalkhas* (1887), contains, among many excerpts lifted without alteration from the dramatic repertoire of the Russian stage, excerpts from *King Lear*, *Othello*, and *Hamlet*. The Hamletian references and quotations in the short stories and plays are too numerous to cite. It is not clear whether Chekhov read Shakespeare in the original or in Russian, though evidence available in his own notes and letters would tend to support the latter hypothesis, as he frequently refers admiringly to the Shakespeare translations of Peter Isaevich Veynberg (1830–1908), the dramatic theoretician and translator of Shakespeare, Goethe and Heine. At no point in Chekhov's writings is Shakespeare quoted in the original, nor could any reference to his knowledge of English be found.

What are some of the most striking characteristics of the use of Hamletian themes which permeate *The Sea Gull*? First the intensity of the Hamlet motif must be noted, in contrast to the incidental use of the theme in the other plays. *Hamlet* sounds, as it were, as a

2. PS, I, 490.
3. Cf. Letters No. 218, 322 (1887), PS, XIII.

constant background music to the play and references to Shakespeare's tragedy and its characters are contained not only in quotations and brief references, but in broad dramatic situations, as the play within the play, and in some aspects of the dramatic structure of Chekhov's play as well. Secondly, we must note the frequent identification of Chekhovian characters with characters from *Hamlet*, notably Treplyov with Hamlet and Arkadina with Gertrude. These identifications grow in intensity as they are presented against a background of other Hamletian themes. Particularly striking is the bandaging scene with its clear echoes of the closet scene between Hamlet and Gertrude. While the relationship between Arkadina and Treplyov shows some striking resemblances to the Hamlet-Gertrude relationship, they are by no means exactly parallel.[4] The disparities between the two relationships, as we shall see later, fulfill a definite function in Chekhov's dramatic plan. The relationship between Treplyov and Nina again evokes the echo of Hamlet's frustrated relationship to Ophelia. Nina's resemblance to Ophelia is less obvious, however, than Treplyov's to Hamlet, for, unlike Treplyov, she does not herself express a feeling of identification.

Chekhov's intent and method may be clarified by a chronological analysis of the Hamletian evocations in the play.

We meet Treplyov at the beginning of Act I and learn of his play and his relationship to Nina and his mother. "I love my mother," he tells Sorin, "but she is always running around with this writer." We are reminded of the much stronger words which Hamlet uses concerning the relationship of his uncle to his mother. The Hamletian mood is strengthened, as we learn that Treplyov has recently returned from the university, just as we meet Hamlet upon his return from Wittenberg. When Nina enters in the same scene, we are confronted with the first, yet weak, shadow of the Ophelia motif which also grows in intensity as the play progresses. We learn from her that her father strongly objects to her association with the Arkadina-Treplyov-Sorin household, as Polonius objects to Ophelia's association with Hamlet. We learn that Nina's mother, just like Ophelia's, is dead. More important, however, Nina introduces, for the first time, the symbol of the sea gull, the central symbol of the play. A discussion of the many-levelled significance of this image in relation to Nina and the central idea of the play cannot fall within the scope of this paper. There is, however, one aspect

---

4. David Magarshack (*Chekhov the Dramatist* [London, 1952], pp. 173, 192, 194–95, 198–99) discusses briefly the mother fixation parallel and has suggested some aspects of Chekhov's variations on this theme. Magarshack's analysis of parallels between *The Sea Gull* and *Hamlet*, however, is limited to the mother fixation problem and is not concerned with the many other aspects of the relationship of Chekhov's play to *Hamlet*.

of the sea gull image which we might consider. The sea gull is an image which gently hints at the connection we are to make between Nina and Ophelia. This is how Nina introduces the image: "I am drawn here, to the lake, like a sea gull." Here, there appears to be a combination of two related images: the free-flying, and later to be destroyed bird, and the lake, which also serves as the natural backdrop to Treplyov's symbolic play. As Chekhov's play progresses, we notice that the image of water is frequently associated with Nina. She mentions it as she first enters the stage; she sits against the background of water when she represents the world spirit in Treplyov's abortive play; in Act II she enters and interrupts a joint reading of Maupassant's *Sur l'eau*; she tells Trigorin of her love for the lake on the shores of which she was raised and Trigorin notes it down as "a subject for a small tale. . . ." Finally, her name, Zarechnaya, seems also related to the water image. We are thus led to associate Nina not only with the image of the sea gull, as she does herself, but also with the image of the closeness to water, an image with which the sea gull, as a water bird, is of course closely connected. Are we not again dealing here with a gentle echo from *Hamlet*? For water, so frequently representing the death image in Shakespeare, is closely tied to Ophelia's end.[5] It is my suggestion then, that throughout the play Nina is identified not only with the destroyed sea gull but also, unconsciously, with the fate of Ophelia, an identification which strengthens the premonition of her doom brought about by her relationship to the image of the bird.

We are now led into the central, climactic scene of the "play-within-the-play" which brings to the fore the conflict between Treplyov and his mother. Two quotations from *Hamlet* are introduced, just as Treplyov's play is about to begin, which direct our attention to the Hamlet theme and strengthen the association of the Treplyov-Arkadina and Hamlet-Gertrude relationships, an association which has already formed in our minds. We are thus reminded of *Hamlet*, just before the play begins, by the interplay between Treplyov and his mother. Arkadina quotes directly from Gertrude in the closet scene and Treplyov answers with a weakened paraphrase of Hamlet's remarks about his mother's adultery in the same scene, which further illustrates his conscious identification with Shakespeare's hero.

ARKADINA. [*reciting* Hamlet]
    My son! Thou turn'st my eye into my very soul.
    And there I see such black and grained spots as will not leave
        their tint.
TREPLYOV. [*from* Hamlet] And why did you give yourself to vice

5. Cf. *Hamlet*, IV, 7: after Gertrude informs Laertes of Ophelia's drowning— Laertes: "Too much water hast thou, poor Ophelia."

and sought love in the abyss of vice [*I dlja čego z ty poddalas' poroku, ljubvi iskala v bezdne prestuplen'ja.*][6]

Reminiscent of "The Murder of Gonzago" is Arkadina's assertion, after Treplyov's play has been abruptly terminated, that Treplyov regards it only as a joke, calling to mind Hamlet's answer to Claudius' query as to whether offense is meant in the "play-within-the-play": "No, no! They do but jest, poison in jest, no offence i'th'world."[7] Actually, both plays have, of course, a very serious intent. In objective function the two plays-within-the-play have very little relationship to each other: "The Murder of Gonzago" is the "mousetrap" by which Hamlet desires to entrap Claudius, while Treplyov's play represents his attempt to create a new form of art. But perhaps both plays-within-the-play have satirical elements also. It has been suggested that the "Murder" represents Shakespeare's burlesque of the style of melodramatic acting prevalent in his days.[8] It is clear that Chekhov's play-within-the-play is a parody, a parody on the aimlessness of the "decadent" drama of Chekhov's days. Furthermore, both plays are used as devices to project discussion concerned with the proper role of art: in *Hamlet* through Hamlet's admonition to the players ("Suit your action to your words. . . ." III, 2); in *The Sea Gull* in Nina's conversation with Treplyov,[9] as well as in Dorn's remark to Treplyov about Treplyov's failure to express an important idea in his "play" (Act I).[1] Both plays end abruptly and abortively. "The

<hr/>

6. Magarshack (*op. cit.*, p. 199) incorrectly quotes Hamlet's rejoinder to Gertrude:

HAMLET. Nay, but to live
In the rank sweat of an enseamed bed.
Stew'd in corruption, honeying and making love
Over the nasty sty.

Here Chekhov uses verbatim the *Hamlet* translation of N. A. Polevoj (*Gamlet, princ datskij*). This translation is available in the Folger Library in an edition of 1876 (*Škol'nyi Šekspir*, P. N. Polevoj, ed. [SPB, 1876]). It is interesting to note that among all the Hamlet translations which exised in Chekhov's time and which are available in this country, Polevoj's is the only one which deliberately softens Hamlet's reply to Gertrude. All other translations use a rather accurate translation of Hamlet's angry words hurled at his mother. (Cf. *Gamlet, tragedija v pjati dejstvijax*, M. V., transl. [SPB, 1828]; *Gamlet*, A. Kronenberg, transl., 2nd ed. [Moscow, 1861]; *Gamlet, princ datskij*, M. Zaguljajev, transl. [SPB, 1861]; *Gamlet*, A. L. Sokolovskij, transl. [SPB, 1883]; *Polnoe sobranie sočinenij V. Šekspira*, P. A. Kanshin,

transl. [SPB, 1893], vol. 1.) Whether Chekhov was aware of the softening of the lines in the translation he used and deliberately chose them to hint at the difference between Treplev and Hamlet, or whether he was acquainted only with Polevoj's translation, is unfortunately not clear.

7. *Hamlet*, III, 3.
8. Cf. J. Dover Wilson, *What Happened in Hamlet* (New York, 1935), p. 301.
9. NINA. Your play is hard to act. There are no live characters in it.

TREPLYOV. Live characters! One must depict life not as it is in reality and not as it ought to be, but as it presents itself to us in dreams. (Act I)

1. Both Nina's and Dorn's criticisms represent Chekhov's views. Cf.: "Remember that the writers whom we consider immortal or even just good, possess one very important common characteristic: they get somewhere and call upon us to go with them. We feel not only with our reason but with the whole of our being that they have an aim. . . . The best of them are realists and depict life as it is, but because every line they write is permeated . . . with the consciousness of a

Murder of Gonzago" ends because the "mousetrap," which had been its goal, has been sprung and Claudius has become aware of the parallel between the murder of Gonzago and that of Hamlet's father. The "play" ends with the success which Hamlet had desired. Treplyov's play, however, as an artistic experiment, ends in failure. Both plays end abruptly because of the offense they give to some of the spectators and because of the passions they arouse. The dismal ending of Treplyov's play is perhaps symbolic of Treplyov's inability to cope with a life which is filled with as many meaningless and empty formulae as is his play. The obvious echoes of the Hamlet "play-within-a-play" only help in pointing to Treplyov's impotence, which becomes increasingly clear during the course of the play.

At the beginning of Act II we find the ironic identification of Treplyov and Hamlet further strengthened by Masha's elevated vision of Treplyov: "When he reads, his eyes burn, his face turns pale; he has a beautiful, sad voice." Here Masha, whom we have already learned not to take seriously, evokes a pointed image of Hamlet, the "man of pale cast." But lest we forget the satirical element in this association, there is Sorin, acting as a chorus and snoring loudly, having fallen asleep at Masha's words. The very same scene brings to mind a further identification of Nina with Ophelia in Nina's refusal to support the man who loves her and in her attack on Treplyov's play, which she calls "uninteresting" in the presence of Arkadina. It is now, after the collapse of his "play" that Treplyov needs Nina more than ever and just at this crucial point she turns from him and refuses him the solace of love and of the moral support he craves, just as Ophelia fails to give Hamlet the support he needs after the cellarage scene.[2]

During the crucial scene in which the dejected Treplyov presents Nina with the gull he has shot and expresses his weariness of life, there enters the other protagonist, Trigorin, with whom the image of the unhappy bird is also forever connected. Here the use of the Hamlet theme is rather complex. As Trigorin, whom Treplyov has learned to hate and fear as a rival in love as well as art (and the two concepts are here symbolically one), enters reading a book, Treplyov refers to him as walking like Hamlet and bitterly quotes Hamlet's "Words, words, words." To fathom the significance of this passage, we must again turn to *Hamlet* (II, 2). The lines quoted by Treplyov occur after Polonius has plotted with the King and Queen to "loose" Ophelia on Hamlet in order to determine the cause of his distemper. J. Dover Wilson[3] holds that Hamlet has overheard

goal . . . one feels not only life as it is in reality, but as it should be and that is what delights you." (Chekhov, letter to Suvorin, No. 1186, November 25, 1892,

PS, XV, 446.)
2. The cellarage scene occurs in Act I, Scene iv, lines 148–90 [*Editor's note*].
3. Wilson, op cit., p. 106.

this plot and thus he accuses Polonius of being a "fishmonger" (in Elizabethan terms: a procurer) and of prostituting Ophelia to entrap him. This interchange is followed by Hamlet's expression of his weariness of life.[4] Apparently Treplyov is reminded of the Hamlet-Polonius scene as Trigorin enters. He is also in despair over his disintegrating relationship to Nina, which he blames on Trigorin (with only partial justification). His despair is accentuated by his realization that his play has been an artistic failure. While he would like openly to taunt Trigorin, as Hamlet had taunted Polonius, he—unlike Hamlet—satisfies himself with a sneer and walks away, thus avoiding decisive action.

After Treplyov's first suicide attempt, of which we hear in Act III, Trigorin tells us that Treplyov plans to challenge him to a duel. Here the double meaning of the Treplyov-Hamlet identification becomes more pronounced, since Treplyov of course never challenges his opponent. While Hamlet fulfills the challenge of his life by killing Claudius, Treplyov only meekly suggests a duel and is ready to forgive and forget at his mother's behest.

The scene which bears the closest single reference to *Hamlet* and which sheds further light on Chekhov's skillful manipulation of the Hamlet theme, is the bandaging scene in the third act, presented in a manner which must remind us of the closet scene (III, 4), in which Hamlet, in passionate tones, accuses his mother of adultery. We are the more let down when Treplyov gives further illustration of his immature emotions. He feels sorry for himself and asks from his mother the sympathy which he no longer can get from Nina. He is incapable of a mature relationship with his mother, or with anyone else, just as he is incapable of producing real works of art. And when he chides his mother over her affair with Trigorin, his is a childish complaint. His squabble with his mother never attains the tragic; it remains on the level of the petty: a silly, name-calling duel, soon patched up by a sentimental reconciliation and an acceptance by Treplyov of Arkadina's request to be reconciled with Trigorin. When the latter appears, again in the Hamletian pose of reading a book as he walks on the stage, Treplyov flees, embarrassed and afraid of meeting his rival. Hamlet, in the end of the closet scene, breaks down Gertrude's defenses and forces her to speak the very words which Arkadina quotes to Treplyov before the beginning of his play. Hamlet, unlike Treplyov, never weakens in his tirade against Gertrude. And when, after the ghost's disappear-

---

4. POL. What are you reading, my lord?
H. Words, words, words.
  and then . . .
POL. . . . Will you walk out of the air, my lord?
H. Into my grave?

POL. . . . I most humbly take my leave of you.
H. You cannot, sir, take from me anything that I will more willingly part withal—except my life, except my life, except my life.

ance, he speaks kind words to his mother ("I must be cruel only to be kind"), these are the result of his conviction that his argument has been at least partially successful. Hamlet thus can afford to be tender from a mature conviction of the righteousness of his cause. Treplyov, however, can be tender only when he assumes the position of a child.

It is the events in Act IV which point to the true significance of the Hamlet theme in *The Sea Gull*. The complex relationship of the characters of *The Sea Gull* with their Hamletian counterparts has been built up in the minds of the audience. While Treplyov continues to think of himself as a Hamlet, charged with the task of righting the wrongs in the state of literature, the audience has become increasingly aware of the contradictions and irony of this identification. The Nina-Ophelia association is also strongly suggested by now, though with none of the ironic overtones with which Chekhov tempers the Treplyov-Hamlet self-identification.

During the final dialogue between Treplyov and Nina the intent of Chekhov's use of the *Hamlet* motif becomes more than clear. For, in the final interview between Treplyov and Nina, which brings us to what we might term a Chekhovian peripetia,[5] we are forcibly made to realize that the two protagonists are not what they had pictured themselves to be. Nina, far from being an unhappy Ophelia, who is destroyed as the unhappy bird was destroyed, is actually the only one in the play who has had the strength to realize her convictions and to achieve the aim for which Treplyov has suffered: true art. She has outgrown her youthful romanticism and conquered the sufferings of her earlier unsuccessful attempts to act; and while Treplyov has only talked, she has finally met reality. "Know how to bear your cross and have faith," she tells Treplyov, "I have faith and I no longer hurt. And when I think of my profession, I am not afraid of life." How very unlike Ophelia and the sea gull symbol as Nina had applied it to herself! "I am a sea gull," she keeps repeating to Treplyov in the state of semi-hysteria into which she has been brought by walking back into past memories. But no, she interrupts herself, "that is not so" (*ne to*). And Treplyov suddenly realizes that the table of symbols has been turned: Nina is neither a sea gull nor an Ophelia. And it comes to him with terrifying force that he is not a Hamlet, but that a part of the sea gull symbol actually applies to him.

Thus what we have is a Hamlet in the wrong key. Treplyov does not, as does Hamlet, end in grandeur; instead, he ends "not with a bang, but a whimper,"[6] as a total failure, walking quietly out of

5. Or reversal [*Editor's note*].
6. The final four lines of a poem, "The Hollow Men" (1925), by T. S. Eliot

(1888–1965), British poet and essayist who was born in the United States: "This is the way the world ends/This is the

life, his last remarks being concern lest his mother be irritated by Nina's visit. The hero is an artist who failed, instead of a defender of kingdoms. For Treplyov does what Chekhov, in his early essay, had asserted that the Prince of Denmark never did: he whines; he *is* a coward who poses as the bearer of Hamlet's indecision to hide from himself his inability to act in the creation of the new art which he craves.

The finale in *Hamlet*, beginning with the graveyard scene, is death. So is Treplyov's finale. But what difference in deaths. There is no *catharsis* in Treplyov's death as there is in Hamlet's. Hamlet, in the end, has abandoned his suicidal ideas. His antic disposition and indecision are gone and he has his mind on revenge. He is noble, though he has a weak strain, while Treplyov is weak, though we cannot deny him a noble strain.

It is vital, says J. D. Wilson,[7] to Shakespeare's purpose that we maintain our sympathy with Hamlet right to the end. "Rob us of our respect for the hero and *Hamlet* ceases to be a tragedy." Yet, this is essentially what Chekhov has done with his hero. We cannot respect this self-styled Hamlet, though we cannot deny him our sympathy. While *Hamlet* is a tragedy about genius, perhaps we might call Treplyov's, in so far as it is a tragedy, a tragedy about mediocrity, a mediocrity which is sharpened in our minds by the constant allusions to *Hamlet*.

Thus, the use of the *Hamlet* theme in *The Sea Gull* has fulfilled a dual purpose. It has acted as an ironic commentary on Treplyov's pretensions. By suggesting to us somewhat parallel situations and thus playing with our expectations, it has also been used by Chekhov as a device for heightening the tension, as we are led, in Act IV, into a variant of the Aristotelian perpetia.

ERIC BENTLEY

Craftsmanship in *Uncle Vanya*

The Anglo-American theatre finds it possible to get along without the services of most of the best playwrights. Aeschylus, Lope de Vega, Racine, Molière, Schiller, Strindberg—one could prolong indefinitely the list of great dramatists who are practically unknown in England and America except to scholars. Two cases of popularity in spite of greatness are, of course, Shakespeare and Shaw, who have this in common: that they can be enjoyed without being taken seriously. And then there is Chekhov.

---

way the world ends/This is the way the world ends/Not with a bang but a whim-

per" [*Editor's note*].
7. Wilson, p. 102.

It is easy to make over a play by Shaw or by Shakespeare into a Broadway show. But why is Chekhov preserved from the general oblivion? Why is it that scarcely a year passes without a major Broadway or West End production of a Chekhov play? Chekhov's plays—at least by reputation, which in commercial theatre is the important thing—are plotless, monotonous, drab, and intellectual: find the opposites of these four adjectives and you have a recipe for a smash hit.

Those who are responsible for productions of Chekhov in London and New York know the commodity theatre. Some of them are conscious rebels against the whole system. Others are simply genuine artists who, if not altogether consciously, are afflicted with guilt; to do Chekhov is for them a gesture of rebellion or atonement, as to do Shakespeare or Shaw is not. It is as if the theatre remembers Chekhov when it remembers its conscience.

The rebels of the theatre know their Chekhov and love him; it is another question whether they understand him. Very few people seem to have given his work the careful examination it requires. Handsome tributes have been paid Chekhov by Stanislavsky, Nemirovich-Danchenko, and Gorky, among his countrymen; and since being taken up by Middleton Murry's circle thirty years ago, he has enjoyed a high literary reputation in England and America. The little book by William Gerhardi[1] and the notes and *obiter dicta*[2] of such critics as Stark Young and Francis Fergusson are, however, too fragmentary and impressionistic to constitute a critical appraisal. They have helped to establish more accurate general ideas about Chekhov's art. They have not inquired too rigorously in what that art consists.

I am prompted to start such an enquiry by the old Vic's engrossing presentation of *Uncle Vanya* in New York. Although *Vanya* is the least well known of Chekhov's four dramatic masterpieces, it is—I find—a good play to start a critical exploration with because it exists in two versions—one mature Chekhov, the other an immature draft. To read both is to discover the direction and intention of Chekhov's development. It is also to learn something about the art of rewriting when not practiced by mere play-doctors. There is a lesson here for playwrights. For we are losing the conception of the writer as an artist who by quiet discipline steadily develops. In the twentieth century a writer becomes an event with his first best-seller, or smash hit, and then spends the rest of his life repeating the performance—or vainly trying to.

Chekhov's earlier version—*The Wood Demon*—is what Holly-

1. W. Gerhardi, *Anton Chekhov: A Critical Study*. New York, 1923 [*Editor's note*].

2. Literally, "a word or speech in passing" [*Editor's note*].

wood would call a comedy drama: that is, a farce spiced with melodrama. It tells the story of three couples: a vain Professor,[3] and his young second wife, Yelena; Astrov, the local doctor, who is nicknamed the Wood Demon because of his passion for forestry, and Sonya, the Professor's daughter by his first marriage; finally, a young man and woman named Fyodor and Julia. The action consists to a great extent in banal comedic crisscrossing of erotic interests. Julia's brother seems for a time to be after Sonya. Yelena is coveted rather casually by Fyodor and more persistently by Uncle Vanya, the brother of the Professor's first wife. Rival suitors, eternal triangles, theatric adultery! It is not a play to take too seriously. Although in the third act there is a climax when Uncle Vanya shoots himself, Chekhov tries in the last and fourth act to re-establish the mode of light comedy by pairing off all three couples before bringing down the curtain on his happy ending.

Yet even in *The Wood Demon* there is much that is "pure Chekhov." The happy ending does not convince, because Chekhov has created a situation that cannot find so easy an outcome. He has created people who cannot possibly be happy ever after. He has struck so deep a note that the play cannot quite, in its last act, become funny again.

The death of Vanya is melodrama, yet it has poignancy too, and one might feel that, if it should be altered, the changes should be in the direction of realism. The plot centers on property. The estate was the dowry of Vanya's sister, the Professor's first wife. Vanya put ten years' work into paying off the mortgage. The present owner is the daughter of the first marriage, Sonya. The Professor, however, thinks he can safely speak of "our estate" and propose to sell it, so he can live in a Finnish villa on the proceeds. It is the shock of this proposal, coming on top of his discovery that the Professor, in whom he has so long believed, is an intellectual fraud—coming on top of his infatuation with Yelena—that drives Vanya to suicide. And if this situation seems already to be asking for realistic treatment, what are we to say to the aftermath? Yelena leaves her husband, but is unable to sustain this "melodramatic" effort. She comes back to him, defeated yet not contrite: "Well, take me, statue of the commander, and go to hell with me in your twenty-six dismal rooms!"[4]

The Wood Demon is a conventional play trying, so to speak, to be something else. In *Uncle Vanya*, rewritten, it succeeds. Perhaps

3. In cases where Chekhov changed the name of a character for his later version, I have used the later name only, to avoid confusion. And I have called each person by the designation that non-Russians most easily remember: "the Professor," "Waffles," "Astrov," "Sonya."

4. In general I quote from published translations of Chekhov: the English of *The Wood Demon* is S. S. Koteliansky's; of *Uncle Vanya*, Constance Garnett's. But I have altered these versions, consulting the Russian original wherever alteration seemed desirable.

Chekhov began by retouching his ending and was led back and back into his play until he had revised everything but the initial situation. He keeps the starting-point of his fable, but alters the whole outcome. Vanya does not shoot himself; he fires his pistol at the Professor, and misses. Consequently the last act has quite a different point of departure. Yelena does not run away from her husband. He decides to leave, and she goes with him. Astrov, in the later version, does not love Sonya; he and she end in isolation. Vanya is not dead or in the condemned cell; but he is not happy.

To the Broadway script-writer, also concerned with the rewriting of plays (especially if in an early version a likable character shoots himself), these alterations of Chekhov's would presumably seem unaccountable. They would look like a deliberate elimination of the dramatic element. Has not Prince Mirsky told us that Chekhov is an undramatic dramatist? The odd thing is only that he could be so dramatic *before* he rewrote. The matter is worth looking into.

Chekhov's theatre, like Ibsen's, is psychological. If Chekhov changed his story, it must be either because he later felt that his old characters would act differently or because he wanted to create more interesting characters. The four people who emerge in the later version as the protagonists are different from their prototypes in *The Wood Demon*, and are differently situated. Although Sonya still loves Astrov, her love is not returned. This fact is one among many that make the later ending Chekhovian: Sonya and Astrov resign themselves to lives of labor without romance. Vanya is not resolute enough for suicide. His discontent takes form as resentment against the author of his misery. And yet, if missing his aim at such close quarters be an accident, it is surely one of those unconsciously willed accidents that Freud wrote of. Vanya is no murderer. His outburst is rightly dismissed as a tantrum by his fellows, none of whom dreams of calling the police. Just as Vanya is the kind of man who does not kill, Yelena is the kind of woman who does not run away from her husband, even temporarily.

In the earlier version the fates of the characters are settled; in the later they are unsettled. In the earlier version they are settled, moreover, not by their own nature or by force of circumstance, but by theatrical convention. In the later, their fate is unsettled because that is Chekhov's view of the truth. Nobody dies. Nobody is paired off. And the general point is clear: life knows no endings, happy or tragic. (Shaw once congratulated Chekhov on the discovery that the tragedy of the Hedda Gablers is, in real life, precisely that they do *not* shoot themselves.) The special satiric point is also familiar: Chekhov's Russians are chronically indecisive people. What is perhaps not so easy to grasp is the effect of a more mature psychology upon dramaturgy. Chekhov has destroyed the climax in his third act and the happy consummation in his fourth. These two alterations alone presuppose a radically different dramatic form.

The framework of the new play is the attractive pattern of arrival and departure: the action is what happens in the short space of time between the arrival of the Professor and his wife on their country estate and their departure from it. The unity of the play is discovered by asking the question: what effect has the visit upon the visited—that is, upon Vanya, Sonya, and Astrov? This question as it stands could not be asked of *The Wood Demon,* for in that play the Professor and Yelena do not depart, and Vanya is dead before the end. As to the effect of the Professor's arrival, it is to change and spoil everything. His big moment—the moment when he announces his intention to sell the estate—leads to reversal in Aritotle's sense, the decisive point at which the whole direction of the narrative turns about. This is Uncle Vanya's suicide. Vanya's futile shots, in the later version, are a kind of mock reversal. It cannot even be said that they make the Professor change his mind, for he had begun to change it already—as soon as Vanya protested. Mechanical, classroom analysis would no doubt locate the climax of the play in the shooting. But the climax is an anticlimax. If one of our scriptwriters went to work on it, his "rewrite" would be *The Wood Demon* all over again, his principle of revision being exactly the opposite of Chekhov's. What Chekhov is after, I think, is not reversal but recognition—also in Aristotle's sense, "the change from ignorance to knowledge." In Aristotle's sense, but with a Chekhovian application.

In the Greeks, in much French drama, and in Ibsen, recognition means the discovery of a secret which reveals that things are not what all these years they have seemed to be. In *Uncle Vanya,* recognition means that what all these years seemed to be so, though one hesitated to believe it, really is so and will remain so. This is Vanya's discovery and gradually (in the course of the ensuing last act) that of the others. Thus Chekhov has created a kind of recognition which is all his own. In Ibsen the terrible thing is that the surface of everyday life is a smooth deception. In Chekhov the terrible thing is that the surface of everyday life is itself a kind of tragedy. In Ibsen the whole surface of life is suddenly burst by volcanic eruption. In Chekhov the crust is all too firm; the volcanic energies of men have no chance of emerging. *Uncle Vanya* opens with a rather rhetorical suggestion that this *might* be so. It ends with the knowledge that it certainly *is* so, a knowledge shared by all the characters who are capable of knowledge—Astrov, Vanya, Sonya, and Yelena. This growth from ignorance to knowledge is, perhaps, our cardinal experience of the play (the moment of recognition, or experimental proof, being Vanya's outburst *before* the shooting).

Aristotle says that the change from ignorance to knowledge produces "love or hate between the persons destined by the poet for good or bad fortune." But only in *The Wood Demon*, where there is no real change from ignorance to knowledge, could the outcome be stated in such round terms. Nobody's fortune at the end of *Uncle Vanya* is as good or bad as it might be; nobody is very conclusively loving or hating. Here again Chekhov is avoiding the black and the white, the tragic and the comic, and is attempting the halftone, the tragicomic.

If, as has been suggested, the action consists in the effect of the presence of the Professor and Yelena upon Sonya, Vanya, and Astrov, we naturally ask: what *was* that effect? To answer this question for the subtlest of the characters—Astrov—is to see far into Chekhov's art. In *The Wood Demon* the effect is nil. The action has not yet been unified. It lies buried in the chaos of Chekhov's materials. In *Uncle Vanya*, however, there is a thread of continuity. We are first told that Astrov is a man with no time for women. We then learn (and there is no trace of this in *The Wood Demon*) that he is infatuated with Yelena. In *The Wood Demon*, Sonya gets Astrov in the end. In *Uncle Vanya*, when Astrov gives up Yelena, he resigns himself to his old role of living without love. The old routine—in this as in other respects—resumes its sway.

The later version of this part of the story includes two splendid scenes that were not in *The Wood Demon*, even embryonically. One is the first of the two climaxes in Act III—when Yelena sounds out Astrov on Sonya's behalf. Astrov reveals that it is Yelena he loves, and he is kissing her when Vanya enters. The second is Astrov's parting from Yelena in the last act, a scene so subtle that Stanislavsky himself misinterpreted it: he held that Astrov was still madly in love with Yelena and was clutching at her as a dying man clutches at a straw. Chekhov had to point out in a letter that this is not so. What really happens is less histrionic and more Chekhovian. The parting kiss is passionless on Astrov's side. This time it is Yelena who feels a little passion. Not very much, though. For both, the kiss is a tribute to the Might-Have-Been.

Astrov's failure to return Sonya's love is not a result of the Professor's visit; he had failed to return it even before the Professor's arrival. The effect of the visit is to confirm (as part of the general Chekhovian pattern) the fact that what seems to be so is so; that what has been will be; that nothing has changed. How much difference has the visit made? It has made the case much sadder. Beforehand Astrov had maintained, and presumably believed, that he was indifferent to women. Afterward we know that it is Sonya in particular to whom he is indifferent. The "wood demon," devoted to the creative and the natural, can love only Yelena the artificial, the sterile, the useless. To Sonya, the good, the competent, the constructive, he is indifferent.

The Professor's visit clarifies Astrov's situation—indeed, his whole nature. True, he had already confessed himself a failure in some of the opening speeches of the play. The uninitiated must certainly find it strange (despite the august precedent of *Antony and Cleopatra*) that the play starts with a summary of the whole disaster. Yet the rest of the play, anything but a gratuitous appendix, is the proof that Astrov, who perhaps could not quite believe himself at the beginning, is right after all. The action of the play is his chance to disprove his own thesis—a chance that he misses, that he was bound to miss, being what he was. What was he, then? In the earlier version he had been known as the Wood Demon or Spirit of the Forest, and in *Uncle Vanya* the long speeches are retained in which he advances his ideal of the natural, the growing, the beautiful. Because he also speaks of great ennobling changes in the future of the race (not unlike those mentioned in the peroration of Trotsky's *Literature and Revolution*), he has been taken to be a prophet of a great political future for Russia in the twentieth century. But this would be wrenching his remarks from their context. Astrov is not to be congratulated on his beautiful dreams; he is to be pitied. His hope that mankind will some day do something good operates as an excuse for doing nothing now. It is an expression of his own futility, and Astrov knows it. Even in the early version he was not really a Wood Demon. That was only the ironical nickname of a crank. In the later version even the nickname has gone,[5] and Astrov is even more of a crank. When Yelena arrives, he leaves his forests to rot. Clearly they were no real fulfillment of his nature, but an old-maidish hobby, like Persian cats. They were *ersatz*; and as soon as something else seemed to offer itself, Astrov made his futile attempt at seduction. Freud would have enjoyed the revealing quality of his last pathetic proposal that Yelena should give herself to him in the depth of the forest.

The actor, of course, should not make Astrov *too* negative. If one school of opinion romanticizes all Chekhov characters who dream of the future, another, even more vulgar, sees them as weaklings and nothing else. Chekhov followed Ibsen in portraying the average mediocre man—*l'homme moyen sensuel*—without ever following the extreme naturalists in their concern with the utterly downtrod-

---

5. From the title as well as from the dialogue. For not only does the center of interest shift from Astrov to Vanya, but Chekhov deliberately drops from his masthead the evocative *demon* in favor of the utterly banal *uncle*. If the name *Vanya* sounds exotic to non-Russian ears, one has to know that it is the equivalent of *Jack*.

den, the inarticulate, the semihuman. His people are no weaker than ninety-nine out of every hundred members of his audience. That is to say, they are very weak, but there are also elements of protest and revolt in them, traces of will-power, some dim sense of responsibility. If his characters never reach fulfillment, it is not because they were always without potentialities. In fact, Chekhov's sustained point is precisely that these weeping, squirming, suffering creatures *might have been men*. And because Chekhov feels this, there is emotion, movement, tension, interplay, dialectic, in his plays. He never could have written a play like Galsworthy's *Justice*, in which the suffering creature is as much an insect as a man.

The Might-Have-Been is Chekhov's *idée fixe*. His people do not dream only of what could never be, or what could come only after thousands of years; they dream of what their lives actually could have been. They spring from a conviction of human potentiality—which is what separates Chekhov from the real misanthropes of modern literature. Astrov moves us because we can readily feel how fully human he might have been, how he has dwindled, under the influence of "country life," from a thinker to a crank, from a man of feeling to a philanderer. "It is strange somehow," he says to Yelena in the last scene, "we have got to know each other, and all at once for some reason—we shall never meet again. So it is with everything in this world." Such lines might be found in any piece of sentimental theater. But why is it that Chekhov's famous "elegiac note" is, in the full context, deeply moving? Is it not because the sense of death is accompanied with so rich a sense of life and the possible worth of living?

Chekhov had a feeling for the unity of the drama, yet his sense of the richness of life kept him clear of formalism. He enriched his dramas in ways that belong to no school and that, at least in their effect, are peculiar to himself. While others tried to revive poetic drama by putting symbolist verse in the mouths of their characters, or simply by imitating the verse drama of the past, Chekhov found poetry within the world of realism. By this is meant not only that he used symbols. Symbolism of a stagy kind was familiar on the boulevards and still is. The Broadway title *Skylark* is symbolic in exactly the same way as *The Wild Duck* and *The Sea Gull*. It is rather the use to which Chekhov puts the symbol that is remarkable. We have seen, for instance, what he makes of his "wood demon." This is not merely a matter of Astrov's character. Chekhov's symbols spread themselves, like Ibsen's, over a large territory. They are a path to the imagination and to those deeper passions which in our latter-day drama are seldom worn on the sleeve. Thus if a symbol in Chekhov is explained—in the manner of the *raisonneur*—the explanation blazes like a denunciation. Yelena says: "As Astrov was just saying,

you are all recklessly destroying the forests and soon there will be
nothing left on the earth. In the same way you recklessly destroy
human beings, and soon, thanks to you, there will be no fidelity, no
purity, no capacity for sacrifice left on the earth either! Why is it
you can never look at a woman with indifference unless she is
yours? That doctor is right: it's because there is a devil of destruction in all of you. You have no mercy on woods or birds or women
or one another."

What a paradox: our playwrights, who plump for the passions
(like O'Neill) are superficial, and Chekhov, who pretends to show
us only the surface (who, as I have said, writes the tragedy of the
surface), is passionate and deep! No modern playwright has presented elemental passions more truly. Both versions of *Uncle Vanya*
are the battleground of two conflicting impulses—the impulse to
destroy and the impulse to create. In *The Wood Demon* the conflict
is simple: Vanya's destructive passion reaches a logical end in suicide, Astrov's creative passion a logical end in happiness ever after.
In *Uncle Vanya* the pattern is complex: Vanya's destructive passion
reaches a pseudo-climax in his pistol-shots, and a pseudo-culmina-
tion in bitter resignation. Astrov's creative passion has found no
outlet. Unsatisfied by his forests, he is fascinated by Yelena. His
ending is the same as Vanya's—isolation. The destructive passions
do not destroy; the creative passions do not create. Or, rather, both
impulses are crushed in the daily routine, crushed by boredom and
triviality. Both Vanya and Astrov have been suffering a gradual
erosion and will continue to do so. They cry out. "I have not lived,
not lived . . . I have ruined and wasted the best years of my life." "I
have grown old, I have worked too hard, I have grown vulgar, all
my feelings are blunted, and I believe I am not capable of being
fond of anyone." Chekhov's people never quite become wounded
animals like the Greek tragic heroes. But through what modern
playwright does suffering speak more poignantly?

At a time when Chekhov is valued for his finer shades, it is
worth stressing his simplicity and strength, his depth and intensity—
provided we remember that these qualities require just as prodigious
a technique for their expression, that they depend just as much on
details. Look at the first two acts of *Uncle Vanya*. While the later
acts differ from *The Wood Demon* in their whole narrative, the first
two differ chiefly in their disposition of the material. Act I of *The
Wood Demon* is a rather conventional bit of exposition: we get to
know the eleven principals and we learn that Vanya is in love with
Yelena. In *Uncle Vanya* Chekhov gives himself more elbow-room
by cutting down the number of characters: Julia and her brother,
Fyodor and his father are eliminated. The act is no longer mere

exposition in the naturalistic manner (people meeting and asking questions like "Whom did you write to?" so that the reply can be given: "I wrote to Sonya"). The principle of organization is what one often hears called "musical." (The word *poetic* is surely more accurate, but music is the accepted metaphor.) The evening opens, we might say, with a little overture in which themes from the body of the play are heard. "I may well look old!" It is Astrov speaking. "And life is tedious, stupid, dirty. Life just drags on." The theme of human deterioration is followed by the theme of aspiration: "Those who will live a hundred or two hundred years after us, for whom we are struggling now to beat out a road, will they remember and say a good word for us?" The overture ends; the play begins.

Analyses of the structure of plays seldom fail to tell us where the climax lies, where the exposition is completed, and how the play ends, but they often omit a more obtrusive factor—the *principle of motion*, the way in which a play copes with its medium, with time-sequence. In general, the nineteenth-century drama proceeded upon the principles of boulevard drama (as triumphantly practiced by Scribe).[6] To deal with such a play, terms like *exposition, complication*, and *denouement* are perfectly adequate because the play is, like most fiction, primarily a pattern of suspense. The "musical" principle of motion, however, does not reflect a preoccupation with suspense. That is why many devotees of popular drama are bored by Chekhov.

Consider even smaller things than the use of overture. Consider the dynamics of the first three lines in *Uncle Vanya*. The scene is one of Chekhov's gardens. Astrov is sitting with the Nurse. She offers him tea. She offers him vodka, but he is not a regular vodka-drinker. "Besides, it's stifling," he says; and there is a lull in the conversation. To the Broadway producer this is a good opening because it gives latecomers a chance to take their seats without missing anything. To Chekhov these little exchanges, these sultry pauses, are the bricks out of which a drama is built.

What makes Chekhov seem most formless is precisely the means by which he achieves strict form—namely, the series of tea-drinkings, arrivals, departures, meals, dances, family gatherings, casual conversations, of which his plays are made. As we have seen, Chekhov works with a highly unified action. He presents it, however, not in the centralized, simplified manner of Sophocles or Ibsen, but obliquely, indirectly, quasi-naturally. The rhythm of the play is

6. Eugène Scribe (1791–1861), probably the most popular playwright of all time (that is, he achieved complete adoration from the public in his own lifetime), wrote more than three hundred plays, almost every one of which was described as a *pièce bien faite*, or "well-made play," the usual fare produced at theatres located on the boulevards in Paria—outside the established, subsidized theatres like the Comédie Française; hence the term "boulevard drama," which appealed to the middle and lower classes [*Editor's note*].

leisurely yet broken and, to suspense-lovers, baffling. It would be an exaggeration to say that there is no story and that the succession of scenes marks simply an advance in our knowledge of a situation that does not change. Yet people who cannot interest themselves in this kind of development as well as in straightforward story-telling will not be interested in Chekhov's plays any more than they would be in Henry James's novels. Chekhov does tell a story—the gifts of one of the greatest raconteurs are not in abeyance in his plays—but his method is to let both his narrative and his situation leak out, so to speak, through domestic gatherings, formal and casual. This is his principle of motion.

The method requires two extraordinary gifts: the mastery of "petty" realistic material and the ability to go beyond sheer *Sachlichkeit*—materiality, factuality—to imagination and thought. (Galsworthy, for example, seems to have possessed neither of these gifts—certainly not the second.) Now, the whole Stanislavsky school of acting and directing is testimony that Chekhov was successfully *sachlich*—that is, not only accurate, but significantly precise, concrete, ironic (like Jane Austen). The art by which a special importance is imparted to everyday objects is familiar enough in fiction; on the stage, Chekhov is one of its few masters. On the stage, moreover, the *Sachlichkeit* may more often consist in a piece of business—I shall never forget Astrov, as played by Olivier, buttoning his coat—than in a piece of furniture. Chekhov was so far from being the average novelist-turned-dramatist that he used the peculiarly theatrical *Sachlichkeit* with the skill of a veteran of the footlights. The first entrance of Vanya, for instance, is achieved this way (compare it with the entrance of the matinee idol in a boulevard comedy):

VANYA. [*comes out of the house; he has had a nap after lunch and looks rumpled; he sits down on the garden-seat and straightens his fashionable tie*] Yes. . . . [*Pause*] Yes. . . .

(Those who are used to the long novelistic stage-directions of Shaw and O'Neill should remember that Chekhov, like Ibsen, added stage-directions only here and there. But the few that do exist show an absolute mastery.)

How did Chekhov transcend mere *Sachlichkeit* and achieve a drama of imagination and thought? Chiefly, I think, by combining the most minute attention to realistic detail with a rigorous sense of form. He diverges widely from all the Western realists—though not so widely from his Russian predecessors such as Turgenev, whose *Month in the Country* could be palmed off as a Chekhov play on more discerning people than most drama critics—and his divergences are often in the preservation of elements of style and stylization, which naturalism prided itself it had discarded. Most obvious among these is the soliloquy. Chekhov does not let his people confide in the audience, but he does use the kind of soliloquy in which the character thinks out loud; and where there is no traditional device for achieving a certain kind of beginning or ending, he constructs for himself a set piece that will do his job. In *Uncle Vanya*, if there may be said to be an overture, played by Astrov, there may also be said to be a finale, played by Sonya. For evidence of Chekhov's theatrical talents one should notice the visual and auditory components of this final minute of the play. We have just heard the bells jingling as the Professor and his wife drive off, leaving the others to their desolation. "Waffles"—one of the neighbors—is softly tuning his guitar. Vanya's mother is reading. Vanya "passes his hand over" Sonya's hair:

> SONYA. We must go on living! [*Pause*] We shall go on living, Uncle Vanya! We shall live through a long, long chain of days and weary evenings; we shall patiently bear the trials that fate sends us; we shall work for others, both now and in our old age, and have no rest; and when our time comes we shall die without a murmur, and there beyond the grave we shall say that we have suffered, that we have wept, that our life has been bitter to us, and God will have pity on us, and you and I, uncle, dear uncle, shall see a life that is bright, lovely, beautiful. We shall rejoice and look back at these troubles of ours with tenderness, with a smile—and we shall have rest. I have faith, uncle, fervent, passionate faith. [*Slips on her knees before him and lays her head on his hands; in a weary voice.*] We shall rest! [WAFFLES *softly plays on the guitar.*] We shall rest! We shall hear the angels; we shall see all heaven lit with radiance, we shall see all earthly evil, all our sufferings, drowned in mercy, which will fill the whole world, and our life will be peaceful, gentle, sweet like a caress. I have faith, I have faith. [*Wipes away his tears with her handkerchief.*] Poor, poor Uncle Vanya, you are crying. [*Through her tears.*] You have had no joy in your life, but wait, Uncle Vanya, wait. We shall rest. [*Puts her arm around him.*] We shall rest! [*The* WATCHMAN *taps;* WAFFLES *plays softly;* VANYA'S *mother makes notes on the margin of her pamphlet; the* NURSE *knits her stocking.*] We shall rest! [*Curtain drops slowly.*]

The silence, the music, the watchman's tapping, the postures, the gestures, the prose with its rhythmic repetitions and melancholy import—these compose an image, if a stage picture with its words and music may be called an image, such as the drama has seldom known since Shakespeare. True, in our time the background music of movies and the noises-off in radio drama have made us see the dangers in this sort of theatricality. But Chekhov knew without these awful examples where to draw the line

A weakness of much realistic literature is that it deals with inarticulate people. The novelist can of course supply in narrative and description what his milieu lacks in conversation, but the dramatist has no recourse—except to the extent that drama is expressed not in words but in action. Chekhov's realistic milieu, however, is, like Ibsen's, bourgeois and "intellectual"; a wide range of conversational styles and topics is therefore plausible enough. But Chekhov is not too pedantic about plausibility. He not only exploits the real explicitness and complication and abstractness of bourgeois talk; he introduces, or re-introduces, a couple of special conventions.

The first is the tirade or long, oratorically composed speech. Chekhov's realistic plays—unlike Ibsen's—have their purple patches. On the assumption that a stage character may be much more self-conscious and aware than his counterpart in real life, Chekhov lets his people talk much more freely than any other modern realist except Shaw. They talk on all subjects from book-keeping to metaphysics. Not always listening to what the other man is saying, they talk about themselves and address the whole world. They make what might be called self-explaining soliloquies in the manner of Richard III—except for the fact that other people are present and waiting, very likely, to make soliloquies of their own.

This is the origin of the second Chekhovian convention: each character speaks his mind without reference to the others. This device is perhaps Chekhov's most notorious idea. It has been used more crudely by Odets and Saroyan; and it has usually been interpreted in what is indeed its primary function: to express the isolation of people from one another. However, the dramaturgic utility of the idea is equally evident: it brings the fates of individuals before the audience with a minimum of fuss.

In Chekhov, as in every successful artist, each device functions both technically and humanly, serves a purpose both as form and as content. The form of the tirade, which Chekhov reintroduces, is one of the chief means to an extension of content; and the extension of content is one of the chief means by which Chekhov escapes from stolid naturalism into the broader realities that only imagination can uncover. Chekhov's people are immersed in facts, buried in circumstances, not to say in trivialities, yet—and this is what differentiates them from most dramatic characters—aware of the realm of ideas and imagination. His drama bred a school of acting which gives more attention to exact detail than any other school in history; it might also have bred a school of dramaturgy which could handle the largest and most general problems. Chekhov was a master of the particular and the general—which is another sign of the richness and balance of his mind.

Obviously Chekhov is not a problem playwright in the vulgar sense. (Neither is Ibsen; neither is Shaw. Who is?) Nor is his drama *about* ideas. He would undoubtedly have agreed with Henry Becque: "The serious thing about drama is not the ideas. It is the absorption of the ideas by the characters, the dramatic or comic force that the characters give to the ideas." It is not so much the force Chekhov gives to any particular ideas as the picture he gives of the role of ideas in the lives of men of ideas—a point particularly relevant to *Uncle Vanya*. If Vanya might be called the active center of the play (in that he precipitates the crisis), there is also a passive center, a character whose mere existence gives direction to the action as a whole.

This is Professor Serebryakov. Although this character is not so satisfactory a creation as the professor in Chekhov's tale *A Tiresome Story*, and though Chekhov does too little to escape the cliché stage professor, the very crudeness of the characterization has dramatic point. Serebryakov is a simple case placed as such in contrast to Vanya and Astrov. His devotion to ideas is no more than a gesture of unearned superiority, and so he has become a valetudinarian whose wife truly says: "You talk of your age as though we were all responsible for it." Around this familiar and, after all, common phenomenon are grouped the others, each of whom has a different relation to the world of culture and learning. The Professor is the middle of the design; characters of developed awareness are, so to say, above him; those of undeveloped awareness below him. Above him are Vanya and Astrov, Yelena and Sonya—the men aware to a great extent through their superior intellect, the women through their finer feeling. Below him are three minor characters—Waffles, Vanya's mother, and the Nurse.

The Nurse, who is not to be found in *The Wood Demon*, stands for life without intellectuality or education. She sits knitting, and the fine talk passes her by. She stands for the monotony of country life, a monotony that she interprets as beneficent order. One of the many significant cross-references in the play is Vanya's remark at the beginning that the Professor's arrival has upset the household routine and the Nurse's remark at the end that now the meals will be on time again and all will be well.

Vanya's mother stands on the first rung of the intellectual ladder. She is an enthusiast for certain ideas, and especially for reading about them, but she understands very little. Less intelligent, less sensitive than Vanya, she has never seen through the Professor. Her whole character is in this exchange with her son:

MOTHER. . . . he has sent his new pamphlet.

VANYA. Interesting?

MOTHER. Interesting but rather queer. He is attacking what he himself maintained seven years ago. It's awful.

VANYA. There's nothing awful in that. Drink your tea, *maman*.

MOTHER. I want to talk.

VANYA. We have been talking and talking for fifty years and reading pamphlets. It's about time to leave off.

MOTHER. You don't like listening when I speak; I don't know why. Forgive my saying so, Jean, but you have so changed in the course of the last year that I hardly know you. You used to be a man of definite convictions, brilliant personality. . . .

On a slightly higher plane than the tract-ridden Mother is the friend of the family, Waffles. If Vanya is the ruin of a man of principle, Waffles is the parody of one. Listen to his account of himself (it is one of Chekhov's characteristic thumbnail autobiographies):

> My wife ran away from me with the man she loved the day after our wedding on the ground of my unprepossessing appearance. But I have never been false to my vows. I love her to this day and am faithful to her. I help her as far as I can, and I gave her all I had for the education of her children by the man she loved. I have lost my happiness, but I still have my pride left. And she? Her youth is over, her beauty, in accordance with the laws of nature, has faded, the man she loved is dead. . . . What has she left?

Just how Waffles is able to keep his equilibrium and avoid the agony that the four principals endure is clear enough. His "pride" is a form of stupidity. For him, as for the Professor, books and ideas are not a window through which he sees the world so much as obstacles that prevent him seeing anything but themselves. The Professor's response to the crisis is a magnanimity that rings as false as Waffles's pride:

> Let bygones be bygones. After what has happened. I have gone through such a lot and thought over so many things in these few hours, I believe I could write a whole treatise on the art of living. . . .

Waffles also finds reflections of life more interesting than life itself. In *The Wood Demon* (where his character is more crudely drawn), having helped Yelena to run away, he shouts:

> If I lived in an intellectual center, they could draw a caricature of me for a magazine, with a very funny satirical inscription.

And a little later:

Your Excellency, it is I who carried off your wife, as once upon
a time a certain Paris carried off the fair Helen. I! Although
there are no pockmarked Parises, yet there are more things in
heaven and earth, Horatio, than are dreamt of in your philosophy!

In the more finely controlled *Uncle Vanya* this side of Waffles is
slyly indicated in his attitude to the shooting:

NURSE. Look at the quarreling and shooting this morning—
shameful!
WAFFLES. Yes, a subject worthy of the brush of Ayvazovsky.

Aside from this special treament of the modern intellectual and
semi-intellectual, aside from explicit mention of various ideas and
philosophies, Chekhov is writing "drama of ideas" only in the sense
that Sophocles and Shakespeare and Ibsen were—that is to say, his
plays are developed thematically. As one can analyze certain Shakespeare plays in terms of the chief concepts employed in them—such
as Nature and Time—so one might analyze a Chekhov play in
terms of certain large antitheses, such as (the list is compiled from
Uncle Vanya) love and hate, feeling and apathy, heroism and
lethargy, innocence and sophistication, reality and illusion, freedom
and captivity, use and waste, culture and nature, youth and age, life
and death. If one were to take up a couple of Chekhov's key
concepts and trace his use of them through a whole play, one would
find that he is a more substantial artist than even his admirers
think.

Happiness and work, for instance. They are not exactly antitheses, but in *Uncle Vanya* they are found in by no means harmonious
association. The outsider's view of Chekhov is of course that he is
"negative" because he portrayed a life without happiness. The amateur's view is that he is "positive" because he preached work as a
remedy for boredom. Both views need serious qualification. The
word *work* shifts its tone and implication a good deal within the one
play *Uncle Vanya*. True, it sometimes looks like the antidote to all
the idleness and futility. On the other hand, the play opens with
Astrov's just complaint that he is worked to death. Work has been
an obsession, and is still one, for the Professor, whose parting word
is: "Permit an old man to add one observation to his farewell
message: you must work, my friends! you must work!"[7] Vanya and
Sonya obey him—but only to stave off desperation. "My heart is
too heavy," says Vanya. "I must make haste and occupy myself
with something. . . . Work! Work!" To Sonya, work is the noblest

7. So Constance Garnett. Actually Chekhov does not here use the Russian word
for "to work" (*rabotat'*), which is his
leitmotiv; he uses an idiom meaning
"You must do something!" (*Nado delo
delat'!*) [See note 2, p. 61, *Uncle Vanya*,
for a second meaning of this sentence—
Editor's note.]

mode of self-destruction, a fact that was rather more than clear in *The Wood Demon:*

ASTROV. Are you happy?

SONYA. This is not the time, Mikhail Lvovich, to think of happiness.

ASTROV. What else is there to think of?

SONYA. Our sorrow came only because we thought too much of happiness. . . .

ASTROV. So! [*Pause.*]

SONYA. There's no evil without some good in it. Sorrow has taught me this—that one must forget one's own happiness and think only of the happiness of others. One's whole life should consist of sacrifices. . . .

ASTROV. Yes . . . [*After a pause.*] Uncle Vanya shot himself, and his mother goes on searching for contradictions in her pamphlets. A great misfortune befell you and you're pampering your self-love, you are trying to distort your life and you think this is a sacrifice. . . . No one has a heart. . . .

In the less explicit *Uncle Vanya* this passage does not appear. What we do have is Sonya's beautiful lyric speech that ends the play. In the thrill of the words perhaps both reader and playgoer overlook just what she says—namely, that the afterlife will so fully make up for this one that we should learn not to take our earthly troubles too seriously. This is not Chekhov speaking. It is an overwrought girl comforting herself with an idea. In *The Wood Demon* Astrov was the author's mouthpiece when he replied to Sonya: "You are trying to distort your life and you think this is a sacrifice." The mature Chekhov has no direct mouthpieces. But the whole passage, the whole play, enforces the meaning: work for these people is not a means to happiness, but a drug that will help them to forget. Happiness they will never know. Astrov's yearnings are not a radical's vision of the future any more than the Professor's doctrine of work is a demand for a workers' state. They are both the daydreams of men who Might Have Been.

So much for *The Wood Demon* and *Uncle Vanya.* Chekhov wrote five other full-length plays. Three—*Ivanov, That Worthless Fellow Platonov,* and *The Wood Demon*—were written in his late twenties, and are experimental in the sense that he was still groping toward his own peculiar style. Two plays—*The Sea Gull* and *Uncle Vanya*—were written in his middle thirties; the last two plays—*The Three Sisters* and *The Cherry Orchard*—when he was about forty. Chekhov's development as a playwright is quite different from that of Ibsen, Strindberg, or any of the other first-rate moderns. While they pushed tempestuously forward, transforming old modes and inventing new ones, perpetually changing their approach, endlessly inventing new forms, Chekhov moved quietly, slowly, and along one straight road. He used only one full-length structure: the four-act drama; and one set of materials: the rural middle class. For all that, the line that stretches from *Ivanov* (1887–89) to *The Cherry Orchard* (1903) is of great interest.

The development is from farce and melodrama to the mature Chekhovian *drame*. The three early plays are violent and a little pretentious. Each presents a protagonist (there is no protagonist in the four subsequent plays) who is a modern variant upon a great type or symbol. Ivanov is referred to as a Hamlet, Platonov as a Don Juan, Astrov as a Wood Demon. In each case it is a "Russian" variant that Chekhov shows—Chekhov's "Russians" like Ibsen's "Norwegian" Peer Gynt and Shaw's "Englishman" representing modern men in general. Those who find Chekhov's plays static should read the three early pieces: they are the proof that, if the later Chekhov eschewed certain kinds of action, it was not for lack of dramatic sense in the most popular meaning of the term. Chekhov was born a melodramatist and farceur; only by discipline and development did he become the kind of playwright the world thinks it knows him to be. Not that the later plays are without farcical and melodramatic elements; only a great mimic and caricaturist could have created Waffles and Gaev. As for melodrama, the pistol continues to go off (all but the last of the seven plays have a murder or suicide as climax or pseudo-climax), but the noise is taken further off-stage, literally and figuratively, until in *The Three Sisters* it is "the dim sound of a far-away shot." And *The Cherry Orchard*, the farthest refinement of Chekhov's method, culminates not with the sharp report of a pistol, but with the dull, precise thud of an ax.

These are a few isolated facts, and one might find one hundred others to demonstrate that Chekhov's plays retain a relationship to the cruder forms. If, as Jacques Barzun has argued, there is a Balzac in Henry James, there is a Sardou[8] in Chekhov. Farce and melodrama are not eliminated, but subordinated to a higher art, and have their part in the dialectic of the whole. As melodrama, *The Sea Gull*, with its tale of the ruined heroine, the glamorous popular novelist, the despairing artist hero, might have appealed to Verdi or Puccini.[9] Even the story of *The Cherry Orchard* (the elegant lady running off to Paris and being abandoned by the object of her grand passion) hardly suggests singularity, highbrowism, or rarefaction.

In the later plays life is seen in softer colors; Chekhov is no longer eager to be the author of a Russian *Hamlet* or *Don Juan*.

8. Victorien Sarodu (1831–1908), playwright and director, who as a dramatist was Scribe's successor as a maker of the "well-made play" [*Editor's note*]
9. Giuseppe Verdi (1813–1901) and Gia-

como Puccini (1858–1924), Italian operatic composers whose libretti often consisted of characters similar to those described by Bentley [*Editor's note*].

The homely Uncle Vanya succeeds on the title page the oversuggestive Wood Demon, and Chekhov forgoes the melodrama of a forest fire. Even more revealing: overexplicit themes are deleted. Only in *The Wood Demon* is the career of the Professor filled in with excessive detail (Heidelberg and all) or Astrov denounced as a socialist. Only in the early version does Vanya's mother add to her remark that a certain writer now makes his living by attacking his own former views: "It is very, very typical of our time. Never have people betrayed their convictions with such levity as they do now." Chekhov deletes Vanya's open allusion to the "cursed poisonous irony" of the sophisticated mind. He keeps the substance of Yelena's declaration that "the world perishes not beceause of murderers and thieves, but from hidden hatred, from hostility among good people, from all those petty squabbles," and deletes the end of the sentence: ". . . unseen by those who call our house a haven of intellectuals." He does not have Yelena explain herself with the remark: "I am an episodic character, mine is a canary's happiness, a woman's happiness." (In both versions Yelena has earlier described herself as an "episodic character." Only in *The Wood Demon* does she repeat the description: In *The Wood Demon* the canary image also receives histrionic reiteration. In *Uncle Vanya* it is not used at all.)

Chekhov does not tone things down because he is afraid of giving himself away. He is not prim or precious. Restraint is for him as positive an idea as temperance was for the Greeks. In Chekhov the toned-down picture—as I hope the example of *Uncle Vanya* indicates—surpasses the hectic color scheme of melodrama, not only in documentary truth, but also in the deeper truth of poetic vision. And the truth of Chekhov's colors has much to do with the delicacy of his forms. Chekhov once wrote in a letter: "When a man spends the least possible number of movements over some definite action, that is grace"; and one of his critics speaks of a " 'trigger' process, the release of enormous forces by some tiny movement." The Chekhovian form as we find it in the final version of *Uncle Vanya* grew from a profound sense of what might be called the *economy* of art.

We have seen how, while this form does not by any means eliminate narrative and suspense, it reintroduces another equally respectable principle of motion—the progress from ignorance to knowledge. Each scene is another stage in our discovery of Chekhov's people and Chekhov's situation; also in their discovering of themselves and their situation (in so far as they are capable of doing so). The apparent casualness of the encounters and discussions on the stage is Chekhov linking himself to "the least possible number of movements." But as there is a "definite action," as "large forces have been brought into play," we are not cheated of drama.

The "trigger effect" is as dramatic in its way as the "buried secret" pattern of Sophocles and Ibsen. Of course, there will be people who see the tininess of the movements and do not notice the enormousness of the forces released—who see the trigger-finger move and do not hear the shot. To them, Chekhov remains a mere manufacturer of atmosphere, a mere contriver of nuance. To others he seems a master of dramatic form unsurpassed in modern times.

ROBERT BRUSTEIN

[Chekhov's Dramaturgy in *The Three Sisters*]

Anton Chekhov is the gentlest and the most impersonal of all the great modern dramatists, but there is one sense in which he does align himself on the side of his characters—insofar as they are cultured individuals, constituting the last stronghold of enlightenment against the encroaching mediocrity, vulgarity, and illiteracy of Russian life. For against these forces of darkness—the environment of his plays—he directs a vigorous personal revolt. Chekhov himself was passionately addicted to "culture"—by which he meant not intellectuality (he finds the intelligentsia "hypocritical, false, hysterical, poorly educated, and indolent"), but rather a mystical compound of humanity, decency, kindness, intelligence, education, accomplishment, and will. It is by these standards that he usually measures the worth of human beings. In a long letter to his brother Nikolay, Chekhov begins by accusing him of an "utter lack of culture," and then proceeds to define the characteristics of truly cultured people in a revelatory manner. Such people, he notes, "respect the human personality, and are therefore always forbearing, gentle, courteous, and compliant. They will overlook noise, and cold, and overdone meat, and the presence of strangers in their house. . . . They are sincere and fear untruth like the very devil. . . . They do not make fools of themselves in order to arouse sympathy. . . . They are not vain. . . . They develop an esthetic sense." Cautioning Nikolay "not to fall below the level of your environment," Chekhov counsels him, "What you need is constant work, day and night, eternal reading, study, willpower."

Chekhov, who had peasant blood himself, foresaw that cultured individuals might arise from any class of society, however humble, but he did not (like Tolstoy) idealize the peasantry, and the crude utilitarianism of the middle class filled him with disgust. If he is aggrieved by any general fact of Russian life, it is the cancerous growth of slovenliness, filth, stupidity, and cruelty among the mass of men; and if he despises the sluggishness and indolence of his upper-class characters, then this is because they, too, are gradually being overwhelmed by the tide, lacking the will to stem it. For if the Russian gentry represents beauty without use, the Russian environment is characterized by use without beauty; and those with the necessary willpower are often utterly without the necessary culture or education. It is this conflict between the cultured upper classes and their stupefying environment—between the forces of light and the forces of darkness—that provides the basic substance of most of Chekhov's plays.

Thus, while David Magarshack, the author of *Chekhov, The Dramatist*,[1] somewhat overstates the case by saying that Chekhov's mature plays are dramas of "courage and hope," he is perfectly right to emphasize the moral purpose behind Chekhov's imitation of reality. Chekhov never developed any program for "life as it should be." His revolt, like that of most great artists, is mainly negative. And it is a mistake to interpret the occasional expressions of visionary optimism that conclude his plays as evidence of "courage and hope" (they are more like desperate defenses against nihilism and despair). Yet it is also wrong to assume that Chekhov shares the pessimism that pervades his plays or the despondency of his defeated characters. Everyone who knew him testified to his gaiety, humor, and buoyancy, and if he always expected the worst, he always hoped for the best. Chekhov the realist was required to transcribe accurately the appalling conditions of provincial life without false affirmations or baseless optimism; but Chekhov the moralist has a sneaking belief in change. In short, Chekhov expresses his revolt not by depicting the ideal, which would have violated his sense of reality, and not by merely imitating the real, which would have violated his sense of moral purpose, but by criticizing the real at the same time that he is representing it. He will not comment on reality; he will permit reality to comment on itself. And so it is that while the surfaces of his plays seem drenched with *tedium vitae* and spiritual vapors, the depths are charged with energy and dissent.

These depths are also charged with melodrama. For although this is a mode that Chekhov deplores as unnatural, he smuggles his personal commentary into his plays by means of a hidden melodramatic configuration. Actually, Chekhov uses melodramatic devices all through his career—suicides, duels, attempted murders, love triangles, interrupted love scenes—and, trying to combat his weakness for exciting act curtains, he is constantly working to excise the unnatural from his art. (After *The Cherry Orchard*, he crows triumphantly that there is "not a single pistol shot in it.") On

1. Gloucester, Mass.: Peter Smith, 1960.

the other hand, all of his mature dramatic works, and especially *The Cherry Orchard*, are constructed on the same melodramatic pattern —the conflict between a despoiler and his victims—while the action of the plays follows the same melodramatic development—the gradual dispossession of the victims from their rightful inheritance.

This external conflict can be more easily observed if we strip away everything extraneous to the (hidden) plot, ignoring for a moment Chekhov's explorations of motive and character. In *The Sea Gull*, Trigorin seduces and ruins Nina; Mme. Arkadina spiritually dispossesses Treplyov, her Hamlet-like son. In *Uncle Vanya*, Yelena steals Sonya's secret love, Astrov, while Serebryakov robs Sonya of her inheritance and produces in Vanya a soul-killing disillusionment. In *The Three Sisters*, Natasha gradually evicts the Prozorov family from their provincial house. And in *The Cherry Orchard*, Lopakhin dipossesses Mme. Ranevskaya and Gaev, taking over their orchard as acreage for summer cottages. In each case, the central act of dispossession is symbolized through some central image, representing what is being ravished, stolen, or destroyed. In *The Sea Gull*, it is the bird that Treplyov kills, identified with Nina, who is also destroyed by a man with "nothing better to do." In *Uncle Vanya*, it is the forest, "a picture of gradual and unmistakable degeneration," associated with the lives of the family, degenerating through sheer inertia. In *The Three Sisters*, it is the Prozorov house, eventually hollowed out by Natasha as though by a nest of termites. And in *The Cherry Orchard*, of course, it is the famous orchard, hacked to pieces by the commercial ax. With the possible exception of *The Sea Gull*, each play dramatizes the triumph of the forces of darkness over the forces of enlightenment, the degeneration of culture in the crude modern world.

What prevents us from seeing these melodramatic configurations is the extraordinary way in which they have been concealed. Technically, Chekhov's most effective masking device is to bury the plot (Magarshack's concept of the "indirect action") so that violent acts and emotional climaxes occur offstage or between the acts. In this way, he manages to avoid the melodramatic crisis and to obscure the external conflict, ducking the event and concentrating on the denouement. Secondly, Chekhov concludes the action before the conventional melodramatic reversal—the triumphant victory of virtue over vice; in its place, he substitutes a reversal of his own invention, in which the defeated characters, shuffling off the old life, begin to look forward to the new. Most important, however, he refuses to cast his characters in conventional hero-villain roles. In the buried plot, Chekhov's despoilers act while his victims suffer; but by subordinating plot to character, Chekhov diverts our attention from process to motive and makes us suspend our judgment of the action.

Chekhov also dilutes the melodramatic pathos by qualifying our sympathy for the victims. In most cases, they seem largely responsible for whatever happens to them. This is not to say, as some have said, that we do not sympathize with their unhappy lot; we do, but since Chekhov highlights their inertia, irresponsibility, and waste, we also deplore their helpless inability to resist their fate. Carefully balancing pathos with irony, Chekhov avoids the stock responses of conventional theatre, deflecting the emphasis from the melodramatic to the natural and the atmospheric, wrapping layers of commonplace detail around extremely climactic events.

And this is precisely the effect that Chekhov aims to achieve. "Let the things that happen onstage," he writes, "be just as complex and yet just as simple as they are in life. For instance, people are having a meal at table, just having a meal, but at the same time their happiness is being created, or their lives are being smashed up." The placid surface of existence, then, is to be a masking device for his controlled manipulation of human fatality; the trivial course of the daily routine is to disguise his sense of process, development, and crisis. Chekhov is so successful in achieving these goals that English and American critics often condemn his plays as vague, actionless, and formless. They have been blinded by Chekhov's extraordinary atmospheric power and his capacity to evoke, through rhythmic sound effects (scratching pens, guitar music, sneezes, songs, etc.), a poetic illusion of fluid reality.

Beneath this surface, Chekhov's work has the tensile strength of a steel girder, the construction being so subtle that it is almost invisible. And while his characters seem to exist in isolated pockets of vacancy, they are all integral parts of a close network of interlocking motives and effects. Thus, while the dialogue seems to wander aimlessly into discussions of cold samovars, the situation in Moscow, and the temperature of the earth, it is economically performing a great number of essential dramatic functions: revealing character, furthering the action, uncovering the theme, evoking in the spectators a mood identical with that of the characters, and diverting attention from the melodramatic events that are erupting under the smooth surface of life. Through this original and inimitable technique, Chekhov manages to exercise his function both as a realist and as a moralist, and to express his resistance to certain aspects of modern life in enduring esthetic form.

All of Chekhov's mature works are masterpieces, but *The Three Sisters* perhaps provides the most stunning example of his dramatic approach. Completed late in 1900, almost four years after *Uncle*

Vanya, it was written mostly in the Crimea, where Chekhov had retired to recuperate from the tuberculosis that was soon to prove fatal to him. One year before, he had published "In the Ravine," a short story with enough similarities to the play to suggest that it was a preparatory sketch. The location of the story is a provincial village called Ukleyevo, so ordinary and banal that it is identified to visitors as the place "where the deacon ate all the caviare at the funeral"—nothing more stimulating has ever happened there. Yet, as usual with Chekhov, extraordinary events take place in this commonplace setting. The most important development, for our purposes, is the progress of the woman, Aksinya—married to one of the two sons of Tsybukin, an elderly, generous shopkeeper. Aksinya, contemptuous of the family, parades wantonly about the town in low-necked dresses and is openly conducting an affair with a rich factory owner. When Tsyvukin's unmarried son weds a girl named Lipa—a quiet, frightened, gentle peasant woman—Aksinya becomes intensely jealous; when Lipa gives birth to a baby boy, Aksinya scalds it with a ladle of boiling water, killing both the infant and the hopes of the family. Instead of being punished, however, Aksinya continues to flourish in the town, finally turning her father-in-law and his family out of their own house.

From this story, Chekhov apparently derived his idea for Natalya Ivanovna, the lustful, ambitious, and predatory woman who eventually disinherits the gentle Prozorovs—an action played out against the background of a provincial town so petty, vulgar, and boring that it has the power to degrade its most cultured inhabitants. *The Three Sisters* is richer, more complex, and more ambiguous than "In the Ravine"; Chekhov smooths the melodramatic wrinkles of the story by toning down the adulterous villainy of Natasha-Aksinya; he enriches the story by adding a military background and transforming the petit-bourgeois Tsybukins into the leisured, upper-class Prozorovs. But the basic outline is the same; and so is Chekhov's careful balancing of the internal and external influences on character, an element of all his mature work. In *Ivanov*, the decline of the hero was mostly determined from within, and Borkin's theory that "it's your environment that's killing you" was rejected as a thoughtless cliché. But in *The Three Sisters*, environment plays a crucial role in the gradual defeat of the central characters, while their own psychological failings are kept relatively muted.

The forces of evil, in fact, are quite inexorable in this work, making the Chekhovian pathos more dominant than usual. Chekhov, according to Stanislavsky, was amazed at the first reading of the play by the Art Theatre, because, in the producer's words, "he had written a happy comedy and all of us considered the play a tragedy and even wept over it." Stanislavsky is probably exaggerating Chekhov's response. Rather than considering it a "happy comedy," he was very careful to call *The Three Sisters* a "drama," the only such classification, as Magarshack notes, among his works. The play is certainly no tragedy, but it is the gloomiest Chekhov ever wrote. Certainly, the author introduces very little of his customary buffoonery. Though the play has its pantaloons, they are too implicated in the events of the house to evoke from us more than occasional smiles: Kulygin, for example, with his genial pedantry and maddening insensitivity to sorrow, is nevertheless a rather pathetic cuckold; and the alcoholic Chebutykin, for all his absurdity, eventually develops into a withdrawn and nihilistic figure. Furthermore, an atmosphere of doom seems to permeate the household, lifted only during brief festive moments; even these are quickly brought to an end by the ominous Natasha. Despite Magarshack's desire to read the play as "a *gay* affirmation of life," there is little that is gay or affirmative about it. Chekhov displays his usual impatience with the delusions of his central characters, but they are more clearly victims than most such figures. And while they undoubtedly are partially responsible for their fates (which explains why Chekhov did not want Stanislavsky's actors to grow maudlin over them), much of the responsibility belongs to Natasha, who represents the dark forces eating away at their lives.

For Natasha is the most malevolent figure Chekhov ever created —a pretentious bourgeois *arriviste* without a single redeeming trait. Everyone emphasizes her vulgarity, vengefulness, and lack of culture, and even Andrey, who leans over backward to be fair, sees in her "a small, blind, sort of thick-skinned animal. In any case, she's not a human being." Natasha is a malignant growth in a benevolent organism, and her final triumph, no matter how Chekhov tries to disguise it, is the triumph of pure evil. Despite the thick texture of the play, then, neatly woven into the tapestry is an almost invisible thread of action: the destruction of the Prozorovs by Natasha. From the moment she enters the house, at the end of Act I, to accept Andrey's proposal of marriage, until she has secured her control at the end of the play, the process of dispossession continues with relentless motion.

It takes place, however, by steady degrees. Andrey has mortgaged the house to the bank in order to pay his gambling debts, but Natasha, a much more dangerous adversary than a bank, takes over from there. Not only has she "grabbed all the money" (presumably the mortgage money), but she is engaged, throughout the play, in shifting the family from room to room, until she has finally shifted them out of the house entirely. Natasha's ambitions proceed under the guise of maternal solicitude and love of order; and never have such qualities seemed so thoroughly repellent. In the second act, she is planning to move Irina into Olga's room so that little Bobik will have a warmer nursery; in the third act, she offers to evict Anfisa, the old family servant, because she has outlived her usefulness (Natasha's unfeeling utilitarianism is among her most inhuman traits); and in the last act—with Olga and Anfisa installed in a government flat and Irina having moved to a furnished room—she is preparing to move Andrey out of his room to make way for baby Sophie. Since Sophie is probably the child of Protopopov, Natasha's lover, the dispossession has been symbolically completed. It will not be long before it is literally completed, and Andrey, the last of the Prozorovs, is ejected from the house altogether.

Chekhov illustrates this process through a careful manipulation of the setting. The first three acts take place in interiors that grow progressively more confined, the third act being laid in the room of Olga and Irina, cramped with people, screens, and furniture. But the last act is laid outdoors. The exterior setting tells the story visually: the family is now out of their own home; Andrey pushes the baby carriage around the house in widening circles; and Protopopov (never seen) is comfortably installed *inside*, in the drawing room with Natasha. Natasha, however, has not yet finished, for she is determined to violate the outdoors as well. Popping out of the house for a moment, she expresses her determination to cut down the fir and maple trees that Tuzenbakh admires so much, an act of despoliation that foreshadows a similar act in *The Cherry Orchard*.

The contrast between Natasha and the Prozorovs is demonstrated by the difference in their manners—Natasha's vulgarity is amply documented by her French affectations and her abuse of the servants. An even better contrast is provided during the fire that is raging in town at the beginning of the third act. In this scene, Chekhov sets off Natasha's *arriviste* pretensions against the instinctual humanity of the Prozorovs by comparing their attitudes toward the victims of the conflagration. In accordance with Chekhov's description of the cultured in his letter to Nikolay ("They will overlook . . . the presence of strangers in their house"), the sisters generously offer their hospitality to those without homes, but Natasha is more occupied with fears that her children will catch some disease. When she considers the homeless, she thinks of them as objects to be patronized—"Indeed, we should always be ready to help the poor, that's the duty of the rich"—and talks about joining a committee for the assistance of the victims, that impersonal, dehumanized approach to charity invented by the middle class less out of generosity than out of status-seeking and guilt.

Since the fire is an external crisis introduced to heighten (and at the same time draw attention from) the crisis occurring within, it also illustrates Natasha's destructive tendencies. The fire is closely identified with that conflagration that is destroying the Prozorov household; the fate of the victims anticipates that of the family (they are out on the street); and Natasha symbolically links the two events. As Natasha marches through her room with a candle, Masha suggests this link by saying: "She goes about looking as if it were she who had started the fire." But at the same time that Natasha is a symbolic arsonist, she is also a symbolic fire extinguisher. Always on the lookout for fear something goes wrong, she stalks through the house, snuffing out candles—snuffing, too, all laughter and pleasure in the family. Pleading baby Bobik's health, she puts an end to the Carnival party; for like Serebryakov (who similarly throws cold water on the musical interlude planned by Yelena and Sonya in *Uncle Vanya*), she functions to extinguish joy, and to spread gloom and despair.

The conflict between Natasha and the Prozorovs, needless to say, is always kept indistinct. Andrey and the sisters are either too polite or too deeply involved in their own problems to comment much on Natasha's activities, and while she and the family brush each other frequently throughout the play, they never break into open argument. Instead of dramatizing the Prozorovs' relations with Natasha, Chekhov defines them against the background of their surroundings, concentrating on the wasting away of this potentially superior family in a coarse and sordid environment. On the other hand, Natasha is really the personification of this environment—a native of the town who lives in the house—and so both she and the environment are actually related forces converging on the same objects. Thus, the surface and the depths of *The Three Sisters* follow parallel lines of development. The gradual dispossession of the Prozorovs by Natasha is the buried action, while their gradual deterioration in their surroundings proceeds above. In each case, the conflict between culture and vulgarity provides the basic theme.

This conflict is clear from the opening lines of the play, when the three sisters—a doleful portrait in blue, black, and white—first reveal their dissatisfaction with the present by reflecting, nostalgically, on the life of the past. A highly educated Moscow family, the Prozorovs were geographically transplanted eleven years before when their father, a brigadier general, took command of an artillery unit in the provinces. As the action proceeds, Chekhov shows how the family, following the father's death, has tried to adapt to their new surroundings: Olga by teaching school, Masha by marrying the local schoolmaster, Irina by working in a variety of civil jobs, Andrey by marrying Natasha and joining the District Board. All these attempts at assimilation are, however, unsuccessful. And regarding their present life as a kind of involuntary banishment, they are now uncomfortably suspended between their idealization of the past and resentment over their depressing provincial existence.

The past, of course, is closely identified with Moscow, seen through a haze of memory as a city of sun, flowers, refinement, and sensibility—in short, of *culture*—as opposed to the cold, stupidity, and dreariness of their town. Their vision of Moscow, like their hopes of returning, is, of course, delusionary—an idle dream with which we are meant to have little patience—and their endless complaining is neither courageous nor attractive. Still, their shared apprehension of the pettiness, drabness, and conformity of their provincial district is terrifyingly accurate. As Andrey describes it:

> Our town has been in existence now for two hundred years, there are a hundred thousand people in it, and not one who isn't exactly like all the others, not one saint, either in the past or in the present, not one scholar, not one artist, no one in the least remarkable who could inspire envy or a passionae desire to imitate him. . . . and an overwhelmingly vulgar influence weighs on the children, the divine spark is extinguished in them, and they become the same pitiful, identical corpses as their fathers and mothers. . . .

In this speech—which may have been intended as an attack on the audience (Chekhov stipulated that Andrey, while speaking it, "must almost threaten the audience with his fists")—Andrey is clearly expressing Chekhov's revolt against the appalling conditions of the provincial town. It is a place in which any man of sensibility is bound to feel "a stranger, and lonely," for it is without culture, without art, without humanity, without excellence; its "overwhelmingly vulgar influence" has the power to brutalize all who live within its circumference. The influence of the town, in its most extreme state, is shown on Chebutykin, who takes refuge from his disillusionment in alcohol and newspapers and from his professional incompetence in a profound nihilism: "Maybe it only appears that we exist, but, in fact, we are not here." For just as the Prozorovs respond to their surroundings by weaving the illusion of Moscow, so Chebutykin responds by declaring that nothing in the world is real, and that "it doesn't matter."

The Prozorovs are aware that the town is brutalizing them, too, which accounts for their growing despair. Masha—dressed in black to illustrate her depression—is perpetually bored; Irina is perpetually tired; Olga suffers from perpetual headaches. As for Andrey, their gifted brother, he trails his life along with no apparent aim, followed by the senile Ferapont, as by an ignominious Nemesis. In this lifeless atmosphere, they are drying up, their culture falling from them like shreds of dead skin—each, in turn, will ask, "Where has it all gone?" For whatever might have made them seem unusual in Moscow is here merely a superfluous layer—useless, unnecessary, and gradually being forgotten. Andrey, carefully trained for a distinguished university career, holds a position in which his education is meaningless. Masha, once an accomplished pianist, now "has forgotten" how to play—just as Chebutykin has "forgotten" his medical training—just as the entire family is forgetting the accomplishments of their hopeful youth. Thus, the Prozorovs alternate between hysteria and despair, their hopes disintegrating in an environment where everything is reduced to zero:

> IRINA. [*sobbing*] Where? Where has it all gone? Where is it? Oh, my God, my God! I have forgotten everything, I've forgotten . . . it's all muddled in my head. . . . I can't remember how to say window or floor in Italian. I'm forgetting everything, every day I forget, and life is slipping by, never to return, never, we shall never go to Moscow. . . . I see that we shall never go. . . .

Life is slipping by, and time, like a cormorant, is devouring hopes, illusions, expectations, consuming their minds, souls, and bodies in its tedious-rapid progress toward death.

While their culture is being forgotten, however, the Prozorovs do try to preserve a pocket of civilization in this dreary wasteland; their house is open to limited forms of intellectual discussion and artistic activity. Generally, the discussions at the Prozorovs' reflect the banality of the surrounding area (Solyony's and Chebutykin's heated argument over *chehartma* and *cheremsha* is typical), but occasionally, genuine ideas seem to come out of these soirées. Attending the discussions are the Prozorovs' cultural allies, the military officers stationed in town. Chekhov, according to Stanislavsky, looked on the military as "the bearers of a cultural mission, since, coming into the farthest corners of the provinces, they brought with them new demands on life, knowledge, art, happiness, and joy." Masha suggests Chekhov's attitudes when she observes the difference between the crude townspeople and the more refined soldiers: "Among civilians generally, there are so many coarse, impolite, ill-bred people," but "in our town the most decent, the most honorable and well-bred people are all in the army." Her attraction to Colonel Vershinin is partially explained by his superior refinement, for he is associated in her mind with the old Muscovite charm and glamour. In part, he probably reminds her of her father (also identified with culture), for he lived on the same street, was an officer in her father's brigade, and has now taken command of her father's old battery. Attracted to educated men (she married Kulygin because she mistakenly thought him "the cleverest of men"), Masha unquestionably finds a suitable intellectual companion in Vershinin; even their courtship reveals their cultural affinities—he hums a tune to which she hums a reply. Magarshack calls this "the most original love declaration in the whole history of the stage"—actually, Congreve's Mirabel and Millamant[2] employ much the same device, when he completes a Lovelace verse that she has begun—but in both cases, the couples signify their instinctual rapport and their superior sophistication to other suitors.

While Masha tries to find expression through an extramarital affair that is doomed to failure, Irina tries to discover a substitute commitment in her work. In this, her spiritual partner, though she doesn't love him, is Tuzenbakh, because he too seeks salvation in work, finally, in a Tolstoyan gesture, resigning his commission for a job in a brickyard. Irina's faith in the dignity of labor, however, is gradually destroyed by depressing jobs in a telegraph office and on the Town Council—in this district, work can have no essential meaning or purpose. In the last act, Irina looks forward to "a new life" as a schoolteacher; but we have Olga's enervating academic career as evidence that this "new life" will be just as unfulfilling as the old. And when Tuzenbakh is killed in a duel with Solyony (*his* despoiler), even the minor consolations of a loveless marriage are denied her.

Everything, in fact, fails the family in *The Three Sisters*. And as their culture fades and their lives grow grayer, the forces of darkness and illiteracy move in like carrion crows, ready to pick the last bones. There is some doubt, however, whether this condition is permanent. The question the play finally asks is whether the defeat of the Prozorovs has any ultimate meaning: will their suffering eventually influence their surroundings in any positive way? The question is never resolved in the play, but it is endlessly debated by Vershinin and Tuzenbakh, whose opinions contrast as sharply as their characters. Vershinin—an extremely unhappy soul—holds to optimistic theories, while Tuzenbakh—inexplicably merry—is more profoundly pessimistic.[3] This conflict, though usually couched in general terms, is secretly connected with the fate of the Prozorovs. When Masha, for example, declares, "We know a great deal that is useless," Vershinin takes the opportunity to expound his views:

It seems to me that there is not and cannot be a town so dull and depressing that a clever, educated person would be useless. Let us suppose that among the hundred thousand inhabitants of this

2. William Congreve (1670–1729), English playwright considered by most critics the most polished writer of the type of play called the "comedy of manners." The leading characters in his play *The Way of the World* (1700) are Mirabel and Millamant [*Editor's note*].

3. Chekhov may be dramatizing a paradox here that he once expounded to Lydia Avilova in the course of explaining the alleged gloominess of his themes and characters: "It has always been pointed out to me that somber, melancholy people always write gaily, while the works of cheerful souls are always depressing." Chekhov, like Tuzenbakh, is a cheerful soul with a gloomy point of view.

town, which, of course, is backward and uncouth, there are only three people such as you. It goes without saying that you cannot vanquish the ignorant masses around you; in the course of your life, little by little, you will have to give way and be lost in that crowd of a hundred thousand; life will stifle you, but all the same, you will not disappear, you will not be without influence. After you there may appear perhaps six like you, then twelve, and so on, until finally, your kind will become the majority. In two or three hundred years life on this earth will be unimaginably beautiful, wonderful.

Vershinin, in short—anticipating the eventual transformation of the surrounding area by people like the Prozorovs—believes in the progressive march of civilization toward perfection. And this perfection will be based on the future interrelationship of the benighted mass and the cultured elite ("If, don't you know, we could add culture to the love of work, and love of work to culture.")—a synthesis of beauty and utility.

Tuzenbakh, on the other hand, is more skeptical. Seeing no special providence in the fall of a sparrow or the flight of migratory cranes, he doubts the ability of anyone to influence anything:

Not only in two or three hundred years, but in a million years, life will be just the same . . . it doesn't change, it remains constant, following its own laws, which do not concern us, or which, in any case, you will never get to know.

Vershinin's view awakens hope that there is some ultimate meaning to life. Tuzenbakh's leads to stoicism and tragic resignation. It is the recurrent conflict between the progressive and the static interpretation of history, and its outcome remains insoluble.

In the last act, in fact, both views are recapitulated without being reconciled. The military is leaving the town—a sad departure, because it signifies not only the end of Masha's affair with Vershinin but also the disintegration of the last cultural rampart. Tuzenbakh anticipates that "dreadful boredom" will descend upon the town, and Andrey notes (reminding us of Natasha's symbolic role) that "it's as though someone put a hood over it." The end of the Prozorov way of life has almost come. Masha has turned obsessive and hysterical; Olga is installed in a position she loathes; Andrey, likened to an expensive bell that has fallen and smashed, has become hag-ridden and mediocre. Only Irina preserves some hope, but even these hopes are soon to be dashed. The entire family is finally facing the truth: "Nothing turns out as we would have it"—the dream of Moscow will never be realized, the mass of darkness has overwhelmed them. In the requiem that concludes the play, the three sisters meditate on the future, just as, in the beginning of the play, they reflected on the past, while Andrey pushes the carriage, Kulygin bustles, and Chebutykin hums softly to himself.

Their affirmations, showing the strong influence of Vershinin's view of life, are inexplicably hopeful and expectant. Masha expresses her determination to endure; Irina has faith that a "time will come when everyone will know what all this is for"; and Olga affirms that "our sufferings will turn into joy for those who live after us, happiness and peace will come to this earth, and then they will remember kindly and bless those who are living now." The gay band music played by the military evokes in the three sisters the will to live. But the music slowly fades away. Will hope fade away as well? Olga's anxious questioning of life ("If only we knew—if only we knew!") is—as if to suggest this—antiphonally answered by Chebutykin's muttered denials ("It doesn't matter, it doesn't matter!"), the skepticism of Tuzenbakh reduced to its most nihilistic form. And on this double note—the dialectic of hope and despair in a situation of defeat—Chekhov's darkest play draws to its close.

In *The Three Sisters*, Chekhov depicts the prostration of the cultured elite before the forces of darkness; in *The Cherry Orchard*, he examines the same problem from a comic-ironic point of view. Written while he was dying and with great difficulty, *The Cherry Orchard* is the most farcical of Chekhov's full-length works, and so it was intended. In 1901, when the play was just beginning to take shape in his mind, he wrote to Olga Knipper: "The next play I write for the Art Theatre will definitely be funny, very funny—at least in intention." The last phrase was probably a sally aimed at Stanislavsky (Chekhov deplored his tendency to turn "my characters into crybabies"), and though Stanislavsky did, in fact, eventually misinterpret *The Cherry Orchard* as a somber study of Russian life, Chekhov always insisted on calling it "not a drama but a comedy; in places almost a farce."

The importance of the comic element in the play suggests that Chekhov is emphasizing the other side of his revolt. Instead of merely evoking sympathy for the victims of the social conflict, he is now satirizing them as well; instead of blackening the character of the despoiler, he is drawing him with a great deal more depth and balance. The change is one of degree—Chekhov has not reversed his earlier position, he has merely modified it—and the dispossession of the victims still evokes strains of pathos that we should not ignore. But in *The Cherry Orchard* Chekhov is more impatient with his cultured idlers; and their eventual fate seems more fitting and more just.

In all of his plays, on the other hand, Chekhov's revolt remains two-edged, for it is directed both against his leisured characters, too will-less to resist their own liquidation, and also against the dark environment that drags them under. Thus Chekhov's revolt may change in emphasis and attack, but it is always fixed on the fate of the cultured classes in the modern world. This is the great "problem" of his plays—and it is a problem that, in keeping with his artistic creed, he undertakes not to solve but simply to present correctly. Confronting the same world as the other modern dramatists—a world without God and, therefore, without meaning—Chekhov has no remedy for the disease of contemporary life. Ibsen speaks of the importance of one's calling, and Strindberg of resignation. But even Chekhov's panacea of work is ultimately ineffectual before the insupportable fact of death.

Still, despite the bleakness of his vision, Chekhov possesses a deeper humanity than any other modern dramatist. For while he never fails to examine the desperate absurdity of his characters, he never loses sight of the qualities that make them fully alive: "My holy of holies," he writes, "are the human body, health, intelligence, talent, inspiration, love, and the most absolute freedom—freedom from despotism and lies." Chekhov himself embodies these qualities so perfectly that no one has even been able to write of him without the most profound affection and love; and he, the author, remains the most positive character in his fiction. Because of his hatred of untruth, Chekhov will not arouse false hopes about the future of mankind—but because he is humane to the marrow of his bones, he manages to increase our expectations of the human race. Coupling sweetness of temper with toughness of mind, Chekhov makes his work an extraordinary compound of morality and reality, rebellion and acceptance, irony and sympathy—evoking a singular affirmation even in the darkest despair. There are more powerful playwrights in the modern theatre—artists with greater range, wider variety, more intellectual power—but there are none more warm and generous, and none who bring the drama to a higher realization of its human role.

FRANCIS FERGUSSON

[*The Cherry Orchard*: A Theatre-Poem
of the Suffering of Change]

* * *

The Plot of The Cherry Orchard

The Cherry Orchard is often accused of having no plot whatever, and it is true that the story gives little indication of the play's content or meaning; nothing happens, as the Broadway reviewers so often point out. Nor does it have a thesis, though many attempts have been made to attribute a thesis to it, to make it into a Marxian tract, or into a nostalgic defense of the old regime. The play does not have much of a plot in either of these accepted meanings of the word, for it is not addressed to the rationalizing mind but to the poetic and histrionic sensibility. It is an imitation of an action in the strictest sense, and it is plotted according to the first meaning of this word which I have distinguished in other contexts: the incidents are selected and arranged to define an action in a certain mode; a complete action, with a beginning, middle, and end in time. Its freedom from the mechanical order of the thesis or the intrigue is the sign of the perfection of Chekhov's realistic art. And its apparently casual incidents are actually composed with most elaborate and conscious skill to reveal the underlying life, and the natural, objective form of the play as a whole.

In *Ghosts*, the action is distorted by the stereotyped requirements of the thesis and the intrigue. That is partly a matter of the mode of action which Ibsen was trying to show; a quest "of ethical motivation" which requires some sort of intellectual framework, and yet can have no final meaning in the purely literal terms of Ibsen's theatre. *The Cherry Orchard*, on the other hand, is a drama "of pathetic motivation," a theatre-poem of the suffering of change; and this mode of action and awareness is much closer to the skeptical basis of modern realism, and to the histrionic basis of all realism. Direct perception before predication is always true, says Aristotle; and the extraordinary feat of Chekhov is to predicate nothing. This he achieves by means of his plot: he selects only those incidents, those moments in his characters' lives, between their rationalized efforts, when they sense their situation and destiny most directly. So he contrives to show the action of the play as a whole—the unsuccessful attempt to cling to the Cherry Orchard—in many diverse reflectors and without propounding any thesis about it.

The slight narrative thread which ties these incidents and characters together for the inquiring mind, is quickly recounted. The family that owns the old estate named after its famous orchard—Lyubov, her brother Gaev, and her daughters Varya and Anya—is all but bankrupt, and the question is how to prevent the bailiffs from selling the estate to pay their debts. Lopakhin, whose family were formerly serfs on the estate, is now rapidly growing rich as a businessman, and he offers a very sensible plan: chop down the orchard, divide the property into small lots, and sell them off to make a residential suburb for the growing industrial town nearby. Thus the cash value of the estate could be not only preserved, but increased. But this would not save what Lyubov and her brother find valuable in the old estate; they cannot consent to the destruction of the orchard. But they cannot find, or earn, or borrow the money to pay their debts either; and in due course the estate is sold at auction to Lopakhin himself, who will make a very good thing of it. His workmen are hacking at the old trees before the family is out of the house.

The play may be briefly described as a realistic ensemble pathos: the characters all suffer the passing of the estate in different ways, thus adumbrating this change at a deeper and more generally significant level than that of any individual's experience. The action which they all share by analogy, and which informs the suffering of the destined change of the Cherry Orchard, is "to save the Cherry Orchard": that is, each character sees some value in it—economic, sentimental, social, cultural—which he wishes to keep. By means of his plot, Chekhov always focuses attention on the general action: his crowded stage, full of the characters I have mentioned as well a half a dozen hangers-on, is like an implicit discussion of the fatality which concerns them all; but Chekhov does not believe in their ideas, and the interplay he shows among his *dramatis personae* is not so much the play of thought as the alternation of his characters' perceptions of their situation, as the moods shift and the time for decision comes and goes.

Though the action which Chekhov chooses to show onstage is "pathetic," i.e., suffering and perception, it is complete: the Cherry Orchard is constituted before our eyes, and then dissolved. The first act is a prologue: it is the occasion of Lyubov's return from Paris to try to resume her old life. Through her eyes and those of her daughter Anya, as well as from the complementary perspectives of Lopakhin and Trofimov, we see the estate as it were in the round, in its many possible meanings. The second act corresponds to the agon; it is in this act that we become aware of the conflicting values of all the characters, and of the efforts they make (offstage) to save each one *his* Orchard. The third act corresponds to the pathos and peripety of the traditional tragic form. The occasion is a rather hysterical party which Lyubov gives while her estate is being sold at auction in the nearby town; it ends with Lopakhin's announcement, in pride and the bitterness of guilt, that he was the purchaser. The last act is the epiphany: we see the action, now completed, in a new and ironic light. The occasion is the departure of the family: the windows are boarded up, the furniture piled in the corners, and the bags packed. All the characters feel, and the audience sees in a thousand ways, that the wish to save the Orchard has amounted in fact to destroying it; the gathering of its denizens to separation; the homecoming to departure. What this "means" we are not told. But the action is completed, and the poem of the suffering of change concludes in a new and final perception, and a rich chord of feeling.

The structure of each act is based upon a more or less ceremonious social occasion. In his use of the social ceremony—arrivals, departures, anniversaries, parties—Chekhov is akin to James. His purpose is the same: to focus attention on an action which all share by analogy, instead of upon the reasoned purpose of any individual, as Ibsen does in his drama of ethical motivation. Chekhov uses the social occasion also to reveal the individual at moments when he is least enclosed in his private rationalization and most open to disinterested insights. The Chekhovian ensembles may appear superficially to be mere pointless stalemates—too like family gatherings and arbitrary meetings which we know offstage. So they are. But in his miraculous arrangement the very discomfort of many presences is made to reveal fundamental aspects of the human situation.

That Chekhov's art of plotting is extremely conscious and deliberate is clear the moment one considers the distinction between the stories of his characters as we learn about them, and the moments of their lives which he chose to show directly onstage. Lopakhin, for example, is a man of action like one of the new capitalists in Gorky's plays. Chekhov knew all about him, and could have shown us an exciting episode from his career if he had not chosen to see him only when he was forced to pause and pathetically sense his own motives in a wider context which qualifies their importance. Lyubov has been dragged about Europe for years by her ne'er-do-well lover, and her life might have yielded several surefire erotic intrigues like those of the commercial theatre. But Chekhov, like all the great artists of modern times, rejected these standard motivations as both stale and false. The actress Arkadina, in *The Sea Gull*, remarks, as she closes a novel of Maupassant's, "Well, among the French that may be, but here with us there's nothing of the kind, we've no set program." In the context the irony of her remark is deep: she is herself a purest product of the commercial theatre, and at that very time she is engaged in a love affair of the kind she objects to in Maupassant. But Chekhov, with his subtle art of plotting, has caught her in a situation, and at a brief moment of clarity and pause, when the falsity of her career is clear to all, even herself.

Thus Chekhov, by his art of plot-making, defines an action in the opposite mode to that of *Ghosts*. Ibsen defines a desperate quest for reasons and for ultimate, intelligible moral values. This action falls naturally into the form of the agon, and at the end of the play Ibsen is at a loss to develop the final pathos, or bring it to an end with an accepted perception. But the pathetic is the very mode of action and awareness which seems to Chekhov closest to the reality of the human situation, and by means of his plot he shows, even in characters who are not in themselves unusually passive, the suffering and the perception of change. The "moment" of human experience which *The Cherry Orchard* presents thus corresponds to that of the Sophoclean chorus, and of the evenings in the *Purgatorio*. *Ghosts* is a fighting play, armed for its sharp encounter with the rationalizing mind, its poetry concealed by its reasons. Chekhov's poetry, like Ibsen's, is behind the naturalistic surfaces; but the form of the play as a whole is "nothing but" poetry in the widest sense: the coherence of the concrete elements of the composition. Hence the curious vulnerability of Chekhov on the contemporary stage: he does not argue, he merely presents; and though his audiences even on Broadway are touched by the time they reach the last act, they are at a loss to say what it is all about.

It is this reticent objectivity of Chekhov also which makes him so difficult to analyze in words: he appeals exclusively to the histrionic sensibility where the little poetry of modern realism is to be found. Nevertheless, the effort of analysis must be made if one is to understand this art at all; and if the reader will bear with me, he is asked to consider one element, that of the scene, in the composition of the second act.

ACT II: THE SCENE AS A BASIC ELEMENT IN THE COMPOSITION

Jean Cocteau writes, in his preface to *Les Mariés de la Tour Eiffel*:[1] "The action of my play is in images (*imagée*) while the text is not: I attempt to substitute a 'poetry of the theatre' for 'poetry in the theatre.' Poetry in the theatre is a piece of lace which it is impossible to see at a distance. Poetry of the theatre would be coarse lace; a lace of ropes, a ship at sea. *Les Mariés* should have the frightening look of a drop of poetry under the microscope. The *scenes* are integrated like the *words* of a poem."

1. *The Eiffel Tower Wedding Party* (1924), a surrealist play by Jean Coc- teau (1889–1963) [*Editor's note*].

This description applies very exactly to *The Cherry Orchard*: the larger elements of the composition—the scenes or episodes, the setting, and the developing story—are composed in such a way as to make a poetry of the theatre; but the "text," as we read it literally, is not. Chekhov's method, as Stark Young puts it in the preface to his translation of *The Sea Gull*, "is to take actual material such as we find in life and manage it in such a way that the inner meanings are made to appear. On the surface the life in his plays is natural, possible, and at times in effect even casual."

Young's translations of Chekhov's plays, together with his beautifully accurate notes, explanations, and interpretations, have made the text of Chekhov at last available for the English-speaking stage, and for any reader who will bring to his reading a little patience and imagination.[2] Young shows us what Chekhov means in detail: by the particular words his characters use; by their rhythms of speech; by their gestures, pauses, and bits of stage business. In short, he makes the text transparent, enabling us to see through it to the music of action, the underlying poetry of the composition as a whole—and this is as much as to say that any study of Chekhov (lacking as we do adequate and available productions) must be based upon Young's work. At this point I propose to take this work for granted; to assume the translucent text; and to consider the role of the setting in the poetic or musical order of Act II.

The second act, as I have said, corresponds to the agon of the traditional plot scheme: it is here that we see most clearly the divisive purposes of the characters, the contrasts between their views of the cherry orchard itself. But the center of interest is not in these individual conflicts, nor in the contrasting versions for their own sake, but in the common fatality which they reveal: the passing of the old estate. The setting, as we come to know it behind the casual surfaces of the text, is one of the chief elements in this poem of change: if Act II were a lyric, instead of an act of a play, the setting would be a crucial word appearing in a succession of rich contexts which endow it with a developing meaning.

Chekhov describes the setting in the following realistic terms. "A field. An old chapel, long abandoned, with crooked walls, near it a well, big stones that apparently were once tombstones, and an old bench. A road to the estate of Gaev can be seen. On one side poplars rise, casting their shadows, the cherry orchard begins there. In the distance a row of telegraph poles; and far, far away, faintly traced on the horizon, is a large town, visible only in the clearest weather. The sun will soon be down."

2. The quotations from *The Cherry Orchard* are taken from the translation by Stark Young (New York: Samuel French). Copyright 1947 by Stark Young. All rights reserved. Reprinted by permission of the author and Samuel French.

To make this set out of a cyclorama, flats, cut-out silhouettes, and lighting effects would be difficult, without producing that unbelievable but literally intended—and in any case indigestible—scene which modern realism demands; and here Chekhov is uncomfortably bound by the convention of his time. The best strategy in production is that adopted by Robert Edmond Jones in his setting for *The Sea Gull*: to pay lip service only to the convention of photographic realism, and make the trees, the chapel, and all the other elements as simple as possible. The less closely the setting is defined by the carpenter, the freer it is to play the role Chekhov wrote for it: a role which changes and develops in relation to the story. Shakespeare did not have this problem; he could present his setting in different ways at different moments in a few lines of verse:

> Alack! the night comes on, and the bleak winds
> Do sorely ruffle; for many miles about
> There's scarce a bush.

Chekhov, as we shall see, gives his setting life and flexibility in spite of the visible elements on-stage, not by means of the poetry of words but by means of his characters' changing sense of it.

When the curtain rises we see the setting simply as the country at the sentimental hour of sunset. Yepikhodov is playing his guitar and other hangers-on of the estate are loafing, as is their habit, before supper. The dialogue which starts after a brief pause focuses attention upon individuals in the group: Charlotta, the governess, boasting of her culture and complaining that no one understands her; the silly maid Dunyasha, who is infatuated with Yasha, Lyubov's valet. The scene, as reflected by these characters, is a satirical period-piece like the "Stag at Eve" or "The Maiden's Prayer";[3] and when the group falls silent and begins to drift away (having heard Lyubov, Gaev, and Lopakhin approaching along the path) Chekhov expects us to smile at the sentimental clichés which the place and the hour have produced.

But Lyubov's party brings with it a very different atmosphere: of irritation, frustration, and fear. It is here we learn that Lopakhin cannot persuade Lyubov and Gaev to put their affairs in order; that Gaev has been making futile gestures toward getting a job and borrowing money; that Lyubov is worried about the estate, about her daughters, and about her lover, who has now fallen ill in Paris. Lopakhin, in a huff, offers to leave; but Lyubov will not let him go—"It's more cheerful with you here," she says; and this group in

---

3. "The Maiden's Prayer" (1856), a piece for the pianoforte by Tekla Badarzewska-Baranowska (1838–61), Polish composer. The piece was extremely popular through-out Europe, and Chekhov uses it as a piece played probably by Natasha off-stage in Act IV of *The Three Sisters* [See p. 147—*Editor's note.*]

its turn falls silent. In the distance we hear the music of the Jewish orchestra—when Chekhov wishes us to raise our eyes from the people in the foreground to their wider setting, he often uses music as a signal and an inducement. This time the musical entrance of the setting into our consciousness is more urgent and sinister than it was before: we see not so much the peace of evening as the silhouette of the dynamic industrial town on the horizon, and the approach of darkness. After a little more desultory conversation, there is another pause, this time without music, and the foreboding aspect of the scene in silence is more intense.

In this silence Firs, the ancient servant, hurries on with Gaev's coat, to protect him from the evening chill, and we briefly see the scene through Firs's eyes. He remembers the estate before the emancipation of the serfs, when it was the scene of a way of life which made sense to him; and now we become aware of the frail relics of this life: the old gravestones and the chapel "fallen out of the perpendicular."

In sharpest contrast with this vision come the young voices of Anya, Varya, and Trofimov, who are approaching along the path. The middle-aged and the old in the foreground are pathetically grateful for this note of youth, of strength, and of hope; and presently they are listening happily (though without agreement or belief) to Trofimov's aspirations, his creed of social progress, and his conviction that their generation is no longer important to the life of Russia. When the group falls silent again, they are all disposed to contentment with the moment; and when Yepikhodov's guitar is heard, and we look up, we feel the country and the evening under the aspect of hope—as offering freedom from the responsibilities and conflicts of the estate itself:

> YEPIKHODOV *passes by at the back, playing his guitar.*
> LYUBOV. [*lost in thought*] Yepikhodov is coming—
> ANYA. [*lost in thought*] Yepikhodov is coming.
> GAEV. The sun has set, ladies and gentlemen.
> TROFIMOV. Yes.
> GAEV. [*not loud and as if he were declaiming*] Oh, Nature, wonderful, you gleam with eternal radiance, beautiful and indifferent, you, whom we call Mother, combine in yourself both life and death, you give life and take it away.
> VARYA. [*beseechingly*] Uncle!

Gaev's false, rhetorical note ends the harmony, brings us back to the present and to the awareness of change on the horizon, and produces a sort of empty stalemate—a silent pause with worry and fear in it.

All sit absorbed in their thoughts. There is only the silence.
FIRS *is heard muttering to himself softly. Suddenly a distant*
sound is heard, as if from the sky, like the sound of a snap-
ped string, dying away, mournful.

This mysterious sound is used like Yepikhodov's strumming to
remind us of the wider scene, but (though distant) it is sharp,
almost a warning signal, and all the characters listen and peer
toward the dim edges of the horizon. In their attitudes and guesses
Chekhov reflects, in rapid succession, the contradictory aspects of
the scene which have been developed at more length before us:

LYUBOV. What's that?
LOPAKHIN. I don't know. Somewhere far off in a mine shaft a
    bucket fell. But somewhere very far off.
GAEV. And it may be some bird—like a heron.
TROFIMOV. Or an owl—
LYUBOV. [*shivering*] It's unpleasant, somehow. [*A pause.*]
FIRS. Before the disaster it was like that. The owl hooted and the
    samovar hummed without stopping, both.
GAEV. Before what disaster?
FIRS. Before the emancipation. [*A pause.*]
LYUBOV. You know, my friends, let's go. . . .

Lyubov feels the need to retreat, but the retreat is turned into flight
when "the wayfarer" suddenly appears on the path asking for
money. Lyubov in her bewilderment, her sympathy, and her bad
conscience, gives him gold. The party breaks up, each in his own
way thwarted and demoralized.

Anya and Trofimov are left onstage; and, to conclude his theatrical poem of the suffering of change, Chekhov reflects the setting in
them:

ANYA. [*a pause*] It's wonderful here today!
TROFIMOV. Yes, the weather is marvelous.
ANYA. What have you done to me, Petya, why don't I love the
    cherry orchard any longer the way I used to? I loved it too
    tenderly; it seemed to me there was not a better place on earth
    than our orchard.
TROFIMOV. All Russia is our garden. The earth is immense and
    beautiful. . . .

The sun has set, the moon is rising with its chill and its ancient
animal excitement, and the estate is dissolved in the darkness as
Nineveh[4] is dissolved in a pile of rubble with vegetation creeping

4. Capital of ancient Assyria on the Tigris, opposite modern Mosul in Northern Iraq
[*Editor's note*].

over it. Chekhov wishes to show the Cherry Orchard as "gone"; but for this purpose he employs not only the literal time-scheme (sunset to moonrise) but, as reflectors, Anya and Trofimov, for whom the present in any form is already gone and only the bodiless future is real. Anya's young love for Trofimov's intellectual enthusiasm (like Juliet's "all as boundless as the sea") has freed her from her actual childhood home, made her feel "at home in the world" anywhere. Trofimov's abstract aspirations give him a chillier and more artificial, but equally complete, detachment not only from the estate itself (he disapproves of it on theoretical grounds) but from Anya (he thinks it would be vulgar to be in love with her). We hear the worried Varya calling for Anya in the distance; Anya and Trofimov run down to the river to discuss the socialistic *Paradiso Terrestre*; and with these complementary images of the human scene, and this subtle chord of feeling, Chekhov ends the act.

The "scene" is only one element in the composition of Act II, but it illustrates the nature of Chekhov's poetry of the theatre. It is very clear, I think, that Chekhov is not trying to present us with a rationalization of social change *à la* Marx, or even with a subtler rationalization *à la* Shaw. On the other hand, he is not seeking, like Wagner,[5] to seduce us into one passion. He shows us a moment of change in society, and he shows us a "pathos"; but the elements of his composition are always taken as objectively real. He offers us various rationalizations, various images, and various feelings, which cannot be reduced either to one emotion or to one idea: they indicate an action and a scene which is "there" before the rational formulations, or the emotionally charged attitudes, of any of the characters.

The surrounding scene of *The Cherry Orchard* corresponds to the significant stage of human life which Sophocles' choruses reveal, and to the empty wilderness beyond Ibsen's little parlor. We miss, in Chekhov's scene, any fixed points of human significance, and that is why, compared with Sophocles, he seems limited and partial—a bit too pathetic even for our bewildered times. But, precisely because he subtly and elaborately develops the moments of pathos with their sad insights, he sees much more in the little scene of modern realism than Ibsen does. Ibsen's snowpeaks strike us as rather hysterical; but the "stage of Europe" which we divine behind the Cherry Orchard is confirmed by a thousand impressions derived from other sources. We may recognize its main elements in a cocktail party in Connecticut or Westchester: someone's lawn full of voluble people; a dry white clapboard church (instead of an Orthodox chapel) just visible across a field; time passing, and the muffled roar of a four-lane highway under the hill—or we may be reminded of it in the

5. Richard Wagner (1813–83), German operatic composer [*Editor's note*].

final section of *The Waste Land*,[6] with its twittering voices, its old gravestones and deserted chapel, and its dim crowd on the horizon foreboding change. It is because Chekhov says so little that he reveals so much, providing a concrete basis for many conflicting rationalizations of contemporary social change: by accepting the immediacy and unintelligibility of modern realism so completely, he in some ways transcends its limitations, and prepares the way for subsequent developments in the modern theatre.

CHEKHOV'S HISTRIONIC ART: AN END AND A BEGINNING

Era già l'ora che volge il disio
　　ai naviganti e intenercisce il core,
　　lo dì ch'han detto ai dolci amici addio;
e che lo nuovo peregrin d'amore
　　punge, se ode squilla di lontano,
　　che paia il giorno pianger che si more.[7]

—*Purgatorio*, Canto VIII

The poetry of modern realistic drama is to be found in those inarticulate moments when the human creature is shown responding directly to his immediate situation. Such are the many moments—composed, interrelated, echoing each other—when the waiting and loafing characters in Act II get a fresh sense (one after the other, and each in his own way) of their situation on the doomed estate. It is because of the exactitude with which Chekhov perceives and imitates these tiny responses, that he can make them echo each other, and convey, when taken together, a single action with the scope, the general significance or suggestiveness, of poetry. Chekhov, like other great dramatists, has what might be called an ear for action, comparable to the trained musician's ear for musical sound.

The action which Chekhov thus imitates in his second act (that of lending ear, in a moment of freedom from practical pressures, to impending change) echoes, in its turn, a number of other poets: Laforgue's "poetry of waiting-rooms"[8] comes to mind, as well as other works stemming from the period of hush before the First World War. The poets are to some extent talking about the same thing, and their works, like voices in a continuing colloquy, help to explain each other: hence the justification and the purpose of seek-

6. A poem by T. S. Eliot (1888–1965), American-born British poet and critic [*Editor's note*].
7. "It was now the hour that turns back the desire of those who sail the seas and melts their heart, that day when they have said to their sweet friends adieu, and that pierces the new pilgrim with love, if from afar he hears the chimes which seem to mourn for the dying day."
8. Jules Laforgue (1860–87), French Symbolist poet said to have introduced *vers libra* (free verse) in poetry [*Editor's note*].

ing comparisons. The eighth canto of the *Purgatorio* is widely separated from *The Cherry Orchard* in space and time, but these two poems unmistakably echo and confirm each other. Thinking of them together, one can begin to place Chekhov's curiously nonverbal dramaturgy and understand the purpose and the value of his reduction of the art to histrionic terms, as well as the more obvious limitations which he thereby accepts. For Dante accepts similar limitations at this point but locates the mode of action he shows here at a certain point in his vast scheme.

The explicit coordinates whereby Dante places the action of Canto VIII might alone suffice to give one a clue to the comparison with *The Cherry Orchard*: we are in the Valley of Negligent Rulers who, lacking light, unwillingly suffer their irresponsibility, just as Lyubov and Gaev do. The *ante-purgatorio* is behind us, and purgatory proper, with its hoped-for work, thought, and moral effort, is somewhere ahead, beyond the night which is now approaching. It is the end of the day; and as we wait, watch, and listen, evening moves slowly over our heads, from sunset to darkness to moonrise. Looking more closely at this canto, one can see that Dante the Pilgrim and the Negligent Rulers he meets are listening and looking as Chekhov's characters are in Act II: the action is the same; in both, a childish and uninstructed responsiveness, an unpremeditated obedience to what is actual, informs the suffering of change. Dante the author, for his elaborate and completely conscious reasons, works here with the primitive histrionic sensibility; he composes with elements sensuously or sympathetically, but not rationally or verbally, defined. The rhythms, the pauses, and the sound effects he employs are strikingly similar to Chekhov's. And so he shows himself—Dante "the new Pilgrim"—meeting this mode of awareness for the first time: as delicately and ignorantly as Gaev when he feels all of a sudden the extent of evening, and before he falsifies this perception with his embarrassing apostrophe to Nature.

If Dante allows himself as artist and as protagonist only the primitive sensibility of the child, the naïf, the natural saint, at this point in the ascent, it is because, like Chekhov, he is presenting a threshold or moment of change in human experience. He wants to show the unbounded potentialities of the psyche before or between the moments when it is morally and intellectually realized. In Canto VIII the pilgrim is both a child, and a child who is changing; later moments of transition are different. Here he is virtually (but for the Grace of God) lost; all the dangers are present. Yet he remains uncommitted and therefore open to finding himself again and more truly. In all of this the parallel to Chekhov is close. But because Dante sees this moment as a moment only in the ascent, Canto VIII is also composed in ways in which Act II of *The Cherry Orchard* is not—ways which the reader of the *Purgatorio* will not understand until he looks back from the top of the mountain. Then he will see the homesickness which informs Canto VIII in a new light, and all of the concrete elements, the snake in the grass, the winged figures that roost at the edge of the valley like night-hawks, will be intelligible to the mind and, without losing their concreteness, take their places in a more general frame. Dante's fiction is laid in the scene beyond the grave, where every human action has its relation to ultimate reality, even though that relation becomes explicit only gradually. But Chekhov's characters are seen in the flesh and in their very secular emotional entanglements: in the contemporary world as anyone can see it—nothing visible beyond the earth's horizon, with its signs of social change. The fatality of the *Zeitgeist*[9] is the ultimate reality in the theatre of modern realism; the anagoge is lacking. And though Ibsen and Chekhov are aware of both history and moral effort, they do not know what to make of them—perhaps they reveal only illusory perspectives, "masquerades which time resumes." If Chekhov echoes Dante, it is not because of what he ultimately understood but because of the accuracy with which he saw and imitated that moment of action.

If one thinks of the generation to which Anya and Trofimov were supposed to belong, it is clear that the new motives and reasons which they were to find, after their inspired evening together, were not such as to turn all Russia, or all the world, into a garden. The potentialities which Chekhov presented at that moment of change were not to be realized in the wars and revolutions which followed: what actually followed was rather that separation and destruction, that scattering and destinationless trekking, which he also sensed as possible. But, in the cultivation of the dramatic art after Chekhov, renewals, the realization of hidden potentialities, did follow. In Chekhov's histrionic art, the "desire is turned back" to its very root, to the immediate response, to the movements of the psyche before they are limited, defined, and realized in reasoned purpose. Thus Chekhov revealed hidden potentialities, if not in the life of the time, at least in ways of seeing and showing human life; if not in society, at least in the dramatic art. The first and most generally recognized result of these labors was to bring modern realism to its final perfection in the productions of the Moscow Art Theatre and in those who learned from it. But the end of modern realism was also a return to very ancient sources; and in our time the fertilizing effect of Chekhov's humble objectivity may be traced in a number of dramatic forms which cannot be called modern realism at all.

The acting technique of the Moscow Art Theatre is so closely connected, in its final development, with Chekhov's dramaturgy,

9. "Spirit of the age" [*Editor's note*].

that it would be hard to say which gave the more important clues. Stanislavsky and Nemirovich-Danchenko from one point of view, and Chekhov from another, approached the same conception: both were searching for an attitude and a method that would be less hidebound, truer to experience, than the cliché-responses of the commercial theatre. The Moscow Art Theatre taught the performer to make that direct and total response which is the root of poetry in the widest sense: they cultivated the histrionic sensibility in order to free the actor to realize, in his art, the situations and actions which the playwright had imagined. Chekhov's plays demand this accuracy and imaginative freedom from the performer; and the Moscow Art Theatre's productions of his works were a demonstration of the perfection, the reticent poetry, of modern realism. And modern realism of this kind is still alive in the work of many artists who have been more or less directly influenced either by Chekhov or by the Moscow Art Theatre. In our country, for instance, there is Clifford Odets; in France, Vildrac and Bernard, and the realistic cinema, of which *Symphonie Pastorale* is an example.[1]

But this cultivation of the histrionic sensibility, bringing modern realism to its end and its perfection, also provided fresh access to many other dramatic forms. The Moscow technique, when properly developed and critically understood, enables the producer and performer to find the life in any theatrical form; before the revolution the Moscow Art Theatre had thus revivified *Hamlet, Carmen*, the interludes of Cervantes, Neoclassic comedies of several kinds, and many other works which were not realistic in the modern sense at all. A closely related acting technique underlay Reinhardt's virtuosity; and Copeau, in the Vieux Colombier,[2] used it to renew not only the art of acting but, by that means, the art of playwriting also. * * *

After periods when great drama is written, great performers usually appear to carry on the life of the theatre for a few more generations. Such were the Siddonses and Macreadys[3] who kept the great Shakespearian roles alive after Shakespeare's theatre was gone, and such, at a further stage of degeneration, were the mimes of the

---

1. Charles Messager Vildrac (b. 1882), French poet and dramatist. Jean-Jacques Bernard (b. 1888), French playwright. *La Symphonie Pastorale* (1919) by André Gide (1869–1951) was adapted by Jean Aurenche (b. 1904) and Pierre Bost into a scenario for the movie (1946) directed by Jean Delannoy (b. 1908) and starring Michèle Morgan and Pierre Blanchar [*Editor's note*].
2. Max Reinhardt (1873–1943), German stage director who achieved international renown as one of the finest directors of his day. Jacques Copeau (1879–1949) founded his Théâtre du Vieux Colombier in Paris in 1913. Dominating the French theatre between the wars, Copeau was a critic and stage director but received his highest praise for training perhaps the best company of actors in France after World War I—a company that ranked among the best in the world [*Editor's note*].
3. Sarah Kemble Siddons (1755–1831) during the period from 1782 to 1812 was considered by critics as the finest English actress in tragedy. William Charles Macready (1793–1873), was an English actor-manager who received praise for restoring much of the original text in his productions of Shakespeare's plays [*Editor's note*].

Commedia dell'Arte, improving on the themes of Terence and Plautus when the theatre had lost most of its meaning. The progress of modern realism from Ibsen to Chekhov looks in some respects like a withering and degeneration of this kind: Chekhov does not demand the intellectual scope, the ultimate meanings, which Ibsen demanded, and to some critics Chekhov does not look like a real dramatist but merely an overdeveloped mime, a stage virtuoso. But the theatre of modern realism did not afford what Ibsen demanded, and Chekhov is much the more perfect master of its little scene. If Chekhov drastically reduced the dramatic art, he did so in full consciousness, and in obedience both to artistic scruples and to a strict sense of reality. He reduced the dramatic art to its ancient root, from which new growths are possible.

Legacy

SIEGFRIED MELCHINGER

Stage Productions in Europe

Chekhov was and is still the great dramatist of the Moscow Art Theatre. To this day its emblem is the sea gull. On its foreign tours, the Moscow Art Theatre still presents Chekhov productions that have been in its repertoire, almost unchanged, for decades. * * * It was Chekhov's view that Stanislavsky was "ruining" his plays. But Stanislavsky's productions of Chekhov did not simply remain as they were being played during Chekhov's lifetime or shortly after his death. Meyerhold reported that Stanislavsky's mania for stage detail reached absurd proportion in his second production of *The Sea Gull*, and that in his second production of *The Cherry Orchard*, in the departure scene of the third act, he had a real troika and horses brought onto the stage.

Yet Stanislavsky's memoirs make it clear that he became more and more concerned with bringing out "the line of the inner dialogue" (rhythm and melody), and with cutting down on his old tendency to scenic naturalism. In the last of the many chapters he devotes to Chekhov, Stanislavsky himself demands a revision of the traditional style of producing Chekhov—"a new Chekhov." What degree of perfection the Moscow Art Theatre ensemble achieved in their interpretation of Chekhov's "art of the quiet truth" may be gathered from a review written by the German critic Alfred Kerr in 1922—only a few years before the publication of Stanislavsky's memoirs.

Here is Kerr's reaction to a guest performance of the Moscow Art Theatre then on tour in Berlin:

> A true performance. . . . Simply wonderful. . . . How the people come and go (they don't seem to be characters making stage entrances) . . . how they stroll through the rooms! One comes from here, another from there, and so there they are. . . . The whole thing is superb, superb, superb. . . . It's a jewel, and truly human. A reflection of life on earth. . . . It is not the individual actor who matters but the marvelous meshing together, one into another. . . .

For the Russian revolutionaries who, around 1919, proclaimed their anti-illusionism, the Chekhov theatre—just because it was

Stanislavsky's theatre—became the prototype of the dated style they opposed. On the tenth anniversary of Chekhov's death (in 1914), Mayakovsky[1] had saluted the author as a master of language—of "laconism, concentration, and precision." In 1921, for the prologue to the second version of his futuristic play *Mysterium Buffo*, he wrote:

> In other theatres too they have representation, but for them the scene is merely a keyhole. One sits still and watches how in this play a highly developed alien life is dismembered. One sits still and watches and hears Uncle Vanya snuffle and converse with Aunt Marya. But we are not interested in uncles and aunts, secretly we ourselves have our dear relatives at home. Surely we show plays taken from common and real life only to let the theatre heighten it into the realm of the uncommon.

After the Revolution it was the official judgment that Chekhov was "too objective," and therefore dated (to quote Lunacharsky, commissar for art and education in 1922). In the 1934 edition of the Soviet encyclopedia this negative judgment was formulated in such terms as "static," "lacking in action," "without ideas," and "a translation of the art of impressionist painting, of the accidental, into drama." Even Meyerhold now disavowed the playwright he had once loved so dearly.

It was not until the period in which the theatre put itself at the service of promulgating the objectives of the 1917 revolution ended that a change came about. And this indeed was a strange change. Now Chekhov was proclaimed the precursor and prophet of the Revolution. His plays were interpreted as optimistic; he was discovered (especially by Yermilov) as the great writer who had swept away the cobwebs of the old. After Stalin's death, this kind of Chekhov fashion also came to an end.

Characteristic of the present Soviet attitude toward Chekhov is the 1961 essay by Ilya Ehrenburg, "On Re-reading Chekhov" * * * . This is a splendid analysis and an unreserved acknowledgement of Chekhov.

Outside Russia, usually following the immensely successful tours of the Moscow Art Theatre, Chekhov's work has found a warm reception. Especially in northern Europe, in Holland, and in the English-speaking countries, there has developed a lively Chekhov tradition, modeled after Stanislavsky. This Chekhov tradition has greatly influenced both dramatic writing and the performing arts. Clearly, the concept of "the understatement" is rooted in Chekhov's "art of the quiet truth," as it was developed by the Moscow Art

1. V. V. Mayakovsky (1893–1930), famous poet and dramatist whose major plays are ranked among the best Russian plays written since 1913, the year of his short Futurist verse play *Vladimir Mayakovsky: A Tragedy* [*Editor's note*].

Theatre. G. B. Shaw called himself a Chekhov disciple. The relationship of such contemporary English dramatists as Harold Pinter, John Arden, John Mortimer, and Arnold Wesker to Chekhov's indirect method has been pointed out by John R. Taylor in his book *Angry Theatre: New British Drama.* To this day the major Chekhov roles are among the favorites of such distinguished actors as Lawrence Olivier. Such great Swedish and Finnish directors as Olof Molander and Eino Kalina whose Chekhov productions have been highly praised, have called themselves disciples of Stanislavsky.

In France, as late as 1939, however, Pitoëff[2]—who had gone there from Russia via Switzerland—was to find out that Chekhov was a little-known author. The Pitoëffs' contribution was decisive in radically changing this situation. In 1961 the French magazine *Arts* spoke of Chekhov as the most often produced playwright in France! Chekhov clearly has influenced Giraudoux and Anouilh. François Mauriac compared him with Mozart. Jean-Louis Barrault said that in Chekhov "every moment is full. And this fullness does not lie in the dialogue but in the silence, in the sense of life." It was Jean Vilar who first brought *Platonov* onto the stage, and he himself played the title role. It would be interesting to seek out Chekhov's trail in the works of Samuel Beckett.

The German theatre, too, around 1918, had a short Chekhov period. Surprisingly, the only Chekhov play ever directed by Max Reinhardt was *The Bear*, in 1905. The theatres he managed, however, sponsored Chekhov productions that left deep impressions, such as the impression the 1917 production of *The Sea Gull* (directed by Eugen Robert) made on the critic Siegfried Jacobson. Jacobson wrote: "One follows with compassionate interest, a response that makes one more attentive than the suspense that is elicited by the usual obvious plot, how bonds of love and suffering are tightened and undone between all these people. Chords, are sounded that are familiar to us all."

In 1919, at the Volksbühne,[3] Jacobson saw *The Cherry Orchard* (directed by Kayssler). He wrote:

> This artlessness will survive the artfulness (of an Ibsen) and literary fashions. It's an example of timeless poetry. . . . *The Cherry Orchard* is inhabited by a dozen people who itch and squirm, quarrel and love, rise and fall, rule and serve, are full of desire and full of resignation—are born and die. It is a moving

2. Georges Pitoëff (1884–1939) and his wife Ludmilla (1896–1951) were native-born Russians who met and married in Switzerland during the first World War, founded their acting company there in 1918, and toured throughout Europe in the 1920s and 1930s but eventually settled in Paris.

3. Friedrich Kayssler (1874–1945), one of Max Reinhardt's best actors, was manager of the Berlin Volksbühne (literally, "People's Theatre") in 1919 when Siegfried Jacobson saw the production of *The Cherry Orchard* [*Editor's note*].

reflection of our own existence. . . . They are all little people with everyday destinies. Their conversations do not strive to be intellectually representative. How great must have been Chekhov's genius, his sensitivity, his knowledge of the human soul, his ability to illuminate it, his gift to feel his brother's suffering and capture it.

But Chekhov did not take root in the German-speaking theatre. And this, although he was loved deeply by Jürgen Fehling,[4] who directed the premiere of *The Three Sisters* in 1926, and Heinz Hilpert,[5] whose last production, in 1967 in Munich, was that of a Chekhov play. This, in part, can be attributed to the difficulty of translating Chekhov into German. But the main reason is that "the art of the quiet truth," as Stanislavsky was presenting it in his later years (German productions, directed by Stanislavsky's student Peter Scharoff, were also being offered) arrived on the German stage at the time when Brecht's theatre demanded that the truth be made "spectacular" in order to prevail. And Thomas Mann's "Anton Chekhov: An Essay," published in 1954, did not succeed in bringing Chekhov any closer to the German audience.

It is possible that there now will be a change. For throughout the world, theatre people are beginning to realize the need for a long overdue revision of the Chekhov theatre.

I have already mentioned five productions as examples of such new interpretations. High standards for a new Chekhov theatre have been set by Giorgio Strehler's 1959 Milan production of *Platonov* and by Ingmar Bergman's 1961 Stockholm production of *The Sea Gull*.

In 1967, the Czech director Otomar Krejča created a sensation with his production of *The Three Sisters* at Prague's Theatre Before the Gate.

Krejča says that Chekhov is "cool like a surgeon." Because of the relentless objectivity and "extreme justice" with which Chekhov treats his characters' attitudes, thoughts, and emotions (also their hardly conscious and unconscious ones), Krejča believes he has the right to move his actors about as if they were driven in harness. It is he, the director, who causes them to move about, clearly against their own will—and this subjugation mirrors how the play's events affect the characters. And the effect of this subjugation is that the actors are put into a state of high tension. Here Chekhov's silence is hardly part of the stage directions. It is rather a dismantling of the spoken words through that which happens behind, between, and

4. Jürgen Fehling (1885–1968), stage director at the Berlin Volksbühne after World War I whose reputation was established by his direction of German ex-   pressionist drama [*Editor's note*].
5. Heinz Hilpert (1890-1967), German stage director [*Editor's note*].

beyond them. Krejča does use Stanislavsky's method of direction, but his objective is not to create a constant and noisy atmosphere or to express "inner" dialogue through silent acting. Here the sounds thicken, jelling into surrealist music. The gestures, the walking, swing in its rhythm, and the constant play of movement and expression that underlies the dialogue becomes high-tension choreography. The Prague *Three Sisters* so far is the richest example of a revision of the Chekhov theatre.

In his Stuttgart production of *The Three Sisters* in 1965, Rudolf Noelte interpreted, with admirable consistency, "the quiet truth" quite differently from Stanislavsky. Noelte saw the play not in terms of scenic detail but as a distillation. Some critics said, and quite rightly so, that he had projected a Beckett world. Peter Zadek, again quite differently, and also in Stuttgart, in his 1968 production of *The Cherry Orchard,* uncovered another Chekhov truth that Gorky already had spoken of: coolness and cruelty. (One could have done without his rearrangement of the second act, which tampered with the play's characters and its structure.)

Recently, there has been a revealing controversy about the interpretation of Chekhov in Moscow. A production of *The Three Sisters,* directed by Anatoli Efros, was closed down because its unconventional style was clearly opposed to the Stanislavsky tradition and so to socialist realism. W. Bronska-Pampuch reported on this production (in the *Stuttgarter Zeitung,* 1968, No. 50):

> Chekhov has been newly discovered. He has, of course, been presented on the Russian stage for decades, but it seems that only now has he been rightly understood. Anatoli Efros, a young director, has produced *The Three Sisters* without the old obligatory sets projecting heavy mood and atmosphere. Gone now is the avenue of birch trees, gone the naturalistic room decor. On the empty stage stands merely a single, stylized tree with copper leaves, which also serves as a coat rack. From the very beginning, Chekhov's characters are now isolated and lonely, and their relationship to the world around them is full of frustration. The ending of the play that in past productions, like many lines of the dialogue, sounded melodramatic, now is farcelike. "Chekhov always wanted to be understood as a writer of farces and comedies," said the Moscow theatre critic Maya Turovskaya. "But people didn't take serious notice of such remarks and declared that Chekhov had merely been joking. For this attitude did not fit into the tradition of our Russian theatre." Now, finally, there is an effort to do justice to Chekhov, the great renewer. And now the development of the Chekhov tradition, which stopped in the year 1900, begins anew.

JOHN GASSNER

The Duality of Chekhov

Two diametrically opposed interpretations of Chekhov have appeared in the English-speaking world, and they have been proclaimed with special fervor in the world of the theatre. The first dominant view, while conceding his talent for vaudeville humor in a number of short stage pieces, lauded an artist of half-lights, a laureate of well-marinated futility, and a master of tragic sensibility even if his work failed to conform to classic standards of tragedy. This view came to be challenged with considerable vigor in England and America after World War II, particularly in the academic world. Without any ideological impetus, such as one could expect in Eastern Europe, to favor a new image of Chekhov as the prophet of a new society, there arose a tendency to discard the old image in favor of a tinsel view of Chekhov as a paragon of breezy extroversion. Young academicians were particularly eager to divest him of the atmosphere of gloom and soulfulness ("Slavic soulfulness," at that!) which he had accumulated in Western criticism and stage productions. Moreover, so many journalistic sources gave their support to proponents of this view that it became the prevailing one whether or not it was applicable to any particular work in whole or in part.

It must become evident, though, upon reflection, that this view has its inadequacies, if not indeed dangers—inadequacies even with respect to a brief humorous story such as the often-printed "A Work of Art," in which a physician is embarrassed in his provincial milieu by the gift of a nude statuette, let alone with respect to the great plays upon which rests much of Chekhov's reputation in the West. The advocates of a blithely extrovert interpretation or the image of a Chekhov purified of "Chekhovianism" are constrained to omit or at least play down too many facets, not to mention nuances, of his work to make it conform to a simplistic definition of comedy; the work thus becomes too thin and elementary, and would therefore have to be rated as little more than clever second-rate histrionics. The proponents of this recently "discovered" image have not known what to make of their extroverted Chekhov, just as their predecessors didn't quite know what to make of their introverted one. For the former, it seems sufficient that Chekhov, according to his biographer, David Magarshack, claimed that he wrote "comedies" and that in his original Moscow Art Theatre stage productions Stanislavsky distorted the plays. For the latter, it was sufficient that

Stanislavsky, who was after all known to be the scion of a wealthy merchant family and a gentleman of the Russian *ancien régime*, laved the plays in a tragical atmosphere until they could be read as rueful epitaphs for a vanishing upper class.

The latter view (though not without comic touches—or what the British weather forecasters call "bright intervals") has prevailed in England, where there has been a decaying upper class now for more than half a century. And British playwrights have long been prone to turn their "country houses" into "Heartbreak Houses," although hardly with the buoyancy of Bernard Shaw, the author of *Heartbreak House*, who felt no sentimental attachment to country houses or their upper-class occupants. In the United States we lacked the country houses that would afford a class basis for mournful Chekhovianism and therefore fared less well with it. Thus the Broadway director Joshua Logan had to go to the deep South for a Chekhovian country house in his *Cherry Orchard* adaptation, *The Wisteria Tree*, and even this sensible recourse did not quite secure Chekhovian introversion against Broadway's cosmopolitan (or merely deracinated) diffidence.

What the old tendency in Chekhovian production failed to perceive (the Lunt–Theatre Guild production of *The Sea Gull* in the 1930s may be considered a happy exception) was that Chekhov himself was not dispirited even if a good many of his characters are, and that even the latter are not altogether willing to wallow in hopelessness. If this old-guard view of Chekhov had been entirely tenable, it would have been easy to advance claims for him as one of the progenitors of the Theatre of the Absurd,[1] and it is perhaps significant that no such claims have been advanced. What the "new-generation" view of the extrovert–Chekhov has failed to take into account is precisely the large area of stalemate against which Chekhov rebelled, and the fact that what he exposed in his plays plainly existed in turn-of-the-century provincial life. It was pervasive and oppressive enough, in fact, to arouse his scorn and indignation. It comprised a world abundantly present in his plays and stories, for a good writer does not launch an attack on something that lacks reality and he also does not tilt against anything to which he has

---

1. The label popularized by British critic Martin Esslin (author of *The Theatre of the Absurd*, 1961; revised in 1968) and given to playwrights and plays of the avant-garde after World War II. One source for the absurdist movement was Albert Camus's essay "Le Mythe de Sisyphe" ("The Myth of Sisyphus," 1942), in which he wrote: "This universe in itself is not rational. . . . What is absurd is the confrontation of this irrational and the mad desire for clarity whose appeal reverberates most deeply in man" (thus, *absurd* in the meaning of "out of harmony"). Among the chief characteristics common to plays labeled *absurd*, like Eugène Ionesco's *La Cantatrice chauve* (*The Bald Soprano*, 1950) and Samuel Beckett's *Waiting for Godot* (1952), are: non-traditional form in terms of structured action, story, characters, language; illogical, unrelated, and grotesque dialogue and action; often circular and repetitive action, story, language [*Edior's note*].

failed to give existence as an artist. And Chekhov could not have done what he did if he had been a wholly detached naturalist, an intellectual snob, a blithely sneering sophisticate, or a superficial propagandist thundering against a crumbling *ancien régime*. It is absurd to assume that he had no empathy with his stalemated characters, no share in the sensibility that makes them so alive and appealing, as it would be to claim that he felt no ambivalence in portraying them sensitively or even sympathetically.

It is ambivalence translated into art (and that means into *artistic reality*) that distinguishes the writer even in laughter from the non-artist and that separates the poet from the poetaster. Chekhov's sensibility for stalemate as well as his attack on it is an important element in his artistry, and Stanislavsky was enough of an artist to discern it in the plays he brought to the stage. To this undertaking, of course, Stanislavsky also brought his own sensibility, as did the Moscow Art Theatre actors, and there is reason to believe that before the Bolshevik revolution the Moscow Art Theatre could not have entertained absolute hostility to the life represented by its greatest playwright. Surely Stanislavsky and his associates could not have been naïve enough to think that the closing scenes of *The Sea Gull, Uncle Vanya, The Three Sisters,* and *The Cherry Orchard* were "funny." Surely they could not be insensible to the presence of heartbreak in whatever affirmativeness is explicit or discoverable in the plays.

Most important of all, however, is the fact that both our old-generation and new-generation viewpoints have tended to fail on the very same ground. They have been almost equally remiss in over-looking the *positive* element in his work, which has its basis not simply in the natural buoyancy of his character, but in his *positivist* outlook as a physician and as a "man of the people" to whom "soul-sickness" seems largely self-indulgence and suffering seems essen-tially the result of individual and societal bumbling. Chekhov was surely the most positivist and least Dostoevskian of the Russian literary masters. The *old* generation of Chekhov admirers in the English-speaking theatre tended to ignore or glide over this fact. The *new* generation, which became articulate after World War II, has tended to overlook the same fact in the very process of raising paeans to him as a writer of comedies. To publicize him without substantial qualification as a humorist is an insult to his engaged intelligence and passionateness.

Chekhov is passionate in both his scorn and his sympathy even when he displays a cool surface of detachment, a surface of natu-ralistic objectivity. This is often only his literary façade, so to speak. If anyone undertakes to appraise Chekhov seriously, he will, it is true, find much humor in the major works of fiction and drama. Chekhov may be a comic master, though hardly that alone (only ignorance of such works as "The Peasants" and "Ward No. 6" could allow such an unqualified generalization); he is far from being one of those clever jesters for whom a jest of any consequence is not, in Shaw's famous words, "an earnest in the womb of time." Only when this is realized can the critic do justice to Chekhov as a major figure of the literary world. Only then, too, can a theatrical production of a major Chekhov play find the ncessary mean between its farcicality and tragicality.

The same kind of writer appears in the mature artistry of both his stories and his plays, and the style is intrinsically the *man* in both despite the more formal demands of the dramatic medium. Chekhov places wonderfully alive characters in the center of his work whether he gives them independence in a character sketch such as "The Darling" or the full but dependent reality of a dramatically involved person. If he relates them to their environment, he does not diminish them as individuals even when the milieu oppresses them, as it does in *Uncle Vanya* and *The Three Sisters*. The dissonances of social reality do not drown out the resonant singularity of the human voice. It is agreed that Chekhov supplants the external action of commonplace fiction and drama with *inner* action, thus producing the so-called plotless work we associate importantly with modern literature and theatre. In reducing the role of plot, however, he does not diminish—he actually enlarges and intensifies—character revelation.

Chekhov performed the extremely difficult feat of maintaining the reality of character and the reality of environment in delicate equilibrium. Chekhov is a naturalist who did not content himself with observing surfaces but created in depth and consequently escaped the aridity of most naturalistic writing. And if, like other naturalists, he provided many a slice of life in his stories and plays, each slice was alive, whereas the naturalist's *"tranche de vie"* too often possesses everything but abounding life.

Chekhov, moreover, wrote with the simplicity of a person who is constitutionally incapable of imposing on anyone. He was that rare literary naturalist who wrote *naturally*. It is not only that his writing flowed easily but that he managed to write masterly stories and a number of major plays in which the characters behave and speak as if they were unaware of having been snared in the net of literature. They seem immersed in the stream of their own life. They feel for themselves, think their own thoughts, and dream their own dreams; so much so, in fact, that they seem to fly off from the center of the action and contribute to a play a centrifugal action (or, on occasion, *inaction*[2]) of their own. Although he wrote neither verse nor purple prose, his mature writing, full of delicate shadings of characterization and emotion, has the effect of poetry. In his chief work, moreover, the "poetry" is of such complex design that his writing has been described as virtually contrapuntal.

And one more technical point must be mentioned: It has often been noted that Chekhov is a great humorist yet also a profoundly moving writer. What this amounts to in terms of artistry is that his writing simply possesses a rich texture, that it exists on several levels of sensibility at the same time, and that his often limpid simplicity masks considerable complexity. Chekhov is especially modern in this one respect: that his mature work belongs, in the main, to a mixed genre. Whereas in past ages comedy and tragedy tended to exist separately, they tend to blend in modern writing. In his work, comedy may infiltrate tragedy, and tragedy may infiltrate comedy, producing controversy on the part of those who like to busy themselves with the fine points of literary classification. Chekhov is the master of the double mode, of what for want of a better term we may call tragicomedy or simply "drama." He was so effective in this genre partly because his various attitudes and moods blended so naturally. He was so effective also because he had such high spirits that disenchantment or depression could not often overcome him as it evidently did in such stories as "The Peasants" and "Ward No. 6."

A romantic half-truth has designated Chekhov as the Jeremiah[3] of soul-bankruptcy. We can perhaps best approach this contention by noting that there have indeed been two major modes of modernism, as there have been *two* Chekhovs in literary tradition. It seems as if modernity has been divided between a modernism of *Thanatos* and a modernism of *Eros*.[4] Chekhov belongs to the *positive* mode of modernism in spite of the widespread tendency to associate him with moribund, negativistic modernity. We have barely begun to do justice, whether in criticism or stage production, to one of the most buoyantly vital of European writers. Chekhov appears to have possessed "the even-tempered soul" Matthew Arnold attributed to Sophocles, although that soul moved through life modestly and never teetered on "high tragic" stilts to survey the landscape of our muddied existence. He was equable with a twinkle and sometimes with a sob, but he was equable. Yet he was not *so* equable that he

2. A fine example of dramatic *inaction* in Chekhovian dramaturgy is the normally hyperactive merchant Lopakhin's unsuccessful wooing scene in *The Cherry Orchard*.
3. A Hebrew prophet of the seventh and sixth centuries B.C. whose work included the Biblical Book of Lamentations. The name is usually applied to persons who are pessimistic about the future [*Editor's note*].
4. In Greek mythology, Thanatos is death personified, Eros the god of love [*Editor's note*].

was devoid of passion and a critical faculty. He was critical of the old regime in Russia, of the general lack of progress in that country, of its dispirited intelligentsia and its ignorant peasantry; and he deplored the inhumanity of the law, including the barbaric penal system in Siberia. Chekhov did not allow himself to be overpowered by the enervation he attributed to provincial gentry. As Gorky observed, Chekhov "was always himself inwardly free." And he did not believe that anyone was doomed to triviality if he did not doom *himself*. Stanislavsky, who has been blamed for filling Chekhov's plays with gloom, also felt that affirmativeness and made a point of it in his autobiography. And Chekhov himself made a point of it even if he disdained the obvious and the unironic in his stories and plays. He believed, as he once declared with unwonted didacticism, that each man must work for the good of mankind despite his private misfortunes, and this idea is indeed the plangent refrain, though not unmixed with irony, of *The Three Sisters*, the darkest of the plays. He himself had known suffering and privation, but he also brought characteristically, much resolve and energy to his difficult family situation. "In my childhood," he once wrote, "I had no childhood"; and he assumed the burden of supporting his parents and brothers with his writing at an early age even while he was studying medicine. As Lillian Hellman puts it in her introduction to a collection of his letters, Chekhov "became the father of his family and remained the father the rest of his life."

Throughout his life he possessed that sense of responsibility and outward direction that produces major writers who belong to all humanity rather than to the minor fellowship of writers engaged in the pursuit of purely private sensibility. "Writers," he wrote to his editor Suvorin "who are immortal or just plain good . . . have one very important trait in common: they are going somewhere and they call us with them." Passiveness, despite his frequent concern with characters who suffer stalemate, was the one fault he could not tolerate in a writer, declaring that "he who wants nothing, hopes for nothing, and fears nothing cannot be an artist." It is for that reason as well as because of his social sympathies and medical training that he also rejected the indifference to science common among turn-of-the-century art-for-art's-sake coteries. "Science and letters," he declared, "should go hand in hand. Anatomy and *belles lettres* have the same enemy—the devil."

It can be said truly that much of his work is a marvelous combination of compassion and buoyant intelligence; he noted the darkness of the Russian milieu but also found many flecks of light in the darkness. Stanislavsky noted how intensely Chekhov's submerged characters reject total defeat, how "they dream, they rebel, and they reach out for what they want." Two significant lines originally in *The Sea Gull* reveal Chekhov's impatience with weakling intellectualism. When the comic schoolmaster Medvedenko declares that "The earth is round," Dr. Dorn asks him, "Why do you say it with so little conviction?"

Characters with whom Chekhov is in obvious sympathy often carry Chekhov's favorite work theme, based upon the belief that salvation for the individual or at least balm for his suffering lies in creativity. Nina, in *The Sea Gull*, is going to make a good actress of herself even after the failure of her love-affair with the novelist Trigorin; and while Uta Hagen played the role in the attractive Theatre Guild production of the 1930s, there could be no doubt that Nina would become one. "If only one could live the remnant of one's life in some new way," cries Uncle Vanya and adds, "we must make haste and work, make haste and do something." Irina, in *The Three Sisters*, cries out at the end, "I will give all my life to those to whom it may be of use," and her fiancé, the Baron, pathetically rejoices at the prospect of exchanging his aristocratic profession of arms for useful employment. "Something formidable is threatening us," he says. "The strong cleansing storm is gathering . . . it will soon sweep our world clean of laziness, indifference, prejudice against work, and wretched boredom." Regardless of Chekhov's dissatisfaction with the early Moscow Art Theatre productions of his plays, Stanislavsky came to appreciate the fact that Chekhov's characters possessed a high degree of resilience. In *My Life in Art*, Stanislavsky denied that they were moribund: "Like Chekhov, [they] seek life, joy, laughter, courage . . . [they try] to overcome the hard and unbearable impasses into which life has plunged them."

Chekhov himself continued his exertions as long as his health permitted; he practiced medicine among the peasants and on one famous occasion took an arduous trip to the Siberian peninsula of Sakhalin for the purpose of investigating Russia's prison camps. Outstanding in his mind were the two necessities: social reform and the application of scientific knowledge to human suffering. "God's earth is good," he once wrote with characteristic simplicity after his travels. "It is only we on it who are bad. Instead of knowledge, there is insolence and boundless conceit; instead of labor, idleness and caddishness; there is no justice, the understanding of honor does not go beyond the honor of the uniform! . . . the important thing is that we must be just and all the rest will follow from this." He was equally plain-spoken on the subject of science. "Surgery alone," he once declared, "has accomplished so much that the very thought of it is frightening. The period of twenty years ago appears just pitiful to anyone studying medicine nowadays . . . . If I were presented the choice of one of the two, the 'ideals' of the sixties or the worst community hospital of the present time, I wouldn't hesitate a moment in choosing the latter." He reminds us in this respect of another great devotee of art whose roots lay in the nineteenth century—Ibsen's English champion and translator, William Archer —who expressed his gratitude for the scientists who discovered anesthetics, "balsam anodyne," who did more for man than religion did in reducing the amount of pain in the world. Chekhov spoke plainly on this subject when he wrote "I am not in the same camp with literary men who take a skeptical attitude toward science."

The activism of social reform and science, moreover, made it possible for Chekhov to pursue a naturalistic style of literature— more apparent in his fiction than in his plays—which constitutes the other side of his richly nuanced and atmospheric art. He could face reality without being coarsened by it, and he knew that he could. Scorning moral censorship, he wrote that "there are people who can be corrupted even by children's literature," and that on the contrary, there are people "like good jurists and physicians who become purer the more they acquaint themselves with the sordidness of life." A responsible artist must conquer his squeamishness, must soil his imagination with the grime of life." We also meet Chekhov in a characteristic posture when we find him maintaining that a man of letters should be as objective as a chemist for whom "there is nothing unclean on the earth," that a writer has to realize "that dungheaps play a very respectable role in a landscape."

Too often in our century, modernism has been almost programatically identified with morbidity, negativism, and nihilism. Modernism, especially after the first and second world wars, became infatuated with this negative attitude in a variety of briefly fashionable temper tantrums, from dada-ism and expressionism to dramatic "absurdism," on the one hand, and with a mystique, on the other hand, ranging from the cult of the spirit absolute to the cult of the flesh absolute. Chekhov the man and the writer, on the contrary, belongs to the clear and broad, if by no means untroubled, stream of progressive modernism, to the modernism of hope rather than despair, and of activism rather than supine passiveness.

For Chekhov, who suffered from tuberculosis during half his lifetime and who died at the age of forty-four, the vivacity of health was not an easy possession. His health of spirit was hard-won and heroically maintained. Sympathy combined with skepticism helped him to maintain his balance under tension. He was a master of irony, and irony was in his case a sensible defense against excessive expectation on the part of one who believed in the possibility of progress. When his characters (such as Colonel Vershinin in *The Three Sisters*) spout optimism unbounded, it is plain that they are *troubled*. They do not speak the sentiments of their author, who remains more or less ironically aloof, although by no means hostile or indifferent toward them. It is plain that he did not share their protestations of deferred hope without a substantial discount.

Chekhov, to sum up, transcended the superficiality that often adheres to optimistic literature and at the same time escaped the morbidity that besets pessimistic profundity; and he kept a characteristic balance in other important respects. He stood virtually alone among the modern literary masters after 1890 in being complex without some mystique and subtle without obscurity. He was, so to speak, Olympian and yet also thoroughly companionable. It is chiefly by bearing these polarities in mind, and remembering especially the plain yet somehow elusive fact that there was ever sympathy in his comedy and some degree of comedy in his sympathy, that we may hope to bring his plays authentically to the stage.

Selected Bibliography

Since the references cited in the footnotes have received complete documentation, very few of those references are repeated in this selected bibliography.

BIOGRAPHICAL AND CRITICAL STUDIES

Avilov, Lydia. *Chekhov in My Life: A Love Story.* Translated with an Introduction by David Magarshack. Drawings by Lynton Lamb. London: J. Lehman, 1950.

Bruford, W. H. *Anton Chekhov.* Studies in Modern European Literature and Thought. London: Bowes & Bowes, 1957.

Charques, Richard. *The Twilight of Imperial Russia.* New York: Oxford University Press, 1947.

Eekman, T., ed., *Anton Čechov, 1860–1960: Some Essays.* Leiden: E. J. Brill, 1960.

Friedland, Louis S., ed. *Anton Chekhov, Letters on the Short Story, the Drama and Other Literary Topics.* 1924. Reprinted New York: Dover Publications, 1966.

Garnett, Constance, ed. and tr. *Letters of Anton Chekhov to His Family and Friends, with a Biographical Sketch.* New York: Macmillan, 1920.

————. *The Letters of Anton Pavlovitch Tchekhov to Olga Leonardovna Knipper.* 1925. Reprinted New York: B. Blom, 1966.

Jackson, Robert Louis, ed. *Chekhov: A Collection of Critical Essays.* Twentieth-Century Views. Englewood Cliffs, N.J.: Prentice-Hall, 1967.

Karlinsky, Simon, ed. *Anton Chekhov's Life and Thought: Selected Letters and Commentary.* Translated by Henry Heim and Simon Karlinsky. Selection, Introduction, and Commentary by Simon Karlinsky. Berkeley: University of California Press, 1973.

Koteliansky, S. S., tr. and ed. *Anton Chekhov, Literary and Theatrical Reminiscences.* 1927. Reprinted New York: B. Blom, 1965.

Koteliansky, S. S. and Philip Tomlinson, tr. and ed. *The Life and Letters of Anton Tschekhov.* New York: George H. Doran, 1925.

Koteliansky, S. S., and Leonard Woolf, tr. *Note-Book of Anton Chekhov.* New York: B. W. Huebsch, 1921.

————. *The Personal Papers of Anton Chekhov.* Introduction by Matthew Josephson. New York: Lear, 1948.

————. *Reminiscences of Anton Chekhov.* By Maxim Gorky, Alexander Kuprin, and I. A. Bunin. New York: B. W. Huebsch, 1921.

Heifetz, Anna, ed. *Chekhov in English: A List of Works by and about Him.* Foreword by Avrahm Yarmolinsky. New York, 1949.

Hellman, Lillian, ed. *The Selected Letters of Anton Chekhov.* Translated by Sidonie Lederer. New York: Farrar, Straus, 1955.

Hingley, Ronald. *Chekhov: A Biographical and Critical Study.* Revised edition. London: George Allen & Unwin, 1966.

Laffitte, Sophie. *Tchékhov 1860–1904.* Paris: Librairie Hachette, 1971.

Magarshack, David. *Chekhov the Dramatist.* New York: Hill & Wang, 1960.

————. *Chekhov: A Life.* New York: Grove Press, 1955.

————. *The Real Chekhov: An Introduction to Chekhov's Last Plays.* London: George Allen & Unwin, 1972.

Meister, Charles W. "Chekhov's Reception in England and America." *The American Slavic and East European Review,* XII (February 1953), 109–21.

Nemirovitch-Dantchenko, Vladimir. *My Life in the Russian Theatre.* Translated by John Cournos. With an Introduction by Joshua Logan, a Foreword by Oliver M. Sayler, and A Chronology by Elizabeth Reynolds Hapgood. 1936. Reprinted New York: Theatre Arts Books, 1968.

Pitcher, Harvey. *The Chekhov Play: A New Interpretation.* New York: Barnes & Noble, 1973.

Rayfield, Donald. *Chekhov: The Evolution of His Art.* New York: Barnes & Noble, 1975.

Simmons, Ernest J. *Chekhov: A Biography.* Boston: Atlantic Monthly Press, 1962.

Smith, Virginia Llewellyn. *Anton Chekhov and the Lady with the Dog.* Foreword by Ronald Hingley. London: Oxford University Press, 1973.
Stanislavsky, Konstantin. *Stanislavsky on the Art of the Stage.* Translated with an Introductory Essay on Stanislavsky's "System" by David Magarshack. London, 1950.
Styan, J. L. *Chekhov in Performance: A Commentary on the Major Plays.* Cambridge: Cambridge University Press, 1971.
Toumanova, Princess Nina Andronikova. *Anton Chekhov: The Voice of Twilight Russia.* New York: Columbia University Press, 1937.
Valency, Maurice. *The Breaking String: The Plays of Anton Chekhov.* New York: Oxford University Press, 1966.
Winner, Thomas. *Chekhov and His Prose.* New York: Holt, Rinehart & Winston, 1966.
Yachnin, Rissa, compiler. *The Chekhov Centennial Chekhov in English: A Selective List of Works by and about Him, 1949–1960.* New York: New York Public Library, 1960.
Yarmolinsky, Avraham, ed. and tr. *Letters of Anton Chekhov.* New York: Viking, 1973.'

MATERIALS IN RUSSIAN CONSULTED IN THE PREPARATION OF THIS VOLUME

Aleksandrov, B. I. *A. P. Čexov, seminarij* . . . [A. P. Chekhov, seminar]. Moscow: Prosvešenie, 1964.
Vsevolodskij [Gerngross], V. *Istorija russkogo teatra* [History of the Russian theatre]. 2 vols. Leningrad: Tea-Kino Pečat', 1929.
Gitovič, N. I. *Letopis žisni i tvorčestva A. P. Čexova* [A chronicle of the life and creative work of A. P. Chekhov]. Moscow: Goslitizdat, 1955.
Nemirovič-Dančenko, V. I. *Iz prošlogo* [Out of the past]. Moscow: Academia, 1936.
Nemirovič-Dančenko vedet repeticiju "Tri sestry" A. P. Čexova v postanovke MXAT 1940 goda: rabota Vl. I. Nemiroviča-Dančenko s aktorom [Nemirovich-Danchenko conducts the rehearsal of Chekhov's *Three Sisters* in the 1940 production at the Moscow Art Theatre: the work of Vladimir Nemirovich-Danchenko with the actors]. Moscow: Iskusstvo, 1965.
Stanislavskij, K. S. *Moja zizn' v isksusstve* [My life in art]. In Stanislavskij, *Sobranie sočinęnij* [Collected works], Vol. I. Moscow: Iskusstvo, 1954.
Stroeva, M. N. *Čexov i Xudožestvennyj teatr* [Chekhov and the art theatre]. Moscow: Iskusstvo, 1955.
Surkov, E. D., ed. *Čexov i teatr: pis'ma, fel'etony, sovremenniki o Čexove-dramaturge* [Chekhov and theatre: letters, newspapers (topical satire), contemporaries on Chekhov—Playwright]. Moscow: Gos-izd. Iskusstvo, 1961.
Teatral'naja Enciklopedija [Theatrical encyclopaedia]. Editor-in-chief P. A. Markov. 5 vols. Moscow: Sovetskaja Enciklopedija, 1961–1967.
A. P. Čexov v vospominanijax sovremennikov [A. P. Chekhov in the recollections of (his) contemporaries]. Edited by N. I. Gitovič. Moscow: Goslitizdat, 1960.
Šax-Azizova, T. K. *Čexov i zapadno-evropejskaja drama ego vremeni* [Chekhov and Western European drama of his time.] Moscow: Nauka, 1966.

NORTON CRITICAL EDITIONS